This dictionary, and all the words inside it, belong to:

Violette

This Student Dictionary has been provided to you by
The (Rotary Club) Santa Barbara Sunrise in the name of

Ruth Alpert

We want to thank the individuals who made contributions to this dictionary by sending in their suggestions and comments. They made this edition better than the last one.

Darian Afkami, Mohammad Alansari, Doug Anthony, Lew and Lynda Aston, Dr. Richard Barshinger, John Beiter, Gael E.Bohannon, George Bozic, Caroline Brost, Dahmen Brown, David Carr, Emily Cowen, Nick Cowie, Noreen Crawford, Laurie David, Stanley Dixon, Lois Dobish, Stanley Doore, Evan Eckersley, Phil Ferrara, Ryan Fiorillo, Arlyne French, Mary Gallagher, Stella Guenther, Avery Harrison, Chris Hope, Tammy Hoeppner, Anthony Huber, Elizabeth Jewell, Arman Kandarian, Timothy Knight, Ruth Kent, Mary Lavarnway, Ann Macaluso, Kaitlin MacAulay, Phyllis Makinster, Nikita Matthews, Richard McArthur, Larry Margolis, Claude and Isaac Mertzenich, Colista Moore, Joan Morgan, Constance Mote, Mark Nabb, Skylar Nugent, Emma Oliver, Wanda Parker, Judith Pendleton, Molly President, Lianna Prill, Linda Qualters, Sasha Sagan, Sergey Szekunov, Storrs Warinner, Trudie Weiden, Don White, Dorothy Willard, Melise Williams, Betty Williford, Natalie Wolfe, Cynthia Xia.

We are grateful for your ideas and contributions. Please write to us, to let us know what you would like to see in the next edition of the dictionary.

Cover design by Julia Sokolow.
We want to thank NASA for providing the images of the Earth and the astronauts on the cover.

This dictionary is one of your most valuable, interesting, and fun learning tools. Keep it handy! It will help you do your very best work in school, and you will also learn many new words to use every day. Communication is the key to learning, and this dictionary was written to help you use words to share your thoughts and articulate your feelings so that you can communicate them with other people.

A dictionary this size cannot contain the 300,000 words in our language. This book has more than 35,000 words and their meanings that will help you better understand our world.

To succeed in school and in life, you must be able to use the English language effectively. You simply cannot learn all that you need to know without being able to understand the words you hear and read, and without knowing how to use the right words to convey your thoughts and ideas clearly. A dictionary is an essential tool for a quality education, you cannot do your best work without one. Use it to look up the spelling, meaning, and pronunciation of words. You will also find that it is fun spending time looking for new and useful words to expand your vocabulary. Learning new words gives you a feeling of satisfaction.

The English language is a living language that is constantly changing, and dictionaries must change, too. Our technology is driven by words that weren't in the dictionary ten years ago. If there are words or meanings you would like to see added to our new dictionaries, please send them to The Dictionary Project for consideration. You will receive a timely response to the suggestions and comments you send. You can help us make sure that this is The Best Dictionary for Students.

www.The Dictionary Project.com

A STUDENT'S DICTIONARY
& GAZETTEER, 22nd edition

©2014, The Dictionary Project, Inc.
Sullivan's Island, SC 29482

Printed and made in the U.S.A.
ISBN 978-1-934669-27-3
        1-934669-27-X

ABCDEFGHIJKLMNOPQRSTUVWXY

Table of Contents

abcdefghijklmnopqrstuvwxyz

ABCDEFGHIJKLMNOPQRSTUVWXYZ

It is truly amazing that out of twenty-six letters there can be thousands of combinations of letters to make up the words in our vocabulary.

This little dictionary touches on between 32,000 and 33,000 of the most commonly used words.

Words have power and can govern our lives. Whether talking to a friend or a family member, making a speech, or in the world of business, it is to your advantage to have a storehouse of words to convey your thoughts to whoever is listening. It builds strong self-confidence.

As you carry this book with you through your school years and use it, your vocabulary will grow along with you. New technical words and phrases will be abreast of the times, but the basics will live on to be uttered by you and upcoming generations.

This dictionary is given to you with best wishes for a word-endowed future.

Colista Moore
Rogue River, OR

Aa Bb Cc Dd Ee Ff Gg Hh Ii Jj Kk
Ll Mm Nn Oo Pp Qq Rr Ss Tt Uu
Vv Ww Xx Yy Zz

NINE PARTS OF SPEECH

Three little words you often see,
Are Articles – *a, an,* and *the*.
A Noun's the name of anything,
As *school*, or *garden*, *hoop*, or *swing*.
Adjectives tell the kind of Noun,
As *great, small, pretty, white*, or *brown*.
Instead of Nouns the Pronouns stand-
Her head, *his* face, *your* arm, *my* hand.
Verbs tell of something to be done –
To *read, count, sing, laugh, jump*, or *run*.
How things are done, the Adverbs tell,
As *slowly, quickly, ill*, or *well*.
Conjunctions join the words together
As man *and* woman, wind *or* weather.
The Preposition stands before
A noun, as *in*, or *through* a door.
The Interjection shows surprise,
As *oh!* How pretty – *ah*! How wise.
The whole are called Nine Parts of Speech,
Which reading, writing, speaking teach.

Dr. Chase , 1867

Punctuation

Punctuation marks and pauses are used to separate written or printed information into sentences and parts of sentences to assist the reader in understanding the meaning of the writer.

A **Period (.)** is placed at the end of a sentence; as,
> *I admit I made a mistake.*
> Or is used after an abbreviation; as
> *Dr. Johnson   Jan. 1, 2004*

A **question mark (?)** indicates a question; as
> *What is your opinion?*

An **Exclamation Point (!)** denotes humor or strong feeling; as,
> *Facing it—always facing it – that's the way to get through it. Face it!*
> Joseph Conrad, 1924

The **Comma (,)**, **Semicolon (;)**, and **Colon (:)** mark grammatical division in a sentence; as,
> *There are three genders: feminine, masculine, and neuter; in language they are referred to as she, he, and it, respectively.*

A **comma** is used to list items in a series. The **colon** may separate two clauses when the second explains the first, and is also used before an explanatory list. The **semicolon** is used to separate two independent clauses when there is no conjunction. Sometimes it is called a weak period.

A **Hyphen (-)** is used between syllables in a word divided at the end of a line; as,
> *knowl-edge   pow-er*
> And between the parts of a compound word, as
> *self-improvement   absent-minded*

4

The Dash (--) is used where there is a sudden break or pause in a sentence; as,

Individual commitment to a group effort-- that is what makes a team work, a company work, a society work, a civilization work.
Vince Lombardi, 1970

Quotation marks (" ") denote the words of another; as

"My name is Margalo," said the little bird softly in a musical voice. "I come from fields once tall with wheat, from pastures deep in fern and thistle; I come from vales of meadow-sweet, and I love to whistle." <u>Stuart Little</u>, *E.B. White, 1985*

An apostrophe (') denotes that a letter or letters are left out; as,

I'd be better off if I had gone to school longer, and so will you.
Joe Louis

And is also used to show ownership; as

There are spaces between our fingers so that another person's fingers can fill them in. Anonymous

Pronunciation Key

ă, for ŏ, as in	want	ў, for ĭ, as in	chlorophyll
ê, " â, "	tear	e, " k, "	character
ę, " ā, "	eight	ç, " s, "	city
ï, " ē, "	police	çh, " sh, "	chivalry
ī, " ẽ, "	sir	eh, " k, "	chorus
ȯ, " ŭ, "	ton	ġ, " j, "	general
ǫ, " ōō, "	do	ṇ, " ng, "	sang
ọ, " ŏŏ, "	book	ṣ, " z, "	hands
ô, " ạ, "	pork	s, " sh, "	sure
õ, " û, "	worm	x, " ḡz, "	example
u, " ōō, "	pull	gh, " f, "	laugh
u̱, " ōō, "	rule	ph, " f, "	phone
ȳ, " ī, "	try	qu, " k. "	plaque

qu, for kw, as in quiet

A schwa "ə" in the pronunciation guide indicates an unstressed vowel, as in "the" or "someone"

Guide to the Dictionary

entry word   **re-spect** [rˈ-spµktˮ] *noun*, 1) an aspect
2) consideration for someone, *verb*, 3) to have a good opinion of someone, to look up to, to hold in esteem

spelling   **cour-te-ous** [kûrˮt¶-…s] *adjective*, showing good manners, polite

meaning   **com-pas-sion** [k…m-p²shˮ…n] *noun*, kindness, tenderness, pity, sympathy for suffering

more than one meaning   **char-ac-ter** [k²rˮ…k-t…r] *noun*
1) the moral makeup of a person
2) a person in a book or movie or play
3) a symbol, sign, or written letter used in a language

part of speech   **hon-or** [¼nˮ…r] *noun*, 1) fame or a rank of high esteem, *verb*, 2) to hold in high respect 3) to keep an agreement

no plural   **cour-age** [kûrˮ¹j] *noun, no plural*, the strength to face danger when overwhelmed by fear

persevere   phrase

guide words   **per-se-vere** [pûrˮs…-vîrˮ] *verb*, to work to accomplish a goal despite difficulty

per-sist [p…r-s¹stˮ] *verb*, to keep doing something, to persevere

phrase [fr³z] *noun*, 1) a part of a sentence 2) an expression, a saying, *verb*, 3) to express in words or a particular way

syllabic pronunciation   **in-teg-ri-ty** [¹n-tµgˮrˈ-t¶] *noun*, honesty ,uprighteousness

phonetic spelling   **in-spire** [¹n-sp⁰rˮ] *verb*, to stimulate to think and to act, to influence

6

a [ā] *article*, used to indicate one before a noun

a-ba-cus [ăb′ə-kəs] *noun*, a frame holding parallel rods with beads, used for doing arithmetic

ab-a-lo-ne [ăb′ə-lō′nē] *noun*, a shell sea mollusk animal whose shell is lined with mother-of-pearl

a-ban-don [ə-băn′dən] *verb*, to leave or give up completely, to walk away from

a-bash [ə-băsh′] *verb*, to cause to feel embarrassed or ashamed

a-bate [ə-bāt′] *verb*, to gradually become less in amount or degree

ab-bre-vi-ate [ə-brē′vē-āt′] *verb*, to shorten, to cut down, to contract

ab-di-cation [ăb′dĭ-kā-shŭn] *noun*, a surrender, abandonment

ab-do-men [ăb′də-mən] *noun*, the digestive system in the body, belly

ab-duct [ăb-dŭkt′] *verb*, to kidnap

ab-er-ra-tion [ăb′ə-rā′shən] *noun*, a departure from what is right, correct or natural

a-bet [ə-bĕt′] *verb*, to encourage or assist, especially in wrongdoing

ab-hor [ăb-hôr′] *verb*, to withdraw in disgust or horror

a-bide [ə-bīd′] *verb,* 1) to put up with, tolerate 2) to wait patiently for

a-bil-i-ty [ə-bĭl′ĭ-tē] *noun*, 1) skill, expertise 2) capability or power

a-ble [ā′bəl] *adjective*, having the strength or knowledge to do something

ab-nor-mal [ăb-nôr′məl] *adjective*, irregular, unusual, peculiar

a-board [ə-bôrd′] *preposition*, on, in, upon (a ship)

a-bode [ə-bōd′] *noun*, home; a place of residence; a habitation

a-bol-ish [ə-bŏl′ĭsh] *verb*, to do away with entirely

ab-o-li-tion [ăb′ə-lĭsh′ən] *noun*, complete destruction

a-bom-i-na-ble [ə-bŏm′ə-nə-bəl] *adjective*, detestable, odious

ab-o-rig-i-ne [ăb′ə-rĭj′ə-nē] *noun*, a person, animal or plant that has been in a country or region from earliest times

a-bor-tive [ə-bôr′tĭv] *adjective*, unsuccessful, fruitless, unfinished

a-bound [ə-bound′] *verb*, to exist in large numbers, to overflow

a-bout [ə-bout′] *adverb*, 1) concerning 2) approximately 3) here or there, everywhere

a-bove [ə-bŭv′] *adverb*, 1) at a higher level, *preposition*, 2) over, in a higher place

a-bra-sion [ə-brā′zhən] *noun*, a wearing away or rubbing that causes scratches

a-bridge [ə-brĭj′] *verb*, to shorten by using fewer words

a-bridg-ment [ə-brĭj′mənt] *noun*, abbreviation, shortening

a-broad [ə-brôd′] *adverb*, in a foreign country, overseas

ab-rupt [ə-brŭpt′] *adjective*, suddenly, without warning,

ab-scess [ăb′sĕs′] *noun*, an accumulation of pus due to an infection from bacteria

ab-sence [ăb′səns] *noun*, 1) the state of being away from someplace or someone 2) lack

ab-sent [ăb′sənt] *adjective*, missing, not present, unavailable

ab-sent-mind-ed [ăb′səntmīn′dĭd] *adjective*, forgetful, not paying attention

ab-so-lute [ăb′sə-lōōt′] *adjective*, complete, perfect, total

ab-solve [əb-zŏlv′, -sŏlv′] *verb*, to pardon, to forgive

ab-sorb [əb-sôrb′, -zôrb′] *verb*, 1) to soak up a fluid or moisture 2) to hold someone's attention 3) to dissolve a debt completely and accept the loss 4) to assimilate information

ab-sorb-ent [əb-sôr′bənt] *adjective*, absorbing moisture, fluid or light rays

ab-stain [ăb-stān′] *verb*, to deliberately avoid doing something

ab-sti-nence [ăb′stə-nəns] *noun*, the act of depriving oneself of some indulgence, voluntary denial

ab-stract [ăb-străkt′] *adjective*, difficult to describe or qualify

ab-surd [əb-sûrd′, -zûrd′] *adjective*, outrageous, silly, untrue

ab-surd-i-ty [əb-sûrd′ĭ ē] *noun*, that which is ridiculous or unreasonable

a-bun-dance [ə-bŭn′dəns] *noun*, large quantity, plenty

a-bun-dant [ə-bŭn′dənt] *adjective*, plentiful, more than enough

a-buse [ə-byōō′s] *noun*, 1) hurtful treatment, *verb* [ə-byōōz′], 2) to hurt someone or something intentionally

a-bu-sive [ə-byōō′sĭv, -zĭv] *adjective*, using insulting words or bad treatment

a-but [ə-bŭt′] *verb*, to border upon, to be next to or touching

a-bys-mal [ə-bĭz′məl] *adjective*, 1) immeasurably bad 2) bottomless

a-byss [ə-bĭs′] *noun*, a very deep crack in the earth, a bottomless gulf, a deep chasm

ac-a-dem-ic [ăk′ə-dĕm′ĭk] *adjective*, 1) of or relating to an education in the arts 2) having no practical importance

a-cad-e-my [ə-kăd′ə-mē] *noun*, a school offering specialized training and education

ac-cel-er-a-tion [ăk-sĕl′ə-rā′shən] *noun*, an increase in the speed of something

ac-cent [ăk′sĕnt′] *noun*, 1) the sound and tone of a foreign language, *verb*, 2) to emphasize a sound or letter when pronouncing a word 3) to emphasize something

ac-cept [ăk-sĕpt′] *verb*, 1) to agree with 2) to receive

ac-cep-tance [ăk-sĕp′təns] *noun*, the act of receiving something graciously

ac-cess [ăk′sĕs] *noun*, a way to get to a person, place, or thing

achieve

ac-ces-si-ble [ăk-sĕs′ə-həl] *adjective*, easy to reach or use, approachable

ac-ces-so-ry [ăk-sĕs′ə-rē] *noun*, 1) an accomplice, connected as a subordinate 2) an article or decoration worn to complete an outfit, such as a belt, scarf, hat, etc.

ac-ci-dent [ăk′sĭ-dənt] *noun*, 1) an incident involving bodily injury or death 2) a mistake

ac-claim [ə-klām′] *verb*, to applaud, to announce with great approval

ac-cli-mate [ə-klī′mĭt] *verb*, to change or adjust to a different temperature or environment

ac-com-mo-date [ə-kŏm′ə-dāt′] *verb* 1) to adapt or make fit 2) to do a favor 3) to provide lodging

ac-com-mo-da-tion [ə-kŏm′ə-dā′shən] *noun*, an adaptation, an adjustment made to assist someone

ac-com-pa-ny [ə-kŭm′pə-nē] *verb*, to go with, to join

ac-com-plice [ə kŏm′plĭs] *noun*, someone who goes along with something, usually something wrong

ac-com-plish [ə-kŏm′plĭsh] *verb*, to finish, to complete a task or reach a goal

ac-com-plish-ment [ə-kŏm′plĭsh-mənt] *noun*, something done, a goal that has been reached, a finished task

ac-cord [ə-kôrd′] *noun*, 1) mutual agreement, *verb*, 2) to be in harmony, to conform

ac-cor-di-on [ə-kôr′dē-ən] *noun*, a musical instrument that is played by fingering a keyboard on one side and squeezing bellows in and out on the other side

ac-cost [ə-kôst′] *verb*, to approach abruptly and speak to first

ac-count [ə-kount′] *noun*, 1) an explanation, a statement of money or inventory, *verb*, 2) to give a reason, to explain

ac-crue [ə-krōō′] *verb*, to be added on to, to increase

ac-cu-mu-late [ə-kyōōm′yə-lāt′] *verb*, to collect, to amass

ac-cu-mu-la-tion [ə-kyōōm′yə-lā′shən] *noun*, gathering a quantity of something

ac-cu-ra-cy [ăk′yər-ə-sē] *noun*, exactness, correctness, precision

ac-cu-rate [ăk′yər-ĭt] *adjective*, having no mistakes

ac-cu-sa-tion [ăk′yōō-zā′shən] *noun*, a claim that someone has done something wrong

ac-cuse [ə-kyōōz′] *verb*, to say someone has committed an offense or crime

ac-cus-tom [ə-kŭs′təm] *verb*, to become familiar with something through use or habit

ace [ās] *noun*, 1) a playing card 2) a fighter pilot who was shot down

ache [āk] *noun*, 1) a painful or sore spot, *verb*, 2) to hurt, to feel pain

a-chieve [ə-chēv′] *verb*, to do what one sets out to do

achievement

a-chieve-ment [ə-chēv′mənt] *noun*, something that a person has done to reach a goal

ac-id [ăs′ĭd] *noun*, a chemical substance soluble in water, sour in taste, that reddens litmus paper

ac-knowl-edge [ăk-nŏl′ĭj] *verb*, 1) to look at someone and speak to him or her 2) to admit the truth

ac-knowl-edg-ment [ăk-nŏl′ĭj-mənt] *noun*, 1) admission, recognition of an achievement 2) an expression of thanks

a-corn [ā′kôrn′, ā′kərn] *noun*, the seed of an oak tree

a-cous-tic [ə-kōō′stĭk] *adjective*, of or relating to the ability to carry a sound without distortion

ac-quaint [ə-kwānt′] *verb*, to cause to know or be aware of someone or something

ac-quaint-ance [ə-kwān′təns] *noun*, a person with whom one is familiar

ac-qui-esce [ăk′wē-ĕs′] *verb*, to submit, to consent, to agree

ac-quire [ə-kwīr′] *verb*, to get or to buy, to gain possession of

ac-qui-si-tion [ăk′wĭ-zĭsh′ən] *noun*, something gained or acquired

ac-quit [ə-kwĭt′] *verb*, to render a verdict that an accused person is not guilty of a crime, to exonerate

ac-quit-tal [ə-kwĭt′l] *noun*, a setting free from a charge, a finding of "not guilty"

a-cre [ā′kər] *noun*, a plot of land measuring 43,560 square feet

ac-ri-mo-ny [ăk′rə-mō′nē] *noun*, bitterness or caustic temper or speech, bad feelings

ac-ro-bat [ăk′rə-băt′] *noun*, a person skilled in tumbling or in using gymnastics equipment

ac-ro-nym [ăk′rə-nĭm′] *noun*, a word formed from the initial letters of a series of words, e.g. AIDS: *Acquired Immune Deficiency Syndrome*

a-cross [ə-krôs′, ə-krŏs′] *adverb*, 1) from one side of a place to the other, *preposition*, 2) on the opposite side from something

act [ăkt] *noun*, 1) something that has been done, a deed 2) a part of a play containing different scenes, *verb*, 3) to pretend to be something or someone 4) to behave 5) to carry out, to perform

ac-tion [ăk′shən] *noun*, 1) something done 2) the process of doing

ac-tive [ăk′tĭv] *adjective*, 1) always busy doing something 2) taking part

ac-tiv-i-ty [ăk-tĭv′ĭ-tē] *noun*, state of action, energy, a task

ac-tor [ăk′tər] *noun*, a male or female performer in a play, a film or television program

ac-tu-al [ăk′chōō-əl] *adjective*, real, existing in fact

ac-tu-al-ly [ăk′chōō-əl-ē] *adverb*, really, truly, in reality

a-cu-i-ty [ə-kyōō′ĭ-tē] *noun*, keenness, as of thought and vision

a-cute [ə-kyōōt′] *adjective*, 1) sharp, pointed, keen, sensitive

2) describing an angle formed by intersecting lines that is less than 90 degrees

A.D. abbreviation for the Latin words **Anno Domini**, the time after the birth of Christ

ad-age [ăd′ĭj] *noun*, a proverb or a saying with a moral message

ad-a-mant [ăd′ə-mənt] *adjective*, inflexible, unyielding

a-dapt [ə-dăpt′] *verb*, to change to fit the environment

ad-ap-ta-tion [ăd′ăp-tā′shən] *noun*, a change to improve the way things work

add [ăd] *verb*, 1) to put together with something else 2) to count

ad-der [ăd′ər] *noun*, a snake with a poisonous bite, a viper

ad-dict [ə-dĭkt′] *noun*, someone who has a strong habit or a physical despendency, as for drugs

ad-dic-tion [ə-dĭk′shən] *noun*, a dependency, such as a physical craving for a drug

ad-di-tion [ə-dĭsh′ən] *noun*, 1) the act of putting or joining things together 2) an annexation

ad-di-tion-al [ə-dĭsh′ən-əl] *adjective*, added on, extra

ad-dress [ə-drĕs′] *noun*, 1) the location of something, usually the street number, city, and state, *verb*, 2) to speak or write to someone 3) to direct in writing, as in a letter 4) to speak to an audience, as in a speech

a-dept [ə-dĕpt′] *adjective*, proficient, expert, highly skilled

ad-e-quate [ăd′ĭ kwĭt] *adjective*, just enough, sufficient, all right

ad-here [ăd-hîr′] *verb*, to hold, to be attached, to stick to

ad-her-ent [ăd-hîr′ənt] *adjective*, 1) sticking securely, *noun*, 2) a supporter or follower

ad-he-sive [ăd-hē′sĭv, -zĭv] *noun*, a sticky substance that holds things in place

a-dieu [ə-dyōō′, ə-dōō′] *noun and interjection*, farewell, goodbye

ad in-fi-ni-tum [ăd ĭn′fə-nī′təm] *adverb*, to infinity, endlessly

ad-ja-cent [ə-jā′sənt] *adjective*, next to, lying near or touching

ad-jec-tive [ăj′ĭk-tĭv] *noun*, a word that describes a person, place or thing

ad-join [ə-join′] *verb*, to be next to and connected to something

ad-journ [ə-jûrn′] *verb*, to put off a meeting until later, to postpone

ad-just [ə-jŭst′] *verb*, to reposition or reset something

ad-just-a-ble [ə-jŭst′ə-bəl] *adjective*, capable of being arranged or altered

ad-just-ment [ə-jŭst′mənt] *noun*, a minor modification or change

ad lib [ăd lĭb′] *verb*, to make up words or actions at the moment, not before

ad-min-is-ter [ăd-mĭn′ĭ-stər] *verb*, 1) to look after or tend 2) to distribute, to disperse 3) to manage, to run

ad-min-is-tra-tion [ăd-mĭn′ĭ-strā′shən] *noun*, those who are empowered to make decisions, management

administrator

ad-min-is-tra-tor [ăd-mĭn′ĭ-strā′tər] *noun*, a person authorized to carry out certain duties

ad-mi-ra-ble [ăd′mər-ə-bəl] *adjective*, excellent, deserving the highest praise

ad-mi-ral [ăd′mər-əl] *noun*, the highest ranking officer in the navy

ad-mi-ra-tion [ăd′mə-rā′shən] *noun*, appreciation, esteem

ad-mire [ăd-mīr′] *verb*, 1) to look up to someone, to revere 2) to look at with pleasure

ad-mis-si-ble [ăd-mĭs′ə-bəl] *adjective*, that may be allowed

ad-mis-sion [ăd-mĭsh′ən] *noun*, 1) access, admittance 2) acknowledgment, confession

ad-mit [ăd-mĭt′] *verb*, 1) to allow someone to enter 2) to acknowledge as true

a-do [ədo͞o] *noun*, fuss, excitment

a-do-be [ə-dō′bē] *noun*, 1) a type of clay or the sun-dried bricks made from it, 2) a home made with baked mud, usually in the Southwest

ad-o-les-cent [ăd′l-ĕs′ənt] *noun*, a teenager

a-dopt [ə-dŏpt′] *verb*, 1) to use someone else's idea 2) to make someone a member of your family, legally

a-dore [ə-dôr′, ə-dōr′] *verb*, to like or love very much

a-dorn [ə-dôrn′] *verb*, to decorate, to add beauty, to embellish

a-drift [ə-drĭft′] *adverb*, out in water or space without means of control, drifting

a-dult [ə-dŭlt′] *noun*, a grown person or animal

ad-vance [ăd-văns′] *adjective*, 1) ahead of time, done beforehand, *noun*, 2) a positive change, progress *verb*, 3) to move forward

ad-van-tage [ăd-văn′tĭj] *noun*, something that helps a person

ad-van-ta-geous [ăd′văn-tā′jəs,] *adjective*, profitable, useful, beneficial, favorable

ad-vent [ăd′vĕnt′] *noun*, the arrival of someone or something

ad-ven-ture [ăd-vĕn′chər] *noun*, 1) a bold or hazardous undertaking, 2) an exciting or extraordinary experience

ad-verb [ăd′vûrb] *noun*, a word that tells how, when, or where something is done

ad-ver-sar-y [ăd′vər-sĕr′ē] *noun*, a rival, foe, or opponent

ad-verse [ăd-vûrs′] *adjective*, opposed, hostile

ad-ver-si-ty [ăd-vûr′sĭ-tē] *noun*, hard times, trouble

ad-ver-tise [ăd′vər-tīz′] *verb*, 1) to announce publicly 2) to try to sell something by promoting it

ad-ver-tise-ment [ăd′vər-tīz′mənt] *noun*, a notice or short film about something that is for sale

ad-vice [ăd-vīs′] *noun*, counsel, opinion given for acceptable conduct, guidance

ad-vis-a-ble [ăd-vī′zə-bəl] *adjective*, proper, recommended, prudent

ad-vise [ăd-vīz′] *verb*, to suggest to someone what to do, to

12

inform, to recommend, to counsel

ad-vis-er [ăd-vī′zər] *noun*, one who advises, one who gives counsel or information

ad-vo-cate [ăd′və-k t′] *noun*, 1) one who pleads the cause of another or himself, [ăd′və-kāt′] *verb*, 2) to defend, to urge, to support, to endorse

aer-i-al [âr′ē-əl] *adjective*, pertaining to or inhabiting the air

aer-o-bic [â-rō′bĭk] *adjective*, requiring the presence of free oxygen to live

aer-o-dy-nam-ics [âr′ō-dī-năm′ĭks] *noun*, the science of the movement of flying bodies in air

aer-o-sol [âr′ə-sôl′] *noun*, a gaseous suspension of fine particles, a mist

aer-o-space [âr′ō-spās′] *adjective*, having to do with the atmosphere and space

aes-thet-ic [ĕs-thĕt′ĭk] *adjective*, relating to beauty or the arts

af-fair [ə-fâr′] *noun*, matter, concern, business of any kind

af-fect [ə-fĕkt′] *verb*, 1) to act upon to bring about a change 2) to move the feelings of someone 3) to pretend to do something

af-fec-ta-tion [ăf′ĕk-tā′shən] *noun*, insincerity, pretense

af-fec-tion [ə-fĕk′shən] *noun*, tenderness, warmth, love, devotion, kindness

af-fec-tion-ate [ə-fĕk′shə-nĭt] *adjective*, feeling or showing love

af-fec-tion-ate-ly [ə-fĕk′shə-nĭt-lē] *adverb*, showing love and care

af-fi-da-vit [ăf′ĭ-dā′vĭt] *noun*, a written declaration, an oath

af-fil-i-ate [ə-fĭl′ē-āt′] *verb*, to closely connect or associate with someone or groups of people

af-fil-i-a-tion [ə-fĭl-ē-ā′shən] *noun*, an association, a connection

af-fin-i-ty [ə-fĭn′ĭ-tē] *noun*, a feeling of attraction to a person or thing

af-firm [ə-fûrm′] *verb*, to approve, to confirm, to endorse

af-fir-ma-tion [ăf′ər-mā′shən] *noun*, a solemn pledge

af-firm-a-tive [ə-fûr′mə-tĭv] *adjective*, 1) being positive and helpful, *noun*, 2) a word or phrase expressing a positive reply

af-flict [ə-flĭkt′] *verb*, to hurt, to torment, to cause pain

af-flic-tion [ə-flĭk′shən] *noun*, state or cause of distress, pain or misery

af-flu-ence [ăf′lōō-əns] *noun*, an abundant supply, wealth

af-ford [ə-fôrd′] *verb*, to have enough money to buy something

a-float [ə-flōt′] *adjective*, on or above the water, buoyant

a-fraid [ə-frād′] *adjective*, scared

Af-ri-ca [ăf′rĭ-kə] *noun*, one of the seven continents, surrounded by the Atlantic and Indian Oceans, containing 12.7% of the world's population

af-ter [ăf′tər] *adverb*, 1) following, next, *preposition*, 2) behind

af-ter-math [ăf′tər-măth′] *noun*, the end result, outcome, consequence

afternoon

af-ter-noon [ăf′tər-nōōn′] *noun*, time between noon and evening

af-ter-ward [ăf′tər-wərd] *adverb*, later

a-gain [ə-gĕn′] *adverb*, once more

a-gainst [ə-gĕnst′] *preposition*, 1) in opposition to 2) in contact with, touching 3) in the other direction, opposite

age [āj] *noun*, 1) the amount of time something has lived 2) a particular period of time, *verb*, 3) to grow or cause to become old

aged [ā′jĭd] *adjective*, old

a-gen-cy [ā′jən-sē] *noun*, an organization designed to distribute funds and services to people

a-gen-da [ə-jĕn′də] *noun*, a list of items that need attention

a-gent [ā′jənt] *noun*, 1) a person who represents a group 2) a force of change

ag-gran-dize [ə-grăn′dīz′] *verb*, to make greater in power, rank or riches

ag-gra-vate [ăg′rə-vāt′] *verb*, to make worse, to annoy

ag-gre-gate [ăg′rĭ-gĭt] *noun*, the sum total of a group of things

ag-gres-sion [ə-grĕsh′ən] *noun*, anger in an attack

ag-gres-sive [ə-grĕs′ĭv] *adjective*, forceful, likely to attack

ag-ile [ăj′əl, -īl′] *adjective*, swift, nimble, able to move easily

ag-i-tate [ăj′ĭ-tāt′] *verb*, to shake up

ag-i-ta-tion [ăj′ĭ-tā′shən] *noun*, confusion, frenzy, excitement

ag-nos-tic [ăg-nŏs′tĭk] *noun*, a person who believes that the human mind cannot comprehend the beginning of the universe or the existence of God

a-go [ə-gō′] *adverb*, in the past

ag-o-ny [ăg′ə-nē] *noun*, very bad physical or emotional pain

a-gree-a-ble [ə-grē′ə-bəl] *adjective*, easy to get along with

a-gree-ment [ə-grē′mənt] *noun*, a mutual understanding

ag-ri-cul-ture [ăg′rĭ-kŭl′chər] *noun*, the science and art of cultivating soil and growing crops

a-head [ə-hĕd′] *adverb*, 1) in front, preceding 2) into the future

aid [ād] *noun*, 1) a form of help 2) assistance, support, *verb*, 3) to help or assist

aide [ād] *noun*, an assistant, a helper

ail-ment [āl′mənt] *noun*, a sickness,

aim [ām] *noun*, 1) target, direction 2) intention, purpose, goal, *verb*, 3) to point toward a target when ready to throw something, fire something, or take a picture

air [âr] *noun* 1) the mixture of gases surrounding the earth 2) an appearance or atmosphere, *verb*, 3) to refresh or ventilate

air-borne [âr′bôrn′] *adjective*, carried by or through the air

air-craft [âr′krăft′] *noun*, a machine capable of flying

air force [âr′fôrs′]*noun*, a group of soldiers trained to fight and destroy using aircraft

air-plane [âr′plān′] *noun*, a flying machine used to transport people or cargo moving through the air by means of motor driven propellers or engines and kept aloft by the upward thrust of the air on its fixed wings

air pol-lu-tion [âr - pə-lōō'shən] *noun*, particles that contaminate the air and make it unsafe to breathe

air-port [âr'pôrt'] *noun*, a place where aircraft land and take off

aisle [īl] *noun*, the passageway between seats in a bus, auditorium, church, etc., or between shelves in a store

a-jar [ə-jär'] *adjective and adverb*, slightly open

Al-a-bama [ăl'ə-băm'ə] *noun*, one of the southern United States the capital is Montgomery. The state flower for **Alabama** is the camellia and the motto is "We dare to defend our rights."

a-lac-ri-ty [ə-lăk'rĭ-tē] *noun*, 1) cheerful willingness or readiness 2) speed

a-larm [ə-lärm'] *noun*, 1) a feeling of fear or danger 2) a programmed sound to awaken persons from sleep or warn of danger, *verb*, 3) to worry or frighten

a-las [ə-lăs'] *interjection*, an expression of pity or concern

Alas-ka [ə-lăs'kə] *noun*, one of the 50 United States located in the North. The capital city is Juneau. The state flower of **Alaska** is the forget me-not, and the motto is "North to the Future."

al-ba-tross [ăl'bə-trôs'] *noun*, a large bird with long narrow wings

found near the ocean, especially in the South Seas

al-bi-no [ăl-bī'nō] *noun*, a person or animal lacking pigmentation, and therefore extraordinarily pale

al-bum [ăl'bəm] *noun*, 1) a book that holds a collection of pictures, stamps or autographs 2) a collection of recordings

al-che-my [ăl'kə-mē] *noun*, medieval chemistry that attempted to turn ordinary things into gold

al-co-hol [ăl'kə-hôl'] *noun*, 1) an intoxicating beverage, such as wine, beer or liquor, the result of fermentation 2) an organic compound used as an antiseptic

al-co-hol-ic [ăl'kə-hô'lĭk] *adjective*, 1) containing alcohol as an ingredient, *noun*, 2) a person with the disease of alcoholism

al-der-man [ôl'dər-mən] *noun*, a member of a city council

a-lert [ə-lûrt'] *adjective*, 1) awake and ready to act, *noun*, 2) a warning of danger

al-fal-fa [ăl-făl'fə] *noun*, a plant in the pea family

al-ga [ăl'gə] *noun*, *plural*, **algae**, an organism, often one-celled, that continuously divides itself, with no root or stem that lives in water

al-ge-bra [ăl'jə-brə] *noun*, a branch of mathematics in which the expressions of quantity are in symbols that express general relationships

a-li-as [ā'lē-əs] *noun*, an assumed name, a fake name, incognito

al-i-bi [ăl′ə-bī′] *noun*, the plea of having been elsewhere at the time a crime was committed

al-ien [ā′lē-ən] *adjective*, 1) strange, wholly different in nature, *noun*, 2) a person from another country

al-ien-ate [āl′yə-nāt′] *verb*, to separate, to make hostile

a-light [ə-līt′] *verb*, to come from, to get off

a-lign-ment [ə-līn′mənt] *noun*, 1) arrangement in a line 2) the condition of cooperation

a-like [ə-līk′] *adjective*, 1) similar, *adverb*, 2) in the same manner

al-i-men-ta-ry [ăl′ə-měn′tə-rē] *adjective*, supplying nourishment

al-i-mo-ny [ăl′ə-mō′nē] *noun*, an allowance given to a spouse for his or her support after a divorce

a-live [ə-līv′] *adjective*, 1) living, not dead 2) active, moving

al-ka-li [ăl′kə-lī′] *noun*, any soluble substance having marked basic qualities as a mineral salt or mixture of salts that can neutralize acids and turns litmus blue

all [ôl] *adjective*, the whole of, any, 2) *adverb*, 2) completely, totally, *pronoun*, 3) everyone, the whole thing

al-lay [ə-lā′] to ease, to calm, to appease

al-le-ga-tion [ăl′ĭ-gā′shən] *noun*, the statement of something that is to be proved, an accusation

al-lege [ə-lěj′] *verb*, to urge as a reason, to assert, to suggest

al-le-giance [ə-lē′jəns] *noun*, strong support of something, an obligation to a government or ruler, loyal support

al-le-go-ry [ăl′ĭ-gôr′ē] *noun*, a story with a moral in which characters are used as symbols, a fable

al-ler-gy [ăl′ər-jē] *noun*, an abnormal reaction to substances in the environment such as pollen, dust or insect bites

al-le-vi-ate [ə-lē′vē-āt′] *verb*, to lighten or lessen pressure

al-ley [ăl′ē] *noun*, a very narrow road between buildings

al-li-ance [ə-lī′əns] *noun*, a partnership based on trust, common objectives, etc.

al-li-ga-tor [ăl′ĭ-gā′tər] *noun*, a large reptile that lives near water and is a carnivore

al-lit-er-a-tion [ə-lĭt′ə-rā′shən] *noun*, repetition of the beginning sound, e.g., *Peter Piper picked a peck of pickled peppers*

al-lo-cate [ăl′ə-kāt′] *verb*, to set something aside for a special use

al-lot [ə-lŏt′] *verb*, to divide something and then to give someone his or her portion

al-lot-ment [ə-lŏt′mənt] *noun*, the portion given to each

al-low [ə-lou′] *verb*, to permit someone to do something

al-low-ance [ə-lou′əns] *noun*, a definite sum granted, an abatement or deduction

al-loy [ăl′oi′] *noun*, a substance composed of two or more metals mixed together

al-lude [ə-lōōd′] *verb*, to hint or suggest indirectly

al-lu-sion [ə-lōō′zhən] *noun*, an indirect reference, knowledge of something not actually mentioned

al-ly [ə-lī′] *noun*, 1) someone who helps you fight against someone else, a person or group who has the same purpose or cause, *verb*, 2) to unite, to join

al-ma ma-ter [ăl′mə mä′tər] *noun*, a school from which a person has graduated

al-ma-nac [ôl′mə-năk′] *noun*, a book containing a calendar and certain statistics

al-might-y [ôl-mī′tē] *adjective*, having very great power

al-mond [ä′mənd] *noun*, a nut-like kernel of the fruit of the almond tree

al-most [ôl′mōst′] *adverb*, nearly, not quite

alms [ämz] *noun, plural*, money or items given to charity

a-lo-ha [ə-lō-ha′] *noun and interjection*, Hawaiian word used for greeting or parting

a-lone [ə-lōn′] *adjective and adverb* without others, singular

a-long [ə-lông′] *adverb*, 1) following the length of something from end to end 2) moving forward 3) as a companion, *preposition*, 4) over, through, by the course of

a-loof [ə-l ōōf] *adjective*, 1) reserved in social relationships, *adverb* 2) away in place or time

a-loud [ə-loud′] *adverb*, in a clear voice that can be easily heard

al-pha-bet [ăl′fə-hĕt′] *noun*, the letters of a language arranged in customary order

al-pha-bet-i-cal [ăl′fə-bĕt′ĭ-kəl] *adjective*, arranged in the same order as the letters of the alphabet

al-read-y [ôl-rĕd′ē] *adverb*, even now, before a certain time

al-so [ôl′sō] *adverb*, in addition, too

al-tar [ôl′tər] *noun*, a table in a holy place where religious rites are performed

al-ter [ôl′tər] *verb*, to change

al-ter-a-tion [ôl′tə-rā′shən] *noun*, a change or an adjustment

al-ter-nate [ôl′tər-nāt′] *verb*, to take turns, to switch off

al-ter-na-tive [ôl-tûr′nə-tĭv] *adjective*, 1) other, *noun*, 2) something you can choose

al-though [ôl-thō′] *conjunction*, supposing that, notwithstanding

al-ti-tude [ăl′tĭ-tōōd′] *noun*, extent upward, the height of something measured in relation to a reference level, such as sea level

al-to [ăl′tō] *noun*, a singing voice between tenor and soprano

al-to-geth-er [ôl′tə-gĕth′ər] *adverb*, wholly, completely, including everyone, united

al-tru-is-tic [ăl′trōō-ĭs′tĭk] *adjective*, unselfish, concerned about others

al-u-mi-num [ə-lōō′mə-nəm] *noun*, a very soft silver metal made chiefly of bauxite ore

al-ways [ôl′wāz] *adverb*, at all times, forever

am

am [ăm] *verb*, the part of the verb **be** used with **I**

a.m. in the morning, the hours between midnight and noon, from the Latin ante meridiem "before midday"

a-mass [ə-măs′] *verb*, to collect, to accumulate

am-a-teur [ăm′ə-tûr′] *adjective*, 1) for enjoyment rather than money, not professional, *noun*, 2) someone who is not paid for doing something but does it for pleasure

a-maze [ə-māz′] *verb*, to surprise or bewilder

a-maze-ment [ə-māz′mənt] *noun*, a state of surprise, awe, wonder

am-a-zon [ăm′ə-zŏn′] *noun*, a mythical female warrior

am-bas-sa-dor [ăm-băs′ə-dər] *noun*, an appointed official who represents his or her country in another country

am-ber [ăm′bər] *noun*, the fossilized sap from a pine tree

am-bi-dex-trous [ăm′bĭ-děk′strəs] *adjective*, capable of using either hand with equal ease

am-bi-ence [ăm′bē-əns] *noun*, the environment, the atmosphere in a room or building

am-big-u-ous [ăm-bĭg′yoo-əs] *adjective*, capable of more than one interpretation, unclear

am-bi-tion [ăm-bĭsh′ən] *noun*, a strong desire to achieve

am-bi-tious [ăm-bĭsh′əs] *adjective*, wanting to have power, driven to achieve

am-biv-a-lent [ăm-bĭv′ə-lənt] *adjective,* having conflicting emotional attitudes

am-bu-lance [ăm′byə-ləns] *noun*, a vehicle equipped to carry the injured or sick

am-bush [ăm′boosh] *noun*, a surprise attack

a-mel-io-rate [ə-mēl′yə-rāt′] *verb*, to improve a deplorable condition

A-men [ā-měn′, ä-měn′] *interjection*, an expression of approval, to say I agree

a-mend [ə-měnd′] *verb*, to correct, to change generally for the better

a-mend-ment [ə-měnd′mənt] *noun*, a change made in a bill or motion

a-men-i-ty [ə-měn′ĭ-tē] *noun*, a courtesy, a thoughtful action of consideration, a convenience

A-mer-i-ca [ə-měr′ĭ-kə]*noun*, a country in North America with a democratic form of government

A-mer-i-can In-di-an [ə-měr′ĭ-kən ĭn′dē-ən] *noun*, the people whose ancestors lived in North America for thousands of years

am-e-thyst [ăm′ə-thĭst] *noun*, a purple or bluish-violet stone

a-mi-a-ble [ā′mē-ə-bəl] *adjective*, friendly, easy to get along with

a-mid [ə-mĭd′] *preposition*, among, surrounded by

am-mo-nia [ə-mōn′yə] *noun*, a colorless compound of hydrogen and nitrogen

am-mu-ni-tion [ăm′yə-nĭsh′ən] *noun*, rockets, bombs and bullets used in loading or charging guns and rifles

am·ne·sia [ăm-nē′zhə] *noun*, loss of memory

am·nes·ty [ăm′nĭ-stē] *noun*, a pardon that absolves or discounts past offenses

a·mok [əmə′k]*adverb*, behave uncontrollably and disruptively

a·mong [ə-mŭng′] *preposition*, between, surrounded by

a·mount [ə-mount′] *noun*, 1) a sum, the total number 2) quantity, mass, *verb*, 3) to add up

am·phib·i·an [ăm-fĭb′ē-ən] *noun*, 1) a cold-blooded animal living both on land and in the water 2) an airplane designed to take off on the water or on land

am·phib·i·ous [ăm-fĭb′ē-əs] *adjective*, able to live or operate on land or in water

am·phi·the·a·ter [ăm′fə-thē′ə-tər] *noun*, a theater with seats all around the stage or arena

am·ple [ăm′pəl] *adjective*, abundant, plentiful, more than enough

am·pli·fy [ăm′plə-fī′] *verb*, to increase in size, to make louder

am·pu·tate [ăm′pyōō-tāt′] *verb*, to cut off

am·u·let [ăm′yə-lĭt] *noun*, a good luck charm, a talisman

a·muse [ə-myōōz′] *verb*, to entertain or delight, to make someone smile

a·muse·ment [ə-myōōz′mənt] *noun*, entertainment, a distraction

an [ən; ăn when stressed] *article*, used instead of a in front of a vowel

an·aer·o·bic [ăn′ə-rō′bĭk] *adjective*, able to live only in the absence of free oxygen

a·nal·o·gous [ə-năl′ə-gəs] *adjective*, similar, comparable, resembling

a·nal·o·gy [ə-năl′ə-jē] *noun*, an explanation based on resemblances between different objects or cases

a·nal·y·sis [ə-năl′ĭ-sĭs] *noun*, a thorough examination

an·a·lyze [ăn′ə-līz′] *verb*, to examine critically elements or constituent parts

an·ar·chist [ăn′ər-kĭst] *noun*, a person who rebels against the established order or laws

an·ar·chy [ăn′ər-kē] *noun*, a lawless condition of society, chaos

a·nat·o·my [ə-năt′ə-mē] *noun*, the study of the structure of people, animals or plants

an·ces·tor [ăn′sĕs′tər] *noun*, a person from whom one is descended

an·ces·try [ăn′sĕs′trē] *noun*, family members or ethnic descent

an·chor [ăng′kər] *noun*, 1) a heavy piece of metal on the end of a rope or chain lowered into the water to keep a boat from drifting, *verb*, 2) to secure or fasten firmly, to fix in place

an·cient [ān′shənt] *adjective*, belonging to a remote period of time, very old

and [ənd, ən; ănd when stressed] *conjunction*, a word that adds or joins other words

an-ec-dote [ăn′ĭk-dōt′] *noun*, a short story or fact of an interesting nature

a-ne-mi-a [ə-nē′mē-ə] *noun*, a condition marked by a low red blood cell count

an-e-mom-e-ter [ăn′ə-mŏm′ĭ-tər] *noun*, an instrument to measure the force or speed of wind

an-es-the-sia [ăn′ĭs-thē′zhə] *noun*, the loss of sensation or consciousness, especially when caused by anesthetic

an-es-thet-ic [ăn′ĭs-thĕt′ĭk] *noun*, a substance that causes loss of sensation or consciousness

an-gel [ān′jəl] *noun*, 1) a messenger of God 2) a kind, loveable person

an-ger [ăng′gər] *noun*, feelings of hostility and hurt, a desire to fight or argue

an-gle [ăng′gəl] *noun*, 1) the shape made when two lines or planes intersect 2) a point of view, *verb*, 3) to fish with a hook and line

an-gry [ăng′grē] *adjective*, feeling extreme emotion due to hurt feelings, hostile

an-guish [ăng′gwĭsh] *noun*, extreme pain either of body or mind, acute suffering, deep sadness

an-i-mal [ăn′ə-məl] *noun*, a living creature that is not a plant

an-i-mate [ăn′ə-māt′] *verb*, to inspire with energy, to enliven

an-i-mos-i-ty [ăn′ə-mŏs′ĭ-tē] *noun*, a feeling of hatred leading to opposition, hostility

an-kle [ăng′kəl] *noun*, the joint connecting the foot to the leg

an-nals [ăn′əlz] *noun*, records, history, chronicles, accounts

an-neal [ə-nēl′] *verb*, to subject to high heat, with subsequent cooling, for the purpose of softening thoroughly and making less brittle

an-nex [ə-nĕks′] *noun*, 1) a building added onto a larger building, *verb*, 2) to add on, to attach a smaller thing to something larger

an-nex-a-tion [ăn′ĭk-sā′shən] *noun*, the territory or thing that has been added

an-ni-hi-late [ə-nī′ə-lāt′] *verb*, to reduce to nothing, to destroy entirely, to obliterate

an-ni-ver-sa-ry [ăn′ə-vûr′sə-rē] *noun*, a day celebrated each year to remember something important from the past

an-no-tate [ăn′ō-tāt′] *verb*, to write comments or explanatory notes

an-nounce [ə-nouns′] *verb*, to give notice of the arrival of something, to proclaim, to declare

an-nounce-ment [ə-nouns′mənt] *noun*, 1) act of making something publicly known 2) a printed notice

an-noy [ə-noi′] *verb*, to disturb or irritate, to bother

an-noy-ance [ə-noi′əns] *noun*, anything that irritates

an-nu-al [ăn′yōō-əl] *adjective*, 1) occurring once a year, *noun*, 2) a plant that lives for one year

a-noint [ə-noint'] *verb*, to baptize, to purify, to sprinkle with oil or holy water

a-nom-a-ly [ə-nŏm'ə-lē] *noun*, an irregularity, a deviation from the normal, one of a kind

a-non-y-mous [ə-nŏn'ə-məs] *adjective*, of unknown name

an-o-rex-i-a [ăn'ə-rĕk'sē-ə] *noun*, a lack of appetite and inability or refusal to consume food

an-oth-er [ə-nŭth'ər] *adjective, and pronoun*, 1) an additional, one more 2) someone else

an-swer [ăn'sər] *noun*, 1) a reply to a question, *verb*, 2) to make a response, to reply

ant [ănt] *noun*, a small insect that lives in colonies, known for its social order and industry

an-tag-o-nist [ăn-tăg'ə-nĭst] *noun*, one who opposes with active resistance, an opponent

Ant-arc-ti-ca [ănt-ärk'tĭ-kə] *noun*, one of the seven continents in the world, the area containing the South Pole

an-te-ced-ent [ăn'tĭ-sēd'nt] *adjective*, going before, preceding

an-te-lope [ăn'tl-ōp'] *noun*, a wild animal, similar to a deer, which runs fast and usually has antlers

an-ten-na [ăn-tĕn'ə] *noun, plural*, **antennae**, 1) the sensory organ of an insect or crustacean 2) wire supported in the air for directly transmitting and receiving electromagnetic waves

an-them [ăn'thəm] *noun*, a song or hymn of praise

an-thro-po-log-ist [ăn'thrə-pŏl'ə-jĭst] *noun*, a student of the history and science of mankind

an-thro-po-mor-phic [ăn'thrə-pə-môr'-fĭk] *adjective*, having human form or characteristics

an-ti-bi-ot-ic [ăn'tĭ-bī-ŏt'ĭk] *noun*, a substance such as penicillin, effective in fighting destructive microorganisms and used for treatment of diseases

an-tic-i-pate [ăn-tĭs'ə-pāt'] *verb*, to look forward to

an-ti-dote [ăn'tĭ-dōt'] *noun*, 1) a remedy to counteract poison 2) anything that counteracts evil

an-tip-a-thy [ăn-tĭp'ə-thē] *noun*, a strong dislike, a natural aversion

an-ti-quat-ed [ăn'tĭ-kwā'tĭd] *adjective*, old-fashioned, obsolete

an-tique [ăn-tēk'] *adjective*, 1) old-fashioned, from another time, *noun*, 2) something made long ago and valued for its age

an-ti-sep-tic [ăn'tĭ-sĕp'tĭk] *adjective*, 1) clean, sterile, *noun*, 2) a substance that tends to prevent harmful effects of bacteria growth

an-tith-e-sis [ăn-tĭth'ĭ-sĭs] *noun*, the exact opposite

ant-ler [ănt'lər] *noun*, one of a pair of branched horns on the head of a deer

an-to-nym [ăn'tə-nĭm'] *noun*, a word that has the opposite meaning to another

anx-i-e-ty [ăng-zī′ĭ-tē] *noun*, uneasiness of mind, concern about future events

anx-ious [ăngk′shəs] *adjective*, worried, concerned, nervous

any [ĕn′ē] *adjective*, 1) some, an uncertain number, quantity, volume or degree 2) every 3) one

an-y-bod-y [ĕn′ē-bŏd′ē] *pronoun*, any person

an-y-one [ĕn′ē-wŭn′] *pronoun*, anybody

an-y-thing [ĕn′ē-thĭng′] *noun*, something

an-y-way [ĕn′ē-wā′] *adverb*, 1) no matter what happens, in any case, 2) haphazardly, in any fashion

an-y-where [ĕn′ē-hwâr′] *adverb*, in, at, or to any place

a-part [ə-pärt′] *adverb*, separately in place or time

a-part-ment [ə-pärt′mənt] *noun*, rooms or a part of a building where someone lives

ap-a-thy [ăp′ə-thē] *noun*, lack of interest or concern

ape [āp] *noun*, 1) a large mammal similar to a monkey without a tail, for example, a gorilla, chimpanzee, etc., *verb*, 2) to copy, to imitate

aph-o-rism [ăf′ə-rĭz′əm] *noun*, a statement of truth, an adage

a-poc-a-lyp-tic [ə-pŏk′ə-lĭp′tĭk] *adjective*, prophetic, pertaining to revelations about the end of the world

a-pol-ogize [ə-pŏl′ə-jīz′] *verb*, to say you're sorry for what you have done, to express regret

a-pol-o-gy [ə-pŏl′ə-jē] *noun*, an explanation by way of asking for forgiveness

a-pos-tle [ə-pŏs′əl] *noun*, any person zealously advocating a cause

a-pos-tro-phe [ə-pŏs′trə-fē] *noun*, a mark (′) used to indicate an omission of a letter, i.e. *I'll*, or letters, or to denote the possessive case i.e. *Kara's*

ap-o-thegm [ăp′ə-thĕm′] *noun*, a pithy, compact saying, a proverb

a-poth-e-o-sis [ə-pŏth′ē-ō′sĭs] *noun*, deification, glorification, making into a god

ap-pall [ə-pôl′] *verb*, to fill with horror or dismay, to shock

ap-pa-rat-us [ăp′ə-rā′təs] *noun*, equipment, a collection or set of implements for a specific purpose

ap-par-el [ə-păr′əl] *noun*, clothing, garments

ap-par-ent [ə-păr′ənt] *adjective*, capable of seeming or appearing to be evident, easily understood

ap-par-ent-ly [ə-păr′ənt] *adverb*, clearly, evidently, obviously

ap-pa-ri-tion [ăp′ə-rĭsh′ən] *noun*, a ghost, a phantom

ap-peal [ə-pēl′] *noun*, 1) the proceeding by which a case is brought to a superior court for reexamination or review 2) a request, *verb*, 3) to plead, to ask urgently 4) to seem attractive

ap-pear [ə-pîr′] *verb*, 1) to come into view unexpectedly 2) to seem to be

ap-pear-ance [ə-pîr′əns] *noun,* 1) the act of appearing or becoming visible 2) the way something or someone looks

ap-pease [ə-pēz′] *verb,* to satisfy or often by granting demands

ap-pel-lant [ə-pĕl′ənt] *noun,* one who asks for a judicial decree

ap-pel-la-tion [ăp′ə-lā′shən] *noun,* a name or title

ap-pen-di-ci-tis [ə-pĕn′dĭ-sī′tĭs] *noun,* inflammation of the appendix

ap-pen-dix [ə-pĕn′dĭks] *noun,* 1) information added to a section at the end of a book 2) a small tube-like part growing out from the intestine

ap-pe-tite [ăp′ĭ-tīt′] *noun,* craving, the desire for food

ap-plaud [ə-plôd′] *verb,* to show approval especially by clapping hands together in praise

ap-plause [ə-plôz′] *noun,* praise for someone, usually expressed by clapping hands

ap-ple [ăp′əl] *noun,* the firm-fleshed, round, juicy fruit of an apple tree

ap-pli-ance [ə-plī′əns] *noun,* an apparatus or device, a machine

ap-pli-ca-ble [ăp′lĭ-kə-bəl] *adjective,* relevant, appropriate

ap-plic-ant [ăp′lĭ-kənt] *noun,* one who makes a request, a petitioner

ap-pli-ca-tion [ăp′lĭ-kā′shən] *noun,* 1) work or effort 2) a use 3) a form used to make a request

ap-pli-que [ăp′lĭ-kā′] *noun,* ornamental patterns put on textiles

ap-ply [ə-plī′] *verb,* 1) to seek or ask 2) to put on 3) to pertain to

ap-point [ə-point′] *verb,* to choose for a job

ap-point-ment [ə-point′mənt] *noun,* 1) a meeting, a date, a rendezvous 2) a selection, a nomination

ap-prais-al [ə-prā′zəl] *noun,* value or worth, assessment

ap-praise [ə-prāz′] *verb,* to evaluate something to establish its worth

ap-pre-ci-ate [ə-prē′shē-āt′] *verb,* 1) to recognize the value of something, 2) to increase in value

ap-pre-ci-a-tion [ə-prē′shē-ā′shən] *noun,* grateful recognition

ap-pre-hend [ăp′rĭ-hĕnd′] *verb,* 1) to arrest a criminal 2) to anticipate with anxiety, dread, or, fear, 3) to understand

ap-pre-hen-sion [ăp′rĭ-hĕn′shən] *noun,* 1) the ability to understand 2) fear, anxiety, dread

ap-pren-tice [ə-prĕn′tĭs] *noun,* a novice or learner who works with a master to learn a skill

ap-prise [ə-prīz′] *verb,* to give notice to, to inform

ap-proach [ə-prōch′] *noun,* 1) a way of dealing with something, 2) the way that leads to a place, *verb,* 3) to move toward

ap-proach-able [ə-prō′chə-bəl] *adjective,* friendly, easy to talk to

ap-pro-pri-ate [ə-prō′prē-ĭt] *adjective,* 1) suitable, proper,

appropriation

[ə-prō′prē-āt] *verb*, 2) to allocate, to set aside for a purpose

ap-pro-pri-a-tion [ə-prō′prē-ā′shən] *noun*, a setting apart for a particular purpose

ap-prov-al [ə-prōō′vəl] *noun*, 1) praise, 2) the go-ahead or okay to proceed, permission

ap-prove [ə-prōōv′] *verb*, to say that something is favorable

ap-prox-i-mate [ə-prŏk′sə-mĭt] *adjective*, 1) almost accurate or exact, near, [ə-prŏk′sə-māt] *verb*, 2) to estimate or guess

ap-prox-i-mate-ly [ə-prŏk′sə-mĭt-lē] *adverb*, closely, nearly

ap-pur-te-nance [ə-pûr′tn-əns] *noun*, something connected but not as important, accessory

A-pril [ā′prəl] *noun*, the fourth month of the year, having 30 days

a-pron [ā′prən] *noun*, a cover worn over the front of one's clothing to protect it

ap-ro-pos [ăp′rə-pō′] *adjective*, appropriate, pertinent

apt [ăpt] *adjective*, 1) suited to, fitting, 2) likely or almost certain

ap-ti-tude [ăp′tĭ-tōōd′] *noun*, natural ability, fitness, talent

a-quar-i-um [ə-kwâr′ē-əm] *noun*, a container, usually with glass sides, to keep animals or plants in water

a-quat-ic [ə-kwăt′ĭk] *adjective*, occurring on or in the water

aq-ue-duct [ăk′wĭ-dŭkt′] *noun*, a passage used to bring water from a distant source

aq-ui-fer [ăk′wə-fər] *noun*, an underground geologic formation in which the cracks in rock, sand, soil, or gravel are filled with water

Ar-ab [ăr′ə-b] 1) an inhabitant of Arabia, 2) any of a Semitic people originating in Arabia

Ar-a-bic [ăr′ə-bĭk] *adjective*, 1) relating to the Arab language and culture, *noun*, 2) the Semitic language of the Arabs

ar-a-ble [ăr′ə-bəl] *adjective*, suitable to be used for growing crops

ar-bi-ter [är′bĭ-tər] *noun*, a judge, an umpire or referee, a mediator

ar-bi-trar-y [är′bĭ-trĕr′ē] *adjective*, chosen without any qualifications

ar-bi-tra-tion [är′bĭ-trā′shən] *noun*, the hearing and determination of a matter in dispute by a third party

ar-bor [är′bər] *noun*, a place shaded by trees or shrubs

ar-bo-re-tum [är′bər ′ē-təm] *noun*, a botanical garden devoted to trees

arc [ärk] *noun*, a segment of a circle, a curve in an arch

ar-cade [är′kād] *noun*, a covered walk with stores along one or both sides

arch [ärch] *noun*, a curved part of a structure sometimes supporting weight above it, as in bridges, doorways, etc

ar-chae-ol-o-gist [är′kē-ŏl′ə-jĭst] *noun*, an expert in the study of past civilizations and ancient cultures, mainly through digging up remains

ar-chae-ol-o-gy [är'kē-ŏl'o-jē] *noun*, the study of ancient things made by man from an earlier civilization

ar-cha-ic [är-kā'ĭk] *adjective*, antiquated, ancient, very old

arch-bish-op [ärch-bĭsh'əp] *noun*, the chief bishop in the Christian church

ar-cher-y [är'chə-rē] *noun*, the practice or art of shooting with a bow and arrow

ar-chi-pel-a-go [är'kə-pěl'ə-gō'] *noun*, a group or chain of islands

ar-chi-tect [är'kĭ-těkt'] *noun*, one who draws plans and specifications for buildings

ar-chi-tec-ture [är'kĭ-těk'chər] *noun*, the art and study of building design and structure

ar-chive [är'kīv'] *noun*, a place in which public records and historic documents are kept

arc-tic [ärk'tĭk, är'tĭk] *adjective*, relating to the area around the North Pole

ar-dent [är'dnt] *adjective*, zealous, passionate, very excited

ar-dor [är'dər] *noun*, passion, zeal, enthusiasm, great excitement

ar-du-ous [är'jōō-əs] *adjective*, difficult, attended with great labor or exertion, strenuous

are [är] *verb*, the part of the *verb* **is** used with we, you and they

ar-e-a [âr'ē-ə] *noun*, 1) a location or vicinity, 2) a surface measured by multiplying the width times the length

a-re-na [ə-rē'nə] *noun*, a playing field or a stadium surrounded by coats used for sports or entertainment

aren't [ärnt, är'ənt] the *contraction*, for the two words **are** and **not**

ar-gon [är'gŏn'] *noun*, one of the noble gases, a colorless, odorless, inert gas

ar-gue [är'gyōō] *verb*, to fight by using words, to disagree, to debate, to dispute

ar-gu-ment [är'gyə-mənt] *noun*, a disagreement, a dispute

ar-id [är'ĭd] *adjective*, dry, parched, dusty

a-rise [ə-rīz'] *verb*, to come up, to issue, to spring forth, to get up

a-ris-to-crat [ə-rĭs'tə-krăt'] *noun*, a man or woman of fashion, a member of the nobility

a-rith-me-tic [ə-rĭth'mĭ-tĭk] *noun*, the science of numbers

Ar-i-zo-na [ăr'ĭ-zō'nə] *noun*, one of the 50 United States, located in the Southwest, the capital is Phoenix. The state flower of **Arizona** is the blossom of the saguaro cactus and the motto is "God enriches."

ark [ärk] *noun*, a large flat-bottomed ship

Ar-kan-sas [är'kən-sô'] *noun*, a state in the southern part of the United States, the capital is Little Rock. The **Arkansas** state flower is the apple blossom and the motto is "The people rule."

arm [ärm] *noun*, 1) the part of the body between the shoulder and the hand, *verb*, 2) to provide with weapons, to prepare for combat

ar-ma-ments [är'mə-mənts] *noun, plural,* military forces and weapons

ar-mi-stice [är'mĭ-stĭs] *noun,* a treaty of peace, a truce

ar-mor [är'mər] *noun,* a covering of metal worn by soldiers for protection

ar-mor-y [är'mə-rē] *noun,* a military storehouse

arms [ärmz] *noun, plural,* weapons, such as bombs and guns

ar-my [är'mē] *noun,* a large number of soldiers training for war on land, ground troops

a-ro-ma [ə-rō'mə] *noun,* smell, scent, fragrance

a-round [ə-round'] *adverb,* 1) in a circle, surrounding all sides, 2) nearby 3) approximately, *preposition,* 4) on every side

a-rouse [ə-rouz'] *verb,* 1) to awaken, to animate, to coax 2) to excite, to provoke, to stimulate

ar-raign [ə-rān'] *verb,* to call to account, to bring into court to answer charges, to accuse publicly

ar-range [ə-rānj'] *verb,* to put in proper order or sequence

ar-range-ment [ə-rānj'mənt] *noun,* 1) the act of putting in an orderly condition 2) plan

ar-ray [ə-rā'] *noun,* 1) a display, an exhibition, *verb,* 2) to arrange in a display, to place, to order

ar-rest [ə-rĕst'] *noun,* 1) the act of taking someone into custody, *verb,* 2) to stop the movement or progress of 3) to seize by legal

authority and charge with breaking the law

ar-ri-val [ə-rī'vəl] *noun,* the moment when a place or object is reached

ar-rive [ə-rīv'] *verb,* to reach a destination or a goal

ar-ro-gance [ăr'ə-gəns] *noun,* an overbearing sense of self-importance. excessive pride

ar-ro-gant [ăr'ə-gənt] *adjective,* having a high opinion of oneself

ar-row [ăr'ō] *noun,* 1) a pointed stick that is shot from a bow 2) a mark shaped like an arrow that shows direction

ar-se-nal [är'sə-nəl] *noun,* a collection of weapons, a storehouse of ammunition

ar-son [är'sən] *noun,* the crime of purposely setting property on fire

art [ärt] *noun,* the creation of beautiful or significant things through music, drawing, painting, sculpture, cooking, dancing, etc.

art-ful [ärt'fəl] *adjective,* a clever or skillful person or action, typically in a crafty or cunning way

ar-ter-y [är'tə-rē] *noun,* the thick blood vessels that carry blood from the heart

ar-te-sian well [är-tē'zhən] *noun,* a well that taps ground water that is under pressure and therefore does not require a pump, so called from Artois, France

ar-thri-tis [är-thrī'tĭs] *noun,* inflammation of the joints

ar-ti-cle [är'tĭ-kəl] *noun,* 1) a particular thing 2) a section, provision, item 3) a brief written composition, as in a newspaper or magazine 4) one of the limiting articles, *a*, *an*, or *the*

ar-tic-u-late [är-tĭk′yə-lĭt] *adjective*, 1) effective, distinct, able to express ideas clearly, [är-tĭk′yə-lāt] *verb*, 2) to speak clearly to express an idea

ar-ti-fact [är′tə-făkt′] *noun*, something made by humans from an earlier civilization

ar-ti-fice [är′tə-fĭs] *noun*, skill, scheme, ability, trick

ar-ti-fi-cial [är′tə-fĭsh′əl] *adjective*, 1) made of or contrived by art 2) not natural, not made by nature, made by humans 3) assumed, affected

ar-t-il-ler-y [är-tĭl′ə-rē] *noun*, the mounted guns in an army, the soldiers in charge of such guns

art-ist [är′tĭst] *noun*, a person skilled in the techniques of the fine arts, such as painting, dancing, drama, etc.

as [ăz] conjunction, 1) when, while 2) because, *preposition*, 3) in such a way, like

ascend [ə-sĕnd′] *verb*, to climb, to go upward, to rise

as-cen-sion [ə-sĕn′shən] *noun*, the act of going up, a rising

as-cent [ə-sĕnt′] *noun*, the act of climbing up an incline, a slope

as-cer-tain [ăs′ər-tān′] *verb*, to determine, to establish

as-cet-ic [ə-sĕt′ĭk] *adjective*, self-denying, austere, disciplined

ash [ăsh] *noun*, 1) the gray powder residue left after something has burned 2) a tree of the olive family, with hard wood

a-shamed [ə-shāmd′] *adjective*, upset because you have done something that you think is silly, not good enough or wrong, embarrassed, feeling inadequate

a-shore [ə-shôr′] *adverb*, on to land

A-sia [ā′zhə] *noun*, one of the seven continents in the world, holding 57% of the population

a-side [ə-sīd′] *adverb*, 1) to or toward one side, away, *noun*, 2) departure from the main topic, 3) a whisper

ask [ăsk] *verb*, 1) to pose or speak a question, to inquire 2) to request something

a-skew [ə-skyo͞o′] *adjective*, out of line, crooked

a-sleep [ə-slēp′] *adjective*, sleeping, not awake

as-pect [ăs′pĕkt] *noun*, 1) appearance, look 2) part, or point of view

as-phalt [ăs′fôlt′] *noun*, a tar like material mixed with sand or gravel for highway surfaces or pavement,

as-phyx-i-a-tion [ăs-fĭk′sē-ā′-shən] *noun*, death by lack of oxygen

as-pi-ra-tion [ăs′pə-rā′shən] *noun*, an ambition, a strong desire

as-pire [ə-spīr′] *verb*, to desire, to strive, to hope for

as-pi-rin [ăs′pər-ĭn, -prĭn] *noun*, a medicine used to relieve pain, acetylsalicylic acid

as-sas-si-nate [ə-săs′ə-nāt′] *verb*, to murder a public official or other important person

assault

as-sault [ə-sôlt′] *noun*, 1) an attack, *verb*, 2) to strike, to hit

as-sem-ble [ə-sĕm′bəl] *verb*, to gather or put together

as-sem-bly [ə-sĕm′blē] *noun*, 1) a gathering, for educational, religious, or entertainment programs of students and teachers 2) a legal body such as Congress or a legislature

as-sert [ə-sûrt′] *verb*, to declare, to state forcefully

as-sess [ə-sĕs′] *verb*, to evaluate

as-sess-ment [ə-sĕs′mənt] *noun*, an appraisal, an estimation

as-set [ăs′ĕt′] *noun*, something of value or worth

as-sign [ə-sīn′] *verb*, 1) to give out or allot 2) to delegate a task

as-sign-ment [ə-sīn′mənt] *noun*, homework, an obligation, work given to someone to accomplish

as-sim-i-late [ə-sĭm′ə-lāt′] *verb*, to take in food or knowledge, to make part of oneself

as-sist [ə-sĭst′] *verb*, to aid or help

as-sis-tance [ə-sĭs′təns] *noun*, help or aid given

as-sis-tant [ə-sĭs′tənt] *noun*, a helper, an aide, a subordinate,

as-so-ci-ate *noun*, [ə-sō′shē-ĭt] 1) a colleague or co-worker, [ə-sō′shē-āt′] *verb*, 2) to think of something in relation with something else 3) to keep company, to socialize with someone

as-so-ci-a-tion [ə-sō′sē-ā′shən,] *noun*, a group of people joined together for one purpose

as-sort-ment [ə-sôrt′mənt] *noun*, a variety of things

as-suage [ə-swāj′] *verb*, to lessen, to ease, to comfort

as-sume [ə-soōm′] *verb*, to think something is true without proof

as-sump-tion [ə-sŭmp′shən] *noun*, something taken for granted

as-sur-ance [ə-shoŏr′əns] *noun*, a promise, a pledge

as-sure [ə-shoŏr′] *verb*, to tell someone firmly, to promise

as-ter-isk [ăs′tə-rĭsk′] *noun*, the sign *

as-ter-oid [ăs′tə-roid′] *noun*, small planets, most of which are located between Mars and Jupiter, that revolve around the sun

asth-ma [ăz′mə] *noun*, a respiratory disorder that causes difficulty in breathing accompanied by wheezing

a-stig-ma-tism [ə-stĭg′mə-tĭz′əm] *noun*, an eye defect that prevents proper focus

as-ton-ish [ə-stŏn′ĭsh] *verb*, to give a feeling of surprise, amaze

as-ton-ish-ment [ə-stŏn′ĭsh-mənt] *noun*, complete surprise, amazement

as-tound [ə-stound′] *verb*, to amaze, to shock, to surprise

as-tral [ăs′trəl] *adjective*, relating to the stars

a-stray [ə-strā′] *adverb*, off course, in error

as-trin-gent [ə-strĭn′jənt] *adjective*, capable of drawing tissue together

as-trol-o-gy [ə-strŏl′ə-jē] *noun*, the study of the assumed influence of planets and stars on the course of human affairs

as-tro-naut [ăs′trə-nôt′] *noun*, a person who travels in space

as-tron-o-mer [ə-strŏn′ə-mər] *noun*, a person who studies the stars and the heavens

as-tro-nom-i-cal [ăs′trə-nŏm′ĭ-kəl] *adjective*, enormously large or extensive, huge

as-tron-o-my [ə-strŏn′ə-mē] *noun*, the study of the sun, moon, stars, and the heavens

as-tute [ə-stōōt′] *adjective*, having a clever, shrewd, or cunning mind, perceptive, insightful

a-sy-lum [ə-sī′ləm] *noun*, protection from persecution

at [ăt] *preposition*, 1) showing where 2) showing when 3) showing how much

ate [āt] *verb*, the *past tense* of **eat**

a-the-ism [ā′thē-ĭz′əm] *noun*, the belief that there is no God

ath-lete [ăth′lēt′] *noun*, someone who is good at sports

ath-let-ic [ăth-lĕt′ĭk] *adjective*, strong, vigorous, having to do with sports

at-las [ăt′ləs] *noun*, a book or section of a book that has maps

at-mos-phere [ăt′mə-sfîr′] *noun*, 1) the mass of air surrounding the earth 2) the mood or feeling of a place, a tone conveyed

at-om [ăt′əm] *noun*, the smallest particle of an element

a-tom-ic [ə-tŏm′ĭk] *adjective*, tiny, infinitesimal, having to do with atoms

at-om-iz-er [ăt′ə-mī′zər] *noun*, an instrument for reducing a liquid to a fine spray

a-tri-um [ā′trē-əm] *noun*, **atria** or **atriums**, *plural*, 1) one of the chambers of the heart 2) the central court in a Roman building

a-tro-cious [ə-trō′shəs] *adjective*, very bad, outrageously cruel

a-troc-i-ty [ə-trŏs′ĭ-tē] *noun*, a brutal deed, a cruel act

a-tro-phy [ăt′rə-fē] *verb*, to stop the development of an organ, to wither from lack of use

at-tach [ə-tăch′] *verb*, 1) to connect something with something else 2) to feel affection toward someone 3) to ascribe

at-tach-ment [ə-tăch′mənt] *noun*, 1) an affection, fondness 2) an additional part for a machine

at-tack [ə-tăk′] *noun*, 1) fight, an attempt to harm someone, *verb*, 2) to assail, to try to injure someone, to assault

at-tain [ə-tān′] *verb*, to succeed in getting something done, to reach a goal

at-tempt [ə-tĕmpt′] *noun*, 1) a try, an endeavor, *verb*, 2) to try, to endeavor, to make an effort

at-tend [ə-tĕnd′] *verb*, 1) to be present at 2) to take care of 3) to pay attention to

at-tend-ance [ə-tĕn′dəns] *noun*, the act of showing up or putting in an appearance, presence

attendant

at-tend-ant [ə-tĕn′dənt] *noun*, one who accompanies or attends, as a companion, a servant

at-ten-tion [ə-tĕn′shən] *noun*, application of the mind to something, concentration

at-ten-tive [ə-tĕn′tĭv] *adjective*, careful to notice little things

at-tic [ăt′ĭk] *noun*, the top floor of a house, right under the roof

at-tire [ə-tīr′] *noun*, anything that dresses or adorns, clothing

at-ti-tude [ăt′ĭ-tōōd′] *noun*, a mood or feeling, a way of thinking

at-tor-ney [ə-tûr′nē] *noun*, one legally authorized to act for another, a lawyer

at-tract [ə-trăkt′] *verb*, 1) to draw the attention of someone or something 2) to cause someone or something to come near

at-trac-tion [ə-trăk′shən] *noun*, 1) the power to bring things together 2) a fascination that holds someone's attention

at-trac-tive [ə-trăk′tĭv] *adjective*, pleasing to look at, appealing

at-trib-ute *noun*, [ə-trăb′yōōt] 1) a distinguishing feature that belongs to someone, [ətrĭb′yōōt] *verb*, 2) to explain how one thing is associated with another

at-tri-tion [ə-trĭsh′ən] *noun*, a gradual wearing down

auc-tion [ôk′shən] *noun*, a public sale at which buyers bid on items to be sold

auc-tion-eer [ôk′shə-nîr′] *noun*, one licensed to hold a public sale at which items go to the highest bidder

au-dac-i-ty [ô-dăs′ĭ-tē] *noun*, impertinence, boldness, self-assurance, daring

au-di-ble [ô′də-bəl] *adjective*, capable of being heard

au-di-ence [ô′dē-əns] *noun*, 1) a group gathered to watch or listen to a performance 2) a formal hearing

au-di-o [ô′dē-ō′] *adjective*, relating to sound or sound reproduction

au-dit [ô′dĭt] *noun*, 1) a special examination of accounting records, *verb*, 2) to examine or investigate, to evaluate

au-di-tion [ô-dĭsh′ən] *noun*, a tryout for a performance

au-di-to-ri-um [ô′dĭ-tôr′ē-əm] *noun*, an assembly hall with a stage and seats

au-ger [ô′gər] *noun*, a tool for making holes, a drill

aug-ment [ôg-mĕnt′] *verb*, to make larger, to increase, to add on to

au-gur [ô′gər] *verb*, to foretell, to see into the future, to portend, to be an omen

Au-gust [ô′gəst] *noun*, the eighth month of the year, having 31 days

aunt [ănt, änt] *noun*, the sister of one of your parents or the wife of the brother of one parent

aus-pices [ô′spĭ-sēz′] *noun*, *plural*, 1) patronage, protection 2) omens

aus-pi-cious [ô-spĭsh′əs] *adjective*, fortunate, showing signs that promise success

aus-tere [ô-stîr′] *adjective*, 1) severe or strict in judging,

harsh, rough or bitter acting,
2) very plain, simple, bare, ascetic

Aus-tra-lia [ô-strāl′yə] *noun*, one of
the seven continents in the
world, the only continent that is
also a country containing .5% of
the world's population

au-then-tic [ô-thĕn′tĭk] *adjective*,
genuine, known to be true

au-then-ti-cate [ô-thĕn′tĭ-kāt′]
verb, to prove genuine

au-thor [ô′thər] *noun*, a person
who writes books, articles, etc.

au-thor-i-ta-tive [ə-thôr′ĭ-tā′tĭv]
adjective, reliably accurate

au-thor-i-ty [ə-thôr′ĭ-tē] *noun*, 1) a
person who runs something or
controls it 2) command, prestige,
influence, control 3) an expert

au-thor-ize [ô′thə-rīz′] *verb*, 1) to
empower 2) to make legal 3) to
give permission to act

au-to-bi-og-ra-phy
[ô′tō-bī-ŏg′rə-fē] *noun*, a story
written about the author's life

au-to-crat [ô′tə-krăt′] *noun*, a ruler
with supreme power

au-to-graph [ô′tə-grăf′] *noun*,
a person's signature

au-to-mat-ic [ô′tə-măt′ĭk]
adjective, acting mechanically
without human direction

au-to-mat-i-cal-ly [ô′tə-măt′ĭk-lē]
adverb, 1) by a machine
2) without trying or thinking first

au-tom-a-tion [ô′tə-mā′shən]
noun, a machine that imitates
the actions of humans, a robot

au-to-mo-bile [ô′tə-mō-bēl′] *noun*,
a vehicle on wheels, powered by

an engine to transport people on
roads, a car

au-ton-o-mous [ô-tŏn′ə-məs]
adjective, self-governing, acting
independently from government

au-top-sy [ô′tŏp′sē] *noun*, the
dissection of a dead body to
determine the cause of death

au-tumn [ô′təm] *noun*, the third
season of each year, between
summer and winter, September
22-December 21, known as fall

aux-il-ia-ry [ôg-zĭl′yə-rē] *adjective*,
additional, serving alongside
another, supporting

a-vail-a-ble [ə-vā′lə-bəl] *adjective*,
capable of being used,
accessible

av-a-lanche [ăv′ə-lănch′] *noun*, a
large overwhelming quantity of
snow, rocks, or mud that falls
from a mountain suddenly,
gaining size as it falls

av-a-rice [ăv′ə-rĭs] *noun*, greed for
money or power

a-venge [ə-vĕnj′] *verb*, to punish in
kind, to retaliate, to get even

av-e-nue [ăv′ə-nōō′] *noun*, a wide
road, often with many roads
intersecting at right angles

av-er-age [ăv′ər-ĭj] *adjective*,
1) ordinary, usual, typical, *noun*,
2) the mean value of a set of
numbers, *verb*, 3) to find the
mean

a-ver-sion [ə-vûr′zhən] *noun*, a
dislike, antipathy, opposition

a-vert [ə-vûrt′] *verb*, to avoid, to
prevent or turn away

a-vi-a-tion [ā′vē-ā′shən, ăv′ē-]
noun, air transportation

aviator

a-vi-a-tor [ā'vē-ā'tər] *noun*, an airplane or helicopter pilot

av-id [ăv'ĭd] *adjective*, eager, enthusiastic, excited

av-o-ca-tion [ăv'ō-kā'shən] *noun*, a hobby

a-void [ə-void'] *verb*, to stay away from, to evade, to shun

a-wait [ə-wāt'] *verb*, to expect, to wait, to anticipate

a-wake [ə-wāk'] *adjective*, not sleeping, alert

a-ward [ə-wôrd'] *noun*, 1) a prize or an honor to recognize exceptional service, achievement, etc., *verb*, 2) to present a certificate or plaque or trophy in recognition of an honor

a-ware [ə-wâr'] *adjective*, knowing, conscious, informed

a-way [ə-wā'] *adverb*, 1) off in a different direction 2) from one's possession

awe [ô] *noun*, a solemn wonder

aw-ful [ô'fəl] *adjective*, very bad, appalling, frightful, horrible

awk-ward [ôk'wərd] *adjective*, 1) clumsy, ungraceful 2) embarrassing

awl [ôl] *noun*, a pointed tool used to make holes in wood or leather

awn-ing [ô'nĭng] *noun*, a sunshade, a canvas covering for a porch, patio, deck, etc.

a-wry [ə-rī'] *adjective*, 1) amiss, crooked, wrong, *adverb*, 2) distorted, twisted to one side

ax or axe [ăks] *noun*, a tool with a metal blade fixed onto a handle, used for chopping

ax-i-om [ăk'sē-əm] *noun*, a self-evident truth or principle

ax-is [ăk'sĭs] *noun*, a real or imaginary line around which something rotates

ax-le [ăk'səl] *noun*, the rod on which a wheel revolves

B

ba-by [bā'bē] *noun*, an infant, a very young child or animal

bach-e-lor [băch'ə-lər] *noun*, a man who has never been married

back [băk] *adverb*, 1) to or in a place where something or someone was before 2) toward the back part, away from the front, *noun*, 3) the part of the body opposite the face, extending from the neck to the hips, *verb*, 4) to move in the opposite direction from 5) to give support to

back-ground [băk'ground'] *noun*, 1) the surroundings behind something 2) past experience, culture

back-ward [băk'wərd] *adjective*, 1) having the part designed for the back in the front 2) following tradition and resisting progress, *adverb*, 3) in reverse 4) beginning at the end

ba-con [bā'kən] *noun*, meat from the back and sides of a pig, salted and smoked

bac-te-ri-um [băk-tîr'ē-əm] *noun*, **bacteria**, *plural*, a single-celled living thing that cannot be seen without a microscope, reproducing rapidly and sometimes causing diseases

bad [băd] *adjective*, 1) not good, rotten 2) severe, unpleasant

badge [băj] *noun*, a pin or emblem worn to show authority or accomplishment

baf-fle [băf/əl] *verb*, to mix up, to confuse, to puzzle

bag [băg] *noun*, a container made of paper, cloth, plastic, or leather that has an opening at the top or in the side

bag-gage [băg/ĭj] *noun, no plural*, suitcases, bags, or trunks one takes along on a journey

bail [bāl] *noun*, 1) a bond or pledge backed with money or property, *verb*, 2) to ladle or empty out

bail-iff [bā/lĭf] *noun*, an official who keeps order in the court

bait [bāt] *noun*, 1) food used to lure or entice fish or animals, *verb*, 2) to annoy or taunt

bake [bāk] *verb*, to cook by dry heat, usually in an oven

bak-er [bā/kər] *noun*, someone who makes pastries, cakes and breads for a living

bak-er-y [bā/kə-rē] *noun*, a place where pastries, cakes, and breads are made and sold

bal-ance [băl/əns] *noun*, 1) steadiness 2) an instrument used to weigh something 3) the difference between the debits and credits of an account, *verb*, 4) to keep oneself steady 5) to make equal and stable, to compensate for

bal-co-ny [băl/kə-nē] *noun*, a porch outside of a building and above the first floor

bald [bôld] *adjective*, having no hair

bale [bāl] *noun*, 1) a large amount of materials bundled tightly together, *verb*, 2) to bundle into a package

balk [bôk] *verb*, 1) to hesitate, to refuse to act 2) to hinder

ball [bôl] *noun*, 1) a round object used in games or as a toy 2) a large party for dancing

bal-lad [băl/əd] *noun*, a poem or song that tells a story

bal-last [băl/əst] *noun*, 1) heavy material carried by a ship to balance it 2) crushed stones

bal-let [bă-lā/] *noun*, a play without speech in which the story is told through dance

bal-loon [bə-lōōn/] *noun*, a rubber bag that expands as it is filled with air or gas

bal-lot [băl/ət] *noun*, 1) a printed ticket used in voting to make a choice 2) the whole vote cast

balm [bäm] *noun*, 1) something that relieves pain 2) a soothing ointment

balm-y [bä/mē] *adjective*, mild, refreshing, soft and warm

bam-boo [băm-bōō/] *noun*, a woody grass with hollow stems, abundant in the tropics

ban [băn] *noun*, 1) an order that does not allow something, *verb*, 2) to not allow something or to prevent it from taking place

ba-nal [bə-năl/, bā/nəl] *adjective*, ordinary, commonplace, trite

ba-nan-a [bə-năn′ə] *noun*, a long yellow tropical fruit having a tasty soft pulp

band [bănd] *noun*, 1) a group of musicians who get together to play their instruments, usually brass, percussion, and woodwinds 2) a strip of something 3) a group 4) a piece that wraps around something, *verb*, 5) to join together

band-age [băn′dĭj] *noun*, 1) a piece of cloth or adhesive strip put over a wound, *verb*, 2) to cover a wound with a cloth or adhesive strip

ban-dan-na [băn-dăn′ə] *noun*, a cotton scarf or handkerchief

ban-dit [băn′dĭt] *noun*, a robber

ban-dy [băn′dē] *verb*, to exchange, to pass to and fro

bane [bān] *noun*, the cause of ruin

bane-ful [bān′fəl] *adjective*, ruinous, having poisonous qualities, causing misery

bang [băng] *noun*, 1) a startling loud sound, *verb*, 2) to produce a loud sound by striking one thing against another

ban-ish [băn′ĭsh] *verb*, 1) to send away, to dismiss 2) to exile as a form of punishment

ban-is-ter [băn′ĭ-stər] *noun*, a railing that guards the edges of stairs to prevent someone from falling

ban-jo [băn′jō] *noun*, a stringed musical instrument, like a ukulele or guitar, but with a circular sound box

bank [băngk] *noun*, 1) the land along a body of water, the side of a hill 2) a commercial institution where money is kept and loaned

bank-er [băng′kər] *noun*, one who conducts the business of a bank

bank-rupt [băngk′rŭpt] *adjective*, broke, out of business

ban-ner [băn′ər] *noun*, a flag, a cloth bearing an emblem

ban-quet [băng′kwĭt] *noun*, a feast or ceremonious dinner

ban-ter [băn′tər] *noun*, 1) good-natured ridiculing or teasing 2) to speak or to address in a witty or teasing manner

bap-tism [băp′tĭz′əm] *noun*, the ceremony of initiation into Christianity

bap-tize [băp-tīz′] *verb*, to sprinkle someone with holy water and bestow a name

bar [bär] *noun*, 1) a counter where drinks are sold 2) a long solid object made of wood or metal 3) the legal profession, *verb*, 4) to exclude or block

barb [bärb] *noun*, the sharp projections from a fishhook, arrow, etc.

bar-ber [bär′bər] *noun*, a person who cuts men's hair

bare [bâr] *adjective*, 1) uncovered, naked 2) unadorned, empty

bare-ly [bâr′lē] *adverb*, almost, not, hardly, only, scarcely

bar-gain [bär′gĭn] *noun*, 1) something bought at a lower price than expected 2) an agreement or compact between two parties, *verb*, 3) to haggle for a lower price

barge [härj] *noun*, a large boat with a flat bottom, used to carry things on a river or a canal

bar-i-um [bâr/ē-əm] *noun*, one of the elements of the alkaline earth group

bark [bärk] *noun*, 1) the outer covering of a tree trunk and branches 2) a sound made by a dog or a brusque voice, *verb*, 3) to speak like a dog

bar-ley [bär/lē] *noun*, one of the cereal grains

barn [bärn] *noun*, a farm building where animals and harvested crops are kept

bar-na-cle [bär/nə-kəl] *noun*, a marine crustacean that attaches itself to rocks and boats

ba-rom-e-ter [bə-rŏm/ĭ-tər] *noun*, a device that measures air pressure in the atmosphere

bar-on [băr/ən] *noun*, a nobleman, an aristocrat, a tycoon

ba-roque [bə-rōk/] *adjective*, an ornate style of the 17th and 18th centuries

bar-racks [băr/əks] *noun*, *plural*, buildings for lodging soldiers

bar-rage [bär/ĭj] *noun*, an artillary attack covering a wide area

bar-rel [băr/əl] *noun*, 1) a large container shaped like a cylinder 2) the long metal tube forming part of a gun

bar-ren [băr/ən] *adjective*, 1) bleak, lacking in good things 2) unable to bear children, unable to support growth

bar-ri-cade [băr/ĭ-kād] *noun*, 1) an obstruction or means of defense, a barrier, *verb*, 2) to block, to fortify, to bar

bar-ri-er [băr/ē-ər] *noun*, 1) a stumbling block, a deterrent, an obstacle, something blocking the way 2) a fence or wall to mark the limits of a place

bar-ris-ter [băr/ĭ-stər] *noun*, in England, a counselor at law, a lawyer

bar-ter [bär/tər] *verb*, to trade

base [bās] *adjective*, 1) low, menial, inferior, *noun*, 2) the bottom on which something stands 3) an area designated safe, in baseball one of four sandbags

base-ball [bās/bôl/] *noun*, a game played with a bat and a ball by two teams with nine players on a side, on a field with four bases at the corners of a diamond

base-ment [bās/mənt] *noun*, storage or living space in the foundation of a building

ba-sic [bā/sĭk] *adjective*, 1) forming a starting point, fundamental 2) plain, simple

ba-sin [bā/sĭn] *noun*, 1) a low, bowl-shaped area, a depression in the land 2) a shallow sink

ba-sis [bā/sĭs] *noun*, the starting point or central idea of something, the core

bask [băsk] *verb*, to lay in the sun

bas-ket [băs/kĭt] *noun*, a container woven from reeds or twigs and used to carry things

bas-ket-ball [băs/kĭt-bôl/] *noun*, a game in which two teams of five players each compete to throw a ball through a hoop

bass [bās] *adjective*, 1) the lowest range of the male voice, as in sound, [băs] *noun*, 2) a fresh-water fish

bas-tion [băs′chən] *noun*, a fortress, a defense

bat [băt] *noun*, 1) a piece of wood used to hit a ball in a game 2) a flying mammal, *verb*, 3) to hit a ball with a piece of wood

batch [băch] *noun*, a number of things in a group

bath [băth, bäth] *noun*, 1) a container large enough to hold water to wash a body 2) the act of washing one's body

bathe [bāth] *verb*, to wash with water, usually a part of a body

bath-room [băth′rōōm] *noun*, a room with a toilet and a sink where people wash

ba-ton [bə-tŏn] *noun*, a wand, a night-stick, a rod, a stick used for conducting an orchestra

bat-tal-ion [bə-tăl′yən] *noun*, a large group of army soldiers ready for battle

bat-ter [băt′ər] *noun*, 1) the person holding the bat in baseball 2) a mixture of flour, eggs, and milk, *verb*, 3) to hit repeatedly

bat-ter-y [băt′ə-rē] *noun*, an apparatus for storing chemical energy and converting it to electrical power

bat-tle [băt′l] *noun*, 1) a fight or skirmish between people or different groups, *verb*, 2) to fight

bay [bā] *adjective*, 1) reddish-brown, *noun*, 2) part of a sea that stretches into land 3) a recess in a room 4) a tree or shrub of the laurel family, *verb*, 5) to howl, to bark at

bay-o-net [bā′ə-nĭt] *noun*, a blade on the end of a rifle

ba-zaar [bə-zär′] *noun*, a marketplace where miscellaneous articles are sold

B.C., signifying a time before the birth of Christ

be [bē] *verb*, 1) used to give information about people or things and to join words for people or things to the qualities or position they have 2) the present indicative of verb **be**

Singular	Plural
I **am**	We **are**

*I **am** proud of you.*
*We **are** happy to see you.*

You **are**	You **are**

*You **are** what you eat.*
*You **are** the students in the class.*

He/she/it **is**	They **are**

*He **is** a gentleman, he **is** kind.*
*They **are** all our friends.*

Past Tense

I **was**	We **were**

*I **was** waiting for you.*
*We **were** hoping you could stay.*

You **were**	You **were**

*You **were** a true friend.*
*You **were** good children.*

He/she it **was**	They **were**

*It **was** time to go.*
*They **were** our heroes.*

beach [bēch] *noun*, a shore of sand or pebbles along a lake or ocean

bea-con [bē′kən] *noun*, a lantern, a beam of light, a signal

bead [bēd] *noun*, a small ball of glass or other material, with a small hole for string or wire to pass through

beak [bēk] *noun*, the hard, pointed mouth of a bird

beak-er [bē′kər] *noun*, 1) a deep, open-mouthed, thin, glass vessel with a lip 2) a tall wide-mouthed cup

beam [bēm] *noun*, 1) a large piece of timber used to brace or support a ceiling 2) a ray, a shaft of light, *verb*, 3) to smile happily 4) to send or transmit, to shine

bean [bēn] *noun*, the seed of any bean plant, often used for food

bear [bâr] *adjective*, 1) referring to unfavorable market conditions. *noun*, 2) a large, furry mammal with four feet, *verb*, 3) to carry 4) to suffer or endure 5) to produce, to bring forth, to yield 6) to exhibit, to show, to relate

beard [bîrd] *noun*, hair on the face below the mouth

beast [bēst] *noun*, an animal, especially a savage animal

beat [bēt] *noun*, 1) a stroke or movement that is part of a rhythm, *verb*, 2) to pound, to tap 3) to conquer, to defeat

beau-ti-ful [byōō′tə-fəl] *adjective*, charming and delightful to the senses, very pretty, lovely

beau-ty [byōō′tē] *noun*, qualities pleasing to the eye or ear, charm

bea-ver [bē′vər] *noun*, an amphibious rodent with brown fur that builds dams as homes

be-cause [bĭ-kôz] *conjunction*, since, for the reason that

beck-on [bĕk′ən] *verb*, to signal, call or summon to come over by motioning silently

be-come [bĭ-kŭm′] *verb*, to change or to grow to be, to suit

bed [bĕd] *noun*, 1) a piece of furniture on which someone sleeps 2) the bottom of something 3) a garden plot

bed-lam [bĕd′ləm] *noun*, confusion, noise, uproar

bed-room [bĕd′rōōm] *noun*, the room for sleeping in

bee [bē] *noun*, an insect with a stinger and wings that makes honey and carries pollen from flower to flower

beech [bēch] *noun*, a family of hardwood trees that includes oak and elm

beef [bēf] *noun*, the meat from cattle

bee-hive [bē′hīv′] *noun*, a house made for bees to live in

been [bĭn] the *past tense* of the *verb* **to be**

beer [bîr] *noun*, an alcoholic beverage made of grain and hops

beet [bēt] *noun*, a purplish root vegetable, used for dye and eaten like a turnip

bee-tle [bēt′l] *noun*, an insect whose outside wings make a hard, protective cover for its body

be-fore [bĭ-fôr] *adverb*, 1) happening in advance of, earlier than, *preposition*, 2) in front of, ahead of

be-fore-hand [bĭ-fôr′hănd] *adverb*, ahead of, in advance

beg [bĕg] *verb*, to ask as a favor

be-gan [bĭ-găn′] *verb, past tense* of **begin**

beg-gar [bĕg′ər] *noun*, one who asks for favors or money

be-gin [bĭ-gĭn′] *verb*, to start, to commence

be-gin-ning [bĭ-gĭn′ĭng] *noun*, the start of something, the origin

be-guile [bĭ-gīl′] *verb*, to divert or to entertain, to trick, to charm

be-gun [bĭ-gŭn′] *verb, past tense* of **begin**

be-half [bĭ-hăf] *noun*, interest, side

be-have [bĭ-hāv′] *verb*, to act, to conduct yourself

be-hav-ior [bĭ-hāv′yər] *noun*, manner of acting or bearing oneself, conduct

be-he-moth [bĭ-hē′məth] *noun*, a huge creature

be-hind [bĭ-hīnd′] *adverb*, 1) further away from, late, *preposition*, 2) following, at the back of, remaining after

be-hoove [bĭ-ho͞ov′] *verb*, to be fitting or proper, to require

be-ing [bē′ĭng] *noun*, 1) a living thing, *verb*, 2) *present participle of the verb* to **be**

be-la-bor [bĭ-lā′bər] *verb*, to repeat over and over

be-lat-ed [bĭ-lā′tĭd] *adjective*, too late, delayed, tardy

be-lea-guered [bĭ-lē′gərd] *adjective*, in a difficult position, besieged, attacked

bel-fry [bĕl′frē] *noun*, a tower where bells hang above a building

be-lie [bĭ-lī′] *verb*, to contradict, to give a false impression

be-lief [bĭ-lēf′] *noun*, faith, acceptance, conviction

be-lieve [bĭ-lēv′] *verb*, 1) to have faith or confidence 2) to think

be-lit-tle [bĭ-lĭt′l] *verb*, to tease, to make fun of

bell [bĕl] *noun*, a round, hollow object of metal or glass that sounds when it is struck

bel-li-cose [bĕl′ĭ-kōs′] *adjective*, warlike, ready to fight

bel-lig-er-ent [bə-lĭj′ər-ənt] *adjective*, hostile, pugnacious, preparing to fight, aggressive

bel-low [bĕl′ō] *verb*, to make a loud deep sound like a bull

bel-lows [bĕl′ōz] *noun, plural,* a machine that draws air through a valve and expels it through a tube by alternate expansion and contraction, used in an organ or to blow air on a fire

bel-ly [bĕl′ē] *noun*, stomach, gut,

be-long [bĭ-lông] *verb*, 1) to be a part of, to be a member 2) to own or have possession of

be-long-ings [bĭ-lông′ĭngs] *noun, plural*, one's personal possessions

be-lov-ed [bĭ-lŭv′ĭd] *adjective*, cherished, highly valued, adored

be-low [bĭ-lō′] *adverb*, 1) at a lower level, *preposition*, 2) at a lower place or rank

belt [bĕlt] *noun*, 1) a band worn around the waist, often made of cloth or leather 2) a band or strip indicating a region or zone, *verb*, 3) to hit or smack, to clobber 4) to strap, to surround, to attach by wrapping a cord around something

bench [bĕnch] *noun*, 1) a long seat often wooden 2) the table at which someone works 3) a judge's seat in court

bend [bĕnd] *noun*, 1) a curve, *verb*, 2) to shape into a curve or make crooked 3) to stoop

be-neath [bĭ-nēth′] *preposition*, below, under, at a lower level than

ben-e-dic-tion [bĕn′ĭ-dĭk′shən] *noun*, a blessing

ben-e-fac-tor [bĕn′ə-făk′tər] *noun*, a gift-giver, a patron

be-nef-i-cent [bə-nĕf′ĭ-sənt] *adjective*, performing acts of kindness and charity, generous

ben-e-fi-cial [bĕn′ə-fĭsh′əl] *adjective*, useful, profitable

ben-e-fi-ci-ar-y [bĕn′ə-fĭsh′ē-ĕr′ē] *noun*, one who is going to receive something valuable

ben-e-fit [bĕn′ə-fĭt] *noun*, 1) an advantage, 2) a fundraiser *verb*, 3) to be helpful, to aid

be-nev-o-lence [bə-nĕv′ə-ləns] *noun*, goodwill or kindness, charity given, generosity

be-nev-o-lent [bə-nĕv′ə-lənt] *adjective*, generous, kind-hearted

be-nign [bĭ-nīn′] *adjective*, harmless, not cancerous

bent [bĕnt] *past tense* of **bend**

be-quest [bĭ-kwĕst′] *noun*, the act of leaving by a written will, a legacy for the next generation

be-rate [bĭ-rāt′] *verb*, to criticize or scold vigorously

be-reave-ment [bĭ-rēv′-mĕnt] *noun*, the state of being deprived of something, sorrow, mourning

be-reft [bĭ-rĕft′] *adjective*, lacking, deprived of, doing without

ber-ry [bĕ-rē′] *noun*, a small, round fruit from a bush

ber-serk [bər-sûrk] *adjective*, frenzied with rage, crazy

be-seech [bĭ-sēch′] *verb*, to ask or entreat, to implore, to beg

be-side [bĭ-sīd′] *preposition*, next to, at the side of, adjacent

be-sides [bĭ-sīdz′] *adverb*, also, in addition to, as an extra

be-siege [bĭ-sēj′] *verb*, to surround with armed forces, to harass, to encircle, to crowd around

best [bĕst] *adjective*, finest, exceeding all others in quality

be-stow [bĭ-stō′] *verb*, to give something, to confer

bet [bĕt] *noun*, 1) an agreement to risk money on the odds of winning, *verb*, 2) to risk money on a gamble, to wager

be-tray [bĭ-trā′] *verb*, to break a trust, to reveal a secret

bet-ter [bĕt′ər] *adjective*, 1) superior, *adverb*, 2) more, larger, *verb*, 3) to improve

bet-ween [bĭ-twēn′] *adverb*, 1) showing where in relation to things or places on either side 2) showing when in relation to events before and after, preposition, 3) showing how things are joined 4) showing how things are divided

bev-er-age [bĕv'ər-ij] *noun*, a drink, a liquid refreshment

bev-y [bĕv'ē] *noun*, 1) a large group, 2) a group of birds

be-ware [bĭ-wâr']*verb*, to be wary, to be careful, to be on guard of

be-wild-er-ed [bĭ-wĭl'dərd] *adjective*, confused, puzzled, perplexed

be-yond [bē-ŏnd] *preposition*, past, on the other side, at a distance farther away

bi-as [bī'əs] *adjective*, 1) in a slanting manner, obliquely, diagonally, *noun*, 2) inclination, tendency, *verb*, 3) to influence, to show prejudice, to sway

Bi-ble [bī'bəl] *noun*, the holy book of the Christian faith containing Old and New Testaments. The Old Testament is composed of Jewish sacred scripture

bib-li-og-ra-phy [bĭb'lē-ŏg'rə-fē] *noun*, a list of books on any subject usually found at the end of a manuscript

bick-er [bĭk'ər] *verb*, to quarrel about petty things

bi-cy-cle [bī'sĭk'əl] *noun*, a two wheeled vehicle propelled by pedals

bid [bĭd] *noun*, 1) an offer to buy something, *verb*, 2) to offer a price for something 3) to ask, plea 4) to utter a greeting

bi-en-ni-al [bī-ĕn'ē-əl] *adjective*, happening every two years

big [bĭg] *adjective*, large in size, weight, importance, etc.

big-ot [bĭg'ət] *noun*, a person filled with stubborn hatred

big-ot-ry [bĭg'ə-trē] *noun*, prejudice, intolerance

bi-lin-gual [bī-lĭng'gwəl] *adjective*, able to speak two languages

bill [bĭl] *noun*, 1) a piece of paper stating what you owe 2) a plan for a new law 3) the beak of a bird, *verb*, 4) to send a list of charges to someone

bil-liards [bĭl'yərdz] *noun, plural*, a game similar to pool

bil-lion [bĭl'yən] *noun, adjective*, a thousand million, written 1,000,000,000

bil-low [bĭl'ō] *noun*, 1) a wave, a surge of water or smoke, *verb*, 2) to surge, to swell

bin [bĭn] *noun*, a large container with a lid, for flour, grain, etc.

bind [bīnd] *verb*, 1) to tie with rope or string 2) to constrict 3) to put under an obligation

bind-er [bīn'dər] *noun*, that which fastens or binds together, such as a notebook with large rings to hold paper

binge [bĭnj] *noun*, a spree, uncontrolled eating

bin-oc-u-lars [bə-nŏk'yə-lərz] *noun, plural*, a pair of special glasses that make things in the distance look closer

bi-o-de-grad-a-ble [bī'ō-dĭ-grā'də-bəl] *adjective*, capable of being broken down by microorganisms into simple, stable compounds such as carbon dioxide and water

bi-og-ra-phy [bī-ŏg′rə-fē] *noun,* a written history of a person's life

bi-ol-o-gy [bī-ŏl′ə-jē] *noun,* the branch of knowledge that studies all living things

bi-ome [bī-ōm] noun, a naturally occurring community of flora and fauna occupying a major habitat, e.g., forest or tundra

birch [bûrch] *noun,* a hardwood tree known for its thin, peeling bark and yellow leaves in the fall

bird [bûrd] *noun,* any of a class of warm-blooded, two-legged, egg-laying vertebrates with feathers and wings

birth [bûrth] *noun,* the act of being born, the beginning of existence

birth-day [bûrth′dā′] *noun,* the day someone is born

bis-cuit [bĭs′kĭt] *noun,* a small soft bread

bish-op [bĭsh′əp] *noun,* a senior member of the Christian clergy

bi-son [bī′sən, -zən] *noun,* a large mammal native to North America and Europe, including the buffalo

bit [bĭt] *noun,* 1) a very small amount 2) the metal mouthpiece on a bridle used to control a horse 3) the cutting edge of a tool, *verb,* 4) *past tense* of **bite**

bite [bīt] *noun,* 1) a wound made by biting or stinging, *verb,* 2) to seize or cut with teeth

bit-ter [bĭt′ər] *adjective,* 1) having a sharp, sour taste 2) grievous, painful 3) piercingly cold

bi-zarre [bĭ-zär′] *adjective,* very strange or unusual, weird

black [blăk] *adjective,* 1) lacking color or light, the opposite of white, *noun,* 2) a Negro or person of African descent

black-mail [blăk′māl′] *noun,* 1) compliance with another person's terms, hush money, *verb,* 2) to threaten to reveal a secret unless money is paid or favors given

blad-der [blăd′ər] *noun,* a sack attached to the kidneys to hold urine

blade [blād] *noun,* 1) the flat cutting part of anything sharp 2) a long flat leaf of grass, or anything with such a shape

blame [blām] *noun,* 1) responsibility for something bad, *verb,* 2) to say that someone is the cause of something unfortunate

blanch [blănch] *verb,* 1) to bleach, to whiten, to fade 2) to cook briefly in boiling water

bland [blănd] *adjective,* mild, almost tasteless, neutral

blank [blăngk] *adjective,* 1) without writing or other marks 2) without expression

blan-ket [blăng′kĭt] *noun,* a warm cloth cover used on a bed

blas-phe-my [blăs′fə-mē] *noun,* speech or actions that are disrespectful to God or sacred things

blast [blăst] *noun,* 1) a strong gust of wind 2) an explosion, *verb,* 3) to launch into space 4) to use explosions to break something apart 4) to make a loud sound

bla-tant [blāt′nt] *adjective,* loudly offensive, very obvious

blaze

blaze [blāz] *noun*, 1) a strong fire, *verb*, 2) to burn, to burst into flame 3) to shine brightly

blaz-er [blā'zər] *noun*, a light sports jacket of wool or silk

bleach [blēch] *noun*, 1) a substance used to whiten or remove color, *verb*, 2) to make white, to remove color

bleach-ers [blē'chərs] *noun*, *plural*, seats for spectators

bleak [blēk] *adjective*, cold and unpleasant, empty

bleed [blēd] *verb*, 1) to lose blood 2) to become mixed or run (e.g., dyes in wet cloth)

blem-ish [blĕm'ĭsh] *noun*, a flaw, an imperfection, a pimple

blend [blĕnd] *noun*, 1) a thorough mixture, *verb*, 2) to mix together into one 3) to go together

bless [blĕs] *verb*, to make holy, to ask God's favor, to praise

bless-ing [blĕs'ĭng] *noun*, 1) words that thank God for His gifts 2) good fortune

blew [bloo] *verb*, *past tense* of **blow**

blight [blīt] *noun*, 1) a disease on plants that makes the leaves dry up, *verb*, 2) to injure, to damage, to ruin a crop

blind [blīnd] *adjective*, 1) unable to see, without the sense of sight 2) concealed, hard to see 3) oblivious, unaware, ignorant, *noun*, 4) a window covering to keep out light, *verb*, 5) to make unable to see

blink [blĭngk] *noun*, 1) the quick opening and closing of an eyelid, *verb*, 2) to open and shut the eyes quickly

bliss [blĭs] *noun*, complete joy, happiness, or delight

blis-ter [blĭs'tər] *noun*, a sack under the skin filled with water or blood, from a burn or rubbing

bliz-zard [blĭz'ərd] *noun*, a snow storm with strong winds and cold temperatures

block [blŏk] *noun*, 1) a cube, a chunk 2) the area bounded by four city streets 3) something that stands in the way and prevents movement, *verb*, 4) to hinder, clog or jam, to impede, prevent, stop, or obstruct 5) to form, shape, or press

block-ade [blŏ'kād] *noun*, the closure of an area , port, etc.

blond or blonde [blŏnd] *adjective*, a light hair color the shade of straw or wheat

blood [blŭd] *noun*, a red fluid in the veins of people and animals

blood ves-sel [blŭd vĕs'əl] *noun*, any of the tubes in the body that carry blood, veins, arteries, capillaries

bloom [bloom] *noun*, 1) a flower, *verb*, 2) to have a flower

blos-som [blŏs'əm] *noun*, 1) a flower, *verb*, 2) to bloom or open from a bud to come in to a flower

blot [blŏt] *noun*, 1) a spot or stain, *verb*, 2) to absorb a liquid with cloth or a sponge to remove it

blouse [blous] *noun*, a garment similar to a shirt covering the top of a woman's body, from the neck to the waist

blow [blō] *noun,* 1) a sudden strike with a hand or weapon, *verb,* 2) to force air into a current, to expel air from the mouth

blue [bloō] *adjective,* 1) having the color of a cloudless sky, 2) unhappy, depressed, *noun,* 3) one of the three primary colors: red, blue, yellow 3) a feeling of unhappiness, sadness

bluff [blŭf] *noun,* 1) a high, steep bank, *verb,* 2) to try to trick or fool someone 3) to pretend

blun-der [blŭn′dər] *noun,* a stupid mistake, an error

blunt [blŭnt] *adjective,* 1) not sharp 2) frank, candid, abrupt, *verb,* 3) to deaden, insensitize, dull

blur [blûr] *verb,* to make unreadable or indistinct, to obscure

blush [blŭsh] *verb,* to become red in the face from embarrassment

board [bôrd] *noun,* 1) a long flat piece of wood 2) a group of directors who act as a body 3) a piece of cardboard or wood on which a game is played, *verb,* 4) to cover with wood 5) to climb onto a vessel or vehicle

board-er [bôr′dər] *noun,* a paying guest who receives meals

boast [bōst] *verb,* to brag, to praise oneself, to show off

boat [bōt] *noun,* a small ship or vessel that floats on water

bode [bōd] *verb,* to predict, to portend, to foretell

bod-y [bŏd′ē] *noun,* 1) the form of a person or animal or object 2) a group of persons who act as a unit 3) a corpse

bog [bôg] *noun,* a swamp, a marsh

boil [boil] *noun,* 1) a painful sore under the skin, *verb,* 2) to heat to 212 degrees Fahrenheit 3) to be angered, to be enraged

bold [bōld] *adjective,* brave, assertive, forward, fearless

bolt [bōlt] *noun,* 1) a metal screw used with a nut to hold something in place, a metal bar 2) a stroke of lightning, a thunderbolt, *verb,* 3) to lock with a bar across a doorway 4) to run quickly from the scene

bomb [bŏm] *noun,* 1) a device of explosive materials, *verb,* 2) to bombard with explosives

bom-bard [bŏm-bärd] *verb,* to attack repeatedly

bond [bŏnd] *noun,* 1) a mutual feeling of trust that joins people together 2) a written promise to pay money, *verb,* 3) to join together, to unite

bond-age [bŏn′dĭj] *noun,* confinement, servitude

bone [bōn] *noun,* a hard white substance forming the skeleton of an animal

bon-fire [bŏn′fīr′] *noun,* a large controlled fire

bo-nus [bō′nəs] *noun,* a sum paid in addition to a salary

book [boŏk] *noun,* 1) sheets of paper bound together for reading or writing, a long work of literature, etc., in electronic form, *verb,* 2) to make reservations for a future date

book-keep-ing [boŏk′kē′pĭng] *noun,* a systematic record of business transactions

boomerang

boo-mer-ang [boo'mə-răng'] *noun*, an angular shaped object that returns after it is thrown

boor [boor] *noun*, a rude person, a jerk, a brash individual

boost [boost] *noun*, 1) a lift, a helping hand, *verb*, 2) to support, to encourage

boot [boot] *noun*, 1) a shoe that covers above the ankle, *verb*, 2) to kick 3) to load the operating system on a computer

booth [booth] *noun*, an enclosure, a cubicle, a compartment

bor-der [bôr'dər] *noun*, 1) the dividing line between two countries or territories 2) an edge or trim, *verb*, 3) to lie along the edge of a geographic boundary

bore [bôr] *noun*, 1) a tiresome person, a nuisance, *verb*, 2) to drill a hole, to penetrate 3) to make someone feel disinterested

bore-dom [bôr'dəm] *noun*, dullness, lack of interest

boring [bôr'ĭng] *adjective*, not interesting, dull, tedious

born [bôrn] *adjective*, having been given life, existing as a result of birth

bor-ough [bûr'ō] *noun*, a self-governing incorporated town

bor-row [bŏr'ō] *verb*, 1) to use a thing that does not belong to you, then return it 2) to adopt or use as one's own

bos-om [booz'əm] *adjective*, 1) relating to the closeness between friends or family, *noun*, 2) chest area 3) a woman's breast

boss [bôs] *noun*, 1) the person in charge, someone in control, the employer, *verb*, 2) to give orders in a domineering way

bot-a-nist [bŏt'n-ĭst] *noun*, one who studies plants

bot-a-ny [bŏt'n-ē] *noun*, the science of plants

both [bōth] *adjective*, *pronoun*, the two together in conjunction

both-er [bŏth'ər] *noun*, *no plural*, 1) trouble or difficulty, a nuisance, *verb*, 2) to trouble or annoy, to harass or pester

bot-tle [bŏt'l] *noun*, 1) a container with a narrow neck, usually made of glass or plastic, used to hold liquids *verb*, 2) to store in a glass container

bot-tom [bŏt'əm] *noun*, 1) the lowest part or end of something 2) the buttocks, seat

bough [bou] *noun*, a tree branch

bouil-lon [bool'yŏn', -yən] *noun*, a broth, consommé

boul-der [bōl'dər] *noun*, a very large stone or rock

bounce [bouns] *verb*, to spring back from a surface, to jump

bound [bound] *adjective*, 1) constrained, restricted, confined 2) going to, destined for, *noun*, 3) a jump, a leap

bound-a-ry [boun'də-rē] *noun*, a real or imaginary limit, especially between two properties

boun-ti-ful [boun'tə-fəl] *adjective*, generous, plentiful, provided freely, abundant

bow [bō] *noun*, 1) a ribbon worn as a hair ornament 2) a piece of wood bent with a string, used to ohoot arrows 3) a piece of wood with hairs fastened, to create vibrations when pulled across the strings of an instrument, such as a violin, [bou] 4) the front of a boat, *verb*, 5) to bend the body forward to show respect 6) to submit to another, to consent

bowl [bōl] *noun*, a round deep dish

box [bŏks] *noun*, 1) a container like a cube, constructed from wood, cardboard, metal, etc. *verb*, 2) to fight with clenched fists

boy [boi] *noun*, a male child

boy-cott [boi/kŏt'] *noun*, 1) the refusal to purchase the products of an individual, corporation, or nation as a way to bring economic pressure for social or political change, *verb*, 2) to refuse to deal with or trade with, to desert, to abandon

brace [brās] *noun*, 1) a support, a vise, 2) two like items, a pair, *verb*, 3) to fortify

brack-et [brăk/ĭt] *noun*, 1) a shelf supported against a wall 2) one of the signs [ ] in a sentence that encloses additional information

brack-ish [brăk/ĭsh] *adjective*, a mixture of fresh and salt water

brag [brăg] *verb*, to praise oneself, to sound conceited, to boast

braid [brād] *noun*, 1) a rope, twine, *verb*, 2) to weave hair or rope

Braille [brāl] *noun*, a system of writing for people who are blind using raised dots as letters and numbers to be read with the fingertips

brain [brān] *noun*, 1) the mass of nerve tissue in the heads of people and animals, the center of the nervous system 2) the intellect, where we get our thoughts and ideas

brake [brāk] *noun*, 1) a mechanical device used to stop a bicycle, car, train, etc., *verb*, 2) to stop with the help of a mechanical device

branch [brănch] *noun*, 1) a part of a tree that extends from the trunk 2) an office that is located some distance from the headquarters 3) a stream or river that flows into a larger one, *verb*, 4) to move away or divide from the main body into branches

brand [brănd] *noun*, 1) a label indicating the name of a product and the manufacturer, *verb*, 2) to make a permanent mark on an animal to identify it

brass [brăs] *noun*, 1) a yellow metal that is a copper and zinc alloy 2) musical instruments, such as a trumpet, that are made out of metal and that give a loud sound when blown

bra-va-do [brə-vä/dō] *noun*, an air of defiance, fake bravery

brave [brāv] *adjective*, willing to make a personal sacrifice

brav-er-y [brā/və-rē] *noun*, courage, daring, boldness

brawl [brôl] *noun*, 1) a fight, an altercation, a dispute, *verb*, 2) to argue and wrestle or fight

breach [brēch] *noun*, the breaking of a contract, a gap in a fence

bread

bread [brĕd] *noun*, a food made of flour, water, and yeast that is baked

breadth [brĕdth] *noun*, the distance from one side to the other, width

break [brāk] *noun*, 1) an opening made when something is torn or broken, 2) a pause, a rest, a time away from school or work, *verb*, 3) to cause to fall apart 4) to violate, to disobey

break-fast [brĕk'fəst] *noun*, the first meal of the day, eaten in the morning

breast [brĕst] *noun*, 1) one of the two parts on the front of a woman's body that can give milk 2) the top part of the front of the body

breath [brĕth] *noun*, air inhaled and exhaled in respiration

breathe [brēth] *verb*, to inhale air into the lung and then exhale

bred [brĕd] *verb*, *past tense and past participle* of **breed**

breed [brēd] *noun*, 1) a type or group of animals descended from a common ancestor, *verb*, 2) to reproduce, to multiply 3) to train and raise animals

breed-ing [brē'dĭng] *noun*, values a person learns, upbringing

breeze [brēz] *noun*, a gentle wind

brev-i-ty [brĕv'ĭ-tē] *noun*, shortness, ability to say something briefly, succinctly

brew [brōō] *verb*, to make drinks such as tea, coffee, or beer

bribe [brīb] *noun*, 1) money given to buy cooperation, *verb*, 2) to get someone's cooperation by paying them, to pay off

brick [brĭk] *noun*, a block of baked clay used in construction

brid-al [brīd'əl]*adjective*, referring to the bride in a wedding

bride [brīd] *noun*, a woman about to be married, is in the process of being married, or who has just been married

bride-groom [brīd'grōōm] *noun*, a man who is going to be married, is in the process of being married, or has just been married

bridge [brĭj] *noun*, 1) an elevated structure such as a viaduct or an overpass that crosses over water or a highway 2) a card game 3) a link, a connection, *verb*, 4) to join, connect, bring together

bri-dle [brīd'l] *noun*, 1) a leather band on the head of a horse used for control, *verb*, 2) to show anger or resentment

brief [brēf] *adjective*, 1) for a short period of time, *noun*, 2) a summary of a case for the court, *verb*, 3) to inform

bri-er [brī'ər] *noun* prickly vegetation

bri-gade [brĭ-gād'] *noun*, a large group of soldiers

bright [brīt] *adjective*, 1) giving light 2) shining, not dull 3) smart, intelligent 4) cheerful

bril-liant [brĭl'yənt] *adjective*, 1) very bright, glittering, splendid 2) very clever

brim [brĭm] *noun*, 1) the edge of a cup, glass, or bowl 2) the part of the hat that is the edge

46

bring [brĭng]*verb*, to carry something or to lead someone

brink [brĭngk] *noun*, the edge of a steep slope, the verge

brisk [brĭsk] *adjective*, 1) quick and active, energetic 2) curt

bris-tle [brĭs'əl] *noun*, 1) a coarse brush, *verb*, 2) to feel irritated or annoyed, to show indignation

brit-tle [brĭt'l] *adjective*, hard but easily broken or snapped

broach [brōch] *verb*, to bring up, to begin discussion of

broad [brôd] *adjective*, 1) wide, extensive 2) tolerant

broad-cast [brôd'kăst'] *noun*, 1) a program aired on television or radio, *verb*, 2) to convey a message through radio or television or other electronic media

broad-en [brôd'n] *verb*, to expand

bro-chure [brō-shŏŏr'] *noun*, a pamphlet dealing with a subject of passing interest, a leaflet

broc-co-li [brŏk'ə-lē] *noun*, a plant with dense green flowers eaten as a vegetable

broil [broil] *verb*, to cook by exposing to direct, intense heat

broke [brōk] *adjective*, 1) without money, bankrupt, *verb*, 2) *past tense* of **break**

bro-ker [brō'kər] *noun*, an agent who buys and sells for others

bron-chi-tis [brŏn-kī'tĭs] *noun*, an inflammation of the lungs that causes chronic coughing

bronze [brŏnz] *noun*, a hard metal made by mixing copper and tin

brooch [brōch] *noun*, an ornamental dress-clasp, a decorative pin

brood [brōōd] *noun*, 1) a group of animals born together, or the children of a family, *verb*, 2) to think deeply and sadly about something

brook [brŏŏk] *noun*, 1) a small river or stream, *verb*, 2) to allow

broom [brōōm] *noun*, a brush with a long handle

broth [brôth] *noun*, watery soup, bouillon

broth-er [brŭth'ər] *noun*, a boy or man with the same parents as another person

brought [brôt] *verb*, *past tense* of **bring**

brow [brou] *noun*, the part of the face between the eyes and the hair, the forehead

brown [broun] *adjective*, a dark color like coffee or earth

browse [brouz] *verb*, to leaf through, to scan, to pass over

bruise [brōōz] *noun*, 1) a red or blue mark left on damaged skin caused by blood vessels breaking beneath the skin, *verb*, 2) to injure in such a way that the blood vessels beneath the skin are broken

brunch [brŭnch] *noun*, a meal between breakfast and lunch

bru-nette [brōō-nĕt'] *noun*, a woman with brown hair

brush [brŭsh] *noun*, 1) a device with wires or plastic bristles spread from a handle for combing, or cleaning, or

painting, *verb*, 2) to clean,
straighten, or paint with a brush

brusque [brŭsk] *adjective*, rough
and short in manner, blunt,

bru-tal [brōōt′l] *adjective*, fierce,
harsh, destructive

brute [brōōt] *noun*, a cruel person
who acts like a wild animal

bub-ble [bŭb′əl] *noun*, 1) a sphere
containing liquid or gas, *verb*,
2) to boil, to froth

buck [bŭk] *noun*, a male deer,
goat, or rabbit

buck-et [bŭk′ĭt] *noun*, a container,
usually with a curved handle to
carry something, a pail

buck-le [bŭk′əl] *noun*, a device for
uniting two loose ends of a belt
or to fasten shoes, etc.

bu-col-ic [byōō-kŏl′ĭk] *adjective*,
rustic, pastoral, in the country

bud [bŭd] *noun*, a sprout on a stem
that becomes a flower or branch

Bud-dhism [bōō′dĭz′əm] *noun*,
one of the world's major
religions, practiced primarily in
Asia and taught by monks

budge [bŭj] *verb*, to make
something heavy move a little

budg-et [bŭj′ĭt] *noun*, a plan that
indicates how money will be
spent

buf-fa-lo [bŭf′ə-lō′] *noun*, a large,
shaggy, wild ox

buff-er [bŭf′ər] *noun*, 1) a solution
that neutralizes different
substances 2) a person or thing
between two opposing forces
that softens the impact of their
collision, *verb*, 3) to lessen

buf-fet [bə-fā′] *noun*, 1) a counter
or table for refreshments, [bə-fĭt]
verb, 2) to batter, to flap, to hit

buf-foon [bə-fōōn′] *noun*, one who
clowns around

bug [bŭg] *noun*, 1) an insect that
drinks juices from plants or
animals 2) an error in data, *verb*,
3) to eavesdrop electronically

bug-gy [bŭg′ē] *noun*, 1) a hand-
pushed carriage for babies 2) a
one-horse carriage for two
people

bu-gle [byōō′gəl] *noun*, a musical
instrument, a horn used mainly
in the military

build [bĭld] *verb*, 1) to create or
construct 2) to increase

build-ing [bĭl′dĭng] *noun*, a
structure with a foundation, roof,
and walls

built [bĭlt] *verb, past tense* of **build**

bulb [bŭlb] *noun*, 1) the
underground part of a plant
formed by thick leaves, which
separates and becomes a new
plant 2) any object of this shape,
such as a light bulb

bulge [bŭlj] *noun*, 1) a swelling
shape, *verb*, 2) to swell outwards

bulk-head [bŭlk′hĕd′] *noun*, a
partition separating the
compartments of a vessel

bull [bŏŏl] *adjective*, 1) describing
the stock market when prices are
going up and the economy is
strong, *noun*, 2) male animal of
the ox, cow, whale, or other
animals

bull-doz-er [bŏŏl′dō′zər] *noun*, a
heavy machine that moves earth

bul-let [bŏŏl'ĭt] *noun*, a piece of metal fired from a gun

bul-le-tin [bŏŏl'ĭ-tn] *noun*, an announcement made by an organization, a newsletter

bul-lion [bŏŏl'yən] *noun*, a block of metal such as gold or silver

bul-ly [bŏŏl'ē] *noun*, 1) a person who likes to hurt or tease weaker people, *verb*, 2) to intimidate someone, to make someone feel afraid or overpowered

bul-wark [bŏŏl'wərk] *noun*, protection, a defensive wall

bum-ble-bee [bŭm'bəl-bē'] *noun*, a large yellow and black hairy social bee

bump [bŭmp] *noun*, 1) a sudden blow 2) a raised round lump due to swelling 3) an elevated place in the road or on a surface, *verb*, 4) to knock against, to strike

bun [bŭn] *noun*, 1) a small sweet roll or dinner roll 2) a hairstyle in which the hair is lifted off the neck and wrapped into a circle

bunch [bŭnch] *noun*, 1) a cluster of similar things grouped together, *verb*, 2) to gather together in a mass

bun-dle [bŭn'dl] *noun*, 1) a group of things tied together to make a package, *verb*, 2) to make into a bunch by tying things together

bu-oy [bŏŏ'ē] *noun*, an anchored floating device used as a navigation marker

buoy-ant [boi'ənt] *adjective*, 1) having the quality of rising or floating in fluid 2) light-hearted

bur-den [bûr'dn] *noun*, 1) a heavy thought or object that is carried, *verb*, 2) to load

bu-reau [byŏŏr'ō] *noun*, 1) a chest of drawers 2) a satellite office for a news agency

bu-reauc-ra-cy [byŏŏ-rŏk'rə-sē] *noun*, a system of government through agencies to which tasks and authority are delegated

bur-geon [bûr'jən] *verb*, to grow and develop rapidly

bur-glar [bûr'glər] *noun*, one who breaks into other people's property to rob them

bur-i-al [bĕr'ē-əl] *noun*, the act of putting a dead body in the ground, internment

burn [bûrn] *noun*, 1) a wound caused by fire or heat, or friction, *verb*, 2) to be destroyed by fire, heat or acid

burnt [bûrnt] *adjective*, showing damage by fire

burr [bûr] *noun*, a round seed covered with spurs or barbs

bur-ro [bûr'ō] *noun*, a donkey

bur-row [bûr'ō] *noun*, 1) a tunnel or hole dug by an animal as a den, *verb*, 2) to dig or hide in a hole

burst [bûrst] *noun*, 1) a sudden action, *verb*, 2) to break due to force from inside, to combust

bury [bĕr'ē] *verb*, to dig a hole to conceal something underground, to cover, to conceal

bus [bŭs] *noun*, a large vehicle that carries many people to a destination by a road

bush [bŏŏsh] *noun*, a shrub

bush-el [bŏosh'əl] *noun*, dry measure equal to 64 pints or 32 quarts

busi-ness [bĭz'nĭs] *noun*, 1) regular occupation, work, profession 2) something to be transacted 3) affairs involving money

bust [bŭst] *noun*, a sculpture of a person from the chest up

bus-y [bĭz'ē] *adjective*, 1) having a lot to do, *verb*, to work actively

but [bŭt; bət when unstressed] *adverb*, 1) only, merely, *conjunction*, 2) yet, however, *preposition*, 3) except, save 4) other than

butch-er [bŏoch'ər] *noun*, a person who cuts meat for sale

but-ter [bŭt'ər] *noun*, a substance made from churning cream

but-ter-fly [bŭt'ər-flī'] *noun*, an insect with four colorful wings and a slender body

but-ton [bŭt'n] *noun*, 1) a variety of forms or materials used to fasten a dress, pants, shirt, etc. 2) a badge, a form of identification, 3) a knob pressed to operate a device, *verb*, 4) to secure with a button or snap

but-ton-hole [bŭt'n-hōl'] *noun*, the hole in a piece of clothing that a button goes through in order to fasten two sides together

but-tress [bŭt'rĭs] *noun*, a support projecting outwards to strengthen the walls of a building

buy [bī] *verb*, to acquire something by giving an accepted price, to purchase with money

buy-er [bī'ər] *noun*, a customer, one who makes a purchase

by [bī] *adverb*, 1) near, aside, past *preposition*, 2) near, beside 3) through, by way of, via 4) before 5) past

by-pro-duct [bī'prŏd'əkt] *noun*, anything produced in the process of making something else

byte [bīt] *noun*, 1) a small unit of information 2) a fixed number of bits (usually eight)

C

cab [kăb] *noun*, 1) a vehicle for hire, a taxi 2) the part of a truck or train where the driver sits

cab-bage [kăb'ĭj] *noun*, a vegetable with a short stem and thick green or purple overlapping leaves that form a dense head

cab-in [kăb'ĭn] *noun*, 1) a small wooden house 2) a room for living quarters on a ship 3) the passenger area on an airplane

cab-i-net [kăb'ə-nĭt] *noun*, 1) a cupboard with drawers or shelves for keeping items 2) a group of people who advise the head of state

ca-ble [kā'bəl] *noun*, 1) a strong, large diameter wire or rope 2) a bundle of insulated wires that carry electrical current 3) a system delivering television signals by cable

ca-boose [kə-bŏos'] *noun*, the last car used on a freight train, containing facilities for the crew

cache [kăsh] *noun*, 1) a hiding place for food or treasures, *verb*, 2) to hide or store something

cack-le [kăk'əl] *noun*, 1) a loud laugh, *verb*, 2) to laugh loudly to sound like a hen

ca-coph-o-ny [kə-kŏf'ə-nē] *noun*, harsh or dissonant noise, a discordant mixture of sounds

cac-tus [kăk'təs] *noun*, *plural*, **cacti or cactuses,** a prickly, succulent plant with thick stems that grows in hot, dry climates

ca-dav-er [kə-dăv'ər] *noun*, a dead body

ca-det [kə-dĕt'] *noun*, a student at a military school

caf-e-te-ri-a [kăf'ĭ-tîr'ē-ə] *noun*, a place to eat where customers select food from a serving line

caf-feine [kă-fēn] *noun*, a stimulant found especially in coffee, tea, or some sodas

cage [kāj] *noun*, a box-like enclosure with bars in which birds or animals are kept, a pen

cake [kāk] *noun*, 1) a sweet, baked food made of flour, fat, and eggs, *verb*, 2) to harden from a wet substance into a solid crust

ca-lam-i-ty [kə-lăm'ĭ-tē] *noun*, an unfortunate event, a disaster

cal-ci-um [kăl'sē-əm] *noun*, a silver-white, rather soft metal that occurs in bones, shells, etc.

cal-cu-late [kăl'kyə-lāt'] *verb*, to find the answer using arithmetic, to plan using reasoning

cal-cu-la-tion [kăl'kyə-lā'shən] *noun*, the result of numbers added together, subtracted, etc.

cal-cu-la-tor [kăl'kyə-lā'tər] *noun*, a small computer used to perform math problems

cal-cu-lus [kăl'kyə-ləs] *noun*, 1) a branch of mathematics that provides a method for describing change 2) a buildup of materials within the body, such as a gallstone

cal-en-dar [kăl'ən-dər] *noun*, a table of the days and the months of the year

calf [kăf] *noun*, 1) the newborn or young of any large mammal, such as a cow, whale, or elephant 2) part of the leg between the knee and the ankle, the back of the shin

cal-i-ber [kăl'ə-bər] *noun*, 1) the diameter of a cylinder or tube 2) a person's degree of ability

Cal-i-for-nia [kăl'ĭ-fôr'nyə] *noun*, a state on the Pacific coast of the United States, the capital is Sacramento. The state flower of **California** is the golden poppy and the motto is "Eureka!"

cal-lis-then-ics [kăl'ĭs-thĕn'ĭks] *noun*, *plural*, exercise to promote strength and grace

call [kôl] *noun*, 1) the act of reaching someone on the telephone or paying a visit 2) a shout or plea, *verb*, 3) to name 4) to shout 5) to ask someone to come 6) to telephone 7) to visit

cal-lig-ra-phy [kə-lĭg'rə-fē] *noun*, beautiful writing, the art of hand lettering

cal-lous [kăl'əs] *adjective*, 1) lacking feeling, hard-hearted, feeling no pity 2) thick skinned

callus

cal-lus [kăl′əs] noun, a hard thickened spot (of skin)

calm [käm] *adjective*, quiet, not excited

cal-o-rie [kăl′ə-rē] *noun*, a unit used to measure the amount of energy produced

cam-el [kăm′əl] *noun*, a large animal with one or two humps on its back, used for transportation

cam-e-o [kăm′ē-ō′] *noun*, a piece of jewelry with a stone or shell on which figures are carved

cam-er-a [kăm′ər-ə] *noun*, an instrument used to take photographs or film pictures

cam-ou-flage [kăm′ə-fläzh] *noun*, 1) special clothing for people or colors in an animal that help them blend into their surroundings, *verb*, 2) an organism's ability to blend in with the environment

camp [kămp] *noun*, 1) a place with tents or cabins for temporary shelter, *verb*, 2) to live outdoors and sleep in a tent under the stars, etc.

cam-paign [kăm-pān′] *noun*, 1) activities organized to gain or win something, *verb*, 2) to create a connected series of operations to achieve a desired result

cam-pus [kăm′pəs] *noun*, the grounds surrounding a college, school, or organization

can [kăn] *noun*, 1) a metal container, *verb*, 2) able to, to know how to 3) to preserve food in a can

ca-nal [kə-năl′] *noun*, 1) an artificial waterway designed for navigation 2) a duct in the body

ca-nar-y [kə-nâr′ē] *noun*, a songbird, usually yellow

can-cel [kăn′səl] *verb*, to annul, to revoke, to end or stop

can-cel-la-tion [kăn′sə-lā′shən] *noun*, a stop or end to something, withdrawal

can-cer [kăn′sər] *noun*, a serious illness in which abnormal cells multiply rapidly

can-di-date [kăn′dĭ-dāt′] *noun*, one who is being considered or who applies for a certain job

can-dle [kăn′dl] *noun*, a cylinder of wax with a wick embedded in it designed to burn to give off light

can-dor [kăn′dər] *noun*, the quality of being fair, unprejudiced, and honest

cane [kān] *noun*, 1) a hollow stick made from some plants 2) a stick with a curved handle used for support when walking

ca-nine [kā′nīn] *adjective*, relating to dogs

can-is-ter [kăn′ĭ-stər] *noun*, a small box or container, often of metal, for holding tea, coffee, etc.

can-ni-bal [kăn′ə-bəl] *noun*, a person who eats people or an animal who eats one of its own kind

can-non [kăn′ən] *noun*, a mounted gun or piece of artillery

can-not [kăn′ŏt] unable to

ca-noe [kə-nōō′] *noun*, a narrow light boat tapered at the ends, moved with paddles

can-o-py [kăn′ə-pē] *noun*, a covering from the sun, an awning or umbrella

cant [kănt] *noun*, 1) empty talk, deceit, 2) jargon, slang, *verb*, 3) to speak insincerely

can't [kănt] the *contraction* of the words **can** and **not**

can-ta-loupe [kăn′tl-ōp′] *noun*, a variety of muskmelon with an orange-red color fruit

can-tan-ker-ous [kăn-tăng′kər-əs] *adjective*, irritable, cross

can-vas [kăn′vəs] *noun*, 1) a strong, coarse, water-repellant cloth used to make tents, sails, etc. 2) a piece of heavy cloth, stretched over a frame, on which pictures are painted

can-vass [kăn′vəs] *verb*, 1) to examine thoroughly, scrutinize 2) to solicit votes or opinions

can-yon [kăn′yən] *noun*, a valley with high, steep sides between hills or mountains

cap [kăp] *noun*, 1) a soft hat 2) the covering for a bottle or tube

ca-pa-ble [kā′pə-bəl] *adjective*, able to do things well, having ability, competent or efficient

ca-pac-i-ty [kə-păs′ĭ-tē] *noun*, 1) the maximum amount of liquid a container can hold, 2) the ability or aptitude for a specified task

cape [kāp] *noun*, 1) a piece of land that goes out into the sea 2) a coat without sleeves that covers shoulders, arms, and back

cap-il-lar-y [kăp′ə-lĕr′ē] *noun*, one of the tiniest blood vessels

cap-i-tal [kăp′ĭ-tl] *adjective*, 1) first, chief, 2 punishable by death, *noun*, 3) resources, means or money 4) the city where the rules for a state or county or country are made 5) a letter that begins a sentence or a proper noun

cap-i-tal-ism [kăp′ĭ-tl-ĭz′əm] *noun*, an economic system based on profit and private ownership

cap-i-tal-ize [kăp′ĭ-tl-īz′] *verb*, 1) to finance or invest in for profit 2) to use a capital letter

Cap-i-tol [kăp′ĭ-tl] *noun*, 1) the building in which the Congress of the United States meets to create laws, **capitol** 2) the building in which a state legislature meets to create laws

ca-price [kə-prēs′] *noun*, a silly thought, a notion, whimsy

cap-size [kăp′sīz′] *verb*, to upset or overturn as of a boat

cap-sule [kăp′səl] *noun*, 1) a container with a matching top and bottom that holds medicine 2) a small spacecraft

cap-tain [kăp′tən] *noun*, the leader of a team or a company of soldiers, or the commander of a ship or aircraft

cap-tion [kăp′shən] *noun*, 1) a short title heading 2) text under an illustration

cap-tive [kăp′tĭv] *adjective*, 1) unable to escape, *noun*, 2) a prisoner

cap-ture [kăp′chər] *verb*, 1) to seize and hold as a prisoner 2) to take hold of something

car [kär] *noun*, an automobile, a form of transportation with four wheels and an engine, usually fueled by gasoline

ca-rafe [kə-răf′] *noun*, a glass bottle, a decanter

car-at [kăr′ət] *noun*, a unit of weight for precious stones

car-a-van [kăr′ə-văn′] *noun*, 1) a group of people traveling together with vehicles or animals 2) a mobile home

car-bo-hy-drate [kär′bō-hī′drāt′] *noun*, a class of foods, that supply energy to the body

car-bon [kär′bən] *noun*, a nonmetallic element, symbolized as C, the required common substance in organic chemistry

car-bo-nate [kär′bə-nāt′] *noun*, a salt of carbonic acid

car-bon di-ox-ide [kär′bən dī-ŏk′sīd] *noun*, a colorless, odorless gas that is absorbed by plants

car-bon mon-ox-ide [kär′bən mə-nŏk′sīd′] *noun*, a colorless, odorless poisonous gas

car-cass [kär′kəs] *noun*, the dead body of an animal or bird

car-cin-o-gen [kär-sĭn′ə-jən] *noun*, a substance that causes cancer

card [kärd] *noun*, a small, flat piece of thick, stiff paper (e.g., a playing card, a postcard, a greeting or business card)

car-di-ac [kär′dē-ăk′] *adjective*, pertaining to the heart, stimulating the heart action

car-di-gan [kär′dĭ-gən] *noun*, a sweater that buttons or opens down the front

car-di-nal [kär′dn-əl] *adjective*, 1) chief, most important, *noun*, 2) an important leader of the Roman Catholic church, appointed by the pope as one of his advisors 3) a bright red bird common in North America

care [kâr] *noun*, 1) thought or interest 2) worry, anxiety, *verb*, 3) to show concern for others 4) to look after someone and tend to his or her needs 5) to show affection or love

ca-reen [kə-rēn′] *verb*, to sway or lean over to one side

ca-reer [kə-rîr′] *noun*, a profession, a chosen pursuit

care-ful [kâr′fəl] *adjective*, cautious, watchful

care-ful-ly [kâr′fə-lē] *adverb*, cautiously, with much care

care-less [kâr′lĭs] *adjective*, neglectful, reckless

ca-ress [kə-rĕs′] *noun*, 1) a tender or loving touch, *verb*, 2) to stroke with affection, to touch in a loving way

car-et [kăr′ĭt] *noun*, a mark used by writers to indicate something – like a word – to be inserted

car-go [kär′gō] *noun*, the goods or freight carried by a ship, train, plane, or any vehicle

car-i-bou [kăr′ə-boo′] *noun*, a type of reindeer

car-i-ca-ture [kăr′ĭ-kə-choŏr′] *noun*, a representation of a person or thing in which the peculiarities are exaggerated to produce a ridiculous effect

car-nage [kär′nĭj] *noun*, the killing of many people, a massacre

car-na-tion [kär-nā′shən] *noun*, a garden flower of the pink family

car-ni-val [kär′nə-vəl] *noun*, a festival with parades and dancing, a fair

car-ni-vore [kär-nĭv′ər] *adjective*, a meat-eating mammal

car-ol [kăr′əl] *noun*, a song of joy

ca-rouse [kə-rouz′] *verb*, to drink and be merry, especially with a group

carp [kärp] *noun*, 1) a kind of fish, *verb*, 2) to find fault, to criticize

car-pen-ter [kär′pən-tər] *noun*, a builder or repairer of wooden structures or objects

car-pen-try [kär′pən-trē] *noun*, the art of making things out of wood

car-pet [kär′pĭt] *noun*, a woven or felted floor covering of wool, cotton, or a synthetic, a rug

car-riage [kăr′ĭj] *noun*, 1) a wheeled vehicle 2) a manner of bearing or posture

car-ri-er [kăr′ē-ər] *noun*, 1) a messenger 2) one engaged in the business of carrying goods for others for hire

car-rot [kăr′ət] *noun*, a plant with an edible root of orange color used as a vegetable

car-ry [kăr′ē] *verb*, 1) to transport something, to convey, to move, to haul 2) to support a weight

cart [kärt] *noun*, a small wagon used to carry goods

car-ti-lage [kär′tl-ĭj] *noun*, elastic animal tissue attached to bones near the joints

car-tog-ra-pher [kär-tŏg′rə-fûr] *noun*, a maker of maps or charts

car-ton [kär′tn] *noun*, a box or container made of cardboard

car-toon [kär-tōōn′] *noun*, a comical drawing of a person, event, or place

car-tridge [kär′trĭj] *noun*, a case holding something that is dispensed mechanically

cart-wheel [kärt′hwēl′] *noun*, a sideways flip that is done by springing the body onto one hand and then the other, followed by the feet

carve [kärv] *verb*, 1) to reshape in an artistic or decorative manner by cutting 2) to cut meat for serving

cas-cade [kă-skăd′] *noun*, a small waterfall, a profusion

case [kās] *noun*, 1) a container to hold things 2) a condition, an example of an illness 3) a question of law decided in court 4) something that has happened, an instance

cash [kăsh] *noun*, 1) money consisting of dollars or loose change, *verb*, 2) to receive bills and coins in exchange for a check

cash-ier [kă-shîr′] *noun*, one who has charge of payments, etc., as at a store

cas-ket [kăs′kĭt] *noun*, a coffin

cas-se-role [kăs′ə-rōl′] *noun*, a dish consisting of several different foods combined together

cas-sette [kə-sĕt′, kă-] *noun*, a magnetic tape used for electronic recording enclosed in a plastic case that can fit directly into a recorder

cast [kăst] *noun*, 1) the performers in a play 2) a plaster dressing used to hold surgery in place, *verb*, 3) to direct a glance at someone or something 4) to assign a role in a play 5) to form a shape from clay on a potter's wheel 6) to throw or toss 7) the act of throwing a fishing line 8) to overshadow 9) to register a vote 10) to discard or shed

caste [kăst] *noun*, 1) one of the hereditary classes in Hindu society 2) any exclusive social class

cas-tle [kăs′əl] *noun*, 1) a fortress or palace usually the residence of nobility 2) a chess piece also known as the rook

cas-u-al [kăzh′o͞o-əl] *adjective*, 1) not planned or prearranged 2) informal 3) careless

cas-u-al-ty [kăzh′o͞o-əl-tē] *noun*, one injured or killed, as in a battle

cat [kăt] *noun*, a furry animal kept in the house as a pet or to catch mice

cat-a-combs [kăt′ə-kōmz′] *noun*, *plural*, a burial ground of underground rooms

cat-a-log [kăt′l-ôg′] *noun*, 1) a list of names, titles, or articles arranged in order, *verb*, 2) to list

names and objects with a description of each one

cat-a-lyst [kăt′l-ĭst] *noun*, an agitator or force of change

cat-a-pult [kăt′ə-pŭlt′] *noun*, 1) a device that uses tension to throw objects, a weapon, *verb*, 2) to hurl or make an object go as far as possible

cat-a-ract [kăt′ə-răkt′] *noun*, 1) a great waterfall 2) an eye abnormality, cloudiness on the lens of the eye resulting in blurry vision

ca-tas-tro-phe [kə-tăs′trə-fē] *noun*, a sudden calamity, a disaster

catch [kăch, kĕch] *noun*, 1) something that has been captured 2) the metal clasp that connects a door to a door frame, *verb*, 3) to get hold of something and not let go, to grasp 4) to get someone's attention 5) to trap

cat-e-chism [kăt′ĭ-kĭz′əm] *noun*, a set of questions and answers, especially for teaching about religion

cat-e-go-ry [kăt′ĭ-gôr′ē] *noun*, division or class to which something belongs

ca-ter [kā′tər] *verb*, to provide food or personal attention, to serve up

ca-ter-pil-lar [kăt′ər-pĭl′ər] *noun*, the larva of a butterfly

ca-thar-sis [kə-thär′sĭs] *noun*, 1) purging or cleansing of any part of the body 2) a release of tension or strong feelings

ca-the-dral [kə-thē′drəl] *noun*, a very large church, the main church of a diocese

Cath-o-lic [kăth/ə-lĭk] *noun*, a member of the church that recognizes the pope as its leader

cat-tle [kăt/l] *noun*, livestock such as cows, bulls, or steer kept for meat, milk, or skins

cau-cus [kô/kəs] *noun*, a group of politicians who gather to decide a policy or select a candidate

caught [kôt] *verb*, *past tense* of **catch**

caulk [kôk] *verb*, to make water-tight, to seal cracks

cause [kôz] *noun*, 1) the reason, the thing that made something happen 2) something you believe in strongly enough to take action, *verb*, 3) to bring about, to make something happen

caus-tic [kô/stĭk] *adjective*, 1) burning 2) sarcastically biting

cau-tion [kô/shən] *noun*, care and watchfulness, a warning

cau-tious [kô/shəs] *adjective*, wary, prudent, careful, watchful

cave [kāv] *noun*, a hollow place under the ground or in the side of a mountain or rock, sheltered from the elements

ca-ve-at [kā/vē-ăt/] *noun*, an indication of limitations

cav-ern [kăv/ərn] *noun*, a hollow place in a rock, a cave

cav-i-ar [kăv/ē-är/] *noun*, the prepared and salted eggs of the sturgeon or other large fish

cav-i-ty [kăv/ĭ-tē] *noun*, 1) a hollow place or a hole 2) a hole in the tooth caused by decay

cease [sēs] *verb*, to end, to stop

cease-less [sēs/lĭo] *adjective*, without end or interruption

ce-dar [sē/dər] *noun*, a large evergreen tree with reddish, fragrant wood

ceil-ing [sē/lĭng] *noun*, 1) the covering of a room 2) the top of a space 3) upper limit

cel-e-brate [sĕl/ə-brāt/] *verb*, to do certain things because of a special occasion, to rejoice

cel-e-bra-tion [sĕl/ə-brā/-shən] *noun*, a festive occasion

ce-leb-ri-ty [sə-lĕb/rĭ-tē] *noun*, fame, renown, a famous person

ce-ler-i-ty [sə-lĕr/ĭ-tē] *noun*, speed,

cel-er-y [sĕl/ə-rē] *noun*, a plant of the parsley family, whose leaf - stalks are eaten raw or cooked

ce-les-tial [sə-lĕs/chəl] *adjective*, in the stars, heavenly

cel-i-ba-cy [sĕl/ə-bə-sē] *noun*, the state of being unmarried

cell [sĕl] *noun*, 1) a small room where a prisoner is kept or where a nun or monk lives 2) a small, microscopic piece of a living organism

cel-lar [sĕl/ər] *noun*, a room under a house, partly or completely underground, a basement

cel-lu-lar [sĕl/yə-lər] *adjective*, 1) formed of cells 2) relating to a mobile telephone system

Cel-si-us [sĕl/sē-əs] *noun*, a scale on which the freezing point is 0

ce-ment [sĭ-mĕnt/] *noun*, a substance that consists of burned lime and clay, which is mixed with water and sand to make concrete

cem-e-ter-y [sĕm′ĭ-tĕr′ē] *noun*, a burial place, a graveyard

cen-sor [sĕn′sər] *noun*, 1) one who filters inappropriate material from books, movies, etc., before they are published or released, *verb*, 2) to filter out information considered unsuitable

cen-sus [sĕn′səs] *noun*, an official count of a population

cent [sĕnt] *noun*, a metal coin equal to one penny or 1/100 of a dollar

cen-ten-ni-al [sĕn-tĕn′ē-əl] *adjective,* of or pertaining to a hundredth anniversary

cen-ter [sĕn′tər] *noun*, 1) the middle, a point equidistant from all sides 2) a place where people gather 3) a hub of activity

cen-ti-grade [sĕn′tĭ-grād′] *noun*, the temperature scale in which 0 degrees is the freezing point and 100 degrees is the boiling point of water

cen-ti-me-ter [sĕn′tə-mē′tər] *noun*, a measure of length somewhat less than ½ an inch, a standard unit in the metric system

cen-tral [sĕn′trəl] *adjective*, located in the middle

cen-trif-u-gal [sĕn-trĭf′yə-gəl] *adjective*, relating to forces caused by rotation directed outward from the center

cen-trip-e-tal [sĕn-trĭp′ĭ-tl] *adjective*, directed toward the center

cen-tu-ry [sĕn′chə-rē] *noun*, a period of one hundred years

ce-re-al [sîr′ē-əl] *noun*, any edible grain, including oats, rye, rice

cer-e-bel-lum [sĕr′ə-bĕl′əm] *noun*, the part of the brain related to muscular movements and coordination

ce-re-bral [sĕr′ə-brəl] *adjective*, appealing to the intellect and not the emotions

cer-e-mo-ni-al [sĕr′ə-mō′nē-əl] *adjective*, following a tradition or certain rituals, formal

cer-e-mo-ny [sĕr′ə-mō′nē] *noun*, a special occasion that honors traditions or rituals

cer-tain [sûr′tn] *adjective*, 1) sure 2) unquestionable 3) not named, but thought to be known

cer-tain-ty [sûr′tn-tē] *noun*, a state of being sure of something

cer-tif-i-cate [sər-tĭf′ĭ-kĭt] *noun*, a document verifying qualification or ability or fact

cer-ti-fy [sûr′tə-fī′] *verb*, to authorize the validity of something, to guarantee

chafe [chāf] *verb*, 1) to rub together leaving a sore 2) to annoy

chaff [chăf] *noun*, 1) a worthless or trivial thing 2) the outer coating of wheat

cha-grin [shə-grĭn′] *noun*, a feeling of embarrassment because one has failed, deep disappointment

chain [chān] *noun*, 1) links or rings joined together, *verb*, 2) to hold with a chain, to restrain

chair [châr] *noun*, furniture with four legs and a back used to seat someone

chal-ice [chăl′ĭs] *noun*, a goblet

chalk [chôk] *noun*, a soft white limestone substance used to write on a blackboard

chal-lenge [chăl'ənj] *noun*, 1) an offer to test ability or skill 2) a formal objection, *verb*, 3) to call or invite to a contest of any kind

cham-ber [chām'bər] *noun*, 1) a room 2) a space surrouded by walls 3) a compartment in a firearm that holds the ammunition

cham-pi-on [chăm'pē-ən] *noun*, the winner of a competition

cham-pi-on-ship [chăm'pē-ən-shĭp'] *noun*, a competition among people or teams to decide who is best

chance [chăns] *noun*, 1) luck, fate 2) possibility or probability 3) risk 4) a turn to do something, an opportunity 5) a coincidence

chan-de-lier [shăn'də-lîr'] *noun*, a branched lighting fixture that hangs from the ceiling in a frame

change [chānj] *noun*, 1) a transformation, the process of becoming different 2) loose coins, *verb*, 3) to make or become different 4) to transform

change-a-ble [chān'jə-bəl] *adjective*, variable, adaptable

chan-nel [chăn'əl] *noun*, 1) a narrow stream of flowing water that connects two large bodies of water, *verb*, 2) to make something, such as energy or water, flow in a certain direction

chant [chănt] *noun*, 1) words repeated in rhythm, *verb*, 2) to speak in a singing way

cha-os [kā'ŏs'] *noun*, disorder, confusion, upheaval

chap-el [chăp'əl] *noun*, a small room within a larger building set aside for religious purposes

chap-er-one [shăp'ə-rōn'] (also **chaperon**) *noun*, an older person who accompanies as a protector

chap-lain [chăp'lĭn] *noun*, a clergyman, minister priest or rabbi serving in a hospital, the armed forces, etc.

chap-ter [chăp'tər] *noun*, a division of a book

char [chär] *verb*, to burn, to scorch

char-ac-ter [kăr'ək-tər] *noun*, 1) the moral makeup of a person 2) a person in a book or movie or play 3) a symbol, sign, or written letter used in a language

char-ac-ter-is-tic [kăr'ək-tə-rĭs'tĭk] *noun*, a trait, an attribute

char-ac-ter-ize [kăr'ək-tə-rīz'] *verb*, to describe, to indicate details or traits of someone or something

char-ac-ter-i-za-tion [kăr'ək-tə-rīz'ā'-shən] *noun*, a description of someone or something

char-coal [chär'kōl'] *noun*, a black porous material made by partially burning wood

charge [chärj] *noun*, 1) an accusation 2) care or instruction given 3) the cost, expense, *verb*, 4) to request money 5) to accuse someone of doing something wrong 6) to rush or attack 7) to fill with power 8) to control

char-i-ot [chăr'ē-ət] *noun*, a horse-drawn cart

charisma

cha-ris-ma [kə-rĭz′mə] *noun*, attraction, charm, and allure, having a strong effect on others

char-i-ta-ble [chăr′ĭ-tə-bəl] *adjective*, 1) giving freely and generously 2) lenient, kind

char-i-ty [chăr′ĭ-tē] *noun*, 1) goodness, generosity, and kindness 2) an agency that provides a service to those in need, especially the poor

charm [chärm] *noun*, 1) a pleasant, courteous manner 2) a thing like a talisman or a group of words spoken to cause good luck, *verb*, 3) to please someone

charm-ing [chär′mĭng] *adjective*, pleasing, beautiful, enchanting

chart [chärt] *noun*, 1) a piece of paper or spreadsheet with information on it indicating, patterns, information, or changes, *verb*, 2) to plan a route on a map of the ocean or other large area

char-ter [chär′tər] *noun*, 1) a document establishing the creation of an entity 2) a reservation of a vehicle, ship, etc., *verb*, 3) to hire a ship, bus, plane, etc.

chase [chās] *noun*, 1) the act of running after someone, *verb*, 2) to follow someone while trying to capture them, to pursue

chasm [kăz′əm] *noun*, a deep hole

chas-sis [shăs′ē] *noun*, the under part of a car, consisting of the frame with the wheels and machinery

chaste [chāst] *adjective*, 1) pure, celibate 2) simple in style

chat [chăt] *noun*, 1) a pleasant conversation, *verb*, 2) to make conversation or small talk

chat-tel [chăt′təl] *noun*, a moveable article of personal property

chauf-feur [shō′fər] *noun*, a person employed as a driver of a car

chau-vin-ist [shō′və-nĭst] *noun*, a belief in the superiority of your own race, sex, etc.

cheap [chēp] *adjective*, low in price, inexpensive, poorly made

cheat [chēt] *verb*, to do something that is not honest, to deceive

check [chĕk] *noun*, 1) an order for money, *verb*, 2) to make sure everything is in order

check-ers [chĕk′ərz] *noun*, *plural*, a board game played by two people, each with twelve pieces

cheek [chēk] *noun*, 1) the fleshy skin covering the bone beneath the eye socket on both sides of the face 2) impudent speech

cheer [chîr] *noun*, 1) a shout of support 2) gladness, a joyful state of mind, *verb*, 3) to make happy 4) to encourage with shouts

cheese [chēz] *noun*, the consolidated curd of milk, used as food

chee-tah [chēNt′ə] *noun*, a swift, animal of Africa and Asia, like a leopard, with a small head, long legs, and black-spotted, tan coat

chef [shĕf] *noun*, a head cook

chem-i-cal [kĕm′ĭ-kəl] *noun*, a substance or mixture of substances used in or produced by changes in atoms or molecules

chem-ist [kĕm/ĭst] *noun*, a person who studies matter such as gases, metal, and liquids to see what they do and what they are made of

chem-is-try [kĕm/ĭ-strē] *noun*, the study of the composition, properties, and reactions of matter, particularly at the level of atoms and molecules

cher-ish [chĕr/ĭsh] *verb*, to love dearly, to adore

cher-ry [chĕr/ē] *noun*, an edible, fleshy, red fruit containing a pit

chess [chĕs] *noun*, a game of skill played on a checkered board by two players each with 16 pieces

chest [chĕst] *noun*, 1) the front of the body between the shoulders and the waist 2) a large box made of metal, wood, etc.

chew [chōo] *verb*, to grind food between the teeth

chic [shēk] *noun*, great artistic cleverness or skill, style

chick-en [chĭk/ən] *noun*, fowl kept for eggs or meat

chide [chīd] *verb*, to scold

chief [chēf] *adjective*, 1) highest in office or rank, *noun*, 2) the leader of a group or organization

chif-fon [shĭ-fŏn/] *noun*, 1) a soft gauzy silk material used for dresses 2) a light airy dessert made with egg whites

child [chīld] *noun*, *plural* **children**, a young person, offspring

child-ish [chīl/dĭsh] *adjective*, to be selfish and inconsiderate

chil-i or chili con carne [chĭl/ē] *noun*, a dish of tomatoes, meat, and sometimes beans, flavored with hot spices

chill [chĭl] *adjective*, 1) cold, frosty, *noun*, 2) coldness, freezing, *verb*, 3) to make or become cold

chime [chīm] *verb*, to make a tinkling sound like a bell

chim-ney [chĭm/nē] *noun*, a structure by which smoke passes from a building to the outdoors

chim-pan-zee [chĭm/păn-zē/] *noun*, an ape native to Africa larger than a monkey, without a tail

chin [chĭn] *noun*, the part of the face below the lips

chi-na [chī/nə] *noun*, *no plural*, dishes, such as plates, cups, and saucers, made of fine clay or porcelain, used to serve a meal

chip [chĭp] *noun*, 1) a small piece of something that has broken off 2) a cracker or a thinly sliced fried food 3) the small silicon object that enables the computer to process information, *verb*, 4) to break off small pieces from the main part

chip-munk [chĭp/mŭngk/] *noun*, a tan rodent like a small squirrel with a black stripe from its head to the tip of its tail

chirp [chûrp] *noun*, 1) a high pitched sound, *verb*, 2) to warble, to tweet like a bird

chis-el [chĭz/əl] *noun*, 1) a metal tool with a cutting edge at the end of a blade, *verb*, 2) to carve

a sculpture or use a chisel as a
tool 3) to swindle, to cheat

chiv-al-ry [shĭv′əl-rē] *noun*,
bravery, heroism, courtesy

chlo-ride [klôr′īd] *noun*, a
compound of chlorine with
another substance

chlo-rine [klôr′ēn′] *noun*, a yellow-
green gas added to water
supplies as a disinfectant

chlo-ro-form [klôr′ə-fôrm′] *noun*, a
colorless, sweetish liquid used
as an anesthetic

chlo-ro-phyll [klôr′ə-fĭl] *noun*, a
green pigment in plants,
essential for photosynthesis

choc-o-late [chô′kə-lĭt] *noun*, a
candy made from cocoa, the
roasted seeds of cacao

choice [chois] *adjective*, 1) first
rate, *noun*, 2) an act of making a
selection or choosing

choir [kwīr] *noun*, a band of
singers, especially in church

choke [chōk] *verb*, 1) to feel
suffocated because the throat is
obstructed 2) to repress

chol-er [kŏl′ər] *noun*, anger

choose [chooz] *verb*, to pick or
select from a group, to make a
choice

chop [chŏp] *noun*, 1) a piece of
meat near the bone, *verb*, 2) to
cut with a sharp blade

cho-ral [kôr′əl] *adjective*, for or
relating to a chorus

chord [kôrd] *noun*, a combination
of three or more tones sounded
together in harmony

chore [chôr] *noun*, a job or
distasteful task

cho-re-og-ra-phy
[kôr′ē-ŏg′rə-fē, kōr′-] *noun*,
1) the plan of the steps and
movements in dancing 2) the
creation of ballets or dances

chor-tle [chôr′tl] *verb*, to make a
chuckling or snorting noise

cho-rus [kôr′əs] *noun*, 1) a
company of singers singing in
concert 2) the part of a song that
is repeated, the refrain

chow-der [chou′dər] *noun*, a thick
soup or stew usually featuring
fish, corn, etc.

chris-ten [krĭs′ən] *verb*, to give a
name to someone who is
baptized into the Christian faith

Chris-tian [krĭs′chən] *noun*, a
person who believes in Jesus
Christ

chromosome [krō′mə-sōm′] *noun*,
a thread-like structure in the
nucleus of a cell that carries the
genes

chron-ic [krŏn′ĭk] *adjective*,
continuing for a long time,
habitual, prolonged

chron-i-cle [krŏn′ĭ-kəl] *noun*, 1) a
historical register of facts in
order of their occurence, *verb*,
2) to record in a factual and
detailed way

chron-o-log-i-cal [krŏn′ə-lŏj′ĭ-kəl]
adjective, documented according
to the order of time

chuck-le [chŭk′əl] *noun*, 1) a quick
laugh or giggle, *verb*, 2) to laugh
softly, in a gentle manner

chunk [chŭngk] *noun*, a thick piece
of something, a block, a slab

church [chûrch] *noun*, a building in which Christians meet to worship and pray

churn [chûrn] *verb*, to move about with force, to turn violently

ci-der [sī'dər] *noun*, a drink made from pressed apples

ci-gar [sĭ-gär'] *noun*, tobacco leaves rolled together in paper for smoking

cig-a-ret-te [sĭg'ə-rĕt'] *noun*, a cylinder of finely cut tobacco rolled in paper

cin-der [sĭn'dərz] *noun*, a hot coal, an ember

cin-e-ma [sĭn'ə-mə] *noun*, 1) a building where films are shown 2) the movie business

cin-na-mon [sĭn'ə-mən] *noun*, the bark of an East Indian tree, ground into a spice

cir-cle [sûr'kəl] *noun*, 1) a closed curve in which all points are equidistant from the center, a ring 2) a group of people

cir-cuit [sûr'kĭt] *noun*, the circumference or distance around an area

cir-cuit-ous [sər-kyōo'ĭ-təs] *adjective*, roundabout, indirect, meandering, winding

cir-cu-lar [sûr'kyə-lər] *adjective*, 1) round, *noun*, 2) a leaflet, a pamphlet, a newsletter

cir-cu-late [sûr'kyə-lāt'] *verb*, to move about or around

cir-cu-la-tion [sûr'kyə-lā'shən] *noun*, 1) the act of moving around, especially of blood through the body 2) the extent or amount of distribution, dissemination

cir-cum-fer-ence [sər-kŭm'fər-əns] *noun*, the distance around a circle or circular figure

cir-cum-lo-cu-tion [sûr'kəm-lō-kyōo'shən] *noun*, an indirect or roundabout way of expressing something

cir-cum-spec-tion [sûr'kəm-spĕk'shən] *noun*, caution, care, forethought

cir-cum-stance [sûr'kəm-stăns'] *noun*, a particular incident, a state of affairs, events

cir-cum-stan-tial [sûr'kəm-stăn'shəl] *adjective*, relating to evidence that tends to prove a fact at issue by proving other basic events

cir-cum-vent [sûr'kəm-vĕnt'] *verb*, to find a way around, to evade a difficulty

cir-cus [sûr'kəs] *noun*, a traveling show usually performed by clowns and acrobats and tamed animals presented in an arena

cit-a-del [sĭt'ə-dəl] *noun*, fortress

ci-ta-tion [sī-tā'shən] *noun*, 1) a summons to appear in court, a ticket 2) a quote or reference to a document 3) honorary mention to receive an award or degree for meritorious service

cite [sīt] *verb*, 1) to quote or refer to a document 2) to recognize someone for commendable service 3) to write a ticket for violating the law

cit-i-zen [sĭt'ĭ-zən] *noun*, a person whose legal home is a certain place or nation

cit-i-zen-ship [sĭt′ĭ-zən-shĭp′] *noun*, 1) the fact of being a citizen 2) community participation

cit-y [sĭt′ē] *noun*, a large important town, a metropolis

civ-ic [sĭv′ĭk] *adjective*, pertaining to a community or city

civ-il [sĭv′əl] *adjective*, 1) polite 2) relating to a government employee who is not in the armed forces

ci-vil-ian [sĭ-vĭl′yən] *noun*, a person not in the armed forces

ci-vil-i-ty [sĭ-vĭl′ĭ-tē] *noun*, good manners, courtesy

civ-i-li-za-tion [sĭv′ə-lĭ-zā′shən] *noun*, 1) the condition of being civilized or having culture 2) people sharing their way of life and living in one place at a time, any human society

civ-i-lize [sĭv′ə-līz′] *verb*, to reclaim from a savage state

civ-il war *noun*, a war fought in a country between two different groups of the same nation

claim [klām] *noun*, 1) a statement, an assertion, *verb*, 2) to say and demand possession of something by demonstrating ownership

claim-ant [klā′mənt] *noun*, a person submitting an application or making a claim

clair-voy-ant [klâr-voi′ənt] *adjective*, having foresight

clam [klăm] *noun*, a shellfish similar to an oyster

clam-or [klăm′ər] *noun*, 1) a loud steady noise, an outcry, *verb*, 2) to make a lot of noise

clan [klăn] *noun*, a group of people sharing one ancestor

clan-des-tine [klăn-dĕs′tĭn] *adjective*, secret, concealed

clang [klăng] *noun*, the sound of one piece of metal hitting another, a ringing sound

clap [klăp] *noun*, 1) a loud noise, as in thunder, *verb*, 2) to make a sound by hitting your hands together, applause

clar-i-fy [klăr′ə-fī′] *verb*, to make or become clear, to explain

clar-i-on [klăr′ē-ən] *adjective*, shrill, loud and clear

clar-i-ty [klăr′ĭ-tē] *adjective*, clearness

clash [klăsh] *noun*, 1) a fight or angry dispute 2) the sound of metal on metal, *verb*, 3) to hit or fight 4) of colors, to look awful together 5) to collide noisily

clasp [klăsp] *noun*, 1) a fastening, *verb*, 2) to hold tightly

class [klăs] *noun*, 1) a group of similar things or people 2) students meeting together for instruction, *verb*, 3) to classify

clas-sic [klăs′ĭk] *adjective*, showing excellence, exemplary

clas-si-cal [klăs′ĭ-kəl] *adjective*, 1) pertaining to ancient Greeks and Romans 2) excellent in a traditional style, esp. of music

clas-si-fi-ca-tion [klăs′ə-fĭ-kā′shən] *noun*, categorizing, grouping

clas-si-fy [klăs′ə-fī′] *verb*, to sort, to form into classes or groupings

clause [klôz] *noun*, 1) a group of words in a sentence that

contains a subject and a verb
2) a single part in a contract, law, or treaty

claus-tro-pho-bi-a
[klô′strə-fō′bē-ə] *noun*, a fear of being in a close space

claw [klô] *noun*, 1) the sharp, hard nails on the foot of an animal or bird, *verb*, 2) to tear or scratch with the hand or nails

clay [klā] *noun*, a common earth used for making pottery and bricks when baked

clean [klēn] *adjective*, 1) free from dirt, neat, *verb*, 2) to remove dirt and soil or impurities

clean-li-ness [klĕn′lē-nĭs] *noun*, the state of being clean, neatness of person, good hygiene

cleanse [klĕnz] *verb*, 1) to scrub, to wash, to disinfect 2) to absolve

clear [klîr] *adjective*, 1) easily understood 2) transparent 3) distinct or easy to hear, *verb*, 4) to remove items 5) to remove an obstacle, to bring into focus

clear-ance [klîr′əns] *noun*, 1) the act of removing whatever may obstruct 2) permission

clear-ly [klîr′lē] *adverb*, plainly

cleave [klēv] *verb*, 1) to cling, to adhere to 2) to separate or split

cleft [klĕft] *noun*, a space or opening made by or as if by splitting, a crack, a fissure

clem-en-cy [klĕm′ən-sē] *noun*, mildness, leniency, mercy

clench [klĕnch] *verb*, to hold tightly, to grip, to grasp

cler-gy [klûr′jj] *noun,* ministers of the church as a group

clerk [klûrk] *noun*, a person who does office work, a salesperson

cle-ver [klĕv′ər] *adjective*, quick at learning, smart, good at doing things, resourceful, intelligent

cli-ché [klē-shā′] *noun*, a phrase repeated often, e.g. *down and out*

click [klĭk] *verb*, 1) to make a small noise like a tick on a clock 2) to press the mouse button once

cli-ent [klī′ənt] *noun*, a customer who uses the professional help of another, a patron

cliff [klĭf] *noun*, a high, steep wall of rock or bank on a coast

cli-mac-tic [klī-măk′tĭk] *adjective*, relating to the highest point or climax

cli-mate [klī′mĭt] *noun*, the typical weather or atmosphere of a place year after year

cli-max [klī′măks′] *noun*, the crucial point when everything comes together, culmination

climb [klīm] *noun*, 1) the distance traveled up a hill or mountain, *verb*, 2) to go up, to ascend

clime [klīm] *noun*, region, climate

cling [klĭng] *verb*, to hold on tightly, to clutch, to grip

cling-ing [klĭng′ĭng] *adjective*, 1) devoted 2) holding fast 3) dependent

clin-ic [klĭn′ĭk] *noun*, a place that provides medical treatment

clin-ic-al [klĭn′ĭ-kəl] *adjective*, 1) related to observation and treatment of patients 2) scientific and observable

clip [klĭp] *noun*, 1) an object used to fasten things 2) a brisk pace, *verb*, 3) to cut or trim

clique [klēk] *noun*, a small group with joint interests, an exclusive set of friends, a gang

cloak [klōk] *noun*, 1) a loose piece of clothing, usually sleeveless, worn as an outer garment, *verb*, 2) to conceal

clock [klŏk] *noun*, an instrument used to measure time

clog [klôg] *noun*, 1) a blockage 2) a thick-soled shoe with an open back, *verb*, 3) to dance in the shoes 4) to hinder or obstruct, to be blocked up

close [klōs] *adjective*, 1) near 2) alike, similar, *verb*, 3) to shut out 4) to end

clos-et [klŏz′ĭt] *noun*, a small room or space where clothes are hung and items are stored

clot [klŏt] *noun*, a thickened mass of blood tissue

cloth [klôth] *noun*, a piece of fabric made of natural or synthetic fibers, such as cotton or rayon

cloth-ing [klō′thĭng] *noun*, *no plural*, garments, apparel, things worn as clothes, articles of dress

cloud [kloud] *noun*, 1) a visible mass of water droplets floating in the sky 2) a mass of dust

cloud-y [klou′dē] *adjective*, filled with clouds, overcast

clown [kloun] *noun*, someone who is paid to make people laugh, usually wearing a costume and makeup

club [klŭb] *noun*, 1) a group of people who meet for a common purpose 2) a heavy stick

clue [kloo] *noun*, information or evidence that helps you find the answer to a puzzling question

clum-sy [klŭm′zē] *adjective*, awkward, unhandy, unwieldy

clus-ter [klŭs′tər] *noun*, 1) a clump, a bunch, a small, close group, *verb*, 2) to gather together into a small group

clutch [klŭch] *noun*, 1) the part of a machine that connects and disconnects the power from the rest of the machine, *verb*, 2) to hold something tightly, to grip, to cling to

clut-ter [klŭt′ər] *noun*, things lying about, a mess

coach [kōch] *noun*, 1) one who trains athletes, actors, or singers 2) a part of a train or bus that carries passengers 3) a carriage drawn by horses, *verb*, 4) to assist talented people develop their capability, to train

co-ag-u-late [kō-ăg′yə-lāt′] *verb*, to form into a dense mass, solidify from a liquid, to congeal

coal [kōl] *noun*, a fossil fuel in solid form that gives off heat when burned

co-a-lesce [kō′ə-lĕs′] *verb*, to combine, to fuse, to join together

co-a-li-tion [kō′ə-lĭsh′ən] *noun*, a union of people of differing views in a single body or group

coarse [kôrs, kōrs] *adjective*, 1) rough in surface or texture 2) crude, ill-mannered

coast [kōst] *noun*, 1) the edge of land that touches the ocean, *verb*, 2) to slide or glide

coat [kōt] *noun*, a piece of clothing with sleeves, worn over everything else, a jacket

coax [kōks] *verb*, to gently persuade

cob-bler [kŏb'lər] *noun*, someone who makes and repairs shoes

cob-web [kŏb'wĕb'] *noun*, threads woven by a spider in which it catches insects

co-caine [kō-kān'] *noun*, a bitter, crystalline alkaloid used as a local anesthetic and illegally as a stimulant

cock [kŏk] *noun*, a male bird

cock-pit [kŏk'pĭt'] *noun*, the compartment in a vehicle where the driver of a race car or the pilot of an airplane sits

co-co-nut [kō'kə-nŭt'] *noun*, the fruit of a variety of palm tree

co-coon [kə-kōōn'] *noun*, the silky case insects live in during the pupa stage

cod [kŏd] *noun, no plural*, a family of sea fish used for food

cod-dle [kŏd'l] *verb*, to treat gently, to pamper, to spoil

code [kōd] *noun*, 1) a collection of laws 2) a system of symbols given certain meanings

co-erce [kō-ûrs'] *verb*, to persuade by force

co-er-cion [kō-ûr'zhən] *noun*, persuasion by force or threats, pressuring

cof-fee [kô'fē] *noun*, the hot beverage made from the seeds of a coffee plant, a pale brown color

cof-fin [kô'fĭn] *noun*, a box in which a dead body is placed

cog [kŏg] *noun*, the tooth projecting from a wheel rim or a bar

cog-ni-zant [kŏg'nĭ-zənt] *adjective*, conscious, aware, knowledgeable

co-her-ent [kō-hîr'ənt] *adjective*, 1) able to be understood 2) forming a connection

co-he-sion [kō-hē'zhən] *noun*, the act of sticking together

coil [koil] *noun*, 1) a wire in a continuous circling shape, *verb*, 2) to wrap up around in a ring

coin [koin] *noun*, 1) a piece of money made of metal, legally authorized by a government 2) a quantity of value, *verb*, 3) to make coins 4)to invent

co-in-cide [kō'ĭn-sīd'] *verb*, to occur at the same time, to correspond exactly

co-in-cid-ence [kō-ĭn'sĭ-dəns] *noun*, random events that happen at the same time, chance, luck

col-an-der [kŭl'ən-dər] *noun*, a bowl-shaped container that is perforated for use as a strainer

cold [kōld] *adjective*, 1) feeling no heat, not warm 2) unfriendly, *noun*, 3) a virus with symptoms of a sore throat and runny nose

col-lab-o-rate [kə-lăb'ə-rāt'] *verb*, to work together as a group

col-lab-o-ra-tion [kə-lăb'ə-rā'shən] *noun*, a project that includes ideas from two or more people working together

col-lapse [kə-lăps'] *noun,* 1) any sudden or complete breakdown, *verb,* 2) to break down suddenly 3) to fall down

col-lar [kŏl'ər] *noun,* 1) a band worn around the neck of an animal 2) the part of a shirt around the neck

col-late [kə-lāt'] *verb,* 1) to examine in order to verify a special authenticity 2) to combine and arrange in order

col-lat-er-al [kə-lăt'ər-əl] *adjective,* 1) secondary, *noun,* 2) security in the form of property for repayment of a loan

col-league [kŏl'ēg'] *noun,* an associate from work, a friend or a peer, a co-worker

col-lect [kə-lĕkt'] *verb,* 1) to accumulate, to compile, to · scrape together 2) to gather, to meet, to flock, to convene

col-lec-tion [kə-lĕk'shən] *noun,* an accumulation of things of a similar nature

col-lec-tive [kə-lĕk'tĭv] *adjective,* gathered, compiled, joint

col-lege [kŏl'ĭj] *noun,* a place where people study after high school that gives degrees

col-lide [kə-līd'] *verb,* to come together with great force

col-li-sion [kə-lĭzh'ən] *noun,* the act of striking or dashing together, a crash

co-lon [kō'lən] *noun,* 1) the sign [:] which is used before a listing or examples 2) the part of the large intestine extending to the rectum

colo-nel [kûr'nəl] *noun,* the commanding officer of a regiment, below brigadier general

co-lo-ni-al [kə-lō'nē-əl] *adjective,* relating to a period in America before independence

col-o-nist [kŏl'ə-nĭst] *noun,* someone who settles a territory

col-o-ni-za-tion [kŏl'ə-nĭ-zā'shən] *noun,* the act of setting up homes and starting a community in a new place with the purpose of living there a long time

col-o-ny [kŏl'ə-nē] *noun,* a country, area, etc. under the jurisdiction of another country and occupied by settlers

col-or [kŭl'ər] *noun,* 1) any of the hues of the rainbow, including white, *verb,* 2) to paint, dye, tint, to change the hue 3) to affect

Col-o-rado [kŏl'ə-răd'ō] *noun,* one of the United States, the capital city is Denver. The state flower of Colorado is the rocky mountain columbine, and the motto is "Nothing without the divine will."

co-los-sal [kə-lŏs'əl] *adjective,* huge, gigantic, immense

colt [kōlt] *noun,* a young male horse

col-umn [kŏl'əm] *noun,* 1) a supporting pillar 2) a perpendicular set of lines of a text in a book or periodical or newspaper or web page

col-um-nist [kŏl'əm-nĭst] *noun,* a writer who is featured regularly in a newspaper, or magazine, or Web site

co-ma [kō'mə] *noun*, state of being unresponsive, unconsciousness

comb [kōm] *noun*, 1) a piece of plastic, wood, or metal with teeth to smooth and adjust hair, *verb*, 2) to tidy hair with a comb

com-bat [kəm-băt'] *noun*, 1) an armed battle, *verb*, 2) to fight

com-bi-na-tion [kŏm'bə-nā'shən] *noun*, the act or result of combining, a union, a mixture

com-bine [kəm-bīn'] *verb*, to mix together, to blend, to unite

com-bus-ti-ble [kəm-bŭs'tə-bəl] *adjective*, apt to catch fire and burn, flammable

come [kŭm] *verb*, 1) to arrive, to approach 2) to happen

com-e-dy [kŏm'ĭ-dē] *noun*, a funny performance that makes the audience laugh, humor

come-ly [kŭm'lē] *adjective*, attractive, beautiful, or handsome

com-et [kŏm'ĭt] *noun*, a celestial object of a frozen mass of dust that vaporizes as it nears the sun

com-fort [kŭm'fərt] *noun*, 1) consolation in trouble, *verb*, 2) to show kindness to someone, to console

com-fort-a-ble [kŭm'fər-tə-bəl] *adjective*, relaxed, content

com-ic [kŏm'ĭk] *adjective,* funny, humorous

com-ma [kŏm'ə] *noun*, a punctuation mark (,) used to indicate pauses and to separate elements within a sentence

com-mand [kə-mănd'] *noun*, 1) an order 2) mastery, rule, *verb*, 3) to be in charge of, to order someone to do something

com-man-deer [kŏm'ən-dîr'] *verb*, to take, often for military use

com-mem-o-rate [kə-měm'ə-rāt'] *verb*, to honor, to memorialize

com-mence-ment [kə-měns'mənt] *noun*, 1) the beginning 2) the ceremony of graduation

com-mend [kə-měnd'] *verb*, to praise, to compliment, to support

com-men-su-rate [kə-měn'sər-ĭt] *adjective*, equal in extent, in proportion, corresponding

com-ment [kŏm'ĕnt] *noun*, 1) a remark or something said, *verb*, 2) to make a remark about something, to express an opinion

com-ment-ary [kŏm'ĕntrĕr'ē] *noun,* remarks or observations about something, an explanation

com-merce [kŏm'ərs] *noun*, business, the buying and selling of goods, all forms of trade

com-mer-cial [kə-mûr'shəl] *adjective*, 1) for business purposes, having profit as an aim, *noun*, 2) an advertisement on television or radio

com-mis-er-ate [kə-mĭz'ə-rāt'] *verb*, to feel or express sorrow

com-mis-sion [kə-mĭsh'ən] *noun*, 1) a committee or board that studies an issue 2) the percentage paid to an agent

com-mit [kə-mĭt'] *verb*, 1) to entrust 2) to pledge 3) to act out, to perform 4) to put into custody

com-mit-ment [kə-mĭt'mənt] *noun*, a pledge, a promise, a responsibility

committee

com-mit-tee [kə-mǐt'ē] *noun*, a group appointed or formed to consider or accomplish some matter or business

com-mod-i-ty [kə-mǒd'ǐ-tē] *noun*, an item that can be bought and sold, merchandise

com-mon [kǒm'ən] *adjective*, 1) ordinary, found everywhere, general 2) joint, shared, *noun*, 3) a public outdoor space

com-mon-wealth [kǒm'ən-wĕlth'] *noun*, 1) a group of independent states in a country 2)a self-governed nation or state

com-mo-tion [kə-mō'shən] *noun*, noise, confusion, disruption,

com-mune [kǒm'yo͞on'] *noun*, a living arrangement in which everyone shares possessions, work, etc.

com-mu-ni-ca-ble [kə-myo͞o'nǐ-kə-bəl] *adjective*, contagious, infectious

com-mu-ni-cate [kə-myo͞o'nǐ-kāt'] *verb*, 1) to give or exchange information 2) to transmit

com-mu-ni-ca-tion [kə-myo͞o'nǐ-kā'shən] *noun*, 1) exchange of information between people 2) that which is made known 3) transmission

com-mun-ion [kə'myo͞onyən] *noun*, 1) the mutual sharing of feelings and thoughts 2) a religious fellowship among members of a church

com-mu-nism [kǒm'yə-nǐz'əm] *noun*, a political system in which property is owned by the state

com-mu-nist [kǒm'yə-nǐst] *noun*, a person who believes the state should own all industry and land

com-mu-ni-ty [kə-myo͞o'nǐ-tē] *noun*, a town, city, suburb, or other place where people live and work, a society

com-mute [kə-myo͞ot'] *verb*, 1) to make a sentence of punishment less severe 2) to travel, to go back and forth to work

com-pact [kəm-pǎkt'] *adjective*, 1) taking up a small amount of space, *noun*, 2) a small case with makeup and a mirror 3) an agreement, *verb*, 4) to press close together

com-pan-ion [kəm-pǎn'yən] *noun*, a friend or associate, one who accompanies another

com-pa-ny [kǔm'pə-nē] *noun*, 1) an association for business or social purposes 2) a corporation or firm 3) guests, visitors 4) a subdivision of a regiment

com-pa-ra-ble [kǒm'pər-ə-bəl] *adjective*, similar, equivalent

com-pare [kəm-pâr'] *verb*, to look at similarities and differences

com-par-i-son [kəm-pǎr'ǐ-sən] *noun*, an examination of two or more objects with the view to discovering the similarities or differences, contrast

com-pass [kǔm'pəs] *noun*, 1) an instrument using a magnetic needle that always points to the north 2) a tool used to draw a circle 3) a range, scope, or limits

com-pas-sion [kəm-pǎsh'ən] *noun*, sympathy for suffering, kindness

com-pat-i-ble [kəm-pat′ə-bəl] *adjective*, in harmony with something, well-suited

com-pel [kəm-pĕl′] *verb*, 1) to drive or urge with force 2) to coerce

com-pen-di-um [kəm-pĕn′dē-əm] *noun*, an abridgement, collection, summary of information

com-pen-sate [kŏm′pən-sāt′] *verb*, to make up for something, to make amends, to pay

com-pen-sa-tion [kŏm′pən-sa/shən] *noun*, an amount paid to make up for something, payment

com-pete [kəm-pēt′] *verb*, to try to win a race, contest, etc.

com-pe-tent [kŏm′pĭ-tənt] *adjective*, capable, qualified, adequate, proficient, able

com-pe-ti-tion [kŏm′pĭ-tĭsh′ən] *noun*, 1) rivalry, free market conditions 2) a contest to see who performs better, a game

com-pet-i-tor [kəm-pĕt′ĭ-tər] *noun*, a rival, one who competes

com-pile [kəm-pīl′] *verb*, to gather information

com-pla-cen-cy [kəm-plā′sən-sē] *noun*, self-satisfaction, smugness

com-plac-ent [kəm-plā′sənt] *adjective*, 1) self-satisfied, smug 2) agreeable, lazy

com-plain [kəm-plān′] *verb*, 1) to express unhappiness or dissatisfaction or resentment 2) to make a formal accusation

com-plaint [kəm-plānt′] *noun*, 1) a criticism, reproach 2) an illness

com-ple-ment [kŏm′plə-mənt] *noun*, that which fills up, completes, or balances

com-plete [kəm-plēt′] *adjective*, 1) lacking nothing, full, whole, 2) finished, *verb*, 3) to finish

com-plex [kəm-plĕks′] *adjective*, 1) complicated, puzzling 2) consisting of connected parts, *noun*, 3) a group of buildings

com-plex-ion [kəm-plĕk′shən] *noun*, 1) the color or hue of the skin of the face 2) general appearance or aspect

com-pli-ance [kəm-plī′əns] *noun*, the act of yielding to demand, consent, agreement

com-plic-ate [kŏm′plĭ-kāt′] *verb*, to confuse, to perplex, to make more difficult or complex

com-pli-ment [kŏm′plə-mənt] *noun*, 1) nice words said about someone, praise, *verb*, 2) to express admiration, to laud

com-ply [kəm-plī′] *verb*, to follow, to conform, to go along with an order or a rule

com-po-nent [kəm-pō′nənt] *noun*, an essential part, a fundamental piece, a constituent part

com-port [kəm-pôrt′] *verb*, , to carry oneself in a specified way

com-pose [kəm-pōz′] *verb*, 1) to write or create music, literature, etc. 2) to blend the ingredients or components of something

com-pos-ite [kəm-pŏz′ĭt] *adjective*, 1) made up of separate distinctive parts 2) relating to a combination of the Corinthian and Ionic styles of architecture.

composition

com-po-si-tion [kŏm′pə-zĭsh′ən] *noun,* 1) something written, such as a story or music 2) a creation

com-post [kŏm′pōst′] *noun,* the product from the decomposition of organic materials, such as yard waste or dead plants

com-po-sure [kəm-pō′zhər] *noun,* a settled state, calmness

com-pound [kŏm-pound′] *noun,* 1) a composite, a mixture 2) a fenced-in area with one or more buildings in it, *verb,* 3) to make by mixing together 4) to increase

com-pre-hend [kŏm′prĭ-hĕnd′] *verb,* to understand

com-pre-hen-sive [kŏm′prĭ-hĕn′sĭv] *adjective,* thorough, all-inclusive

com-press [kŏm′prĕs′] *noun,* 1) a bandage, a pad, *verb,* [kŭm′prĕs] 2) to pack, to squeeze

com-prise [kəm-prīz′] *verb,* to include, consisting of

com-pro-mise [kŏm′prə-mīz′] *noun,* 1) the result of adjustments made by concessions to make a mutual agreement, *verb,* 2) to adjust by making concessions

com-pul-sion [kəm-pŭl′shən] *noun,* 1) duress, urgency, duty 2) an obsession, a fixation

com-pul-so-ry [kəm-pŭl′sə-rē] *adjective,* required, mandatory

com-pute [kəm-pyōōt′] *verb,* to figure mathematically

com-put-er [kəm-pyōōt′ər] *noun,* an electronic device for storing and processing data, typically in binary form, according to instructions given to it in a software program

com-rade [kŏm′răd′] *noun,* a faithful friend, a colleague

con-cave [kŏn-kāv′] *adjective,* sunken, as the inside of a sphere or a spoon

con-ceal [kən-sēl′] *verb,* to hide, to disguise, to keep from sight

con-cede [kən-sēd′] *verb,* to surrender, to grant, to allow

con-ceit [kən-sēt′] *noun,* vanity, an exaggerated opinion of oneself, self-importance

con-ceive [kən-sēv′] *verb,* 1) to imagine, to take into one's mind 2) to become pregnant

con-cen-trate [kŏn′sən-trāt′] *verb,* 1) to focus all one's thoughts and efforts on 2) to bring or come together in one place to increase the strength of

con-cen-tra-tion [kŏn′sən-trā′shən] *noun,* 1) density, consistency 2) close attention, intense thought

con-cen-tric [kən-sĕn′trĭk] *adjective,* having a common center

con-cept [kŏn′sĕpt′] *noun,* an abstract idea, a thought

con-cep-tion [kən-sĕp′shən] *noun,* 1) the act of conceiving life 2) the beginning or understanding of an idea

con-cern [kən-sûrn′] *noun,* 1) anxiety 2) something that involves a person or people, *verb,* 3) to be about, to interest 4) to trouble or worry

con-cert [kŏn′sûrt′] *noun,* 1) music played for an audience, [kŏn′sûrt] *verb* 2) to plan or arrange together

con-ces-sion [kən-sĕsh′ən] *noun*, the act of yielding, a grant

con-cil-i-ate [kən-sĭl′ē-āt] *verb*, to gain goodwill, to placate

con-cil-i-a-to-ry [kən-sĭl′ē-ə-tôr′ē] *adjective*, making less angry or hostile to overcome animosity

con-cise [kən-sīs′] *adjective*, short, to the point, brief, succinct

con-clude [kən-klo͞od′] *verb*, 1) to form an opinion after thinking about something 2) to finish to bring or come to an end

con-clu-sion [kən-klo͞o′zhən] *noun*, 1) the end, an outcome 2) a decision, a judgment

con-coct [kən-kŏkt′] *verb*, 1) to prepare by combining different ingredients 2) to devise a plan or scheme, to invent

con-cor-dant [kən-kôr′dant] *adjective*, in agreement, harmonious

con-crete [kŏn-krēt′] *adjective*, 1) not abstract, particular, *noun*, 2) a compound mass of cement, sand, gravel, and water used for building

con-cus-sion [kən-kŭsh′ən] *noun*, a head injury that is the result of a blow or a fall, a shock

con-demn [kən-dĕm′] *verb*, 1) to pronounce sentence against someone 2) to disapprove of or censure, to denounce

con-dem-na-tion [kŏn′dĕm-nā′shən] *noun*, criticism, blame, an objection

con-den-sa-tion [kŏn′dĕn-sā′shən] *noun*, 1) the act, process, or state of compressing or being compressed into a smaller enclosed space 2) the process by which a substance changes from its gaseous state to a liquid state 3) the liquid formed by this process

con-dense [kən-dĕns′] *verb*, to shorten or compress

con-de-scend [kŏn′dĭ-sĕnd′] *verb*, to act superior to someone else

con-di-ment [kŏn′də-mənt] *noun*, a type of relish or seasoning

con-di-tion [kən-dĭsh′ən] *noun*, 1) a stipulation or provision 2) the state in which a person or thing exists, *verb*, 3) to prepare, to adapt, to train, to influence

con-di-tion-ing [kən-dĭsh′ən-ing] *noun*, preparation, training

con-dol-ence [kən-dō′ləns] *noun*, an offering of sympathy, an expression of regret

con-done [kən-dōn′] *verb*, to pardon, to forgive, to overlook

con-du-cive [kən-do͞o′sĭv] *adjective*, tending to promote, helpful, beneficial

con-duct *noun*, [kən-dŭkt′] 1) behavior, [kən-dŭkt′] *verb*, 2) to lead or guide 3) to direct

con-duc-tor [kən-dŭk′tər] *noun*, 1) someone who sells tickets on a train 2) something that transmits energy 3) the leader of a musical ensemble

con-duit [kŏn′do͞o-ĭt] *noun*, a channel or passage through which electrical wires run

cone [kōn] *noun*, 1) a cylinder that tapers to a point at the end 2) the reproductive structures of the conifer trees, a pine cone 3) a cylindrical wafer on which a scoop of ice cream is placed

con-fed-er-ate [kən-fĕd′ər-ĭt] *noun*, 1) an ally, an accomplice **Confederate** 2) someone who fought for the Confederacy during the Civil War

con-fed-er-a-tion [kən-fĕd′ə-rā′shən] *noun*, an alliance, a coalition

con-fer [kən-fûr′] *verb*, 1) to give as a gift 2) to meet and discuss

con-fer-ence [kŏn′fər-əns] *noun*, a meeting for an exchange of ideas, a conversation with someone to share information

con-fess [kən-fĕs′] *verb*, to acknowledge or admit a fault

con-fes-sion [kən-fĕsh′ən] *noun*, an admission of guilt or wrongdoing

con-fet-ti [kən-fĕt′ē] *noun*, small pieces of colorful paper scattered at celebrations

con-fi-dant [kŏn′fĭ-dănt′] *noun*, one to whom secrets are entrusted, a friend

con-fide [kən-fīd′] *verb*, to trust, to disclose a secret, to reveal

con-fi-dence [kŏn′fĭ-dəns] *noun*, complete trust, a secret

con-fi-dent [kŏn′fĭ-dənt] *adjective*, assured beyond doubt, self-reliant, feeling certain, sure

con-fi-den-tial [kŏn′fĭ-dĕn′shəl] *adjective*, secret, private, trusted

con-fine [kən-fīn′] *verb*, to restrain, within a specific place

con-firm [kən-fûrm′] *verb*, to give proof of something, to ratify

con-fir-ma-tion [kŏn′fər-mā′shən] *noun*, 1) proof, collaboration 2) a ceremony recognizing a member of the church

con-fis-cate [kŏn′fĭ-skāt′] *verb*, to seize, to take without consent

con-flict [kŏn′flĭkt′] *noun*, 1) a fight or argument, a disagreement, *verb*, 2) to disagree or clash

con-form [kən-fôrm′] *verb*, to comply, to obey social norms

con-form-i-ty [kən-fôr′mĭ-tē] *noun*, harmony, agreement

con-fuse [kən-fyōōz′] *verb*, to mix up in the mind, to perplex

con-fu-sion [kən-fyōō′zhən] *noun*, a state of disorder, chaos, bewilderment

con-geal [kən-jēl′] *verb*, 1) to change from a fluid state to a solid state 2) to thicken

con-gen-ial [kən-jēn′yəl] *adjective*, naturally adapted, pleasant and sympathetic, good-natured

con-gen-i-tal [kən-jĕn′ĭ-tl] *adjective*, existing at birth

con-ges-tion [kən-jĕs′shən] *noun*, 1) a gathering or accumulation 2) an overcrowded state

con-glom-er-a-tion [kən-glŏm′ə-rā′shən] *noun*, material sticking together

con-grat-u-la-tions [kən-grăch′ə-lā′shənz] *noun, plural*, expressions of good wishes for a happy event or achievement

oon grc gate [kŏng'grĭ-gāl'] *verb*, to gather together, to assemble

con-gre-ga-tion [kŏng'grĭ-gā'shən] *noun*, a gathering or assembly

con-gress [kŏng'grĭs] *noun*, 1) a meeting of a group of people **Congress** 2) the legislature of the United States consisting of the Senate and the House of Representatives

con-gru-ent [kŏng'grōō-ənt] *adjective*, in agreement, exactly alike, matching, equal

con-jec-ture [kən-jĕk'chər] *noun*, theory, an unfounded remark

con-ju-gate [kŏn'jə-gāt'] *verb*, to change the form of a verb depending on the subject and the tense, e.g. *I am, you are, he is, we are, you are, they are*

con-junc-tion [kən-jŭngk'shən] *noun*, a word that joins two other words or phrases together

con-jure [kŏn'jər] *verb*, 1) to seem to create out of thin air as if by magic 2) to entreat, to summon

con-nect [kə-nĕkt'] *verb*, to join or bring together, to link, to unite

Con-nect-i-cut [kə-nĕt'ĭ-kət] *noun*, one of the 50 United States, the capital is Hartford. The state flower of **Connecticut** is the mountain laurel, and the motto is "He who transplanted still sustains."

con-nec-tion [kə-nĕk'shən] *noun*, the act of joining, a relationship

con-nive [kə-nīv'] *verb*, to cooperate in a crime or fault, to secretly allow, to deceive

con-nois-seur [kŏn'ə-sur'] *noun*, one who is an expert judge of art and style or taste

con-no-ta-tion [kŏn'ə-tā'shən] *noun*, suggested meaning

con-quer [kŏng'kər] *verb*, 1) to gain or acquire by force, to be victorious, to win, to defeat 2) to master, to overcome

con-quest [kŏn'kwĕst'] *noun*, a takeover, a triumph, a victory

con-science [kŏn'shəns] *noun*, a sense of moral goodness

con-sci-en-tious [kŏn'shē-ĕn'shəs] *adjective*, influenced by conscience, careful, thoughtful

con-scious [kŏn'shəs] *adjective*, aware of, awake, alert

con-scious-ly [kŏn'shəs-lē] *adverb*, after thorough consideration, with full awareness

con-se-crate [kŏn'sĭ-krāt'] *verb*, to dedicate, to declare sacred

con-sec-u-tive [kən-sĕk'yə-tĭv] *adjective*, one after another

con-sen-sus [kən-sĕn'səs] *noun*, agreement in opinion, custom, or function, the popular choice

con-sent [kən-sĕnt'] *noun*, 1) an agreement, permission, *verb*, 2) to agree, to comply

con-se-quence [kŏn'sĭ-kwĕns'] *noun*, 1) that which follows as a result, outcome 2) importance

con-se-quen-tial [kŏn'sĭ-kwĕn'shəl] *adjective*, significant, very important

con-ser-va-tion [kŏn'sûr-vā'shən] *noun*, the planned management of natural resources to prevent loss, destruction, or waste

con-serv-a-tive [kən-sûr′və-tĭv] *adjective*, 1) opposed to change or innovation 2) traditional 3) a low estimated number

con-ser-va-tor-y [kən-sûr′və-tôr′ē] *noun*, 1) a small greenhouse for growing plants 2) a college of music, an academy

con-serve [kən-sûrv′] *verb*, to keep from loss or waste, to preserve

con-sid-er [kən-sĭd′ər] *verb*, 1) to think about carefully, 2) to take into account 3) to believe

con-sid-er-a-ble [kən-sĭd′ər-ə-bəl] *adjective*, important, great, large

con-sid-er-ate [kən-sĭd′ər-ĭt] *adjective*, caring about a person's feelings, courteous

con-sid-er-a-tion [kən-sĭd′ə-rā′shən] *noun*, 1) thought and attention 2) a payment

con-sign [kən-sīn′] *verb*, 1) to ship something to an agent in another place, to deliver 2) to assign

con-sign-ment [kən-sīn′mənt] *noun*, 1) the entrusting of something to another's care 2) a quantity of goods for delivery

con-sist [kən-sĭst′] *verb*, to be made of or composed of

con-sist-ent [kən-sĭs′tənt] *adjective*, sticking to the same principles, the same throughout

con-so-la-tion [kŏn′sə-lā′shən] *noun*, comfort, sympathy

con-sole [kən-sōl′] *verb*, to comfort, to calm, to soothe

con-sol-i-date [kən-sŏl′ĭ-dāt′] *verb*, to unite, to bring together , to strengthen, to make solid

con-so-nant [kŏn′sə-nənt] *adjective*, 1) in agreement, *noun*, 2) a letter in the alphabet other than a vowel

con-spic-u-ous [kən-spĭk′yōō-əs] *adjective*, plainly visible, prominent, attracting attention

con-spir-a-cy [kən-spîr′ə-sē] *noun*, a combination of people often for an evil purpose, a secret plan

con-stant [kŏn′stənt] *adjective*, continuous, unceasing, faithful

con-stel-la-tion [kŏn′stə-lā′shən] *noun*, an arrangement of stars that resembles a figure

con-sti-tute [kŏn′stĭ-tōot′] *verb*, to make up, to empower

con-sti-tu-tion [kŏn′stĭ-tōo′shən] *noun*, the fundamental law of a nation, state, or society

con-sti-tu-tion-al [kŏn′stĭtōo′shənl] *adjective*, according to law

con-strain [kən-strān′] *verb*, to force, to restrain unnaturally

con-struct [kən-strŭkt′] *verb*, to build a structure, to erect

con-struc-tion [kən-strŭk′shən] *noun*, 1) something that is built, a structure 2) the arrangement of words in parts of a sentence

con-struc-tive [kən-strŭk′tĭv] *adjective*, helpful, useful, productive, beneficial

con-strue [kən-strōo′] *verb*, to interpret, to try to understand

con-sult [kən-sŭlt′] *verb*, to ask for help looking for more information, to confer

con-sult-ant [kən oŭl′tənt] *noun*, an expert hired to study data to resolve a problem or give advice

con-sume [kən-soōm′] *verb*, 1) to eat 2) to exhaust, to expend 3) to make use of, to apply 4) to destroy

con-sum-er [kən-soō′mər] *noun*, 1) a higher level organism that gets its food from other living things 2) someone who buys products, a customer

con-sum-mate [kŏn′sə-māt′] *verb*, to bring to completion, to perfect

con-sump-tion [kən-sŭmp′shən] *noun*, 1) the use of goods 2) a disease of the lungs, such as tuberculosis 3) the eating of food

con-tact [kŏn′tăkt′] *noun*, 1) a physical touch 2) a connection through writing or speaking, *verb*, 3) to talk or write to, to touch

con-ta-gi-ous [kən-tā′jəs] *adjective*, of a disease passed from one person to another by touch or proximity

con-tain [kən-tān′] *verb*, 1) to have inside, to hold 2) to include

con-tain-er [kən-tā′nər] *noun*, anything that can hold and carry something, eg., a box, jar, basket

con-tam-i-nant [kən-tăm′ə-nənt] *noun*, a compound that pollutes, making the original substance impure, a poison, a toxin

con-tam-i-nate [kən-tăm′ə-nāt′] *verb*, to soil, to stain or corrupt by contact, to pollute, to infect

con-tam-i-na-tion [kən-tăm′ə-nā′shən] *noun*, the act of making a substance impure or unusable

con-tem-plate [kŏn′təm-plāt′] *verb*, to consider with continued attention, to think about, to ponder

con-tem-po-rar-y [kən-tĕm′pə-rĕr′ē] *adjective*, 1) of the present day, current, *noun*, 2) a person of the same age, a peer

con-tempt [kən-tĕmpt′] *noun*, a feeling that someone or something is bad

con-tempt-i-ble [kən-tĕmp′tə-bəl] *adjective*, despicable, vile

con-tent [kən-tĕnt′] *adjective*, 1) happy, satisfied, [kŏn′-tĕnt] *noun*, 2) that which is inside 3) the subject matter of a book

con-ten-tion [kən-tĕn′shən] *noun*, a struggle, an argument, a dispute

con-ten-tious [kən-tĕn′shəs] *adjective*, argumentative, quarrel-some, causing disagreement

con-test [kŏn′tĕst] *noun*, 1) a game in which there is a winner [kən-tĕst′] *verb*, 2) to disagree, to object to, to challenge

con-text [kŏn′tĕkst′] *noun*, the words or actions that provide a necessary link or explanation to the meaning of a word or event

con-tig-u-ous [kən-tĭg′yoō-əs] *adjective*, adjoining, touching

con-ti-nent [kŏn′tə-nənt] *noun*, a major land area in the world unbroken by major oceans

contingent

con-tin-gent [kən-tĭn′jənt]
adjective, conditional, relying on
chance or something happening

con-tin-u-al [kən-tĭn′yōō-əl]
adjective, happening repeatedly

con-tin-ue [kən-tĭn′yōō] *verb*, 1) to
go on, to resume 2) to persevere

con-tin-u-ous [kən-tĭn′yōō-əs]
adjective, uninterrupted

con-tor-tion [kən-tôr′shən] *noun*,
something bent or twisted out of
shape, a distortion

con-tour [kŏn′tōōr′] *noun*, the
outline of a figure, body, hill,
coastline, etc.

con-tra-band [kŏn′trə-bănd′] *noun*,
illegal goods, smuggled
materials

con-tract [kŏn′trăkt′] *noun*, 1) a
written agreement between two
or more persons that has the
force of law, [kən′-trăkt′] *verb*,
2) to draw closer together 3) to
make a binding agreement

con-trac-tion [kŏn′trăk′ shən]
noun, 1) the shortening of a
word or group of words by
omitting a letter or letters and
replacing them with an
apostrophe, e.g. y*ou'll* 2) the act
of drawing together like muscles

con-tra-dict [kŏn′trə-dĭkt′] *verb*, to
say the opposite, to oppose in
words, to conflict with

con-trar-y [kŏn′trĕr′ē] *adjective,*
opposite, perverse, wayward

con-trast [kən-trăst′] *noun*, 1) the
difference, *verb*, 2) to compare in
order to show the differences
between two things

con-trib-ute [kən-trĭb′yōōt] *verb*, to
give as part of a group effort, to
help in causing

con-tri-bu-tion [kŏn′trĭ-byōō′shən]
noun, an offering, a donation

con-trite [kən-trīt′] *adjective*,
asking forgiveness, remorseful

con-trive [kən-trīv′] *verb*, to invent
or make a clever device

con-trol [kən-trōl′] *noun*, 1) power,
guidance, *verb*, 2) to manage or
oversee a situation or machine

con-tro-ver-sy [kŏn′trə-vûr′sē]
noun, a disagreement or debate

con-tu-sion [kən-tōō′zhən] *noun*, a
wound or bruise that does not
break the skin

con-va-les-cent [kŏn′və-lĕs′ənt]
adjective, recovering from
sickness

con-vene [kən-vēn′] *verb*, to
assemble, to call together

con-ven-ience [kən-vēn′yəns]
noun, the state of being easily
used or immediately available

con-ven-ient [kən-vēn′yənt]
adjective, adapted to one's
comfort or ready use, handy

con-vent [kŏn′vənt] *noun*, a home
where nuns live

con-ven-tion [kən-vĕn′shən] *noun*,
1) an assembly of members of a
delegation 2) a practice or
custom 3) a formal agreement

con-ven-tion-al [kən-vĕn′shə-nəl]
adjective, contemporary

con-verge [kən-vûrj′] *verb*, to
come together, to assemble

con-ver-sant [kən-vûr′sənt]
adjective, familiar with

con-ver-sa-tion [kŏn′vər-sā′shən] *noun*, an informal discourse, a chat or familiar talk

con-verse *noun*, [kən- vûrs′] 1) the contrary or opposite, [kŏn′vûrs′] *verb*, 2) to talk or exchange ideas

con-ver-sion [kən-vûr′zhən] *noun*, a change from one thing, state, or religion to another

con-vert [kən-vûrt′] *verb*, to change into something else

con-vex [kŏn′vĕks′] *adjective*, curved out like the outside of a sphere or ball or spoon

con-vey [kən-vā′] *verb*, 1) to take or transport, to carry 2) to communicate, to pass on, to impart, to give 3) to transmit

con-vict [kən-vĭkt′] *noun*, 1) a person who has been judged guilty of a crime, and sentenced *verb*, 2) to decide in court that someone has committed a crime

con-vic-tion [kən-vĭk′shən] *noun*, a strong belief, the state of being convinced, complete confidence

con-vince [kən vĭns′] *verb*, to satisfy by proof

con-vo-lut-ed [kŏn′və-loo′tĭd] *adjective*, coiled around, intricate, complicated

con-vul-sions [kŏn′və-loo′shənz] *noun, plural*, strong and uncontrolled involuntary muscle contractions

cook [kŏok] *noun*, 1) someone who prepares food to eat, *verb*, 2) to prepare food for eating on the stove or in an oven, to bake

cool [kool] *adjective*, 1) moderately cold 2) calm, *verb*, 3) to lower temperature 4) to calm down

coop [koop] *noun*, a pen, a hen-house, a cage for poultry

co-op-er-ate [kō-ŏp′ə-rāt′] *verb*, to work together, to collaborate

co-op-er-a-tion [kō-ŏp′ə-rā′shən] *noun*, the process of working together toward a common goal

co-op-er-a-tive [kō-ŏp′ər-ə-tĭv] *adjective*, willing to join together to help other people

co-or-di-nate [kō-ôr′dn-āt′] *verb*, to make the parts of something work together, to harmonize

co-or-di-na-tion [kō-ôr′dn-ā′shən] *noun*, 1) the organization of separate elements working together 2) dexterity

cope [kōp] *verb*, to deal successfully with something

cop-per [kŏp′ər] *noun*, a common metal of a reddish color, a good conductor of heat and electricity

cop-y [kŏp′ē] *noun*, 1) an imitation, reproduction, *verb*, 2) to make something that is the same as something else

cop-y-right [kŏp′ē-rīt′] *noun*, the exclusive right to publish and sell the matter and form of a literary or artistic work

cor-al [kôr′əl] *noun*, 1) a pink reddish color, salmon 2) a stony substance formed from the skeletons of tiny animals that live on reefs in the ocean

cord [kôrd] *noun*, thin rope

cor-dial [kôr′jəl] *adjective*, sincere, friendly, encouraging, gracious

core [kôr] *noun*, 1) the heart, essence 2) the center of focus

cork [kôrk] *noun*, a light substance that comes from the outer bark of a tree

corn [kôrn] *noun*, 1) a sore that sometimes grows on toes when shoes are tight 2) a grain grown on a stalk as an ear (maize)

cor-ner [kôr′nər] *noun*, 1) a nook, a niche 2) where two lines, edges or streets meet, *verb*, 3) to put someone in a place they cannot escape 4) to monopolize

cor-nu-co-pi-a [kôr′nə-kō′pē-ə] *noun*, 1) a horn containing an abundantly overflowing supply of food 2) abundance, plenty

cor-ol-lary [kôr′ə-lĕr-ē] *noun*, what follows logically, the consequence or effect

cor-o-na-tion [kôr′ə-nā′shən] *noun*, a ceremony to crown a king or queen

cor-po-ra-tion [kôr′pə-rā′shən] *noun*, a business that operates as a person under the law

corps [kôr] *noun*, a troop, a main subdivision of an army

corpse [kôrps] *noun*, a dead body

cor-pu-lent [kôr′pyə-lənt] *adjective*, very fat

cor-pus-cle [kôr′pə-səl] *noun*, a minute particle of matter, a cell, a red or white blood cell

cor-ral [kə-răl′] *noun*, a pen for livestock

cor-rect [kə-rĕkt′] *adjective*, 1) without error, *verb*, 2) to point out an error 3) to make right

cor-rec-tion [kə-rĕk′shən] *noun*, a change or revision, to remove error, to make right

cor-rel-ate [kôr′ə-lāt′] *verb*, to be linked to something

cor-re-la-tion [kôr′ə-lā′shən] *noun*, a mutual relationship, a connection

cor-re-spond [kôr′ĭ-spŏnd′] *verb*, 1) to communicate by writing and receiving letters 2) to fit in with, to match, to agree

cor-re-spond-ence [kôr′ĭ-spŏn′dəns] *noun*, an exchange of letters

cor-ri-dor [kôr′ĭ-dər] *noun*, a hallway connecting rooms or apartments opening onto it

cor-rob-o-rate [kə-rŏb′ə-rāt′] *verb*, to confirm or support with facts,

cor-ro-sive [kə-rō′sĭv] *adjective*, 1) eating away gradually by chemicals 2) sarcastic

cor-ru-gat-ed [kôr′ə-gā′tĭd] *adjective*, bent into a series of alternate ridges and grooves for added stiffness

cor-rupt [kə-rŭpt′] *adjective*, 1) crooked, dishonest, *verb*, 2) to cause to become dishonest

cor-rup-tion [kə-rŭp′shən] *noun*, dishonesty, depravity

cort-ege [kôr-tĕzh′] *noun*, a funeral procession

cos-met-ic [kŏz-mĕt′ĭk] *noun*, a beauty product

cos-mic [kŏz′mĭk] *adjective*, universal, vast

cost [kôst] *noun*, 1) the price you pay when you buy something, *verb*, 2) to have as a price

cos-tume [kŏs′tōōm′] *noun*, clothes worn for a special occasion to represent a particular period in history, traditions of a country, or an assumed character

cot [kŏt] *noun*, a lightweight collapsible bed that usually folds up to a smaller size

cot-tage [kŏt′ĭj] *noun*, a small country house, a bungalow

cot-ton [kŏt′n] *noun*, 1) the white part of the cotton plant used to make cloth 2) the fabric made from this

couch [kouch] *noun*, an upholstered piece of furniture that seats several people

cough [kôf] *noun*, 1) a hacking sound made when air is expelled from the lungs, *verb*, 2) to make a sharp noise when air comes up from the lungs

could [kŏŏd] *verb past tense* of **can**

could-n't [kŏŏd′nt] the *contraction* of the words **could** and **not**

coun-cil [koun′səl] *noun*, an assembly of men and women convened for consultation

coun-sel [koun′səl] *noun*, 1) an attorney, a lawyer 2) an interchange of opinions, advice, *verb*, 3) to advise

coun-se-lor [koun′sə-lər] *noun*, someone who helps you make the best choice

count [kount] *noun*, 1) the total number added together, *verb*, 2) to add up 3) to recite numbers in the correct order 4) to list

coun-te-nance [koun′tə-nəns] *noun*, a facial expression, aspect, appearance, composure

coun-ter [koun′tər] *noun*, 1) the table between customers and workers in a business, *verb*, 2) to make an offer against another

coun-ter-act [koun′tər-ăkt′] *verb*, to act against, to neutralize, to prevent the effects of

coun-ter-clock-wise [koun′tər-klŏk′wīz′] *adjective*, in the opposite direction from the movement of the hands of a clock

coun-ter-feit [koun′tər-fĭt′] *noun*, 1) an imitation intended to deceive, *verb*, 2) to imitate or make a copy of

coun-ter-part [koun′tər-pärt′] *noun*, a thing that completes another, a mate

coun-try [kŭn′trē] *noun*, 1) the land ruled by a government, a nation 2) the land outside of a city, usually farmland or forests

coun-ty [koun′tē] *noun*, an administrative division of a state

coup [kōō] *noun*, a successful sudden attack to seize power

coupe [kōōp] *noun*, a sports car with a sloping back

cou-ple [kŭp′əl] *noun*, 1) two people or things that are usually thought of together, a pair, *verb*, 2) to fasten

cou-pon [kōō′pŏn′] *noun*, a certificate that gives a discount on a purchase, a rebate

cour-age [kûr′ĭj] *noun*, *no plural*, the strength to face danger when overwhelmed by fear

courageous

cou·ra·geous [kə-rā′jəs] *adjective*, brave or bold in danger

cour·i·er [ko͝or′ē-ər] *noun*, a messenger who carries documents

course [kôrs] *noun*, 1) the path of something, the sequence of events 2) a portion of a meal 3) a series of lessons in a school

court [kôrt] *noun*, 1) a place where judges decide how people who break laws should be punished and civil cases heard 2) an open space next to a house in an enclosed area 3) the members of a royal family 4) a royal palace *verb*, 5) to date

cour·te·ous [kûr′tē-əs] *adjective*, showing good manners, polite

cour·te·sy [kûr′tĭ-sē] *noun*, politeness, civility, consideration

court·ship [kôrt′shĭp′] *noun*, going steady, a period of dating before marriage

cous·in [kŭz′ĭn] *noun*, the son or daughter of your uncle or aunt

cove [kōv] *noun*, an inlet

cov·e·nant [kŭv′ə-nənt] *noun*, 1) a legal undertaking to do or to refrain from doing some act or thing 2) a contract under seal

cov·er [kŭv′ər] *noun*, 1) something that is placed over something to protect it, *verb*, 2) to protect by placing a lid, wrapping, etc., around or on top of 3) to hide 4) to go over

co·vert [kŭv′ərt] *adjective*, concealed, hidden, or sheltered

cov·et [kŭv′ĭt] *verb*, to want to have a thing belonging to another person

cow [kou] *noun*, a grown female cattle or certain other large animals

cow·ard [kou′ərd] *noun*, someone who is easily frightened, a person who lacks courage

cow·ard·ice [kou′ər-dĭs] *noun*, lack of courage to face danger, timidity, fearfulness

cow·ard·ly [kou′ərd-lē] *adjective*, timid, afraid, scared, fearful

cow·boy [kou′boi′] *noun*, a man who rides a horse and looks after livestock on a ranch

cow·er [kou′ər] *verb*, to shrink from as if from fear, to tremble

coy·o·te [kī-ō′tē] *noun*, a North American, wolflike dog

co·zy [kō′zē] *adjective*, snug, warm

crab [krăb] *noun*, a sea animal with eight legs, a pair of pincers and a hard shell that lives in a hole

crack [krăk] *noun*, 1) a line showing where something is broken, a crevice 2) a sharp noise, such as a gunshot or thunder, *verb*, 3) to break while separating

cra·dle [krād′l] *noun*, 1) a small bed for an infant 2) the holder for a telephone, *verb*, 3) to rock or shelter an infant or comfort a crying baby

craft [krăft] *noun*, 1) something made by hand to be used as a decoration 2) a boat or plane 3) guile, slyness, skill

cram [krăm] *verb*, to fill or force in

cramp [krămp] *noun*, 1) a painful muscle spasm, *verb*, 2) to keep within narrow limits, to confine

82

crane [krān] *noun*, a machine designed to lift heavy loads from one place to another

cra-ni-um [krā'nē-əm] *noun*, the skull of a vertebrate animal

crank [krăngk] *noun*, a handle that is attached to a machine and that turns, causing motion

crash [krăsh] *noun*, 1) a loud noise caused by a collision or something falling, *verb*, 2) to shatter violently, scattering pieces everywhere

crass [krăs] *adjective*, grossly insensible, rude coarse

crate [krāt] *noun*, a large usually wooden box or container, a case

cra-ter [krā'tər] *noun*, a bowl-shaped cavity, a hole

crave [krāv] *verb*, to want something badly

crawl [krôl] *verb*, to move on one's hands and knees, to move slowly

cray-on [krā'ŏn'] *noun*, a small pencil of colored wax used for drawing or writing

craze [krāz] *noun*, a fad, a popular idea, a trend

cra-zy [krā'zē] *adjective*, insane, wild, daft, very foolish

creak [krēk] *verb*, to make the sound of a door that has not been oiled, a long squeak

cream [krēm] *adjective*, 1) the color yellowish white, ivory 2) a thick lotion, *noun*, 3) the fatty part of milk

crease [krēs] *noun*, the mark or line left by a fold, a wrinkle, a furrow

cre-ate [krē-at'] *verb*, to make, to bring into being, to produce for the first time

cre-a-tion [krē-ā'shən] *noun*, the act of causing to exist, that which is produced

cre-a-tive [krē-ā'tĭv] *adjective*, having new or original ideas

cre-a-tiv-i-ty [krē-ā'tĭv-ĭ-tē] *noun*, the ability to make or invent things, originality

crea-ture [krē'chər] *noun*, an animal or insect or person

cre-den-tials [krĭ-dĕn'shəlz] *noun*, a document verifying a person's ability or authority, references

cred-i-ble [krĕd'ə-bəl] *adjective*, 1) believable 2) reliable or trustworthy

cred-it [krĕd'ĭt] *noun*, 1) a system in which merchandise is given with the understanding that it will be paid for later 2) attention and praise received for doing something

cred-o [krē'dō] *noun*, creed, a belief

cred-u-lous [krĕj'ə-ləs] *adjective*, easily imposed upon, gullible

creed [krēd] *noun*, a statement of religious or ethical beliefs, principles

creek [krēk, krĭk] *noun*, a stream smaller than a river and larger than a brook, an inlet of water

creep [krēp] *verb*, to move slowly and quietly, to move furtively

cre-o-sote [krē'ə-sōt'] *noun*, an oily liquid obtained from coal tar and used as a wood preservative

cre-scen-do [krə-shĕn′dō] *noun*, a musical direction used to indicate increasing loudness

cres-cent [krĕs′ənt] *noun,* a curved shape like a new moon

crest [krĕst] *noun*, 1) the feathers that stick up on top of a bird's head 2) the top of something

crev-ice [krĕv′ĭs] *noun*, a narrow opening in a surface resulting from a split, a cleft, a gap

crew [krōō] *noun*, a group of people who work together

crib [krĭb] *noun*, 1) a bed made for an infant 2) a container for grain

crick-et [krĭk′ĭt] *noun*, 1) a ball game played with two teams of eleven players 2) a small brown insect that makes a shrill chirping noise at night

cried [krīd] *verb, past tense* of **cry**

crime [krīm] *noun*, something that is against the law, illegal acts

crim-i-nal [krĭm′ə-nəl] *adjective*, 1) illegal, wrong, *noun*, 2) one who has broken the law and is guilty of a crime

cringe [krĭnj] *verb*, to shrink back in fear, to cower in fear

crip-ple [krĭp′əl] *verb*, to disable or make lame

cri-sis [krī′sĭs] *noun*, *plural*, **crises** [krī′-sēz], a stressful time when something serious is happening

crisp [krĭsp] *adjective*, 1) dry, brittle, easily broken 2) firm and fresh 3) very clean and pressed

criss cross [krĭs′krôs′] *noun*, a pattern of intersecting lines

cri-te-ri-on [krī-tîr′ē-ən] *noun*, *plural*, **criteria**, a standard for judgment, a benchmark

crit-ic [krĭt′ĭk] *noun*, 1) a person who is paid to review a performance or art 2) one who finds faults

crit-i-cal [krĭt′ĭ-kəl] *adjective*, 1) very important, able or inclined to pass judgment 2) crucial, pivotal, key

crit-i-cism [krĭt′ĭ-sĭz′əm] *noun*, faultfinding, review

crit-i-cize [krĭt′ĭ-sīz′] *verb*, to examine as a critic, to censure

croak [krōk] *noun*, 1) a hoarse sound like that made by frogs, *verb*, 2) to make a low hoarse sound in the throat

croc-o-dile [krŏk′ə-dīl′] *noun*, a large reptile, like an alligator, that lives in tropical climates

crook-ed [krŏŏk′ĭd] *adjective*, 1) bent, not straightened 2) dishonest, deceitful

crop [krŏp] *noun*, food that is planted and grown in a field

cross [krôs] *adjective*, 1) irritated, angry, *noun*, 2) a shape with four arms, *verb*, 3) to go over, to extend across

crouch [krouch] *verb*, to stoop

crow [krō] *noun*, 1) any of a genus of large black birds including the raven, *verb*, 2) to make a sound like a rooster

crowd [kroud] *noun*, 1) a large gathering of people or things, *verb*, 2) to press or cram

crown [kroun] *noun*, 1) a circular head covering, often made of metal with precious stones, worn by royalty, *verb*, 2) to top, to culminate, to climax

cru-ci-al [kroō′shəl] *adjective*, important or essential as decisive in determining a doubtful crisis

cru-ci-ble [kroō′sə-bəl] *noun*, a vessel used for melting substances

cru-ci-fix-ion [kroō′sə-fĭk′shən] *noun*, the killing of someone by nailing them to a cross

crude [kroōd] *adjective*, 1) roughly made 2) rude, ill-mannered

cru-el [kroō′əl] *adjective*, mean, deliberately causing pain

cru-el-ty [kroō′əl-tē] *noun*, unkindness, oppression

cruise [kroōz] *noun*, 1) a holiday on ship, *verb*, 2) to sail or drive around

crum-ble [krŭm′bəl] *verb*, to fall or break apart into small pieces

cru-sade [kroō-sād′] *noun*, 1) a campaign conducted by a band of people devoted to advancing a cause, *verb*, 2) to battle for a cause

crush [krŭsh] *verb*, to hurt or flatten by applying pressure

crust [krŭst] *noun*, a hard surface on the outside of something that often preserves what is inside, such as bread, pie, or the earth

crutch [krŭch] *noun*, a piece of wood or metal extending from under the arm to the ground, to support a person who cannot walk unaided

crux [krŭks] *noun*, the crucial point

cry [krī] *noun*, 1) a shout or call for help, *verb*, 2) to call out loudly 3) tears flowing from the eyes

crypt [krĭpt] *noun*, a vault where bodies are buried, a tomb

cryp-tic [krĭp′tĭk] *adjective*, having a hidden meaning, puzzling

crys-tal [krĭs′təl] *adjective*, 1) clear, transparent, *noun*, 2) a clear mineral 3) a high-quality clear glass

crys-tal-lize [krĭs′tə-līz′] *verb*, 1) to form crystals 2) to become clear

cub [kŭb] *noun*, a young animal of certain mammals, such as a bear, lion, or fox

cube [kyoōb] *noun*, a solid shape with six equal square sides

cu-bic-le [kyoō′bĭ-kəl] *noun*, a small space for work partitioned off in a larger room

cu-cum-ber [kyoō′kŭm′bər] *noun*, a long, green-skinned fruit, pickled or eaten green as a salad

cue [kyoō] *noun*, 1) a signal or hint 2) a rod used to hit a billiard ball

cul-de-sac [kŭl′dĭ-săk′] *noun*, a small dead end off the main road

cu-li-nar-y [kyoō′lə-nĕr′ē] *adjective*, relating to cooking

cull [kŭl] *verb*, to select or gather, to pick out from others

cul-mi-nate [kŭl′mə-nāt′] *verb*, to reach the highest point of altitude, power, climax

cul-pa-ble [kŭl′pə-bəl] *adjective*, deserving blame, liable

culprit

cul-prit [kŭl′prĭt] *noun*, a person charged with or found guilty of a crime or misdeed

cul-ti-vate [kŭl′tə-vāt′] *verb*, 1) to improve or develop, to refine 2) to foster and promote healthy growth, as in crops, to farm

cul-tur-al [kŭl′chər-əl] *adjective*, relating to culture, the arts, good taste, etc.

cul-ture [kŭl′chər] *noun*, 1) advancement of knowledge of a civilization 2) a level of education that appreciates art and style 3) a growth of micro-organisms and bacteria

cum-ber-some [kŭm′bər-səm] *adjective*, heavy, hard to manage, unwieldy

cu-mu-la-tive [kyōōm′yə-lā′tĭv] *adjective*, increasing by successive additions

cun-ning [kŭn′ĭng] *noun*, cleverness, craftiness, skill

cup [kŭp] *noun*, 1) a bowl-shaped drinking container with a handle 2) a unit of measure equal to 8 ounces

cup-board [kŭb′ərd] *noun*, a small closet or recessed shelf

cu-ra-tor [kyōō-rā′tər] *noun*, one who has the care of a museum, a custodian, keeper

curb [kûrb] *noun*, 1) control, restraint 2) a ledge, a boundary, especially that along a street

cur-dle [kûr′dl] *verb*, to sour and coagulate from liquid to a solid, e.g., milk to cheese

cure [kyōōr] *noun*, 1) the remedy that made someone who was sick well again, *verb*, 2) to make

someone who is ill, healthy, to heal

cur-few [kûr′fyōō] *noun*, a set time enforced by law when people are to be off the streets

cu-ri-os-i-ty [kyōōr′ē-ŏs′ĭ-tē] *noun*, 1) the feeling of wanting to know about something 2) something that is strange or unusual

cu-ri-ous [kyōōr′ē-əs] *adjective*, 1) eager to know about all things 2) singular, unusual, odd

curl [kûrl] *noun*, 1) a ringlet or spiral shape, *verb*, 2) to make straight hair wavy and curly

cur-mudg-eon [kər-mŭj′ən] *noun*, a mean, bad-tempered person

cur-rant [kûr′ənt] *noun*, a small berry, similar to a raisin

cur-ren-cy [kûr′ən-sē] *noun*, money in circulation

cur-rent [kûr′ənt] *adjective*, 1) up to date, pertaining to the present, *noun*, 2) the powerful flow of water or electricity or air

cur-ric-u-lum [kə-rĭk′yə-ləm] *noun*, the classes that a school requires or offers

cur-ry [kûr′ē, kûr′ē] *noun*, 1) a yellow powder containing several spices, including turmeric, used to flavor cooking, *verb*, 2) to seek favor by flattery 3) to brush or groom a horse

curse [kûrs] *noun*, 1) something said hoping harm will come to someone, *verb*, 2) to wish bad luck or injury on someone 3) to use profanity

cur-sive [kûr′sĭv] *adjective*, characteristic of handwriting in which the letters flow together

cur-tail [kər tāl'] *verb*, to cut short, to reduce, to decrease

cur-tain [kûr'tn] *noun*, a piece of cloth hung over a window or doorway as a screen or cover

cur-tsy [kûrt'sē] *noun*, 1) a formal bow made with bent knees by a woman, *verb*, 2) to make a bow with one foot forward, as a gesture of respect

cur-va-ture [kûr'və-chŏŏr'] *noun*, a curve, a bend

curve [kûrv] *noun*, a bend or arch

curv-ed [kûrvd] *adjective*, having a line with no part straight or flat

cush-ion [kŏŏsh'ən] *noun*, a case or bag stuffed with some soft and elastic material

cus-tard [kŭs'tərd] *noun*, a pudding made of milk and eggs

cus-to-di-an [kŭ-stō'dē-ən] *noun*, a caretaker or porter, a janitor

cus-to-dy [kŭs'tə-dē] *noun*, safe-keeping under penalty or under a judge's ruling, imprisonment

cus-tom [kŭs'təm] *noun*, a tradition passed on from one generation to the next

cus-tom-ar-y [kŭs'tə-mĕr'ē] *adjective*, established by common usage, habitual

cus-tom-er [kŭs'tə-mər] *noun*, one who makes regular purchases from a business, a patron

cut [kŭt] *noun*, 1) a wound or injury that may cause the skin to bleed 2) an insult, a derogatory remark 3) something that has been made shorter, *verb*, 4) to break with a knife or blade

cute [kyōōt] *adjective*, lovable, adorable, delightful

cu-ti-cle [kyōō'tĭ-kəl] *noun*, the skin surrounding the fingernail

cy-cle [sī'kəl] *noun*, 1) events that happen in the same order over and over again 2) a bicycle, *verb*, 3) to move in a circuit controlled by alternating negative and positive currents

cy-clone [sī'klōn'] *noun*, a violent windstorm, sometimes called a typhoon or hurricane, depending on location and intensity

cyl-in-der [sĭl'ən-dər] *noun*, a solid spherical figure with two faces that are circles

cy-lin-dri-cal [sə-lĭn'drĭ-kəl] *adjective*, a circular or spherical shape with straight sides

cym-bal [sĭm'bəl] *noun*, a large round metal plate used as a percussion instrument

cyn-ic [sĭn'ĭk] *noun*, a doubter, a skeptic, an unbeliever

cyn-i-cism [sĭn'ĭ-sĭz'əm] *noun*, an attitude given to sneering at honesty or virtue, a belief that people are self-interested

cy-press [sī'prĭs] *noun*, an evergreen tree with scale-like needles

cyst [sĭst] *noun*, a fluid-filled pouch attached to a body part

czar [zär, tsär] *noun*, the supreme ruler of an empire, especially the ruler of Russia before 1917

D

dad [dăd] *noun*, father

daffodil

daf-fo-dil [dăf′ə-dĭl] *noun*, a spring flowering bulb, yellow or white, with a trumpet-like center

dag-ger [dăg′ər] *noun*, a weapon used specifically for stabbing, a knife

dai-ly [dā′lē] *adjective*, done or occurring every day

dain-ty [dān′tē] *adjective*, delicate, fragile, small, pretty, refined

dair-y [dâr′ē] *noun*, a place where milk is produced and pasteurized

da-is [dā′ĭs] *noun*, a raised platform for honored guests

dai-sy [dā′zē] *noun*, a flower with a yellow or brown center surrounded by petals

dal-ly [dăl′ē] *verb*, to loiter, to fiddle around, to flirt

dam [dăm] *noun*, 1) a wall built across a river or lake that controls water flow, *verb*, 2) to construct a wall in a lake to retain the water and to regulate its flow

dam-age [dăm′ĭj] *noun*, 1) loss or detriment due to injury or harm, *verb*, 2) to hurt or cause harm or injury to something, to destroy

damp [dămp] *adjective*, humid, somewhat wet, moist

dance [dăns] *noun*, 1) a set of movements designed to accompany music, *verb*, 2) to move in rhythm with music, to skip or leap, to perform

dan-de-li-on [dăn′dl-ī′ən] *noun*, a bitter herb with yellow flowers, often cooked and eaten

dan-ger [dān′jər] *noun*, the possibility of harm

dan-ger-ous [dān′jər-əs] *adjective*, full of risk, perilous, hazardous, likely to harm

dan-gle [dăng′gəl] *verb*, to hang, to suspend loosely

dap-pled [dăp′əld] *adjective*, spotted with color or shade

dare [dâr] *verb*, to be brave, bold

dark [därk] *adjective*, 1) without light, not reflecting light, shadowy, *noun*, 2) a space without light

dark-ness [därk′nĕs] *noun*, no plural, a lack of light

darl-ing [där′lĭng] *adjective*, 1) a term of affection for someone who is loved, *noun*, 2) a sweetheart, the favorite

darn [därn] *verb*, to mend socks

dart [därt] *noun*, 1) a small weapon like a tiny arrow that can be thrown by hand, *verb*, 2) to move quickly or suddenly

dash [dăsh] *noun*, 1) a punctuation mark used to indicate a pause 2) a small amount, *verb*, 3) to move quickly 4) to hit, to shatter, to break, to strike

da-ta [dā′tə, dăt′ə, dä′tə] *noun*, information collected on a subject for reference

da-ta-base [dā′tə-bās′, dăt′ə-] *noun*, information arranged for computer access

date [dāt] *noun*, 1) the date, month, and year 2) a small, sweet, brown fruit grown in tropical climates, *verb*, 3) to measure, to mark 4) to court

daub [dôb] *verb*, to dab, to smear, to spread paint or another liquid

daugh-ter [dô'tər] *noun*, a human female considered with reference to her parents

daunt [dônt] *verb*, to intimidate

daunt-less [dônt'lĭs] *adjective*, bold

daw-dle [dôd'l] *verb*, to dilly dally, to waste time

dawn [dôn] *noun*, the break of day when the sun rises

day [dā] *noun*, 1) the period of 24 hours when the earth completes one rotation on its axis 2) the opposite of night, when the sun is in the sky

daze [dāz] *noun*, 1) a stupor, amazement, *verb*, 2) to cause to feel stunned

daz-zle [dăz'əl] *verb*, to awe, to impress with splendor

dead [dĕd] *adjective*, 1) not alive, inactive, *noun*, 2) referring to people who are no longer alive

dead-line [dĕd'līn'] *noun*, a set time when an assignment is to be finished, a time limit

dead-lock [dĕd'lŏk'] *noun*, a stalemate, a state in which no progress can be made

dead-ly [dĕd'lē] *adjective*, dangerous, possibly fatal, causing death, mortal

deaf [dĕf] *adjective*, 1) not able to hear 2) not listening

deal [dēl] *noun*, 1) a business agreement 2) an unspecified amount 3) a bargain, *verb*, 4) to barter, or buy and sell 5) to be concerned, to cope 6) to pass out or to distribute, i.e. playing cards

deal-er [dē'lər] *noun*, 1) a person who buys and sells things 2) in a card game, the person who holds the cards and passes them out

dear [dîr] *adjective*, 1) beloved 2) costly

dear-ly [dîr'lē] *adverb*, very much

death [dĕth] *noun*, the end of life

de-ba-cle [dĭ-bä'kəl] *noun*, a sudden downfall

de-bat-a-ble [dĭ-bā'tə-bəl] *adjective*, disputable, open to question

de-bate [dĭ-bāt'] *noun*, 1) a public discussion of a topic in which opposing points of view are presented, *verb*, 2) to argue different points of view

de-bil-i-tate [dĭ-bĭl'ĭ-tāt'] *verb*, to weaken

deb-it [dĕb'ĭt] *noun*, an entry on an account for a sum owed

de-bris [də-brē', dā'brē'] *noun*, rubbish, especially such as results from destruction

debt [dĕt] *noun*, money owed

debt-or [dĕt'ər] *noun*, one who owes something, especially money

de-but [dā-byoō'] *noun*, 1) a beginning 2) first public appearance

dec-ade [dĕk'ād'] *noun*, a period of ten years

de-cay [dĭ-kā'] *noun*, 1) the condition of being rotten or degenerating, *verb*, 2) to rot, to decompose 3) to decline

de-ceased [dĭ-sēst'] *adjective*, dead, defunct, without life

deceit

de-ceit [dǐ-sēt′] *noun*, fraud, trickery, deception, lie

de-ceit-ful [dǐ-sēt′fəl] *adjective*, dishonest, deceptive, false

de-ceive [dǐ-sēv′] *verb*, to lead into error, to mislead, to delude, to lie to

De-cem-ber [dǐ-sĕm′bər] *noun*, the twelfth month of the year, having 31 days

de-cen-cy [dē′sən-sē] *noun*, behavior that is proper and moral

de-cent [dē′sənt] *adjective*, honorable, good, fitting, ethical

de-cep-tion [dǐ-sĕp′shən] *noun*, the act of deceiving, fraud, false representation, dishonesty

de-cide [dǐ-sīd′] *verb*, to determine, to make a choice, to resolve, to choose

de-cid-u-ous [dǐ-sǐj′ōō-əs] *adjective*, falling out at a certain stage of development (as some leaves, antlers, insect wings, or milk teeth)

dec-i-mal [dĕs′ə-məl] *adjective,* pertaining to or founded on the number ten

de-ci-pher [dǐ-sī′fər] *verb*, 1) to translate from coded characters 2) to make out or read

de-ci-sion [dǐ-sǐzh′ən] *noun*, act or result of deciding or settling, a conclusion, a resolution

de-ci-sive [dǐ-sī′sǐv] *adjective*, positive, able to decide quickly

de-ci-sive-ly [dǐ-sī′sǐv-lē] *adverb*, in a clean manner, precisely

deck [dĕk] *noun*, 1) the floor on each level of a ship 2) a pack of playing cards 3) a flat structure without a roof attached to a house

dec-la-ra-tion [dĕk′lə-rā′shən] *noun*, an announcement or statement, a proclamation

de-clare [dǐ-klâr′] *verb*, to formally announce, to state firmly and solemnly

de-cline [dǐ-klīn′] *noun*, 1) a gradual lessening of strength or numbers, *verb*, 2) to refuse 3) to steadily become less

de-com-pose [dē′kəm-pōz′] *verb*, 1) to rot or decay 2) to separate a chemical into constituent parts

de-com-po-si-tion [dē-kŏm′pə-zǐsh′ən] *noun*, the process of decay

dec-o-rate [dĕk′ə-rāt′] *verb*, to beautify, to adorn, to enhance

dec-o-ra-tion [dĕk′ə-rā′shən] *noun*, 1) an ornament 2) an award such as a ribbon or a medal

dec-o-rous [dĕk′ər-əs] *adjective*, proper, correct, polite

de-coy [dē′koi′] *noun*, something used as a lure or bait

de-crease [dǐ-krēs′] *noun*, 1) the amount by which something has been made smaller, *verb*, 2) to diminish and lessen the amount, to reduce

de-cree [dǐ-krē′] *noun*, 1) a pronouncement, a declaration, *verb*, 2) to proclaim, to order

de-crep-it [dǐ-krĕp′ǐt] *adjective*, broken down with age, feeble, worn out, dilapidated

de-cry [dǐ-krī′] *verb*, to discredit, to denounce publicly

ded-i-cate [dĕd'ĭ-kāt'] *verb*, 1) to recognize in a solemn ceremony 2) to devote oneself to something 3) to inscribe a message in the front of a book

ded-i-ca-tion [dĕd'ĭ-kā'shən] *noun*, 1) devotion to something 2) an acknowledgement of another person by an author

de-duce [dĭ-dōōs'] *verb*, to reach a conclusion by reasoning

de-duct [dĭ-dŭkt'] *verb*, to subtract, to take away

deed [dēd] *noun*, 1) an action taken, something someone has done 2) a legal document proving that someone owns a piece of land or property

deep [dēp] *adjective*, 1) extending or reaching a long distance beneath the surface of the earth 2) intense, heart-felt, feelings

deer [dîr] *noun*, an animal with hooves that eats grass and leaves; the males have antlers

de-face [dĭ-fās'] *verb*, to mar, to vandalize, to destroy the appearance of

def-a-ma-tion [dĕf'ə-mā'shən] *noun*, harm to a person's good reputation, slander, libel

de-fault [dĭ-fôlt'] *noun*, 1) failure to fulfill an obligation 2) a computer setting that is used if the user does not make another choice

de-feat [dĭ-fēt'] *noun*, 1) a loss to be overcome, *verb*, 2) to beat, to conquer, to cause to fail

de-fect [dē'fĕkt'] *noun*, 1) a fault, a failing, a drawback, *verb*, 2) to desert your country or cause

de-fec-tive [dĭ-fĕk'tĭv] *adjective*, faulty, broken, imperfect

de-fend [dĭ-fĕnd'] *verb*, to fight to protect something, to guard

de-fend-ant [dĭ-fĕn'dənt] *noun*, a person required to make an answer in a lawsuit or a criminal case

de-fense [dĭ-fĕns'] *noun*, 1) protection from harm 2) justification for an action 3) protection of the goal in sports

de-fen-sive [dĭ-fĕn'sĭv] *adjective*, guarding, protective

de-fer [dĭ-fûr'] *verb*, 1) to put off, to postpone 2) to submit respectfully

de-fer-ence [dĕf'ər-əns] *noun*, a yielding of judgment with respect to another, courtesy

de-fi-ance [dĭ-fī'əns] *noun*, a state of open opposition, a challenge

de-fi-ant [dĭ-fī'ənt] *adjective*, opposing or resisting power or authority, disobedient

def-i-cit [dĕf'ĭ-sĭt] *noun*, an amount that falls short of a goal or perfect balance

de-fine [dĭ-fīn'] *verb*, 1) to determine the boundaries of something 2) to give the meaning of

def-i-nite [dĕf'ə-nĭt] *adjective*, fixed, having certain limits, precise, clearly defined

def-i-nite-ly [dĕf'ə-nĭt-lē] *adverb*, precisely, clearly stated, certainly

def-i-ni-tion [dĕf'ə-nĭsh'ən] *noun*, an explanation of the meaning of a word or term

definitive

de-fin-i-tive [dǐ-fǐn′ǐ-tǐv] *adjective*, final, conclusive, decisive

de-flate [dǐ-flāt′] *verb*, 1) to let the air out 2) to dishearten, to discourage

de-flect [dǐ-flěkt′] *verb*, 1) to turn aside 2) to cause something to change direction

de-form-i-ty [dǐ-fôr′mǐ-tē] *noun*, a lack of proper form or symmetry, distortion

de-fraud [dǐ-frôd′] *verb*, to deprive someone of a right or property through deceit, to swindle

de-fray [dǐ-frā′] *verb*, to meet the cost of something, to pay

de-frost [dē-frôst′] *verb*, to melt, to thaw, to remove ice by melting

deft [děft] *adjective*, able, skillful,

de-funct [dǐ-fŭngkt′] *adjective*, ended, dead, no longer existing

de-fy [dǐ-fī′] *verb*, to challenge a stronger force, to disobey

de-gen-er-ate [dǐ-jěn′ər-āt′] *verb*, to become worse physically, mentally or morally, to decay

de-grade [dǐ-grād′] *verb*, to lower someone's reputation or character, to treat disrespectfully

de-gree [dǐ-grē′] *noun*, 1) a unit for measuring temperature or angles 2) a grade or rank conferred by colleges or un graduates or other scholars 3) a measured portion determined on a scale 4) a proportion

de-i-fy [dē′ə-fī′] *verb*, to idolize or worship as a god

de-jec-tion [dǐ-jěk′shən] *noun*, sadness, depression, low spirits

Del-a-ware [děl′ə-wâr′] *noun*, a state on the east coast of the United States; the capital is Dover. The state flower of **Delaware** is the peach blossom and the motto is "Liberty and Independence."

de-lay [dǐ-lā′] *noun*, 1) a period of waiting, *verb*, 2) to postpone, to make something take longer

de-lec-ta-ble [dǐ-lěk′tə-bəl] *adjective*, delicious

del-e-gate [děl′ǐ-gāt′] *noun*, 1) one sent and empowered to act for another, a deputy, *verb*, 2) to entrust a duty or task to another, to assign

de-lete [dǐ-lēt′] *verb*, to erase, to mark for omission, to remove

de-lib-er-ate [dǐ-lǐb′ər-ǐt] *adjective*, 1) planned or done on purpose, *verb*, [dǐ-lǐb′ər-āt] 2) to think carefully in or to make up one's mind, to consider reasons for and against

de-lib-er-ate-ly [dǐ-lǐb′ər-ǐt-lē] *adverb*, after mature consideration, consciously, intentionally, on purpose

del-i-ca-tes-sen [děl′ǐ-kə-těs′ən] *noun*, a shop where meat, cheese, and salads are sold

del-i-ca-cy [děl′ǐ-kə-sē] *noun*, 1) good taste, tact 2) choice food

de-li-cious [dǐ-lǐsh′əs] *adjective*, giving pleasure to the senses, especially taste

de-light [dǐ-līt′] *noun*, 1) a joy, *verb*, 2) to please, to cause joy or happiness

de-light-ful [dǐ-līt′fəl] *adjective*, pleasing, causing pleasure and satisfaction

de-lin-quent [dǐ-lǐng′kwənt] *adjective*, 1) failing to do what is required 2) past due, *noun*, 3) a child who persistently breaks the law

de-lir-i-ous [dǐ-lîr′ē-əs] *adjective*, wandering in mind, light-headed

de-liv-er [dǐ-lǐv′ər] *verb*, 1) to carry or take to a person to whom something is addressed 2) to assist in the birth of a baby 3) to utter, to speak 4) to rescue or set free

de-liv-er-y [dǐ-lǐv′ə-rē] *noun*, the act of delivering goods, a letter, etc. 2) goods that have been brought to be handed over

del-ta [děl′tə] *noun*, a fan-shaped area of land where a river splits into channels at its mouth

de-lude [dǐ-lōōd′] *verb*, to deceive, to fool, to mislead

de-lu-sion [dǐ-lōō′zhən] *noun*, 1) a mirage, a fantasy 2) a mistake, a misconception, a false belief

delve [dělv] *verb*, to examine, to probe, to look through, to search

dem-a-gogue [děm′ə-gôg′] *noun*, a person who wins support by appealing to popular feelings and prejudices especially in speeches

de-mand [dǐ-mǎnd′] *noun*, 1) a strong request, *verb*, 2) to ask for something very strongly, to insist or require, to claim

de-mean [dǐ-mēn′] *verb*, to humiliate, to lower

de-mean-or [dǐ-mē′nər] *noun*, a person's posture or conduct, behavior, attitude

de-mise [dǐ-mīz′] *noun*, the death of a person, the end of something, a failure

de-moc-ra-cy [dǐ-mŏk′rə-sē] *noun*, a form of government in which people exercise power by electing representatives

Dem-o-crat [děm′ə-krăt′] *noun*, a person who advocates democracy, one who believes in government in which all people have a vote

dem-o-crat-ic [děm′ə-krăt′ ĭk] *adjective*, 1) favoring equality, considerate of humanity 2) representative

de-mol-ish [dǐ-mŏl′ĭsh] *verb*, to destroy, to ruin, to take down

dem-o-li-tion [děm′ə-lĭsh′ən] *noun*, destruction

dem-on-strate [děm′ən-strāt′] *verb*, to establish beyond doubt, to show

dem-on-stra-tion [děm′ən stra′shən] *noun*, 1) a presentation of evidence, proof 2) an exhibit, a display 3) a peaceful march, a protest

de-mor-al-ize [dǐ-môr′ə-līz′] *verb*, 1) to corrupt, to destroy the morals of someone 2) to discourage 3) to confuse

de-mur [dǐ-mûr′] *noun*, 1) hesitation, objection, refusal, *verb*, 2) to make an objection, to delay

de-mure [dǐ-myōōr′] *adjective*, quietly modest, reserved

den [dĕn] *noun*, 1) a place in which a wild animal lives, a lair 2) a quiet, private room

den-i-grate [dĕn'ĭ-grāt'] *verb*, to ridicule, to belittle, to defame

den-im [dĕn'ĭm] *noun*, a heavy cotton fabric, usually blue, used to make clothing such as jeans

de-nom-i-na-tion [dĭ-nŏm'ə-nā'shən] *noun*, 1) classification, identification, 2) a branch of a religion 3) the value of a banknote, stamp, etc.

de-nom-i-na-tor [dĭ-nŏm'ə-nā'tər] *noun*, the number base or the quantity below the line of a fraction

de-nounce [dĭ-*nouns*'] *verb*, to attack as deserving of punishment or censure

dense [dĕns] *adjective*, compact, closely packed together

den-si-ty [dĕn'sĭ-tē] *noun*, 1) mass per unit of volume 2) the number of people in a specified area

dent [dĕnt] *noun*, 1) an indentation, a nick, *verb*, 2) to make a gouge

den-tal [dĕn'tl] *adjective*, referring to teeth or dentistry

de-nun-ci-a-tion [dĭ-nŭn'sē-ā'shən] *noun*, a public accusation, condemnation

de-ny [dĭ-nī'] *verb*, to declare something untrue

de-part [dĭ-pärt'] *verb*, to leave, to go away from 2) deviate, to withdraw 3) to die

de-part-ment [dĭ-pärt'mənt] *noun*, a separate division of a government or a business

de-par-ture [dĭ-pär'chər] *noun*, the act of leaving a place or the subject

de-pend [dĭ-pĕnd']*verb*, to be determined, to be a result of 2) to need, to trust, to rely on

de-pend-a-ble [dĭ-pĕnd'ā'bəl] *adjective*, reliable

de-pend-ant or de-pend-ent [dĭ-pĕn'dənt] *noun*, a person supported by another

de-pend-ent [dĭ-pĕn'dənt] *adjective*, relying on something else for support, contingent

de-pict [dĭ-pĭkt'] *verb*, to portray

de-plete [dĭ-plēt'] *verb*, to use up

de-plor-able [dĭ-plôr'ə-bəl] *adjective*, shockingly bad, vile, horrible, unfortunate

de-plore [dĭ-plôr'] *verb*, to feel or express disapproval

de-ploy [dĭ-ploi'] *verb*, to move troops to the battle line to make it stronger, to position strategically

de-port [dĭ-pôrt'] *verb*, to force someone to leave a country

de-pose [dĭ-pōz'] *verb*, 1) to remove from office or power 2) to testify under oath

de-pos-it [dĭ-pŏz'ĭt] *noun*, 1) money placed in a bank for safekeeping 2) money to hold something until the full price is paid 3) sediment that has settled on the bottom, *verb*, 4) to put aside for safekeeping

de-po-si-tion [dĕp'ə-zĭsh'ən] *noun*, testimony under oath

de-pot [dē'pō] *noun*, a railroad or bus station 2) a warehouse

de-praved [dǐ-prāvd′] *adjective*, morally corrupt

de-pre-ci-ate [dǐ-prē′shē-āt′] *verb*, to diminish in value

de-pre-ci-a-tion [dǐ-prē′shē-ā′shən] *noun*, a decrease in value

dep-re-da-tion [děp′rǐ-dā′shən] *noun*, stealing, pillage, plundering, destruction

de-press [dǐ-prěs′] *verb*, 1) to make someone feel sad and despondent 2) to hold down

de-pres-sion [dǐ-prěsh′ən] *noun*, 1) a feeling of sadness 2) a mental illness characterized by hopelessness and despair 3)a low place or hole or basin 4) a major slump in the economy, a long recession

de-prive [dǐ-prīv′] *verb*, to deny, to keep from having, to prevent from enjoying something

depth [děpth] *noun*, 1) wisdom, intellect 2)the distance from the top downward

de-ranged [dǐ-rānjd′] *adjective*, insane, mad, crazy

der-by [dûr′bē] *noun*, 1) a contest or race, a horserace 2) a round hat with a narrow brim

der-e-lict [děr′ə-lǐkt′] *adjective*, 1) abandoned 2) failing in one's duty, *noun* 3) a vagrant

de-ride [dǐ-rīd′] *verb*, to scoff at

de-ri-sion [dǐ-rǐzh′ən] *noun*, ridicule, scorn, mockery

de-riv-a-tive [dǐ-rǐv′ə-tǐv] *noun*, something derived from another source

de-rive [dǐ-rīv′] *verb*, to obtain or issue from a source

de-rog-a-to-ry [dǐ-rǒg′ə-tôr′ē] *adjective*, negative, mean, detracting, disparaging

der-rick [děr′ǐk] *noun*, 1) a tall tower that fits over an oil well, that supports drilling machinery 2) a large hoisting crane

dearth [dûrth] *noun*, a scarcity, lack, too small a supply

de-scend [dǐ-sěnd′] *verb*, to go or move down, to fall, to drop

de-scend-ant [dǐ-sěn′dənt] *noun*, a person descended from a particular ancestor, such as a child or a grandchild

de-scent [dǐ-sěnt′] *noun*, a change from higher to lower, a downward movement

de-scribe [dǐ-skrīb′] *verb*, 1) to set forth in words, to tell about, to recount 2) to mark out, to draw

de-scrip-tion [dǐ-skrǐp′shən] *noun*, act or result of representing by words, a narration

des-e-crate [děs′ǐ-krāt′] *verb*, to destroy something sacred or of religious significance

des-ert [děz′ərt] *noun*, 1) a dry region that is sandy and without trees, [dǐ-zûrt′] *verb*, 2) to leave, to leave the armed forces without permission, to abandon

de-ser-tion [dǐ-zûr′shən] *noun*, 1) abandonment 2)the act of leaving service in the armed forces without permission

de-serve [dǐ-zûrv′] *verb*, to merit or be worthy of, to earn by service

design

de-sign [dĭ-zīn′] *noun*, 1) a plan, 2) a pattern, *verb*, 3) to conceive, to invent 4) to create a plan for something, to scheme

des-ig-nate [dĕz′ĭg-nāt′] *verb*, 1) to point out, to indicate 2) to give a name 3) to appoint

de-sign-er [dĭ-zī′nər] *noun*, a person who creates plans for clothes, buildings, products, etc.

de-sire [dĭ-zīr′] *noun*, 1) a want, wish, craving, *verb*, 2) to long for, to set your heart on

desk [dĕsk] *noun*, a work table usually with drawers for paper, pencils, etc.

des-o-late [dĕs′ə-lĭt] *adjective*, deserted, forsaken, comfortless, dismal, abandoned

des-o-la-tion [dĕs′ə-lā′shən] *noun*, 1) emptiness, extinction 2) extreme sadness

de-spair [dĭ-spâr′] *noun*, 1) the state of being without hope, *verb*, 2) to have no hope or optimism

des-per-ate [dĕs′pər-ĭt] *adjective*, hopeless, downcast, frantic, reckless because of despair

des-per-a-tion [dĕs′pə-rā′shən] *noun*, a great need, an anxious feeling out of hopelessness

de-spise [dĭ-spīz′] *verb*, to look down upon with contempt, to consider unworthy of respect

de-spite [dĭ-spīt′] *preposition*, 1) in spite of, notwithstanding, *noun* 2) insult, injury

de-spoil [dĭ-spoil′] *verb*, to plunder

de-spond-ent [dĭ-spŏn′dənt] *adjective*, discouraged, without hope

des-pot-ic [dĭ-spŏt′ĭk] *adjective*, 1) possessing unlimited power 2) tyrannical

des-pot-ism [dĕs′pə-tĭz′əm] *noun*, tyranny, dictatorship, repression

des-sert [dĭ-zûrt′] *noun*, usually sweet, the last course of a meal

des-ti-na-tion [dĕs′tə-nā′shən] *noun*, the place someone is going, a goal, the end of a journey

des-ti-ny [dĕs′tə-nē] *noun*, fate, a condition predetermined by divine will, providence

des-ti-tute [dĕs′tĭ-tōōt′] *adjective*, without means of existence, extremely poor, penniless

de-stroy [dĭ-stroi′] *verb*, to put an end to, to ruin or annihilate

de-struc-tion [dĭ-strŭk′shən] *noun*, the act of tearing down, causing harm or damage

de-struc-tive [dĭ-strŭk′tĭv] *adjective*, harmful, ruinous, causing damage

de-tach [dĭ-tăch′] *verb*, to separate, to remove, to disconnect, to undo

de-tail [dĭ-tāl′] *noun*, a small part of a larger whole, an item

de-tain [dĭ-tān′] *verb*, 1) to restrain, to confine, to hold back, 2) to delay, to hinder, to impede

de-tect [dĭ-tĕkt′] *verb*, to discover the presence of, to find

de-tec-tive [dĭ-tĕk′tĭv] *noun*, 1) a special policeman who is trained to investigate crimes 2) a person whose job it is to obtain information for clients

de-ter-gent [dĭ-tûr′jənt] *noun*, a chemical substance like soap used to wash clothes or dishes

de-te-ri-o-rate [dĭ-tîr′ē-ə-rāt′] *verb*, to grow worse, to rot, to decay

de-te-ri-o-ra-tion [dĭ-tîr′ē-ə-rā′shən] *noun*, a process of getting worse

de-ter-mi-na-tion [dĭ-tûr′mə-nā′shən] *noun*, a firm purpose, resolve, willpower

de-ter-mine [dĭ-tûr′mĭn] *verb*, to come to a decision, to realize

de-test [dĭ-tĕst′] *verb*, to hate

de-tour [dē′tŏŏr′] *noun*, a temporary way around a blockage in the road

de-tract [dĭ-trăkt′] *verb*, to belittle, to take away from

det-ri-men-tal [dĕt′rə-mĕn′tl] *adjective*, harmful, injurious

dev-as-tate [dĕv′ə-stāt′] *verb*, 1) to lay waste, to destroy 2) to cause someone sorrow

de-vel-op [dĭ-vĕl′əp] *verb*, unfold gradually, to evolve, to mature

de-vel-op-ment [dĭ-vĕl′əp-mənt] *noun*, 1) expansion, growth 2) a new piece of information

de-vi-ate [dē′vē-āt′] *verb*, to turn away from an accepted course of action or standard, to stray

de-vice [dĭ-vīs′] *noun*, 1) an instrument used for a particular purpose 2) a scheme, a trick

dev-il [dĕv′əl] *noun*, 1) an evil spirit, thought to cause destruction and bad things 2) a wicked or mischievous person

de-vi-ous [dē′vē-əs] *adjective*, crafty, dishonest, gone astray

de-vise [dĭ-vīz′] *verb*, to contrive, to invent, to plan, to create

de-void [dĭ-void′] *adjective*, empty, entirely without, lacking

de-vote [dĭ-vōt′] *verb*, to dedicate, to give entirely, to use for a specific purpose

de-vo-tion [dĭ-vō′shən] *noun*, 1) dedication, affection, love 2) religious worship

de-vour [dĭ-vour′] *verb*, to consume greedily, to eat

de-vout [dĭ-vout′] *adjective*, sincere, dedicated, having religious feeling

dew-drop [dōō′drŏp′] *noun*, drops of water that form on anything exposed to air overnight

dex-ter-i-ty [dĕk-stĕr′ĭ-tē] *noun*, the ability to operate skillfully by hand, adroitness

di-a-be-tes [dī′ə-bē′tĭs] *noun*, a metabolic disorder in which one is very thirsty, produces excessive urine, and is unable to produce or use sufficient insulin

di-a-bol-ic-al [dī′ə-bŏl′ĭ-kəl] *adjective*, evil, devilish

di-ag-no-sis [dī′əg-nō′sĭs] *noun*, an identification of a disease based on signs or symptoms

di-ag-o-nal [dī-ăg′ə-nəl] *adjective*, a line extending from one corner of a polygon to another corner, that is not adjacent

di-a-gram [dī′ə-grăm′] *noun*, 1) a figure, or plan drawn to show how something works, *verb*, 2) to represent by a drawing

dial

di-al [dī′əl] *noun*, a round face on a machine, often with numbers on it, that sets the instrument to perform a specific task 2) the face of a clock, watch, etc. 3) to make a telephone call

di-a-lect [dī′ə-lĕkt′] *noun*, a form of speech characterized by local peculiarities

di-a-logue [dī′ə-lôg′] *noun*, 1) a conversation between two or more people, especially in a play or narrative 2) a discussion

di-am-e-ter [dī-ăm′ĭ-tər] *noun*, any straight line passing from side to side, through the center of a figure or body

dia-mond [dī′ə-mənd] *noun*, 1) a hard clear stone that is very precious 2) a plane shape with four equal sides with two acute angles and two obtuse angles 3) a baseball field

di-a-phragm [dī′ə-frăm′] *noun*, the muscle for breathing located between the lungs and the stomach

di-ar-rhe-a [dī′ə-rē′ə] *noun*, a purging or looseness of the bowels

di-a-ry [dī′ə-rē] *noun*, a journal in which a person makes daily entries of observations and personal experiences

di-a-tribe [dī′ə-trīb′] *noun*, a tirade, a scolding, a forceful and bitter verbal attack against someone or something

dice, [dīs] *noun, plural* 1) a small square cube with a different number of dots on each side ranging from 1-6, often used in games of chance, 2) *verb*, to cut into small cubes

di-chot-o-my [dī-kŏt′ə-mē] *noun*, a division into two parts

dic-tate [dĭk′tāt′] *verb*, 1) to speak into a recording device or so that someone else can write or type what is said 2) to impose, to decree, to command

dic-ta-tor [dĭk′tā′tər] *noun*, an absolute ruler, a tyrant

dic-tion [dĭk′shən] *noun*, enunciation of words

dic-tion-ar-y [dĭk′shə-nĕr′ē] *noun*, a word list, usually with definitions, pronunciations, etc.

did [dĭd] *past tense* of **do**

did-n't [dĭd′nt] the *contraction* of the words **did** and **not**

die [dī] *verb*, 1) to stop living or existing 2) to fade away

die-sel [dē′zəl, -səl] *noun*, 1) an engine that burns oil instead of gasoline 2) the petroleum fuel used in a diesel engine

di-et [dī′ĭt] *noun*, 1) the food someone eats, *verb*, 2) to reduce the intake of food

dif-fer [dĭf′ər] *verb*, to be unlike, to vary, to disagree

dif-fer-ence [dĭf′ər-əns] *noun*, 1) contrast, unlikeness 2) disagreement, dissension 3) the answer in subtraction

dif-fer-ent [dĭf′ər-ənt] *adjective*, 1) not alike 2) not the same as the rest, strange 3) separate

dif-fer-ent-ial [dĭf′ə-rĕn′shəl] *adjective*, 1) showing or making a difference, *noun* 2) a gear that allows two wheels to rotate at different speeds

dif-fi-cult [dĭf′ĭ-kŭlt′] *adjective*, hard to manage or please, tough

dif-fi-cul-ty [dĭf′ĭ-kŭl′tē] *noun*, a hardship, a problem

dif-fuse *adjective*, [dĭ-fyoo′ s′] 1) not concentrated, [dĭ-fyooz′] *verb*, 2) to spread or circulate 3) to cause to flow on all sides

dif-fu-sion ən] *noun*, the process of spreading in all directions like gas

dig [dĭg] *verb*, 1) to unearth dirt with tools or a machine to make a hole 2) to search, to probe

di-gest [dī-jĕst′]*noun*, 1) a condensed literary work, article, etc. *verb*, 2) to convert food into an absorbable form 3) to think over and arrange in the mind

di-ges-tion [dī-jĕs′chən] *noun*, the process by which food is converted into a source of energy that can be assimilated by the body

di-ges-tive tract *noun*, the alimentary canal where food is processed and broken down into sugars for energy and wastes are eliminated

dig-it [dĭj′ĭt] *noun*, 1) a finger or toe 2) any number 0 through 9

dig-it-al [dĭj′ĭtəl] *adjective*, using signals or information represented by values of a physical quantity, such as voltage or magnetic polarization, to represent arithmetic numbers from logical expressions

dig-ni-fy [dĭg′nə-fī] *verb,* to give honor to

dig-ni-tar-y [dĭg′nĭ tŏr′ē] *noun*, 1) a person who is well-known and respected 2) a person holding high rank or position

dig-ni-ty [dĭg′nĭ-tē] *noun*, 1) an office or rank 2) nobleness of manner 3) the quality of being respected and respecting oneself

di-gres-sion [dī-grĕsh′ən, dĭ-] *noun*, an act or instance of wandering away from the subject temporarily

dike [dīk] *noun*, a dam or wall that holds back water

di-lap-i-dat-ed [dĭ-lăp′ĭ-dā′tĭd] *adjective*, falling into ruin, decaying, in disrepair

di-late [dī-lāt′] *verb*, to expand, to enlarge or become wider

dil-a-to-ry [dĭl′ə-tôr′ē] *adjective*, delaying, wasting time

di-lem-ma [dĭ-lĕm′ə] *noun*, a case in which a person must make a difficult choice, a quandary

dil-i-gence [dĭl′ə-jəns] *noun*, careful attention and application to work, a constant effort to accomplish something

dil-i-gent [dĭl′ə-jənt] *adjective*, careful, tireless in work

di-lute [dī-loot′] *verb*, to make thinner or weaker by mixing in something else

dim [dĭm] *adjective*, 1) poorly lit, 2) becoming less bright or distinct

dime [dīm] *noun*, a coin worth ten cents in the United States

di-men-sion [dĭ-mĕn′shən] *noun*, size in a particular direction such as length or width, scope, extent

diminish

di-min-ish [dǐ-mǐn′ǐsh] *verb*, to make or grow less, to reduce

dim-i-nu-tion [dǐm′ə-noo′shən] *noun*, a lessening, a reduction in size or duration

dim-ple [dǐm′pəl] *noun*, a small dent in a surface

dine [dīn] *verb*, to eat supper

din-gy [dǐn′jē] *adjective*, dirty, soiled, dull and drab, shabby

din-ner [dǐn′ər] *noun*, the main meal of the day served in the evening

di-no-saur [dī′nə-sôr′] *noun*, extinct gigantic reptiles of the Mesozoic era that were either herbivores, carnivores, or omnivores

dip [dǐp] *noun*, 1) a decline 2) a plunge, a soaking, an immersion 3) a mixture into which foods are dunked, *verb*, 4) to put something into a liquid and then take it out again 5) to slope

diph-thong [dǐf′thông′] *noun*, a combination of two vowels forming a compound sound

di-plo-ma [dǐ-plō′mə] *noun*, a document under seal attesting a degree conferred on a person

di-plo-ma-cy [dǐ-plō′mə-sē] *noun*, the business of conducting international negotiations

dip-lo-mat [dǐp′lə-mǎt′] *noun*, 1) an ambassador 2) a tactful person

dire [dīr] *adjective*, disastrous, serious, threatening

di-rect [dǐ-rěkt′, dī-] *adjective*, 1) straight to something without stopping, *verb*, 2) to aim 3) to guide, to control, to manage

di-rec-tion [dǐ-rěk′shən] *noun*, 1) the way in which someone is going or pointing 2) **di-rec-tions** instructions explaining how to do something

di-rect-ly [dǐ-rěkt′lē] *adverb*, 1) at once, immediately 2) in a forthright manner

di-rec-to-ry [dǐ-rěk′tə-rē] *noun*, 1) a list of people and their addresses 2) a computer file listing other files

dirge [dûrj] *noun*, sorrowful music, a lament for someone who has died

dir-i-gi-ble [dǐr′ə-jə-bəl] *noun*, an airship, a blimp

dirt [dûrt] *noun*, loose soil, something which causes filth

dirt-y [dûr′tē] *adjective*, 1) not clean, soiled 2) obscene

dis-a-bil-i-ty [dǐs′ə-bǐl′ǐ-tē] *noun*, a physical or mental incapacity, an inability to do something

dis-a-ble [dǐs-ā′bəl] *verb*, to impair the activity of something, to make incapable

dis-ad-van-tage [dǐs′əd-văn′tǐj] *noun*, something that makes things more difficult, a detriment

dis-a-gree [dǐs′ə-grē′] *verb*, to be of a different opinion, to differ

dis-a-gree-a-ble [dǐs′ə-grē′ə-bəl] *adjective*, unpleasant, irritating, obnoxious, bad-tempered

dis-a-gree-ment [dǐs′ə-grē′mənt] *noun*, an argument, a dispute

dis-ap-pear [dĭs′ə-pîr′] *verb*, to vanish, to go away or become hidden, to fade away

dis-ap-point [dĭs′ə-point′] *verb*, to frustrate the hopes of someone

dis-ap-point-ment [dĭs′ə-point′mənt] *noun*, failure, frustration, a feeling of being let down

dis-ap-prove [dĭs′ə-prōōv′] *verb*, to object, to have a bad opinion of

dis-arm [dĭs-ärm′] *verb*, 1) to take weapons away from someone, to subdue 2) to win over

dis-as-ter [dĭ-zăs′tər] *noun*, something very bad that happens, a catastrophe

dis-be-lief [dĭs′bĭ-lēf′] *noun*, doubt, skepticism

dis-burse [dĭs-bûrs′] *verb*, to pay out money

dis-burse-ment [dĭs-bûrs′mənt] *noun*, 1) the act of paying out money 2) money paid out

dis-card [dĭ-skärd′] *verb*, to shed, to eliminate, to throw away

dis-cern [dĭ-sûrn′] *verb*, to distinguish, to perceive

dis-charge [dĭs-chärj′] *noun*, 1) something that is sent out from its source, *verb*, 2) to unload 3) to send away, to dismiss from duty or a job

dis-ci-ple [dĭ-sī′pəl] *noun*, a follower, an apostle

dis-ci-pline [dĭs′ə-plĭn] *noun*, 1) strict training to teach self-control 2) an advanced area of knowledge *verb*, 3) to instruct, to prepare 4) to punish

dis-close [dĭ-sklōz′] *verb*, to reveal, to make known, to uncover

dis-com-fort [dĭs-kŭm′fərt] *noun*, 1) annoyance, embarrassment 2) ache

dis-con-nect [dĭs′kə-nĕkt′] *verb*, to cut off, to detach, to sever

dis-con-tent [dĭs′kən-tĕnt′] *noun*, dissatisfaction, restlessness, unhappiness

dis-con-tin-ue [dĭs′kən-tĭn′yōō] *verb*, to cease, to stop

dis-cord [dĭs′kôrd′] *noun*, a conflict, opposition, differences

dis-count [dĭs′kount′] *noun*, 1) a reduction in the price of something, *verb*, 2) to disregard or disbelieve someone

dis-cour-age [dĭ-skûr′ĭj] *verb*, to dishearten, to deter

dis-course [dĭs′kôrs′] *noun*, a talk, a long written or verbal discussion

dis-cov-er [dĭ-skŭv′ər] *verb*, 1) to make known the existence of something 2) to find out through study or observation

dis-cov-er-y [dĭ-skŭv′ə-rē] *noun*, something seen or learned for the first time

dis-cred-it [dĭs-krĕd′ĭt] *verb*, to destroy confidence in, to cause to disbelieve

dis-creet [dĭ-skrēt′] *adjective*, prudent, careful, tactful, unobtrusive

dis-crep-an-cy [dĭ-skrĕp′ən-sē] *noun*, inconsistency between facts or figures, failure to match

discretion

dis-cre-tion [dĭ-skrĕsh'ən] *noun*, discernment, wise conduct and management, freedom to decide something, the act of being discreet

dis-crim-i-nate [dĭ-skrĭm'ə-nāt'] *verb*, to make a difference or distinction, to treat differently

dis-crim-i-na-tion [dĭ-skrĭm'ə-nā'shən] *noun*, no plural, 1) the ability to make fine distinctions 2) treatment based on differences, prejudice

dis-cuss [dĭ-skŭs'] *verb*, to talk about, to exchange ideas

dis-cus-sion [dĭ-skŭsh'ən] *noun*, the exchange of ideas, a debate

dis-dain [dĭs-dān'] *noun*, scorn or contempt

dis-ease [dĭ-zēz'] *noun*, 1) any mental or physical disorder 2) any quality or social condition considered harmful

dis-en-gage [dĭs'ĕn-gāj'] *verb*, to release, to detach, to become free

dis-fig-ure [dĭs-fĭg'yər] *verb*, to deform, to injure, to spoil

dis-grace [dĭs-grās'] *noun*, 1) something to feel ashamed of *verb*, 2) to shame, to discredit

dis-grace-ful [dĭs-grās'fəl] *adjective*, causing shame

dis-grunt-led [dĭs-grŭn'tld] *adjective*, resentful, annoyed, discontented, angry

dis-guise [dĭs-gīz'] *noun*, 1) things worn to change the appearance, *verb*, 2) to change the appearance of someone or something, to cover up

dis-gust [dĭs-gŭst'] *noun*, 1) a strong feeling of dislike, revulsion, *verb*, 2) to cause someone a strong feeling of dislike or offense

dish [dĭsh] *noun*, 1) a container used at a meal to serve food 2) food served

dis-hon-est [dĭs-ŏn'ĭst] *adjective*, deceitful, lying, corrupt

disk [dĭsk] *noun*, any flat round object, a circular plate

dis-like [dĭs-līk'] *noun*, 1) distaste, hostility *verb*, 2) to detest, to hate

dis-mal [dĭz'məl] *adjective*, dark or gloomy, dreary, depressing

dis-man-tle [dĭs-măn'tl] *verb*, to take apart, to break down to basic parts to see how something is made

dis-may [dĭs-mā'] *noun*, 1) an uneasy feeling of alarm, *verb*, 2) to feel alarm and distress

dis-miss [dĭs-mĭs'] *verb*, to send away, to cause or permit to go

dis-obed-i-ent [dĭs'ə-bē'dē-ənt] *adjective*, refusing to obey

dis-o-bey [dĭs'ə-bā'] *verb*, not to do what you are told, to resist

dis-or-der [dĭs-ôr'dər] *noun*, 1) sickness, ailment 2) confusion, chaos

dis-or-gan-ized [dĭs-ôr'gə-nīzd'] *adjective*, not properly planned

dis-par-age [dĭ-spăr'ĭj] *verb*, to belittle, to criticize

dis-pa-rate [dĭs'pər-ĭt] *adjective*, very different in kind, containing unrelated elements

dis-par-i-ty [dĭ-spăr′ĭ-tē] *noun*, a noticeable difference, inequality

dis-patch [dĭ-spăch′] *noun*, 1) a message 2) promptness, *verb*, 3) to send off to a destination

dis-pel [dĭ-spĕl′] *verb*, to drive or clear away

dis-pense [dĭ-spĕns′] *verb*, to distribute, to give out medicine

dis-perse [dĭ-spûrs′] *verb*, to scatter, to distribute in different directions, to disseminate

dis-per-sion [dĭ-spûr′zhən] *noun*, scattering, diffusion, distribution

dis-place [dĭs-plās′] *verb*, 1) to rearrange, to move around 2) to force people from their homes 3) to take the place of

dis-play [dĭ-splā′] *noun*, 1) a show, an exhibit, *verb*, 2) to show or exhibit something, to present

dis-pose [dĭ-spōz′] *verb*, 1) to get rid of 2) to adjust, to settle 3) to place or arrange 4) to influence in favor of

dis-po-si-tion [dĭs′pə-zĭsh′ən] *noun*, 1) nature, personality, makeup 2) arrangement

dis-pro-por-tion-ate [dĭs′prə-pôr′shə-nĭt] *adjective*, relatively too large or too small, uneven, out of proportion

dis-prove [dĭs-prōōv′] *verb*, to refute, to prove false

dis-pute [dĭ-spyōōt′] *noun*, 1) an argument, a strong difference of opinion, *verb*, 2) to call into question, to debate

dis-qual-i-fy [dĭs-kwŏl′ə-fī′] *verb*, to invalidate, to judge ineligible

dis-re-gard [dĭs′rĭ gärd′] *noun*, 1) indifference, disrespect, neglect, *verb*, 2) to fail to notice

dis-re-spect-ful [dĭs′rĭ-spĕkt′fəl] *adjective*, rude, lacking respect

dis-rupt [dĭs-rŭpt′] *verb*, to interrupt, to disturb

dis-sat-is-fac-tion [dĭs-săt′ĭs-făk′shən] *noun*, discontent, uneasiness

dis-sat-is-fied [dĭs-săt′ĭs-fīd′] *adjective*, displeased, fed up, disgruntled, unhappy

dis-sect [dĭ-sĕkt′] *verb*, 1) to divide into separate parts 2) to analyze

dis-sec-tion [dĭ-sĕk′shən] *noun*, analysis, the act of cutting apart in order to examine internal structure

dis-sem-i-nate [dĭ-sĕm′ə-nāt′] *verb*, to scatter, to spread around

dis-sem-i-na-tion [dĭ-sĕm′ə-nā′shən] *noun*, a scattering or spreading around, diffusion

dis-sen-sion [dĭ-sĕn′shən] *noun*, a disagreement causing strife

dis-sent [dĭ-sĕnt′] *noun*, disagreement, a quarrel

dis-sim-i-lar [dĭ-sĭm′ə-lər] *adjective*, not alike, different

dis-si-pate [dĭs′ə-pāt′] *verb*, 1) to lessen, to diminish, to scatter 2) to fritter away

dis-solve [dĭ-zŏlv′] *verb*, 1) to make a solid disappear into a liquid solution 2) to break up an assembly, to end an agreement

dis-so-nance [dĭs′ə-nəns] *noun*, discord, noise, harsh sounds

dissuade

dis-suade [dǐ-swād′] *verb*, to discourage by persuasion, to deter

dis-tance [dǐs′təns] *noun*, 1) the space between two points, an interval 2) a place far away

dis-tant [dǐs′tənt] *adjective*, 1) far 2) cool, reserved in manner

dis-tend [dǐ-stěnd′] *verb*, to expand, to bloat, to stretch

dis-tinct [dǐ-stǐngkt′] *adjective*, 1) distinguished by nature or station 2) individual, unique 3) well-defined, very clear

dis-tinc-tion [dǐ-stǐngk′shən] *noun*, 1) notable difference as in a feature 2) excellence, recognition of an accomplishment

dis-tin-guish [dǐ-stǐng′gwǐsh] *verb*, 1) to stand out, to be different 2) to recognize as different

dis-tort [dǐ-stôrt′] *verb*, to twist out of shape, to bend, to falsify

dis-tract [dǐ-străkt′] *verb*, to take one's attention from something

dis-trac-tion [dǐ-străk′shən] *noun*, 1) mental distress 2) something that distracts or amuses

dis-traught [dǐ-strôt′] *adjective*, very worried, disturbed, overcome with anxiety, upset

dis-tress [dǐ-strěs′] *noun*, 1) a feeling of worry, sadness or difficulty, *verb*, 2) to make someone sad or worried

dis-trib-ute [dǐ-strǐb′yo͞ot] *verb*, 1) to allot or divide among several 2) to spread out over an area, to give out

dis-tri-bu-tion [dǐs′trə-byo͞o′shən] *noun*, the passing out of things, circulation

dis-trict [dǐs′trǐkt] *noun*, 1) a division of territory 2) a defined portion of a state, county, or city

dis-trust [dǐs-trŭst′] *noun*, 1) suspicion, doubt, *verb*, 2) to lack confidence or trust in

dis-turb [dǐ-stûrb′] *verb*, to bother or interrupt, to make anxious

ditch [dǐch] *noun*, 1) a long narrow channel, a shallow waterway *verb*, 2) to discard

dive [dīv] *noun*, 1) a downward plunge, *verb*, 2) to plunge head first into water 3) to move downward, to drop sharply

div-er [dī′vər] *noun*, 1) a person who dives into water 2) a person who works underwater

di-verge [dǐ-vûrj′] *verb*, to go off in different directions from the same starting point

di-verse [dǐ-vûrs′] *adjective*, various, many and different

di-ver-sion [dǐ-vûr′zhən] *noun*, amusement, play, distraction

di-ver-si-ty [dǐ-vûr′sǐ-tē] *noun*, variety, a wide range

di-vert [dǐ-vûrt′] *verb*, to distract, to draw aside, to entertain, to change the course of

di-vest [dǐ-věst′] *verb*, to strip, to take away from, to get rid of

di-vide [dǐ-vīd′] *verb*, 1) to calculate how many times one number can go into another 2) to separate 3) to share or distribute

div-i-dend [dǐv′ǐ-děnd′] *noun*, 1) the share of profits earned by any policy or company 2) a number to be divided by another number 3) a benefit from an action

di-vine [dĭ-vīn'] *adjective*, of or relating to God, holy, sacred

di-vis-i-ble [dĭ-vĭz'ə-bəl] *adjective*, capable of being divided or separated

di-vi-sion [dĭ-vĭzh'ən] *noun*, 1) the act or result of separating anything into parts 2) a difference in opinion or feeling 3) an operation on two numbers that results in a quotient 4) a military group 5) a section of a company

di-vorce [dĭ-vôrs'] *noun*, 1) a legal end of a marriage, *verb*, 2) to arrange by law for a husband and wife to separate and end their marriage

di-vulge [dĭ-vŭlj'] *verb*, to reveal

do [doō] *verb*, 1) to act, to produce 2) to travel 3) to be enough 4) to give 5) used with another verb to ask a question

doc-ile [dŏs'əl] *adjective*, easy to control, gentle, submissive

dock [dŏk] *noun*, 1) a pier where ships load and unload cargo, *verb*, 2) to tie a ship up at a port or wharf or boat landing 3) to deduct from someone's wages

doc-tor [dŏk'tər] *noun*, a person trained and licensed to practice medicine

doc-trine [dŏk'trĭn] *noun*, a tenet, a principle of faith or religion

doc-u-ment [dŏk'yə-mənt] *noun*, 1) an original or official paper 2) any writing that conveys

information, *verb*, 3) to write down or put on paper 4) to provide information as proof

dodge [dŏj] *verb*, to avoid something by moving out of the way, to evade, to escape

doe [dō] *noun*, a female deer

does [dŭz] *verb*, the part of the verb **do** used with he, she and it

does-n't [dŭz'ənt] the *contraction* of the words **does** and **not**

dog [dôg] *noun*, a domesticated mammal four legs that eats meat

dog-ma [dôg'mə] *noun*, 1) opinion or beliefs widely held but not based on facts 2) doctrine

dol-drums [dōl'drəmz'] *noun*, 1) listlessness, an inactive period, depression 2) an ocean region near the equator with calm waters and little wind

dol-lar [dŏl'ər] *noun*, 1) currency used in the United States and Canada, valued at 100 cents 2) the basic unit of currency used in many countries

dol-phin [dŏl'fĭn] *noun*, 1) any of various small cetaceans with the snout in the shape of a beak and the neck vertebrae partially fused like a whale 2) any of various fish

do-main [dō-mān'] *noun*, specialty, area ruled over, jurisdiction, field

dome [dōm] *noun*, a roof that resembles a half circle

do-mes-tic [də-mĕs'tĭk] *adjective*, found in the home or in one's home land

dom-i-nant [dŏm'ə-nənt] *adjective*, governing, controlling, bossy

dominate

dom-i-nate [dŏm′ə-nāt′] *verb*, to have control over someone

dom-i-no [dŏm′ə-nō′] *noun*, a game played with uniform blocks with one side divided into two halves, each half showing any number from 0 to 6

do-nate [dō′nāt′] *verb*, to make a contribution, to bestow, to give

do-na-tion [dō-nā′shən] *noun*, a gift of money or goods given to a charitable organization

done [dŭn] *adjective*, 1) finished or complete 2) cooked, *verb*, 3) the *past tense* of **do**

don-key [dŏng′kē] *noun*, an animal like a small horse with long ears

do-nor [dō′nər] *noun*, a person who gives money or something of value

don't [dōnt] the *contraction* of the words **do** and **not**

doom [do͞om] *noun,* 1) a grim fate, *verb*, 2) to make certain that something fails or is destroyed

door [dôr] *noun*, the moveable piece of wood or metal standing at an entrance, a portal

door-way [dôr′wā′] *noun*, the opening for an entrance to a building or a room

dor-mant [dôr′mənt] *adjective*, sleeping, inactive, inert

dor-mi-to-ry [dôr′mĭ-tôr′ē] *noun*, a building containing rooms for sleeping, a residence hall 2) a large room with many beds

dor-sal [dôr′səl] *adjective*, of or on the back of an animal

dose [dōs] *noun*, the amount of medicine that is to be taken at one time to be effective

dot [dŏt] *noun*, a very small round spot or mark, a point, a fleck

dou-ble [dŭb′əl] *adjective*, 1) twice as much, *noun,* 2) a stand in or look alike 3) a two-base hit in baseball, *verb*, 4) to make twice as much, to fold in two

doubt [dout] *noun*, 1) a question, a feeling of uncertainty, mistrust, *verb*, 2) to question, to wonder 3) to hesitate, to ponder

doubt-ful [dout′fəl] *adjective*, 1) questionable, unlikely 2) feeling uncertain

dough [dō] *noun*, a mixture of mostly flour and a liquid to be baked to make bread or cake

douse [dous] *verb*, to drench, to saturate, to put out a light

dove [dŭv] *noun*, 1) one of many of a small type of pigeon, *verb*, [dōv] 2) *past tense* of **dive**

down [doun] *adverb*, 1) toward the ground, *noun*, 2) soft feathers, *preposition*, 3) in or to a lower place

down-stairs [doun′stârz′] *adverb*, 1) on or to a lower floor, *noun*, 2) a lower floor of a building

downtown [doun′toun′] *noun*, the main business area of a city or town

down-ward [doun′wərd] *adverb*, descending from a higher to a lower level, moving toward the ground

doze [dōz] *verb*, to take a nap, to sleep for a brief time, to sleep lightly

doz-en [dŭz/ən] *noun*, twelve

Dr. the abbreviation of doctor

drab [drăb] *adjective*, dull in color, dreary, dingy, not interesting

draft [drăft] *noun*, 1) the first unedited copy of a manuscript 2) an order for payment of money 3) a current of air 4) forced military service

drag [drăg] *verb*, to pull along with effort, to haul

drag-on [drăg/ən] *noun*, a mythical creature that breathes fire

drain [drān] *noun*, 1) a pipe used to transport water into a sewer, *verb*, 2) to relieve the pressure of fluid in a wound 3) to become dry as water flows away 4) to make weak

dra-ma [drä/mə] *noun*, 1) a story that can be performed on stage 2) excitement

dra-mat-ic [drə-măt/ĭk] *adjective*, theatrical, exciting, stirring

dra-mat-i-cal-ly [drə-măt/ĭk-lē] *adverb*, in a sudden or alarming way, impressively

drank [drăngk] *past tense* of **drink**

drape [drāp] *noun*, 1) a heavy curtain, *verb*, 2) to cover with a piece of cloth

dra-per-y [drā/pə-rē] *noun*, a heavy curtain or fabric designed to cover a window

dras-tic [drăs/tĭk] *adjective*, forceful, severe, extreme

draw [drô] *noun*, 1) a tie score, *verb*, 2) to get, to take, to understand 3) to pull along 4) to make a picture with a writing instrument 5) to choose at random 6) to formulate, to prepare 7) to suck

draw-bridge [drô/brĭj/] *noun*, a bridge that can be raised or turned to allow boats and ships to pass

drawl [drôl] *noun*, a manner of speaking that stretches out the sound of a word or vowels

drawn [drôn] *adjective*, thin, gaunt

dread [drĕd] *noun*, 1) fear, horror, terror, *verb*, 2) to anticipate with anxiety, to fear greatly

dream [drēm] *noun*, 1) images seen while you sleep 2) desires, goals, *verb*, 3) to picture something with your imagination 4) to see images while sleeping

drear-y [drîr/ē] *adjective*, gloomy, depressing

dredge [drĕj] *verb*, 1) to remove something from deep water 2) to cover food with sugar, flour, etc.

drench [drĕnch] *verb*, to make completely wet, to soak

dress [drĕs] *noun*, 1) a piece of clothing that covers the bust, waist and thighs 2) a general term for clothing or attire, *verb*, 3) to put clothes on 4) to adorn

dress-er [drĕs/ər] *noun*, 1) a chest of drawers, a bureau 2) a person who helps another to dress 3) a person who dresses a certain way

drew [drōō] *past tense* of **draw**

drift [drĭft] *noun*, 1) the general meaning 2) a pile of snow, leaves, etc. *verb*, 3) to float

drill [drĭl] *noun*, 1) a tool made of hard material used to make holes in something 2) a practice,

drink

an exercise, *verb*, 3) to make a hole in something with a special machine 4) to be trained

drink [drĭngk] *noun*, 1) liquid refreshment, a beverage, *verb*, 2) to consume liquid through the mouth, to swallow, to imbibe

drip [drĭp] *verb*, to fall in drops

drive [drīv] *noun*, 1) a short journey or trip made in a vehicle, *verb*, 2) to steer and control a moving vehicle 3) to force to go, to push through 4) to make, to compel, to urge

driv-er [drī/vər] *noun*, 1) the person steering and controlling a moving vehicle 2) a golf club for hitting long shots

droll [drōl] *adjective*, odd, strange and amusing

drone [drōn] *noun*, 1) a male bee with no stinger that mates with the queen bee, *verb*, 2) to talk dully, to buzz or murmur like a bee

drop [drŏp] *noun*, 1) a small amount of a liquid, *verb*, 2) to let something fall 3) to decrease

dross [drŏs] *noun*, waste, impurity

drought [drout] *noun*, a long period without rain

drown [droun] *verb*, to suffocate by immersion under water

drow-sy [drou/zē] *adjective*, sleepy, sluggish

drudg-er-y [drŭj/ə-rē] *noun*, dull routine work

drug [drŭg] *noun*, 1) a substance that changes the body's chemistry, medicine 2) a narcotic

drug-gist [drŭg/ĭst] *noun*, a pharmacist, one who is licensed to sell drugs

drum [drŭm] *noun*, 1) a percussion instrument consisting of a hollow cylinder with a taut covering 2) a cylindrical metal container, *verb*, 3) to make music or beat on a drum

drunk [drŭngk] *adjective*, showing the effect of too much alcohol, losing control of one's movement or speech because of alcohol

dry [drī] *adjective*, 1) without moisture or water, *verb*, 2) to expel or remove moisture

dry-er [drī/ər] *noun*, a machine that adds heat and tumbles clothes to evaporate and remove moisture

dual [dōō/əl] *adjective*, having two purposes or parts

duch-ess [dŭch/ĭs] *noun*, the wife or widow of a duke

duck [dŭk] *noun*, 1) a bird that swims and is hunted for its eggs and meat, *verb*, 2) to crouch or lower one's head to avoid something, to dodge

duct [dŭkt] *noun*, a tube or channel, a ventilation shaft

due [dōō] *adjective*, 1) owed, unpaid 2) expected, appropriate, *noun*, 3) a charge or fee for membership

duel [dōō/əl] *noun*, 1) a fight or competition, *verb*, 2) to fight

du-et [dōō-ĕt/] *noun*, a song or a piece of music for two people

duke [dōōk] *noun*, the title of a man who is a high-ranking nobleman

dull [dŭl] *adjective*, 1) not sharp, blunt 2) boring, slow, dim

dumb [dŭm] *adjective*, 1) unable to speak, mute, silent 2) unintelligent, stupid

dump [dŭmp] *noun*, 1) a public place where garbage is collected and usually buried, *verb*, 2) to leave, to drop or throw away

dune [dōōn] *noun*, a rounded hill of sand heaped up by the wind

dun-geon [dŭn′jən] *noun*, a close, dark prison, an underground cell

dupe [dōōp] *verb*, to fool, to trick

du-pli-cate [dōō′plĭ-kĭt] *adjective*, 1) alike, twin, *noun*, 2) a copy, a reproduction, [dōō′pl ī-kāt′] *verb*, 3) to reproduce, to remake, to do again

du-ra-ble [dōōr′ə-bəl] *adjective*, able to endure, lasting

du-ra-tion [dōō-rā′shən] *noun*, the length of time something continues or exists

dur-ing [dōōr′ĭng] *preposition*, in the course of a period of time, throughout the course of

dusk [dŭsk] *noun*, evening, the time just after the sun has set, twilight

dust [dŭst] *noun*, 1) fine particles or powder of matter, *verb*, 2) to remove the powder by cleaning or wiping

du-ty [dōō′tē] *noun*, 1) an obligation or a commitment 2) the responsibilities of one's job 3) a tax on goods, especially imports and exports

dwarf [dwôrf] *noun*, 1) an unusually small person, *verb*,

2) to make something look small by comparison

dwell [dwĕl] *verb*, 1) to inhabit, to live in 2) to emphasize, to think about for a long time, to ponder

dwell-ing [dwĕl′ĭng] *noun*, a home to live in, a residence, an abode

dwin-dle [dwĭn′dl] *verb*, to reduce

dye [dī] *noun*, 1) a substance used to color cloth, hair, etc. *verb*, 2) fixing colors permanently in the fibers of materials, to change the color

dy-na-mic [dī-năm′ĭk] *adjective*, relating to the forces producing motion, forceful, energetic

dy-na-mite [dī′nə-mīt′] *noun*, an explosive of nitroglycerin absorbed in porous matter

dy-nas-ty [dī′nə-stē] *noun*, a series of rulers from the same family

dys-func-tion-al [dĭs-fŭngk′shən-əl] *adjective*, functioning abnormally

E

each [ēch] *adjective*, every, one of two or more things, all

ea-ger [ē′gər] *adjective*, very willing to do something, enthusiastic

ea-gle [ē′gəl] *noun*, a very large keen-sighted bird of prey

ear [îr] *noun*, 1) the organ, one on each side of the head, used to hear 2) the sleeve in a cereal plant used to hold seeds or flowers

ear-ly [ûr′lē] *adjective*, 1) near the beginning of a time period, *adverb*, 2) before the set time

earn [ûrn] *verb*, 1) to get something through work, to achieve, to gain money 2) to achieve by one's own efforts

ear-nest [ûr′nĭst] *adjective*, fervent, serious, sincere

ear-ring [îr′rĭng, îr′ĭng] *noun*, an ornament worn on the earlobe

Earth [ûrth] *proper noun*, 1) the name of the planet on which we live, our world, 2) **earth** *common noun*, soil, dirt, ground

earth-quake [ûrth′kwāk′] *noun*, a shaking movement of the earth caused by underground movement

ease [ēz] *noun*, 1) relaxation, relief, *verb*, 2) to move carefully 3) to make less painful or difficult

ea-sel [ē′zəl] *noun*, a tripod frame used to support an artist's canvas

eas-i-ly [ē′zə-lē] *adverb*, without difficulty, effortlessly

east [ēst] *noun*, one of the four points of a compass, pointing right of north, where the sun rises

east-ern [ē′stərn] *adjective*, 1) belonging to or characteristic of the east 2) Asian

eas-y [ē′zē] *adjective*, 1) effortless, not difficult 2) relaxed, comfortable 3) free from pain or worry 4) not strict

eat [ēt] *verb*, 1) to put food in the mouth, chewing it and swallowing it 2) to corrode

eaves [ēvz] *noun*, *plural*, the lower edges of a roof that overhang a building

ebb [ĕb] *noun*, 1) the receding of the tide, *verb*, 2) to fall back

eb-on-y [ĕb′ə-nē] *adjective*, 1) black, *noun*, 2) a hard, heavy and durable wood 3) a tropical Asian tree

ec-cen-tric [ĭk-sĕn′trĭk] *adjective*, 1) off-center from the regular or normal, *noun*, 2) an odd person

ec-cle-si-as-tic [ĭ-klē′zē-ăs′tĭk] *adjective*, pertaining to the Christian church or clergy

ech-o [ĕk′ō] *noun*, 1) a series of reflected sound waves that repeat as they bounce back from an object, repeating the sound *verb*, 2) to reverberate, to reflect a sound back

e-clipse [ĭ-klĭps′] *noun*, 1) a period of time when the light from one celestial object is blocked another, *verb*, 2) to overshadow and cause a loss of light

e-col-o-gy [ĭ-kŏl′ə-jē] *noun*, the study of how plants and animals interact with the environment

e-co-nom-ic [ĕk′ə-nŏm′ĭk] *adjective*, related to business and the production of goods

e-co-nom-i-cal [ĕk′ə-nŏm′ĭ-kəl] *adjective*, affordable, inexpensive

e-co-nom-ics [ĕk′ə-nŏm′ĭks] *noun*, the study of the way people secure goods and services and the necessities of life

e-con-o-my [ĭ-kŏn′ə-mē] *noun*, 1) the careful or thrifty management of resources 2) a system for the management of resources, money, and jobs

ec-o-sys-tem [ĕk′ō-sĭs′təm] *noun*, living things that work together and their environment

ec-u-men-i-cal [ĕk′ə- mĕn′ĭ′-kəl] *adjective*, representing a number of different Christian churches

ec-sta-sy [ĕk′stə-sē] *noun*, an overwhelming feeling of delight

ec-ze-ma [ĕk′sə-mə] *noun*, a rash, inflammatory disease of the skin

edge [ĕj] *noun*, 1) the segment where two surfaces meet 2) the rim or brink of something 3) the sharp blade of a cutting instrument such as a knife 4) the point farthest from the middle of a surface 5) an advantage, *verb*, 6) to take small, cautious steps 7) to put a border on something

ed-i-ble [ĕd′ə-bəl] *adjective*, fit to be eaten as food

ed-i-fice [ĕd′ə-fĭs] *noun*, a large, imposing building or structure

ed-i-fy [ĕd′ə-fī′] *verb*, to educate, to instruct, to guide spiritually

ed-it [ĕd′ĭt] *verb*, to revise and correct, to prepare something for publication, to cut a part of

e-di-tion [ĭ-dĭsh′ən] *noun*, an issue of a book, newspaper or magazine

ed-i-tor [ĕd′ĭ-tər] *noun*, one who reads and revises books or newspapers before they are published

ed-u-cate [ĕj′ə-kāt′] *verb*, to teach people, to provide knowledge

ed-u-ca-tion [ĕj′ə-kā′shən] *noun*, the process of teaching and learning, acquired knowledge

eel [ēl] *noun*, a long fish that looks like a snake that lives in freshwater and the sea

ee-rie [îr′ē] *adjective*, spooky, strange, causing dread

ef-fect [ĭ-fĕkt′] *noun*, a result, consequence, outcome

ef-fec-tive [ĭ-fĕk′tĭv] *adjective*, having a positive result, helpful

ef-fer-ves-cence [ĕf′ər-vĕs′sĭns] *noun*, 1) the process of gas escaping in innumerable small bubbles 2) vivacious, enthusiasm

ef-fi-ca-cious [ĕf′ĭ-kā′shəs] *adjective*, producing a desired result, effective, efficient

ef-fi-cien-cy [ĭ-fĭsh′ən-sē] *noun*, productivity with little or no wasted effort

ef-fi-cient [ĭ-fĭsh′ənt] *adjective*, working well with no waste of money or effort, capable

ef-fi-gy [ĕf′ə-jē] *noun*, a likeness in the form of a dummy, an image of a hated person usually hung

ef-fort [ĕf′ərt] *noun*, an attempt, an action, strenuous exertion

ef-fu-sion [ĭ-fyōō′zhən] *noun*, a pouring forth of liquid, light, etc.

e.g. for example

egg [ĕg] *noun*, 1) a shell covered fetus of a baby bird, fish or insect 2) an ovum, a female reproductive cell

e-go [ē′gō, ĕg′ō] *noun*, a person's self-importance, self-esteem

e-go-tist [ē′gə-tĭst] *noun*, one who is excessively interested in herself or himself

eight [āt] *noun*, the number 8

eight-een [ā-tēn′] *noun*, the number 18, ten plus eight

eight-eenth [ā-tēnth′] *noun*, *adjective*, the number eighteen in order, 18th

eighth [ātth] *noun*, *adjective*, the number eight in order, one of eight equal parts

eight-i-eth [ā′tē-ĭth] *noun*, the number 80 in order, one of eighty equal parts

eight-y [ā′tē] *adjective*, *noun*, the number 80, eight times ten

ei-ther [ē′thər, ī′thər] *adjective*, *pronoun*, one or the other of two

e-ject [ĭ jĕkt′] *verb*, to exit suddenly and forcefully, to expel

e-lab-o-rate [ĭ-lăb′ər-ĭt] *adjective*, 1) made with great care, carefully planned, complicated, [ĭ-lă-bə-rāt′] *verb*, 2) to explain in detail

e-lapse [ĭ-lăps′] *verb*, to pass by

e-las-tic [ĭ-lăs′tĭk] *adjective*, 1) able to return to an original size and shape after having been stretched completely, *noun*, 2) fabric with fine strings of rubber woven in it

e-la-tion [ĭ-lā′ shən] *noun*, excitement, joy

el-bow [ĕl′bō′] *noun*, the joint in the arm that allows it to bend in the middle

eld-er [ĕl′dər] *adjective*, 1) older, more aged, *noun*, 2) one who is older than others 3) an influential older person

e-lect [ĭ-lĕkt′] *verb*, to choose by vote, to decide a course of action or representative

e-lec-tion [ĭ-lĕk′shən] *noun*, the process of making a choice by voting

e-lec-tor-ate [ĭ-lĕk′tər-ĭt] *noun*, the people qualified to vote

e-lec-tric [ĭ-lĕk′trĭk] *adjective*, relating to or powered by electricity

e-lec-tri-cian [ĭ-lĕk-trĭsh′ən] *noun*, one who is licensed to install and repair electrical equipment

e-lec-tric-i-ty [ĭ-lĕk-trĭs′ĭ-tē] *noun*, a form of energy resulting from the activity of electrons and protons

e-lec-tro-cute [ĭ-lĕk′trə-kyōōt′] *verb*, to kill by electric shock

e-lec-trode [ĭ-lĕk′trōd′] *noun*, a conductor by which an electric unit enters or leaves a region or object

e-lec-tron [ĭ-lĕk′trŏn′] *noun*, a particle smaller than an atom and having a negative electric charge

e-lec-tron-ic [ĭ-lĕk′trŏnĭk] *adjective*, operating by transistors, microchips, etc. that control an electric current

el-e-gant [ĕl′ĭ-gənt] *adjective*, lovely, gorgeous, refined

el-e-ment [ĕl′ə-mənt] *noun*, 1) a basic substance of which the universe is composed, *plural*, 2) the forces that constitute the weather

el-e-men-ta-ry [ĕl′ə-mĕn′tə-rē] *adjective*, of or related to the first principles or basic facts of a subject

el-e-phant [ĕl′ə-fənt] *noun*, a huge, herbivore mammal that lives in Africa and India, weighs 3-7 tons, stands 8-13 feet high, has thick skin, two tusks and a long nose called a trunk

el-e-vate [ĕl′ə-vāt′] *verb*, to raise to a higher level, to lift up

el-e-va-tion [ĕl′ə-vā′shən] *noun*, the altitude, the height of something from a reference point such as sea level

el-e-va-tor [ĕl′ə-vā′tər] *noun*, a machine with hoisting equipment for conveying persons, goods, etc. to or from different levels

e-lev-en [ĭ-lĕv′ən] *noun*, the number 11, one plus ten

e-lev-enth [ĭ-lĕv′ənth] *noun*, the number 11 in order, 11ᵗʰ

elf [ĕlf] *noun*, an imaginary small person with pointed ears who makes mischief

elic-it [ĭ-lĭs′ĭt] *verb*, to draw forth, to evoke a response

el-i-gi-ble [ĕl′ĭ-jə-bəl] *adjective*, qualified to be chosen

e-lim-i-nate [ĭ-lĭm′ə-nāt′] *verb*, to get rid of, to exclude from consideration, to leave out

e-lite [ĭ-lēt′] *adjective*, choice, select, superior, considered best

elk [ĕlk] *noun*, an animal similar to a moose, a large deer

elm [ĕlm] *noun*, a tall hardwood shade tree

e-lope [ĭ-lōp′] *verb*, to run away to marry secretly

el-o-quence [ĕl′ə-kwəns] *noun*, persuasive use of language

else [ĕls] *adverb*, 1) otherwise, instead of 2) more, in addition

else-where [ĕls′hwâr′] *adverb*, in some other place

e-lude [ĭ-lōōd′] *verb*, to get away from, to avoid, to escape

e-lu-sive [ĭ-lōō′sĭv] *adjective*, hard to grasp or catch, hard to remember

em-a-nate [ĕm′ə-nāt′] *verb*, to flow out, to radiate, to come out

e-man-ci-pate [ĭ-măn′sə-pāt′] *verb*, to set free from restrictions or slavery

e-man-ci-pa-tion [ĭ-măn′sə-pā′shən] *noun*, the act or condition of being freed from oppression or slavery

em-bar-go [ĕm-bär′gō] *noun*, a law that prevents a country from trading with another

em-bark [ĕm-bärk′] *verb*, 1) to board an airplane or boat 2) to begin an undertaking

em-bar-rass [ĕm-băr′əs] *verb*, to make ill at ease or self-conscious

em-bar-rass-ment [ĕm-băr′əs-mənt] *noun*, a feeling of self-consciousness, distress or shame

em-bas-sy [ĕm′bə-sē] *noun*, the building in which people work to represent their own country in another country

em-bed [ĕm-bĕd′] *verb*, to implant into something, to fix firmly

em-bel-lish [ĕm-bĕl′ĭsh] *verb*, to adorn, to make beautiful by adding decoration

embezzle

em-bez-zle [ĕm-bĕz′əl] *verb*, to steal money from one's company or from savings accounts entrusted to one

em-blem [ĕm′bləm] *noun*, a badge or symbol of something

em-bod-y [ĕm-bŏd′ē] *verb*, 1) to include as a part of a whole 2) to represent

em-brace [ĕm-brās′] *verb*, 1) to hold closely in one's arms, to hug 2) to accept something, to include 3) to take up seriously

em-broi-der [ĕm-broi′dər] *verb*, 1) to sew ornamental patterns on fabric 2) to embellish, to add false details

em-bry-o [ĕm′brē-ō′] *noun*, an early stage of development of an animal or plant organism

em-bry-on-ic [ĕm′brē-ŏn′ĭk] *adjective*, in an early stage of development of an organism

em-er-ald [ĕm′ər-əld] *noun*, a precious stone of rich, bright green color, a variety of beryl

e-merge [ĭ-mûrj′] *verb*, to come out or become visible, to appear

e-mer-gen-cy [ĭ-mûr′jən-sē] *noun*, an unexpected event that calls for immediate action, a crisis

em-i-grant [ĕm′ĭ-grənt] *noun*, a person leaving one country to live in another

em-i-grate [ĕm′ĭ-grāt′] *verb*, to leave one country to go and live in another

em-i-nent [ĕm′ə-nənt] *adjective*, high, lofty, noted, famous

e-mis-sion [ĭ-mĭsh′ən] *noun*, a substance given off into the air

e-mo-tion [ĭ-mō′shən] *noun*, feelings, passion, excitement

e-mo-tion-al [ĭ-mō′shə-nəl] *adjective*, excitable, showing emotions more than usual, fervent

em-pa-thize [ĕm′pə-thīz′] *verb*, to relate to the feelings of others

em-pa-thy [ĕm′pə-thē] *noun*, the ability to share the feelings of another person

em-per-or [ĕm′pər-ər] *noun*, the male ruler of a country or empire

em-pha-sis [ĕm′fə-sĭs] *noun*, importance or stress given to something

em-pha-size [ĕm′fə-sīz′] *verb*, to call to someone's attention, to bring out clearly, to stress

em-pire [ĕm′pīr′] *noun*, a group of nations or states united under a single sovereign power

em-pir-i-cal [ĕm-pîr′ĭ-kəl] *adjective*, based on observation and experience rather than theory

em-ploy [ĕm-ploi′] *verb*, to put into use, to engage, to hire for work

em-ploy-ee [ĕm-ploi′ē] *noun*, one who works for another for wages

em-ploy-er [ĕm-ploi′ər] *noun*, a person or business that employs or hires one or more persons

em-ploy-ment [ĕm-ploi′mənt] *noun*, a job, an occupation

em-pow-er [ĕm-pou′ər] *verb*, to authorize, to enable

emp-ty [ĕmp′tē] *adjective*, 1) having nothing inside, without content or meaning, *verb*, 2) to remove the contents completely, to make vacant, to unload

em-u-late [ĕm′yə-lāt′] *verb*, to follow or copy in the hope of equaling

en-a-ble [ĕ-nā′bəl] *verb*, to make possible, to empower

en-act [ĕn-ăkt′] *verb*, 1) to make into law 2) to act, to perform

e-nam-el [ĭ-năm′əl] *noun*, 1) a smooth glossy surface finish 2) a hard glassy colored substance fused to metal, glass or pottery 3) the outer covering of the teeth

en-chant [ĕn-chănt′] *verb*, 1) to put a spell on 2) to captivate, to delight

en-chant-ment [ĕn-chănt′mənt] *noun*, 1) a magical spell, 2) a fascination, appeal, charm

en-clave [ĕn′klāv′] *noun*, territory enclosed in a foreign land

en-close [ĕn-klōz′] *verb*, to put something inside of something else, to shut in on all sides

en-clo-sure [ĕn-klōz′hər] *noun*, something that surrounds on all sides

en-com-pass [ĕn-kŭm′pəs] *verb*, 1) to enclose in a circle, to surround 2) to include as a part of

en-core [ŏn′kôr′] *noun*, an additional performance given in response to calls from the audience, as by applause

en-coun-ter [ĕn-koun′tər] *noun*, 1) a casual meeting 2) a skirmish, *verb*, 3) to meet by chance 4) to confront in battle

en-cour-age [ĕn-kûr′ĭj] *verb*, to give praise or hope to someone, to urge

en-cour-age-ment [ĕn-kûr′ĭj-mənt, -kŭr′-] *noun*, support, assurance

en-croach-ment [ĕn-krōch′mənt] *noun*, the act of overstepping boundaries or someone's rights

en-cy-clo-pe-di-a [ĕn-sī′klə-pē′dē-ə] *noun*, a comprehensive summary of knowledge on many subjects or a specialilzed subject written in a set of volumes

end [ĕnd] *noun*, 1) the farthest point or edge of anything 2) completion, finish 3) the aim, reason, design, *verb*, 4) to finish

en-dan-ger [ĕn-dān′jər] *verb*, to put in danger, to hazard

en-deav-or [ĕn-dĕv′ər] *noun*, 1) an attempt, a serious effort, *verb*, 2) to try, to make an earnest effort, to strive

end-less [ĕnd′lĭs] *adjective*, without end, infinite, ceaseless

en-dorse [ĕn-dôrs′] *verb*, 1) to write on the back of a check to cash it or give it to another person 2) to sanction, to declare approval of

en-dow [ĕn-dou′] *verb*, 1) to provide or bestow income or property 2) to give a quality to

en-dow-ment [ĕn-dou′mənt] *noun*, giving of money to provide a regular income

en-dur-ance [ĕn-dŏŏr′əns] *noun*, the ability to survive, the will to persevere

en-dure [ĕn-dŏŏr′] *verb*, to bear, to put up with, to tolerate, to suffer

enemy

en·e·my [ĕn'ə-mē] *noun*, a hostile person or group or country, a foe

en·er·gize [ĕn'ər-jīz'] *verb*, to make active, to invigorate, to give energy to

en·er·gy [ĕn'ər-jē] *noun*, 1) the capacity for performing work 2) power that makes machines work

en·fold [ĕn-fōld'] *verb*, to envelope, to enclose

en·force [ĕn-fôrs'] *verb*, to impose by force, to require compliance

en·gage [ĕn-gāj'] *verb*, 1) to put in gear 2) to fight 3) to hire 4) to become involved 5) to be busy or occupied 6) to promise

en·gage·ment [ĕn-gāj'mənt] *noun*, 1) an encounter, a military action 2) a promise by two people to marry 3) an appointment

en·gen·der [ĕn-jĕn'dər] *verb*, to cause, to give rise to

en·gine [ĕn'jĭn] *noun*, 1) a machine that converts energy into motion 2) a locomotive 3) a source of power

en·gi·neer [ĕn'jə-nîr'] *noun*, 1) one who designs machines 2) one who drives an engine, *verb*, 3) to bring about an event

Eng·lish [ĭng'glĭsh] *adjective*, 1) the language of the people of Britain, America, Canada, Australia, and other countries 2) relating to or belonging to the people of England

en·grave [ĕn-grāv'] *verb*, 1) to cut into a surface 2) to leave an impression

en·gulf [ĕn-gŭlf'] *verb*, to cover completely, to close over

en·hance [ĕn-hăns'] *verb*, to make better, to increase the value or quality of something

e·nig·ma [ĭ-nĭg'mə] *noun*, something hard to explain, a puzzle, a mysterious person

en·joy [ĕn-joi'] *verb*, to take pleasure in

en·joy·ment [ĕn-joi'mənt] *noun*, delight, satisfaction, happiness, pleasure

en·large [ĕn-lärj'] *verb*, to increase

en·light·en [ĕn-līt'n] *verb*, to educate, to inform, to give spiritual insight

en·list [ĕn-lĭst'] *verb*, to sign up, to enroll in the armed forces

en·mi·ty [ĕn'mĭ-tē] *noun*, hatred

e·nor·mous [ĭ-nôr'məs] *adjective*, monstrous, huge, immense

e·nough [ĭ-nŭf'] *adjective*, 1) as much as is needed, ample, *adverb*, 2) to an adequate or sufficient degree, *noun*, 3) the required amount

en·rage [ĕn-rāj'] *verb*, to anger, to inflame, to make furious

en·rich [ĕn-rĭch'] *verb*, to improve, to make rich, to enhance

en·roll [ĕn-rōl'] *verb*, to register in a list or as a student in a school, to become a member

en·roll·ment [ĕn-rōl'mənt] *noun*, the total number registered

en·sem·ble [ŏn-sŏm'bəl] *noun*, the whole, all the parts taken together as a group

en·sue [ĕn-sōō'] *verb*, to make sure or certain, to follow up

en-sure [ĕn-shoor'] *verb*, to guarantee, to make sure of, to insure

en-ter [ĕn'tər] *verb*, to go into, to become involved in

en-ter-prise [ĕn'tər-prīz'] *noun*, a bold undertaking, a project or business activity, a venture

en-ter-tain [ĕn'tər-tān'] *verb*, 1) to hold the interest of the people you are talking to or performing for, 2) to amuse, to delight 3) to have in mind

en-ter-tain-ment [ĕn'tər-tān'mənt] *noun*, a performance that tries to interest an audience

en-thrall [ĕn-thrôl'] *verb*, to fascinate, to mesmerize

en-thu-si-asm [ĕn-thoō'zē-ăz'əm] *noun*, eager interest, excitement

en-thu-si-as-tic [ĕn-thoō'zē-ăs'tĭk] *adjective*, showing a passionate and devoted interest in a belief or idea

en-tice [ĕn-tīs'] *verb*, to lure, to attract, to tempt, to persuade

en-tire [ĕn-tīr'] *adjective*, whole, complete, with no parts missing

en-ti-tle [ĕn-tīt'l] *verb*, 1) to give as a right 2) to give a title to

en-ti-ty [ĕn'tĭ-tē] *noun*, a being, an individual, an existence

en-trance [ĕn'trəns] *noun*, 1) a means of entry or access 2) the act of coming in

en-tree [ŏn'trā] *noun*, the main dish of a meal

en-tre-pre-neur [ŏn'trə-prə-nûr'] *noun*, a businessman, one who starts a business and assumes financial risk for it

en-truct [ŏn trūot'] *verb*, to confide, to give to for safekeeping

en-try [ĕn'trē] *noun*, 1) entrance, a way in 2) an item in a log

e-nun-ci-ate [ĭ-nŭn'sē-āt'] *verb*, to pronounce, to state clearly

en-vel-op [ĕn-vĕl'əp] *verb*, to cover, to enclose, to surround

en-vel-ope [ĕn'və-lōp'] *noun*, a folded paper cover like a pocket for a letter

en-vi-ous [ĕn'vē-əs] *adjective*, jealous, full of envy

en-vi-ron-ment [ĕn-vī'rən-mənt] *noun*, the surroundings or place in which something lives

en-vy [ĕn'vē] *noun*, 1) a feeling of anger or bitterness because someone has more of something, or a better life, *verb*, 2) to want something someone has, to be jealous

e-on [ē'ŏn', ē'ən] *noun*, a billion years, a long time

e-phem-er-al [ĭ-fĕm'ər-əl] *adjective*, short-lived, fleeting

ep-ic [ĕp'ĭk] *noun*, a long poem about a hero and his deeds

ep-i-dem-ic [ĕp'ĭ-dĕm'ĭk] *adjective*, 1) affecting many in the community, widespread, *noun*, 2) a contagious disease infecting many among the population

ep-i-der-mis [ĕp'ĭ-dûr'mĭs] *noun*, the outer layer of the skin

ep-i-gram [ĕp'ĭ-grăm'] *noun*, a pithy phrase, a witty saying

ep-i-lep-sy [ĕp'ə-lĕp'sē] *noun*, a disorder of the nervous system accompanied by convulsions and loss of consiousness

ep-i-logue [ĕp′ə-lôg′] *noun*, a short conclusion added to the end of a book, play, etc.

ep-i-sode [ĕp′ĭ-sōd′] *noun*, 1) a distinctive occurrence 2) a separate incident in a longer story or poem

ep-i-taph [ĕp′ĭ-tăf′] *noun*, an inscription on a monument in memory of a dead person who is buried there

e-pit-o-me [ĭ-pĭt′ə-mē] *noun*, a typical or perfect example of a group or type

ep-och [ĕp′ək] *noun*, 1) a time period characterized by a distinctive development 2) a date marking the beginning of a new period of history 3) a division of geological time

e-qual [ē′kwəl] *adjective*, 1) being the same as 2) alike, *noun*, 3) something valued as the same 4) a symbol = that shows both sides have the same value, *verb*, 5) to be as good as someone or something else

e-qual-i-ty [ĭ-kwŏl′ĭ-tē] *noun*, the state of being the same as

e-qual-ize [ē′kwə-līz′] *verb*, to make even, to balance

e-qual-ly [ē′kwə-lē] *adverb*, in an equal way, to an equal degree

e-qua-tion [ĭ-kwā′shən] *noun*, 1) the act or process of considering or making equal 2) a statement that the values of two mathematical expressions are equal (=)

e-qua-tor [ĭ-kwā′tər] *noun*, the imaginary band circling the middle of the earth, at an equal distance from the North and South Poles

e-ques-tri-an [ĭ-kwĕs′trē-ən] *adjective*, 1) relating to horseback riding, *noun*, 2) a rider on horseback

e-qui-lib-ri-um [ē′kwə-lĭb′rē-əm] *noun*, a state of balance between opposing forces

e-qui-lat-er-al tri-angle [ē′kwə-lăt′ər-əl trī′ăng′gəl] *noun*, a triangle with 60 degree angles and three equal sides

e-qui-nox [ē′kwə-nŏks′] *noun*, either of two times in the year when night and day are of equal length: March 20; September 22

e-quip [ĭ-kwĭp′] *verb*, to provide what is needed, to outfit

e-quip-ment [ĭ-kwĭp′mənt] *noun*, tools, supplies, etc., needed for a job or a special activity

eq-ui-ty [ĕk′wĭ-tē] *noun*, 1) the value of property or stock after subtracting liens against it 2) just, impartial, fairness

e-quiv-a-lent [ĭ-kwĭv′ə-lənt] *noun*, 1) equal in value or worth 2) similar in force, measure, meaning or effect, identical

e-quiv-o-cate [ĭ-kwĭv′ə-kāt′] *verb*, to use deliberately evasive language

e-ra [îr′ə, ĕr′ə] *noun*, a distinct period of time, or history

e-rad-i-cate [ĭ-răd′ĭ-kāt′] *verb*, to destroy completely, to get rid of

e-rase [ĭ-rās′] *verb*, to rub out, to remove all traces of

e-rect [ĭ-rĕkt′] *adjective*, 1) standing straight, upright, *verb*, 2) to build or construct

er-mine [ûr'mĭn] *noun*, a small weasel with white fur and black-tipped tail in winter

e-rode [ĭ-rōd'] *verb*, 1) to wear away gradually 2) to destroy slowly

e-ro-sion [ĭ-rō'zhən] *noun*, the process of wearing down, breaking up, and carrying off land, soil, and rock, by wind and water

err [ûr, ĕr] *verb*, to be mistaken

er-rand [ĕr'ənd] *noun*, a short trip to accomplish a task

er-rat-ic [ĭ-răt'ĭk] *adjective*, irregular, inconsistent

er-ro-ne-ous [ĭ-rō'nē-əs] *adjective*, false, incorrect

er-ror [ĕr'ər] *noun*, 1) a belief in what is untrue 2) an act involving a departure from truth and accuracy, a mistake

er-satz [er'säts] *adjective*, 1) made or used as a substitute 2) not real or genuine

er-u-dite [ĕr'yə-dīt] *adjective*, learned, well-educated, scholarly

e-rupt [ĭ-rŭpt'] *verb*, 1) to burst out suddenly, to explode 2) to express an emotion suddenly and forcefully

es-ca-la-tor [ĕs'kə-lā'tər] *noun*, moving stairs attached to a circulating belt

es-cape [ĭ-skāp'] *noun*, 1) a means to get away from danger or unpleasantness, *verb*, 2) to free oneself

es-chew [ĕs-chōō'] *verb*, to avoid, to keep away from, to evade

es-cort [ĕs'kôrt'] *noun*, 1) a guide, an attendant, *verb*, 2) to accompany someone, to go with them as protection or an honor

es-crow [ĕs'krō'] *noun*, money, a bond or a deed held by a third person until a specified condition is met

Es-ki-mo [ĕs'kə-mō'] *noun*, a member of a people living in Russia, Alaska, Canada, and Greenland, the Inuit

e-soph-a-gus [ĭ-sŏf'ə-gəs] *noun*, the tube that leads from the pharynx to the stomach

es-o-ter-ic [ĕs'ə-tĕr'ĭk] *adjective*, understood only by a chosen few

es-pe-cial-ly [ĕ-spĕsh'ə-lē] *adverb*, particularly, to a great extent

es-pi-o-nage [ĕs'pē-ə-näzh'] *noun*, of spying, the practice of spying

es-prit de corps [ĕ-sprē' də kôr'] *noun*, the spirit of the group

es-say [ĕs'ā', ĕ-sā'] *noun*, 1) a literary composition expressing personal observations, *verb*, 2) to try out, to test, to attempt

es-sence [ĕs'əns] *noun*, 1) the real character or nature of something 2) perfume

es-sen-tial [ĭ-sĕn'shəl] *adjective*, 1) indispensable 2) of or pertaining to the essential nature, *noun*, 3) a necessity, the basic elements

es-tab-lish [ĭ-stăb'lĭsh] *verb*, 1) to make stable or firm, to settle or set up, *verb*, 2) to prove to be true

es-tab-lish-ment [ĭ-stăb'lĭsh-mənt] *noun*, 1) a place of business or residence 2) an organization

estate

es-tate [ĭ-stāt′] *noun*, 1) a property
2) property left at someone's
death

es-teem [ĭ-stēm′] *noun*, 1) respect,
honor, *verb*, 2) to regard
favorably

es-ti-mate [ĕs′tə-mĭt′] *noun*, 1) an
educated guess, an
approximation, [ĕs′tə-māt′] *verb*,
2) to calculate the approximate
value or amount of something
3) to give an approximate rather
than an exact answer, to guess

et cet-er-a [ĕt sĕt′ər-ə] abbr. **etc.**,
and so on

etch [ĕch] *verb*, to engrave by
biting out with an acid

e-ter-nal [ĭ-tûr′nəl] *adjective*,
endless, infinite, forever

e-ter-ni-ty [ĭ-tûr′nĭ-tē] *noun*, forever

eth-i-cal [ĕth′ĭ-kəl] *adjective*,
having or relating to morals

eth-ics [ĕth′ĭks] *noun*, *plural*, rules
of moral principles governing a
group

eth-nic [ĕth′nĭk] *adjective*, relating
to different races or culture

eth-nol-o-gy [ĕth-nŏl′ə-jē] *noun*,
the study of different races and
their characteristics

et-i-quette [ĕt′ĭ-kĕt′] *noun*, the
rules for polite behavior, good
manners

et-y-mol-o-gy [ĕt′ə-mŏl′ə-jē] *noun*,
the study of the origin and
derivation of words

eu-gen-ics [yōō-jĕn′ĭks] *noun*, the
study of genetic traits by
controlling breeding

eu-lo-gy [yōō′lə-jē] *noun*, a speech
or written tribute lauding a
deceased person

eu-phe-mism [yōō′fə-mĭz′əm]
noun, a mild expression to
replace an offensive remark

eu-re-ka [yōō-rē′kə] *exclamation*,
an expression of triumph
concerning a discovery

Eu-ro [yōōr′ŏ], *noun*, a unit of
money used by most of the
countries belonging to the
European Union

Eu-rope [yōōr′əp] *noun*, one of the
seven continents, the second
smallest continent

eu-tha-na-sia [yōō′thə-nā′zhə]
noun, mercy killing

e-vac-u-ate [ĭ-văk′yōō-āt′] *verb*, to
abandon, to empty out

e-vade [ĭ-vād′] *verb*, to avoid, to
escape by cleverness

e-val-u-ate [ĭ-văl′yōō-āt′] *verb*, to
measure the value, to appraise

e-vap-o-rate [ĭ-văp′ə-rāt′] *verb*,
1) to turn from solid or liquid into
vapor 2) to lose moisture, to dry
up 3) to vanish

e-vap-o-ra-tion [ĭ-văp′ə-rā′shən]
noun, the process in which water
disappears from a surface as it
becomes vapor, the loss of water
into the air

e-va-sive [ĭ-vā′sĭv] *adjective*,
1) avoiding something, elusive
2) intentionally not answering

eve [ĕv] *noun*, the night before

e-ven [ē′vən] *adjective*, 1) level,
flat, smooth 2) able to be divided
by two 3) equal, *adverb*, 4) more

than expected 5) indeed 6) exactly

eve-ning [ēv′nĭng] *noun*, the time between the end of the afternoon and bedtime, dusk

e-ven-ly [ē′vən-lē] *adverb*, in an equal way, smoothly

e-vent [ĭ-vĕnt′] *noun*, something that takes place, an activity

e-ven-tu-al-ly [ĭ-vĕn′chōō-ə-lē] *adverb*, at long last, after the passing of some time

ev-er [ĕv′ər] *adverb*, 1) always, at all times 2) at any time

ev-er-green [ĕv′ər-grēn′] *noun*, a plant that keeps its leaves all year long, including holly, rhododendrons, and pine trees

eve-ry [ĕv′rē] *adjective*, each, all possible

eve-ry-bod-y [ĕv′rē-bŏd′ē] *pronoun*, every person

eve-ry-day [ĕv′rē-dā′] *adjective*, ordinary, commonplace, normal

eve-ry-one [ĕv′rē-wŭn′] *pronoun*, each person, everybody

eve-ry-thing [ĕv′rē-thĭng′] *pronoun*, all together, all things

eve-ry-where [ĕv′rē-hwâr′] *adverb*, in every place

ev-i-dence [ĕv′ĭ-dəns] *noun*, 1) one or more facts or items 2) testimony 3) the basis on which one believes something to be true

ev-i-dent [ĕv′ĭ-dənt] *adjective*, clear, apparent, obvious

e-vil [ē′vəl] *adjective*, very bad, corrupt, immoral, wicked

e-voke [ĭ-vōk′] *verb*, 1) to call forth, 2) to bring to mind

ev-o-lu-tion [ĕv′ə-lōō′shən] *noun*, the natural process of growth and change, development

e-volve [ĭ-vŏlv′] *verb*, to come into being, to develop gradually

ex-ac-er-bate [ĭg-zăs′ər-bāt′] *verb*, to make worse

ex-act [ĭg-zăkt′] *adjective*, precise, correct, completely accurate

ex-ag-ger-ate [ĭg-zăj′ə-rāt′] *verb*, to enlarge beyond the bounds of truth, to overstate

ex-alt [ĭg-zôlt′] *verb*, to praise, to elevate, to raise in rank

ex-am-i-na-tion [ĭg-zăm′ə-nā′shən] *noun*, scrutiny, inquiry, a test

ex-am-ine [ĭg-zăm′ĭn] *verb*, 1) to inspect carefully, to look at every point 2) to scrutinize 3) to question

ex-am-ple [ĭg-zăm′pəl] *noun*, 1) a model, a sample of what others are like 2) a person punished as a warning to others

ex-as-per-ate [ĭg-zăs′pə-rāt′] *verb*, to irritate, to provoke, to enrage

ex-ceed [ĭk-sēd′] *verb*, 1) to pass beyond the measure of something, 2) to surpass

ex-cel [ĭk-sĕl′] *verb*, to be better than others at something, to do well

ex-cel-lent [ĕk′sə-lənt] *adjective*, superior, very good

ex-cel-si-or [ĕk′sə-l′sē′ər] *adjective*, higher, always upward

ex-cept [ĭk-sĕpt′] *preposition*, 1) apart from, not including, *verb*, 2) to exclude

exception

ex-cep-tion [ĭk-sĕp′shən] *noun*,
1) a circumstance not
conforming to the general rule
2) an omission

ex-cep-tion-al [ĭk-sĕp′shə-nəl]
adjective, superior, unusually
good

ex-cerpt [ĕk′sûrpt′] *noun*, section
that has been removed from a
longer text

ex-cess [ĭk-sĕs′] *adjective*,
1) extra, more than expected,
noun, 2) an amount that is more
than enough 3) immoderate
behaivor

ex-change [ĭks-chānj′] *noun*, 1) the
process of settling accounts or
trading items between parties,
verb, 2) to change something for
something else, to replace, to
trade

ex-cise [ĕk′sīz′] *noun*, a tax levied
upon specific articles and
services within a country

ex-cite [ĭk-sīt′] *verb*, to be
energized or to have strong
feeling

ex-cit-ement [ĭk-sīt′mənt] *noun*,
1) ado, commotion 2) a thrill

ex-claim [ĭk-sklām′] *verb*, to speak
suddenly and with strong feeling

ex-cla-ma-tion mark
[ĕk′sklə-mā′shən märk] *noun*, the
sign ! used to show surprise,
humor, or strong feeling

ex-clude [ĭk-sklōōd′] *verb*, to keep
out

ex-clu-sive [ĭk-sklōō′sĭv] *adjective*,
restricted to particular group of
people

ex-cru-ci-at-ing
[ĭk skrōō′shē-ā′tĭng] *adjective*,
very painful, agonizing

ex-cur-sion [ĭk-skûr′zhən] *noun*, a
journey chiefly for recreation, a
brief tour, an outing

ex-cuse [ĭk′skyōōs] *noun*, 1) a
reason, a defense, [ĭk-skyōōz′]
verb, 2) to free, to allow an
interruption 3) to give a reason
for a fault

ex-e-cute [ĕk′sĭ-kyōōt′] *verb*, 1) to
kill someone legally as
punishment for a crime 2) to take
action

ex-e-cu-tion [ĕk′sĭ-kyōō′shən]
noun, 1) accomplishment,
implementation 2) the act of
putting to death a condemned
person

ex-ec-u-tive [ĭg-zĕk′yə-tĭv] *noun*,
1) a business person responsible
for making decisions, a manager
2) one of the three branches of
the United States government

ex-em-pla-ry [ĭg-zĕm′plə-rē]
adjective, commendable, serving
as a desirable model

ex-em-pli-fy [ĭg-zĕm′plə-fī′] *verb*,
to show or illustrate by example

ex-empt [ĭg-zĕmpt′] *verb*, to
excuse from an obligation or
rule, to make immune

ex-er-cise [ĕk′sər-sīz′] *noun*, 1) an
activity used to train the body,
verb, 2) to train the body by
using one's muscles

ex-ert [ĭg-zûrt′] *verb*, 1) to make an
effort 2) to bring to bear

ex-er-tion [ĭg-zûr′shən] *noun*, hard
work, a strong effort

ex-hale [ĕks-hāl′] *verb*, to breathe out, to blow, to emit

ex-haust [ĭg-zôst′] *verb*, 1) to be thorough covering all points 2) to use up 3) the waste fumes from an engine

ex-haus-tion [ĭg-zôs′chən] *noun*, fatique, tiredness

ex-haus-tive [ĭg-zô′stĭv] *adjective*, complete, thorough, attending to every detail, comprehensive

ex-hib-it [ĭg-zĭb′ĭt] *noun*, 1) a display of a collection, *verb*, 2) to display

ex-hi-bi-tion [ĕk′sə-bĭsh′ən] *noun*, a public display of art or other items

ex-hil-a-ra-tion [ĭg-zĭl′ə-rā′shən] *noun*, a feeling of excitement and joy

ex-i-gen-cy [ĕk′sə-jən-sē] *noun*, a pressing necessity, a case demanding immediate action

ex-ile [ĕg′zīl′] *noun*, 1) one who is not allowed to live in his or her own country as a form of punishment, *verb*, 2) to be forced out of a place and not allowed to return

ex-ist [ĭg-zĭot′] *verb*, 1) to be, to live, to be present, to occur

ex-ist-ence [ĭg-zĭs′təns] *noun*, 1) state of being actual, life 2) reality 3) all that which lives

ex-it [ĕg′zĭt] *noun*, 1) a way to go out, the door leading out of a building 2) the ramp leading off a major highway, *verb*, 3) to leave, to go out, to depart

ex-o-dus [ĕk′sə-dəs] *noun*, mass departure of people, migration

ex-o-skel-e-ton [ĕk′sō-ɔkŏl′ĭ tn] *noun*, an outer structure that provides protection to an insect, shellfish, turtle, etc.

ex-ot-ic [ĭg-zŏt′ĭk] *adjective*, strange, interesting, or unusual

ex-pand [ĭk-spănd′] *verb*, to grow or make larger, to extend

ex-panse [ĭk-spăns′] *noun*, a large open space, an area of land

ex-pa-tri-ate [ĕk-spā′trē-āt′] *noun*, someone who left his native land

ex-pect [ĭk-spĕkt′] *verb*, to wait for something that is supposed to happen, to anticipate

ex-pec-ta-tion [ĕk′spĕk-tā′shən] *noun*, anticipation, calculation

ex-pe-di-en-cy [ĭk-spē′dē-ən-sē] *noun*, that which is practical

ex-pe-di-tion [ĕk′spĭ-dĭsh′ən] *noun*, a journey or excursion for a specific purpose, a trip

ex-pe-di-tious [ĕk′spĭ-dĭsh′əs] *adjective*, efficient and speedy

ex-pel [ĭk-spĕl′] *verb*, to drive out

ex-pend-i-ture [ĭk-spĕn′də-chər] *noun*, a laying out, as of money or labor, the cost

ex-pense [ĭk-spĕns′] *noun*, 1) cost, payment 2) detriment, sacrifice

ex-pen-sive [ĭk-spĕn′sĭv] *adjective*, costing a lot of money

ex-pe-ri-ence [ĭk-spîr′ē-əns] *noun*, 1) an encounter that provokes a reaction 2) knowledge gained by observation or trial, *verb*, 3) to live, to feel by participating

ex-per-i-ment [ĭk-spĕr′ə-mənt] *noun*, 1) a test done to see if something is valid or true, *verb*,

2) to carry out a plan in order to test a prediction

ex-pert [ĕk′spûrt′] *noun*, a very knowledgeable person in his or her particular field, an authority

ex-per-tise [ĕk′spûr-tēz′] *noun*, specialized knowledge or skill

ex-pi-ra-tion [ĕk′spə-rā′shən] *noun*, 1) a coming to a close 2) death, the end

ex-pire [ĭk-spīr′] *verb*, 1) to end, to cease to exist 2) to breath out

ex-plain [ĭk-splān′] *verb*, to clarify or to give a reason, to account for

ex-pla-na-tion [ĕk′splə-nā′shən] *noun*, the act of interpreting an action or giving a description

ex-ple-tive [ĕk′splĭ-tĭv] *noun*, a curse word, an obscenity

ex-plic-it [ĭk-splĭs′ĭt] *adjective*, plain, definite, expressed clearly

ex-plode [ĭk-splōd′] *verb*, 1) to release energy with a loud noise as something is destroyed by bursting outward 2) to increase suddenly

ex-ploit [ĕk′sploit′] *noun*, 1) a deed or act, especially one of renown, *verb*, 2) to make use of for one's own profit

ex-plo-ra-tion [ĕk′splə-rā′shən] *noun*, a search in order to discover, an investigation

ex-plore [ĭk-splôr′] *verb*, 1) to look into closely, to examine or investigate 2) to go into new or unknown places to find new things and learn about them

ex-plo-sion [ĭk-splō′zhən] *noun*, a blast, a bomb bursting

ex-plo-sive [ĭk-splō′sĭv] *adjective*, 1) likely to explode, *noun*, 2) a substance that explodes

ex-port [ĭk-spôrt′] *noun*, 1) goods sold abroad as part of international trade, *verb*, 2) to convey merchandise to another country for sale

ex-pose [ĭk-spōz′] *verb* 1) to make easy to see 2) to reveal something hidden, to make known 3) to leave unprotected

ex-po-si-tion [ĕk′spə-zĭsh′ən] *noun*, 1) a statement of intent, 2) a public exhibition or display

ex-po-sure [ĭk-spō′zhər] *noun*, the state of not being sheltered from the elements, such as cold, sun, rain, wind, etc.

ex-press [ĭk-sprĕs′] *adjective*, 1) by the fastest means available, without many stops *verb*, 2) to show, to state

ex-pres-sion [ĭk-sprĕsh′ən] *noun*, 1) the look on someone's face, a facial gesture 2) a remark, a cliché 3) voice, articulation, 4) wording language, 5)a way of showing feelings or emotion

ex-pul-sion [ĭk-spŭl′shən] *noun*, a driving or forcing out

ex-punge [ĭk-spŭnj′] *verb*, to erase, to remove

ex-quis-ite [ĕk′skwĭ-zĭt] *adjective*, 1) carefully crafted or executed, delicate 2) lovely, very beautiful

ex-tend [ĭk-stĕnd′] *verb*, 1) to stretch out, to lengthen 2) to offer

ex-ten-sion [ĭk-stĕn′shən] *noun*, 1) the act of extending 2) a part added on

ex-ten-sive [ĭk-stĕn′sĭv] *adjective*, having wide reach, broad

ex-tent [ĭk-stĕnt′] *noun*, the area covered or affected by something, the amount or degree

ex-ten-u-ate [ĭk-stĕn′yōō-āt′] *verb*, to make something seem less serious

ex-te-ri-or [ĭk-stîr′ē-ər] *adjective*, 1) external, outward, 2) of the surface or appearance, *noun*, 3) the outer surface

ex-ter-mi-nate [ĭk-stûr′mə-nāt′] *verb*, to destroy completely

ex-ter-nal [ĭk-stûr′nəl] *adjective*, 1) on or relating to the outside of the subject 2) outward

ex-tinct [ĭk-stĭngkt′] *adjective*, no longer existing or living

ex-tin-guish [ĭk-stĭng′gwĭsh] *verb*, to put out, to suppress, to kill

ex-tort [ĭk-stôrt′] *verb*, to get by making threats and by intimidation or coercion

ex-tor-tion [ĭk-stôr′shən] *noun*, the act of demanding money by making threats, blackmail

ex-tra [ĕk′strə] *adjective*, 1) more than needed, *noun* 2) a surplus, *adverb*, 3) unusually

ex-tract [ĭk-străkt′] *verb*, 1) to take out 2) to distill or remove

ex-tra-di-tion [ĕk′strə-dĭsh′ən] *noun*, the surrender of a prisoner by a country or state to another

ex-tra-ne-ous [ĭk-strā′nē-əs] *adjective*, not essential

ex-traor-di-nar-y [ĭk-strôr′dn-ĕr′ē, ĕk′strə-ôr′-] *adjective*, beyond the common order, unusual, rare

ex-tra-ter-res-tri-al [ĕkstrətə′ restrēəl] *adjective*, 1) of or from outside the earth's atmosphere 2) a person from another planet

ex-trav-a-gant [ĭk-străv′ə-gənt] *adjective*, wasteful, exceeding reasonable limits, spending too much, very expensive

ex-treme [ĭk-strēm′] *adjective*, 1) to the highest or a very high degree 2) to or of the utmost limit or degree, radical 3) final

ex-trem-i-ty [ĭk-strĕm′ĭ-tē] *noun*, 1) farthest point or part 2) an appendage such as a hand or foot

ex-tri-cate [ĕk′strĭ-kāt′] *verb*, to free, to untangle

ex-trin-sic [ĭk-strĭn′sĭk] *adjective*, from outside, nonessential

ex-u-ber-ant [ĭg-zōō′bər-ənt] *adjective*, displaying high spirits

ex-ude [ĭg-zōōd′] *verb*, 1) to ooze, to discharge 2) to display a strong feeling

ex-ul-ta-tion [ĕk′səl-tā′shən] *noun*, joy, celebration, delight

eye [ī] *noun*, 1) either of the pair of organs located in the head used to see 2) the tiny hole at the end of a needle

eye-lash [ī′lăsh′] *noun*, one of the hairs growing on the eyelid

eye-lid [ī′lĭd′] *noun*, the skin that covers the eye

F

fa-ble [fā′bəl] *noun*, a fictitious short story with a moral, often with animals that talk

fabric

fab-ric [făb′rĭk] *noun*, 1) any cloth that is woven or knit from fibers 2) make up, substance

fab-ri-cate [făb′rĭ-kāt′] *verb*, 1) to build, to construct 2) to lie

fab-u-lous [făb′yə-ləs] *adjective*, marvelous, wonderful, amazing

fa-cade [fə-säd′] *noun*, the decorated front of a building

face [fās] *noun*, 1) the front of the head, with the eyes, nose and mouth 2) the front of something 3) a flat surface of an object, *verb*, 4) to stand in front of or turn to confront

fac-et [făs′ĭt] *noun*, 1) one of the polished plane surfaces of a precious stone 2) an aspect of a subject, a feature

fa-ce-tious [fə-sē′shəs] *adjective*, joking, sportive, not serious

fac-ile [făs′əl] *adjective*, 1) easy, superficial 2) speaking fluently

fa-cil-i-tate [fə-sĭl′ĭ-tāt′] *verb*, to make easier, to aid, to help

fac-sim-i-le [făk-sĭm′ə-lē] *noun*, a reproduction or a likeness

fact [făkt] *noun*, an indisputable piece of information, a certainty

fac-tion [făk′shən] *noun*, a dissenting party, an inner circle, a clique, a group within a group

fac-tious [făk′shəs] *adjective*, relating to internal dissension

fac-tor [făk′tər] *noun*, 1) a condition that contributes to a result 2) the numbers multiplied to give a product

fac-to-ry [făk′tə-rē] *noun*, a building where products are manufactured

fac-ul-ty [făk′əl-tē] *noun*, 1) the teachers in an institution of learning 2) a physical or mental ability, talent, capacity

fad [făd] *noun*, temporary fashion or style, the "in" thing

fade [fād] *verb*, 1) to lose light or color 2) to become dim or less visable

Fahr-en-heit [făr′ən-hīt′] *adjective*, of or relating to the temperature scale on which the freezing point of water is 32 degrees and the boiling point of water is 212 degrees under normal atmospheric pressure

fail [fāl] *verb*, 1) to not accomplish what you set out to 2) to stop working

fail-ure [fāl′yər] *noun*, 1) lack of success 2) state of not working

faint [fānt] *adjective*, 1) hard to see, dim 2) inaudible, indistinct, soft, *noun*, 3) a loss of consciousness, *verb*, 4) to collapse unconscious

fair [fâr] *adjective*, 1) treating everyone equally, not favoring one more than another, 2) so-so, mediocre 3) pale, light-skinned *noun*, 4) a place for buying and selling goods 5)an entertainment with rides, games, and food

fair-y [fâr′ē] *noun*, an imaginary person with magical powers

faith [fāth] *noun*, 1) a belief in something that is not seen, relying on trust 2) belief in a religion

faith-ful [fāth′fəl] *adjective*, loyal, trustworthy, full of faith

fake [fāk] *noun*, 1) a forgery, an imitation, *verb*, 2) to pretend, to falsify 3) to counterfeit

fall [fôl] *noun*, 1) autumn, 2) a dropping downward, *verb*, 3) to come down, to tumble or topple, 4) to lose power

fal-lacy [făl′ə-sē] *noun*, an error in reasoning, an erroneous idea

fal-li-ble [făl′ə-bəl] *adjective*, liable to err

false [fôls] *adjective*, 1) not true 2) artificial, not real

fal-ter [fôl′tər] *verb*, to hesitate

fame [fām] *noun*, *no plural*, wide recognition, renown

fa-mil-iar [fə-mĭl′yər] *adjective*, having some knowledge of something or someone

fam-i-ly [făm′ə-lē] *noun*, 1) a parent or parents and children 2) all of a person's relatives

fam-ine [făm′ĭn] *noun*, 1) general scarcity of food 2) extreme scarcity of something

fam-ish-ed [făm′ĭshd] *adjective*, extremely hungry

fa-mous [fā′məs] *adjective*, well known, celebrated, noted

fan [făn] *noun*, 1) a device designed to circulate air 2) an ardent follower or supporter, *verb*, 3) to move air, to cool with a fan 4) to spread out

fa-nat-ic [fə-năt′ĭk] *adjective*, 1) carrying an interest or enthusiasm to extremes, *noun*, 2) a person with a very strong enthusiasm for something

fan-cy [făn′sē] *adjective*, elaborate, unusually decorated, not plain

fang [făng] *noun*, 1) a long sharp tooth 2) the often hollow tooth through which a snake injects poison

fan-tas-tic [făn-tăs′tĭk] *adjective*, 1) imaginary, fanciful, unreal 2) very good

fan-ta-sy [făn′tə-sē] *noun*, a daydream, an imaginary situation, make-believe

far [fär] *adjective*, 1) at a great distance, not near or close by, *adverb*, 2) exceedingly 3) at or to or by a great distance in time or space

fare [fâr] *noun*, 1) money paid for a trip by bus or train 2) food and drink, *verb* 3) to get along well

fare-well [fâr-wĕl′] *noun*, a goodbye, the act of parting

farm [färm] *noun*, buildings and land where people grow food or raise animals to sell

farm-er [fär′mər] *noun*, a person who cultivates crops or raises animals for sale

far-ther [fär′thər] *adjective*, 1) more distant in time, space or degree *adverb*, 2) to or at a greater distance in space or time

fas-ci-nate [făs′ə-nāt′] *verb*, to attract and hold interest, to captivate

fas-ci-na-tion [făs′ə-nā′shən] *noun*, personal attraction, infatuation

fash-ion [făsh′ən] *noun*, 1) clothing or articles that are in style, *verb*, 2) to shape or form

fast [făst] *adjective*, 1) quick, rapid 2) fixed in place, unable to move,

fastidious

verb, 3) to go for a long period of time without eating

fas-tid-i-ous [făst'ĭd'ē-əs] *adjective*, hard to please, very critical

fat [făt] *adjective*, 1) having a wide round shape 2) thick, *noun*, 3) a greasy substance in meat

fa-tal [fāt'l] *adjective*, resulting in death, lethal

fate [fāt] *noun*, an invisible hand that seems to cause certain things to happen over which people have no control, destiny

fa-ther [fä'thər] *noun*, the male parent

fa-ther-in-law [fä'thər-ĭn-lô'] *noun*, the father of your wife or husband

fath-om [făth'əm] *noun*, 1) a measurement of water depth, *verb*, 2) to understand, to comprehend

fa-tigue [fə-tēg'] *noun*, 1) the condition of being very tired or exhausted, *verb*, 2) to become or make tired

fau-cet [fô'sĭt] *noun*, a fixture for drawing liquid from a pipe and regulating the flow

fault [fôlt] *noun*, 1) mistake, failure 2) a defect, 3) responsibility for a failure, 4) a fracture in the earth's surface causing a displacement

fa-vor [fā'vər] *noun*, 1) an act of kindness, *verb*, 2) to prefer, to patronize, to fancy, to like

fa-vor-ite [fā'vər-ĭt] *adjective*, something preferred above others, liked the best

fawn [fôn] *noun*, a young deer less than a year old

fear [fîr] *noun*, 1) expecting harm, *verb*, 2) to dread or be afraid of

fear-ful [fîr'fəl] *adjective*, afraid

fea-si-ble [fē'zə-bəl] *adjective*, capable of being done, practical, possible, achievable

feast [fēst] *noun*, 1) an elaborate meal, a banquet, *verb*, 2) to eat large amounts of food and drink

feat [fēt] *noun*, an accomplishment, a remarkable achievement

feath-er [fĕth'ər] *noun*, a soft thing which covers birds, like a toothpick covered with fine hairs

fea-ture [fē'chər] *noun*, 1) a distinctive aspect of a person's face, a characteristic 2) an article in the newspaper

Feb-ru-ar-y [fĕb'rōō-ĕr'ē] *noun*, the second month in the year, usually having 28 days but 29 every four years on the leap year

fed [fĕd] *past tense* of **feed**

fed-er-al [fĕd'ər-əl] *adjective*, belonging or pertaining to a state formed by the consolidation of several states

fed-er-a-tion [fĕd'ə-rā'shən] *noun*, an alliance, an association in which members retain autonomy

fee [fē] *noun*, money charged for something, the cost or expense

fee-ble [fē'bəl] *adjective*, frail

feed [fēd] *noun*, 1) food for animals, *verb*, 2) to give someone food, to nourish

feel [fēl] *verb*, 1) to perceive in a way other than your five senses, to sense with emotions 2) to examine with the sense of touch 3) to form an opinion

feign [fān] *verb*, to pretend

feist-y [fī′stē] *adjective*, 1) spirited, lively, exuberant 2) quarrelsome

fell [fĕl] *adjective*, 1) cruel, deadly, *verb*, 2) *past tense* of **fall**

fel-low [fĕl′ō] *noun*, 1) a man 2) a companion, a comrade

fel-on [fĕl′ən] *noun*, a person convicted of a serious crime

fel-o-ny [fĕl′ə-nē] *noun*, any offense that is punishable by confinement in prison for one year or more or death

felt [fĕlt] *noun*, 1) a soft synthetic fabric of compressed, matted animal fibers, such as wool 2) the *past tense* of **feel**

fe-male [fē′māl′] *adjective*, 1) referring to a woman, feminine, *noun*, 2) a woman, a person who belongs to the sex that can have babies

fem-i-nine [fĕm′ə-nĭn] *adjective*, of or pertaining to the female sex

fence [fĕns] *noun*, 1) a partition that encloses an area made of wood or wire 2) a person who receives stolen goods, *verb*, 3) to put in an enclosure 4) to duel with a sword

fend-er [fĕn′dər] *noun*, the strip of metal over the wheels of a car, bicycle, or other vehicle to protect against mud or water

fer-ment [fər-mĕnt′] *verb*, to change chemically with bacteria or yeast

fern [fûrn] *noun*, a plant that does not have flowers or seeds that grows in shady places

fer-ret [fĕr′ĭt] *noun*, 1) a small mammal of the weasel family, *verb*, 2) to drive or hunt out of hiding 3) to find something out by persistent investigation

fer-ry [fĕr′ē] *noun*, a boat used to transport people or goods across a body of water

fer-tile [fûr′tl] *adjective*, fruitful, able to produce abundantly

fer-ti-lize [fûr′tl-īz′] *verb*, to make ready for planting or encourage growth by providing proper amounts of nitrogen, potash, etc.

fer-vent [fûr′vənt] *adjective*, hot, showing intense feeling

fes-ter [fĕs′tər] *verb*, to become worse due to infection or anger

fes-ti-val [fĕs′tə-vəl] *noun*, 1) a big party that takes place on a holiday or at another special time 2) a program of cultural events 3) a carnival

fetch [fĕch] *verb*, 1) to go after something and bring it back, to retrieve 2) to bring a certain price

fet-ish [fĕt′ĭsh] *noun*, 1) a quirky habit based on a belief in magic 2) a compulsion 3) an object believed to be magical

feud [fyood] *noun*, 1) a prolonged fight, a quarrel, lasting hostility

fe-ver [fē′vər] *noun*, a body temperature higher than 98.6 degrees, often because the body is trying to fight off infection

few [fyoo] *adjective*, *noun*, *pronoun*, three or more

fi-an-cé [fē′än-sā′, fē-än′sā′] *noun*, a man engaged to be married

fiancée

fi-an-cée [fē′än-sā′] *noun*, a woman engaged to be married

fi-as-co [fē-ăs′kō] *noun*, a total failure, an upheaval, a collapse

fi-ber [fī′bər] *noun*, 1) thread-like structures combined with others to create tissue 2) a filament 3) material in food that is not easily digested

fick-le [fĭk′əl] *adjective*, moody, inconsistent, not loyal, flighty

fic-tion [fĭk′shən] *noun*, that which is not true or based in fact, make-believe literature that is based on imagination

fic-ti-tious [fĭk-tĭsh′əs] *adjective*, imaginary, unreal, false

fid-dle [fĭd′l] *noun*, 1) another word for a violin, *verb*, 2) to tinker with something

fid-dler [fĭd′l-ər] *noun*, a person who plays a hand-held stringed instrument

fi-del-i-ty [fĭ-dĕl′ĭ-tē, fī-] *noun*, 1) faithfulness, loyalty, honesty 2) degree to which electronics accurately reproduce sound

field [fēld] *noun*, 1) land put to special use for sports or farming 2) a sphere or range of activities, *verb*, 3) to receive a ball in a game and pass it to another player

fiend [fēnd] *noun*, 1) a person who is wicked, cruel, or malicious 2) an evil sprit, a demon

fierce [fîrs] *adjective*, furious, violent or aggressive, intense

fier-y [fîr′ē] *adjective*, burning, heated, impassioned

fif-teen [fĭf-tēn′] *adjective, noun*, the number 15, ten plus five

fif-teenth [fĭf-tēnth′] *adjective, noun*, number 15 in order, 15th

fifth [fĭfth] *adjective, noun*, number five in order, 5th

fif-ti-eth [fĭf′tē-ĭth] *adjective, noun*, the ordinal of fifty, 50th

fif-ty [fĭf′tē] *adjective, noun*, the number 50, 5 times 10

fig [fĭg] *noun*, a small fruit grown in warm climates, full of seeds

fight [fīt] *noun*, 1) the use of the body or weapons against someone, *verb*, 2) to engage in a physical struggle 3) to quarrel 4) to struggle in any way

fig-ment [fĭg′mənt] *noun*, an imaginary thing

fig-ur-a-tive [fĭg′yər-ə-tĭv] *adjective*, 1) not literal, metaphorical 2) featuring human or animal figures

fig-ure [fĭg′yər] *noun*, 1) shape or outline of something, 2) digits or numbers in an equation, *verb*, 3) to calculate numbers or simplify something hard to understand

fig-ure-head [fĭg′yər-hĕd′] *noun*, 1) a carved figure set at the front of a sailing ship 2) a leader in name only who has no authority

fil-a-ment [fĭl′ə-mənt] *noun*, a slender threadlike structure, fiber, or wire

filch [fĭlch] *verb*, to steal

file [fīl] *noun*, 1) a drawer for papers 2) a metal tool with a rough edge for making things smooth 3) a line of people 4) a stored collection of data, *verb*,

5) to organize papers or other items into a system 6) to make a surface smooth through friction with a tool 7) to walk in a straight and orderly line 8) to register with a public agency

fil-i-al [fĭl′ē-əl] *adjective*, referring to having a relationship like a son or daughter

fill [fĭl] *verb*, 1) to occupy as much as possible 2) to make full

fil-let or fi-let [fĭl′ĭt] *noun*, 1) a boneless piece of meat or fish, *verb*, 2) to remove bones from and slice into fillets

film [fĭlm] *noun*, 1) a sensitized material that receives photographic impressions 2) a movie shown in a theater or on television, *verb*, 3) to photograph something on film 4) to make a movie using a camera

filth-y [fĭl′thē] *adjective*, 1) very dirty, nasty, squalid 2) obscene

fil-tra-tion [fĭl-trā′shən] *noun*, purification of a liquid by passing it through a filter

fin [fĭn] *noun*, part of a fish that sticks out, may be fan-shaped, used for steering or balance

fi-nal [fī′nəl] *adjective*, last, not to be changed

fi-na-le [fə-năl′ē] *noun*, the last part of a show or musical composition

fi-nal-ly [fī′nə-lē] *adverb*, at last, reaching the end, concluding

fi-nance [fə-năns′] *noun*, 1) money management of, *verb*, 2) to use money to pay for something

find [fīnd] *verb*, to uncover or see something after a search

fine [fīn] *adjective*, 1) pleasant, nice 2) having small grains or particles, *noun*, 3) a penalty, *verb*, 4) to punish someone by making them pay money

fin-esse [fə-nĕs′] *noun*, 1) a delicate skill, dexterity 2) tact, grace

fin-ger [fĭng′gər] *noun*, 1) one of five digits on a hand, *verb*, 2) to handle, to touch or feel

fin-ger-nail [fĭng′gər-nāl′] *noun*, the horny protective material on the end of a finger

fin-ick-y [fĭn′ĭ-kē] *adjective*, fussy

fin-ish [fĭn′ĭsh] *noun*, 1) a surface appearance or texture, *verb*, 2) to end or complete 3) to use up

fi-nite [fī′nīt′] *adjective*, 1) limited in number 2) having boundaries

fir [fûr] *noun*, an evergreen tree

fire [fīr] *noun*, 1) excitement 2) the state or process of burning, *verb*, 3) to dismiss from a job 4) to discharge from a gun

firm [fûrm] *adjective*, 1) solid, hard, *noun*, 2) a company managing a business

firm-ly [fûrm′lē] *adverb*, solidly, resolutely, unwaveringly

first [fûrst] *adjective*, 1) initial, beginning, *noun*, 2) the most important, the highest

first aid [fûrst′ād′] *noun*, the emergency help given someone who has been hurt or who suddenly becomes ill

fish [fĭsh] *noun*, 1) any cold-blooded vertebrate that lives in water, *verb*, 2) to try to catch a fish 3) to try to get something from someone

fis-sure [fĭsh/ər] *noun*, a crack, a narrow groove, a cleft

fist [fĭst] *noun*, the hand with fingers closed tightly together and folded into the palm

fit [fĭt] *adjective*, 1) healthy, active, vibrant 2) good enough, *verb*, 3) to be the right size 4) to conform in shape and size

five [fīv] *adjective*, *noun*, the number 5, one plus four

fix [fĭks] *noun*, 1) a dilemma, a predicament, *verb*, 2) to repair 3) to set, to arrange, to put in place 4) to focus on

fix-ture [fĭks/chər] *noun*, that which is attached to something permanently, apparatus

flac-cid [flăk/sĭd, flăs/ĭd] *adjective*, flabby, hanging loosely

flag [flăg] *noun*, 1) cloth with a special pattern on it, used as the sign of a country, club, etc., *verb*, 2) to wave to someone as a signal to stop 3) to droop

flag-rant [flā/grənt] *adjective*, plainly wicked, unashamed

flail [flāl] *verb*, to move wildly as if beating something, to thrash

flair [flâr] *noun*, an aptitude or talent for doing something well

flake [flāk] *noun*, 1) a small sliver of something, *verb*, 2) to peel off in shavings or tiny bits

flam-boy-ant [flăm-boi/ənt] *adjective*, showy, flashy

flame [flām] *noun*, burning gas seen in a fire

flam-ma-ble [flăm/ə-bəl] *adjective*, capable of igniting easily and burning quickly

flank [flăngk] *noun*, a side of the body between the ribs and the hip, *verb*, 2) to be on one or either side of something

flan-nel [flăn/əl] *noun*, a very soft woolen or cotton cloth

flap [flăp] *noun*, 1) the covering of an opening, that hangs loose, *verb*, 2) to wave to and fro

flare [flâr] *noun*, 1) a torch or brilliant light, *verb*, 2) to shine, to burn brightly 3) to spread out like a fan, to expand outward

flash [flăsh] *noun*, 1) a split second, an instant, 2) a burst of light, *verb*, 3) to show a bright light

flash-back [flăsh'băk] *noun*, an interruption in the continuity of a story, play, etc. by the presentation of an earlier episode

flat [flăt] *adjective*, level and horizontal, smooth

flat-ter-y [flăt/ə-rē] *noun*, *no plural*, excessive compliments

flaunt [flônt] *verb*, to show off

fla-vor [flā/vər] *noun*, 1) seasoning of food, the taste of something, *verb*, 2) to give a taste to food

flaw [flô] *noun*, a defect, a weak spot, an imperfection

flax [flăks] *noun*, a slender plant with blue flowers whose stalks are used to make thread

flay [flā] *verb*, to whip or beat so as to strip off the skin

flea [flē] *noun*, a small jumping insect that sucks blood from people and animals

fled [flĕd] *verb*, *past tense* of **flee**

flee [flē] *verb*, to run away

fleece [flēs] *noun*, 1) the wool on sheep 2) a soft fabric with a deep pile, *verb*, 3) to shake someone down for money 4) to swindle

fleet [flet] *noun*, a group of ships sailing together, or vehicles, or aircraft under one command

fleet-ing [flē/tĭng] *adjective*, swift in motion, passing quickly

flex [flĕks] *verb*, to bend, to contract

flex-i-ble [flĕk/sə-bəl] *adjective*, 1) willing to change a course of action, easily adaptable 2) moving or bending easily

flick-er [flĭk/ər] *verb*, 1) to change unsteadily from bright to dim light, *noun*, 2) a brief sensation

flight [flīt] *noun*, 1) flying, a trip by plane 2) an act of fleeing

flim-sy [flĭm/zē] *adjective*, 1) weak and easily broken 2) ineffectual, without substance

flinch [flĭnch] *verb*, to hesitate, to make a nervous movement away

flint [flĭnt] *noun*, a kind of quartz

flip [flĭp] *adjective*, 1) sarcastic, kidding, joking, *noun*, 2) a somersault in the air, *verb*, 3) to turn swiftly in the air

flip-pant [flĭp/ənt] *adjective*, glib, sarcastic, disrespectful

flirt [flûrt] *verb*, to show romantic interest, to tease affectionately

float [flōt] *noun*, 1) a portable display in a parade, 2) a soda with ice cream in it, *verb*, 3) to be supported by liquid or gas

flock [flŏk] *noun*, 1) a company of birds, animals, or people 2) to gather, to congregate, to huddle

flood [flŭd] *noun*, 1) water that stays on land that is normally dry, *verb*, 2) to cover or overflow with water

floor [flôr] *noun*, 1) the part of the room you walk on 2) a level of a building, *verb*, 3) to knock down 4) to surprise

flo-ral [flôr/əl] *adjective*, decorated with or containing flowers

Flor-i-da [flôr/ĭ-də] *noun*, one of the 50 United States, located in the Southeast, the capital is Tallahassee. The **Florida** state flower is the orange blossom, the motto: "In God we trust."

floss [flôs] *noun*, 1) a soft silky substance found in the husks of some plants 2) a thin silk thread used for embroidery 3) a thread covered with wax used to clean between the teeth, *verb*, 4) to run thread through the teeth to remove food and tartar

flo-til-la [flō-tĭl/ə] *noun*, a small fleet of ships

floun-der [floun/dər] *noun*, 1) a member of the flatfish family, *verb*, 2) to flail about

flour [flour] *noun*, the finely ground meal of wheat or other cereal plants like oats, rice, corn

flour-ish [flûr/ĭsh] *noun*, 1) a handwritten decoration, 2) a sweeping, showy gesture, *verb*, 3) to prosper, to grow well

flout

flout [flout] *verb*, to scoff at, to ridicule, to disobey a law

flow [flō] *noun, no plural*, 1) a current, a steady stream, *verb*, 2) to move in the manner of gases or fluid

flow-er [flou′ər] *noun*, the part of a plant that bears the seeds, the blossom where fruit develops

flu [floo] *noun*, an illness caused by a virus and characterized by fever, body aches and coughing, influenza

fluc-tu-ate [flŭk′choo-āt′] *verb*, 1) to move back and forth like a wave, 2) to vary in degree or value

fluc-tu-a-tion [flŭk′choo-ā′ shən] *noun*, 1) wavering 2) the change of the level or degree of something

flu-ent [floo′ənt] *adjective*, able to speak smoothly and easily

flu-id [floo′ĭd] *adjective*, 1) not fixed or settled, able to flow, *noun*, 2) a liquid that flows

fluo-res-cent [floo-rĕs′ənt] *adjective*, giving off light after absorbing radiation from another source

flur-ry [flûr′ē] *noun*, 1) a brief, quick movement, 2) a light, windy snowfall

flush [flŭsh] *adjective*, 1) even, *noun*, 2) in poker, five cards of the same suit, *verb*, 3) to turn red in the face 4) to wash out

flust-er [flŭs′tər] *verb*, to confuse

flute [floot] *noun*, a musical instrument, a woodwind, like a pipe with keys to control the flow of air

flut-ter [flŭt′ər] *verb*, to flap, to move up and down or back and forth hurriedly

flux [flŭks] *noun*, a flowing series of continuous changes

fly [flī] *noun*, 1) a small flying insect, *verb*, 2) to move through the air 3) to move very fast

foam [fōm] *noun*, 1) froth formed on the surface of liquids by agitation, 2) a soft material produced by putting gas bubbles into a solid

fo-cal [fō′kəl] *adjective*, central

fo-cus [fō′kəs] *noun*, 1) a central point, 2) the clarity of a photgraph or other optical object, *verb*, 3) to concentrate, to pay attention to something

foe [fō] *noun*, an enemy, an adversary, an opponent

fog [fôg] *noun*, a cloud of fine water drops of vapor found close to the ground or sea

foil [foil] *noun*, 1) a paper-like sheet of metal, 2) a long, thin sword used in fencing, *verb*, 3) to throw off someone's plans

fo-li-age [fōlē′ĭj] *noun*, the leaves of trees and other plants

fold [fōld] *noun*, 1) a part of something that has been wrapped or doubled over, *verb*, 2) to double or bend over, to envelope 3) to quit

fol-low [fŏl′ō] *verb*, 1) to go after, to pursue 2) to come after or behind 3) to pay close attention

fond [fŏnd] *adjective*, having feelings of affection

fon-dle [fŏn′dl] *verb*, to caress, to stroke lovingly

food [fŏod] *noun*, a source of nourishment, what you eat

fool [fŏol] *noun*, 1) a silly person, *verb*, 2) to trick or deceive

fool-ish [fŏo′lĭsh] *adjective*, unwise, silly, senseless

foot [fŏot] *noun*, *plural*, **feet**, 1) the part of the leg that touches the ground 2) a measure of length equal to 12 inches 3) any base that resembles a foot

foot-ball [fŏot′bôl′] *noun*, 1) a game in which two teams of eleven players try to score points by passing a ball to each other in a period of time 2) an oval-shaped inflated ball 3) soccer used outside of the US

for [fôr, fər when unstressed] *conjunction*, 1) because, *preposition*, 2) in favor of 3) on behalf of or used by 4) at a certain price 5) having as a destination 6) showing the meaning of as in an example

for-age [fôr′ĭj] *verb*, to look for food or supplies

for-ay [fôr′ā′] *noun*, a raid, an attempt at something unfamiliar

for-bear [fôr-bâr′] *verb*, to hold back, to wait, to refrain from

for-bear-ance [fôr-bâr′əns] *noun*, the act of refraining from anything, self-restraint

for-bid [fər-bĭd′] *verb*, to prohibit, to order someone not to do something

force [fôrs, fōrs] *noun*, 1) power, energy 2) police or military personel, *verb*, 3) to cause to

happen by strength or compulsion

fore-bod-ing [fôr-bō′dĭng] *noun*, a sense of evil to come

fore-cast [fôr′kăst′] *noun*, 1) a prediction that something will happen, especially in reference to the weather, *verb*, 2) to anticipate, or expect

fore-close [fôr-klōz′] *verb*, to take away property from a person who owes money on it

for-eign [fôr′ĭn] *adjective*, belonging to another country

for-eign-er [fôr′ə-nər] *noun*, someone from another country

fore-man [fôr′mən] *noun*, 1) the overseer of a set of workers 2) the spokesman of a jury

fore-most [fôr′mōst′] *adjective*, first in importance, time or place

fo-ren-sic [fə-rĕn′sĭk] *adjective*, suitable for argument in court

fore-see-a-ble [fôr-sē′ə-bəl] *adjective*, predictable, able to be seen as likely to occur

fore-sight [fôr′sīt′] *noun*, the ability to foresee future happenings or needs

for-est [fôr′ĭst] *noun*, a large place where trees grow together

fore-stall [fôr-stôl′] *verb*, to prevent by taking action first

fore-tell [fôr-tĕl′] *verb*, to predict, to make a prophecy, to forecast

for-ev-er [fôr-ĕv′ər] *adverb*, until the end of time, always

for-feit [fôr′fĭt] *verb*, to lose the right, to surrender, to give up

forge [fôrj] *noun*, 1) a furnace where metal is worked, *verb*,

forgery

2) to move ahead deliberately and steadily 3) to mold metal with heat and then hammer it into shapes 4) to invent or create something 5) to counterfeit with intent to defraud

for-ger-y [fôr′jə-rē] *noun*, a false or altered document, art object or other item for the purpose of fraud, counterfeit

for-get [fər-gĕt′] *verb*, 1) to fail to recall or remember 2) to neglect

for-give [fər-gĭv′] *verb*, to accept an apology, to get rid of a grudge, to cease to feel angry

for-got [fər-gŏt′] *verb*, *past tense* of forget

for-got-ten [fər-gŏt′n] *adjective*, left behind

fork [fôrk] *noun*, 1) a utensil with prongs on the end used to stab food 2) a place in a road where it separates in different directions

for-lorn [fər-lôrn′] *adjective*, sad and unhappy, lonely

form [fôrm] *noun*, 1) the shape of something 2) a document with questions that need to be answered, *verb*, 3) to shape or create, to develop, to mold

for-mal [fôr′məl] *adjective*, following the customs of an occasion, ceremonious

for-mal-i-ty [fôr-măl′ĭ-tē] *noun*, adherence to established rules of etiquette and convention

for-ma-tion [fôr-mā′shən] *noun*, 1) a creation, the process of being formed 2) an arrangement

form-er [fôr′mər] *noun*, the first mentioned of two

for-mi-da-ble [fôr′mĭ-də-bəl] *adjective*, 1) causing apprehension, feared 2) impressive because of excellence 3) difficult to overcome

for-mu-la [fôr′myə-lə] *noun*, 1) a representation using chemical symbols of substances mixed together in specific amounts to create something 2) a mathematical statement using symbols

for-mu-late [fôr′myə-lāt′] *verb*, to prepare using a formula 2) to give form to 3) to express precisely in words

fort [fôrt] *noun*, a place for protecting soldiers, a fortified structure

forte [fôrt] *noun*, one's strength

for-ti-eth [fôr′tē-ĭth] *noun*, the ordinal of forty, 40th

for-ti-fy [fôr′tə-fī′] *verb*, 1) to make stronger or more secure 2) to strengthen against attack 3) to add nutrients

for-ti-tude [fôr′tĭ-tood′] *noun*, courage, strength of mind, the ability to withstand hardship

for-tu-nate [fôr′chə-nĭt] *adjective*, lucky, favorable, advantageous

for-tune [fôr′chən] *noun*, 1) whatever good or bad happens to people, luck 2) a large amount of money, wealth, riches

for-ty [fôr′tē] *noun*, the number 40

fo-rum [fôr′əm] *noun*, a public meeting place and market square

for-ward [fôr'wərd] *adjective*, 1) near or at the front part, ahead 2) onward 3) bold, aggressive

fos-sil [fŏs'əl] *noun*, the impression or remains in a rock of a petrified plant or animal

fos-ter [fô'stər] *verb*, to help, to raise children not related to you, to encourage

fought [fôt] *past tense* of **fight**

foul [foul] *adjective*, 1) dirty, filthy, *noun*, 2) an action in a sport that is against the rules

found [found] *verb*, 1) to establish, to lay a foundation 2) *past tense* of **find**

foun-da-tion [foun-dā'shən] *noun*, 1) the base of a building 2) fundamental assumptions 3) a charitable institution

found-er [foun'dər] *noun*, 1) one who begins or establishes an organization, *verb*, 2) to sink

found-ry [foun'drē] *noun*, a plant refining metal or glass, a factory

foun-tain [foun'tən] *noun*, a device that sprays water into the air or pumps it for drinking

four [fôr] *adjective*, *noun*, the number 4, one plus three

four-teen [fôr-tēn'] *noun*, the number 14, four plus ten

four-teenth [fôr-tēnth'] *adjective*, *noun*, number 14 in order, 14th

fourth [fôrth] *adjective*, *noun*, the ordinal number after third, 4th

fowl [foul] *noun*, a bird eaten as food or kept for its eggs

fox [fŏks] *noun*, a carnivorous mammal, the size of a dog with a pointed muzzle and bushy tail

foy-er [foi'ər] *noun*, the entry way in a hall, a hotel lobby

frac-tion [frăk'shən] *noun*, 1) a piece of something 2) a number that names part of a whole or part of a group using equal parts

frac-ture [frăk'chər] *noun*, 1) a break, a fissure, *verb*, 2) to break

frag-ile [frăj'əl, -īl'] *adjective*, easily broken, delicate

frag-ment [frăg'mənt] *noun*, a piece broken off, a particle

fra-grance [frā'grəns] *noun*, a sweet smell, perfume, aroma

frail [frāl] *adjective*, weak, fragile

frame [frām] *noun*, 1) the structure that supports something 2) the outline of something encasing something, *verb*, 3) to enclose in a frame 4) to make someone appear guilty of a crime by arranging false evidence

fran-chise [frăn'chīz'] *noun*, an agreement granted by a company to do business under their name

frank [frăngk] *adjective*, candid, honest in expressing your thoughts

fran-tic [frăn'tĭk] *adjective*, wild with emotion, characterized by nervous activity

fra-ter-ni-ty [frə-tûr'nĭ-tē] *noun*, a fellowship of men in a college

fraud [frôd] *noun*, 1) an imposter, a fake 2) criminal deception

fraud-u-lent [frô'jə-lənt] *adjective*, tricky, deceitful, dishonest

fray

fray [frā] *noun*, 1) a conflict, a commotion, *verb*, 2) to unravel

freak [frēk] *noun*, a strange event or person, an aberration

freck-le [frĕk′əl] *noun*, a small, brownish spot on the skin

free [frē] *adjective*, 1) able to do as you please, unrestrained 2) not costing any money 3) available, *verb*, 4) to release something from captivity

free-dom [frē′dəm] *noun*, liberty, independent, the state of being free

freeze [frēz] *verb*, to become chilled by cold, to change to ice

freez-er [frē′zər] *noun*, an appliance that preserves food by keeping it frozen

freight [frāt] *noun*, transportation of products in bulk, cargo

freight-er [frā′tər] *noun*, a ship or aircraft laden with cargo

fren-zy [frĕn′zē] *noun*, craziness, wild excitement, violent agitation

fre-quen-cy [frē′kwən-sē] *noun*, the number of times something, especially a sound wave, occurs during a particular period of time

fre-quent [frē′kwənt] *adjective*, 1) happening often, repeated many times, *verb*, 2) to go to a place often for visits

fresh [frĕsh] *adjective*, new, unused, arrived recently

fresh-man [frĕsh′mən] *noun*, a person in his first year of high school or college

fret [frĕt] *verb*, to feel anxious

fric-tion [frĭk′shən] *noun*, 1) the force that resists movement

between two things that are in contact with each other 2) an argument caused by differences of opinion, rivalry

Fri-day [frī′dē, -dā′] *noun*, the sixth day of the week

friend [frĕnd] *noun*, a person who knows and likes another

friend-ship [frĕnd- shĭp] *noun*, mutual respect, companionship

fright [frīt] *noun*, sudden fear

fright-en [frīt′n] *verb*, to scare or alarm, to fill with fear

frig-id [frĭj′ĭd] *adjective*, very cold

frill [frĭl] *noun*,1) a doodad, an unnecessary extra feature or luxury 2) a pleated piece of fabric used as a trim

fringe [frĭnj] *noun*, 1) an edge made of short lengths of thread, used to decorate clothes, curtains, etc. 2) an outside edge

frisk-y [frĭs′kē] *adjective*, playful

frit-ter [frĭt′ər] *verb*, 1) to waste 2) friend batter containing fruit, vegetables, or meat

friv-o-lous [frĭv′ə-ləs] *adjective*, 1) of little weight or importance 2) given to trifling, silly

frog [frôg] *noun*, 1) a jumping amphibian that can swim in water or live on land 2) a tool designed to sit in the bottom of a bowl or vase to hold flower stems 3) a decorative braid used to fasten a piece of clothing

frol-ic [frŏl′ĭk] *noun*, 1) merry making, *verb*, 2) to play happily

from [frŭm] *preposition*, 1) used to show a starting point 2) used to show a point of separation

3) used to show material source or cause, given by

front [frŭnt] *adjective*, 1) located ahead of the others, *noun*, 2) the face or the part of something that faces forward 3) the facade

fron-tier [frŭn-tîr'] *noun*, 1) the part of a country facing another country 2) a new field of learning, undiscovered territory, 3) a region at the edge of settled territory

frost [frôst] *noun*, the frozen water that covers the surface of everything outdoors when the temperature goes below freezing

froth [frôth] *noun*, 1) fine bubbles, foam, *verb*, 2) to cause to foam

frown [froun] *noun*, 1) facial expression in which the brow is furrowed and the lips turn down at the edges, *verb*, 2) to look unhappy, to show disapproval

froze [frōz] *past tense* of **freeze**

fro-zen [frō'zən] *adjective*, cooled to the point that liquid turns to solid, icy

fru-gal [frōo'gəl] *adjective*, careful with resources, thrifty

fruit [frōot] *noun*, 1) an edible product of a plant, bearing seeds 2) the results, the outcome

fruit-ful [frōot'fəl] *adjective*, successful, productive

fru-i-tion [frōo-ĭsh'ən] *noun*, fulfillment, realization

frus-trate [frŭs'trāt'] *verb*, to prevent from attaining a purpose

fry [frī] *verb*, to cook in hot oil

fudge [fŭj] *noun*, a soft candy usually made with sugar, milk

and flavoring 2) chocolate candy or sauce, *verb* 3) to deal with in an inadequate or evasive way

fuel [fyōo'əl] *noun*, something that gives off heat when it is burned

fu-gi-tive [fyōo'jĭ-tĭv] *noun*, one who flees pursuit by the law

ful-fill [fōol-fĭl'] *verb*, 1) to satisfy a contract 2) to complete

full [fōol] *adjective*, 1) leaving no empty space, holding as much as possible, *adverb*, 2) entirely

fumes [fyōomz] *noun*, *plural*, gases

fu-mi-gate [fyōo'mĭ-gāt'] *verb*, to apply smoke or vapor as a means of disinfecting or killing bugs

fun [fŭn] *noun*, *no plural*, amusement, enjoyment

func-tion [fŭngk'shən] *noun*, 1) the natural and proper action of anything 2) a service, purpose 3) the way in which something works 4) a large social gathering

fund [fŭnd] *noun*, 1) a sum of money collected for a special purpose, *verb*, 2) to provide money to support a cause

fun-da-men-tal [fŭn'də-měn'tl] *adjective*, 1) of first importance, essential 2) elementary, basic

fu-ner-al [fyōo'nər-əl] *noun*, a ceremony honoring the life of someone who died

fun-gus [fŭng'gəs] *noun*, *plural*, *fungi*, a member of the kingdom of living things, such as mushrooms, mold and yeast, that lack chlorophyll, leaves, and flowers

fun-nel [fŭn/əl] *noun*, an open cone wide at the top with a smaller end to pour liquids from one container to another

fun-ny [fŭn/ē] *adjective*, 1) amusing, entertaining, making someone laugh 2) strange, unusual, odd

fur [fûr] *noun*, a soft hair covering on some animals, the pelt

fu-ri-ous [fyŏŏr/ē-əs] *adjective*, very angry, violent

fur-nace [fûr/nĭs] *noun*, 1) an enclosed place in which heat is produced by the combustion of fuel 2) a large appliance containing a very hot fire

fur-nish [fûr/nĭsh] *verb*, to supply, to stock or provide, to give

fur-ni-ture [fûr/nĭ-chər] *noun*, *no plural*, the articles in a home that make it more comfortable, such as beds, chairs, tables, etc.

fu-ror [fyŏŏr/ôr/] *noun*, frenzy, a state of great public excitement

fur-ther [fûr/thər] *adverb*, at a greater distance, beyond

fur-tive [fûr tĭv] *adjective*, done in a sneaky way, hoping to be unnoticed

fu-ry [fyŏŏr/ē] *noun*, great anger

fur-ry [fûr/ē] *adjective*, covered with hair, like fur

fuse [fyŏŏz] *noun*, 1) a combustible cord that is lit to ignite an explosive device 2) a device to protect an electrical circuit from an electrical surge, *verb*, 3) to combine, to melt together

fu-sion [fyŏŏ/zhən] *noun*, 1) the process of joining two or more

things together as one 2) a nuclear reaction

fuss [fŭs] *noun*, 1) complaint, commotion, *verb*, 2) to behave in an excited, worried way

fu-tile [fyŏŏt/l, fyŏŏ/tīl/] *adjective*, ineffective, fruitless, pointless

fu-ture [fyŏŏ/chər] *adjective*, 1) coming after the present, *noun*, 2) a time that has not yet arrived

G

gadg-et [găj/ĭt] *noun*, a mechanical device or tool, a thingamajig

gag [găg] *noun*, 1) something put in the mouth to keep people from talking, *verb*, 2) to restrain someone from speaking 3) to choke or retch

gai-e-ty [gā/ĭ-tē] *noun*, merriment

gain [gān] *noun*, 1) an increase, *verb*, 2) to win, to acquire

gait [gāt] *noun*, a manner of walking, skipping, or running

gal-ax-y [găl/ək-sē] *noun*, a group of billions of stars held together by mutual gravitation

gale [gāl] *noun*, a strong wind

gall [gôl] *noun*, 1) bitterness, anger, 2) nerve, rudeness, *verb*, 3) to annoy, to anger, to infuriate

gal-lant [găl/ənt] *adjective*, brave, bold, daring, chivalrous

gal-le-on [găl/ē-ən] *noun*, a large sailing ship of earlier times

gal-ler-y [găl/ə-rē] *noun*, 1) a long, narrow, room-like corridor or passageway 2) a room for the exhibition of works of art

gal-ley [găl′ē] *noun*, 1) an oblong tray to hold type which has been set 2) the part of a ship where food is prepared

gal-lon [găl′ən] *noun*, a unit of liquid measure equal to 4 quarts or 128 ounces

gal-lop [găl′əp] *verb*, to trot

gal-lows [găl′ōz] *noun*, apparatus from which criminals are hung

gal-va-nize [găl′və-nīz′] *verb*, 1) to stimulate with shock, to stir up 2) to cover with zinc

gam-ble [găm′bəl] *verb*, to try to win money by betting

gam-bler [găm′blər] *noun*, a bettor

game [gām] *noun*, a form of entertainment played with rules that tests skill, knowledge, or athletic ability

gam-ut [găm′ət] *noun*, the entire range from beginning to end

gan-der [găn′dər] *noun*, male goose

gang [găng] *noun*, 1) an organized group of people who intimidate and harass 2) a group of workers

gan-grene [găng′grēn′] *noun*, the death of body tissue because of infection

gap [găp] *noun*, 1) a hole, an opening 2) the difference between two numbers

ga-rage [gə-räzh′] *noun*, 1) a place for housing automobiles 2) a place where motor vehicles are repaired

gar-bage [gär′bĭj] *noun*, another word for solid waste, especially household waste, trash

gar-den [gär′dn] *noun*, 1) a plot of land where flowers or vegetables grow, *verb*, 2) to look after the plants by watering and pruning

gar-den-er [gärd′nər] *noun*, one who makes and tends a garden

gar-gle [gär′gəl] *verb*, to rinse the throat with a liquid kept in motion by air forced through it from the lungs

gar-goyle [gär′goil′] *noun*, grotesque figures of people or animals carved as a roof spout

gar-ish [gâr′ĭsh, găr′-] *adjective*, in bad taste, gaudy, showy

gar-lic [gär′lĭk] *noun*, a plant like an onion with a strong taste and smell, used to season food

gar-ment [gär′mənt] *noun*, a piece of clothing

gar-ner [gär′nər] *verb*, to gather up, to accumulate, to amass

gar-net [gär′nĭt] *noun*, a semiprecious stone of a red color

gar-nish [gär′nĭsh] *noun*, 1) a decoration for food, *verb*, 2) to adorn 3) to take funds from someone a little at a time by order of the court to pay a debt

gar-ri-son [găr′ĭ-sən] *noun*, troops stationed in a fort or fortified town, a military post

gas [găs] *noun*, 1) a state of matter in which a substance like air is capable of infinitely expanding, has no fixed form or volume and takes the shape of its container 2) the short word for gasoline

gas-e-ous [găs′ē-əs, găsh′əs] *adjective*, in vapor form

gas-ket [găs′kĭt] *noun*, a piece of rubber sealing a joint between metal surfaces

gas-o-line [găs′ə-lēn′] *noun*, petroleum refined and used as motor fuel

gasp [găsp] *noun*, 1) a short intake of breath, *verb*, 2) to pant with a short, excited breath

gas-tron-o-my [gă-strŏn′ə-mē] *noun*, the art of preparing and serving good food

gate [gāt] *noun*, a a hinged door that closes an opening in a wall or fence

gath-er [găth′ər] noun, 1) a fold or pucker in a piece of cloth, *verb*, 2) to bring together or accumulate, to harvest 3) to infer from what someone has said

gauche [gōsh] *adjective*, clumsy, lacking social grace, awkward

gaud-y [gô′dē] *adjective*, showy in a tasteless way, ostentatious

gauge [gāj] *noun*, 1) an instrument used to measure, *verb*, 2) to measure or estimate

gaunt [gônt] *adjective*, 1) thin, lean 2) emaciated as from illness

gauze [gôz] *noun*, 1) a cotton bandage 2) a thin fabric

gaze [gāz] *verb*, to look at steadily, and intently, to stare

gaz-et-teer [gaezə′tir] *noun*, a geographical dictionary

gear [gîr] *noun*, 1) a toothed wheel that passes motion and power along 2) equipment, supplies

gel-a-tin [jĕl′ə-tn] *noun*, a tasteless, transparent substance, obtained from animal tissue such as skin, bones, or horns

gem [jĕm] *noun*, a precious or semiprecious stone used as an ornament

gen-der [jĕn′dər] *noun*, 1) a set of categories applied to nouns as masculine or feminine 2) the state of being male or female

ge-ne-al-o-gy [jē′nē-ŏl′ə-jē] *noun*, a record of family history, a family tree

gen-er-al [jĕn′ər-əl] *adjective*, 1) not particular or definite of or from the whole 2) usual or customary, common, lacking detail, *noun*, 3) the title of the commander in an army

Gen-er-al As-sem-bly *noun*, 1) the law-making body of some of the US states 2) the assembly of the representatives of the United Nations

gen-er-al-i-ty [jĕn′ə-răl′ĭ-tē] *noun*, a vague, nonspecific statement

gen-er-al-ize [jĕn′ər-ə-līz′] *verb*, to make a broad statement

gen-er-al-ly [jĕn′ər-ə-lē] *adverb*, usually, as a rule, normally

gen-er-ate [jĕn′ə-rāt′] *verb*, to make or create, to produce

gen-er-a-tion [jĕn′ə-rā′shən] *noun*, 1) the average time interval between the birth of parents and the birth of their offspring 2) all of the people born at about the same time 3) the act or process of producing something

gen-er-a-tor [jĕn′ə-rā′tər] *noun*, a machine by which mechanical energy is changed into electrical energy

gen-er-os-i-ty [jĕn′ə-rŏs′ĭ-tē] *noun*, the trait of giving freely to others, unselfishness

gen-er-ous [jĕn′ər-əs] *adjective*, liberal, open-handed, abundant

ge-ni-al [jēn′yəl] *adjective*, kind

gen-ius [jēn′yəs] *noun*, mental or creative superiority

gen-re [zhän′rə] *noun*, a category, art or music characterized by a particular style, class

gen-til-i-ty [jĕn-tĭl′ĭ-tē] *noun*, men or women who have high social standing and refined manners

gen-tle [jĕn′tl] *adjective*, 1) kind, courteous, amiable 2) soft and mild 3) not steep, moderate

gen-tle-man [jĕn′tl-mən] *noun*, a well-mannered man

gent-ly [jĕnt′lē] *adverb*, carefully

gen-u-flect [jĕn′yə-flĕkt′] *verb*, to bend one knee and bow in worship or reverence

gen-u-ine [jĕn′yōō-ĭn] *adjective*, real, not false, not pretended

gen-u-ine-ly [jĕn′yōō-ĭn-lē] *adverb*, truly, really

ge-og-ra-phy [jē-ŏg′rə-fē] *noun*, the science that describes the physical surface of the earth, and the effects of human activity on it

ge-ol-o-gist [jē-ŏl′ə-jĭst] *noun*, a person who studies the structure of the earth, its physical changes, and the causes producing these

ge-ol-o-gy [jē-ŏl′ə-jē] *noun*, the science that studies the history and structure of the earth, its physical changes, and the causes producing these changes

ge-om-e-try [jē-ŏm′ĭ-trē] *noun*, the branch of mathematics that studies the relations, properties, and measurement of solids, surfaces, lines, and angles

Geor-gia [jôr′jə] *noun*, a state in the southeastern United States. The capital city is Atlanta. The state flower of **Georgia** is the Cherokee rose and the motto is "Wisdom, justice, and moderation."

ge-ra-ni-um [jə-rā′nē-əm] *noun*, a flower with pink, red, or white blooms and velvety leaves

germ [jûrm] *noun*, a micro-organism that causes disease

ger-mi-nate [jûr′mə-nāt′] *verb*, to cause to grow, develop or sprout

ges-ta-tion [jĕ-stā′shən] *noun*, the period of time a new life is in the womb until it is born, pregnancy

ges-tic-u-late [jĕ-stĭk′yə-lāt′] *verb*, to make a motion, to gesture emphatically

ges-ture [jĕs′chər] *noun*, 1) any action of the hand or head that shows feeling, *verb*, 2) to make a movement, to signal

get [gĕt] *verb*, 1) to receive, have, or buy, to acquire 2) to become or attain

gey-ser [gī′zər] *noun*, a natural hot spring that throws out a spray of steam and water occasionally

ghet-to [gĕt- tō] *noun*, any section of a city in which many members of a minority group live, or to which they are restricted by discrimination

ghost [gōst] *noun,* the appearance of a dead person, an apparition believed to haunt the living

gi-ant [jī'ənt] *adjective,* 1) very large, huge, *noun,* 2) a legendary person or animal who is huge

gift [gĭft] *noun,* 1) a present 2) a person's inborn ability to do something well, talent

gi-gan-tic [jī-găn'tĭk] *adjective,* very big, large, huge, titanic

gig-gle [gĭg'əl] *verb,* to laugh in a silly, undignified way

gill [gĭl] *noun,* respiratory organs in fish that separate dissolved oxygen from water

gi-raffe [jə-răf'] *noun,* a tall African animal with a very long neck and very long legs and large brown spots on its coat

gird-er [gûr'dər] *noun,* an iron or steel beam to span an opening or carry the weight of a building

girl [gûrl] *noun,* a female child

gist [jĭst] *noun,* the main point

give [gĭv] *verb,* 1) to present, to donate, to hand-over 2) to impart something 3) to provide or assign 4) to yield to pressure

giv-en [gĭv'ən] *adjective,* 1) stated, typical 2) habitually inclined

gla-cier [glā'shər] *noun,* a body of ice, formed in a region of perpetual snow, moving slowly across land

glad [glăd] *adjective,* 1) feeling pleasure or joy 2) very willing

glad-i-o-lus [glăd'ē-ō'ləs] *noun, plural,* **gladioli,** a native bulb from Africa of the iris family, with sword-shaped leaves and stems of brightly colored flowers

glad-ly [glăd'lē] *adverb,* happily, willingly, joyfully

glam-or [glăm'ər] *noun,* beauty, attraction, alluring charm

glance [glăns] *noun,* 1) a quick or a brief look, *verb,* 2) to look quickly or briefly, to glimpse

gland [glănd] *noun,* a part of a living organism that secretes a vital substance

glare [glâr] *noun,* 1) a bright light reflecting shine or a gleam 2) an angry stare, *verb,* 3) to stare disapprovingly, to glower

glass [glăs] *noun, no plural,* 1) a hard clear substance that is easily shattered, used for windows 2) a drinking container *plural,* **glass-es** [glăs'ez] *noun,* 3) specially cut lenses made of plastic or glass held in a frame to adjust vision so that a person can see better, spectacles

glaze [glāz] *noun,* 1) a coating that creates a smooth, shiny surface, *verb,* 2) to cover with material or substance that creates a thin shiny surface

gleam [glēm] *noun,* 1) a brief flash of light, *verb,* 2) to shine brightly, to glisten, to glitter

glean [glēn] *verb,* to gather leftovers, to collect

glee [glē] *noun,* joy, merriment

glib [glĭb] *adjective,* flippant, speaking freely, persuasive

glide [glīd] *verb,* to move smoothly and effortlessly, to slide

glid-er [glī'dər] *noun,* an aircraft that flies without an engine

glimpse [glĭmps] *noun*, 1) a brief look at something, *verb*, 2) to get a quick look at something

glit-ter [glĭt′ər] *noun*, 1) something that sparkles or twinkles, *verb*, 2) to sparkle or twinkle as a reflection of light, to shimmer

gloat [glōt] *verb*, to brag, to boast

globe [glōb] *noun*, 1) the round replica of the Earth marked with countries, continents and oceans 2) anything round like a ball

gloom [glōōm] *noun*, 1) near or total darkness 2) a feeling of sadness, dejection, despondency

glo-ri-fy [glôr′ə-fī′] *verb*, to exalt, to acclaim, to worship

glo-ri-ous [glôr′ē-əs] *adjective*, exhibiting qualities that deserve or receive glory or praise

glory [glôr′ē] *noun*, praise given to someone who has accomplished something extraordinary, a state of honor

glos-sa-ry [glô′sə-rē] *noun*, a list of specialized words used in a given text with definitions

gloss-y [glô′sē] *adjective*, smooth and shiny, gleaming bright

glove [glŭv] *noun*, a covering for the hand with separate sections for the fingers and the thumb

glow [glō] *noun*, 1) gentle radiance, light and warmth, *verb*, 2) to radiate, steady, even light or heat

glu-cose [glōō′kōs′] *noun*, 1) sugar created in the body by processing starch 2) a syrup made by processing corn

glue [glōō] *noun*, 1) a substance used to make things stick together, *verb*, 2) to fasten with an adhesive, to attach closely

glut-ton [glŭt′n] *noun*, someone who is greedy for food

glyc-er-in [glĭs′ər-ĭn] *noun*, syrupy liquid used as a softening agent for skin, solvent, and in foods

gnarled [närld] *adjective*, twisted in a knotted form

gnat [năt] *noun*, a very small flying insect that bites

gnaw [nô] *verb*, to bite so as to wear away persistently

go [gō] *noun*, 1) a try, *verb*, 2) to move along 3) to depart

goad [gōd] *verb*, 1) to use some object to make an animal move 2) to provoke into an argument

goal [gōl] *noun*, 1) an intended or desired achievement 2) an objective 3) the cage, line or basket at the end of a playing field that the opposite team tries to penetrate 4) a score in some athletic contests

goat [gōt] *noun*, a small, horned ruminant animal, sometimes raised for its milk, meat, and fur

gob-lin [gŏb′lĭn] *noun*, in folklore, an ugly, grotesque creature that makes trouble

god [gŏd] *noun*, a being to whom people pray and that has control of the forces in the world

God [gŏd] *proper noun*, the supreme being, the creator of the universe

goddess

god-dess [gŏd′ĭs] *noun*, a female diety, a woman who is worshipped

goes [gōz] *present tense* of **go** used in the singular, with *he, she,* or *it*

gog-gles [gŏg′əlz] *noun*, large spectacles for protecting the eyes

gold [gōld] *adjective*, 1) having a bright deep yellow color, *noun*, 2) a precious metallic element

golf [gŏlf] *noun*, a game played by two or more people in which a small ball is hit into 9 or 18 holes arranged on a large piece of land called a course

gone [gôn] *past tense* of **go**,

gong [gông] *noun*, a percussion instrument consisting of a large piece of metal hung up and hit to make a loud noise

good [gŏŏd] *adjective*, 1) right, not wrong 2) appropriate, suitable, useful 3) well-behaved 4) nice, pleasant, *noun, no plural*, 5) what is virtuous and kind

good-ness [gŏŏd′nĭs] *noun*, generosity, kindness, virtue

goods [gŏŏdz] *noun*, merchandise, things made by people

good-will [gŏŏd wĭl] *noun*, the value of kindness in business and relationships

goo-gol [′gŏŏ, gōl] cardinal number equivalent to ten raised to the power of one hundred

goose [gŏŏs] *noun, plural,* **geese**, a large web-footed aquatic bird

gore [gôr] *noun*, clotted blood

gorge [gôrj]*verb*, to stuff yourself

gor-geous [gôr′jəs] *adjective*, strikingly beautiful

go-ril-la [gə-rĭl′ə] *noun*, a very large animal similar to a monkey, the largest ape

gos-pel [gŏs′pəl] *noun*, the first four books of the New Testament of the Bible, which tell the life and teachings of Jesus

gos-sa-mer [gŏs′ə-mər] *adjective*, sheer, like cobwebs

gos-sip [gŏs′əp] *noun*, 1) rumors about people that are often unkind or untrue 2) a person who divulges personal information about others, *verb*, 3) to talk about other people

got [gŏt] *past tense* of **get**

gouge [gouj] *noun*, 1) a chisel with a troughlike blade 2) a groove or hole, *verb*, 3) to cut, scoop, or tear out

gourd [gôrd] *noun*, a large fruit related to squash, with a shell often made into a container

gour-met [gŏŏr-mā′] *noun*, a person who understands and enjoys the finest food and drink

gov-ern [gŭv′ərn] *verb*, to lead or control by authority; to make and enforce laws

gov-ern-ment [gŭv′ərn-mənt] *noun*, the offices, agencies, and people who control a nation, state, or city by making laws and seeing that they are followed

gov-er-nor [gŭv′ər-nər] *noun*, 1) the elected or appointed leader who controls a colony, state, or country 2) an attachment to an engine for controlling its speed

gown [goun] *noun*, 1) a dress worn by a woman that reaches to the floor 2) a covering over the body so that a doctor can examine you without your clothes on or worn by a surgeon during operations

grab [grăb] *verb*, to seize, to clutch, to snatch suddenly

grace [grās] *noun*, 1) elegance, refinement, charm 2) kindness, 3) holiness, devotion, love 4) mercy, pardon, 5) a blessing, giving thanks, *verb*, 6) to beautify, to enhance, to adorn

grace-ful [grās'fəl] *adjective*, having beauty of movement

gra-cious [grā'shəs] *adjective*, kindly, pleasing, courteous

grade [grād] *noun*, 1) a rating of evaluation or class, *verb*, 2) to rate or rank in a group according to size, quantity, or aptitude

grad-u-al [grăj'ōō-əl] *adjective*, progressing slowly, step by step

grad-u-al-ly [grăj'ōō-ə-lē] *adverb*, progressively, in a piecemeal way

grad-u-ate [grăj'ōō-ĭt'] *noun*, 1) someone who has received a diploma to document that he or she has completed a required course of study 2) a cup or cylinder marked for measuring liquid, [grăj'ōō-āt'] *verb*, 3) to get one's degree by finishing school

grad-u-a-tion [grăj'ōō-ā'shən] *noun*, a ceremony to award diplomas to graduates

graf-fi-to [grə-fē'tō] *noun*, *plural*, **graffiti**, words or images drawn or painted in public places to deface a building or surface

graft [grăft] *noun*, 1) a bud or a shoot of a tree inserted into another tree to grow 2) a piece of transplanted living skin, tissue, or an organ 3) use of one's position to make dishonest gains

grain [grān] *noun*, 1) a very small piece of something, a particle 2) seed from a cereal plant such as wheat, corn, or rice 3) the design or pattern of wood

gram [grăm] *noun*, the metric unit of weight used to measure small objects equal to one thousandth of a kilogram

gram-mar [grăm'ər] *noun, no plural* 1) the study of how words make sentences 2) rules that govern the correct use of language

grand [grănd] *adjective*, very large and fine, impressive in size

grand-child [grănd'chīld'] *noun*, *plural* **grandchildren**, the child of someone's son or daughter

grand-daugh-ter [grăn'dô'tər] *noun*, the daughter of a person's son or daughter

gran-deur [grăn'jər] *noun*, magnificence, greatness

grand-fa-ther [grăn'fä'thər] *noun*, 1) the father of one's mother or father 2) the person who founded or originated something, *verb*, 3) to exempt from a new law or rule

grand-moth-er [grăn'mŭth'ər] *noun*, a mother of one's father or mother

grand-par-ent [grăn'pâr'ənt] *noun*, a parent of one's father or mother

grand-son [grănd′sŭn′] *noun*, the son of a person's daughter or son

gran-ite [grăn′ĭt] *noun*, a hard igneous rock, consisting of feldspar, mica, and quartz

grange [grānj] *noun*, 1) a farm with its dwelling house, barns, etc. 2) an association of farmers founded in 1867 for mutual welfare and advancement

grant [grănt] *noun*, 1) money donated by the government *verb*, 2) to allow, to confer, to give

gran-u-late [grăn′yə-lāt′] *verb*, to process a dense solid into grains

grape [grāp] *noun*, a small fruit that grows in clusters on a vine

grape-fruit [grāp′frōōt′] *noun*, a large, round, sour citrus fruit

graph [grăf] *noun*, 1) a picture indicating measurements to show change 2) a drawing used to show information

graph-ic [grăf′ĭk] *adjective*, 1) pertaining to the arts of painting and drawing 2) clearly and vividly described

graph-ite [grăf′ĭt′] *noun*, a soft, black crystallized form of carbon

grap-ple [grăp′əl] *noun*, 1) a tool with several hooks, usually attached to a rope and thrown *verb*, 2) to grab and struggle, to seize in a firm grip

grasp [grăsp] *noun*, 1) a clasp with the hand, *verb*, 2) to hold or seize 3) to understand or learn

grass [grăs] *noun*, 1) a fine ground cover with thin leaves 2) a lawn

grass-hop-per [grăs′hŏp′ər] *noun*, an insect with strong back legs for jumping and wings for flying

grate [grāt] *noun*, 1) a metal frame with wires or bars laid in the shape of a grid, *verb*, 2) to shred or shave into small pieces by rubbing on a jagged surface

grate-ful [grāt′fəl] *adjective*, thankful, appreciative

grat-i-fy [grăt′ə-fī′] *verb*, to please

grat-i-tude [grăt′ĭ-tōōd′] *noun*, no plural, a feeling of thankfulness

gra-tu-i-tous [grə-tōō′ĭ-təs] *adjective*, 1) given freely or without charge 2) unnecessary

gra-tu-i-ty [grə-tōō′ĭ-tē] *noun*, a tip

grave [grāv] *adjective*, 1) serious, *noun*, 2) a hole in the ground where a dead person is buried

grav-el [grăv′əl] *noun*, a mixture of pebbles and rock fragments

grav-i-ty [grăv′ĭ-tē] *noun*, 1) the force that draws everything to the earth's center 2) of a serious nature, a very solemn occasion

gra-vy [grā′vē] *noun*, a sauce made with flour and meat drippings

gray [grā] *noun*, a color between white and black

graze [grāz] *verb*, 1) to eat grass or vegetation 2) to rub against something and scrape against the surface

grease [grēs] *noun*, 1) a soft animal fat 2) any oily matter, *verb*, 3) to lubricate or make slippery with oils, to coat with grease

great [grāt] *adjective*. 1) large in size, quantity, duration 2) awesome, eminent, remarkable

great-er [grā'tər] *adjective*, more than something in comparison to it, bigger, larger, better

great-est [grā'tĭst] *adjective*, most, superior, best, largest

greed [grēd] *noun, no plural*, the feeling that you want more than you need, desire for wealth

green [grēn] *noun*, 1) a color made by combining yellow and blue 2) a plot of grass

green-house [grēn'hous'] *noun*, a house made of glass or clear plastic used to grow plants in a controlled environment all year

greet [grēt] *verb*, to welcome, to say hello

greet-ing [grē'tĭng] *noun*, a friendly expression when meeting someone

gre-gar-i-ous [grĭ-gâr'ē-əs] *adjective*, very social

grew [grōō] *past tense* of **grow**

grey [grā] see **gray**, *noun*, a mixture of black and white

grid [grĭd] *noun*, 1) grate, a metal plate with perforations 2) a network of horizontal and vertical lines used to locate a particular point on a map 3) a system of electrical wires for distributing power in an area

grief [grēf] *noun*, very deep sorrow, sadness caused by someone's death

griev-ance [grō'vəns] *noun*, cause of complaint, a protest expressing resentment

grieve [grēv] *verb*, to be very sorry· and upset about something lost or done, to be filled with sadness

grill [grĭl] *noun*, 1) a cooking unit with a metal rack or a flat heated surface used for broiling food 2) a system of bars forming a lattice, *verb*, 3) to broil food 4) to question intensely

grim [grĭm] *adjective*, dreadful,

grin [grĭn] *noun*, 1) a big smile, *verb*, 2) to smile broadly

grind [grīnd] *verb*, to crush something so hard that it becomes powder

grip [grĭp] *noun*, 1) a hold, a grasp, *verb*, 2) to hold or clench something tightly

gris-ly [grĭz'lē] *adjective*, ghastly, horrible, gruesome, shocking

grist [grĭst] *noun*, grain that is to be or has been ground

grit [grĭt] *noun*, 1) courage, fortitude, bravery 2) sand, gravel, coarse sandstone

grits [grĭts] *noun, plural*, coarsely ground hulled corn

griz-zly [grĭz'lē] *noun*, a big brown bear found in western North America

groan [grōn] *noun*, 1) a moan, a complaint, a cry of distress, *verb*, 2) to emit a low cry in disapproval or pain

groom [grōōm] *noun*, 1) a man about to be or just having been married 2) a person who takes care of horses, *verb*, 3) to make

groove

oneself presentable, neat and trim 4) to train someone for a career

groove [groͦv] *noun*, 1) a channel or furrow cut into something, *verb*, 2) to move to a rhythm

grope [grōp] *verb*, to feel your way blindly or uncertainly

gross [grōs] *adjective*, 1) bulky, coarse, unrefined 2) very fat, *noun*, 3) twelve dozen 4) income earned before deductions

gro-tesque [grō-tĕsk′] *adjective*, strange-looking in shape, bizarre

ground [ground] *noun, no plural,* 1) the surface of the earth, *verb*, 2) past tense of **grind**

ground-wa-ter [ground′wô′tər] *noun*, water beneath the earth's surface that supplies wells and springs

group [groͦp] *noun*, 1) people or things classed together because of similar qualities 2) people who share the same needs and interests

grove [grōv] *noun*, a group of trees without undergrowth

grov-el [grŏv′əl] *verb*, to lie prone, crawl, or creep, to beg

grow [grō] *verb*, 1) to become larger, to increase in size or maturity 2) to change and become 3) to sprout, to germinate, to develop 4) to cultivate plants

growl [groul] *noun*, a low angry or unfriendly noise coming from the throat made by a dog, other animal or person

grown [grōn] *adjective*, having reached maturity or full growth

growth [grōth] *noun* 1) development 2) tumor or other form of swelling

grub [grŭb] *noun*, 1) the larva of certain insects, a maggot, *verb*, 2) to dig, to uproot

grudge [grŭj] *noun*, hatred, lasting resentment

gruel-ing [groͦ′ə-lĭng] *adjective*, exhausting, very difficult

grue-some [groͦ′səm] *adjective*, ghastly, frightening, horrible

grum-ble [grŭm′bəl] *verb*, to complain in a low voice

grunt [grŭnt] *verb*, to make a guttural sound, to snort like a pig

guar-an-tee [găr′ən-tē′] *noun*, 1) a pledge, *verb* 2) to make a promise

guard [gärd] *noun*, 1) a person or thing that provides security or a defense, *verb*, 2) to watch over, to prevent an escape

guard-i-an [gär′dē-ən] *noun*, someone who takes care of another or their property

guer-ril-la [gə-rĭl′ə] *noun*, a member of an irregular military group that carries out surprise attacks and harasses the enemy

guess [gĕs] *noun*, 1) a conjecture, *verb*, 2) to imagine, to think or believe 3) to give an answer without being sure

guest [gĕst] *noun*, 1) a person invited to stay with someone else, a visitor 2) a customer

guid-ance [gīd′ns] *noun; no plural*, help, the act or result of guiding

guide [gīd] *noun*, 1) someone or something that shows the way to find something, *verb*, 2) to show the way or lead 3) to counsel

guile [gīl] *noun*, the ability to trick others, cunning, deceit

guilt [gĭlt] *noun, no plural*, the knowledge that you have done wrong, the acceptance of blame for a wrongdoing

guilt-y [gĭl'tē] *adjective*, 1) legally convicted of a crime 2) full of shame, feeling remorse

guise [gīz] *noun*, general, external appearance, manner, pretense

gui-tar [gĭ-tär'] *noun*, a musical instrument with six strings that you pluck or strum

gulf [gŭlf] *noun*, 1) part of a sea partially surrounded by land, larger and deeper than a bay 2) a large empty space or chasm

gul-li-ble [gŭl'ə-bəl] *adjective*, easily tricked or cheated

gul-ly [gŭl'ē] *noun*, a deep channel made by running water

gulp [gŭlp] *noun*, 1) a mouthful that is swallowed, *verb*, 2) to swallow quickly 3) to choke or gasp nervously

gum [gŭm] *noun*, 1) the tissue in your mouth above or below the teeth to protect the roots of each tooth 2) a sticky substance, like glue, used to hold things together, 3) a soft substance, flavored like candy that can be chewed but it does not dissolve in the mouth

gun [gŭn] *noun*, a weapon consisting of a metal tube used to shoot bullets under pressure

gust [gŭst] *noun*, a sudden rush of wind or strong blast of air

gut [gŭt] *noun*, 1) the stomach, the belly 2) the intestine

gut-ter [gŭt'ər] *noun*, 1) a drainage ditch along the side of the road 2) a trough along the eaves that drains water from a roof

gym-na-si-um [jĭm-nā'zē-əm] *noun*, a place where athletic exercises are performed or sports are played

gym-nas-tics [jĭm-năs'tĭks] *noun, plural,* exercises that develop and train the body and the muscles

gyp-sy [jĭp'sē] *noun*, a group of wandering people originally from Central Asia

H

hab-it [hăb'ĭt] *noun*, a pattern of behavior acquired through repetition

hab-i-tat [hăb'ĭ-tăt'] *noun*, the natural environment in which an animal or plant lives

hab-i-ta-tion [hăb'ĭ-tā'shən] *noun*, home, abode, dwelling

hab-it-u-al [hə-bĭch'ŏŏ-əl] *adjective*, customary, regular

hack-les [hăk'əlz] *plural, noun*, hairs on the back of the neck of a dog

hack-neyed [hăk'nēd] *adjective*, common, dull, overused

had [hăd] *past tense* of **have**

hag-gle [hăg'əl] *verb*, to argue about price, to bargain

hai-ku [hī'kōō] *noun*, a form of Japanese poetry consisting of 3 lines of 5, 7, and 5 syllables each

hail [hāl] *noun*, 1) small lumps of ice and snow that can fall during thunderstorms, *verb*, 2) to shout with enthusiasm, to call out in a greeting, to welcome

hair [hâr] *noun*, a strand of filament that grows out of the skin of mammals

hal-cy-on [hăl'sē-ən] *adjective*, calm, peaceful, happy

half [hăf] *adverb*, 1) partially, *noun*, 2) one of two equal parts of a whole

half-dol-lar [hăf'dŏl'ər] *noun*, a coin equal to fifty cents

half-way [hăf'wā'] *adjective*, midway between two points

hal-i-but [hăl'ə-bət] *noun*, the largest species of marine flatfish

hall [hôl] *noun*, 1) the corridor in a building 2) a large room for entertaining 3) a building at a college or university

hal-low [hăl'ō] *verb*, to bless or make holy or sacred

hal-lu-ci-na-tion [hə-loo'sə-nā'shən] *noun*, something that is seen or heard but is not actually happening, a delusion, a vision

halt [hôlt] *verb*, to cause to stop, to come to a stop

halt-er [hôl'tər] *noun*, 1) a rope or leather straps used to lead or secure a horse 2) a woman's top tied behind the neck and across the back 3) a hangman's noose

halve [hăv] *verb*, to divide in two

ham [hăm] *noun*, the meat from a pig's leg, preserved with salt or smoke 2) an actor who overacts

ham-burg-er [hăm'bûr'gər] *noun*, ground beef often served as a patty on a sandwich

ham-mer [hăm'ər] *noun*, 1) a tool used for driving nails, *verb*, 2) to hit or pound with a hammer or mallet, to strike

ham-mock [hăm'ək] *noun*, a bed of canvas cord hanging between two supports and easily swinging

ham-per [hăm'pər] *noun*, 1) a basket usually with a cover, *verb*, 2) to obstruct, to hinder

ham-ster [hăm'stər] *noun*, a rodent similar to a rat, with large cheek pouches often kept as a pet

hand [hănd] *noun*, 1) the part at the end of the arm used to hold something, *verb*, 2) to deliver or pass on

hand-i-cap [hăn'dē-kăp'] *noun*, an impediment, a physical defect

hand-ker-chief [hăng'kər-chĭf] *noun*, a cloth carried for wiping hands, the face, or the nose

han-dle [hăn'dl] *noun*, 1) the part of a tool or instrument held in the hand, *verb*, 2) to touch, feel, or examine with the hand 3) to control, manage or deal with

han-dle-bar [hăn'dl-bär'] *noun*, the part of a bicycle used to steer when you ride it

hand-shake [hănd'shāk'] *noun*, a greeting made by shaking hands

hand-some [hăn'səm] *adjective*, good-looking, attractive, manly

hand-writ-ing [hănd′rī′tĭng] *noun*, penmanship, writing done with a pen and usually in cursive

hand-y [hăn′dē] *adjective*, 1) easy to use, convenient 2) skillful with one's hands

hang [hăng] *verb*, 1) to fasten so that something can swing freely, to suspend 2) to suspend from a rope until dead 3) to linger, to wait 4) to be contingent

hang-ar [hăng′ər] *noun*, a building for storing aircraft

hang-er [hăng′ər] *noun*, a device on which something hangs

hap-haz-ard [hăp-hăz′ərd] *adjective*, random, by chance

hap-less [hăp′lĭs] *adjective*, unfortunate, unlucky

hap-pen [hăp′ən] *verb*, 1) to occur by chance, 2) to come to pass

hap-pi-ly [hăp′ə-lē] *adverb*, 1) in a joyous way 2) fortunately

hap-pi-ness [hăp′ē-nĭs] *noun*, conscious enjoyment of good fortune, contentment

hap-py [hăp′ē] *adjective*, content, delighted, or pleased

ha-rangue [hə-răng′] *noun*, a loud address to a multitude, a noisy, ranting speech

ha-rass [hăr′əs] *verb*, to trouble by repeated attacks, to annoy

har-bor [här′bər] *noun*, 1) a port where ships or boats can dock safely, *verb*, 2) to hide, to protect or conceal

hard [härd] *adjective*, 1) difficult to understand 2) firm, solid, impenetrable 3) difficult, fatiguing, challenging, *adverb*, 4) intensely, diligently

hard drive [hard-drĭv] *noun*, a nonremovable storage device in a computer

hard-en [här′dn] *verb*, 1) to make solid 2) to become unfeeling to become used to

hard-ly [härd′lē] *adverb*, barely, almost never, scarcely

hard-ship [härd′shĭp′] *noun*, something that causes suffering, extreme privation

hard-ware [härd′wâr′] *noun*, 1) the pieces of equipment that make up a computer 2) the items such as nuts, bolts, tools, and machinery needed to put something together or to do repairs

hare [hâr] *noun*, an animal similar to a rabbit, but larger, and with young born covered with fur

harm [härm] *noun*, 1) injury, damage, *verb*, 2) to hurt or injure

harm-ful [härm′fəl] *adjective*, able or likely to cause damage or injury

harm-less [härm′lĭs] *adjective*, causing no harm or damage

har-mon-i-ca [här-mŏn′ĭ-kə] *noun*, a hand-held rectangular musical instrument played by exhaling and inhaling through a row of metal reeds

har-mo-ni-ous [här-mō′nē-əs] *adjective*, symmetrical, congruous, in agreement

har-mo-nize [här′mə-nīz′] *verb*, 1) to sing in harmony 2) to go together, to coordinate

harmony

har-mo-ny [här′mə-nē] *noun*, 1) a pleasing combination of musical chords 2) agreement, accord

har-ness [här′nĭs] *noun*, the working gear of a horse used to attach it to a cart

harp [härp] *noun*, 1) a large stringed instrument, plucked with fingers, *verb*, 2) to nag

har-poon [här-pōōn′] *noun*, 1) a barbed spear, that is thrown, *verb*, 2) to spear with a harpoon

harsh [härsh] *adjective*, 1) hard to bear, severe, cruel 2) inharmonious, jarring, dissonant

har-vest [här′vĭst] *noun*, 1) the season's crop, the amount gathered, *verb*, 2) to gather or pick a crop, to reap, to gain

has [hăz] the part of the *verb* **have** used with *he, she,* and *it*

haste [hāst] *noun*, hurry

hast-i-ly [hāst′ĭ-lē] *adverb*, hurriedly, quickly, fast

hast-y [hā′stē] *adjective*, swift

hat [hăt] *noun*, a clothing accessory used to cover the head often with a crown and a brim

hatch [hăch] *noun*, 1) a small doorway or opening in a wall or a floor or the deck of a ship, *verb*, 2) to emerge from an egg when born

hatch-et [hăch′ĭt] *noun*, a small ax with a short handle

hate [hāt] *verb*, to dislike, to detest

hate-ful [hāt′fəl] *adjective*, arousing, deserving, or full of hate

ha-tred [hā′trĭd] *noun*, hostility

haugh-ty [hô′tē] *adjective*, snobbish, proud, arrogant

haul [hôl] *verb*, 1) to pull or draw with force, to drag 2) move from one place to another in a vehicle

haunt [hônt] *noun*, 1) a frequently visited place, *verb*, 2) to intrude upon continually, to annoy

have [hăv] *verb*, 1) to hold possession of or keep 2) a word used to indicate the *past tense* 3) need to, must

ha-ven [hā′vən] *noun*, a safe place

hav-oc [hăv′ək] *noun*, widespread destruction, confusion

Ha-waii [hə-wä′ē] *noun*, one of the 50 United States located in the Pacific ocean, the capital city is Honolulu. The state flower of **Hawaii** is the red hibiscus, and the motto is "The life of the land is preserved in righteousness."

hawk [hôk] *noun*, 1) a large bird of prey that kills birds and small animals for food, *verb*, 2) to peddle, to sell on the street

hay [hā] *noun*, grass cut and dried that is eaten by farm animals such as cows, goats, and horses

haz-ard [hăz′ərd] *noun*, a danger

haz-ard-ous [hăz′ər-dəs] *adjective*, dangerous, risky

haze [hāz] *noun, no plural*, widely dispersed dust, smoke, and moisture particles in the air that cloud the view

ha-zel [hā′zəl] *noun*, a color that combines gray, brown, and brownish-yellow

he [hē] *pronoun, plural,* **they**. the male person or animal, who is the subject of the sentence

head [hĕd] *noun,* 1) the bony structure at the top of humans and animals that contains the brain, face, ears, eyes, mouth, and nose 2) the seat of reason 3) the leader 4) the top of something, *verb,* 5) to move in the direction of something 6) to lead, to be the chief of

head-ache [hĕd′āk′] *noun,* 1) pain in the head 2) a dispute, a nuisance

head-ing [hĕd′ĭng] *noun,* the title or caption at the top of a piece of writing

head-line [hĕd′līn′] *noun,* 1) a line of type displayed conspicuously at the top of a page or column of a newspaper, etc.

head-quar-ters [hĕd′kwôr′tərz] *noun,* the center of operations from which orders are issued

heal [hēl] *verb,* to cure, to treat an illness, to remedy, to repair

health [hĕlth] *noun,* 1) the condition of the body or mind free from sickness or disease

health-y [hĕl′thē] *adjective,* 1) having a sound mind and body, strong, vibrant, robust 2) wholesome, nutritious

heap [hēp] *noun,* 1) a pile of things, *verb,* 2) to put into a large pile, to stack

hear [hîr] *verb,* to receive sound through the ears

heard [hûrd] *past tense* of **hear**

hear-ing [hîr′ĭng] *noun,* 1) the ability to hear 2) an opportunity to be heard

hearse [hûrs] *noun,* a car used to carry a coffin to a church or the cemetery

heart [härt] *noun,* 1) an organ in the chest that pumps the blood around the body 2) a feeling of tenderness, compasson, or sympathy, affection, emotions

hearth [härth] *noun,* the floor of a fireplace

heat [hēt] *noun, no plural,* 1) the feeling of warmth from a fire, furnace, or caused by friction, *verb,* 2) to raise the temperature to become hot, to make warmer

heat-er [hē′tər] *noun,* an appliance that warms

heath-en [hē′thən] *noun,* a person who does not acknowledge the god of Christianity, Judaism, or Islam

heave [hēv] *verb,* to lift or pull something of great weight

heav-en [hĕv′ən] *noun,* 1) the home of God, where the saved go to live after death 2) a state of supreme happiness or bliss

heav-en-ly [hĕv′ən-lē] *adjective,* divine, very nice or pleasant

heav-i-er [hĕv′ē-ər] *adjective,* having more weight

heav-y [hĕv′ē] *adjective,* 1) having a lot of weight 2) burdensome

heck-ler [hĕk′əl- ər] *noun,* a person who shouts and bothers a public speaker by asking impertinent questions

hectic

hec-tic [hĕk′tĭk] *adjective*, unsettled, confused, frenzied

hedge [hĕj] *noun*, a dense row of shrubs or bushes to make a wall or border

heed [hēd] *verb*, to notice, to pay careful attention to

heel [hēl] *noun*, 1) the back part of a foot, below the ankle 2) the back, bottom part of a shoe 3) an unpleasant, immoral person, *verb*, 4) to follow closely behind

heif-er [hĕf′ər] *noun*, a young cow

height [hīt] *noun*, distance upwards, how tall something is

hei-nous [hā′nəs] *adjective*, hateful, odious, wicked

heir [âr] *noun*, one who inherits, or has the right to inherit, property after the death of its owner

heir-ess [âr′ĭs] *noun*, a woman who inherits, especially one who inherits a fortune

heir-loom [âr′lo͞om′] *noun*, a valued family possession that is given to a new generation

held [hĕld] *past tense* of **hold**

hel-i-cop-ter [hĕl′ĭ-kŏp′tər] *noun*, a flying machine propelled by rotating blades without supporting wings

he-li-um [hē′lē-əm] *noun*, an inert, gaseous element the lightest of the noble gasses

hell [hĕl] *noun*, a place where Satan lives, and where the wicked are said to go when they die according to Christian belief

helm [hĕlm] *noun*,1) the wheel or other device by which a ship is steered 2) a position of control

hel-met [hĕl′mĭt] *noun*, a hard protective head covering

help [hĕlp] *noun*, 1) assistance, support, guidance, *verb*, 2) to do something for someone, to assist

help-ing [hĕl′pĭng] *adjective*, 1) willing to assist, *noun*, 2) a portion of food, a serving

help-less [hĕlp′lĭs] *adjective*, unable to help oneself

help-ful [hĕlp′fəl] *adjective*, ready to give help, useful

hem [hĕm] *noun*, 1) the edge of a garment that has been folded over and sewn to keep it from fraying and to hang on the body at the correct length, *verb*, 2) to sew the bottom of a garment 3) to confine, to enclose

hem-i-sphere [hĕm′ĭ-sfîr′] *noun*, one of the halves of the Earth

hem-or-rhage [hĕm′ər-ĭj] *noun*, excessive discharge of blood, heavy bleeding

hen [hĕn] *noun*, a female bird

her [hər, ər; hûr when stressed] *pronoun*, 1) belonging to a female 2) referring to a female previously mentioned

her-ald [hĕr′əld] *noun*, 1) a bearer of news, *verb*, 2) to announce publicly, to proclaim

herb [ûrb] *noun*, a plant used for medicine or adding flavor to food or aromatherapy

her-biv-o-rous [hûr-bĭv′ər-əs] *adjective*, plant eating

herd [hûrd] *noun*, 1) a group of animals eating, traveling, or living together, *verb*, 2) to control

or steer a group of animals 3) to
congregate

here [hîr] *adverb*, in this place

he-red-i-tar-y [hə-rĕd′ĭ-tĕr′ē]
adjective, transmitted genetically

he-red-i-ty [hə-rĕd′ĭ-tē] *noun*,
inherited characteristics or traits
passed from parents to offspring

her-e-sy [hĕr′ĭ-sē] *noun*, dissenting
religious view, nonconformity

her-e-tic [hĕr′ĭ-tĭk] *noun*, a person
who holds beliefs opposed to
church dogma

her-it-age [hĕr′ĭ-tĭj] *noun*, practices,
attributes or possessions handed
down from ancestors, traditions

her-mit [hûr′mĭt] *noun*, a recluse

he-ro [hîr′ō] *noun*, a person of
great strength or courage

her-o-ine [hĕr′ō-ĭn] *noun*, a woman
admired for her brave deeds

her-o-ism [hĕr′ō-ĭz′əm] *noun*,
courage, boldness, bravery

her-on [hĕr′ən] *noun*, a large
wading bird with long legs, a
long neck, and a pointed bill

her-ring [hĕr′ĭng] *noun*, a small
food fish abundant in the ocean

hers [hûrz] *pronoun*, indicating
something belonging to a woman
or girl

her-self [hûr-sĕlf′] *pronoun*, *plural*,
themselves, the reflexive form
of **she**, belonging to her

hes-i-tate [hĕz′ĭ-tāt′] *verb*, to act
slowly, as if in doubt, or
uncertain, to falter

hes-i-ta-tion [hĕz′ĭ-tā′shən] *noun*,
pausing because of doubt or
uncertainty

hew [hyōō] *verb*, to cut with an ax

hex-a-gon [hĕk′sə-gŏn′] *noun*, a
plane figure having six sides

hi-a-tus [hī-ā′təs] *noun*, a gap, an
interval in time, a pause

hi-ber-nate [hī′bər-nāt′] *verb*, to
sleep or be dormant in winter

hic-cup [hĭk′əp]*noun*, a spasm of
the diaphragm and other
breathing muscles causing small
gulping or gasping sounds

hid-den [hĭd′n] *adjective*,
concealed from sight

hide [hīd] *noun*, 1) the skin of an
animal, *verb*, 2) to put out of
sight or keep a secret

hid-e-ous [hĭd′ē-əs] *adjective*,
horribly ugly, shocking

hi-er-ar-chy [hī′ə-rär′kē] *noun*, a
pecking order, ranking

hi-er-o-glyph-ics [hī′ər-ə-glĭf′ĭks]
noun, *plural*, characters in the
picture writing of the ancient
Egyptians

high [hī] *adjective*, 1) tall, far above
the ground 2) expensive 3) shrill
in pitch 4) elated, happy

high-land [hī′lənd] *noun*, land that
is high up in the hills

high-ness [hī′nĭs] *noun*, a title of a
member of the royal family

high-way [hī′wā′] *noun*, a main
road connecting two towns

hi-jack [hī′jăk′] *verb*, to force the
driver of a vehicle to go
somewhere, to commandeer

hike [hīk] *noun*, 1) a walk, a trek,
verb, 2) to go on an extended
walk

hi-lar-i-ous [hĭ-lâr′ē-əs] *adjective*,
very funny, boisterously merry

hill [hĭl] *noun*, a natural elevation

him

him [hǐm] *pronoun*, a man or boy previously named

him-self [hǐm-sělf´] *pronoun*, referring to a man or boy as the object of a verb or preposition or reflexively used of the subject *plural*, **themselves**

hind [hīnd] *adjective*, 1) situated in the rear, back, posterior 2) a female deer

hind-er [hīn´dər] *verb*, to make it more difficult for someone to do something, to obstruct

hind-rance [hǐn´drəns] *noun*, an impediment, something that slows you down

Hin-du [hǐn´dōō] *noun*, 1) a native of India or Hindustan 2) an adherent of Hinduism, religion in the culture of India

hinge [hǐnj] *noun*, 1) a joint on which a door or gate turns or swings, *verb*, 2) to hang on or attach to something

hint [hǐnt] *noun*, 1) a suggestion, a clue 2) a slight trace

hip [hǐp] *noun*, the part of your body below the waist where your legs are connected to the rest of your body

hip-po-pot-a-mus[hǐp´ə-pŏt´ə məs] *noun*, a large mammal native to Africa that eats plants and lives mostly in water, with a thick skin and short legs

hire [hīr] *verb*, to pay someone to do work or perform services

his [hǐz] *pronoun*, belonging to a man or a boy, the possessive case of **he**

hiss [hǐs] *noun*, 1) a sound made by forcing air through the teeth,

verb, 2) to make a sound like a defensive cat to express displeasure

his-tol-o-gy [hǐ-stŏl´ə-jē] *noun*, the science that treats of the microscopic structure of animal and vegetable tissues

his-to-ri-an [hǐ-stôr´ē-ən] *noun*, an authority of events in history

his-tor-ic [hǐ-stôr´ǐk] *adjective*, something important in or belonging to the past

his-to-ry [hǐs´tə-rē] *noun*, the story and knowledge of the past

hit [hǐt] *noun*, 1) a blow 2) contact between the ball and the bat 3) a smash, a wow, a success, *verb*, 4) to bring something down hard onto something else, to smack, to strike with the hand

hitch [hǐch] *verb*, to tie something to something else, to attach to a vehicle for hauling

hive [hīv] *noun*, 1) a place in which bees live 2) any place busy with activity 3) a variety of allergic reactions marked by itching welts or a rash

hoard [hôrd] *noun*, 1) a hidden store of something, *verb*, 2) to collect and save, to accumulate, to set aside and hide away

hoarse [hôrs] *adjective*, sounding husky and rough or harsh

hoax [hōks] *noun*, a deceitful trick

hob-by [hŏb´ē] *noun*, an activity outside work that is done for relaxation and pleasure

hock-ey [hŏk´ē] *noun*, a game played on ice (ice hockey) or grass (field hockey) by two teams of several players who use curved sticks to hit a puck or a ball into a net or goal

hoe [hō] *noun*, 1) a tool with a flat blade used to lift and loosen the earth, *verb*, 2) to turn the soil over with a hoe

hog [hôg, hŏg] *noun*, a large pig, warthog, or boar

hoist [hoist] *verb*, to lift up, especially with a pulley

hold [hōld] *noun*, 1) the part of the ship that holds cargo, *verb*, 2) to grasp 3) to contain 4) to host an event 5) to restrain, to keep back 6) to possess 7) to embrace

hole [hōl] *noun*, an empty space in something, a gap, a cavity

hol-i-day [hŏl'ĭ-dā'] *noun*, 1) a day on which a particular event is celebrated 2) a period of time that involves relaxation not work

hol-low [hŏl'ō] *adjective*, 1) not solid, empty inside 2) without significance, *noun*, 3) a valley

hol-ly [hŏl'ē] *noun*, an evergreen tree or shrub, with red berries and prickly and glossy leaves

hol-o-caust [hŏl'ə-kôst'] *noun*, great or total destruction by fire

ho-ly [hō'lē] *adjective*, of God or the gods, divine, sacred

hom-age [hŏm'ĭj] *noun*, honor, public tribute to a person

home [hōm] *noun*, a place where someone lives, a residence

home-less [hōm'lĭs] *adjective*, 1) without a home *noun, plural* 2) (the homeless) people who do not have a home and who live on the streets of a city

home-ly [hōm'lē] *adjective*, unattractive, plain looking, ugly

ho-me-o-path [hō'mē -ə-păth'] *noun*, one who combats disease with remedies producing a similar complaint in a healthy person

home run [hōm rŭn'] *noun*, a run scored on a hit that enables the batter to touch all four bases

home-stead [hōm'stĕd'] *verb*, to claim land by settling on it according to US law

home-work [hōm'wûrk'] *noun*, material from school to be completed at home

hom-i-cide [hŏm'ĭ-sīd'] *noun*, the killing of a person by another

hom-i-ly [hŏm'ə-lē] *noun*, a sermon, a moral lesson

ho-mo-ge-neous [hō'mə-jē'nē-əs] *adjective*, 1) of the same kind or nature 2) consisting of similar parts throughout

ho-mog-e-nize [hə-mŏj'ə-nīz'] *verb*, to reduce particles in liquids such as milk or paint to the same size by mixing and distributing them evenly

hom-o-phone [hŏm'ə-fōn'] *noun*, a word that sounds the same as another, but is spelled differently, and has a different meaning, e.g. *see* and *sea*

hone [hōn] *verb*, to sharpen

hon-est [ŏn'ĭst] *adjective*, truthful, not deceitful, trustworthy

hon-est-ly [ŏn'ĭst-lē] *adverb*, truthfully, openly, candidly

hon-es-ty [ŏn′ĭ-stē] *noun*, the quality of telling the truth, integrity, truthfulness

hon-ey [hŭn′ē] *noun*, a syrup made by bees with nectar gathered from flowers

hon-ey-comb [hŭn′ē-kōm′] *noun*, six-sided wax cells made by bees to store honey or larvae

hon-ey-moon [hŭn′ē-mōōn′] *noun*, a holiday taken by a couple who have just been married

hon-or [ŏn′ər] *noun*, 1) high esteem 2) good reputation 3) an award for bravery or achievement, *verb*, 4) to hold in high respect 5) to keep an agreement

hon-or-a-ble [ŏn′ər-ə-bəl] *adjective*, respectable, honest

hood [hŏŏd] *noun*, 1) a covering for the head, often attached to another piece of clothing 2) an engine cover

hoof [hŏŏf] *noun, plural,* **hooves,** the horny, hard covering on the foot of a horse, cow, goat, etc.

hook [hŏŏk] *noun*, 1) a bent piece of metal or plastic used to catch or hang something, *verb*, 2) to clasp, to hang or fasten with a hook

hoop [hŏŏp] *noun*, a hard circular band, such as a hoola hoop or a basketball hoop

hop [hŏp] *noun*, 1) a short jump, *verb*, 2) to move on one foot 3) to jump with both feet together

hope [hōp] *noun*, 1) a feeling of confidence, expectation *verb*, 2) to look forward to something believing that it will happen

horde [hôrd] *noun*, crowd, a mob, a large multitude, a swarm

ho-ri-zon [hə-rī′zən] *noun*, the line where the earth appears to intersect the sky

hor-i-zon-tal [hôr′ĭ-zŏn′tl] *adjective*, 1) parallel to the horizon 2) flat, level

horn [hôrn] *noun*, 1) one of two hard growths growing out from the heads of some animals such as deer, elk, etc. 2) the device on a car or bicycle used to warn people 3) a musical wind instrument in the brass family with valves to regulate the flow of air

hor-net [hôr′nĭt] *noun*, a large wasp

hor-o-scope [hôr′ə-skōp′] *noun*, 1) a chart of the positions of the stars at the time of someone's birth 2) an astrological prediction

hor-ri-ble [hôr′ə-bəl] *adjective*, shocking, hideous, terrible

hor-rid [hôr′ĭd] *adjective*, vile, disgusting, vulgar, frightful

hor-ri-fy [hôr′ə-fī′] *verb*, to frighten, to terrify, to petrify

hor-ror [hôr′ər] *noun*, great fear and shock caused by something terrible, a feeling of terror

horse [hôrs] *noun*, a mammal with long legs that eats grass and can pull a cart or carry people

horse-back [hôrs′băk′] *adverb*, on the back of a horse

horse-pow-er [hôrs′pou′ər] *noun*, a unit of power, 33,000 foot pounds of work per minute or about 746 watts

horse-shoe [hôrs′chōō′] *noun*, a strip of iron conformed to the rim of a horse's hoof

hor-ti-cul-ture [hôr′tĭ-kŭl′chər] *noun*, the study of growing fruits, vegetables, flowers, or plants

hose [hōz] *noun*, 1) a rubber or plastic tube used to transfer liquid 2) socks, stockings, and tights, *verb*, 3) to water with a hose

hos-pi-tal [hŏs′pĭ-tl] *noun*, a facility where the sick or injured are treated and given medicine

hos-pi-tal-i-ty [hŏs′pĭ-tăl′ĭ-tē] *noun*, *no plural*, a warm welcome or reception to visitors

host [hōst] *noun*, 1) a man who entertains guests 2) an organism harboring a parasite 3) the communion wafer, representing the bread of the last supper, *verb*, 4) to receive guests, to entertain 5) to serve as a master of ceremonies

hos-tage [hŏs′tĭj] *noun*, a person or thing taken prisoner to ensure that others meet specified demands

host-ess [hō′stĭs] *noun*, a woman who entertains guests

hos-til-i-ty [hŏ-stĭl′ĭ-tē] *noun*, unfriendliness, antagonism, ill will, rancor

hot [hŏt] *adjective*, 1) having a very high temperature 2) having a very spicy taste

ho-tel [hō-tĕl′] *noun*, a building where travelers can pay for a place to sleep and other services

hound [hound] *noun*, a breed of dog used for hunting or racing

hour [our] *noun*, 1) sixty minutes, a measure of time, 1/24th of a day 2) a particular time of day

house [hous] *noun*, a building or part of one, where people live

House of Representatives *noun*, the lower house of the legislature of the United States

hov-el [hŭv′əl] *noun*, a shack

hov-er [hŭv′ər] *verb*, to stay in one place flying or floating in the air

hov-er-craft [hŭv′ər-krăft′] *noun*, a vehicle that travels over land or water by floating on air pushed out by its engines

how [hou] *adverb*, 1) used in questions about time, amount, or size 2) used to ask about health 3) used to show surprise or pleasure 4) used to show the way something is done

how-ev-er [hou-ev′ər] *adverb*, 1) nonetheless, despite, though 2) yet, after all 3) in whatever manner

howl [houl] *verb*, 1) to make a long wailing cry like a wolf, 2) to moan loudly in pain

hub [hŭb] *noun*, 1) the center of activity 2) the center part of a wheel or propeller

hud-dle [hŭd′l] *verb*, to cluster

hue [hyōō] *noun*, a shade of a color

hug [hŭg] *noun*, 1) a close embrace with arms around the body, *verb*, 2) to put arms around someone, to hold them closely, to embrace

huge [hyōōj] *adjective*, very large

hulk

hulk [hŭlk] *noun*, 1) a bulky body, a big clumsy person or thing 2) a ship that has been wrecked

hull [hŭl] *noun*, 1) the body of a ship 2) a shell or a husk of fruit, grain, or a seed

hum [hŭm] *noun*, 1) a low, buzzing sound like a bee, *verb*, 2) to sing a melody to yourself with lips closed

hu-man [hyo͞o′mən] *noun*, a person, *Homo sapiens*

hu-mane [hyo͞o-mān′] *adjective*, kind, compassionate, merciful

hu-man-i-ty [hyo͞o-măn′ĭ-tē] *noun*, mankind, people, the human race

hum-ble [hŭm′bəl] *adjective*, 1) modest, not proud, 2) plain 3) respectful, courteous, *verb*, 4) to bring down to defeat, to humiliate

hu-mid-i-ty [hyo͞o-mĭd′ĭ-tē] *noun*, moisture in the air, dampness

hu-mil-i-ate [hyo͞o-mĭl′ē-āt′] *verb*, to treat in a way that takes away a person's pride or self-respect

hu-mil-i-a-tion [hyo͞o-mĭl′ē-ā′shən] *noun*, embarrassment, shame

hu-mil-i-ty [hyo͞o-mĭl′ĭ-tē] *noun*, the state of being modest, meek

hu-mor [hyo͞o′mər] *noun*, *no plural*, 1) the ability to make others laugh, *verb*, 2) to indulge

hu-mor-ous [hyo͞o′mər-əs] *adjective*, full of or characterized by humor, funny, comical

hump [hŭmp] *noun*, a round lump or protuberance

hu-mus [hyo͞o′məs] *noun*, 1) organic material consisting of decayed vegetable matter 2) a thick dip made from mashed chickpeas and flavorings

hunch [hŭnch] *noun*, 1) a premonition or suspicion, *verb*, 2) to sit or stand with the back bent or arched

hun-dred [hŭn′drĭd] *noun*, the number 100, ten times ten

hun-dredth [hŭn′drĭdth] *noun*, 1) the ordinal number after 99th 2) the number two digits to the right of the decimal point

hung [hŭng] *past tense* of **hang**

hun-ger [hŭng′gər] *noun*, 1) the desire for food, craving, *verb*, 2) to feel a strong desire for something, 3) to yearn

hun-gry [hŭng′grē] *adjective*, desiring food

hunt [hŭnt] *verb*, 1) seek out to capture for food or sport, 2) to search for something

hur-dle [hûr′dl] *noun*, 1) a barrier that can be jumped over, 2) an obstacle to overcome, *verb*, 3) to jump over, to vault

hurl [hûrl] *verb*, to throw hard

hur-ri-cane [hûr′ĭ-kān′] *noun*, a severe tropical storm with high winds

hur-ry [hûr′ē] *noun*, 1) haste, *verb*, 2) to move quickly, to rush

hurt [hûrt] *verb*, 1) to injure, to inflict pain or damage 2) to offend 3) to ache, to throb

hur-tle [hûr′tl] *verb*, to move at great speed, to rush headlong

hus-band [hŭz′bənd] *noun*, the male spouse in a marriage

hus-band-ry [hŭz′bən-drē] *noun*, 1) cultivation of plants or animals in a scientific way, 2) home management, careful attention to spending money

hush [hŭsh] *noun*, 1) calm, silence, *verb*, 2) to muffle, to quiet down

hus-tle [hŭs′əl] *verb*, 1) to hurry 2) to trick someone in business

hy-brid [hī′brĭd] *noun*, a new breed created by breeding two different varieties or species

hy-drant [hī′drənt] *noun*, a pipe located at a curb with a valve for fire engines to connect a hose to a source of water to fight fire

hy-drau-lic [hī-drô′lĭk] *adjective*, operated or moved by means of fluid under pressure

hy-dro-gen [hī′drə-jən] *noun*, an element that is normally a tasteless, odorless, and inflammable gas

hy-dro-pho-bi-a [hī′drə-fō′bē-ə] *noun*, 1) fear of water 2) a symptom of rabies

hy-dro-plane [hī′drə-plān′] *noun*, 1) a boat that glides on the surface of water, *verb*, 2) to lose control and slide on a wet road because a vehicle has lost traction

hy-e-na [hī-ē′nə] *noun*, a carnivorous wild doglike mammal that lives in Africa and Asia

hy-giene [hī′jēn′] *noun*, practices that keep people clean and healthy, cleanliness

hymn [hĭm] *noun*, a religious song

hy-per-bo-le [hī-pûr′bə-lē] *noun*, a figure of speech using extravagant exaggeration, e.g., *I've told you at least a million times.*

hy-phen [hī′fən] *noun*, the mark -, used to separate syllables, as at the end of a line e.g. *composition,* or to join the parts of compound words e.g. *self-confidence, self-reliant*

hyp-no-tize [hĭp′nə-tīz′] *verb*, to put in a trance in which the subject is susceptible to suggestion, to mesmerize

hy-po-chon-dri-ac [hī′pə-kŏn′drē-ăk′] *noun*, a person always worrying about the state of their health, especially one with imaginary illnesses

hy-poc-ri-sy [hĭ-pŏk′rĭ-sē] *noun*, the act or practice of feigning to be what one is not, especially the false assumption of virtue or religion

hyp-o-crite [hĭp′ə-krĭt′] *noun*, someone who says one thing especially in regard to values and morals, and does another

hy-poth-e-sis [hī-pŏth′ĭ-sĭs] *noun*, a theory that has not been proven

hy-po-thet-i-cal [hī′pə-thĕt′ĭ-kəl] *adjective*, an assumption based on theory or conjecture

hys-ter-i-cal [hĭ-stĕr′ĭ-kəl] *adjective*, showing excessive or uncontrollable emotion

I

I [ī] *pronoun*, *plural*, **we**, first person singular, the individual speaking

ice [īs] *noun*, 1) frozen water, *verb*, 2) to put frosting on a cake

ice-berg [īs′bûrg′] *noun*, a large mass of ice floating in the sea

ice cream [īs′krēm′] *noun*, cream, sugar, milk, flavoring, and eggs mixed together to make a frozen dessert

i-ch-thy-ol-o-gy [ĭk′thē-ŏl′ə-jē] *noun*, the study of fish

i-ci-cle [ī′sĭ-kəl] *noun*, a piece of ice in the form of a spike made by water dripping and freezing

i-con [ī′kŏn′] *noun*, 1) a religious image painted on wood, found especially in the Eastern Christian Church 2) a graphic symbol used in computing

I'd [īd] the *contraction* of the words **I** and **would**

Ida-ho [ī′də-hō′] *noun*, one of the United States, located in the northwest, the capital city is Boise. The state flower of **Idaho** is the syringa, and the motto is "May it endure forever."

i-de-a [ī-dē′ə] *noun*, 1) a concept, a thought, an impression 2) a belief, an opinion 3) an intention

i-de-al [ī-dē′əl] *adjective*, 1) perfect, ultimate, *noun*, 2) an image of something in its perfect form, a model

i-den-ti-cal [ī-dĕn′tĭ-kəl] *adjective*, being the very same in every way

i-den-ti-fi-ca-tion [ī-dĕn′tə-fī-kā′shən] *noun*, the means to verify who someone is

i-den-ti-fy [ī-dĕn′tə-fī′] *verb*, 1) to classify or name 2) to equate

i-den-ti-ty [ī-dĕn′tĭ-tē] *noun*, who someone is, individuality

i-de-ol-o-gy [ī′dē-ŏl′ə-jē] *noun*, a system of beliefs, political ideas

id-i-om [ĭd′ē-əm] *noun*, a group of words that when used together have a special meaning, different from what they mean individually, e.g., *raining cats and dogs*

id-i-o-syn-cra-sy [ĭd′ē-ō-sĭng′krə-sē] *noun*, a peculiar habit, a quirk

i-dle [īd′l] *adjective*, not busy, unoccupied, inactive, lazy

i-dol [īd′l] *noun*, 1) an image that is worshipped, 2) a person that is adored

i.e. an abbreviation, that is…

if [ĭf] *conjunction*, 1) on condition that 2) whether

ig-loo [ĭg′loō] *noun*, an Eskimo home made of blocks of ice and snow

ig-ne-ous [ĭg′nē-əs] *adjective*, produced by fire, volcanic

ig-nite [ĭg-nīt′] *verb*, 1) to set on fire, to begin to burn 2) to inspire, to inflame

ig-no-ble [ĭg-nō′bəl] *adjective*, unworthy, of low character

ig-no-rance [ĭg′nər-əns] *noun*, no *plural*, lack of knowledge

ig-no-rant [ĭg′nər-ənt] *adjective*, uneducated, lacking knowledge

ig-nore [ĭg-nôr′] *verb*, to pretend something is not there

ill [ĭl] *adjective*, feeling unhealthy

I'll [īl] the *contraction* of the words **I** and **will**

il-le-gal [ĭ-lē′gəl] *adjective*, against the law, prohibited, criminal

il-leg-i-ble [ĭ-lĕj′ə-bəl] *adjective*, so poorly written as to be unreadable

il-le-git-i-mate [ĭl′ĭ-jĭt′ə-mĭt] *adjective*, 1) unlawful, illegal, 2) born of unmarried parents

il-lic-it [ĭ-lĭs′ĭt] *adjective*, not according to law, not permitted or allowed, forbidden

il-lim-it-a-ble [ĭ-lĭm′ĭ-tə-bəl] *adjective*, infinite, vast, limitless

Il-li-nois [ĭl′ə-noi′] *noun*, one of the United States, located in the midwest, the capital is Springfield. The state flower of **Illinois** is the meadow violet, and the motto is "State sovereignty, national union."

il-lit-er-ate [ĭ-lĭt′ər-ĭt] *adjective*, unable to read and write

il-log-i-cal [ĭ-lŏj′ĭ-kəl] *adjective*, not observing the rules of correct reasoning, unreasonable

il-lu-mi-nate [ĭ-lōō′mə-nāt′] *verb*, 1) to fill with light 2) to make understandable, to clarify

il-lu-sion [ĭ-lōō′zhən] *noun*, a false idea, a fallacy, a delusion

il-lu-sive [ĭ-lōō′sĭv] *adjective*, deceptive, false, evasive

il-lus-trate [ĭl′ə-strāt′] *verb*, 1) to explain by examples or verbal images 2) to provide with pictures or designs, to show

il-lus-tra-tion [ĭl′ə-strā′shən] *noun*, 1) a picture or drawing that makes something written clearer 2) an explanation

il-lus-tri-ous [ĭ-lŭs′trē-əs] *adjective*, distinguished, well known, acclaimed, celebrated

I'm [īm] the *contraction* of the words **I** and **am**

im-age [ĭm′ĭj] *noun*, 1) a picture in the mind or in a mirror or on television, etc. 2) a figure made of stone, wood, etc.

im-age-ry [ĭm′-măj′ĕr′ē] *noun*, 1) mental images 2) descriptions and figures of speech

im-ag-i-nar-y [ĭ-măj′ə-nĕr′ē] *adjective*, unreal, fanciful, existing only in the mind

im-ag-i-na-tion [ĭ-măj′ə-nā′shən] *noun*, 1) fantasy, dreams, 2) creativity

im-ag-ine [ĭ-măj′ĭn] *verb*, 1) to develop an idea in your mind or mental picture 2) to suppose

im-bue [ĭm-byōō′] *verb*, 1) to saturate with moisture or color 2) to teach, to inspire

im-i-tate [ĭm′ĭ-tāt′] *verb*, to do something the same way as someone else, to emulate

im-i-ta-tion [ĭm′ĭ-tā′shən] *adjective*, 1) artificial, synthetic, counterfeit, *noun*, 2) a copy of something, a fake, a replica

im-mac-u-late [ĭ-măk′yə-lĭt] *adjective*, without stain or blemish, spotlessly clean

im-ma-te-ri-al [ĭm′ə-tîr′ē-əl] *adjective*, not applicable, irrelevant, not important

im-ma-ture [ĭm′ə-tyŏŏr′] *adjective*, not grown up, childish

immeasurable

im-meas-ur-a-ble
[ĭ-mĕzh′ər-ə-bəl] *adjective*, vast, limitless, endless, infinite

im-me-di-ate [ĭ-mē′dē-ĭt] *adjective*, right away

im-me-di-ate-ly [ĭ-mē′dē-ĭt-lē] *adverb*, at once, without interval of time or delay, now

im-mense [ĭ-mĕns′] *adjective*, huge, very large, enormous

im-men-si-ty [ĭ-mĕn′sĭ-tē] *noun*, enormity, endlessness

im-mi-grant [ĭm′ĭ-grənt] *noun*, a settler from another country

im-mi-gra-tion [ĭm′ĭ-grā′shən] *noun*, the process of traveling to another country to settle there

im-mi-grate [ĭm′ĭ-grāt′] *verb*, to go to a country of which one is not a native to live as a resident

im-mi-nent [ĭm′ə-nənt] *adjective*, impending, near at hand, likely to occur at any moment

im-mo-bil-i-ty [ĭ-mō-bĭl′-ĭ-tē] *noun*, the state of being unable to move, motionlessness

im-mortal [ĭ-môr′tl] *adjective*, undying, everlasting, perpetual

im-mor-tal-i-ty [ĭm′ôr-tăl′ĭ-tē] *noun*, eternal life, unending fame

im-mune [ĭ-myoōn′] *adjective*, 1) not affected by disease 2) exempt from an influence

im-mu-ni-ty [ĭ-myoō′nĭ-tē] *noun*, 1) the ability to resist a disease or infection 2) freedom from legal prosecution

im-mu-nize [ĭm′yə-nīz′] *verb*, to protect the body from diseases by injecting an inactive form of the virus or bacteria

im-mu-ni-za-tion [ĭm′yə-nĭ-zā′shən] *noun*, an injection that protects the body from a virus or disease

im-pact [ĭm′păkt′] *noun*, 1) personal contact, 2) a forceful impression, a strong effect

im-pair [ĭm-pâr′] *verb*, to weaken, to diminish in value, make worse

im-pale [ĭm-pāl′] *verb*, to pierce with something pointed

im-part [ĭm-pärt′] *verb*, to tell, to reveal, to make known, to give

im-par-tial [ĭm-pär′shəl] *adjective*, fair, just, not favoring one more than another, not biased

im-pas-sa-ble [ĭm-păs′ə-bəl] *adjective*, unable to be passed or traversed

im-passe [ĭm′păs′] *noun*, 1) a road with no outlet, a blind alley or dead end, 2) a situation in which no progress can be made or resolution reached

im-pa-tience [ĭm-pā′shəns] *noun*, *no plural*, anticipation, anxious expectancy, irritation with delay

im-pa-tiens [ĭm-pā′shəns] *noun*, a flower with white or red flowers that bloom in summer

im-pa-tient [ĭm-pā′shənt] *adjective*, not wanting to wait

im-peach [ĭm-pēch′] *verb*, to charge with a crime while in office, to discredit

im-pec-ca-ble [ĭm-pĕk′ə-bəl] *adjective*, faultless, perfect, without sin

im-pede [ĭm-pēd′] *verb*, to hinder or obstruct, to slow action

im-ped-i-ment [ĭm-pĕd'ə-mənt]
noun, hindrance, obstacle

im-pel [ĭm-pĕl'] *verb*, to push, to
motivate, to drive forward

im-pend-ing [ĭm-pĕn'dĭng]
adjective, about to happen

im-per-a-tive [ĭm-pĕr'ə-tĭv]
adjective, 1) expressive of
command 2) binding, obligatory

im-per-fect [ĭm-pûr'fĭkt] *adjective*,
1) flawed, defective, faulty, *noun*,
2) a verb tense used for action
that is continuing

im-per-fec-tion [ĭm'pər-fĕk'shən]
noun, 1) a flaw, a defect 2) a
failing, a shortcoming, a fault

im-pe-ri-al [ĭm-pîr'ē-əl] *adjective*,
relating to an empire and its ruler

im-per-il [ĭm-pĕr'əl] *verb*, to put in
danger or peril

im-pe-ri-ous [ĭm-pîr'ē-əs]
adjective, bossy, domineering

im-per-me-a-ble [ĭm-pûr'mē-ə-bəl]
adjective, not allowing other
substances, especially liquid, to
pass through

im-per-son-al [ĭm-pûr'sə-nəl]
adjective, detached, withdrawn

im-per-son-ate [ĭm-pûr'sə-nāt']
verb, to pretend to be someone
by assuming their identity, often
with the intent to defraud

im-per-ti-nent [ĭm-pûr'tn-ənt]
adjective, 1) rude, 2) irrelevant

im-per-vi-ous [ĭm-pûr'vē-əs]
adjective, 1) impenetrable, not
admitting entrance or passage
through 2) unaffected, unharmed

im-pet-u-ous [ĭm-pĕch'ōō-əs]
adjective, impulsive, rash

im-pe-tus [ĭm'pĭ-təs] *noun*, a
driving force, motive, incentive

im-plau-si-ble [ĭm-plô'zə-bəl]
adjective, unlikely, unbelievable

im-ple-ment [ĭm'plə-mənt] *noun*,
1) a tool, a device, *verb*, 2) to
complete, to accomplish, to
make good on an idea

im-pli-ca-tion [ĭm'plĭ-kā'shən]
noun, something that is implied,
hinted at or suggested

im-plic-it [ĭm-plĭs'ĭt] *adjective*,
1) implied although unsaid,
understood, 2) without doubt

im-plore [ĭm'plôr] *verb*, to plead
with much feeling

im-ply [ĭm-plī'] *verb*, 1) to suggest
a meaning not spoken, to hint
2) to include or suggest as a
necessary condition

im-po-lite [ĭm'pə-līt'] *adjective*,
rude, discourteous, disrespectful

im-port [ĭm-pôrt'] *noun*,
1) merchandise brought into
another country 2) the
significance, the meaning, *verb*,
3) to bring goods into another
country 4) to signify

im-por-tance [ĭm-pôr'tns] *noun*,
no plural, great significance or
consequence, prominence

im-por-tant [ĭm-pôr'tnt] *adjective*,
significant, having a great value

im-por-tu-nate [ĭm-pôr'chə-nĭt]
adjective, urging, demanding

im-pose [ĭm-pōz'] *verb*, 1) to take
unfair advantage of, to compel,
to force on others 2) to require
something, such as a tax, be
paid

impossible

im-pos-si-ble [ĭm-pŏs′ə-bəl]
adjective, unrealizable, hopeless

im-pos-tor [ĭm-pŏs′tər] *noun*, one
who practices deception by
assuming a false identity

im-po-tent [ĭm′pə-tənt] *adjective*,
weak, ineffective, powerless

im-prac-ti-cal [ĭm-prăk′tĭ-kəl]
adjective, not easily done

im-pre-cate [ĭm′prĭ-kāt′] *verb*, to
hope evil will happen, to curse

im-preg-na-ble [ĭm-prĕg′nə-bəl]
adjective, invulnerable, able to
withstand attack, unbeatable

im-press [ĭm-prĕs′] *verb*, 1) to
affect someone's feelings or
opinion in a positive way 2) to
leave an imprint, to stamp

im-pres-sion [ĭm-prĕsh′ən] *noun*,
1) a sensation, an effect 2) an
imitation of a person 3) a mark
made on a surface of something

im-pres-sive [ĭm-prĕs′ĭv]
adjective, evoking admiration or
respect because of size, ability,
etc.

im-print [ĭm-prĭnt′] *noun*, a deep
impression left by pressure

im-pris-on [ĭm-prĭz′ən] *verb*, to
hold someone in jail

im-prob-a-ble [ĭm-prŏb′ə-bəl]
adjective, unlikely to happen

im-prop-er [ĭm-prŏp′ər] *adjective*,
rude or inappropriate, contrary to
social convention

im-pro-pri-e-ty [ĭm′prə-prī′ĭ-tē]
noun, an inappropriate or
indecent expression or act

im-prove [ĭm-prōōv′] *verb*, to make
or become better, to uplift, to
refine

im-prove-ment [ĭm-prōōv′mənt]
noun, an act, state, or result of
improving or bettering

im-pro-vise [ĭm′prə-vīz′] *verb*,
1) to make do with whatever is at
hand 2) to perform without
preparation at a moment's notice

im-pru-dent [ĭm-prōōd′nt]
adjective, not wise, indiscreet

im-pu-dent [ĭm′pyə-dənt]
adjective, bold, disrespectful

im-pulse [ĭm′pŭls′] *noun*, 1) a
sudden desire to do something
2) a driving force 3) an electrical
pulse or current

im-pul-sive [ĭm-pŭl′sĭv] *adjective*,
spontaneous, without
forethought

im-pu-ni-ty [ĭm-pyōō′nĭ-tē] *noun*,
freedom from punishment

im-pu-ri-ty [ĭm-pyōōr′ĭ-tē] *noun*,
pollution, contamination

im-pute [ĭm-pyōōt′] *verb*, to credit,
to attribute, to ascribe

in [ĭn] *adjective*, 1) being inside,
preposition, 2) showing where
3) at or inside of something
4) during, before the end
5) wearing 6) at hand or on hand
7) near

in-a-bil-i-ty [ĭn′ə-bĭl′ĭ-tē] *noun,* lack
of ability, power or capacity

in-ac-ces-si-ble [ĭn′ăk-sĕs′ə-bəl]
adjective, 1) out of reach,
unattainable 2) hard to contact

in-ac-cu-ra-cy [ĭn-ăk′yər-ə-sē]
noun, an error, being incorrect

in-ad-e-quate [ĭn-ăd′ĭ-kwĭt]
adjective, not enough

in-ad-ver-tent-ly [ĭn′əd-vûr′tnt-lē]
adverb, accidentally

in-al-ien-a-ble [ĭn-āl′yə-nə-bəl]
adjective, not to be taken away

in-an-i-mate [ĭn-ăn′ə-mĭt]
adjective, lifeless, dull

in-ar-tic-u-late [ĭn′är-tĭk′yə-lĭt]
adjective, lacking the ability to
express oneself in speech

in-au-gu-rate [ĭn-ô′gyə-rāt′] *verb*,
1) to begin 2) to install into office
in a formal manner

In-can-des-cent [ĭn′kən-děs′ənt]
adjective, glowing or luminous
with intense heat or brightness

in-can-ta-tion [ĭn′kăn-tā′shən]
noun, singing or chanting of
words or sounds believed to
have magical effect

In-ca-pa-ble [ĭn-kā′pə-bəl]
adjective, unable, lacking skill,
ability, or temperament

in-ca-pac-i-tate [ĭn′kə-păs′ĭ-tāt′]
verb, to disable

In-car-cer-a-tion [ĭn-kär′sə-rā′
shən] *noun*, imprisonment

In-car-nate [ĭn-kär′nĭt] *adjective*, in
the flesh, in human form

in-car-na-tion [ĭn′kär-nā′shən]
noun, 1) the act of assuming a
human body 2) the embodiment
of a god or spirit 3) one life
among many for those who
believe in reincarnation

in-cen-di-ar-y [ĭn-sĕn′dē-ĕr′ē]
adjective, 1) causing something
to burn, 2) tending to inflame,
noun, 3) a bomb designed to
start fires 4) an arsonist

in-cense [ĭn-sĕns′] *noun*, 1) a
substance that releases a
pleasant scent when burned,
verb, 2) to anger

in-cen-tive [ĭn-sĕn′tĭv] *noun*,
encouragement, stimulus

in-ces-sant [ĭn-sĕs′ənt] *adjective*,
continuing without interruption

inch [ĭnch] *noun*, a measure of
length, 1/12 of a foot

in-ci-dent [ĭn′sĭ-dənt] *noun*, 1) a
happening, a casual occurrence
2) a disturbance, a violent event

in-ci-den-tal-ly [ĭn′sĭ-dĕn′tl-ē]
adverb, casually, by chance

in-cin-er-a-tor [ĭn-sĭn′ə-rā′tər]
noun, a container or furnace
where garbage is burned

in-ci-sion [ĭn-sĭzh′ən] *noun*, a cut
or slit into body tissue, a gash

in-cite [ĭn-sīt′] *verb*, to stir up, to
stimulate to action, to provoke

in-clem-ent [ĭn-klĕm′ənt] *adjective*,
1) stormy 2) lacking mercy,
unkind

in-cli-na-tion [ĭn′klə-nā′shən]
noun, 1) a preference, a
tendency 2) a slant, an angle

in-cline [ĭn-klīn′] *verb*, 1) to lean, to
slant 2) to be likely to, to tend to

in-clude [ĭn-klo͞od′] *verb*, 1) to
have as part of 2) to count or
think of someone or something
as a part of a group, to involve

in-clu-sive [ĭn-klo͞o′sĭv] *adjective*,
not leaving anyone or anything
out

in-cog-ni-to [ĭn′kŏg-nē′tō]
adjective or adverb, 1) with one's
identity concealed, *noun*, 2) a
secret identity

in-co-her-ent [ĭn′kō-hîr′ənt]
adjective, incomprehensible,
lacking meaningful connection

income

in-come [ĭn′kŭm′] *noun*, the money a person earns from work or investments, salary

in-com-par-able [ĭn-kŏm′pər-ə-bəl] *adjective*, excellent, unequaled by comparison, unrivaled

in-com-pat-i-ble [ĭn′kəm-păt′ə-bəl] *adjective*, not capable of getting along or being used together

in-com-pe-tent [ĭn-kŏm′pĭ-tənt] *adjective*, not qualified, not able to do a job or task

in-com-plete [ĭn′kəm-plēt′] *adjective*, unfinished, lacking

in-con-ceiv-a-ble [ĭn′kən-sē′və-bəl] *adjective*, unimaginable, hard to believe

in-con-gru-ous [ĭn-kŏng′grōō-əs] *adjective*, lacking harmony, inconsistent

in-con-se-quen-tial [ĭn-kŏn′sĭ-kwĕn′shəl] *adjective*, having little importance

in-con-ven-ience [ĭn′kən-vēn′yəns] *noun*, a problem or difficulty that interferes with your comfort or ability to do something in a timely manner

in-con-ven-ient [ĭn′kən-vēn′yənt] *adjective*, untimely, awkward

in-cor-po-rate [ĭn-kôr′pə-rāt′] *verb*, 1) to unite into one body 2) to form into a corporation

in-cor-rect [ĭn′kə-rĕkt′] *adjective*, not right in facts, wrong

in-crease [ĭn-krēs′] *noun*, 1) the amount by which something gets larger , *verb*, 2) to become greater in size or quantity

in-cred-i-ble [ĭn-krĕd′ə-bəl] *adjective*, surpassing belief, unlikely, unbelievable

in-cred-u-lous [ĭn-krĕj′ə-ləs] *adjective*, unwilling to believe, skeptical

in-cre-ment [ĭn′krə-mənt, ĭng′-] *noun*, an increase, addition

in-crim-i-nate [ĭn-krĭm′ə-nāt′] *verb*, to accuse or charge with a crime or fault, to implicate

in-crim-i-nat-ing [ĭn-krĭm′ə-nā′tĭng] *adjective*, showing proof of guilt

in-cu-bate [ĭn′kyə-bāt′] *verb*, 1) to apply enough warmth to make something hatch 2) to help develop

in-cum-bent [ĭn-kŭm′bənt] *adjective*, 1) required, obligatory, *noun*, 2) an officeholder

in-cur [ĭn-kûr′] *verb*, to bring something unpleasant upon oneself

in-cur-a-ble [ĭn-kyōōr′ə-bəl] *adjective*, irreparable, incapable of being cured, terminally ill

in-cur-sion [ĭn-kûr′zhən] *noun*, an invasion into enemy territory

in-debt-ed [ĭn-dĕt′ĭd] *adjective*, under obligation to repay money or a favor

in-deed [ĭn-dēd′] *adverb*, really, truly, in fact, certainly

in-def-i-nite [ĭn-dĕf′ə-nĭt] *adjective*, uncertain, inexact

in-def-i-nite-ly [ĭn-dĕf′ə-nĭt-lē] *adverb*, without a set time frame

in-del-i-ble [ĭn-dĕl′ə-bəl] *adjective*, unable to be removed or blotted out, permanent

in-dem-ni-ty [ĭn dĕm′nĭ-tē] *noun*, protection or exemption from loss or damage, security

in-dent [ĭn-dĕnt′] *verb*, 1) to set lines in from the margin 2) to form notches on the edge

in-den-ture [ĭn-dĕn′chər] *noun*, the written work agreement of a servant to a master

in-de-pend-ence [ĭn′dĭ-pĕn′dəns] *noun, no plural*, freedom from the control of others

in-de-pend-ent [ĭn′dĭ-pĕn′dənt] *adjective*, free, not relying on others, without bias

in-de-struct-i-ble [ĭn′dĭ-strŭk′tə-bəl] *adjective*, incapable of being destroyed

in-dex [ĭn′dĕks′] *noun*, a list, usually alphabetical, for finding reference to topics, names, etc.

In-di-an [ĭn′dē-ən] *noun*, 1) a native American 2) a native of the Asian country of India

In-di-ana [ĭn′dē-ăn′ə] *noun*, one of the 50 United States located in the Midwest, the capital is Indianapolis. The state flower of **Indiana** is the peony, and the state motto is "The crossroads of America."

in-di-cate [ĭn′dĭ-kāt′] *verb*, to show or describe, to point out

in-di-ca-tion [ĭn′dĭ-kā′shən] *noun*, something that shows a trait

in-di-ca-tor [ĭn′dĭ-kā′tər] *noun*, 1) something that points to a trait 2) an instrument for automatically showing the pressure of the working fluid in an engine

in-dict [ĭn-dīt′] *verb*, to formally charge with a crime

in-dict-ment [ĭn-dīt′mənt] *noun*, a formal accusation charging someone with a crime

in-dif-fer-ent [ĭn-dĭf′ər-ənt] *adjective*, 1) mediocre 2) unresponsive, unconcerned

in-dig-e-nous [ĭn-dĭj′ə-nəs] *adjective*, native to an area

in-di-gent [ĭn′dĭ-jənt] *adjective*, poor, destitute

in-di-gest-i-ble [ĭn′dĭ-jĕs′tə-bəl] *adjective*, unable to be swallowed, eaten or digested

in-di-ges-tion [ĭn′dĭ-jĕs′chən] *noun*, a stomach-ache, heartburn

in-dig-nant [ĭn-dĭg′nənt] *adjective*, angry because of something that is not right, resentful

in-dig-na-tion [ĭn′dĭg-nā′shən] *noun*, anger about something thought not right, rage

in-dig-ni-ty [ĭn-dĭg′nĭ-tē] *noun*, insulting or humiliating treatment

in-di-go [ĭn′dĭ-gō′] *noun*, a deep blue-violet dye made from plants

in-di-rect [ĭn′dĭ-rĕkt′] *adjective*, in a roundabout way, circuitous

in-di-rect-ly [ĭn′dĭ-rĕkt′lē] *adverb*, inadvertently, not intentionally

in-dis-creet [ĭn′dĭ-skrēt′] *adjective*, lacking prudence or discretion, unwise, not careful, imprudent

in-dis-pen-sa-ble [ĭn′dĭ-spĕn′sə-bəl] *adjective*, absolutely necessary, essential

in-dis-put-a-ble [ĭn′dĭ-spyōō′tə-bəl] *adjective*, undeniable, unquestionable

in-di-vid-u-al [ĭn′də-vĭj′ōō-əl], *adjective*, 1) a person, 2) a single thing, an entity, one

in-di-vid-u-al-ly [ĭn′də-vĭj′ōō-əl-lē] *adverb*, separately, one by one, distinctly

in-di-vis-i-ble [ĭn′də- vĭz′ə-bəl] *adjective*, 1) that cannot be divided 2) cannot be divided without leaving a remainder

in-do-lent [ĭn′də-lənt] *adjective*, lazy, inactive, slothful

in-dom-i-ta-ble [ĭn-dŏm′ĭ-tə-bəl] *adjective*, unconquerable

in-duce [ĭn-dōōs′] *verb*, 1) to persuade, to influence 2) to cause 3) to infer

in-duce-ment [ĭn-dōōs′mənt] *noun*, any motive that leads one to act

in-duc-tive [ĭn-dŭk′tĭv] *adjective*, 1) going from specific to general 2) relating to electric or magnetic induction

in-dulge [ĭn-dŭlj′] *verb*, to allow one to enjoy, to give way to

in-dul-gence [ĭn-dŭl′jəns] *noun*, the act of being too permissive or generous

in-dus-tri-al [ĭn-dŭs′trē-əl] *adjective*, commercial, related to economy, industry, or manufacturing

in-dus-tri-ous [ĭn-dŭs′trē-əs] *adjective*, hard-working

in-dus-try [ĭn′də-strē] *noun*, 1) hard work 2) commerce, enterprise, business activity

in-el-i-gi-ble [ĭn-ĕl′ĭ-jə-bəl] *adjective*, not qualified to be chosen for an office, activity, or relationship

in-ept [ĭn-ĕpt′] *adjective*, incapable of performing a task, unskilled

in-eq-ui-ty [ĭn-ĕk′wĭ-tē] *noun*, unfairness, bias

in-ert [ĭn-ûrt′] *adjective*, 1) without power, inactive 2) unable to react

in-er-tia [ĭ-nûr′shə] *noun*, the state of matter by which it tends to remain at rest unless acted upon by an external force

in-ev-i-ta-ble [ĭn-ĕv′ĭ-tə-bəl] *adjective*, unavoidable

in-fal-li-ble [ĭn-făl′ə-bəl] *adjective*, unfailing, incapable of error

in-fa-mous [ĭn′fə-məs] *adjective*, having a bad reputation

in-fan-cy [ĭn′fən-sē] *noun*, the first part of life, early childhood

in-fant [ĭn′fənt] *noun*, a very young child in the first stage of life, a baby, a newborn

in-fan-try [ĭn′fən-trē] *noun*, the ground forces of the army, foot soldiers

in-fat-u-a-tion [ĭ-făch′ōō-ā′shən] *noun*, a brief but intense romantic attachment

in-fect [ĭn-fĕkt′] *verb*, to share a virus or infection with others

in-fec-tion [ĭn-fĕk′shən] *noun*, any disease caused by germs

in-fec-tious [ĭn-fĕk′shəs] *adjective*, capable of being spread or communicated, contagious

in-fer [ĭn-fûr′] *verb*, to arrive at a conclusion by logic, to deduce

in-fer-ence [ĭn′fər-əns] *noun*, a conclusion drawn from certain premises, a guess

in-fe-ri-or [ĭn-fîr′ē-ər] *adjectivo*,
1) lower 2) of less importance
3) inequal, subordinate

in-fer-nal [ĭn-fûr′nəl] *adjective*,
referring to hell, diabolical

in-fest [ĭn-fĕst′] *verb*, to overrun in
a troublesome manner

in-fil-tra-tion [ĭn′fĭl-trā′shən] *noun*,
1) the act of penetrating the
pores of a substance 2) the
process of joining gradually

in-fi-nite [ĭn′fə-nĭt] *adjective*,
unending, total, without limit

in-fin-i-tes-i-mal
[ĭn′fĭn-ĭ-tĕs′ə-məl] *adjective*,
immeasurably small

in-fin-i-ty [ĭn-fĭn′ĭ-tē] *noun*, the
symbol ~, that which continues
indefinitely, timelessness

in-firm [ĭn-fûrm′] *adjective*, weak,
sick, in poor health, ill, not well

in-fir-ma-ry [ĭn-fûr′mə-rē] *noun*, a
small hospital, a first-aid facility

in-flam-ma-ble [ĭn-flăm′ə-bəl]
adjective, easy to burn, volatile

in-flam-ma-tion [ĭn′flə-mā′shən]
noun, swelling and redness

in-flate [ĭn-flāt′] *verb*, to fill with air,
to expand

in-fla-tion [ĭn-flā′shən] *noun*, a
state in which price levels rise
continually

in-flict [ĭn-flĭkt′] *verb*, to force, to
impose, to deal a blow

in-flu-ence [ĭn′flōō-əns] *noun*,
1) power, authority, or control
2) the gradual or unseen
operation of some cause, *verb*,
3) to act upon 4) to persuade

in-flu-en-tial [ĭn′flōō-ĕn′shəl]
adjective, able to change
people's thoughts on something

in-flu-en-za [ĭn′flōō-ĕn′zə] *noun*,
the flu, a disease characterized
by fever, headaches, and fatigue

in-flux [ĭn′flŭks′] *noun*, the process
of flowing into or coming in

in-form [ĭn-fôrm′] *verb*, 1) to tell, to
notify, to advise 2) to teach

in-for-mal [ĭn-fôr′məl] *adjective*,
casual, not dressy or formal

in-form-ant [ĭn-fôr′mənt] *noun*,
someone who gives information

in-for-ma-tion [ĭn′fər-mā′shən]
noun, facts, data, the things you
need to know, knowledge

in-frac-tion [ĭn-frăk′shən] *noun*, a
violation, the breaking of a law,
rule, etc.

in-fringe-ment [ĭn-frĭnj′mənt]
noun, an act that breaks the
rules of an agreement

in-fu-ri-ate [ĭn-fyōōr′ē-āt′] *verb*, to
make someone furious

in-fuse [ĭn-fyōōz′] *verb*, 1) to instill
a principle or quality 2) to steep
in water or other fluid without
boiling for the purpose of
extracting useful qualities

in-fu-sion [ĭn-fyōō′zhən] *noun*,
1) the act of introducing or
dispersing of properties 2) a
beverage or other solution
obtained by steeping a
substance in water or other liquid

in-ge-nu-i-ty [ĭn′jə-nōō′ĭ-tē] *noun*,
skill in discovering, inventing, or
planning

in-gest [ĭn-jĕst′] *verb*, to take in
food or liquids

in-grat-i-tude [ĭn-grăt′ĭ-tōōd′] *noun*, unthankfulness

in-gre-di-ent [ĭn-grē′dē-ənt] *noun*, 1) a component part of any mixture 2) one of several things that are mixed together to make something

in-hab-it [ĭn-hăb′ĭt] *verb*, to make a place a home, to live or dwell in

in-hab-it-ant [ĭn-hăb′ĭ-tənt] *noun*, an animal or person who lives at a location, a resident

in-hale [ĭn-hāl′] *verb*, to take a deep breath, to breathe in

in-her-ent [ĭn-hîr′ənt] *adjective*, exisling as part of the naturo of a person or thing

in-her-it [ĭn-hĕr′ĭt] *verb*, to receive something, usually from a person by will or succession

in-her-it-ance [ĭn-hĕr′ĭ-təns] *noun*, an estate, heritage, legacy

in-hib-it [ĭn-hĭb′ĭt] *verb*, 1) to intimidate, to make someone hold back in fear 2) to restrain

in-hi-bi-tion [ĭn′hə-bĭsh′ən] *noun*, a painfully self-conscious feeling

in-iq-ui-ty [ĭ-nĭk′wĭ-tē] *noun*, a gross injustice, wickedness

in-i-tial [ĭ-nĭsh′əl] *adjective*, 1) first, *noun*, 2) the first letter of a name, *verb*, 3) to sign with one's initials

in-i-tial-ly [ĭ-nĭsh′ə-lē] *adverb*, at the beginning

in-i-ti-ate [ĭ-nĭsh′ē-āt′] *verb*, to introduce, to begin or start something, to originate

in-i-ti-a-tion [ĭ-nĭsh′ē-ā′shən] *noun*, an induction, an inaugural

in-i-t-ia-tive [ĭ-nĭsh′ə-tĭv] *noun*, 1) an act that begins a series of actions 2) the ability or will to do something because it needs to be done

in-ject [ĭn-jĕkt′] *verb*, 1) to introduce, to insert 2) to give someone a shot 3) to force something into

in-jec-tion [ĭn-jĕk′shən] *noun*, an insertion of medicine through a needle into the body, a shot

in-jure [ĭn′jər] *verb*, to cause harm of any kind, to wound

in-ju-ri-ous [ĭn-jŏŏr′ē-əs] *adjective*, hurtful, harmful

in-ju-ry [ĭn′jə-rē] *noun*, 1) a wound, harm to the body 2) an offense, harm done

in-jus-tice [ĭn-jŭs′tĭs] *noun*, a violation of the rights of another, an unfair or unjust act

ink [ĭngk] *noun*, a colored liquid used with a pen for writing, in a printer, etc.

in-land [ĭn′lənd] *adjective*, away from the shore or coast

in-law [ĭn′lô′] *noun*, a person related through marriage

in-let [ĭn′lĕt′] *noun*, a channel of water extending into the land from a larger body of water

in-mate [ĭn′māt′] *noun*, a prisoner or resident of a mental hospital

inn [ĭn] *noun*, a small hotel that serves meals, a tavern

in-nate [ĭ-nāt′] *adjective*, inborn, inherent

in-ner [ĭn′ər] *adjective*, 1) further in or in the center 2) spiritual

in-ning [ĭn′ĭng] *noun*, the period in a baseball game for each of two teams to get three outs

in-no-cence [ĭn′ə-səns] *noun, no plural*, 1) freedom from guilt, 2) simplicity, naivete

in-no-cent [ĭn′ə-sənt] *adjective*, 1) not guilty of a crime or sin, blameless 2) pure, unsophisticated

in-no-va-tion [ĭn′ə-vā′shən] *noun*, the introduction of a new product or method

in-no-va-tive [ĭn′ə-vā′tĭv] *adjective*, featuring something new, original

in-nu-en-do [ĭn′yōō-ĕn′dō] *noun*, a suggestion, a hint, an insinuation

in-oc-u-late [ĭ-nŏk′yə-lāt′] *verb*, to inject an animal or person with a virus to prevent an infection

in-op-por-tune [ĭn-ŏp′ər-tōōn′] *adjective*, poorly timed

in-or-di-nate [ĭn-ôr′dn-ĭt] *adjective*, excessive, extravagant

in-or-gan-ic [ĭn′ôr-găn′ĭk] *adjective*, relating to matter that does not contain carbon atoms in its main structure

in-put [ĭn′pŏŏt′] *noun*, anything put in, feedback, data entry

in-quest [ĭn′kwĕst′] *noun*, judicial inquiry or examination especially into a death

in-quire [ĭn-kwīr′] *verb*, to ask about, to investigate

in-quir-y [ĭn-kwīr′ē, ĭng′-] *noun*, investigation, study, the act of asking

in-qui-si-tion [ĭn′kwĭ-zĭsh′ən, ĭng′] *noun*, formal questioning

in-quis-i-tive [ĭn-kwĭz′ĭ-tĭv] *adjective*, curious, apt to ask questions, given to research

in-sane [ĭn-sān′] *adjective*, crazy, mentally ill

in-sa-tia-ble [ĭn-sā′shə-bəl] *adjective*, incapable of being satisfied or appeased

in-scrip-tion [ĭn-skrĭp′shən] *noun*, an engraved or carved message

in-scru-ta-ble [ĭn-skrōō′tə-bəl] *adjective*, unexplainable, mysterious

in-sect [ĭn′sĕkt′] *noun*, a bug with six legs and usually one or two pairs of wings

in-sec-ti-cide [ĭn-sĕk′tĭ-sīd′] *noun*, a poison used to kill insects

in-sen-si-ble [ĭn-sĕn′sə-bəl] *adjective*, not aware, unconscious, unable to feel

in-sep-a-ra-ble [ĭn-sĕp′ər-ə-bəl] *adjective*, incapable of being separated or disjoined

in-sert [ĭn-sûrt′] *noun*, 1) an extra piece sewn or put in place, *verb*, 2) to put something into another thing, to inject, to set in place

in-side [ĭn-sīd′] *adjective*, 1) internal, interior, *noun*, 2) the portion that is in the middle or inner surface of something, *preposition*, 3) lying within

in-sid-i-ous [ĭn-sĭd′ē-əs] *adjective*, deceitful, beguiling, hidden

in-sight [ĭn′sīt′] *noun*, understanding, perceptiveness

in-sig-ni-a [ĭn-sĭg′nē-ə] *noun*, an emblem, a symbol, a badge

insignificance

in-sig-nif-i-cance [ĭn′sĭg-nĭf′ĭ-kəns] *noun*, lack of importance, irrelevance

in-sig-nif-i-cant [ĭn′sĭg-nĭf′ĭ-kənt] *adjective*, unimportant, trivial

in-sin-cere [ĭn′sĭn-sîr′] *adjective*, untrue, false, disingenuous

in-sin-u-ate [ĭn-sĭn′yōō-āt′] *verb*, to introduce artfully, to suggest, to imply, to hint slyly

in-sip-id [ĭn-sĭp′ĭd] *adjective*, uninteresting, dull, banal

in-sist [ĭn-sĭst′] *verb*, to say firmly with emphasis 2) to assert or demand persistently

in-so-lence [ĭn′sə-ləns] *noun*, arrogance, rudeness, impudence

in-so-lent [ĭn′sə-lənt] *adjective*, rude, insulting, disrespectful

in-sol-u-ble [ĭn-sŏl′yə-bəl] *adjective*, 1) incapable of being dissolved 2) not able to be solved or explained

in-som-ni-a [ĭn-sŏm′nē-ə] *noun*, the inability to sleep

in-spect [ĭn-spĕkt′] *verb*, to examine carefully and critically, to scrutinize, to look over

in-spec-tion [ĭn-spĕk′shən] *noun*, a careful examination

in-spec-tor [ĭn-spĕk′tər] *noun*, 1) someone who inspects things 2) a high-ranking police official

in-spi-ra-tion [ĭn′spə-rā′shən] *noun*, something that stimulates imagination and goodwill

in-spire [ĭn-spīr′] *verb*, to stimulate to think and to act, to influence

in-sta-bil-i-ty [ĭn′stə-bĭl′ĭ-tē] *noun*, lack of stability, unsteadiness

in-stall [ĭn-stôl′] *verb*, 1) to place in possession of an office, rank, or order 2) to put in place

in-stal-la-tion [ĭn′stə-lā′shən] *noun*, the act of putting something into place

in-stall-ment [ĭn-stôl′mənt] *noun*, one of a number of parts or payments

in-stance [ĭn′stəns] *noun*, an example, a case in point

in-stant [ĭn′stənt] *adjective*, 1) happening or done at once, urgent, immediate, *noun*, 2) the present or current moment

in-stan-ta-ne-ous [ĭn′stən-tā′nē-əs] *adjective*, done at that moment

in-stant-ly [ĭn′stənt-lē] *adverb*, at once, immediately

in-stead [ĭn-stĕd′] *adverb*, in place of someone or something

in-step [ĭn′stĕp′] *noun*, the arched middle portion of the human foot or of a shoe

in-sti-gate [ĭn′stĭ-gāt′] *verb*, to urge, to start, to provoke

in-still [ĭn-stĭl′] *verb*, 1) to teach, to educate, to inform 2) to saturate, to infuse, to permeate

in-stinct [ĭn′stĭngkt′] *noun*, a natural impulse that makes animals know how to take care of themselves, innate aptitude

in-stinc-tive-ly [ĭn-stĭngk′tĭv-lē] *adverb*, naturally, innately, automatically

in-sti-tute [ĭn′stĭ-tōōt′] *noun*, 1) an organization devoted to research and study, *verb*, 2) to form or establish an organization 3) to set in motion

in-sti-tu-tion [ĭn′stĭ-tōō′shən] *noun*, 1) an organization used to serve a group of people 2) a way of life, an established custom

in-struct [ĭn-strŭkt′] *verb*, to teach, to show someone how to do something, to direct

in-struc-tion [ĭn-strŭk′shən] *noun*, teaching, direction, a training manual, knowledge imparted

in-struc-tor [ĭn-strŭk′tər] *noun*, a teacher or mentor

in-stru-ment [ĭn′strə-mənt] *noun*, 1) a device, a mechanism, a tool 2) a device used to make musical sounds 3) a means to an end

in-stru-men-tal [ĭn′strə-měn′tl] *adjective*, 1) helpful, acting to get something done 2) meant to be performed on musical instruments

in-suf-fer-a-ble [ĭn-sŭf′ər-ə-bəl] *adjective*, painful, not to be endured, intolerable

in-suf-fi-cient [ĭn′sə-fĭsh′ənt] *adjective*, not enough for what is needed

in-su-late [ĭn′sə-lāt′] *verb*, to protect from heat, cold, electricity, etc., by means of a layer of protective material

in-su-la-tion [ĭn′sə-lā′shən] *noun*, a material that prevents passage of heat, electricity, or sound

in-sult [ĭn-sŭlt′] *noun*, 1) an unkind or rude remark, *verb*, 2) to treat with abuse or rudeness

in-sur-ance [ĭn-shōōr′əns] *noun*, money paid in return for the promise of payment in the event of an accident, property damage, death, etc.

in-sure [ĭn-shōōr′] *verb*, to guarantee, to protect

in-sur-gent [ĭn-sûr′jənt] *noun*, a person who rebels against the law or leadership

in-sur-rec-tion [ĭn′sə-rěk′shən] *noun*, an uprising, a rebellion

in-tan-gi-ble [ĭn-tăn′jə-bəl] *adjective*, not able to be touched

in-te-ger [ĭn′tĭ-jər] *noun*, 1) a whole number 2) an intact unit

in-te-grate [ĭn′tĭ-grāt′] *verb*, to make into a whole, to combine into one unit, to merge

in-teg-ri-ty [ĭn-těg′rĭ-tē] *noun*, honesty, uprightness

in-tel-lect [ĭn′tl-ĕkt′] *noun*, the power to understand the mind

in-tel-lec-tu-al [ĭn′tl-ĕk′chōō-əl] *adjective*, able to reason, smart

in-tel-li-gence [ĭn-těl′ə-jəns] *noun*, 1) the faculty of understanding and reasoning 2) information communicated

in-tel-li-gent [ĭn-těl′ə-jənt] *adjective*, very smart, clever

in-tel-li-gent-ly [ĭn-těl′ə-jənt-lē] *adverb*, sensibly, skillfully

in-tel-li-gi-ble [ĭn-těl′ĭ-jə-bəl] *adjective*, capable of being understood

in-tend [ĭn-těnd′] *verb*, 1) to plan to do something 2) to design for a particular purpose

in-tense [ĭn-těns′] *adjective*, expressing strong emotion, extreme

in-ten-si-fy [ĭn-těn′sə-fī′] *verb*, to make greater or more intense

intensity

in-ten-si-ty [ĭn-těn′sĭ-tē] *noun*,
great concentration of energy

in-ten-sive [ĭn-těn′sĭv] *adjective*,
thorough, involving special effort

in-tent [ĭn-těnt′] *noun*, 1) purpose
2) meaning

in-ten-tion [ĭn-těn′shən] *noun*, aim,
a plan, a purpose, a meaning

in-ten-tion-al-ly [ĭn-těn′shə-nəl-lē]
adverb, purposely, deliberately

in-tent-ly [ĭn-těnt′lē] *adverb*,
strongly, purposefully

in-ter [ĭn-tûr′] *verb*, to bury

in-ter-act [ĭn′tər-ăkt′] *verb*, to relate
mutually to

in-ter-cede [ĭn′tər-sēd′] *verb*, to act
on another's behalf, to mediate

in-ter-cept [ĭn′tər-sěpt′] *verb*, to
stop or seize something before it
reaches its intended destination

in-ter-est [ĭn′trĭst] *noun*, 1) a
concern or pleasure from
learning something 2) title or
share in a thing 3) a percentage
rate of money paid for the use of
money, *verb*, 4) to involve or gain
the attention of someone

in-ter-est-ing [ĭn′trĭ-stĭng]
adjective, able to hold the
attention or curiosity of someone

in-ter-face [ĭn′tər-fās′] *noun*, 1) a
surface forming a common
boundary between adjacent
areas 2) in computer science,
the software or hardware
connecting one drive or system
to another

in-ter-fere [ĭn′tər-fîr′] *verb*, to
prevent something from
happening, to meddle

in-ter-fer-ence [ĭn′tər-fîr′əns] *noun*,
obstruction, interruption

in-ter-im [ĭn′tər-ĭm] *adjective*,
1) temporary, *noun*, 2) the
meantime

in-te-ri-or [ĭn-tîr′ē-ər] *adjective*,
1) being within any limits, inner,
inside, *noun*, 2) that which is
within, an inner area

in-ter-lude [ĭn′tər-lōōd′] *noun*, 1) a
pause, a lull 2) a brief play or
musical piece performed
between longer pieces

in-ter-me-di-ate [ĭn′tər-mē′dē-ĭt]
adjective, in the middle between
extremes

in-ter-ment [ĭn-tûr′mənt] *noun*, the
burial ceremony

in-ter-mi-na-ble [ĭn-tûr′mə-nə-bəl]
adjective, seemingly endless

in-ter-mis-sion [ĭn′tər-mĭsh′ən]
noun, a break or recess

in-ter-mit-tent [ĭn′tər-mĭt′nt]
adjective, coming and going at
intervals, beginning again

in-ter-nal [ĭn-tûr′nəl] *adjective*,
1) occuriring inside of
something, inner 2) referring to
any function inside the body

in-ter-na-tion-al [ĭn′tər-năsh′ə-nəl]
adjective, universal, global

in-ter-ne-cine [ĭn′tər-něs′ēn′]
adjective, mutually destructive

In-ter-net [ĭn′tûr-nět] *noun*, the link
to other computers, connected
by a network

in-ter-pret [ĭn-tûr′prĭt] *verb*, to
translate, to define, to explain

in-ter-pre-ta-tion
[ĭn-tûr′prĭ-tā′shən] *noun*, an

explanation of someone's art or other work, a translation

in-ter-pret-er [ĭn-tûr′prĭ-tər] *noun*, 1) one who explains or expounds 2) a translator

in-ter-ro-gate [ĭn-tĕr′ə-gāt′] *verb*, to ask questions of someone

in-ter-rupt [ĭn′tə-rŭpt′] *verb*, to stop something from continuing

in-ter-sect [ĭn′tər-sĕkt′] *verb*, to meet to form angles

in-ter-sec-tion [ĭn′tər-sĕk′shən] *noun*, 1) a point formed by two lines meeting 2) a place where two or more roads meet

in-ter-state [ĭn′tər-stāt′] *adjective*, 1) pertaining to commerce between the states, *noun*, 2) a highway that runs through two or more states

in-ter-val [ĭn′tər-vəl] *noun*, the space of time between any two points or events, a break

in-ter-vene [ĭn′tər-vēn′] *verb*, 1) to come or be between 2) to occur between points of time or events

in-ter-view [ĭn′tər-vyoo′] *noun*, a meeting in which one person or several people are questioned often by journalists or a prospective employer

in-ti-ma-cy [ĭn′tə-mə-sē] *noun*, close familiarity or association, a very personal relationship

in-ti-mate [ĭn′tə-mĭt] *adjective*, familiar, close, dear, private

in-tim-i-date [ĭn-tĭm′ĭ-dāt′] *verb*, to make someone afraid, to threaten someone, to scare

in-to [ĭn′too] *preposition*, toward the middle of something to the inside from outside

in-tol-er-a-ble [ĭn-tŏl′ər-ə-bəl] *adjective*, unbearable

in-tol-er-ance [ĭn-tŏl′ər-əns] *noun*, prejudice, bias, bigotry

in-to-na-tion [ĭn′tə-nā′shən] *noun*, 1) the rise and fall of a voice's pitch 2) chanting

in-tox-i-cate [ĭn-tŏk′sĭ-kāt′] *verb*, 1) to enliven, to excite, to elate 2) to make drunk

in-trac-ta-ble [ĭn-trăk′tə-bəl] *adjective*, difficult to control

in-tran-si-tive [ĭn-trăn′sĭ-tĭv] *adjective*, designating a verb in a sentence that does not need a direct object to complete its meaning

in-trep-id [ĭn-trĕp′ĭd] *adjective*, fearless, dauntless

in-tri-cate [ĭn′trĭ-kĭt] *adjective*, complicated, involved, detailed

in-trigue [ĭn′trēg′] *noun*, 1) a conspiracy, a strategy, a secret plan, *verb*, 2) to draw into, to fascinate, to arouse curiosity

in-trin-sic [ĭn-trĭn′zĭk] *adjective*, basic and essential

in-tro-duce [ĭn′trə-doos′] *verb*, 1) to bring into notice 2) to make known by formal announcement 3) to bring into use

in-tro-duc-tion [ĭn′trə-dŭk′shən] *noun*, 1) a piece of writing at the beginning of a book that explains something about the story 2) the exchange of names when two people first meet

in-tro-vert [ĭn′trə-vûrt′] *noun*, a loner, someone who feels self-conscious, a shy person

intrude

in-trude [ĭn-trōod′] *verb*, to trespass, to enter uninvited

in-tru-sion [ĭn-trōo′zhən] *noun*, the act of forcing your way in without right or welcome or permission

in-tu-i-tion [ĭn′tōo-ĭsh′ən] *noun*, instinctive knowledge or feeling

in-un-date [ĭn′ŭn-dāt′] *verb*, to overflow, to flood, to overwhelm

in-ure [ĭn-yōor′] *verb*, to accustom, to harden by use or exposure

in-vade [ĭn-vād′] *verb*, to move by force into another's country, property, house, etc.

in-va-lid [ĭn-văl′ĭd] *adjective*, 1) null and void, insupportable, [ĭn-val′ĭ-d] *noun*, 2) a person who is incapacitated by injury or illness

in-val-i-date [ĭn-văl′ĭ-dāt′] *verb*, 1) to make or show something to be wrong 2) to deprive of legal force

in-var-i-ab-ly [ĭn-vâr′ē-ə-blē] *adverb*, without fail, predictably

in-va-sion [ĭn-vā′zhən] *noun*, an attack, a raid

in-vent [ĭn-vĕnt′] *verb*, to create or design a new product

in-ven-tion [ĭn-vĕn′shən] *noun*, a design or creation of something new

in-ven-to-ry [ĭn′vən-tôr′ē] *noun*, an itemized list of stock on hand often with its estimated worth

in-verse [ĭn-vûrs′] *noun*, the opposite, the reverse in direction

in-vert [ĭn-vûrt′] *verb*, to overturn, to turn upside down

in-ver-te-brate [ĭn-vûr′tə-brĭt] *noun*, any animal without a backbone or spinal column, e.g. *a worm*

in-vest [ĭn-vĕst′] *verb*, 1) to empower 2) to provide time or money, usually in the hope of receiving more in return

in-ves-ti-gate [ĭn-vĕs′tĭ-gāt′] *verb*, to examine, to inquire

in-ves-ti-ga-tion [ĭn-vĕs′tĭ-gā′shən] *noun*, an inquiry into a matter, a thorough exploration or inspection, an examination

in-vest-ment [ĭn-vĕst′mənt] *noun*, money used to create a source of income or profit

in-ves-tor [ĭn-vĕs′tər] *noun*, one who spends money on something with a view of obtaining income or profit

in-vet-er-ate [ĭn-vĕt′ər-ĭt] *adjective*, deep-rooted, habitual

in-vig-o-rate [ĭn-vĭg′ə-rāt′] *verb*, to fill with life and energy

in-vin-ci-ble [ĭn-vĭn′sə-bəl] *adjective*, not capable of being overcome, unyielding

in-vis-i-ble [ĭn-vĭz′ə-bəl] *adjective*, not visible, not able to be seen

in-vi-ta-tion [ĭn′vĭ-tā′shən] *noun*, a request asking for someone to be present or participate in an activity

in-vite [ĭn-vīt′] *verb*, to ask someone to do something or come somewhere

in-voke [ĭn-vōk′] *verb*, 1) to call upon, to ask for 2) to cause

in-vol-un-tar-y [ĭn-vŏl′ən-tĕr′ē] *adjective*, done unwillingly

in-volve [ĭn-vŏlv′] *verb*, to take part in, to make a part of

in-vul-ner-a-ble [ĭn-vŭl′nər-ə-bəl]
adjective, incapable of being
injured

in-ward [ĭn′wərd] *adjective*,
directed toward the center

in-ward-ly [ĭn′wərd-lē] *adverb*,
internally

i-o-dine [ī′ə-dīn′] *noun*, a
nonmetallic element isolated as
a crystalline solid

i-o-ta [ī-ō′tə] *noun*, a very small
quantity or degree, a particle

Io-wa [ī′ə-wə] *noun*, one of the 50
United States located in the
Midwest the capital city is Des
Moines. The state flower of **Iowa**
is the wild rose and the state
motto is "Our liberties we prize
and our rights we will maintain."

i-rate [ī-rāt′] *adjective*, angry

ir-i-des-cent [ĭr′ĭ-dĕs′ənt]
adjective, showing the rainbow-
like play of colors, shimmering

irk-some [ûrk′səm] *adjective*,
tedious, annoying

i-ron [ī′ərn] *noun*, 1) a magnetic
gray metal 2) a heated device
used to smooth the wrinkles from
clothes 3) an element, *verb*, 4) to
press with a heated iron to
remove wrinkles on clothes

i-ron-ic [ī-rŏn′ĭk] *adjective*,
appearing to be false or
contradictory, but in fact true

i-ro-ny [ī′rə-nē, ī′ər-] *noun*, 1) the
outcome of events contrary to
what was expected 2) the
expression of the opposite of
what is meant for humorous or
literary effect

ir-rad-i-ate [ĭ-rā′dē-āt′] *verb*, 1) to
illuminate, to enlighten 2) to
expose to radiation

ir-ra-tion-al [ĭ-răsh′ə-nəl] *adjective*,
absurd, unreasonable

ir-rec-on-cil-a-ble [ĭ-rĕk′ən-sī′lə-bəl]
adjective, not able to be resolved
by compromise, unfriendly

ir-reg-u-lar [ĭ-rĕg′yə-lər]
adjective,1) not conforming to
rule 2) erratic, not uniform

ir-rel-e-vant [ĭ-rĕl′ə-vənt] *adjective*,
not applicable

ir-rep-a-ra-ble [ĭ-rĕp′ər-ə-bəl]
adjective, permanently damaged

ir-re-proach-a-ble
[ĭr′ĭ-prō′chə-bəl] *adjective*,
blameless, above reproach

ir-re-sist-i-ble [ĭr′ĭ-zĭs′tə-bəl]
adjective, too attractive to resist

ir-re-triev-a-ble [ĭr′ĭ-trē′və-bəl]
adjective, lost, gone forever

ir-rev-er-ent [ĭ-rĕv′ər-ənt] *adjective*,
lacking proper respect

ir-rev-o-ca-ble [ĭ-rĕv′ə-kə-bəl]
adjective, unable to be retracted

ir-ri-gate [ĭr′ĭ-gāt′] *verb*, to supply
with water by causing a stream
to flow through, as in channels

ir-ri-tate [ĭr′ĭ-tāt′] *verb*, 1) to annoy,
to excite to anger, to bother 2) to
make skin sore, red, or swollen

ir-ri-ta-tion [ĭr′ĭ-tā′shən] *noun*,
1) something that makes a
person mildly angry 2) something
that causes a painful or inflamed
part of the body

is [ĭz] the part of the *verb* to **be** that
we use with *he, she,* and *it*

Is-lam [ĭs-läm′] *noun*, Muslim
religion founded in Arabia in the

island

7th century based on the teaching of Muhammed as recorded in the Koran

is-land [ĭ′lənd] *noun*, a body of land completely surrounded by water

isle [īl] *noun*, a small island

i-so-late [ī′sə-lāt′] *verb*, 1) to separate and set apart, to place alone 2) to cut off from others

iso-la-tion [ī′sə-lā′shən] *noun*, solitude, detachment

i-sos-ce-les tri-ang-le [ī-sŏs′ə-lēz′ trī′ăng′gəl] *noun*, a triangle with two equal sides

is-sue [ĭsh′o͞o] *noun*, 1) a topic on which there is disagreement 2) the condition or action of being made available, *verb*, 3) to give

isth-mus [ĭs′məs] *noun*, a neck of land bordered by water joining two larger portions of land

it [ĭt] *pronoun, plural*, **they**, 1) used of something previously named 2) used as the subject in sentences about the weather, time, and dates and other phrases

i-tal-ic [ĭ-tăl′ĭk] *noun*, type in which the letters slant

itch [ĭch] *noun*, 1) a tickling feeling in the skin that makes one want to scratch, *verb*, 2) to feel a desire to scratch and rub a sore because it is irritating

i-tem [ī′təm] *noun*, 1) a point 2) a news article 3) a single thing in a list

i-tem-ize [ī′tə-mīz′] *verb*, to list or state by particulars

itin-er-ant [ī-tĭn′ər-ənt] *adjective*, traveling from place to place

itin-er-ar-y [ī-tĭn′ə-rĕr′ē] *noun*, the detailed plan for a journey

its [ĭts] *adjective*, of it, belonging to it, the possessive of the word it

it's [ĭts] the *contraction* of the words it and is

it-self [ĭt-sĕlf′] *pronoun*, *plural*, **themselves**, referring to the subject of the sentence

I've [īv] the *contraction* of the words I and **have**

i-vo-ry [ī′və-rē, īv′rē] *noun*, hard, white substance taken from the tusks of elephants or walruses

i-vy [ī′vē] *noun*, a leafy climbing vine usually with pointed evergreen leaves

J

jack-et [jăk′ĭt] *noun*, 1) a covering worn over clothing, similar to a coat, typically of waist or hip length 2) a covering put over something

jade [jād] *noun*, a stone of a green color, but sometimes whitish, capable of a fine polish

jad-ed [jā′dĭd] *adjective*, tired, weary from having had too much of something

jag-uar [jăg′wär′] *noun*, a wild cat with a spotted coat that lives in Central or South America

jail [jāl] *noun*, a prison

jam [jăm] *noun*, 1) a sweet spread, made of boiled fruit and sugar 2) traffic that is stopped because no one can move 3) a predicament *verb*, 4) to pack tightly together, to compress, to press or push

jan-i-tor [jăn/ĭ-tər] *noun*, one who takes care of the repairs and cleaning of a building

Jan-u-ary [jăn/yoo-ĕr/ē] *noun*, the first month of the year, having 31 days

jar [jär] *noun*, a container like a bottle with a wide opening

jar-gon [jär/gən] *noun*, language used by a particular group, special terminology

jaun-dice [jôn/dĭs] *noun*, a medical condition that makes the skin look yellow

jaunt [jônt] *noun*, a short trip

jave-lin [jăv/lĭn] *noun*, a spear thrown by hand for distance as in an athletic event or used as a weapon

jaw [jô] *noun*, the bony part of the face in which the teeth are set

jazz [jăz] *noun*, a style of music using unusual tone effects on brass instruments improvised by black Americans in the 1900's

jeal-ous [jĕl/əs] *adjective*, to be unhappy because you want what someone else has, envious

jeal-ous-y [jĕl/ə-sē] *noun*, suspicious fear or watchfulness, resentment of someone's success or romantic interest in someone else

jeer [jîr] *verb*, to make fun of someone and laugh in their face, to mock, to scorn

jel-ly [jĕl/ē] *noun, no plural*, 1) any substance between liquid and solid 2) a sweet spread made of fruit and pectin

jel-ly-fish [jĕl/ō fĭoh/] *noun*, a soft gelatinous sea creature that looks like a squishy blob

jeop-ard-ize [jĕp/ər-dīz/] *verb*, to expose to danger or even death

jerk [jûrk] *noun*, 1) a quick pull or twist movement, *verb*, 2) to pull, to push or to twist suddenly

jer-sey [jûr/zē] *noun*, clothing usually made of cotton with elastic that covers the top of the body like a shirt

jest [jĕst] *verb*, to joke, to jeer

jet [jĕt] *noun*, 1) an aircraft propelled through air by an engine, which releases a stream of hot air behind itself as it travels 2) a stream of gas, air, or liquid that spurts from a hole

jet-ti-son [jĕt/ĭ-sən] *verb*, to throw overboard, to discard

jet-ty [jĕt/ē] *noun*, a kind of wall built out into water for protection against the waves

Jew [joo] *noun*, a member of the Jewish religion

jew-el [joo/əl] *noun*, a precious stone used as an ornament, a gem of great value

jew-el-er [joo/ə-lər] *noun*, one who makes, or deals in jewels, gems and precious stones, etc.

jew-el-ry [joo/əl-rē] *noun, no plural*, ornaments like rings, earrings, necklaces made with precious or semiprecious stones, gems and metals

jilt [jĭlt] *verb*, to break up a romantic interest

jingle

jin-gle [jĭng′gəl] *verb*, 1) to make a tingling sound like the sound of bells, *noun*, 2) a catchy verse

job [jŏb] *noun*, 1) a task or responsibility 2) work done for payment 3) a position or duty

jog [jŏg] *verb*, 1) to run for exercise 2) to jolt, to bump, to shake 3) to stir into activity

join [join] *verb*, 1) to connect, to bring together, to meet 2) to become a member

joint [joint] *adjective*, 1) an endeavor involving two or more people, *noun*, 2) the part of the body where bones connect 3) the place where two things are joined or connected 4) a poor quality restaurant or night club

joke [jōk] *noun*, 1) a funny story or funny phrase spoken to amuse people, *verb*, 2) to tell funny stories or say things to make people laugh, to fool around

jolt [jōlt] *noun*, 1) a sudden and unexpected movement, *verb*, 2) to cause a sudden movement

joule [jōol, joul] *noun*, the measurement of force or energy

jour-nal [jûr′nəl] *noun*, a book that records daily thoughts or transactions, a diary

jour-nal-ism [jûr′nə-lĭz′əm] *noun*, no plural, the job of writing for a publication or broadcasting news

jour-nal-ist [jûr′nə-lĭst] *noun*, a professional writer for a newspaper or magazine

jour-ney [jûr′nē] *noun*, the passage from one place to another, a trip

jo-vi-al [jō′vē-əl] *adjective*, joking in a friendly manner, light-hearted, joyous humor

joy [joi] *noun*, no plural, great happiness, delight, elation

joy-ful [joi′fəl] *adjective*, full of joy, very glad, happy

ju-bi-lant [jōo′bə-lənt] *adjective*, thrilled, rejoicing, great joy

Ju-da-ism [jōo′dē-ĭz′əm] *noun*, the religion of people descended from the Israelites in the Bible

judge [jŭj] *noun*, 1) one with legal authority who applies the rules of law in a court 2) the person designated to decide the winner in a contest, *verb*, 3) to make a decision, to form an opinion

judg-ment [jŭj′mənt] *noun*, 1) a decision or opinion 2) intelligence, understanding

ju-di-cial [jōo-dĭsh′əl] *adjective*, providing or relating to justice or a fair decision, just, legal

ju-di-cious [jōo-dĭsh′əs] *adjective*, sound in judgment, wise, discreet, sagacious, fair

ju-do [jōo′dō] *noun*, no plural, a form of martial arts that uses the body as a weapon, and bans throws and blows

jug [jŭg] *noun*, a container with a handle for holding liquids

jug-ger-naut [jŭg′ər-nôt′] *noun*, an overpowering or crushing force

jug-gle [jŭg′əl] *verb*, to throw several things into the air and keep them moving by throwing and catching them as a trick

jug-u-lar [jŭg′yə-lər] *noun*, one of the large veins returning the blood from the head

juice [jōōs] *noun*, the natural fluid that comes from fruit, vegetables or cooked meat

Ju-ly [jōō-lī′] *noun*, the seventh month of the year, having 31 days

jump [jŭmp] *noun*, 1) a spring or leap, *verb*, 2) to lift the feet off the ground into the air, to leap 3) to rise suddenly

jump-er [jŭm′pər] *noun*, a sleeveless dress worn over a blouse

junc-tion [jŭngk′shən] *noun*, a place where roads or lines of railways meet and cross

June [jōōn] *noun*, the sixth month of the year, having 30 days

jun-gle [jŭng′gəl] *noun*, a thick growth of tropical bushes, vines, trees, etc., extending over a large area

jun-ior [jōōn′yər] *adjective*, 1) a student in his third year of a four-year course 2) the son named after his father

junk [jŭngk] *noun*, stuff regarded as unwanted or useless

jun-ket [jŭng′kĭt] *noun*, a trip, a short pleasure excursion

ju-ris-dic-tion [jōōr′ĭs-dĭk′shən] *noun*, the legal authority of a court, to apply the law

ju-ror [jōōr′ər, -ôr′] *noun*, one of a group of peers chosen to judge someone accused of a crime

ju-ry [jōōr′ē] *noun*, a group of people chosen to decide if a person is guilty or innocent of a crime in a court of law

just [jŭst] *adjective*, 1) fair and right 2) normal, *adverb*, 3) to the amount needed, but no more 4) a very short time ago, by a short time 5) only 6) used to compare two things

jus-tice [jŭs′tĭs] *noun*, *no plural*, fairness, equity, impartiality

jus-ti-fy [jŭs′tə-fī′] *verb*, 1) to show or prove to be right 2) to make even or true, as lines of type by proper spacing

ju-ve-nile [jōō′və-nīl′] *adjective*, 1) young, youthful, *noun*, 2) a youth, anyone under the legal adult age of 18

K

ka-lei-do-scope [kə-lī′də-skōp′] *noun*, an optical instrument exhibiting an endless variety of colored forms

kan-ga-roo [kăng′gə-rōō′] *noun*, a marsupial, an animal that eats only plants, lives in Australia, jumps around on its large back legs

Kan-sas [kăn′zəs] *noun*, one of the 50 United States, located in the Midwest, the capital city is Topeka. The state flower of **Kansas** is the sunflower, and the motto is "To the stars through difficulties."

kar-at [kăr′ət] *noun*, the unit measure of the purity of gold

kay-ak [kī′ăk′] *noun*, a canoe that holds one person

keel [kēl] *noun*, the bottom of the boat, the underside

keen [kēn] *adjective*, 1) having a sharp edge 2) mentally aware, quick to understand 3) showing a stong interest, eager

keep [kēp] *verb*, 1) to hold something 2) to store something, to stock it 3) to make someone stay someplace 4) to prevent someone from doing something 5) to continue on

ken-nel [kĕn′əl] *noun*, a place to keep and care for dogs

Ken-tucky [kən-tŭk′ē] *noun*, one of the 50 United States, located in the South, the capital is Frankfort. The state flower of **Kentucky** is the goldenrod, and the state motto is "United We Stand, Divided We Fall."

kept [kĕpt] *past tense* of **keep**

ker-chief [kûr′chĭf] *noun*, a woman's scarf worn as a covering for the head

ker-nel [kûr′nəl] *noun*, a grain or seed, the edible part of a nut

ker-o-sene [kĕr′ə-sēn′] *noun*, thin oil used to ignite a fire

ketch-up [kĕch′ŭp] *noun*, a thick sauce made of tomatoes, flavored with onion, salt, sugar, and spice

ket-tle [kĕt′l] *noun*, a large metal pot with a lid and a handle and a spout

key [kē] *noun*, 1) a metal instrument used for locking and unlocking things 2) a lever on a musical instrument that affects the sound 3) the piece of information needed to make something understood

key-board [kē′bôrd′] *noun*, a common input device

khak-i [kăk′ē] *noun*, a tan or brownish cotton cloth

kick [kĭk] *noun*, 1) an impulsive move with the foot, *verb*, 2) to hit something with the foot, to move the foot suddenly

kid [kĭd] *noun*, 1) a young goat 2) a child, *verb*, 3) to tease or joke

kid-nap [kĭd′năp′] *verb*, to take someone against their will

kid-nap-per [kĭd′nă-pər] *noun*, someone who takes a person against their will

kid-ney [kĭd′nē] *noun*, one of two parts inside the body which remove waste liquid from the blood and excretes uric acid

kill [kĭl] *verb*, to make someone die

kill-er [kĭl′ər] *noun*, a person who murders or takes the life from another

kil-o-gram [kĭl′ə-grăm′] *noun*, a unit of weight equal to 1,000 grams

kil-o-me-ter [kĭ-lŏm′ĭ-tər] *noun*, a distance equal to 1,000 meters, or 3,281feet

kil-o-watt [kĭl′ə-wŏt′] *noun*, a unit of power equal to 1,000 watts

kin [kĭn] *noun*, *no plural*, family members, one's relatives

kind [kīnd] *adjective*, 1) nice, good, helpful, willing to please, *noun*, 2) a sort or particular one

kin-der-gar-ten [kĭn′dər-gär′tn] *noun*, a preschool for children before the first grade

kin dle [kĭn′dl] *verb*, 1) to set fire, to ignite 2) to arouse, to inspire

kind-ness [kīnd/nĭs] *noun, no plural*, goodness, compassion

kin-dred [kĭn′drĭd] *adjective*, 1) similar in nature, comparable, alike 2) related by family

ki-net-ic [kĭ-nĕt′ĭk] *adjective*, the changes of motion produced by forces, the force of motion

king [kĭng] *noun*, a male ruler of a country, especially one who comes from a family of rulers

king-dom [kĭng′dəm] *noun*, the lands owned by a monarchy, an empire, an independent realm

kin-ship [kĭn′shĭp′] *noun*, a relationship or connection between family members

kiss [kĭs] *noun*, 1) a slight touch with the lips, *verb*, 2) to touch with the lips as a sign of affection or love

kit [kĭt] *noun*, a set of instruments needed for doing something or going somewhere

kitch-en [kĭch′ən] *noun*, the room where food is prepared and cooked and eaten

kite [kīt] *noun*, a light frame covered with fabric, plastic or paper, flown in the air at the end of a long string

kit-ten [kĭt′n] *noun*, a baby cat

knap-sack [năp′săk′] *noun*, a supply bag of canvas or leather with shoulder straps, worn on the back

knave [nāv] *noun*, an unscrupulous, dishonest person, a rascal

knead [nēd] *verb*, to manipulate by pressing and stretching to mix and remove air, to massage

knee [nē] *noun*, the joint between the thigh and the lower leg connecting the femur and tibia

kneel [nēl] *verb*, to stand on your knees, to bend down so that your calf is laying on the ground

knew [nōō] *past tense* of **know**

knife [nīf] *noun, plural,* **knives**, a cutting instrument consisting of a sharp blade fastened to a handle

knight [nīt] *noun*, 1) an armed soldier in the Middle Ages 2) a chess piece in the shape of a horse's head 3) an honorary title in Britain

knit [nĭt] *verb*, to join wool into a cloth using long needles

knob [nŏb] *noun*, a handle in the shape of a round lump

knock [nŏk] *noun*, 1) a noise made when something is hit *verb*, 2) to hit or strike with the fist 4) to make a noise by hitting on the surface

knoll [nōl] *noun*, a small round hill

knot [nŏt] *noun*, 1) one or more threads tied together, *verb*, 2) to tie something securely with rope or cord so that it cannot come untied

know [nō] *verb*, 1) to understand clearly, to learn 2) to be skilled in 3) to be acquainted with someone

knowl-edge [nŏl′ĭj] *noun*, something learned and remembered, gained by experience

knowledgeable

know-ledge-a-ble [nŏl′ĭ-jə-bəl] *adjective*, familiar with, learned

known [nōn] past participle of **know**

knuck-le [nŭk′əl] *noun*, one of the joints in the finger or toe

Ko-ran [kə-răn′, -rän′, kô-, kō-] *noun*, the holy book of Islam containing the revelations of God to Muhammad

L

la-bel [lā′bəl] *noun*, 1) a slip of paper indicating contents, ownership, etc. *verb*, 2) to affix a tag or sticker on something naming what it is

la-bor [lā′bər] *noun*, 1) work 2) the pain a woman feels birthing a baby, *verb*, 3) to work hard

lab-o-ra-to-ry [lăb′rə-tôr′ē] *noun*, a place devoted to experiments in natural science

la-bo-ri-ous [lə-bôr′ē-əs] *adjective*, hardworking, tiresome, tedious

lab-y-rinth [lăb′ə-rĭnth′] *noun*, a series of intricate passageways, a maze, an inexplicable difficulty

lace [lās] *noun*, 1) a string used to tie a shoe 2) frilly threadwork used as edging or as an embroidery design, *verb*, 3) to thread through holes with a string or cord

lac-er-a-tion [lăs′ə-rā′shən] *noun*, a cut, a tear made with a knife

lack [lăk] *noun*, 1) not enough, a shortage, *verb* 2) to be without

lack-a-dai-si-cal [lăk′ə-dā′zĭ-kəl] *adjective*, half-hearted, lazy, indifferent, listless

la-con-ic [lə-kŏn′ĭk] *adjective*, brief and to the point

lac-quer [lăk′ər] *noun*, a liquid that hardens into a clear tough film

lac-tic acid [lăk′tĭk-ăs′ĭd] *noun*, a colorless, syrupy liquid, occurring in sour milk

lad [lăd] *noun*, a boy

lad-der [lăd′ər] *noun*, a device used for climbing designed with two side pieces joined together with shorter pieces called rungs that form steps

lad-en [lād′n] *adjective*, heavily loaded, full of cargo

la-dle [lād′l] *noun*, a cup-shaped spoon with a long handle, used for serving or dipping

la-dy [lā′dē] *noun*, 1) a polite and considerate woman 2) in Britain, a title for the wife or daughter of a Lord

lag [lăg] *verb*, to move at a slower pace to stay behind the others

la-goon [lə-gōōn′] *noun*, a shallow body of water near a sea, or pond-like body of water

laid [lād] *past tense* of **lay**

lair [lâr] *noun*, a den, a hole, a hideout for a wild animal

la-i-ty [lā′ĭ-tē] *noun*, someone not connected to the clergy, a layman practicing religion

lake [lāk] *noun*, a body of water with land all around

lamb [lăm] *noun*, a baby sheep

lame [lām] *adjective*, limping or disabled in a hand or joint

la-ment [lə-měnt′] *verb*, to mourn, to express grief or regret

lam-i-nat-ed [lăm′ə-nā′tĭd] *adjective*, arranged in layers of plastic one upon the other

lamp [lămp] *noun*, a device used to project artificial light

lam-poon [lăm-pōon′] *noun*, a cartoon or satire in print

lance [lăns] *noun*, 1) a spear, a harpoon, a javelin, *verb*, 2) to puncture 3) to cut into with a surgical knife

land [lănd] *noun, no plural*, 1) the dry part of the earth, not covered by water 2) a country, region, area, *verb*, 3) to arrive on the ground from the air or water

land-fill [lănd′fĭl′] *noun*, a large outdoor site where solid waste is covered by soil

land-lord [lănd′lôrd′] *noun*, a person who owns a building which he lets others use or live in, in return for money

land-mark [lănd′märk′] *noun*, 1) an achievement, a turning point, benchmark 2) a distinctive building or geographical marker like a bend in the river

land-scape [lănd′skāp′] *noun*, a view of an area with its natural surroundings

lane [lān] *noun*, a short road

lan-guage [lăng′gwĭj] *noun*, 1) any means of conveying or communicating ideas 2) human speech 3) dialect, jargon, vocabulary used by a group

lan-guish [lăng′gwĭsh] *verb*, to lose strength, to weaken

lan-guor [lăng′gər] *noun*, a feeling of depression, nervous exhaustion, weakness of mind or body

lank [lăngk] *adjective*, 1)thin, lean 2) hanging straight or limp

lan-tern [lăn′tərn] *noun*, a portable lamp, with a protective case for lights, carried with a handle often used outdoors for light

lap [lăp] *noun*, 1) the seat created by the legs and chest when sitting 2) the distance once around a track 3) a place of rest, *verb*, 4) to drink water with a tongue, like an animal

lapel [lə-pěl′] *noun*, the flat hanging appendage on a jacket

lapse [lăps] *noun*, 1) an interval of time in which something stops and then starts again 2) termination of policy because of non-payment of premium when due 3) a slip or error

lar-ce-ny [lär′sə-nē] *noun*, taking and carrying away of things, stealing, robbery

lard [lärd] *noun*, grease, fat

large [lärj] *adjective*, greater than average in size, number, etc., immense, big

large-ly [lärj′lē] *adverb*, mostly

lar-ger [lär′jər] *adjective*, bigger

lar-gess [lär-zhěs′] *noun*, the generous giving of gifts

lar-va [lär′və] *noun, plural, **larvae** or **larvas***, the second stage of an insect that goes through complete metamorphosis

laryngitis

lar-yn-gi-tis [lăr′ən-jī′tĭs] *noun*, infection of the larynx or upper end of the windpipe

lar-ynx [lăr′ĭngks] *noun*, the voice organ in the upper throat

la-ser [lā′zər] *noun*, a narrow beam of high-energy light that is all exactly the same color

lash [lăsh] *noun*, 1) a whip, a cane, *verb*, 2) to hit hard 3) to secure something in place with a rope

las-so [lăs′ō] *noun*, 1) a rope with a loop at the end used for catching cattle, *verb*, 2) to catch by throwing the noose of a rope around the neck or torso

last [lăst] *adjective*, 1) the end, final 2) an instance when something happens 3) to come after all others 4) to be a part of for a long time, to endure, *adverb*, 5) to stay in good condition, to be preserved 6) most recently

last-ing [lăs′tĭng] *adjective*, the length of time something continues, enduring

latch [lăch] *noun*, 1) a small bolt used to fasten a door, *verb*, 2) to fasten something shut

late [lāt] *adjective*, 1) after the time agreed on 2) near the end of a day, year, etc. 3) a missed opportunity 4) deceased

late-ly [lāt′lē] *adverb*, recently, a short time ago, not long since

la-tent [lāt′nt] *adjective*, hidden, present but not visible

lat-er [lāt′ər] *adverb*, after a certain amount of time, subsequently

lat-er-al [lăt′ər-əl] *adjective*, coming from the side

lat-est [lā′tĭst] *adjective*, most recent, newest, popular

lath-er [lăth′ər] *noun, no plural*, the bubbles created by soap

lat-i-tude [lăt′ĭ-tōōd′] *noun, no plural*, 1) distance north or south of the equator, indicated by horizontal lines on a map or globe 2) freedom to choose or act

lat-ter [lăt′ər] *adjective*, the second of two things, the last mentioned

laud [lôd] *verb*, to praise, to commend

laugh [lăf] *verb*, to make a sound showing something is funny, to express happiness

laugh-ter [lăf′tər] *noun, no plural*, a giggle, mirth, a chuckle

launch [lônch] *noun*, 1) a small boat propelled by an engine, *verb*, 2) to send off, to put a boat into water or send a space ship into orbit 3) to plunge boldly into action

laun-dry [lôn′drē] *noun*, dirty clothes washed together

lau-rel [lôr′əl] *noun*, an evergreen shrub with pink flowers

la-va [lä′və] *noun*, very hot melted rock that bursts out of a volcano

lav-a-to-ry [lăv′ə-tôr′ē] *noun*, a room with a toilet and a sink

lav-en-der [lăv′ən-dər] *noun*, a fragrant plant with purple flowers, classified as an herb

lav-ish [lăv′ĭsh] *adjective*, 1) extravagant, excessive, 2) giving in great amounts, *verb*, 3) to give generously

law [lô] *noun*, a written rule of conduct made and enforced by the government

law-mak-er [lô′mā′kər] *noun*, a person in government who is part of the legislature

lawn [lôn] *noun*, a piece of ground where grass is grown and is kept short in front of a building

law-yer [lô′yər] *noun*, a professional who practices law, an attorney, barrister

lax-a-tive [lăk′sə-tĭv] *noun*, a medicine or herb that induces a bowel movement

lay [lā] *verb*, 1) to place something in a horizontal position 2) when an adult female produces eggs 3) to remain, to rest

lay-er [lā′ər] *noun*, a covering that is set between two levels

la-zy [lā′zē] *adjective*, disinterested in work, slow-moving, indolent

lead [lĕd] *noun*, 1) a heavy, metallic element, having a bright luster 2) the part of a pencil used for writing, [lēd] *verb*, 3) to guide, to show someone the way

lead-er [lē′dər] *noun*, the chief, the person in charge, the ruler

lead-er-ship [lē′dər-shĭp′] *noun*, the quality of those who take charge or show the way

leaf [lēf] *noun, plural, **leaves**, 1) a green part of a stem that grows off a branch of a plant 2) a sheet of paper

leaf-let [lē′flĭt] *noun*, a brochure or a small sheet of printed matter

league [lēg] *noun*, 1) an association or alliance with other individuals 2) sports teams

organized to compete against each other 3) three nautical miles

leak [lēk] *noun*, 1) a crack or hole through which liquid, gas or light can ooze, *verb*, 2) to let something escape through an unintended opening such as a crack or hole

lean [lēn] *adjective*, 1) thin, without fat, *verb*, 2) to bend or incline toward 3) to rest on something for support to keep from falling, to recline

leap [lēp] *noun*, 1) a jump, *verb*, 2) to jump or spring over a hurdle or through space

leap year *noun*, a year, once every four years, in which February has 29 days instead of 28

learn [lûrn] *verb*, 1) to acquire knowledge or skill through study or experience 2) to find out, to commit to memory

learn-ing [lûr′nĭng] *noun*, knowledge, education

leash [lēsh] *noun*, a restraining device in the form of a rope or cord, chain or strap

least [lēst] *adjective*, the smallest amount, degree or size

leath-er [lĕth′ər] *noun*, skin of a dead animal prepared for use

leave [lēv] *noun*, 1) permission to be absent, *verb*, 2) to go away from, to depart, to exit 3) to allow something to remain untouched 4) to bequeath

lech-er-ous [lĕch′ər-əs] *adjective*, impure in thought and act, lustful, perverted

lectern

lec-tern [lĕk′tərn] *noun*, a podium for public speaking

lec-ture [lĕk′chər] *noun*, 1) a speech on any subject, *verb*, 2) to speak, to talk, to teach

ledge [lĕj] *noun*, a narrow shelf, such as at the bottom of a window, or a narrow, flat piece of rock, on which you can stand

ledg-er [lĕj′ər] *noun*, a book of accounts listing names and debits and credits

left [lĕft] *adjective*, 1) the side of a person or thing that is to the west when facing north, the opposite of the right side, *verb*, 2) the *past tense* of **leave**

leg [lĕg] *noun*, 1) the body part attached to the foot or paw, used for walking 2) one of at least three pieces on a piece of furniture, used to make it stand

leg-a-cy [lĕg′ə-sē] *noun*, a gift of personal property left in a will

le-gal [lē′gəl] *noun*, based upon or in accordance with law

leg-end [lĕj′ənd] *noun*, 1) a story about someone that has no factual basis 2) a description or key accompanying a map or picture 3) an admirable person

leg-er-de-main [lĕj′ər-də-mān′] *noun*, slight of hand, magic

leg-i-ble [lĕj′ə-bəl] *adjective*, capable of being read with ease

le-gion [lē′jən] *noun*, a large group of soldiers, a multitude of people

leg-is-la-ture [lĕj′ĭ-slā′chər] *noun*, persons in a state elected by the people, having power to make, repeal or change laws

le-git-i-mate [lə-jĭt′ə-mĭt] *adjective*, 1) lawful, conforming to accepted standards 2) genuine

leg-ume [leg′yōōm] *noun*, a plant of the pea family grown as a crop

lei-sure [lē′zhər] *noun*, *no plural*, free time from the demand of work or duty, spare time

lem-ming [lĕm′ĭng] *noun*, a small rat-like animal known for its mass migration into the sea

lem-on [lĕm′ən] *noun*, a yellow citrus fruit with a very sour taste, grown in tropical climates

lem-on-ade [lĕm′ə-nād′] *noun*, a beverage of sweetened lemon juice and water

lend [lĕnd] *verb*, 1) to let someone use something for a while, until they return it 2) to offer help

length [lĕngkth] *noun*, 1) the distance from end to end 2) the amount of time

length-en [lĕngk′thən-] *verb*, to make longer, drawn out

le-ni-ent [lē′nē-ənt] *adjective*, mild, merciful, not strict

lens [lĕnz] *noun*, 1) a piece of curved glass or other transparent material by which light rays meet to form an image 2) a part of the eye that focuses light rays to form an image on the retina

leop-ard [lĕp′ərd] *noun*, one of the big cats with a spotted coat, that weighs 100-175 pounds, is seven feet long and lives in Africa

le-sion [lē′zhən] *noun*, a wound, a sore, diseased tissue

less [lĕs] *adjective*, a smaller amount, a reduction

less-en [lĕs′ən] *verb*, to make smaller, to become less

les-son [lĕs′ən] *noun*, something that must be learned or studied

let [lĕt] *verb*, 1) to allow, to permit, to grant 2) to rent, to lease

le-thal [lē′thəl] *adjective*, deadly

le-thar-gy [lĕth′ər-jē] *noun*, fatigue, without energy, feeling tired, drowsy, sluggish

let's [lĕts] the *contraction* of the words **let** and **us**

let-ter [lĕt′ər] *noun*, 1) a message in writing, often sent through the mail 2) one of the characters of the alphabet

let-tuce [lĕt′əs] *noun*, a plant having succulent leaves that are used in salads

lev-ee [lĕv′ē] *noun*, an embankment, dike, dam

lev-el [lĕv′əl] *adjective*, 1) flat, with no higher or lower places, *noun*, 2) a place or position of a particular height, *verb*, 3) to make a surface flat or even

lev-er [lĕv′ər] *noun*, 1) a bar used to exert pressure or sustain weight 2) a means to an end

lev-i-ty [lĕv′ĭ-tē] *noun*, lightness of mind, high spirits, happiness

le-vy [lĕv′ē] *verb*, to put a judgment on property to collect money, to impose a tax

lewd [lōōd] *adjective*, obscene, indecent, lecherous, lustful

lex-i-cog-ra-pher [lĕk′sĭ-kŏg′rə-fər] *noun*, a person who writes dictionaries

lex-i-con [lĕk′sĭ-kŏn′] *noun*, a dictionary, a word list

li-a-bil-i-ty [lī′ə-bĭl′ĭ-tē] *noun*, 1) a responsibility, 2) a monetary obligation, a debt

li-a-ble [lī′ə-bəl] *adjective*, 1) legally responsible 2) likely, prone, inclined, apt

li-ai-son [lē′ā-zŏn′] *noun*, cooperation that facilitates a close working relationship between people or organizations

li-ar [lī′ər] *noun*, someone who does not tell the truth

li-bel [lī′bəl] *noun*, 1) a false statement made about someone

lib-er-al [lĭb′ər-əl] *adjective*, 1) progressive reform 2) generous, ample, abundant

lib-er-ate [lĭb′ə-rāt′] *verb*, to free from constraints, to release

lib-er-a-tion [lĭb′ə-rā′shən] *noun*, freeing, emancipation

lib-er-ty [lĭb′ər-tē] *noun*, freedom, independence from foreign rule

li-bi-do [lĭ-bē′dō] *noun*, emotional urges behind human activity

li-brar-i-an [lī-brâr′ē-ən] *noun*, one who has charge or care of the materials in a library

li-brar-y [lī′brĕr′ē] *noun*, 1) a place where books are kept for reading and research 2) a room or building where books and documents are preserved for future generations

lib-ret-to [lĭ-brĕt′ō] *noun*, the text of an opera or other dramatic musical work

license

li-cense [lī'səns] *noun*, 1) authority given to do any act 2) excess of liberty, *verb*, 3) to authorize

li-cen-tious [lī-sĕn'shəs] *adjective*, unprincipled, unrestrained

li-chen [lī'kən] *noun*, a fungus that grows like algae on rocks and tree bark

lick [lĭk] *noun*, 1) a stroke of the tongue over something *verb*, 2) to touch with the tongue 3) to defeat

lic-o-rice [lĭk'ər-ĭs] *noun*, a dried root, or an extract used in candy

lid [lĭd] *noun*, a cover for a pot or pan, or some other container

lie [lī] *noun*, 1) the intentional statement of an untruth, *verb*, 2) to put oneself in a reclining position 3) to say something that is not true, to fib

lien [lēn] *noun*, a legal claim upon real or personal property

lieu [lōō] *preposition*, in place, as in the phrase "in lieu of"

lieu-ten-ant [lōō-tĕn'ənt] *noun*, 1) a substitute for another in performance of any duty 2) a commissioned officer in the military below captain

life [līf] *noun*, 1) the ability of living organisms to grow and reproduce 2) the period between birth and death

lift [lĭft] *noun*, 1) a free ride in a car or other form of transportation 2) the means by which something is raised, *verb*, 3) to pick up, to raise, to elevate 4) to go up, to ascend

lig-a-ment [lĭg'ə-mənt] *noun*, a tough band of fibrous tissue connecting bones, or to support an organ in place in the body

light [līt] *adjective*, 1) buoyant, not heavy 2) carefree, *noun*, *no plural*, 3) the opposite of darkness, *verb*, 4) to ignite a fire 5) to illuminate, to brighten

light-ning [līt'nĭng] *noun*, *no plural*, flashing of light by electricity discharged from one cloud to another during a storm

like [līk] *adjective*, 1) similar to, equal to, *preposition*, 2) resembling, typical of, *verb*, 3) to enjoy, to find agreeable

like-ly [līk'lē] *adjective*, 1) expected, probable, suitable, *adverb*, 2) probably, certainly

like-ness [līk'nĭs] *noun*, 1) similarity, resemblance, 2) a picture of a person, a portrait

like-wise [līk'wīz'] *adverb*, in the same way, also, similarly

li-lac [lī'lək] *noun*, a shrub in the olive family that has fragrant white or purple flowers

lil-li-pu-tian [lĭl'ə-pyōō'shən] *adjective*, extremely small

lil-y [lĭl'ē] *noun*, a plant with trumpet-like flowers and thick tubular roots

limb [lĭm] *noun*, 1) a part of the body such as an arm or leg or wing 2) the large branch of a tree

lim-ber [lĭm'bər] *adjective*, flexible, elastic, easy to bend

lim-bo [lĭm'bō] *noun*, 1) a place near heaven or hell where certain souls are kept 2) a West Indian dance 3) a state of oblivion

lime [līm] *noun*, a green citrus fruit, similar to a lemon, grown on trees in warm climates

lim-it [lĭm′ĭt] *noun*, 1) that which terminates or confines 2) the full extent, *verb*, 3) to set boundaries, to restrict

lim-i-ta-tion [lĭm′ĭ-tā′shən] *noun*, shortcomings, restriction

lim-ou-sine [lĭm′ə-zēn′] *noun*, a long automobile with many seats and a permanent top

limp [lĭmp] *adjective*, 1) without stiffness, not firm, *noun*, 2) the way you walk when one leg is hurt, *verb*, 3) to walk carefully without putting too much pressure on the leg or foot

lim-pid [lĭm′pĭd] *adjective*, crystal clear, transparent

line [līn] *noun*, 1) the distance between 2 points 2) people or things arranged in a row 3) a business or vocation 4) a streak made with a pencil and ruler 5) a collection of points along a straight path that goes on and on in opposite directions 6) a boundary marker 7) dialogue in performance, *verb*, 8) to put a layer between the container and the product 9) to collect in a row, to watch or wait for something 10) to draw a thin mark

lin-en [lĭn′ən] *noun*, a thread or cloth made of flax

lin-er [lī′nər] *noun*, a first class passenger ship or airplane

lin-ger [lĭng′gər] *verb*, 1) to stay on longer than expected, to dawdle 2) to persist

lin-ge-rie [län′zhə-rā′] *noun*, lacey, silk or cotton underwear worn by women, undergarments

lin-guis-tic [lĭng-gwĭs′tĭk] *adjective*, pertaining to language

lin-i-ment [lĭn′ə-mənt] *noun*, a liquid applied to soothe the skin

lin-ing [lī′nĭng] *noun*, a fold, an overlay that forms a covering

link [lĭngk] *noun*, 1) a connection, a bond, a tie, *verb*, 2) to be joined together, to unite

li-no-le-um [lĭ-nō′lē-əm] *noun*, a washable floor covering having a base of solidified oil on a canvas foundation

lint [lĭnt] *noun*, dirt, dust, fuzz

li-on [lī′ən] *noun*, one of the big cats that lives in Africa

lip [lĭp] *noun*, one of the soft red rims round the mouth

liq-uid [lĭk′wĭd] *adjective*, 1) flowing like water, *noun*, 2) fluid, not solid or gas

liq-ui-date [lĭk′wĭ-dāt′] *verb*, to sell possessions for cash

liq-uor [lĭk′ər] *noun*, any liquid substance, an alcoholic beverage

lisp [lĭsp] *noun*, a speech impediment making it difficult to make an **S** sound

list [lĭst] *noun*, 1) names of different things written down one after another, *verb*, 2) to order things by writing them down in a sequence

lis-ten [lĭs′ən] *verb*, to pay attention to what someone is saying, to heed

list-less [lĭst′lĭs] *adjective*, lacking spirit or energy, languid, tired

lit [lĭt] *past tense* of **light**

lit-a-ny [lĭt′n-ē] *noun*, a prayer in the form of a religious song alternating with the congregation

li-ter [lē′tər] *noun*, a unit in the metric system used to measure liquid equal to 1.057 quarts

lit-er-ac-y [lĭt′ə-r′ə-sē] , *noun* the ability to listen, speak, read, write, view, represent, compute, and solve problems at levels of proficiency necessary to function in the family, in the community, and on the job

li-ter-ate:*adjective,* able to read and write

lit-er-al-ly [lĭt′ər-ə-lē] *adverb*, word for word, as stated, verbatim

lit-er-a-ture [lĭt′ər-ə-chŏŏr′] *noun*, *no plural*, 1) the study of writing and books 2) printed material

lithe [līth] *adjective*, pliable, bendable, limber, supple

lith-i-um [lĭth′ē-əm] *noun*, a soft, silver-white metallic element of the alkali group

lit-i-gant [lĭt′ĭ-gənt] *noun*, a person who wants to sue another

lit-i-ga-tion [lĭt′ĭ-gā′ shən] *noun*, the subject of a lawsuit, any matter before the court or a judge

lit-mus [lĭt′məs] *noun*, a coloring matter obtained from lichens, that is violet-blue, and turns red by an acid, and is restored to blue by an alkali

lit-ter [lĭt′ər] *noun*, 1) newborn baby animals, offspring 2) trash, small pieces of garbage thoughtlessly discarded, *verb*, 3) to throw trash on the ground, not in a garbage can

lit-tle [lĭt′l] *adjective*, 1) a small amount or size 2) a brief period of time

live [līv, lĭv] *adjective*, 1) performed unrehearsed, broadcasted directly 2) full of energy, *verb*, 3) to be, to exist 4) to reside in, to inhabit 5) to be active and to satisfy an ideal

live-li-hood [līv′lē hŏŏd] *noun*, the means of supporting oneself

live-ly [līv′lē] *adverb*, full of energy, very active, full of life

liv-er [lĭv′ər] *noun*, an organ inside the body which cleans the blood

live-stock [līv′stŏk′] *noun*, animals raised on a farm or ranch

liv-id [lĭv′ĭd] *adjective*, 1) angry 2) lead colored, black and blue

liv-ing [lĭv′ĭng] *adjective*, 1) alive, *noun*, 2) a manner of existence

liz-ard [lĭz′ərd] *noun*, a cold blooded reptile with four short legs and a scaly body

lla-ma [lä′mə] *noun*, a South American ruminant animal, related to the camel and raised for its fleecy wool

load [lōd] *noun*, 1) something carried by a person, vehicle or animal 2) a burden, *verb*, 3) to put cargo or materials on a truck or vehicle 4) to fill a gun with ammunition 5) to burden

loaf [lōf] *noun*, 1) the whole amount of bread before it is sliced, *verb*, 2) to take it easy, to idle away time, to waste time

loan [lōn] *noun*, 1) a thing, especially money, lent to another person, *verb*, 2) to let someone borrow something, to lend

loathe [lōth] *verb*, to detest, to feel intense dislike for, to abhor

lob-by [lŏb'ē] *noun*, 1) an entrance way, a foyer, *verb*, 2) to influence, to pressure, to sway

lob-ster [lŏb'stər] *noun*, an edible sea animal with a shell, a tail, and ten legs

lo-cal [lō'kəl] *adjective*, regional, in a confined area or place

lo-cal-i-ty [lō-kăl'ĭ-tē] *noun*, a position, a situation, a place

lo-cate [lō'kāt'] *verb*, to find, to search out, to come across

lo-ca-tion [lō-kā'shən] *noun*, where something is, a certain place

lock [lŏk] *noun*, 1) a device for fastening things like doors that can only be opened or closed with a key or secret code 2) a strand of hair, *verb*, 3) to close and make secure 4) to fasten with a lock

lock-er [lŏk'ər] *noun*, a box often with a lock, for keeping things

lo-co-mo-tive [lō'kə-mō'tĭv] *noun*, a railroad engine that pulls trains

lo-cust [lō'kəst] *noun*, an insect like a grasshopper that travels in swarms and eats plants

lode [lōd] *noun*, vein-like deposit of mineral ore

lodge [lŏj] *noun*, 1) a place to stay where you pay for the service, *verb*, 2) to pay to stay someplace, like a motel or inn

3) to become embedded in something

loft [lôft] *noun*, an upper room, a storage area, an attic

loft-y [lôf'tē] *adjective*, very high

log [lôg, lŏg] *noun*, 1) a piece of wood that was part of the trunk or limb of a tree 2) a book of records, a register of a trip

log-ic [lŏj'ĭk] *noun*, the art of correct reasoning, especially of inference, sound judgment

log-i-cal [lŏj'ĭ-kəl] *adjective*, in a way that is orderly and makes sense, reasonable

lo-go [lō'gō'] *noun*, a slogan or symbol that represents a name

loi-ter [loi'tər] *verb*, to hang around, to linger aimlessly, to proceed slowly, to waste time

loll [lŏl] *verb*, to lounge about

lone [lōn] *adjective*, single, one, standing apart, isolated

lone-li-ness [lōn'lē-nĕs] *noun*, feeling alone, solitude

lone-ly [lōn'lē] *adjective*, 1) a sad, depressing feeling because one is alone 2) desolate, remote

long [lông] *adjective*, 1) measuring a distance from one end to another 2) farther or taller than the others 3) an extended period or time, *adverb*, 4) a time in the distant past 5) conditionally, *verb*, 6) to want something badly, to pine, to yearn

lon-gev-i-ty [lŏn-jĕv'ĭ-tē] *noun*, to live the duration of a long life

long-ing [lông'ĭng] *verb*, desiring, wanting, yearning, craving

lon-gi-tude [lŏn′jĭ-tood′] *noun, no plural,* imaginary lines shown on maps that go from east to west

look [look] *noun,* 1) a glance, a gaze 2) appearance, *verb,* 3) to stare, or glance at 4) to seem or appear 5) to expect, to await

loom [loom] *noun,* 1) a machine used to weave cloth from yarn, *verb,* 2) to hover over 3) likely to will happen in the future

loop [loop] *noun,* a ring made by a rope or string crossing itself

loop-hole [loop′hōl′] *noun,* a way of getting around a law or legal agreement, a means of escape

loose [loos] *adjective,* 1) not fastened tightly or securely 2) free, not confined or shut in

loos-en [loo′sən] *verb,* to become unfastened, to make less tight

loot [loot] *noun,* 1) money or spoils, *verb,* 2) to steal, to rob, to pillage and plunder

lope [lōp] *verb,* to run with long, slow steps, to gallop slowly

lop-sid-ed [lŏp′sī′dĭd] *adjective,* hanging over to one side, uneven

lo-qua-cious [lōkwā′shəs] *adjective,* talkative, chatty, fond of talking

lord [lôrd] *noun,* 1) a person having great power or authority, a master or ruler 2) the title for a judge, bishop, or nobleman

lore [lôr] *noun,* a lesson, a teaching

lose [looz] *verb,* 1) to fail to win 2) to misplace something

loss [lôs] *noun,* 1) damage, injury, ruin 2) deprivation

lost [lôst] *adjective,* 1) confused, bewildered, disoriented 2) wasted 3) the *past tense* of **lose**

lot [lŏt] *noun,* 1) a piece of land or property 2) a large quantity of something 3) a kind or sort

lo-tion [lō′shən] *noun,* a liquid put on the skin to add moisture and make it soft or clean

lot-tery [lŏt′ə-rē] *noun,* a game of gambling in which a prize is given to the person with the matching digits drawn from a pool of numbers

lo-tus [lō′təs] *noun,* a water plant with white, yellow, blue or pink flowers, a water lily

loud [loud] *adjective,* 1) noisy, making or having a loud sound 2) offensively bright colors

Lou-i-si-ana [loo-ē′zē-ăn′ə] *noun,* one of the 50 United States located in the South, the capital is Baton Rouge. The state flower of **Louisiana** is the flower of the magnolia tree, and the motto is "Union, justice, confidence."

lounge [lounj] *noun,* 1) a couch with little or no back 2) a room in a bar where people relax and listen to music, *verb,* 3) to rest or recline comfortably

louse [lous] *noun, plural,* **lice**, a small insect without wings that lives on the skin of animals, birds, and people

lous-y [lou′zē] *adjective,* bad

lov-a-ble [lŭv′ə-bəl] *adjective,* able to be loved, warm, deep feeling

love [lŭv] *noun,* 1) a very strong warm feeling or deep concern for

someone, commitment 2)
darling, sweetheart, *verb*, 3) to
feel passion, or a strong affection
for someone or something

love-ly [lŭv′lē] *adjective*, beautiful,
having pleasing qualities

lov-ing [lŭv′ĭng] *adjective*, showing
affection or fondness

low [lō] *adjective*, 1) close to the
ground, not very high 2) quiet,
not very loud 3) coarse, mean
4) inferior quality

low-er [lou′ər] *adjective*,
1) inferior 2) less 3) under, *verb*,
4) to make something closer to
the ground 5) to diminish the
volume of sound 6) to demean,
to debase in estimation

loy-al [loi′əl] *adjective*, true and
faithful to a person

loy-al-ty [loi′əl-tē] *adjective*,
allegiance, faithfulness

lu-bri-cant [lōō′brĭ-kənt] *noun*,
grease or gear oil

lu-bri-cate [lōō′brĭ-kāt′] *verb*, to
make smooth or slippery

lu-cent [lōō′sənt] *adjective*,
glowing with light, shining

lu-cid [lōō′sĭd] *adjective*, 1) bright,
2) easily understood, clear

luck [lŭk] *noun*, 1) something good
or bad that happens by chance
or accident 2) good fortune

luck-y [lŭk′ē] *adjective*, fortunate

lu-cra-tive [lōō′krə-tĭv] *adjective*,
profitable, money making

lu-cre [lōō′kər] *noun*, money

lu-di-crous [lōō′dĭ-krəs] *adjective*,
funny, ridiculous, absurd

lug-gage [lŭg′ĭj] *noun*, *no plural*,
bags, suitcases, trunks and
traveling accessories, baggage

luke-warm [lōōk′wôrm′] *adjective*,
not very warm, but not cold,
room temperature, tepid

lull [lŭl] *noun*, 1) a quiet interval, a
pause, *verb*, 2) to soothe, to
calm

lull-a-by [lŭl′ə-bī′] *noun*, a soft
song that puts someone to sleep

lum-ba-go [lŭm-bā′gō] *noun*,
rheumatic pain in the loins and
small of the back

lum-ber [lŭm′bər] *noun*, 1) logs or
timber cut into planks or boards,
verb, 2) to move along slowly
and heavily, to plod

lu-mi-nous [lōō′mə-nəs] *adjective*,
1) well lit, bright, radiating light 2)
glowing in the dark

lump [lŭmp] *noun*, 1) a swelling on
the body that becomes a mass
2) a hard form without a special
shape or size, *verb*, 3) to put
together in a pile

lu-nar [lōō′nər] *adjective*, having to
do with the moon

lu-na-tic [lōō′nə-tĭk] *adjective*,
1) crazy, mad, psychotic, *noun*,
2) an insane person

lunch [lŭnch] *noun*, the meal you
eat in the middle of the day

lunch-eon [lŭn′chən] *noun*, a
midday meal enjoyed with others

lung [lŭng] *noun*, one of the two
sac-like organs inside the chest
with which we breathe

lunge [lŭnj] *verb*, to leap, to charge
at someone suddenly

lu-pine [lōō′pən] *noun*, a plant related to peas and beans with tall spikes of flowers

lure [lōōr] *noun*, 1) something appealing, *verb*, 2) to entice, to bait, to attract, to tempt

lu-rid [lōōr′ĭd] *adjective*, horrible, sensational, shocking, gruesome

lurk [lûrk] *verb*, to wait in hiding, to watch someone without their knowledge, to go furtively

lus-cious [lŭsh′əs] *adjective*, appealing to taste or smell

lust [lŭst] *noun*, 1) a strong feeling of wanting something that would be selfish 2) sexual appetite

lus-ter [lŭs′tər] *noun*, shine, brightness, sheen or gloss

lux-u-ri-ous [lŭg-zhōōr′ē-əs] *adjective*, fine and expensive, very nice, sumptuous

lux-u-ry [lŭg′zhə-rē] *noun*, an item that adds to pleasure and comfort

lynch [lĭnch] *verb*, to hang someone in an act of mob violence

lyr-ic [lĭr′ĭk] *noun*, a poem intended to be a song

M

ma-ca-bre [mə-kä′brə] *adjective*, horrible, gruesome, ghastly

mac-a-ro-ni [măk′ə-rō′nē] *noun*, a flour paste dried in long slender tubes, pasta

ma-chet-e [mə-shĕt′ē] *noun*, a long, curved knife used for cutting tall vegetation

mach-i-na-tion [măk′ə-nā′shən] *noun*, a scheme, a plot, or plan

ma-chine [mə-shēn′] *noun*, a device made to consume energy to produce another form of energy to do some kind of work

ma-chin-er-y [mə-shē′nə-rē] *noun*, *no plural*, equipment, devices

mack-er-el [măk′ər-əl] *noun*, a fish found traveling in schools in the North Atlantic

mad [măd] *adjective*, 1) insane, crazy, out of your right mind, reckless 2) angry, enraged

mad-am [măd′əm] *noun*, a respectful way of speaking to or writing to a woman

made [mād] *past tense* of **make**

mad-ri-gal [măd′rĭ-gəl] *noun*, a folk song or ballad of the 16th and 17th century

mael-strom [māl′strəm] *noun*, a powerful whirlpool

maes-tro [mīs′trō] *noun*, an eminent composer, a master

mag-a-zine [măg′ə-zēn′] *noun*, a pamphlet or news summary published periodically

mag-ic [măj′ĭk] *noun*, *no plural*, 1) the art or pretended art of controlling forces through the use of secret charms 2) clever tricks done to outsmart people, using sleight of hand

mag-i-cal [măj′ĭ-kəl] *adjective*, enchanting, marvelous

ma-gi-cian [mə-jĭsh′ən] *noun*, one who uses tricks to do things that seem impossible

mag-is-trate [măj′ĭ-strāt′] *noun*, a public civil officer charged with administering the law, a justice of the peace

mag-nan-i-mous [măg-năn′ə-məs] *adjective*, great of mind, generous and forgiving

mag-nate [măg′nāt′] *noun*, a person of prominence and influence, a tycoon

mag-ne-si-um [măg-nē′zē-əm] *noun*, a ductile silver-white metallic element

mag-net [măg′nĭt] *noun*, 1) a combination of metals that have a force that attract metals like iron 2) something that attracts

mag-net-ic [măg-nĕt′ĭk] *adjective*, 1) possessing the properties of the magnet 2) exerting a moral attractive force or charm

mag-nif-i-cence [măg-nĭf′ĭ-səns] *adjective*, grandeur, splendor

mag-nif-i-cent [măg-nĭf′ĭ-sənt] *adjective*, wonderful, impressive

mag-ni-fy [măg′nə-fī′] *verb*, to increase the size of what you are looking at, to enlarge

mag-ni-fy-ing glass [măg′nə-fī′ĭng glăs] *noun*, a lens that enlarges something small so that it is easier to see

mag-ni-tude [măg′nĭ-tōōd′] *noun*, great in size, or extent

ma-hog-a-ny [mə-hŏg′ə-nē] *noun*, a hard, reddish wood from tropical American trees

maid [mād] *noun*, a female servant

maid-en name [mād′n-nām] *noun*, a woman's last name before she is married

mail [māl] *noun*, letters and packages sent through and delivered by the postal service

maim [mām] *verb*, to injure so that part of the body is useless

main [mān] *adjective*, chief, most important, the center piece

Maine [mān] *noun*, one of the 50 United States located in New England, the capital is Augusta. The state flower of **Maine** is the eastern white pine cone and tassel, and the motto is "Direct or guide."

main-spring [mān′sprĭng′] *noun*, the principal spring in a mechanism, as in a watch

main-stay [mān′stā′] *noun*, 1) pillar, support 2) strength

main-tain [mān-tān′] *verb*, 1) to hold or keep in any particular condition, to preserve 2) to support, to insist

main-te-nance [mān′tə-nəns] *noun, no plural*, support, sustenance, upkeep, preservation

maize [māz] *adjective*, 1) pale yellow, *noun*, 2) corn

ma-jes-ti-cal-ly [mə-jĕs′tĭk-lē] *adverb*, with grandeur and stately dignity, regal

maj-es-ty [măj′ĭ-stē] *noun*, the title of a sovereign power, grandeur

ma-jor [mā′jər] *adjective*, 1) chief, most important, the largest, *noun*, 2) an officer in the military between Captain and Lieutenant Colonel

ma-jor-i-ty [mə-jôr′ĭ-tē] *noun*, the greater number, more than half

make

make [māk] *verb*, 1) to create or produce 2) to force 3) to earn or win 4) to appoint or name

mal-aise [mă-lāz/] *noun*, uneasiness, distress, fatigue

mal-a-prop-ism [măl/ə-prŏp-ĭz/əm] *noun*, comic misuse of a word, *i.e., a verbal agreement isn't worth the paper it is written on*

ma-lar-i-a [mə-lâr/ē-ə] *noun*, a disease produced by the bite of a mosquito causing a fever

male [māl] *adjective*, 1) belonging to men and boys, *noun*, 2) a grown boy, masculine, manly

ma-lev-o-lent [mə-lĕv/ə-lənt] *adjective*, wishing evil or harm

mal-ice [măl/ĭs] *noun*, a desire to inflict bad feelings on another

ma-lign [mə-līn/] *verb*, to say bad things about someone

ma-lig-nant [mə-lĭg/nənt] *adjective*, tending or threatening to produce death as a tumor

mall [môl] *noun*, a public walk, a marketplace, a shopping center

mal-le-a-ble [măl/ē-ə-bəl] *adjective*, 1) capable of being extended or shaped by beating with a hammer 2) easy to influence

mal-let [măl/ĭt] *noun*, a stick, a club, a hammer-like tool

mal-nu-tri-tion [măl/nōō-trĭsh/ən] *noun*, *no plural*, undernourishment caused by poor diet

mam-mal [măm/əl] *noun*, any warm-blooded vertebrate that nurses its young

mam-moth [măm/əth] *adjective*, very large, gigantic, huge

man [măn] *noun*, *plural*, **men**, 1) a full grown male person 2) speaking of mankind in general *verb*, 3) to supply with people

man-age [măn/ĭj] *verb*, 1) to succeed in getting something done, to reach a goal 2) to control or have power over something 3) to function

man-age-a-ble [măn/-ĭ-jə-bəl] *adjective*, governable, submitting to control

man-age-ment [măn/ĭj-mənt] *noun*, people who manage any enterprise, an administration

man-ag-er [măn/ĭ-jər] *noun*, a person who looks after and directs the activities of a business, a supervisor

man-date [măn/dāt/] *noun*, an order, a command

man-da-to-ry [măn/də-tôr/ē] *adjective*, required, imperative

man-drel [măn/drəl] *noun*, an axis inserted to support something

mane [mān] *noun*, the long hair on the back of the neck of an animal, such as a horse or lion

ma-neu-ver [mə-nōō/vər] *noun*, 1) a military movement 2) a scheme or manipulation, *verb*, 3) to move in a skillful way

mange [mānj] *noun*, a contagious skin disease of animals marked by itching and hair loss

man-go [măng/gō] *noun*, a juicy fruit with a large seed that grows on a tree in tropical climates

ma-ni-ac [mā'nē-ăk'] *noun*, a madman, an insane person

man-i-cure [măn'ĭ-kyoōr'] *noun*, a grooming of hands and fingernails

man-i-fest [măn'ə-fĕst'] *adjective*, 1) something obvious or clear, *noun*, 2) an invoice of a ship's, or truck's, or plane's cargo, *verb*, 3) to show, to display, to reveal

man-i-fes-to [măn'ə-fĕs'tō] *noun*, a statement of policy and plans

man-i-fold [măn'ə-fōld'] *adjective*, having many and various kinds or features

ma-nip-u-late [mə-nĭp'yə-lāt'] *verb*, 1) to treat or work with the hands 2) to control the action of something by management

man-kind [măn'kīnd'] *noun*, no plural, all human beings

man-ner [măn'ər] *noun*, 1) the way in which something is done or happens, prevailing customs *plural*, 2) ways of behaving in social situations

man-or [măn'ər] *noun*, a large house, a mansion,

man-sion [măn'shən] *noun*, a large, impressive house, a castle

man-tel [măn'tl] *noun*, 1) the shelf above a fireplace 2) the earth's interior layer between the crust and the core

man-u-al [măn'yoō-əl] *adjective*, 1) done by hand, *noun*, 2) an instruction guide

man-u-fac-ture [măn'yə-făk'chər] *verb*, to assemble parts into a product in a factory

ma-nure [mə-noōr'] *noun*, livestock excrement

man-u-script [măn'yə-skrĭpt'] *noun*, a copy of a work intended for publication

man-y [mĕn'ē] *adjective*, containing a large number of something

map [măp] *noun*, 1) a representation of the physical features of the earth, *verb*, 2) to plan, to chart, to outline

ma-ple [mā'pəl] *noun*, a hardwood tree that produces sweet sap, boiled into syrup

mar [mär] *verb*, to damage, to hurt, to disfigure, to impair, to injure

mar-ble [mär'bəl] *noun*, no plural, 1) a hard stone that polishes well, used in buildings 2) a small glass or stone ball used in a game

March [märch] *noun*, the third month of the year, having 31 days

march [märch] *noun*, 1) the distance of a walk using regular steps 2) a piece of music to which soldiers walk, *verb*, 3) to walk with measured steps, to advance in this manner

mare [mâr] *noun*, a female horse

mar-ga-rine [mär'jər-ĭn] *noun*, no plural, a butter substitute made from vegetable oils

mar-gin [mär'jĭn] *noun*, 1) the border of empty space around the text on paper 2) a deposit of a portion of the value of stocks or bonds

mar-gin-al [mär'jə-nəl] *adjective*, borderline, passable

marigold

mar-i-gold [măr′ĭ-gōld′] *noun*, a yellow or orange flower that is a member of the daisy family

ma-rine [mə-rēn′] *noun*, having to do with the sea

mar-i-on-ette [măr′ē-ə-nĕt′] *noun*, a puppet manipulated by strings

mar-i-time [măr′ĭ-tīm′] *adjective*, bordering on the sea, nautical

mark [märk] *noun*, 1) a spot or a scratch, imprint 2) a point or the total of points indicating how one has scored on an examination or in a class 3) a distinguishing feature, *verb*, 4) to indicate a line or boundary 5) to leave a spot or write something 6) to distinguish

mar-ket [mär′kĭt] *noun*, 1) a store, an outlet, a shop 2) supply and demand, commodity market, *verb*, 3) to develop ways to sell a product by making it attractive

mar-ma-lade [mär′mə-lād′] *noun*, a preserve or jam made of the pulp and rind of fruit

ma-roon [mə-roon′] *verb*, to leave someone isolated

mar-riage [măr′ĭj] *noun*, a wedding ceremony, the state of being married

mar-row [măr′ō] *noun*, soft tissue filling in cavities of bones

mar-ry [măr′ē] *verb*, to take someone as a husband or wife

marsh [märsh] *noun*, a low, wet place where the ground is damp and swampy, a bog

mar-shal [mär′shəl] *noun*, 1) the master of ceremonies of a parade or an event 2) an officer of justice similar to a sheriff, *verb*, 3) to manage, to direct

mar-su-pi-al [mär-soo′pē-əl] *noun*, animals that nurse their offspring in a pouch

mar-tial [mär′shəl] *adjective*, pertaining to military affairs, war or battle, inclined to war

mar-tyr [mär′tər] *noun*, one who suffers persecution, torture or death for a cause or beliefs

mar-vel [mär′vəl] *noun*, 1) something that is remarkable or exciting, *verb*, 2) to be filled with wonder or astonishment

mar-vel-ous [mär′və-ləs] *adjective*, astonishing, causing wonder

Mary-land [mĕr′ə-lənd] *noun*, one of the 50 United States located on the East Coast, the capital is Annapolis. The state flower of **Maryland** is the black-eyed susan and the motto is "Manly deeds, womanly words."

mas-cot [măs′kŏt′] *noun*, an animal or person that represents a school, team, or other group

mas-cu-line [măs′kyə-lĭn] *adjective*, of or pertaining to the male sex, manly

mash [măsh] *verb*, to make into a pulpy mass or mush

mask [măsk] *noun*, 1) a covering that hides a face or its expressions *verb*, 2) to disguise or hide, to cover, to conceal

ma-son [mā′sən] *noun*, a person who builds with brick, stone, etc.

mas-quer-ade [măs′kə-rād′] *noun*, 1) a party at which people wear masks and sometimes costumes, *verb*, 2) to dress in costume, to wear a disguise, to conceal

mass [măs] *noun*, 1) a quantity or amount of something with no particular shape or number 2) the quantity of matter that a body contains as measured by the force of gravity on it 3) a large gathering of people 4) in the Catholic church the celebration of the Eucharist

Mas-sa-chu-setts [măs′ə-chōō′sĭts] *noun*, one of the 50 United States, located on the East Coast, the capital is Boston. The state flower of **Massachusetts** is the mayflower, and the motto is "By the sword we seek peace, but peace only under liberty."

mas-sa-cre [măs′ə-kər] *noun*, 1) the killing of many defenseless people, *verb*, 2) to murder a large number of people

mas-sage [mə-säzh′] *noun*, 1) a rubdown, kneading of the body with the hands, *verb*, 2) to rub to stimulate circulation, to caress

mas-sive [măs′ĭv] *adjective*, heavy, weighty, consisting of a large amount, immense, huge

mast [măst] *noun*, a tall pole that holds up a ship's sail

mas-ter [măs′tər] *noun*, 1) an accomplished artist, a teacher , one in control 2) the title of address in front of a boy's name, *verb*, 3) to accomplish a difficult task

mas-ter-piece [măs′tər-pēs′] *noun*, a fine example of skill or excellence

mat [măt] *noun*, 1) a floor covering made of straw, rubber, vinyl, etc. 2) a tangled hair mass

match [măch] *noun*, 1) a slender piece of wood or cardboard tipped with a flammable mixture 2) a sports contest, 3) a person or thing equal to another, *verb*, 4) to sort similar objects, to pair up

mate [māt] *noun*, 1) an associate, one of a male and female pair of animals, birds, etc., *verb*, 3) to bring together a male and female animal to reproduce

ma-te-ri-al [mə-tîr′ē-əl] *adjective*, 1) pertaining to or composed of matter 2) of consequence, substantial, *noun* 3) data 4) cloth, the fabric something is made of 5) possessions, real things not spiritual things

ma-te-ri-al-ize [mə-tîr′ē-ə-līz′] *verb*, to take form, to emerge

ma-ter-nal [mə-tûr′nəl] *adjective*, motherly, relating to a mother

ma-ter-ni-ty [mə-tûr′nĭ-tē] *noun*, motherhood, the time during pregnancy, or for a mother to care for a newborn infant

math-e-mat-ics [măth′ə-măt′ĭks] *noun*, *plural*, the study of numbers, arithmetic

ma-tin-ee [măt′n-ā′] *noun*, an afternoon theater performance

ma-tri-arch [mā′trē-ärk′] *noun*, the woman who rules a family or social group, clan or tribe

mat-ri-mo-ny [măt′rə-mō′nē] *noun*, marriage, wedlock

ma-trix [mā′trĭks] *noun*, 1) an environment from which

something develops or originates 2) a mold or die

mat-ter [măt′ər] *noun, no plural,* 1) the substance of which something is made 2) a situation or affair *verb,* 3) to be of importance, to signify

mat-tress [măt′rĭs] *noun,* a stuffed cushion to sleep on

ma-ture [mə-tyŏŏr′] *adjective,* fully grown or developed, adult

ma-tu-ri-ty [mə-tyŏŏr′ĭ-tē] *noun,* adulthood, full development

maud-lin [môd′lĭn] *adjective,* tearfully sentimental

maul [môl] *verb,* to handle roughly, to lacerate

mau-so-le-um [mô′sə-lē′əm] *noun,* a stately tomb, an above ground structure for burials

mav-er-ick [măv′ər-ĭk] *noun,* a rebel, a nonconformist

max-im [măk′sĭm] *noun,* a proverb, wise words

max-i-mum [măk′sə-məm] *adjective,* 1) greatest attainable, most, *noun,* 2) the largest amount possible

May [mā] *noun,* the fifth month of the year, having 31 days

may [mā] *verb,* 1) used to show that something is possible 2) to be allowed or permitted to 3) showing a hope that something will happen

may-be [mā′bē] *adverb,* perhaps, possibly

may-hem [mā′hĕm′] *noun,* commotion, disturbance

may-on-naise [mā′ə-nāz′] *noun,* a dressing for salad or

sandwiches, usually made from eggs and oil

may-or [mā′ər, mâr] *noun,* the chief magistrate and leader of a city or town

me [mē] *pronoun,* the form of "I" used as an object, used by a speaker to refer to himself or herself

mead-ow [mĕd′ō] *noun,* a field of grass or flowers, grassland

mea-ger [mē′gər] *adjective,* small in amount, scant

meal [mēl] *noun,* food served and eaten, the occasion for eating

mean [mēn] *adjective,* 1) unkind, cruel, uncaring 2) the middle, *verb,* 3) to be the same as, to have as a definition 4) to intend to do something 5) to denote

me-an-der [mē-ăn′dər] *verb,* to wander around, to follow a path with twists and turns

mean-ing [mē′nĭng] *noun,* 1) the definition of a word 2) the significance of an action , signs or symbols

means [mēnz] *noun, plural,* resources that help us to do what we want to do, wealth

meant [mĕnt] *verb, past tense* of **mean**

mean-while [mēn′hwīl′] *adverb,* at the same time

mea-sles [mē′zəlz] *noun, plural,* a contagious disease marked by distinct red circular spots, accompanied by a fever

meas-ure [mĕzh′ər] *noun,* 1) a standard or test 2) dimension, size, capacity 3) step, action, proceeding, maneuver, *verb,*

4) to take measurements, to gauge, to scale, to calibrate

meas-ure-ment [mĕzh′ər-mənt] *noun*, the size, weight, distance, mass, etc. of something

meat [mēt] *noun*, the parts of an animal's body used as food

me-chan-ic [mĭ-kăn′ĭk] *noun*, 1) one who repairs cars or other machines, 2) *plural,* **mechanics**, the inner workings or things, the study of how machines work

mech-an-ism [mĕk′ə-nĭz′əm] *noun*, 1) the parts of a machine taken collectively 2) any system that works like a machine

med-al [mĕd′l] *noun*, a small, award, often embossed, given for achievement

med-dle [mĕd′l] *verb*, to interfere

me-di-a [mē′dē-ə] *plural, noun*, see **medium**

me-di-an [mē′dē-ən] *adjective*, 1) halfway, central, *noun*, 2) the middle, center, mid-point

me-di-ate [mē′dē-āt′] *verb*, to settle a dispute as an impartial third party

med-i-cal [mĕd′ĭ-kəl] *adjective*, healing, therapeutic

me-dic-i-nal [mĭ-dĭs′ə-nəl] *adjective*, having properties that cure disease or sickness

med-i-cine [mĕd′ĭ-sĭn] *noun*, 1) the study and treatment of illness 2) a remedy to treat disease and restore good health

me-di-e-val [mē′dē-ē′vəl] *adjective*, characteristic of the Middle Ages from about the fifth to the fifteenth centuries

me-di-oc-ri-ty [mē′dē-ŏk′rĭ-tē] *noun*, the average, commonplace, ordinary

med-i-tate [mĕd′ĭ-tāt′] *verb*, to think deeply

med-i-ta-tion [mĕd′ĭ-tā′shən] *noun*, deep, solemn reflection

me-di-um [mē′dē-əm] *adjective*, 1) sized between large and small, *noun*, 2) conditions, the environment 3) a means to communicate with the dead *plural*, **media**, 4) a network of communication such as television, radio, newspapers, etc. that reaches the public

med-ley [mĕd′lē] *noun*, a mixture

meek [mēk] *adjective*, humble, gentle, patient, quiet

meet [mēt] *verb*, to come face to face, to approach, to encounter

meet-ing [mē′tĭng] *noun*, 1) a gathering to discuss an issue or idea 2) point of contact

meg-a-phone [mĕg′ə-fōn′] *noun*, a cone or electric device that amplifies the sound of a voice

mel-an-chol-y [mĕl′ən-kŏl′ē] *adjective*, 1) filled with sorrow, very sad, *noun*, 2) a feeling of sadness characterized by depression

mel-low [mĕl′ō] *adjective*, 1) good-natured, relaxed, *verb*, 2) to soften with maturity

mel-o-dy [mĕl′ə-dē] *noun*, a harmonious tune, music

mel-on [mĕl′ən] *noun*, a large juicy fruit growing on vines

melt [mĕlt] *verb*, to change to a liquid state by applying heat

member

mem-ber [mĕm'bər] *noun*, 1) one of the limbs of the body, such as a leg, arm, hand, etc. 2) a part of a group, a component 3) one that belongs to a certain group

mem-ber-ship [mĕm'bər-shĭp'] *noun*, the state of belonging to a certain group

mem-brane [mĕm'brān'] *noun*, a thin piece or layer of animal or vegetable tissue that serves to cover separate cells, organs, etc.

me-men-to [mə-mĕn'tō] *noun*, a token as a reminder, a souvenir

mem-oir [mĕm'wär', -wôr'] *noun*, an autobiography

mem-o-ra-ble [mĕm'ər-ə-bəl] *adjective*, worthy of remembrance, remarkable

mem-o-ran-dum [mĕm'ə-răn'dəm] *noun*, a note made as a reminder, a written message, a memo

me-mo-ri-al [mə-môr'ē-əl] *noun*, a monument, a marker, a statue

mem-o-rize [mĕm'ə-rīz'] *verb*, to commit to memory, to learn by heart, to remember exactly

mem-o-ry [mĕm'ə-rē] *noun*, something a person remembers, the ability to remember

men-ace [mĕn'ĭs] *noun*, a danger

me-nag-er-ie [mə-năj'ə-rē] *noun*, a varied group or collection of animals, persons, or things that are strange, odd, or startling

mend [mĕnd] *verb*, 1) to repair or fix, to sew a tear, or patch a hole 2) to heal, to improve, to recover from illness 3) to set right a dispute

me-ni-al [mē'nē-əl] *adjective*, suitable for servants, low

men-in-gi-tis [mĕn'ĭn-jī'tĭs] *noun*, an infection of the three membranes that envelop the brain and spinal cord, that could be fatal

men-tal [mĕn'tl] *adjective*, of or existing in the mind

men-tal-ly [mĕn'tl-lē] *adverb*, in or using the mind, intellectually

men-tion [mĕn'shən] *noun*, 1) a reference, a notice, *verb*, 2) to remark, to refer to briefly

men-tor [mĕn'tôr'] *noun*, a trusted teacher, a wise counselor

men-u [mĕn'yōō] *noun*, 1) a list indicating the choice of meals at a restaurant 2) a list of options in a computer program

mer-chan-dise [mûr'chən-dīz'] *noun*, 1) commodities, wares, goods, *verb*, 2) to sell, to promote, to market

mer-chant [mûr'chənt] *noun*, a person who buys and sells goods

mer-ci-ful [mûr'sĭ-fəl] *adjective*, compassionate, kind-hearted

mer-ci-less [mûr'sĭ-lĭs] *adjective*, cruel, unkind, showing no compassion, inhumane

mer-cu-ry [mûr'kyŏŏrē] *noun, no plural,* a heavy, silver-white metallic chemical element, liquid at ordinary temperatures

mer-cy [mûr's *noun*, the act of sparing someone punishment shown to an offender or enemy

mere [mîr] *adjective*, not more than what is specified, only

mere-ly [mîr'lē] *adverb*, simply, hardly, barely

merge [mûrj] *verb*, to combine into one, to blend gradually

me-rid-i-an [mə-rĭd'ē-ən] *noun*, an imaginary great circle on the surface of the earth, passing through the poles and any given place on the earth's surface

mer-it [mĕr'ĭt] *noun*, 1) worth, good qualities, *verb*, 2) to deserve

mer-maid [mûr'mād'] *noun*, a mythical creature that lives in the water, having the head and torso of a woman and the tail of a fish

mer-ry [mĕr'ē] *adjective*, happy, full of laughter, joyful

me-sa [mā'sə] *noun*, a flat-topped hill with steep sides, common in dry areas

mesh [mĕsh] *noun*, 1) a net-like material of cords or wires that interlock with spaces between them, like a screen, *verb*, 2) to blend, to intertwine

mes-mer-ize [mĕz'mə-rīz'] *verb*, to hypnotize, to spellbind

mess [mĕs] *noun*, 1) many things mixed up, a jumble, *verb*, 2) to make something dirty or untidy 3) to make a muddle of

mes-sage [mĕs'ĭj] *noun*, 1) a letter or note 2) a communication transmitted from one person to another 3) a central theme

mes-sen-ger [mĕs'ən-jər] *noun*, one who does an errand, a carrier

mes-sy [mĕs'ē] *adjective*, untidy

met [mĕt] *past tense* of **meet**

me-tab-o-lism [mĭ-tăb'ə-lĭz'əm] *noun*, the chemical and physical changes in living cells that process energy in the body

met-al [mĕt'l] *noun*, 1) a chemical element such as silver or gold, or any combination of metals, such as brass, copper, or nickel

met-al-lic [mə-tăl'ĭk] *adjective*, resembling, pertaining to or consisting of metal

meta-mor-phic [mĕt'ə-môr'fĭk] *adjective*, changed in form

met-a-mor-pho-sis [mĕt'ə-môr'fə-sĭs] *noun*, a change from one form of development or shape into another

met-a-phor [mĕt'ə-fôr'] *noun*, a figure of speech in which one thing is spoken of in terms of another, *i.e., the road was a ribbon of moonlight…*

met-a-phys-ics [mĕt'ə-fĭz'ĭks] *noun*, speculative philosophy

me-te-or [mē'tē-ər'] *noun*, a fragment of solid matter that enters the earth's atmosphere and burns, leaving a bright streak in the sky

me-te-or-ite [mē'tē-ə-rīt'] *noun*, the metallic or stony remains of a body that has entered the earth's atmosphere

me-te-or-ol-o-gist [mē'tē-ə-rŏl'ə-jĭst] *noun*, a person who studies the weather

me-ter [mē'tər] *noun*, 1) a machine used for measuring 2) a measure of length equal to 100 centimeters or approximately 39 inches 3) the rhythm in a poem

method

meth-od [mĕth′əd] *noun*, a process or system used to do something

me-thod-i-cal [mə-thŏd′ĭ-kəl] *adjective*, systematic, orderly

Me-tho-dist [mə-thŏdĭst] *noun*, a member of the Protestant Christian denomination that developed from the teachings of John and Charles Wesley

me-tic-u-lous [mĭ-tĭk′yə-ləs] *adjective*, extremely careful

met-ric sys-tem *noun*, a system that measures length in centimeters, meters, and kilometers; capacity in liters, mass in grams and kilograms; temperature in degrees Celsius

me-trop-o-lis [mĭ-trŏp′ə-lĭs] *noun*, the chief city of a country, state or region, an urban center

met-tle [mĕt′l] *noun*, courage, spirit, fortitude, character

Mich-i-gan [mĭsh′ĭ-gən] *noun*, one of the 50 United States, located in the North, the capital is Lansing. The state flower of **Michigan** is the apple blossom and the motto is "If you seek a pleasant peninsula, look about you."

mi-cro-cosm [mī′krə-kŏz′əm] *noun*, a small world

mi-cro-or-gan-ism [mī′krō-ôr′gə-nĭz′əm] *noun*, an animal , bacterium, plant, or virus that can only be seen with a microscope

mi-cro-phone [mī′krə-fōn′] *noun*, a device that converts sounds into electrical energy signals that can then be amplified

mi-cro-scope [mī′krə-skōp′] *noun*, an optical instrument with a lens that makes it possible to see things too small to be seen with the naked eye

mi-cro-scop-ic [mī′krə-skŏp′ĭk] *adjective*, too small to be seen with a naked eye

mid [mĭd] *adjective*, halfway

mid-dle [mĭd′l] *adjective*, 1) halfway between two points, median, central, *noun*, 2) the center, the point equally distant from two sides

mid-get [mĭj′ĭt] *noun*, a small person who is fully mature

mid-night [mĭd′nīt′] *noun*, 12 o'clock at night

midst [mĭdst, mĭtst] *noun*, the middle, the central point

might [mīt] *noun*, *no plural*, 1) strength or force, *verb*, 2) *past tense* of **may**

might-y [mī′tē] *adjective*, strong, powerful, important, great

mi-grant [mī′grənt] *adjective*, one who travels from place to place in search of work

mi-grate [mī′grāt′] *verb*, 1) to move from one land to settle in another 2) to make a journey each year from one place to another at the same time of year

mi-gra-tion [mī-grā′shən] *noun*, movement to leave one area to live in another

mild [mīld] *adjective*, 1) gentle in feeling 2) not severe or extreme

mile [mīl] *noun*, a measure of length equal to 5,280 feet, 1,760 yards, or 1.6 kilometers

mile-age [mī′lĭj] *noun*, 1) an allowance for the cost per mile traveled 2) the total amount of miles traveled in a given time

mile-stone [mīl′stōn′] *noun*, a turning point, a great achievement or significant event

mil-i-tant [mĭl′ĭ-tənt] *adjective*, 1) warlike, combative, *noun*, 2) a revolutionary, a violent objector, a terrorist

mil-i-tar-y [mĭl′ĭ-tĕr′ē] *noun*, the armed forces of a country

milk [mĭlk] *noun*, 1) the liquid produced by a female mammal to feed her young, *verb*, 2) to force milk from a female mammal

mill [mĭl] *noun*, a building or group of buildings in which resources such as lumber, cotton, corn and steel, are processed

mil-len-ni-um [mə-lĕn′ē-əm] *noun*, a span of one thousand years

mil-li-liter [mĭl′ə-lē′tər] *noun*, a liquid measure equal to 1/1000 of a liter, or less than .04 fluid ounces

mil-li-me-ter [mĭl′ə-mē′tər] *noun*, a measure of length, 1/1000 of a meter, or about .04 inches

mil-lion [mĭl′yən] *noun*, ten times one hundred thousand, 1,000,000

mil-lion-aire [mĭl′yə-nâr′] *noun*, a person whose property and assets total $1,000,000

mime [mīm] *noun*, 1) a performer who only uses motion and facial expression, but no voice, to communicate, *verb*, 2) to use actions instead of speech to communicate

mim-e-o-graph [mĭm′ē-ə-grăf′] *noun*, a stenciling copying device fed by an ink drum

mim-ic [mĭm′ĭk] *verb*, to copy or repeat what someone does or says, to imitate playfully

mim-ic-ry [mĭm′ĭ-krē] *noun*, an imitation, an impersonation

min-a-ret [mĭn′ə-rĕt′] *noun*, a lofty slender tower attached to a mosque

mince [mĭns] *verb*, 1) to cut into very small pieces 2) to moderate or restrain words

mind [mīnd] *noun*, 1) thoughts, a person's reason or way of feeling, *verb*, 2) to watch over, to pay attention to, to obey

mine [mīn] *noun*, 1) a large hole or tunnel deep in the ground made to reach and remove metals or other natural resources from the earth, *pronoun*, 2) something that belongs to the person who is speaking, *verb*, 3) digging into land to remove metal ore or other valuable resources

min-er-al [mĭn′ər-əl] *noun*, any inorganic substance occurring naturally in the earth

min-gle [mĭng′gəl] *verb*, to join or mix together, to blend

min-i-a-ture [mĭn′ē-ə-choͦr′] *adjective*, 1) very small, done on a small scale, *noun*, 2) a very small painting, especially a portrait

min-i-mum [mĭn′ə-məm] *adjective*, 1) smallest, *noun*, 2) the least

minister

quantity possible or allowable in a given case

min-is-ter [mĭn′ĭ-stər] *noun*, 1) the head of a government department in some countries 2) a representative to a foreign country ranking under an ambassador 3) a Christian member of the clergy, *verb*, 4) to give help to someone, to care for, to serve, to attend

min-is-try [mĭn′ĭ-strē] *noun*, 1) a department of government headed by a minister 2) the work of the clergy 3) the act of serving

Min-ne-so-ta [mĭn′ĭ-sō′tə] *noun*, one of the 50 United States located in the North, the capital is St. Paul. The state flower of **Minnesota**, is the pink and white lady slipper and the motto is, "The star of the north."

min-now [mĭn′ō] *noun*, a small fish

mi-nor [mī′nər] *adjective*, 1) smaller, not very important *noun*, 2) a person younger than the legal age

mi-nor-i-ty [mə-nôr′ĭ-tē] *noun*, a number, part or amount forming less than half of a whole

mint [mĭnt] *noun*, 1) a large amount of money 2) any of the plants of the mint family, used to flavor food, gum, etc. 3) a candy

mi-nus [mī′nəs] *preposition*, less

min-ute [mĭn′ĭt] *adjective*, 1) very small, *noun*, 2) a period of time equal to sixty seconds

mi-nu-ti-a [mĭ-nōō′shē-ə] *noun*, *plural*, **minutiae**, very small, petty details, trifling matters

mir-a-cle [mĭr′ə-kəl] *noun*, an occurrence that is unusual and goes beyond the laws of nature

mi-rac-u-lous [mĭ-răk′yə-ləs] *adjective*, supernatural, awesome, incredible

mi-rage [mĭ-räzh′] *noun*, an unreal reflection, an optical illusion

mire [mīr] *noun*, 1) a bog, a swamp, *verb*, 2) to immerse in swampy ground, to entangle

mir-ror [mĭr′ər] *noun*, 1) a looking glass in which one can see reflections 2) something that reflects

mirth [mûrth] *noun*, laughter, glee

mis-be-have [mĭs′bĭ-hāv′] *verb*, to behave badly, to be disruptive

mis-cel-la-ne-ous [mĭs′ə-lā′nē-əs] *adjective*, consisting of several different kinds, mixed, various

mis-chief [mĭs′chĭf] *noun*, an annoying action on the part of a person, havoc, harm or damage

mis-chie-vous [mĭs′chə-vəs] *adjective*, causing petty injury or annoyance to others

mis-con-cep-tion [mĭs′kən-sĕp′shən] *noun*, a misunderstanding, a mistake

mis-con-duct [mĭs-kŏn′dŭkt] *noun*, wrongdoing, improper behavior

mis-con-strue [mĭs′kən-strōō′] *verb*, to misunderstand

mis-cre-ant [mĭs′krē-ənt] *noun*, an evil person, a lawbreaker

mis-de-mean-or [mĭs′dĭ-mē′nər] *noun*, a crime less than a felony, any minor misdeed

212

mi-ser [mī′zər] *noun*, a tightwad, one who hoards money

mis-er-a-ble [mĭz′ər-ə-bəl] *adjective*, unhappy, causing misery

mis-er-y [mĭz′ə-rē] *noun*, great unhappiness, or distress

mis-for-tune [mĭs-fôr′chən] *noun*, bad luck, something bad that happens, an unlucky event

mis-giv-ing [mĭs-gĭv′ĭng] *noun*, a feeling of worry, doubt about a future event, apprehension

mis-hap [mĭs′hăp′] *noun*, an unfortunate accident

mis-in-ter-pret [mĭs′ĭn-tûr′prĭt] *verb*, to confuse, to mistake

mis-judge [mĭs-jŭj′] *verb*, to mistake, to underestimate

mis-lead [mĭs-lēd′] *verb*, to lead astray, to deceive, to lie

mis-lead-ing [mĭs-lē′dĭng] *adjective*, deceptive, vague, unclear, not accurate

mis-no-mer [mĭs-no′mər] *noun*, the wrong name, an incorrect identification

mis-place [mĭs-plās′] *verb*, to lose temporarily, to mislay

Miss [mĭs] *noun*, the title before the name of an unmarried woman

miss [mĭs] *noun*, 1) a failure, an error, a slip, *verb*, 2) to fail to make the most of an opportunity or moment 3) to notice someone's absence, to feel sad someone is gone 4) to avoid, to fail to hit, to escape 5) to omit

mis-sile [mĭs′əl] *noun*, a weapon capable of being hurled

mis-sion [mĭsh′ən] *noun*, a special service, task or duty

mis-sion-ar-y [mĭsh′ə-něr′ē] *noun*, one whose work is to teach others about his religion

Mis-sis-sip-pi [mĭs′ĭ-sĭp′ē] *noun*, one of the 50 United States, located in the South, the capital is Jackson. The state flower of **Mississippi** is the magnolia blossom, and the motto is "By valor and arms."

mis-sive [mĭs′ĭv] *noun*, a letter

Mis-sou-ri [mĭ-zŏŏr′ē] *noun*, one of the 50 Unieted States, located in the Midwest, the capital is Jefferson City. The state flower of **Missouri** is the hawthorn, and the motto is: "Let the welfare of the people be the supreme law."

mis-spell [mĭs-spĕl′] *verb*, to spell incorrectly

mist [mĭst] *noun*, a thin cloud of fine droplets of water vapor or fog near the ground

mis-take [mĭ-stāk′] *noun*, an error, the wrong answer or action

Mis-ter [mĭs′tər] *noun*, a title for a man, abbreviated, 'Mr.'

mis-tle-toe [mĭs′əl-tō′] *noun*, a plant that lives off another, with evergreen leaves and white berries used at Christmas for decoration

mis-tress [mĭs′trĭs] *noun*, a woman who has control over others

mis-trust [mĭs-trŭst′] *noun*, 1) suspicion, uncertainty, doubt, lack of confidence, *verb*, 2) to doubt, to question, to challenge

mist-y [mĭs/tē] *adjective*, hazy, damp, and foggy, consisting of a mass of fine droplets of water vapor in the atmosphere

mis-un-der-stand [mĭs′-ŭn-dər-stănd/] *verb*, to misconstrue, to mistake

mite [mīt] *noun*, 1) a small amount 2) a small, usually parasitic arachnid, related to the tick

mi-ter [mī/tər] *verb*, to bevel the ends for the purpose of matching together, as a picture frame

mitt [mĭt] *noun*, a baseball glove with padding to protect the hand

mit-ten [mĭt/n] *noun*, a glove with a section for covering the thumb and a larger section to cover all four fingers

mix [mĭks] *verb*, to combine different things to make one

mix-ture [mĭks/chər] *noun*, a combination of different substances

moan [mōn] *verb*, to make a sound of pain or suffering, to complain

mob [mŏb] *noun*, a crowd, a horde

mo-bile [mō/bəl, *adjective* 1) moveable, portable, [mō′-bīl/] *noun*, 2) objects attached by a wire that move airily

mo-bi-lize [mō/bə-līz′] *verb*, to put into action, to move

moc-ca-sin [mŏk/ə-sĭn] *noun*, a heelless shoe of deerskin or other soft leather

mock [mŏk] *adjective*, 1) not real, pretended, 2) *verb*, to make fun of, to treat with ridicule

mode [mōd] *noun*, 1) manner 2) fashion, style

mod-el [mŏd/l] *noun*, 1) a person who sets a good example 2) a version of something that can be studied, a copy, 3) someone who wears clothes for advertisement, *verb*, 3) to make a copy of something 4) to wear clothes as part of an exhibit

mod-er-a-tion [mŏd/ər-ā/shən] *noun*, restraint, a happy medium

mod-ern [mŏd/ərn] *adjective*, representative of the current trends and fashions

mod-est [mŏd/ĭst] *adjective*, 1) humble, decent 2) simple

mod-es-ty [mŏd/ĭ-stē] *noun*, *no plural*, humility, decency

mod-i-cum [mŏd/ĭ-kəm] *noun*, a moderate or small amount

mod-i-fi-ca-tion [mŏd/ə-fī-kā/shən] *noun*, a slight change in form, an alteration

mod-i-fy [mŏd/ə-fī′] *verb*, to change, to adjust, to alter

mod-u-late [mŏj/ə-lāt′] *verb*, to adjust the sound

mo-gul [mō/gəl] *noun*, a powerful person, especially in business

moist [moist] *adjective*, a little wet, damp, humid, soggy

mois-ture [mois/chər] *noun*, *no plural*, small drops of water, wetness caused by water

mo-lar [mō/lər] *noun*, one of several back teeth used for chewing

mo-las-ses [mə-lăs/ĭz] *noun*, the thick brown syrup drained from sugar in the refining process

mold [mōld] *noun*, 1) a cast for shapes into which a substance is poured 2) a furry substance that grows on clothing or food if left damp and away from the sun, it is a kind of small fungus, *verb*, 3) to shape something into a form or a mold

mold-ing [mōl′dĭng] *noun*, a plane or curved narrow surface, used for ornamentation

mole [mōl] *noun*, 1) a small insectivore that makes and lives in holes underground 2) a small round brown mark on the skin

mol-e-cule [mŏl′ĭ-kyo͞ol′] *noun*, 1) a unit of matter consisting of two or more atoms combined 2) a particle

mo-lest [mə-lĕst′] *verb*, 1) to touch without permission 2) to annoy

molt [mōlt] *verb*, to shed the outer skin, feathers or exoskeleton

mol-ten [mōl′tən] *adjective*, made liquid by great heat, melted

mo-ment [mō′mənt] *noun*, a very brief period of time, an instant

mo-men-tar-y [mō′mən-tĕr′ē] *adjective*, fleeting, passing

mo-men-tous [mō-mĕn′təs] *adjective*, very important

mo-men-tum [mō-mĕn′təm] *noun*, the force or speed of movement

mon-arch [mŏn′ərk, -ärk′] *noun*, a king or queen 2) an orange and black butterfly

mon-ar-chy [mŏn′ər-kē] *noun*, a government headed by one person, a king or a queen

mon-as-ter-y [mŏn′ə-stĕr′ē] *noun*, a residence in which monks live

Mon-day [mŭn′dē, -dā′] *noun*, the second day of the week

mon-e-tar-y [mŏn′ĭ-tĕr′ē] *adjective*, of or pertaining to money or currency, pecuniary

mon-ey [mŭn′ē] *noun*, currency and coins issued by a government to use in exchange for goods or services

mon-i-tor [mŏn′ĭ-tər] *noun*, 1) a pupil or student given authority 2) a video screen attached to a computer, *verb*, 3) to keep watch over, to supervise, to check

monk [mŭngk] *noun*, a religious man who lives with other men who devote their lives to prayer and religion, a member of a religious order

mon-key [mŭng′kē] *noun*, a primate that usually has a long tail and lives in trees

mon-o-gram [mŏn′ə-grăm′] *noun*, initials consisting of two or more letters interwoven, usually written, embroidered, or engraved

mon-o-logue [mŏn′ə-lôg′] *noun*, a long speech, a soliloquy

mo-nop-o-lize [mə nŏp′ə-līz′] *verb*, to have exclusive possession of something

mo-nop-o-ly [mə-nŏp′ə-lē] *noun*, exclusive control of the supply of any commodity

mon-o-the-ism [mŏn′ə-thē-ĭz′əm] *noun*, belief in one God

mon-o-tone [mŏn′ə-tōn′] *noun*, a voice that never changes in pitch

mo-not-o-nous [mə-nŏt′n-əs] *adjective*, 1) unvarying in pitch 2) repetitiously dull, being the same all the time

mon-soon [mŏn-so͞on′] *noun*, heavy rains and strong winds in southern Asia

mon-ster [mŏn′stər] *noun*, 1) an animal or person with a strange or unusual shape 2) an imaginary and usually frightening creature

Mon-tana [mŏn-tăn′ə] *noun*, one of the 50 United States located in the Northwest, the capital is Helena. The state flower of **Montana** is the bitteroot, and the motto is "Gold and silver."

month [mŭnth] *noun*, a period of 30 days, four weeks, or 1/12 of the year

mon-u-ment [mŏn′yə-mənt] *noun*, a statue or building erected as a tribute to someone who has died

mon-u-men-tal [mŏn′yə-mĕn′tl] *adjective*, massive, enormous, exceptionally great

mood [mo͞od] *noun*, the way a person feels, state of mind

moon [mo͞on] *noun*, the large body in the sky that shines at night, a satellite of a planet

moose [mo͞os] *noun*, a large North American and Eurasian deer

moot [mo͞ot] *adjective*, questionable, debatable

mop [mŏp] *noun*, 1) a tool with a long handle and a sponge or fabric on the bottom used for cleaning floors, *verb*, 2) to clean the floor, usually with soap and water or to remove spilled liquids

mor-al [môr′əl] *adjective*, ethical, honest, concerned with right conduct, virtuous, upright

mo-rale [mə-răl′] *noun*, spirit, confidence, resolve,

mo-ral-i-ty [mə-răl′ĭ-tē] *noun*, virtue, righteousness, ethics

mor-al-ly [môr′ə-lē] *adverb*, in accordance with ethical duty, righteously, respectfully

mor-a-to-ri-um [môr′ə-tôr′ē-əm] *noun*, 1) a suspension, an interval 2) a legal delay of payment

mor-bid [môr′bĭd] *adjective*, depressing, having to do with disease, gruesome

more [môr] *adjective*, 1) larger in amount or number, *adverb*, 2) again, in addition

mo-res [môr′āz′] *noun*, *plural*, the customs of a society, the code of acceptable conduct

morgue [môrg] *noun*, a place where dead bodies go to be identified before burial

Mor-mon [môr mŭn] *noun*, a member of the Church of Jesus Christ of Latter-day Saints founded in the U.S. in 1830 by Joseph Smith

morn-ing [môr′nĭng] *noun*, the time from when the sun rises until noon or the time from midnight to noon

mo-rose [mə-rōs′] *adjective*, sad, dejected, gloomy or sullen

mor-phine [môr′fēn′] *noun*, a narcotic derived from opium

morse code [môrs kōd] *noun*, *no plural*, a way of sending messages using flashing lights or a pattern of sounds

mor-sel [môr′səl] *noun*, a little piece of food, a crumb

mor-tal [môr′tl] *adjective*, 1) destructive to life, fatal 2) human and therefore able to die

mor-tal-i-ty [môr-tăl′ĭ-tē] *noun*, the condition of being mortal

mor-tar [môr′tər] *noun*, 1) a mixture made of cement, lime, sand, and water, used to hold bricks or stone together 2) a short cannon used to fire shells at a high angle 3) a bowl in which substances are crushed to a powder with a pestle

mort-gage [môr′gĭj] *noun*, a legal agreement regarding property between a borrower and a lender

mor-ti-cian [môr-tĭsh′ən] *noun*, an undertaker, a funeral director

mor-ti-fy [môr′tə-fī′] *verb*, to shame, to belittle, to humiliate

mor-tu-ar-y [môr′choo-ĕr′ē] *noun*, a place where dead bodies are kept until burial or cremation

mo-sa-ic [mō-zā′ĭk] *noun*, a surface decoration made by inlaying small pieces of variously colored material such as tile, marble, or glass

Mos-lem [mŏz′ləm] *noun*, *adjective*, see Muslim

mosque [mŏsk] *noun*, a sacred building where Muslims worship

mos-qui-to [mə-skē′tō] *noun*, an insect capable of puncturing the skin of humans and other animals and sucking blood

moss [môs, mŏs] *noun*, a bright green plant that grows flat on wet ground and stones

most [mōst] *adjective*, 1) greatest in amount or number, *adverb*, 2) very, *noun*, 3) the largest amount or number

mote [mōt] *noun*, a small speck

moth [môth] *noun*, an insect with four wings, like a butterfly that flies at night

moth-er [mŭth′ər] *noun*, the female parent

moth-er-in-law [mŭth′ər-ĭn-lô′] *noun*, the mother of one's spouse

mo-tion [mō′shən] *noun*, the action or process of moving

mo-tion-less [mō′shən-lĭs] *adjective*, not moving

mo-ti-vate [mō′tə-vāt′] *verb*, to provide the inner drive that causes one to act

mo-ti-va-tion [mō′tə-vā′shən] *noun*, the feeling that moves one to act

mo-tive [mō′tĭv] *noun*, the reason for doing something, incentive

mo-tor [mō′tər] *noun*, a compact engine that makes things move or work

mo-tor-boat [mō′tər-bōt′] *noun*, a small boat with an engine

mo-tor-cy-cle [mō′tər-sī′kəl] *noun*, a two-wheeled vehicle without a top, moved by a motor

mot-tled [mŏt′ld] *adjective*, spotted with different colors

mot-to [mŏt′ō] *noun*, a saying or catch-phrase that expresses a belief, a guiding principle; the motto of the 4-H Club is, "To make the best better"

mound

mound [mound] *noun*, 1) a heap of earth or a small hill, a knoll 2) any small pile

mount [mount] *noun*, 1) a mountain named after someone, *verb*, 2) to rise 3) to get on 4) to ascend 5) to prepare by putting in place

moun-tain [moun′tən] *noun*, a large hill or raised part of land with steep sides that rises from the earth's surface

mourn [môrn] *verb*, to feel sadness at a loss or death of someone

mourn-ing [môr′nǐng] *noun, no plural*, a period of grief to honor someone who died

mouse [mous] *noun, plural*, **mice**, 1) a small rodent, similar to a rat 2) a hand-held device that guides the cursor or pointer on a computer

mouth [mouth] *noun*, 1) the opening through which all animals consume food 2) an entry

move [mо̄оv] *verb*, 1) to change position or cause something to change position 2) to go to live in a new place 3) to affect, to arouse, or influence 3) to budge, to change opionion, to go on

move-ment [mо̄оv′mənt] *noun*, 1) an inclination, a tendency toward change 2) action, transit, change

mov-ie [mо̄о′vē] *noun*, a film, a motion picture

mov-ing [mо̄о′vǐng] *adjective*, touching, emotional

mow [mо̄] *verb*, to cut grass

Mr. *noun*, a title put before a man's name

Mrs. *noun*, a title put before a married woman's name

Ms. *noun*, a title put before a woman's name

much [mǔch] *adjective*, 1) of a large amount, great. *adverb*, 2) often, to a great degree *noun*, 3) a large amount or a lot of

mucus [myо̄о′kəs] *noun*, spit, of or relating to mucus, a shiny substance coating the inside of the body cavities

mud [mǔd] *noun*, wet soft earth

mud-dy [mǔd′ē] *adjective*, 1) murky, dirty 2) not clear or pure

muf-fin [mǔf′ǐn] *noun*, a quick bread made from batter and baked in a cup-shaped pan

muf-fle [mǔf′əl] *verb*, to cover or suppress a sound, to tone down

muf-fler [mǔf′lər] *noun*, 1) any of various devices to deaden the noise of escaping gases or vapors 2) a scarf worn around the neck

mug [mǔg] *noun*, 1) a cup with a handle, *verb*, 2) to assault someone, usually to rob them

mug-gy [mǔg′ē] *adjective*, warm and very damp, humid

mulch [mǔlch] *noun*, a protective layer of decomposing organic matter

mule [myо̄оl] *noun*, an animal whose parents were a female horse and a male donkey

mul-ti-form [mŭl'tə-fôrm']
adjective, having many shapes
or forms

mul-ti-ple [mŭl'tə-pəl] *adjective*,
1) many 2) having many parts

mul-ti-pli-ca-tion
[mŭl'tə-plĭ-kā'shən] *noun*, no
plural, the process of finding the
number or quantity by repeated
addition of a specified number

mul-ti-ply [mŭl'tə-plɪ'] *verb*, to
increase by a number of times

mul-ti-tude [mŭl'tĭ-tōōd'] *noun*, a
crowd, a large gathering

mum-my [mŭm'ē] *noun*, a dead
body preserved with chemicals
and wrapped in cloth

mumps [mŭmps] *noun, plural*, an
illness that causes fever and
swelling in the neck and throat

mun-dane [mŭn-dān'] *adjective*,
commonplace, worldly as
opposed to spiritual

mu-nic-i-pal [myōō-nĭs'ə-pəl]
adjective, having a local self-
government, as in a city or town

mu-ral [myōōr'əl] *noun*, a picture
painted directly on a wall

mur-der [mûr'dər] *noun*, 1) the act
of killing someone, either after
first planning to do so or during
another crime, such as a
robbery, *verb*, 2) to kill a person
intentionally

mur-der-er [mûr'dər-ər] *noun*, a
person who intends to kill
someone and does so

mur-mur [mûr'mər] *verb*, to speak
very softly, to whisper

mus-cle [mŭs'əl] *noun*, an organ
whose special function is to
produce movement

muse [myōōz] *noun*, 1) one's inner
voice as a source of creativity,
Muse, 2) one of the nine Greek
goddesses, responsible for art,
music, and literature, *verb*, 3) to
ponder, to meditate, to think, to
reflect

mu-se-um [myōō-zē'əm] *noun*, a
building that exhibits a collection
of things of interest

mush-room [mŭsh'rōōm'] *noun*, a
plant that is not green and is a
fungus, it usually has a stem with
a cap on it

mu-sic [myōō'zĭk] *noun*, the art or
science of harmonic sounds

mu-si-cian [myōō-zĭsh'ən] *noun*,
one who plays a musical
instrument and performs

mus-ket [mŭs'kĭt] *noun*, a gun with
a long barrel, used by soldiers
before rifles were invented

musk-rat [mŭs'krăt'] *noun*, a
rodent that lives in or near water

Mus-lim [mŭz'ləm] *noun*, a follower
of the religion that believes in
Allah as the one god and the
teachings of Muhammed as
written in the Koran

must [mŭst] *verb*, 1) used with
another verb to show what is
necessary or what has to be
done 2) showing what is sure or
likely

mus-tache [mŭs'tăsh'] *noun*, the
hair covering an upper lip

mus-tang [mŭs'tăng'] *noun*, a wild
horse of the American plains

mustard

mus-tard [mŭs′tərd] *noun*, 1) a plant with yellow flowers and a seed in pods 2) powder or sauce made of ground mustard seed

mu-ta-ble [myo͞o′tə-bəl] *adjective*, 1) changing in form 2) fickle

mute [myo͞ot] *adjective*, voiceless, speechless, unable to speak

mu-ti-late [myo͞ot′l-āt′] *verb*, to cut off or remove an essential part

mu-ti-nous [myo͞ot′n-əs] *adjective*, unruly, rebellious, insurgent

mu-ti-ny [myo͞ot′n-ē] *noun*, a revolt, a rebellion, an uprising

mu-tual [myo͞o′cho͞o-əl] *adjective*, having a common interest

muz-zle [mŭz′əl] *noun*, 1) a fastening on the mouth of an animal to prevent it from biting or eating 2) the open end of a gun from which the bullet comes out when the gun is fired, *verb*, 3) to gag, to silence, to hush, to restrain speech and expression

my [mī] *adjective*, belonging to the person speaking

my-op-ic [mī-ŏp′ĭk] *adjective*, 1) nearsighted 2) self-centered, small minede

myr-i-ad [mĭr′ē-əd] *noun*, a very large number

my-self [mī-sĕlf′] *pronoun*, the same person as the one speaking

mys-ter-y [mĭs′tə-rē] *noun*, something not explained or beyond human comprehension

mys-ti-cal [mĭs′tĭ-kəl] *adjective*, beyond understanding, spiritual

mys-ti-fy [mĭs′tə-fī′] *verb*, to confuse, to puzzle, to bewilder

myth [mĭth] *noun*, 1) a legendary story used to explain nature or religion and often featuring heroes or supernatural beings

my-thol-o-gy [mĭ-thŏl′ə-jē] *noun*, the study of stories and legends

N

nag [năg] *verb*, to pester, to annoy, to bother, to find faults

nail [nāl] *noun*, 1) a piece of pointed metal to be put into wood with a hammer 2) the horny tip on the ends of fingers and toes, *verb*, 3) to fasten with a hammer and nail

na-ive [nä-ēv′] *adjective*, unsophisticated, innocent

na-ked [nā′kĭd] *adjective*, without clothes, uncovered, nude

name [nām] *noun*, 1) a word given to someone or something for identification, *verb*, 2) to decide what someone or something will be called, to specify

name-ly [nām′lē] *adverb*, that is

name-sake [nām′sāk′] *noun*, one having the same name as another one, named after another

nap [năp] *noun*, 1) a short rest 2) a textured surface on fabric

nap-kin [năp′kĭn] *noun*, a piece of cloth or paper used at a meal to keep one's clothes, hands, and mouth clean while eating

nar-cot-ic [när-kŏt′ĭk] *noun*, a drug that relieves pain, blunts the senses and produces sleep

nar-rate [năr′āt′] *verb*, to make known, to tell a story, to recount

nar-ra-tive [năr′ə-tĭv] *noun*, a story, a history, a recital

nar-ra-tor [năr′āt′ ər] *noun*, a person who relates a story

nar-row [năr′ō] *adjective*, limited in width, breadth, or scope

na-sal [nā′zəl] *adjective*, associated with the nose

nas-cent [năs′ənt] *adjective*, coming into existence, the beginning

na-tion [nā′shən] *noun*, a group of people living in a particular territory under the same government, a federation

na-tion-al [năsh′ə-nəl] *adjective*, of or pertaining to a country or territory

na-tion-al-i-ty [năsh′ə-năl′ĭ-tē] *noun*, the identification of a person based on the country where he or she was born or holds citizenship

na-tive [nā′tĭv] *adjective*, 1) belonging to the place where a person is born, indigenous, *noun*, 2) a person born and raised in a certain place

nat-u-ral [năch′ər-əl] *adjective*, 1) produced by nature, not man-made 2) inborn, an innate ability

nat-u-ral-ly [năch′ər-ə-lē] *adverb*, as one would expect

na-ture [nā′chər] *noun*, *no plural*, 1) that which is not man-made, the physical world 2) traits characteristic of someone, disposition, personality

nau-se-a [nô′zē ə] *noun*, 1) a stomach sickness accompanied by a desire to vomit 2) disgust

nau-se-ate [nô′zē-āt′] *verb*, to cause to become sick, to fill with disgust, causing a sick feeling

nau-ti-cal [nô′tĭ-kəl] *adjective*, having to do with the sea

na-val [nā′vəl] *adjective*, seafaring, nautical, relating to the navy

na-vel [nā′vəl] *noun*, the belly button, where the umbilical cord was attached before birth

nav-i-gate [năv′ĭ-gāt′] *verb*, to control in which direction a vehicle will go on a route

nav-i-ga-tion [năv′ĭ-gā′shən] *noun*, *no plural*, the ability to travel through water or plan and follow a specific route

nav-i-ga-tor [năv′ĭ-gā′tər] *noun*, one who directs and controls the course of a vehicle

na-vy [nā′vē] *noun*, the officers and personnel of warships

near [nîr] *adverb*, 1) a short distance away, *preposition*, 2) close to

near-by [nîr′bī′] *adverb*, close at hand, not far away

near-ly [nîr′lē] *adverb*, almost

near-sight-ed [nîr′sī′tĭd] *adjective*, able to see only things close by

neat [nēt] *adjective*, clean and orderly, well arranged

Ne-bras-ka [nə-brăs′kə] *noun*, one of the 50 United States, centrally located west of the Missouri River, the capital is Lincoln. The state flower of **Nebraska** is the goldenrod, and the motto is "Equality before the law."

nec·es·sar·y [nĕs′ĭ-sĕr′ē] *adjective*, needing to be done, essential

ne·ces·si·tate [nə-sĕs′ĭ-tāt′] *verb*, to demand, to require

ne·ces·si·ty [nə-sĕs′ĭ-tē] *noun*, 1) something indispensable or necessary 2) an urgent matter

neck [nĕk] *noun*, 1) the part of the body connecting the head and the torso 2) a narrow connecting part, as of a bottle

neck·lace [nĕk′lĭs] *noun*, jewelry worn around the neck

nec·tar [nĕk′tər] *noun*, a sweet liquid made by flowers

need [nēd] *noun*, 1) a lack, *verb*, 2) to lack something that is necessary or essential 3) must

nee·dle [nēd′l] *noun*, an instrument for sewing, made of steel, sharp at one end, with an eyehole for thread at the other end

need·y [nē′dē] *adjective*, poor, penniless, impoverished

neg·ate [nĕg′ə-tĭv] verb, 1) to deny the existence of something 2) to nullify, make ineffective

neg·a·tive [nĕg′ə-tĭv] *adjective*, 1) expressing denial, refusal or resistance, not positive, *noun*, 2) an image on developed film

ne·glect [nĭ-glĕkt′] *noun, no plural*, 1) disregard, carelessness, lack of care or attention, *verb*, 2) to not look after something, letting it deteriorate, to ignore

neg·li·gence [nĕg′lĭ-jəns] *noun*, failure to give the care the occasion demands

neg·li·gi·ble [nĕg′lĭ-jə-bəl] *adjective*, very small, insignificant

ne·go·ti·a·ble [nĭ-gō′shə-bəl] *adjective*, 1) transferable or able to be assigned to another person 2) able to be compromised about, open to discussion

ne·go·ti·ate [nĭ-gō′shē-āt′] *verb*, to settle, to work out, to deal or bargain with others, to compromise

neigh·bor [nā′bər] *noun*, a person who lives near another

neigh·bor·hood [nā′bər-hŏŏd′] *noun*, a small part of a community shared by a group of people who live near each other

nei·ther [nē′thər] *adjective, pronoun*, 1) not the one nor the other, *conjunction*, 2) not either

ne·on [nē′ŏn′] *noun*, an inert gaseous element often used in display lights

neph·ew [nĕf′yōō] *noun*, the son of a brother or a sister

nep·o·tism [nĕp′ə-tĭz′əm] *noun*, favoritism to a relative in a business situation

nerve [nûrv] *noun*, a thread in the body that carries feelings and messages to and from the brain

nerv·ous [nûr′vəs] *adjective*, very worried and a little scared

nest [nĕst] *noun*, a temporary home built by an animal or insect

nes·tle [nĕs′əl] *verb*, to be very close to someone else in a comfortable way

net [nĕt] *noun* 1) a fabric made of tying threads together in a

uniform design to form a mesh
2) remaining income after
deducting taxes and expenses

net-tle [nĕt′l] *noun,* 1) a weed with
small thorns, *verb,* 2) to annoy,
to bother, to irritate, to vex

neu-rot-ic [nŏo-rŏt′ĭk] *adjective,*
suffering from a mental disorder
characterized by anxiety and
worry and phobias

neu-ter [nŏo′tər] *verb,* to make
sterile, to spay or castrate

neu-tral [nŏo′trəl] *adjective,*
1) neither positive nor negative
2) not on either side during a war
3) in the middle 4) a position in
which gears are not engaged

neu-tron [nŏo′trŏn′] *noun,* an
uncharged particle in an atomic
nucleus

Ne-va-da [nə-vădʹə] *noun,* one of
the 50 United States, located in
the West, the capital is Carson
City. The state flower of **Nevada**
is the sagebrush, and the motto
is "All for our country."

nev-er [nĕv′ər] *adverb,* not at any
time, absolutely not

nev-er-the-less [nĕv′ər-thə-lĕs′]
adverb, notwithstanding, in spite
of that, yet, however

new [nŏo] *adjective,* 1) not having
been seen or used before
2) additional

New Hampshire [nŏo hămp′shər]
noun, one of the 50 United
States located in New England,
the capital is Concord. The state
flower of **New Hampshire** is the
purple lilac, the motto is "Live
free or die."

New Jersey [nŏo jûr′zē] *noun,* one
of the 50 United States located
in the East, the capital is Trenton.
The state flower of **New Jersey**
is the purple violet and the motto
is "Liberty and prosperity."

New Mexico [nŏo mĕk′sĭ-kō′]
noun, one of the 50 United
States, located in the Southwest,
the capital is Santa Fe. The state
flower of **New Mexico** is the
yucca and the motto is "It grows
as it goes."

news [nŏoz] *noun, plural,* a report
of current events, things that
happened recently

news-pa-per [nŏoz′pā′pər] *noun,* a
publication that appears daily or
weekly, containing recent
information

New York [nŏo yôrk] *noun,* one of
the 50 United States located in
the Northeast, the capital is
Albany. The state flower of **New
York** is the rose and the motto is
"Excelsior", which expresses the
idea of still higher, ever upward.

next [nĕkst] *adverb,* 1) in the
nearest position, without
anything between
2) immediately following

nib-ble [nĭb′əl] *verb,* to eat small
bites of something

nice [nīs] *adjective,* 1) kind, good
2) pleasant, socially agreeable

niche [nĭch] *noun,* 1) a small,
suitable place 2) the position of a
particular population in an
ecological community

nick-el [nĭk′əl] *noun,* 1) five cents,
equal to five pennies 2) a hard,

silvery metallic element of the iron group

nick-name [nĭk′nām′] *noun*, a name given to someone which is not his real name

nic-o-tine [nĭk′ə-tēn′] *noun*, a toxic alkaloid, the addictive property of tobacco

niece [nēs] *noun*, the daughter of one's brother or sister

nig-gard-ly [nĭg′ərd-lē] *adjective*, meanly stingy, meager

night [nīt] *noun*, the time of day after the sun goes down

night-mare [nīt′mâr′] *noun*, a terrifying dream or event

nine [nīn] *adjective*, *noun*, the number 9, eight plus one

nine-teen [nīn-tēn′] *noun*, nine plus ten, written 19

nine-teenth [nīn-tēnth′]*adjective*, the number 19 in order, 19th

nine-ti-eth [nīn′tē-ĭth] *adjective*, the number ninety in order, 90th

nine-ty [nīn′tē] *noun*, written 90, 9 X 10

ninth [nīnth] *noun*, *adjective*, number 9 in order, 9th

nip-ple [nĭp′əl] *noun*, 1) the tip of the breast where the milk ducts discharge 2) the rubber cap on a baby bottle

nir-va-na [nîr-vä′nə] *noun*, in Buddhist teachings, the ideal state, freedom from pain and worry, perfect bliss

ni-tro-gen [nī′trə-jən] *noun*, a gas necessary for life that is colorless, tasteless and odorless

no [nō] *adjective*, 1) not any, *adverb*, 2) a word we use to answer a question, or indicate disagreement

no-bil-i-ty [nō-bĭl′ĭ-tē] *adjective*, a member of the royal circle

no-ble [nō′bəl] *adjective*, 1) aristocratic, born to wealth 2) unselfish, of good character

no-bod-y [nō′bŏd′ē] *pronoun*, no one, a person of no importance

noc-tur-nal [nŏk-tûr′nəl] *adjective*, active or functioning at night

nod [nŏd] *noun*, 1) an inclination of the head, *verb*, 2) to tip the head slightly to acknowledge something

noise [noiz] *noun*, 1) a loud harsh sound, 2) sound of any kind

no-mad [nō′mǎd′] *noun*, a person who travels about with a tribe and has no address or home

nom-i-nate [nŏm′ə-nāt′] *verb*, to name for an office or place

nom-i-na-tion [nŏm′ə-nā′shən] *noun*, to submit a name for an award or appointment

nom-i-nee [nŏm′ə-nē′] *noun*, a person selected or appointed to run for a position

non-cha-lant [nŏn′shə-länt′] *adjective*, showing a jaunty coolness, aloof, unconcerned

none [nŭn] *adjective*, not any, nothing, no one, not one

non-ex-ist-ent [nŏn′ĭg-zĭs′tənt] *adjective*, not real

non-fic-tion [nŏn-fĭk′shən] *noun*, a true story

non-sense [nŏn′sĕns′] *noun*, folly, silliness, absurdity, meaningless

noon [nōōn] *noun*, midday, twelve o'clock, daytime

nor [nôr; nər when unstressed] *conjunction*, a word used between two choices after neither

nor-mal [nôr′məl] *adjective*, not unusual, common, every day

nor-mal-ly [nôr′mə-lē] *adverb*, generally, ordinarily, frequently

north [nôrth] *adjective*, 1) facing or coming from the north, *adverb*, 2) to or toward the north *noun*, 3) the direction to the left of one facing east, the compass point opposite to south, **North**, 4) regions or countries north of a point that is mentioned or understood

North America [nôrth-ə-mĕr′ĭ-kə] *noun*, one of the seven continents containing 7.9% of the world's population

North Carolina [nôrth kăr′ə-lī′nə] *noun*, one of the 50 United States located in the Southeast, the capital is Raleigh. The state flower of **North Carolina** is the dogwood, the state motto is "To be rather than to seem."

North Dakota [nôrth də-kō′tə] *noun*, a state located in the Northwest of the United States, the capital is Bismark. The state flower of **North Dakota** is the wild prairie rose, and the state motto is "Liberty and union, now and forever, one and inseparable."

north-east [nôrth-ēst′] *noun*, the point between north and east on a compass

north-west [nôrth wĕst′] *noun*, the point between north and west on the compass

nose [nōz] *noun*, 1) the part of the face that contains the nostrils and the organs of smell 2) the front of a plane, rocket, etc.

nose-gay [nōz′gā′] *noun*, a small hand-held fragrant bouquet

nos-tal-gia [nŏ-stăl′jə] *noun*, homesickness, a sentimental longing for something in the past

nos-tril [nŏs′trəl] *noun*, either of the external openings of the nose

not [nŏt] *adverb*, a word that forms a contradiction in a sentence

no-ta-ble [nō′tə-bəl] *adjective*, remarkable, worthy of notice

no-ta-ry [nō′tə-rē] *noun*, an officer who witnesses and verifies commercial papers and is authorized to take affidavits

no-ta-tion [nō-tā′shən] *noun*, notes or marks to indicate something

notch [nŏch] *noun*, 1) a nick, a dent, *verb*, 2) to make a notch

note [nōt] *noun*, 1) an observation stuck in the mind 2) a bill, IOU, paper money 3) a single sound of music on the scale 4) a brief written message, *verb*, 5) to make an observation and commit it to memory 6) to mention

noth-ing [nŭth′ĭng] *adjective*, not anything, zero, insignificant

no-tice [nō′tĭs] *noun*, 1) a written warning indicating that something has happened or will happen, *verb*, 2) to observe, to become aware of

no-tice-a-ble [nō′tĭ-sə-bəl] *adjective*, capable of being observed, conspicuous

no-ti-fi-ca-tion [nō′tə-fĭ-kā′shən] *noun*, to inform someone of something, to give notice

no-ti-fy [nō′tə-fī′] *verb*, to let someone know, to inform

no-tion [nō′shən] *noun*, a general or vague idea, a thought, a whim

no-to-ri-e-ty [nō′tə-rī′ĭ-tē] *noun*, fame, renown, celebrity status

no-to-ri-ous [nō-tôr′ē-əs] *adjective*, widely or commonly known, usually unfavorable

not-with-stand-ing [nŏt′wĭth-stăn′dĭng] despite, although, nevertheless *preposition*, 2) in spite of

noun [*noun*] *noun*, a word that refers to a person, place, or thing

nour-ish [nûr′ĭsh] *verb*, 1) to feed or foster the growth of something 2) to keep healthy, to nurture, to strengthen

nour-ish-ment [nûr′ĭsh-mənt] *noun*, food that strengthens the body and helps it grow

nov-el [nŏv′əl] *adjective*, 1) new, unusual, *noun*, 2) a work of fiction or romance

nov-el-ist [nŏv′ə-lĭst] *noun*, a person who writes fictional stories

nov-el-ty [nŏv′əl-tē] *noun*, something new

No-vem-ber [nō-vĕm′bər] *noun*, the eleventh month of the year, having 30 days

nov-ice [nŏv′ĭs] *noun*, 1) a beginner 2) a person admitted to a religious order before taking the final vows

now [nou] *adverb*, at the present time, immediately

no-where [nō′hwâr′] *adverb*, 1) not anywhere, *noun*, 2) a place that does not exist

nox-ious [nŏk′shəs] *adjective*, harmful, deadly fumes

noz-zle [nŏz′əl] *noun*, a short outlet or pipe as of a hose, a spout

nu-ance [nōō′äns′] *noun*, a shade or trace of differences in meaning, or color, or tone

nu-cle-ar [nōō′klē-ər] *adjective*, using the very great power made by splitting an atom or joining atoms in nuclear fission

nu-cle-us [nōō′klē-əs] *noun*, 1) a central mass of an atom about which matter is concentrated 2) the seed of the cell is the positively charged central region of an atom

nude [nōōd] *adjective*, naked, bare

nudge [nŭj] *noun*, 1) a gentle push, *verb*, 2) to push someone lightly

nug-get [nŭg′ĭt] *noun*, a small lump, especially of natural gold

nui-sance [nōō′səns] *noun*, anything which annoys or gives trouble, a disturbance

nul-li-fy [nŭl′ə-fī′] *adjective*, to render invalid or void

numb [nŭm] *adjective*, 1) insensitive from excessive cold 2) unable to feel pain

num-ber [nŭm′bər] *noun*, 1) a symbol representing a quantity

2) abundance, *verb,* 3) to identify with a number 4) to amount to

nu-mer-al [nōo′mər-əl] *noun,* a symbol used to represent a number

nu-mer-ous [nōo′mər-əs] *adjective,* very many, myriad, several

nun [nŭn] *noun,* a woman who gives her life to serving God

nup-tial [nŭp′shəl] *adjective,* marriage vows, a wedding

nurse [nûrs] *noun,* 1) a person who takes care of the sick and dying, *verb,* 2) to look after and attend to the needs of the sick

nurs-er-y [nûr′sə-rē] *noun,* 1) a child's room or playroom 2) a greenhouse for young plants

nur-ture [nûr′chər] *verb,* to care for, to feed and protect

nut [nŭt] *noun,* 1) the edible kernel of a seed 2) a small piece of metal with a hole in it, used to hold a bolt in place

nut-meg [nŭt′mĕg′] *noun,* the aromatic seed of an East Indian tree used as a spice

nu-tri-ent [nōo′trē-ənt] *noun,* vitamins and minerals derived from food, proteins

nu-tri-tion [nōo-trĭsh′ən] *noun,* a healthy diet, that nourishes the body

nu-tri-tious [nōo-trĭsh′əs] *adjective,* wholesome, healthy

ny-lon [nī′lŏn′] *noun,* a strong man-made elastic thread

nymph [nĭmf] *noun,* 1) the young of an insect that has not fully developed the structural

proportions and size of an adult 2) a fairy

O

oaf [ōf] *noun,* a clumsy person

oak [ōk] *noun,* a tree of hard wood bearing the acorn as a fruit

oar [ôr, ōr] *noun,* a paddle with a flat blade at the end, used to row or push a boat

o-a-sis [ō-ā′sĭs] *noun,* a fertile spot in a desert having a spring

oat [ōt] *noun,* a member of the cereal family having edible seeds such as rice, wheat or corn

oath [ōth] *noun,* a promise, a commitment, a solemn appeal

o-be-di-ence [ō-bē′dē-əns] *noun, no plural,* compliance with authority, submission

o-be-di-ent [ō-bē′dē-ənt] *adjective,* willing to do what one is told to do

ob-e-lisk [ŏb′ə-lĭsk] *noun,* a tall 4-sided column tapering and ending in a pyramid apex

o-bese [ō-bēs′] *adjective,* very fat

o-bey [ō-bā′] *verb,* to follow or carry out an order or law

ob-fus-cate [ŏb′fə-skāt′] *verb,* to confuse, to muddle, to obscure

o-bit-u-ar-y [ō-bĭch′ōo-ĕr′ē] *noun,* an announcement of someone's death often with a short biography

ob-ject [ŏb′jĭkt] *noun,* 1) a thing, *verb,* 2) to oppose, to disagree

ob-jec-tion [əb-jĕk′shən] *noun,* a statement, a complaint

objective

ob-jec-tive [əb-jĕk′tĭv] *adjective*,
1) not influenced by emotions,
fair, *noun*, 2) a purpose or goal

ob-jur-gate [ŏb′jər-gāt′] *verb*, to
scold, to rebuke severely

ob-li-ga-tion [ŏb′lĭ-gā′shən] *noun*,
1) the binding power of a
promise 2) a debt of gratitude

ob-lig-a-to-ry [ə-blĭg′ə-tôr′ē]
adjective, necessary, binding in
law or conscience, mandatory

o-blige [ə-blīj′] *verb*, 1) to put
under obligation, to
accommodate 2) to do a favor
for, to help, to assist

o-blique [ō-blēk′] *adjective*,
1) sloping or slanting 2) indirect
or evasive, not explicit

ob-lit-er-ate [ə-blĭt′ə-rāt′] *verb*, to
erase or blot out, to efface

ob-liv-i-on [ə-blĭv′ē-ən] *noun*,
being utterly forgotten

ob-liv-i-ous [ə-blĭv′ē-əs] *adjective*,
forgetful, lost in thought

ob-long [ŏb′lông′] *adjective*, a flat
shape with four straight sides
and four equal angles, that is
longer than it is wide

ob-nox-ious [ŏb-nŏk′shəs]
adjective, annoying, offensive

ob-scure [ŏb-skyo͞or′] *adjective*,
1) unclear, vague, unknown
2) not easily seen or heard
3) dark, hidden

ob-scu-ri-ty [ŏb-skyo͞or′ĭ-tē] *noun*,
oblivion, no where

ob-se-qui-ous [ŏb-sē′kwē-əs]
adjective, submissive, fawning

ob-ser-vance [əb-zûr′vəns] *noun*,
1) noticing with attention

2) compliance as a duty or
custom

ob-ser-va-tion [ŏb′zər-vā′shən]
noun, the noting and recording of
facts and events

ob-serv-a-to-ry [əb-zûr′və-tôr′ē]
noun, a building equipped with
instruments for observing the
heavenly bodies, such as the
stars, moon, etc.

ob-serve [əb-zûrv′] *verb*, 1) to see
or notice 2) to comment 3) to
mark an event or day

ob-ses-sion [əb-sĕsh′ən, ŏb-]
noun, a fixed idea, continued
brooding

ob-so-lete [ŏb′sə-lēt′] *adjective*, no
longer in use, outdated

ob-sta-cle [ŏb′stə-kəl] *noun*,
something that stands in the
way, an obstruction

ob-ste-tri-cian [ŏb′stĭ-trĭsh′ən]
noun, a physician specializing in
the delivery of babies

ob-sti-nate [ŏb′stə-nĭt] *adjective*,
not yielding to reason, stubborn

ob-struct [əb-strŭkt′] *verb*, to get in
the way of something or stop it
completely, to hinder

ob-struc-tion [əb-strŭk′shən]
noun, a barrier, an interference

ob-tain [əb-tān′] *verb*, to acquire or
win through effort or request

ob-tain-a-ble [əb-tān′ə-bəl]
adjective, capable of being
acquired or won

ob-trude [ŏb-tro͞od′] *verb*, 1) to get
in on, to meddle, 2) to stick out

ob-tuse [ŏb-to͞os′] *adjective*, an
angle greater than 90 degrees

ob-vi-ous [ŏb′vē-əs] *adjective*, easily seen or understood, evident, apparent to everyone

ob-vi-ous-ly [ŏb′vē-əs-lē] *adverb*, apparently, clearly, evidently

oc-ca-sion [ə-kā′zhən] *noun*, 1) an event, a happening, an important time 2) a chance, an opportunity

oc-cas-ion-al-ly [ə-kā′zhə-nə-lē] *adverb*, once in a while

oc-cult [ə-kült′] *adjective*, the mysterious, secret, supernatural

oc-cu-pant [ŏk′yə-pənt] *noun*, the inhabitant, a resident, a tenant

oc-cu-pa-tion [ŏk′yə-pā′shən] *noun*, 1) a job, a way of using time, *no plural*, 2) being in a certain place or space

oc-cu-py [ŏk′yə-pī′] *verb*, 1) to make or hold possession of something 2) to live in a place

oc-cur [ə-kûr′] *verb*, 1) to happen 2) to come to mind, to appear

oc-cur-rence [ə-kûr′əns] *noun*, something that happens

o-cean [ō′shən] *noun*, a body of salt water covering three fifths of the earth

o-cea-nog-ra-phy [ō′shə-nŏg′rə-fē] *noun*, the study of life in the sea

o'clock [ə-klŏk′] *adverb*, according to the clock

Oc-to-ber [ŏk-tō′bər] *noun*, the tenth month of the year having 31 days

oc-to-pus [ŏk′tə-pəs] *noun*, a sea creature that has eight long limbs

oc-u-list [ŏk′yə-lĭst] *noun*, a doctor who treats the eyes

odd [ŏd] *adjective*, 1) any number that cannot be evenly divided by two 2) unusual, very different

odds [ŏdz] *noun*, *plural*, uncertain advantages, doubtful chances

odi-ous [ō′dē-əs] *adjective*, hateful, repulsive, repugnant

odi-um [ō′dē-əm] *noun*, repugnance, intense hatred

o-dom-e-ter [ō-dŏm′ĭ-tər] *noun*, a device in a vehicle used to measure distance traveled

o-dor [ō′dər] *noun*, a smell

o-dor-ous [ō′dər-əs] *adjective*, having a strong smell

of [ŭv] *preposition*, 1) belonging to 2) from among 3) made from 4) about 5) in relation to

off [ôf] *adverb*, 1) away from 2) not on or not working, *preposition*, 3) at a distance

of-fend [ə-fĕnd′] *verb*, to hurt someone's feelings, to insult

of-fense [ə-fĕns′] *noun*, a misdeed, an insult, a sense of insult or injury, an act of aggression

of-fen-sive [ə-fĕn′sĭv] *adjective*, 1) insulting, in poor taste, *noun*, 2) the position of an attack

of-fer [ô′fər] *noun*, 1) a proposal, a suggestion, *verb*, 2) to present to be accepted or refused

of-fice [ô′fĭs] *noun*, 1) a place in which business or professional work is done 2) a position that requires certain duties and tasks

of-fi-cer [ô′fĭ-sər] *noun*, a person lawfully invested with a position of trust or authority

of-fi-cial [ə-fĭsh′əl] *adjective*, 1) having the right or permission

officiate

to do something, *noun*, 2) a person who is in charge of something 3) of or pertaining to the holding of an office

of-fi-ci-ate [ə-físh′ē-āt′] *verb*, to act as an officer in performing a duty such as a minister

off-spring [ôf′spríng′] *noun*, descendants, children, progeny

of-ten [ô′fən] *adverb*, many times, frequently, repeatedly

o-ha-na [ōhŏna] *noun*, family, no one left behind

Ohio [ō-hī′ō] *noun*, one of the 50 United States located in the Midwest region, the capital is Columbus. The state flower of **Ohio** is the scarlet carnation and the motto is "With God all things are possible."

ohm [ōm] *noun*, the unit of electrical resistance

oil [oil] *noun*, 1) any liquid substance that does not dissolve in water 2) a nutrient derived from a pressed nut 3) a dark, thick mineral liquid, found deep in the ground 4) a substance used to burn in a lantern or lamp post, *verb*, 5) to lubricate with grease or oil

oint-ment [oint′mənt] *noun*, a lubricant put on the skin, containing medicine

Okla-ho-ma [ō′klə-hō′mə] *noun*, one of the 50 United States located in the Southwest, the capital is Oklahoma City. The state flower of **Oklahoma** is the mistletoe, and the motto is "Labor conquers all things."

old [ōld] *adjective*, 1) not young, having lived a long time 2) the word we use to show our age 3) not new 4) something that has lasted over time, antique

ol-fac-to-ry [ŏl-făk′tə-rē] *adjective*, referring to the nose and the sense of smell

ol-i-gar-chy [ŏl′ĭ-gär′kē] *noun*, a government run by a few leaders

ol-ive [ŏl′ĭv] *noun*, the fruit of an olive tree eaten as a relish

om-i-nous [ŏm′ə-nəs] *adjective*, looking or sounding as if something bad will happen, portending evil or harm

o-mis-sion [ō-mĭsh′ən] *noun*, failure to do something, something that is left out

o-mit [ō-mĭt′] *verb*, to leave something out, to fail to include

om-e-lette [ŏm′ə-lĭt] *noun*, eggs beaten together and cooked in hot fat in a flat pan

om-nip-o-tent [ŏm-nĭp′ə-tənt] *adjective*, having power over all

om-ni-pres-ent [ŏm′nĭ-prĕz′ənt] *adjective*, universally present at the same time, everywhere

om-nis-cient [ŏm-nĭsh′ənt] *adjective*, all-knowing

om-ni-vore [ŏm′nə-vôr′] *noun*, an animal that eats both plants and animals

on [ŏn] *adverb*, 1) to be precise 2) a location 3) to show time or date 4) about 5) to continue, *preposition*, 6) atop

once [wŭns] *adverb*, 1) one time 2) a long time ago

one [wŭn] *adjective*, 1) tho number 1 2) the same, unified 3) act as the same, *noun*, 4) a single thing 5) any person 6) a unit

one-self [wŭn-sĕlf'] *pronoun*, the same person who is the subject of the sentence

on-ion [ŭn'yən] *noun*, a garden vegetable having an edible bulb with pungent taste and odor

on-ly [ōn'lē] *adjective*, 1) sole, no one else, nothing more, 2) but, *adverb*, 3) merely, just

on-o-mat-o-poe-ia [ŏn'ə-măt'ə-pē'ə] *noun*, a term used to describe words that actually sound like the noises they depict such as *boom*

on-slaught [ŏn'slôt'] *noun*, a vicious assault, a massacre

on-to [ŏn'tōō'] *preposition*, to a place, to a position on

o-nus [ō'nəs] *noun*, 1) a burden 2) a responsibility, blame

on-ward [ŏn'wərd] *adverb*, moving toward a point ahead, forward

ooze [ōōz] *verb*, to flow out slowly

o-pal [ō'pəl] *noun*, a precious stone of milky hue, with a play of iridescent colors

o-paque [ō-pāk'] *adjective*, not reflecting or giving out light, not transparent; dull, dark

o-pen [ō'pən] *adjective*, 1) not shut or covered 2) ready for business 3) not surrounded by other things 4) unbiased, free thinking, *verb*, 5) to allow entrance 6) to start, to unfold 7) to remove the cover or door 8) to undo, to untie

o-pe-ra [ŏp'ər-ə] *noun*, a dramatic presentation set to music

op-er-ate [ŏp'ə-rāt'] *verb*, to make something work or function

op-er-a-tion [ŏp'ə-rā'shən] *noun*, 1) any methodical action 2) a plan put into action 3) surgery

op-er-a-tor [ŏp'ə-rā'tər] *noun*, one who operates equipment or works as a manager

o-pi-ate [ō'pē-ĭt] *noun*, a drug which causes rest or sleep, a narcotic or sedative

o-pin-ion [ə-pĭn'yən] *noun*, a belief stronger than an impression, a point of view, a conclusion

o-pos-sum [ə-pŏs'əm] *noun*, a rodent that sleeps upside down hanging from a tree during the day, and travels at night

op-po-nent [ə-pō'nənt] *noun*, a member of the other team, an antagonist, an adversary

op-por-tune [ŏp'ər-tōōn'] *adjective*, timely, well chosen

op-por-tun-ist [ŏp'ər-tōō'nĭst] *noun*, an individual who takes advantage of a situation and ignores ethics to achieve a goal

op-por-tu-ni-ty [ŏp'ər-tōō'nĭ-tē] *noun*, a fit or convenient time, occasion, a good chance

op-pose [ə-pōz'] *verb*, to go against, to defend, to combat, to object, to resist, to fight

op-po-site [ŏp'ə-zĭt] *adjective*, 1) facing, set over against 2) one that is contrary to another

op-po-si-tion [ŏp'ə-zĭsh'ən] *noun*, against, hostile or contrary action, a negative response

oppress

op-press [ə-prĕs'] *verb*, to overpower, to subdue, to treat harshly, to hold down

op-pres-sion [ə-prĕsh'ən] *noun*, hardship, cruelty, persecution

op-pres-sive [ə-prĕs'ĭv] *adjective*, 1) unreasonably burdensome 2) tyrannical, cruel, unfair

op-tic [ŏp'tĭk] *adjective*, pertaining to the eye, light and vision

op-ti-cal [ŏp'tĭ-kəl] *adjective*, visual, seeing

op-ti-cian [ŏp-tĭsh'ən] *noun*, a person who makes glasses, a dealer in optical goods

op-ti-mal [ŏp'tə-məl] *adjective*, most favorable condition

op-ti-mist [ŏp'tə-mĭst] *noun*, one who looks on the bright side of things, positive thinking

op-ti-mis-tic [ŏp'tə-mĭs-tĭk] *adjective*, having a positive outlook, upbeat, hopeful

op-tion [ŏp'shən] *noun*, 1) a choice 2) a stock available at a certain time at a stated price

op-tom-e-trist [ŏp-tŏm'ĭ-trĭst] *noun*, one who examines eyes and fits glasses to help a person see better

op-u-lence [ŏp'yə-ləns] *adjective*, having property, wealthy, rich, affluent, luxurious

o-pus [ō'pəs] *noun*, a great creative literary or musical work

or [ôr;] *conjunction*, used to connect words when given a choice

o-ral [ôr'əl] *adjective*, 1) spoken information 2) of the mouth

or-ange [ôr'ĭnj] *adjective*, 1) a color made when red and yellow are mixed together, *noun*, 2) a sweet, juicy fruit grown on trees in tropical climates

or-a-tor [ôr'ə-tər] *noun*, a public speaker of great eloquence

or-a-to-ri-o [ôr'ə-tôr'ē-ō'] *noun*, a dramatic poem set to music

or-a-to-ry [ôr'ə-tôr'ē] *noun*, a moving or powerful speech

or-bit [ôr'bĭt] *noun*, 1) the course an object follows in space around another, *verb*, 2) to travel through space in a cycle

or-chard [ôr'chərd] *noun*, a grove where fruit trees grow for food

or-ches-tra [ôr'kĭ-strə] *noun*, 1) a band of performers on various instruments 2) the lower floor in a theater for instruments

or-chid [ôr'kĭd] *noun*, an exotic tropical flower with three petals

or-dain [ôr-dān'] *verb*, to appoint, to install, to elect, to decree

or-deal [ôr-dēl'] *noun*, an extremely stressful situation

or-der [ôr'dər] *noun*, 1) a careful arrangement 2) a special system used to organize information 3) grouping, placement 4) a request telling someone to do something, *verb*, 5) to arrange carefully 6) to issue a command, to instruct

or-di-nal num-ber [ôr'dn-əl-nŭm'bər] *noun*, a number expressing degree or order in a series such as 1st, 2nd,

or-di-nance [ôr'dn-əns] *noun*, 1) a local law, an edict or decree 2) a prescribed practice or usage

or-di-nar-i-ly [ôr′dn-âr′ə-lē] *adverb*, usually, generally

or-di-nar-y [ôr′dn-ĕr′ē] *adjective*, 1) according to custom or established order 2) regular, commonplace, normal

ore [ôr, ōr] *noun*, a kind of rock in which metal is found

Or-e-gon [ôr′ĭ-gən] *noun*, one of the 50 United States in the Northwest, the capital is Salem. The state flower of **Oregon** is the Oregon grape, and the motto is "The Union."

or-gan [ôr′gən] *noun*, 1) a musical instrument similar to a piano, with long pipes through which air travels through to make the sound 2) a part of the body that serves a specific function

or-gan-ic [ôr-găn′ĭk] *adjective*, grown naturally without pesticides or fertilizers

or-gan-ism [ôr′gə-nĭz′əm] *noun*, any individual life form

or-gan-i-za-tion [ôr′gə-nĭ-zā′shən] *noun*, an association, a group of people working together for a common purpose

or-gan-ize [ôr′gə-nīz′] *verb*, 1) to plan, to arrange and implement in an orderly way 2) to establish or construct a plan or a scheme

o-ri-en-tal [ôr′ē-ĕn′tl] *adjective*, pertaining to the Orient or East Asia

o-ri-en-ta-tion [ôr′ē-ĕn-tā′shən] *noun*, the act of getting your bearings, an introduction

or-i-fice [ôr′ə-fĭs] *noun*, a mouthlike opening, a slit, any hole in a body

or-i-gin [ôr′ə-jĭn] *noun*, the first use or the beginning

o-rig-i-nal [ə-rĭj′ə-nəl] *adjective*, the first of its kind, new and different, inventive

o-rig-i-nal-i-ty [ə-rĭj′ə-năl′ĭ-tē] *noun*, creativeness, innovation

o-rig-i-nate [ə-rĭj′ə-nāt′] *verb*, 1) to bring into existence, to initiate 2) to produce as new

or-na-ment [ôr′nə-mənt] *noun*, a decoration, beautification

or-na-men-tal [ôr′nə-mĕn′tl] *adjective*, decorative, adorned, beautiful, embellished

or-nate [ôr-nāt′] *adjective*, excessively decorated, adorned

or-ni-thol-o-gist [ôr′nə-thŏl′ə-jĭst] *noun*, one who studies birds

or-phan [ôr′fən] *noun*, a child whose parents are dead

or-phan-age [ôr′fə-nĭj] *noun*, a home for children who have no family

or-tho-dox [ôr′thə-dŏks′] *adjective*, accepted, traditional doctrine, very conservative

or-thog-ra-phy [ôr-thŏg′rə-fē] *noun*, correct spelling

os-cil-late [ŏs′ə-lāt′] *verb*, 1) to swing backward and forward, to vibrate 2) varying above or below a mean value

os-si-fy [ŏs′ə-fī′] *verb*, 1) to change or harden cartilage into bone 2) to set into a repeating pattern

os-ten-si-ble [ŏ-stĕn′sə-bəl] *adjective*, shown, professed, apparent, pretended

ostentatious

os-ten-ta-tious [ŏs'tĕn-tā'shəs] *adjective*, pretentious, conspicuous, showiness as an attempt to attract attention

os-tra-cize [ŏs'trə-sīz'] *verb*, to banish, to cast out from social favor or fellowship

os-trich [ŏs'trĭch] *noun*, a very large bird, with long legs, that is black and white, and cannot fly

oth-er [ŭth'ər] *adjective*, 1) not the same, a different one, *adverb*, 2) differently, *pronoun*, 3) someone or something not mentioned specifically

oth-er-wise [ŭth'ər-wīz'] *adverb*, 1) if not 2) except for that 3) of a different kind

ought [ôt] *verb*, should

ounce [ouns] *noun*, 1) a weight measurement equal to 28.35 grams 2) a tiny bit

our [our] *adjective*, belonging to us

our-selves [our-sĕlvz'] *pronoun*, referring to the subjects in a sentence, we or us

oust [oust] *verb*, to dismiss, to kick out, to expel, to force out

out [out] *adverb*, 1) not in or inside, away from 2) absent, away 3) not shining or burning 4) to bring to a conclusion 5) excluded, omitted

out-cast [out'kăst'] *noun*, a displaced person, an exile

out-come [out'kŭm'] *noun*, a possible result as in an experiment, a final product

out-doors [out-dôrz', -dōrz'] *adjective*, not inside a building, located outside in the open air

out-doors-man [out-dôrz'mən, -dōrz'-] *noun*, a person who enjoys nature and outdoor activities

out-er [ou'tər] *adjective*, on the outside or edge of something

out-fit [out'fĭt'] *noun*, 1) clothing used for a particular purpose, *verb*, 2) to provide clothes or equipment

out-grow [out-grō'] *verb*, to change as one develops

out-growth [out'grōth'] *noun*, development, product

out-ing [ou'tĭng] *noun*, a short trip

out-let [out'lĕt', -lĭt] *noun*, 1) an opening, 2) manufacturer

out-line [out'līn'] *noun*, 1) a line showing the shape of something 2) the plan or format for a composition, *verb*, 3) to give the main points of

out-live [out-lĭv'] *verb*, to outlast, to live or last longer than

out-rage [out'rāj'] *noun*, 1) anger caused by injury or insult 2) anything that causes resentment or anger, a wicked or brutal act or remark *verb*, 2) to fill with anger of resentment

out-side [out-sīd'] *adverb*, 1) on or to the exterior surface, *noun*, 2) the outer part or surface

out-stand-ing [out-stăn'dĭng] *adjective*, 1) very good, excellent 2) not paid or settled

o-val [ō'vəl] *adjective*, a round flat shape like an egg

ov-en [ŭv'ən] *noun*, an electric appliance like a sealed box used to bake food

o-ver [ō′vər] *adjective*, 1) in control of 2) finished, *adverb*, 3) from start to finish again 4) unused, extra 5) to go beyond the top, *preposition*, 6) covering 7) across, from one side to the other 8) in every part

o-ver-all [ō′vər-ôl′] *adjective*, including all things, as a whole

o-ver-alls [ō′vər-ôlz′] *noun*, a kind of loose trousers with a bib

o-ver-board [ō′vər-bôrd′] *adverb*, over the side of a boat into the water

o-ver-cast [ō′vər-kăst′] *adjective*, cloudy, sunless, gloomy

o-ver-coat [ō′vər-kōt′] *noun*, a coat worn over the other clothing

o-ver-come [ō′vər-kŭm′] *verb*, to beat, to conquer, to lick

o-ver-due [ō′vər-dōō′] *adjective*, delinquent, late, past due

o-ver-es-ti-mate [ō′vər-ĕs′tə-māt′] *verb*, to calculate over the actual amount

o-ver-flow [ō′vər-flō′] *verb*, 1) to pour over the edge of a container when filled 2) to flood

o-ver-haul [ō′vər-hôl′] *verb*, to restore, to repair, to rebuild

o-ver-head [ō′vər-hĕd′] *adjective*, 1) above our heads, in the sky, *noun, no plural*, 2) the fixed costs to maintain something

o-ver-lap [ō′vər-lăp′] *verb*, 1) to rest on top of or over something and cover part of it 2) to partially coincide

o-ver-look [ō′vər-lŏŏk′] *verb*, 1) to fail to notice 2) to excuse

o-ver-night [ō′vər-nīt′] *adjective*, 1) from one day to the next, *adverb*, 2) during the night

o-ver-seas [ō′vər-sēz′] *adjective*, across the ocean, abroad

o-ver-seer [ō′vər-sē′ər] *noun*, one who watches over an area or institution, a supervisor

o-ver-sight [ō′vər-sīt′] *noun*, an error, a blunder, a failure

o-vert [ō-vûrt′] *adjective*, open to view, not concealed

o-ver-take [ō′vər-tāk′] *verb*, to chase and catch up to

o-ver-time [ō′vər-tīm′], *noun*, time in addition to what is normally worked, beyond one's scheduled working hours

o-ver-ture [ō′vər-chōŏr′] *noun*, a proposal, an introduction

o-ver-whelm [ō′vər-hwĕlm′] *verb*, 1) to overpower in mind and feeling 2) to engulf, to inundate

owe [ō] *verb*, 1) to have to give or pay 2) to feel grateful to someone for something

owl [oul] *noun*, a large bird that lives in the forest, it flies at night and eats small animals

own [ōn] *adjective*, 1) of or belonging to oneself or itself, *verb*, 2) to have or possess

own-er [ō′nər] *noun*, the person who has the right to something

own-er-ship [ō′nər-shĭp′] *noun*, a right of possession, a lawful claim or title

ox [ŏks] *noun*, *plural*, **oxen,** a full-grown male of domestic cattle used for farm work

oxidize

ox-i-dize [ŏk′sĭ-dīz′] *verb*, to combine with oxygen

ox-y-gen [ŏk′sĭ-jən] *noun*, a colorless, tasteless, odorless, chemically active gas, the part of air that animals, plants and people need to stay alive

oys-ter [oi′stər] *noun*, an edible shellfish, a bivalve mollusk

o-zone [ō′zōn′] *noun*, a faintly blue gas obtained by the silent discharge of electricity in air

P

pace [pās] *noun*, 1) a steady step or speed that is maintained, *verb*, 2) to walk back and forth

pach-y-derm [păk′ĭ-dûrm′] *noun*, a thick-skinned animal

pac-i-fist [pə-sĭf′ĭ-st] *noun*, someone who looks for peaceful means, opposed to force

pac-i-fy [păs′ə-fī′] *verb*, to appease, to calm, to soothe

pack [păk] *noun*, 1) a bundle or a collection of things 2) a group of wild animals that hunt together, *verb*, 3) to bundle or place a group of things into a container

pack-age [păk′ĭj] *noun*, a box or bundle containing one or more objects

pact [păkt] *noun*, an agreement, a contract, a treaty, a bargain

pad [păd] *noun*, 1) a soft material used to protect a wound 2) a number of sheets of paper stuck together at one edge

pad-dle [păd′l] *noun*, 1) an ore or long stick used to row a boat, *verb*, 2) to spank, to whack on the bottom 3) to row a boat 4) to move the hands and feet in shallow water

pad-dock [păd′ək] *noun*, a field or enclosure where horses are kept

pad-dy [păd′ē] *noun*, a field for growing rice

pad-lock [păd′lŏk′] *noun*, a portable lock, jointed at one end

page [pāj] *noun*, 1) one side of a piece of paper in a book 2) a person who delivers messages *verb*, 2) to summon or call indirectly through an intercom or paging system

pag-eant [păj′ənt] *noun*, an exhibition, a show, a parade

paid [pād] *verb*, the *past tense* of **pay**

pail [pāl] *noun*, a bucket or container with a handle

pain [pān] *noun*, physical suffering from injury or illness, distress

pain-ful [pān′fəl] *adjective*, a feeling of hurt, aching

paint [pānt] *noun*, 1) a liquid in a variety of colors that is used to cover a surface to protect or decorate it, *verb*, 2) to coat or color with paint 3) to convey an image by creating it using paints

paint-er [pān′tər] *noun*, a person who paints pictures or buildings

paint-ing [pān′tĭng] *noun*, completed pictures done with paint, a representation

pair [pâr] *noun*, 1) two like things put together as a match 2) an instrument with two parts joined together, e.g. *scissors*, *verb*, 3) to separate into groups of two

pa-ja-mas [pə-jä′mə] *noun, plural,* loose fitting clothes worn to bed

pal [păl] *noun,* a friend, chum

pal-ace [păl′ĭs] *noun,* a beautiful home of a wealthy person

pal-at-a-ble [păl′ə-tə-bəl] *adjective,* 1) tasty 2) acceptable to the mind, pleasing

pa-la-tial [pə-lā′shəl] *adjective,* suitable for a palace, impressively spacious

pale [pāl] *adjective,* 1) light in color, faded, *noun,* 2) the area enclosed by a boundary

pal-ette [păl′ĭt] *noun,* a board on which a painter mixes paints

pal-i-sade [păl′ĭ-sād′] *noun,* a partition formed as a barrier

pal-lid: [păl′id] *adjective,* pale

palm [päm] *noun,* 1) a tree with a long trunk without branches and large leaves at the top 2) the wide part inside the hand

pal-pa-ble [păl′pə-bəl] *adjective,* 1) capable of being touched or felt, obvious 2) tangible

pal-pi-tate [păl′pĭ-tāt′] *verb,* to throb, to pound with emotion or exertion, to quiver, to shake

pal-try [pôl′trē] *adjective,* insignificant, petty, trifling

pam-per [păm′pər] *verb,* to coddle, to indulge, to baby, to spoil

pam-phlet [păm′flĭt] *noun,* a book of a few sheets of printed matter

pan [păn] *noun,* a round metal pot for cooking things over heat

pan-a-ce-a [păn′ə-sē′ə] *noun,* a solution to all problems or sickness, a cure-all

pan-cre-as [păng′krē əs] *noun,* a large gland under and behind the stomach that secretes insulin to the intestine to help digest food

pan-da [păn′də] *noun,* a large black and white animal like a bear restricted to China

pan-de-mo-ni-um [păn′də-mō′nē-əm] *noun,* a wild tumult, an uproar, confusion

pan-der [păn′dər] *verb,* to cater to the low desires of others

pane [pān] *noun,* a piece of glass used in windows or doors

pan-el [păn′əl] *noun,* 1) a sunken compartment with raised margins in a ceiling 2) a complete jury 3) a group assembled to judge a contest or conduct a public discussion

pan-ic [păn′ĭk] *noun,* 1) a sudden fear which can spread quickly, *verb,* 2) to feel frightened or alarmed, filled with terror

pan-sy [păn′zē] *noun,* a flower that blooms through the winter

pant [pănt] *verb,* to breathe quickly

pan-ther [păn′thər] *noun,* one of the large wild cats, a cougar

pan-to-mime [păn′tə-mīm′] *noun,* a play in which actors use gestures without speech

pan-try [păn′trē] *noun,* a small room where food is stored

pants [pănts] *noun, plural,* trousers

pa-pa [pä′pə] *noun,* a father, a dad

pa-per [pā′pər] *noun,* 1) sheets of thin material used for writing, wrapping, etc. 2) a newspaper 3) paper with writing or printing on it verifying identity

paprika

pap-ri-ka [pă-prē′kə] *noun*, a
Turkish red pepper

pa-py-rus [pə-pī′rəs] *noun*, a reed
plant that grows in the Nile Valley
once used as paper

par [pär] *noun*, average, standard,
the norm, equality in value

par-a-ble [păr′ə-bəl] *noun*, a short,
simple story teaching a lesson

par-a-chute [păr′ə-shōōt′] *noun*,
1) a light device made of silk or
nylon, designed in an umbrella
shape, used to retard the free fall
from an aircraft, *verb*, 2) to eject
from an aircraft by jumping out
equipped with a parachute used
to slow something's fall to the
ground from a great height

pa-rade [pə-rād′] *noun*, 1) a
number of people walking or
marching together, a public
procession, *verb*, 2) to walk or
march with a group of people

par-a-digm [păr′ə-dīm′] *noun*, a
model, an example, a pattern

par-a-dise [păr′ə-dīs′] *noun*, a
place of complete happiness or
beauty, like heaven

par-a-dox [păr′ə-dŏks′] *noun*, a
statement that contradicts itself,
but is in fact true

par-af-fin [păr′ə-fĭn] *noun*, a white
wax used to make candles and
seal preserves

par-a-gon [păr′ə-gŏn′] *noun*, a
model of perfection

par-a-graph [păr′ə-grăf′] *noun*, a
subdivision in writing, beginning
with an indent on a new line

par-a-keet [păr′ə-kēt′] *noun*, a
small blue or green domestic
song bird

par-al-lel [păr′ə-lĕl′] *adjective*,
1) lying in the same direction and
always the same distance apart,
never intersecting 2) similar

par-al-lel-o-gram
[păr′ə-lĕl′ə-grăm′] *noun*, a four
sided plane figure with opposite
sides equal and parallel

pa-ral-y-sis [pə-răl′ĭ-sĭs] *adjective*,
loss of sensation and motion of
body parts, a helpless state

par-a-lyze [păr′ə-līz′] *verb*, to
destroy the energy of something,
to stop all movement or feeling

pa-ram-e-ter [pə-răm′ĭ-tər] *noun*,
the limit, a set standard

par-a-mount [păr′ə-mount′]
adjective, most important

par-a-noi-a [păr′ə-noi′ə] *noun*,
insanity marked by delusions of
persecution or glory

par-a-phrase [păr′ə-frāz′] *verb*, to
restate a passage in one's own
words for clarity

par-a-site [păr′ə-sīt′] *noun*, animal
or plant living off another, using it
as its only source of food

par-cel [pär′səl] *noun*, 1) a
package wrapped in paper, for
mailing or carrying, *verb*, 2) to
divide into portions to hand out

parch [pärch] *verb*, to dry in the
sun, to dehydrate, to scorch

parch-ment [pärch′mənt] *noun*, the
skin of a goat or sheep prepared
for writing

par-don [pär′dn] *noun*, *no plural*,
1) forgiveness, *verb*, 2) to
excuse, to forgive, to absolve

par-don-a-ble [pär′dn-ə-bəl]
adjective, excusable, forgivable

pare [pâr] *verb*, 1) to peel, to cut off the outer edge, 2) to reduce

par-ent [pâr/ənt] *noun*, 1) the father or mother 2) the source

pa-ren-the-sis [pə-rĕn/thĭ-sĭs] *noun*, one of the curved lines which enclose an aside ( )

par-ish [păr/ĭsh] *noun*, an area served by one church

park [pärk] *noun*, 1) a place in town designated for recreation, rest, and beauty, *verb*, 2) to put a car or vehicle in place

par-ka [pär/kə] *noun*, a heavy winter coat with a hood

par-ley [pär/lē] *noun*, a conference between two opponents, a discussion to settle a dispute

par-lia-ment [pär/lə-mənt] *noun*, an assembly in Great Britain similar to the United States Congress

par-lor [pär/lər] *noun*, a room that is usually used for talking or entertaining, a living room

pa-ro-chi-al [pə-rō/kē-əl] *adjective*, of or pertaining to a parish, a local area

par-o-dy [păr/ə-dc] *noun*, a humorous imitation, satire

pa-role [pə-rōl/] *noun*, an early conditional release from prison, free on probation

par-rot [păr/ət] *noun*, a brightly colored bird with a short curved beak that can mimic speech

par-si-mo-ny [pär/sə-mō/nē] *noun*, selfishness, stinginess

pars-ley [pär/slē] *noun*, an herb with flat or curled leaves used to flavor soups, etc., or to garnish food

par-snip [pär/snĭp] *noun*, a fleshy white root, in the carrot group

part [pärt] *noun*, 1) some of a thing or things 2) a share in an activity 3) a character in a play or film, *verb*, 4) to separate, to leave from 5) to break apart

par-tial-ly [pär/shə-lē] *adverb*, partly, somewhat, slightly

par-ti-al-i-ty [pär/shē-ăl/ĭ-tē] *adjective*, biased, inclined to favor one side

par-tic-i-pate [pär-tĭs/ə-pāt/] *verb*, to have a share in common with others, to take part, to join in

par-tic-i-pa-tion [pär-tĭs/ə-pā/shən] *noun*, the act of getting involved with others

par-ti-ci-ple [pär/tĭ-sĭp/əl] *noun*, one of two forms of a verb forming the past or future tense

par-ti-cle [pär/tĭ-kəl] *noun*, the smallest form of matter

par-tic-u-lar [pər-tĭk/yə-lər] *adjective*, relating to a part, individual, precise, specific

par-tic-u-lar-ly [pər-tĭk/yə-lər-lē] *adverb*, specifically, in detail

par-ti-san [pär/tĭ-zən] *adjective*, an adherent to a party or faction

par-ti-tion [pär-tĭsh/ən] *noun*, 1) a division, a dividing wall, *verb*, 2) to divide, to separate

part-ly [pärt/lē] *adverb*, to some extent, partially, somewhat

part-ner [pärt/nər] *noun*, 1) an associate in business 2) a companion in dancing or sports

par-ty [pär/tē] *noun*, 1) a meeting of friends to enjoy themselves 2) a group of people who have

pass

the same interests or goals, *verb*, 3) to celebrate

pass [păs] *noun*, 1) a high mountain road 2) a paper allowing you to go somewhere or have something 3) a forward gesture, *verb*, 4) to give something to someone else 5) to be allowed to advance to the next level

pas-sage [păs′ĭj] *noun*, 1) an excerpt from a chapter, a clause or quotation 2) the act or process of passing as through time or from place to place, a journey 3) a path 4) a part of a written work or a piece of music

pass-é [pă-sā′] *adjective*, behind the times, old fashioned

pas-sen-ger [păs′ən-jər] *noun*, a traveler in a vehicle such as a car, boat, bus, etc.

pas-sion [păsh′ən] *noun*, a strong feeling or desire, enthusiasm

pas-sion-ate [păsh′ə-nĭt] *adjective*, ardent in feeling or desire

pas-sive [păs′ĭv] *adjective*, to be unresponsive, not active

pass-port [păs′pôrt′] *noun*, an official permission issued to a person allowing travel out of the country and return, a document of identification

past [păst] *adjective*, 1) referring to time and events in history, *noun*, *no plural*, 2) time gone by, *preposition*, 3) to or on the further side of 4) beyond in time

pas-ta [päs′tə] *noun*, noodles made from flour, water, salt, and eggs

paste [pāst] *noun*, 1) a sticky substance that glues things together, *verb*, 2) to put in place, for example with an adhesive

pas-tel [pă-stĕl′] *noun*, a sketch or drawing of a soft color or hue

pas-teur-ize [păs′chə-rīz′] *verb*, to subject fluids to a high temperature (131 degrees Celsius, 158 degrees Fahrenheit) to prevent the growth of bacteria

pas-time [păs′tīm′] *noun*, something that you do to amuse yourself or to relax, like a hobby

pas-tor [păs′tər] *noun*, a reverend, the clergyman of a church

pas-to-ral [păs′tər-əl] *adjective*, rural, in the country, rustic

pas-try [pā′strē] *noun*, sweet baked foods, such as cakes or pies

pas-ture [păs′chər] *noun*, grassland for grazing livestock

pat [păt] *noun*, 1) a light touch with an open hand, a gentle tap, *verb*, 2) to touch lightly with a hand

patch [păch] *noun*, 1) a small piece of cloth used to mend a tear, *verb*, 2) to put a piece of material on a surface to repair a hole or strengthen a worn area

pat-ent [păt′nt] *adjective*, 1) obvious, plain, *noun*, 2) the right given to an inventor by the government, to exclusively produce a product for a number of years

pa-ter-nal [pə-tûr′nəl] *adjective*, fatherly, kind, devoted

path [păth] *noun*, a track worn by people or animals walking on it

pa·thet·ic [pə-thĕt′ĭk] *adjective*, causing pity or grief, full of pathos and sympathy

pa·thol·o·gy [pă-thŏl′ə-jē] *noun*, the science of treating disease, their natural causes, results, etc.

pa·thos [pā′thŏs′] *noun*, human or animal experience that cause feelings of pity, compassion

pa·tience [pā′shəns] *noun*, no *plural*, the act of waiting calmly for someone or something

pa·tient [pā′shənt] *adjective*, 1) able to bear quietly or wait for something calmly, *noun*, 2) a person under medical treatment

pat·i·o [păt′ē-ō′] *noun*, a paved outdoor space that is used for eating, cooking or relaxing

pa·tri·arch [pā′trē-ärk′] *noun*, 1) father and ruler of a family or tribe 2) a venerable old man

pa·tri·ot [pā′trē-ət] *noun*, one who loves and defends his country

pa·tri·ot·ic [pā′trē-ŏt′ĭk] *adjective*, public-spirited, flag-waving

pa·tri·ot·ism [pā′trē-ə-tĭz′ərn] *adjective*, love of one's country

pa·trol [pə-trōl′] *noun*, 1) a small group of soldiers or police officers, *verb*, 2) to follow a route regularly looking for criminal activity

pa·tron [pā′trən] *noun*, 1) someone who provides financial support to a cause 2) a customer

pa·tron·ize [pā′trə-nīz′] *verb*, 1) to act as a supporter 2) to treat with condescension, to look down on

pat·tern [păt′ərn] *noun*, 1) anything used as a guide or model for making things 2) a repeated sequence 3) to make by following a prototype or model

pau·per [pô′pər] *noun*, destitute, a very poor person, a beggar

pause [pôz] *noun*, 1) a break in action of speech, *verb*, 2) to stop briefly, to delay action or speech

pave [pāv] *verb*, 1) to cover the surface with asphalt bricks or cement 2) to prepare the way

pave·ment [pāv′mənt] *noun*, highway surface, asphalt

paw [pô] *noun*, the foot of a four-legged animal that has claws

pawn [pôn] *noun*, 1) a victim 2) a chess piece, *verb*, 3) to sell

pay [pā] *noun*, 1) the compensation received for work, *verb*, 2) to give someone money for goods and services

pay·ment [pā′mənt] *noun*, compensation, installment

pay·roll [pā′rōl′] *noun*, the money used to pay workers

pea [pē] *noun*, a seed from a pod bearing vine that can be eaten

peace [pēs] *noun*, 1) a period of harmony among nations when there is no war 2) a calm ordered condition

peach [pēch] *noun*, *plural*, **peaches** 1) a juicy yellow-orange fruit with downy skin, from an orchard tree that has pink flowers 2) a yellowish-pink color

pea·cock [pē′kŏk′] *noun*, a bird with a large brightly colored tail

peak [pēk] *noun*, 1) the pointed top of a mountain or ridge 2) the point of greatest development

peal [pēl] *noun*, 1) a loud ringing of bells *verb*, 2) to resound

pea-nut [pē'nŭt'] *noun*, a legume that bears edible pods that taste like nuts

pear [pâr] *noun*, a juicy yellow, brown or green fruit from an orchard tree

pearl [pûrl] *noun*, a precious white substance like a bead found inside an oyster, used in jewelry

peas-ant [pĕz'ənt] *noun*, a person who makes a living from working the soil, especially in poorer countries

peb-ble [pĕb'əl] *noun*, a small stone worn by erosion

pe-can [pĭ-kän'] *noun*, the edible kernel nut from a hickory tree grown in the south

peck [pĕk] *noun*, 1) ¼ of a bushel, *verb*, 2) to cut or lift with the beak

pec-to-ral [pĕk'tər-əl] *adjective*, pertaining to the chest

pe-cu-liar [pĭ-kyo͞ol'yər] *adjective*, oddly different from the usual, strange, distinctive, particular

pe-cu-ni-ar-y [pĭ-kyo͞o'nē-ĕr'ē] *adjective*, pertaining to or consisting of money

ped-a-gogue [pĕd'ə-gŏg'] *noun*, a narrow-minded teacher

ped-al [pĕd'l] *noun*, 1) a lever acted on by the foot, *verb*, 2) to push with the feet when riding a bicycle in order to get the bicycle to move

ped-dle [pĕd'l] *verb*, to sell on the street or door to door

ped-es-tal [pĕd'ĭ-stəl] *noun*, a base or support for a column

pe-des-tri-an [pə-dĕs'trē-ən] *noun*, a person who walks

pe-di-a-tri-cian [pē'dē-ə-trĭsh'ən] *noun*, a doctor who is an expert in children's diseases

ped-i-gree [pĕd'ĭ-grē'] *noun*, a register of a line of ancestors, descent, ancestry, lineage

peek [pēk] *noun*, 1) a glance, *verb*, 2) to look at, to catch sight of

peel [pēl] *noun*, no plural, 1) the outside covering of a fruit or vegetable, *verb*, 2) to cut the outside covering off of a fruit or vegetable to eat the food inside

peer [pîr] *noun*, 1) someone your own age or someone with similar interests, an equal, *verb*, 2) to take a closer look

peg [pĕg] *noun*, a wooden or metal object used as a hook when put on a wall or as a fastening

pe-jo-ra-tive [pĭ-jôr'ə-tĭv] *adjective*, a deteriorating effect on the meaning of a word

pel-i-can [pĕl'ĭ-kän'] *noun*, a large water bird with webbed feet and an expandable pouch in the lower beak for holding fish

pelt [pĕlt] *noun*, 1) the furry skin of an animal 2) to strike over and over with repeated blows

pen [pĕn] *noun*, 1) an instrument for writing using ink 2) an enclosure for animals

pe-nal-ize [pē'nə-līz'] *verb*, to scold, to punish, to chastise

pen-al-ty [pĕn′əl-tē] *noun*, the suffering or fine imposed as a punishment for a violation

pen-chant [pĕn′chənt] *noun*, a strong mental leaning or attraction, a decided taste

pen-cil [pĕn′səl] *noun*, a writing instrument with a gray substance in the middle that marks paper

pend-ant [pĕn′dənt] *noun*, a hanging ornament or piece of jewelry, like a necklace

pend-ent [pĕn′dənt] *adjective*, hanging or suspended

pend-ing [pĕn′dĭng] *adjective*, 1) about to happen, imminent, *preposition*, 2) until 3) during

pen-du-lum [pĕn′jə-ləm] *noun*, a weight which swings from side to side under the combined action of gravity and momentum

pen-e-trate [pĕn′ĭ-trāt′] *verb*, 1) to enter into 2) to affect deeply

pen-guin [pĕng′gwĭn] *noun*, a large flightless sea bird of Antarctica that has flipper-like wings

pen-in-su-la [pə nĭn′syə-lə] *noun*, a piece of land extending from the mainland, surrounded by water on three sides

pen-i-ten-tia-ry [pĕn′ĭ-tĕn′shə-rē] *noun*, a federal prison

pen-nant [pĕn′ənt] *noun*, a flag or banner with an insignia

pen-ni-less [pĕn′ē-lĭs] *adjective*, without any money, destitute

Penn-syl-va-nia [pĕn′səl-vān′yə] *noun*, one of the 50 United States located in the Northeast, the capital is Harrisburg. The state flower of **Pennsylvania** is the mountain laurel and the motto is "Virtue, liberty, and independence."

pen-ny [pĕn′ē] *noun*, a copper coin worth one cent

pen-sion [pĕn′shən] *noun*, an allowance of money given to someone regularly starting at retirement

pen-sive [pĕn′sĭv] *adjective*, a deep thinker, thoughtful with a hint of sadness, reflective

pen-ta-gon [pĕn′tə-gŏn′] *noun*, a shape with five equal sides

pent-house [pĕnt′hous′] *noun*, an apartment on the top floor of a building

pe-on [pē′ŏn′] *noun*, an unskilled laborer, a menial worker

peo-ple [pē′pəl] *noun*, *plural* of **person**, 1) human beings, men, women, and children 2) a nation

pep-per [pĕp′ər] *noun*, *no plural*, 1) a powder made from seeds of some plants and used to flavor food 2) the fruit of pepper plants, which can be used in cooking or eaten raw in salads

pep-per-mint [pĕp′ər-mĭnt′] *noun*, 1) oil from an herb used to give a taste of mint 2) a candy that tastes like mint

per [pûr] *preposition*, for or in each, according to

per-ceive [pər-sēv′] *verb*, to comprehend, to obtain knowledge through the senses

per-cent [pər-sĕnt′] *noun*, a number in proportion to 100

percentage

per-cent-age [pər-sĕn'tĭj] *adjective*, allowance or commission on a hundred

per-cep-ti-ble [pər-sĕp'tə-bəl] *adjective*, capable of being perceived, discernible

per-cep-tion [pər-sĕp'shən] *noun*, viewpoint, observation

perch [pûrch] *noun*, 1) a place for a bird to sit, *verb*, 2) to sit on a narrow branch or stick

per-co-late [pûr'kə-lāt'] *verb*, to pass or ooze through, to trickle through, to filter

per-cus-sion [pər-kŭsh'ən] *noun*, the group of musical instruments, such as a drum, whose sound is produced by striking or hitting

per-emp-to-ry [pə-rĕmp'tə-rē] *adjective*, closed to further discussion or action

per-en-ni-al [pə-rĕn'ē-əl] *adjective*, 1) lasting through the year 2) never failing

per-fect [pûr'fĭkt] *adjective*, 1) beyond improvement, having nothing wrong, *verb*, 2) to improve, to make better

per-fec-tion [pər-fĕk'shən] *noun*, the state of being without fault the highest degree of excellence

per-fect-ly [pûr'fĭkt-lē] *adverb*, completely, ideally, flawlessly

per-fo-rate [pûr'fə-rāt'] *verb*, to make a small hole, to prick

per-form [pər-fôrm'] *verb*, 1) to act in a play or a musical event 2) to do, to carry out a task

per-for-mance [pər-fôr'məns] *noun*, a show or act presented before an audience

per-form-er [pər-fôrm'ər] *noun*, one who entertains before an audience

per-fume [pûr'fyōōm'] *noun*, no *plural*, liquid that has a sweet smell, a fragrant oil 2) a delightful odor

per-func-to-ry [pər-fŭngk'tə-rē] *adjective*, done merely as a duty with little interest or care

per-haps [pər-hăps'] *adverb*, by chance, possibly, maybe

per-il [pĕr'əl] *noun*, a danger, a grave risk, a hazard

pe-rim-e-ter [pə-rĭm'ĭ-tər] *noun*, the measurement of the distance around a two-dimensional figure

pe-ri-od [pĭr'ē-əd] *noun*, 1) an interval of time having a specific length or character 2) a punctuation mark used at the end of a sentence 3) a session in school

pe-ri-od-i-cal [pĭr'ē-ŏd'ĭ-kəl] *noun*, a publication appearing with a fixed interval between issues

pe-riph-er-al [pə-rĭf'ər-əl] *adjective*, having to do with, or situated on the outside

pe-riph-er-y [pə-rĭf'ə-rē] *noun*, the edge, usually of a round surface

per-i-scope [pĕr'ĭ-skōp'] *noun*, an optical instrument that allows observation of objects from a position not in a direct line of sight, used in submarines

per-ish [pĕr'ĭsh] *verb*, to die

per-ish-a-ble [pĕr′ĭ-shə-bəl]
adjective, likely to spoil,
something that rots in air, it has
to be refrigerated to make it last

per-ju-ry [pûr′jə-rē] *noun*, false
testimony under oath

per-ma-nent [pûr′mə-nənt]
adjective, meant to last without
changing, lasting, durable

per-ma-nent-ly [pûr′mə-nənt-lē]
adverb, lasting indefinitely

per-me-a-ble [pûr′mē-ə-bəl]
adjective, 1) capable of receiving
fluids or transmitting magnetic
effects 2) allowing liquids to pass
through

per-me-ate [pûr′mē-āt′] *verb*, to
pass through the pores of, to
spread throughout, to pervade

per-mis-sion [pər-mĭsh′ən] *noun*,
formal consent, authorization

per-mit [pər-mĭt′] *noun*, 1) a written
notice that allows you to do
something, *verb*, 2) to allow

per-ni-cious [pər-nĭsh′əs]
adjective, destructive, ruinous,
causing insidious harm

per-pen-dic-u-lar
[pûr′pən-dĭk′yə-lər] *adjective*,
1) perfectly upright 2) at right
angles to a horizontal plane

per-pe-trate [pûr′pĭ-trāt′] *verb*, to
do or to perform, to carry
through, to commit

per-pet-u-al [pər-pĕch′o͞o-əl]
adjective, never ceasing,
continuing forever, endless

per-pe-tu-ate [pər-pĕch′o͞o-āt′]
verb, to continue, indefinitely

per-plex [pər-plĕks′] *verb*, to
embarrass, to bewilder, to cause
to doubt, to puzzle, to baffle

per-plex-i-ty [pər-plĕk′sĭ-tē] *noun*,
the quality or state of being
puzzled, bewilderment

per-se-cute [pûr′sĭ-kyo͞ot′] *verb*, to
bother, to oppress, to punish

per-se-cu-tion [pûr′sĭ-kyo͞o′shən]
noun, the act of persistently
injuring, harassing or annoying

per-se-ver-ance [pûr′sə-vîr′əns]
noun, the will to keep working
until the job is done, persistence

per-se-vere [pûr′sə-vîr′] *verb*, to
work to accomplish a goal
despite difficulty

per-sist [pər-sĭst′] *verb*, to keep
doing something, to persevere,
to keep trying

per-sist-ence [pər-sĭs′təns] *noun*,
the act of continuing to do
something, not giving up

per-son [pûr′sən] *noun*, **people**,
plural, a human being, such as a
man, woman or child, an
unnamed individual

per-son-a-ble [pûr′sə-nə-bəl]
adjective, good-natured,
agreeable, charming, attractive

per-son-al [pûr′sə-nəl] *adjective*, of
or concerning a particular
person, concerning a person's
private life, confidential

per-son-al-i-ty [pûr′sə-năl′ĭ-tē]
noun, distinctive personal
character, individuality

per-son-al-ly [pûr′sə-nə-lē] *adverb*,
1) from one's own viewpoint 2) in
person

personification

per-son-i-fi-ca-tion
[pər-sŏn′ə-fĭ-kā′shən] *noun*,
1) to think of or represent as a
person 2) an embodiment or
example of someone

per-son-nel [pûr′sə-něl′] *noun*, the
staff of an organization

per-spec-tive [pər-spěk′tĭv] *noun*,
as one sees it, a point of view

per-spi-ra-tion [pûr′spə-rā′shən]
noun, sweat, a salty water fluid
secreted from the sweat glands

per-spire [pər-spīr′] *verb*, to sweat

per-suade [pər-swād′] *verb*, to
influence or gain over by
argument or advice

per-sua-sive [pər-swā′sĭv]
adjective, an influential argument

pert [pûrt] *adjective*, bold, flippant,
forward, impertinent, saucy

per-tain [pər-tān′] *verb*, to relate, to
be connected as a part

per-ti-nent [pûr′tn-ənt] *adjective*,
belonging or relating to the
subject at hand, relevant

per-turb [pər-tûrb′] *verb*, to trouble,
or disturb, to agitate

pe-ruse [pə-rōōz′] *verb*, to read

per-vade [pər-vā′d] *verb*, to pass
through, to permeate

per-va-sive [pər-vā′sĭv] *adjective*,
to become spread throughout all
parts, universal, permeating

per-ver-sion [pər-vûr′zhən] *noun*,
turning from right to wrong

per-vert [pər-vûrt′] *verb*, to make
contrary or obstinate remarks

pes-ky [pěs′kē] *adjective*,
annoying, being like a pest

pes-si-mist [pěs′ə-mĭst] *noun*, one
who looks on the dark side of
things and expects the worst

pes-si-mism [pěs′ə-mĭz′əm]
adjective, belief that life is
basically bad or evil

pest [pěst] *noun*, an annoying and
destructive insect or person

pes-ti-cide [pěs′tĭ-sīd′] *noun*, any
substance designed to kill living
organisms, such as insects,
plants, fungi and rodents

pes-ti-lence [pěs′tə-ləns] *noun*,
any deadly contagious epidemic
of a disease or virus

pet [pět] *noun*, 1) an animal you
look after and keep in your
house, *verb*, 2) to stroke

pet-al [pět′l] *noun*, one of the parts
of the corolla of a flower that are
usually colorful

pe-tite [pə-tēt′] *adjective*, small,
little, a woman or girl of small
size

pe-ti-tion [pə-tĭsh′ən] *noun*, 1) a
formal request accompanied by
signatures as an endorsement,
verb, 2) to request change by
making a written formal request

pet-ri-fy [pět′rə-fī′] *verb*, to turn to
stone, to harden, to deaden

pet-ro-le-um [pə-trō′lē-əm] *noun*,
mineral oil, a dark brown or
green inflammable liquid

pet-ty [pět′ē] *adjective*, a small
matter of little importance,
insignificant, trivial

pew [pyōō] *noun*, one of a number
of fixed benches, like a seat, with
backs in a church

pew-ter [pyōō'tər] *noun*, an alloy consisting mainly of tin and other metals

phan-tom [făn'təm] *noun*, an apparition, a ghost, a vision

phar-ma-cy [fär'mə-sē] *noun*, a place where medicines are dispensed, a drug store

phase [fāz] *noun*, a stage in a process of development

pheas-ant [fĕz'ənt] *noun*, a game bird with long tail feathers that lives in the woods

phe-nom-e-non [fĭ-nŏm'ə-nŏn'] *noun*, *plural*, **phenomena**, a marvel, an event, a happening

phil-an-throp-ic [fĭl'ən-thrŏp'ĭk] *adjective*, love for mankind, benevolent, generous

phi-lol-o-gist [fĭ-lŏl'ə-jĭst] *noun*, the study of languages, their structure and origin

phi-los-o-pher [fĭ-lŏs'ə-fər] *noun*, a wise person, a reflective thinker, a sage

phi-los-o-phy [fĭ-lŏs'ə-fē] *noun*, the study of moral and mental sciences, metaphysics

pho-bi-a [fō'bē-ə] *noun*, dislike, an irrational fear of something

phone [fōn] *noun*, the short term for telephone

pho-net-ic [fə-nĕt'ĭk] *adjective*, the sound of letters in a word that create speech

pho-no-graph [fō'nə-grăf'] *noun*, a record player

phos-pho-res-cence [fŏs'fə-rĕs'əns] *noun*, any bright and luminous radiating light

phos-pho-rus [fŏs'fər oo] *noun*, a nonmetallic element used in matches

pho-to-graph [fō'tə-grăf'] *noun*, 1) a picture produced using film and a camera, *verb*, 2) to take a picture with a camera

pho-to-graph-ic [fō'tə-grăf'ĭk] *adjective*, the process of photography

pho-to-syn-the-sis [fō'tō-sĭn'thĭ-sĭs] *verb*, the process by which chlorophyll-containing cells in green plants use light as an energy source to synthesize carbohydrates from carbon dioxide and water

phrase [frāz] *noun*, 1) a part of a sentence 2) an expression, a saying, *verb*, 3) to express in words or a particular way

phys-i-cal [fĭz'ĭ-kəl] *adjective*, of or pertaining to nature or the human body

phy-si-cian [fĭ-zĭsh'ən] *noun*, a doctor of medicine

phys-ics [fĭz'ĭks] *noun*, the science that deals with matter and energy such as light, motion, sound, heat, electricity, or force, and the laws that govern them

phys-i-ol-o-gy [fĭz'ē-ŏl'ə-jē] *noun*, that part of biology which studies living organisms

phy-sique [fĭ-zēk'] *noun*, the development and bodily structure or appearance of a person, the frame, figure

pi-an-ist [pē-ăn'ĭst] *noun*, a skilled performer on the piano

pi-a-no [pē-ăn'ō] *noun*, a musical instrument played by hitting its keys on a keyboard with fingers, which hit felt-covered hammers which strike metal strings

pick [pĭk] *noun*, 1) a choice or selection 2) a tool used to break the earth, *verb*, 3) to choose 4) to hold with your fingers

pick-et [pĭk/ĭt] *noun*, 1) a stake, a peg, *verb*, 2) to strike, to boycott

pick-le [pĭk/əl] *noun*, 1) any food which has been preserved in brine or in vinegar 2) an awkward situation

pic-nic [pĭk/nĭk] *noun*, a pleasure trip with a meal eaten in the open air

pic-to-graph [pĭk/tə-grăf/] *noun*, a rudimentary diagram or symbol used to represent an idea as the primitive writing of stone tablets and cave drawings

pic-ture [pĭk/chər] *noun*, 1) visual respresentation such as a drawing, painting, photograph, etc., *verb*, 2) to imagine in your mind, to visualize

pic-tur-esque [pĭk/chə-rĕsk/] *adjective*, forming a pleasing picture, graphic, quaint

pie [pī] *noun*, a dish made with fruit, meat or vegetables, surrounded by a pastry crust on the bottom and sometimes on top

piece [pēs] *noun*, 1) a fragment or part separated from the whole, *verb*, 2) to put together, to repair

pier [pîr] *noun*, a wharf or dock extending into the water from the land used as a place to moor ships

pierce [pîrs] *verb*, 1) to pass or break through 2) to make a hole through

pierc-ing [pîrsĭng] *adjective*, very loud and shrill

pig [pĭg] *noun*, any swine raised for pork and bacon

pi-geon [pĭj/ən] *noun*, a plump bird with a small head

pig-ment [pĭg/mənt] *noun*, the color of something, a hue

pile [pīl] *noun*, 1) a heap of things laying one on another 2) the nap of a fabric 3) a post in a pier that goes into the soil beneath the water, *verb*, 4) to amass, to gather together in a heap, to accumulate, to stack

pil-grim [pĭl/grəm] *noun*, a person who journeys to pray at a holy place as an act of religious devotion

pil-grim-age [pĭl/grə-mĭj] *noun*, a journey to a holy place

pill [pĭl] *noun*, a small tablet or capsule of medicine that can be easily swallowed

pil-lage [pĭl/ĭj] *verb*, to strip of money, ransack, rob, destroy

pil-lar [pĭl/ər] *noun*, 1) a strong post 2) a column, a vertical support or structure

pil-low [pĭl/ō] *noun*, a cloth case filled with feathers or other soft material put under the head during sleep

pil-low-case [pĭl/ō-kās/] *noun*, the cloth bag put over a pillow to keep it clean

pi-lot [pī/lət] *noun*, someone who is qualified to guide or navigate a ship or a plane

pin [pĭn] *noun*, 1) a slender piece of metal or wood, sharp on one end round on the other, used to join and fasten things together, *verb*, 2) to fasten with a sharp instrument 3) to hold in a spot

pin-cers [pĭn′sərz] *noun*, an instrument or an appendage having two grasping jaws working on a pivot

pinch [pĭnch] *noun*, 1) a very small amount, *verb*, 2) to squeeze between the finger and thumb 3) to make something feel tight

pine [pīn] *noun*, 1) an evergreen tree with leaves that look like needles, *verb*, 2) to want something very badly

pine-ap-ple [pīn′ăp′əl] *noun*, 1) the fruit of a tropical plant, resembling the shape of a pinecone 2) a symbol of hospitality

pin-ion [pĭn′yən] *noun*, a cogwheel with a small number of teeth, designed to interlock its gear with a larger wheel

pink [pĭngk] *adjective*, 1) a pastel color of red and white
noun, 2) the color made by mixing red and white

pin-na-cle [pĭn′ə-kəl] *noun*, 1) a small turret above the rest of the building 2) a lofty peak

pint [pīnt] *noun*, a liquid measurement equal to 2 cups or 16 fluid ounces

pi-o-neer [pī′ə-nîr′] *noun*, one of the first to explore an area or field of study, an innovator

pi-ous [pī′əs] *adjective*, devout

pipe [pīp] *noun*, 1) a tube, a cylinder used to convey liquid or gas 2) a device with a bowl at the end of a short straw used to smoke tobacco 3) a musical instrument through which air is blown, *verb*, 4) to make a high pitched sound

pi-quant [pē′kənt] *adjective*, 1) pleasantly tart-tasting, spicy 2) provocative

pique [pēk] *noun*, slight anger or resentment, wounded pride

pi-rate [pī′rĭt] *noun*, a person who robs ships at sea

pis-til [pĭs′təl] *noun*, the part of a flower that produces seeds

pis-tol [pĭs′təl] *noun*, a small gun like a revolver, a firearm

pis-ton [pĭs′tən] *noun*, a metal disk which moves up and down in a cylinder exerting pressure

pit [pĭt] *noun*, 1) a deep hole in the ground 2) the seed of a fruit

pitch [pĭch] *noun*, 1) a gummy substance used for sealing roads and caulking 2) a ball thrown or tossed 3) the tone of a voice or a sound, *verb*, 4) to put in place or set up 5) to toss or throw a ball 6) when a boat leans to an angle while traveling in the water

pitch-er [pĭch′ər] *noun*, 1) a container with a lip and a handle to pour liquid 2) the person who throws the ball to the batter in a baseball game

pitch-fork [pĭch′fôrk′] *noun*, a fork with a long handle used to lift and toss hay

pitfall

pit-fall [pĭt′fôl′] *noun*, a trap, a snare or hazard not easily avoided, a manhole

pith-y [pĭth′ē] *adjective*, concise, short and to the point

pit-i-ful [pĭt′ĭ-fəl] *adjective*, something that causes sympathy

pit-tance [pĭt′ns] *noun*, a small amount, next to nothing

pit-y [pĭt′ē] *noun*, 1) the sadness felt when someone else is hurt or in trouble, *verb*, 2) to feel sorry for someone, to feel sympathy

piv-ot [pĭv′ət] *noun*, a fixed pin on which something turns

piz-za [pēt′sə] *noun*, a baked flat crust covered with cheese, tomato sauce, etc.

pla-cate [plā′kāt′] *verb*, to pacify, to satisfy, to please someone

place [plās] *noun*, 1) a designated area or a particular space, *verb*, 2) to put in a particular spot 3) to identify by recalling

plac-id [plăs′ĭd] *adjective*, calm, peaceful, tranquil, untroubled

pla-gia-rism [plā′jə-rĭz′əm] *noun*, the act of copying someone's work and claiming it as your own

plague [plāg] *noun*, 1) anything troublesome 2) an infectious disease, *verb*, 3) to annoy

plaid [plăd] *adjective*, a pattern on cloth with stripes of different colors that cross each other

plain [plān] *adjective*, 1) open to view, clear, easy to understand, 2) simple, *noun*, 3) a stretch of gently rolling land with few trees

plain-ly [plān′lē] *adverb*, clearly

plain-tiff [plān′tĭf] *noun*, one who commences a legal action or suit

plan [plăn] *noun*, 1) a drawing made to scale of a new building or a project 2) a scheme indicating how to accomplish something, *verb*, 3) to design, to scheme or devise

plane [plān] *noun*, 1) a hand tool used to smooth the surface of wood 2) the short term for airplane 3) any flat or level surface

plan-et [plăn′ĭt] *noun*, a large mass like the earth that revolves around the sun

plank [plăngk] *noun*, a long, flat, thin piece of wood

plank-ton [plăngk′tən] *noun*, plant and animal organisms, generally microscopic, that float and or drift in great numbers in fresh or salt water

plant [plănt] *noun*, 1) a living thing that is not a mineral or animal 2) a factory, a work place, *verb*, 3) to put into the ground to grow

plan-ta-tion [plăn-tā′shən] *noun*, a large estate or farm cultivated by workers living on it

plaque [plăk] *noun*, 1) a marker, a tablet with an inscription 2) tarter calcified on the teeth

plas-ma [plăz′mə] *noun*, the fourth state of matter, composed of broken up atoms

plas-tic [plăs′tĭk] *adjective*, 1) referring to any pliable petroleum based product, *noun*, 2) any of a group of substances made chemically and molded by heat to form, fibers, bottles, etc.

plato [plāt] *noun*, a shallow dish from which food is eaten

pla-teau [plă-tō′] *noun*, 1) an elevated plane 2) inactive period

plat-form [plăt′fôrm′] *noun*, 1) a part of a station where you get on and off trains 2) a raised stage or dais so the audience can see the speaker or performers 3) beliefs, principles

plat-i-tude [plăt′ĭ-tōōd′] *noun*, a commonplace statement

pla-ton-ic [plə-tŏn′ĭk] *adjective*, a friendly relationship

pla-toon [plə-tōōn′] *noun*, a military unit of troops

plat-ter [plăt′ər] *noun*, 1) a large serving of food 2) a large shallow plate for serving food

plau-dits [plô′dĭts] *noun, plural*, enthusiastic approval, applause

plau-si-ble [plô′zə-bəl] *adjective*, apparently right, seeming to be reasonable, credible

play [plā] *noun*, 1) the performance of a story on the stage, *verb*, 2) to amuse or entertain 3) to take part in a game 4) to perform on a musical instrument

plea [plē] *noun*, 1) an appeal, an urgent request 2) a defense

plead [plēd] *verb*, 1) to ask for something that is felt to be very important, to appeal earnestly 2) to respond to a charge by a court of law

pleas-ant [plĕz′ənt] *adjective*, 1) agreeable, amiable, friendly 2) fair, mild, comfortable

pleas-ant-ly [plĕz′ənt-lē] *adverb*, agreeably, politely, kindly

please [plēz] *noun*, 1) a word added to a request to make it sound polite, *verb*, 2) to make someone happy 3) to wish

pleased [plēzd] *adjective*, glad

plea-sur-ably [plĕzh′ər-ə-bəl] *adverb*, capable of affording satisfaction, pleasant

pleas-ure [plĕzh′ər] *noun*, enjoyment or satisfaction

pledge [plĕj] *noun*, 1) a promise, a guarantee, *verb*, 2) to take an oath, to bind by a promise

plen-ty [plĕn′tē] *adjective*, enough, all that is needed

pleth-o-ra [plĕth′ər-ə] *noun*, a large or excessive amount of something, an abundance

pli-ant [plī′ənt] *adjective*, bendable

pli-ers [plī′ərz] *noun*, a small pincers with long jaws, used for bending metal rods or wire, or holding small objects

plod [plŏd] *verb*, to walk heavily, to trudge, to work steadily

plot [plŏt] *noun*, 1) a piece of land 2) a secret plan, usually to commit a crime 3) the story of a book, film, etc. *verb*, 4) to plan a secret activity, to conspire

plow [plou] *noun*, 1) a farm tool used to overturn earth for planting *verb*, 2) to turn over the soil to prepare the earth for planting 3) to move forcefully

pluck [plŭk] *verb*, to pull off or pull out 2) to grasp or grab

plug [plŭg] *noun*, 1) a stopper used to keep water from draining out of a basin 2) a device put in a wall socket to conduct electricity,

plum

verb, 3) to put an electric cord into a socket 4) to put a stopper into a drain hole, to fill a hole 5) to persevere

plum [plŭm] *noun*, a sweet juicy red fruit with a pit as a seed

plumb-er [plŭm/ər] *noun*, a tradesman who fits, and repairs gas and water pipes

plumb-ing [plŭm/ĭng] *noun, no plural*, all the water pipes, containers, etc. put in a building so that there can be running water and drainage

plume [plo͞om] *noun*, a large or conspicuous feather

plum-met [plŭm/ĭt] *verb*, to fall straight down quickly

plump [plŭmp] *adjective*, a little fat, rounded in form

plunge [plŭnj] *noun,* 1) a sudden dive or fall, *verb*, 2) to fall quickly from a great height 3) to throw oneself into

plung-er [plŭn/jər] *noun*, 1) a rubber suction cup on a handle, used to clear drains 2) a piston-like part that acts with a thrusting movement in a pump

plu-ral [plo͝or/əl] *adjective*, of or involving more than one

plus [plŭs] *preposition*, in addition to, increased by

ply-wood [plī/wo͝od/] *noun*, sheets of wood arranged in thin layers where the grain is in opposite directions to give it strength

p.m. *adjective*, post meridian, the afternoon, the period between noon and midnight

pneu-mo-nia [no͞o-mōn/yə] *noun*, infection of the lungs caused by bacteria or viruses

poach [pōch] *verb*, 1) to hunt or fish illegally 2) to cook a raw egg in boiling water

pock-et [pŏk/ĭt] *noun*, an envelope made by sewing a piece of cloth into clothing to hold things

pod [pŏd] *noun*, a long, slender part of a vine plant in which the seeds grow, like a pea or bean

po-di-um [pō/dē-əm] *noun*, a pedestal, a raised platform

po-em [pō/əm] *noun*, a composition, usually in verse, with regular rhythm and sounds that express images in powerful or beautiful language

po-et [pō/ĭt] *noun*, one who writes verse in a specific form

po-et-ic [pō-ĕt/ĭk] *adjective*, pertaining to poetry, imaginative

po-et-ry [pō/ĭ-trē] *noun, no plural*, words written in verse

poign-ant [poin/yənt] *adjective*, touching, piercing, sharp, keen, affecting the emotions

point [point] *noun*, 1) the tip of something, usually sharp, 2) the purpose of a verbal illustration, 3) the number of goals for a team, 4) at a particular time, 5) the location of an ordered pair of numbers, *verb*, 6) to indicate

point-less [pointlĕs] *adjective*, meaningless, senseless

poise [poiz] *noun*, 1) composure, self-assurance, confidence, *verb*, 2) to balance, to keep steady

poi-son [poi′zən] *noun*, 1) any substance dangerous to life and health, *verb*, 2) to kill with toxic chemicals, 3) to ruin

poi-son-ous [poi′zə-nəs] *adjective*, deadly, toxic, noxious

poke [pōk] *verb*, to push something pointed into something, to prod

po-lar [pō′lər] *adjective*, 1) of or near the North or South Poles, 2) at opposite ends

pole [pōl] *noun*, 1) a round piece of wood, metal or plastic,etc. a rod, 2) one end of the earth or at the end of the axis of a sphere

po-lice [pə-lēs′] *noun, no plural*, members of a department of government that maintains order and enforces the law

pol-i-cy [pŏl′ĭ-sē] *noun*, 1) a course of action adopted by an individual or group, 2) an insurance contract

po-li-o [pŏl′ē′ō] *noun*, (short for poliomyelitis) a disease caused by a virus that affects the nervous system and can result in paralysis

pol-ish [pŏl′ĭsh] *noun*, 1) a substance such as oil or cleanser used to make a surface shine when rubbed with a cloth, *verb*, 2) rubbing something to make it shine or glossy

po-lite [pə-līt′] *adjective*, showing good manners, courteous

po-lit-i-cal [pə-lĭt′ĭ-kəl] *adjective*, of or pertaining to the conduct of government or politics

po-li-ti-cian [pŏl′ĭ-tĭsh′ən] *noun*, a person who runs for public office

pol-i-tics [pŏl′ĭ-tĭks] *noun*, the conduct of government

pol-i-ty [pŏl′ĭ-tē] *noun*, form of government of a nation or a state

poll [pōl] *noun*, 1) a survey, *verb*, 2) to interview, to canvass

pol-len [pŏl′ən] *noun*, a fine yellow dust on the anthers of seed bearing flowers, which serves as the male agent in reproduction

pol-li-nate [pŏl′ə-nāt′] *verb*, to fertilize a flower so that it will reproduce itself by conveying pollen to the stigma

pol-lute [pə-lōōt′] *verb*, to contaminate, to make dirty or unusable, to make foul

pol-lu-tion [pə-lōō′shən] *noun*, substances in the air, in water and on land that contaminate the earth

pol-y-gon [pŏl′ē-gŏn′] *noun*, a many sided plane or figure

pomp-ous [pŏm′pəs] *adjective*, arrogant, showing off

pon-cho [pŏn′chō] *noun*, a sleeveless cover for the upper body, a waterproof cloak

pond [pŏnd] *noun*, a small body of water, smaller than a lake

pon-der [pŏn′dər] *verb*, to think about something, to contemplate, to consider carefully

po-ny [pō′nē] *noun*, a small horse

pool [pōōl] *noun*, 1) any amount of still liquid, a basin 2) a collection of things 3) billiards 4) to gather or combine resources for mutual benefit

poor [po͞or] *adjective*, 1) not having much money, 2) needing kindness or help, 3) not good

pop [pŏp] *noun, no plural*, 1) a sudden noise made when air is released, 2) part of the popular culture of the 1960s, *verb*, 3) to make a sudden, sharp, explosive sound

pope, Pope [pōp] *noun*, the leader of the Roman Catholic Church

pop-py [pŏp′ē] *noun*, a red flower that has seeds that have a narcotic effect

pop-u-lar [pŏp′yə-lər] *adjective*, pleasing to people in general

pop-u-lar-i-ty [pŏp′yə-lăr′ĭ-tē] *noun, no plural*, a measurement of how happy people are with something

pop-u-late [pŏp′yə-lāt′] *verb*, to occupy, to reside in

pop-u-la-tion [pŏp′yə-lā′shən] *noun*, the count of people or organisms who live in an area

pop-u-lous [pŏp′yə-ləs] *adjective*, crowded with people

por-ce-lain [pôr′sə-lĭn] *noun*, a delicate form of china, made with a special clay

porch [pôrch] *noun*, a covered platform in front of a doorway

por-cu-pine [pôr′kyə-pīn′] *noun*, a small animal that has long spikes all over its body for protection

pore [pôr] *noun*, a small hole in the skin for perspiration

pork [pôrk] *noun, no plural*, the meat from a pig used as food

po-rous [pôr′əs] *adjective*, a rough surface, full of holes or texture

por-ridge [pôr′ĭj] *noun*, food made by boiling grain in water or milk until it is very soft, e.g., oatmeal

port [pôrt] *noun*, 1) a harbor or community where ships and boats dock, 2) the left handed side of a ship when facing forward, 3) a sweet red wine, 4) an opening in a ship for cargo

port-a-ble [pôr′tə-bəl] *adjective*, easily carried by hand

por-tal [pôr′tl] *noun*, an entrance, a large doorway, a gate

por-tend [pôr-těnd′] *verb*, to foretell, to predict, to forecast

por-tent [pôr′těnt′] *noun*, a sign, an omen, forewarning of a threat

por-tent-ous [pôr-těn′təs] *adjective*, ominous, serious

por-ter [pôr′tər] *noun*, a person hired to carry luggage in a hotel or a train station or airport

port-fo-li-o [pôrt-fō′lē-ō′] *noun*, a portable case holding papers, prints, drawings, etc.

por-ti-co [pôr′tĭ-kō′] *noun*, a colonnade at the entrance of a building

por-tion [pôr′shən] *noun*, a part of a whole, a segment, a share

port-ly [pôrt′lē] *adjective*, overweight, heavy set, fat

por-trait [pôr′trĭt] *noun*, a painting or photograph of someone

por-tray [pôr-trā′] *verb*, to describe, to represent

pose [pōz] *noun*, 1) a stance or posture, *verb*, 2) to model, to stand, 3) to ask a question

pound

po·si·tion [pə zǐsh′ən] *noun*, 1) a posture, an attitude 2) a job

pos·i·tive [pǒz′ĭ-tǐv] *adjective*, 1) the affirmative, the opposite of negative 2) confident attitude

pos·sess [pə-zěs′] *verb*, to have as property, to own, to control

pos·ses·sion [pə-zěsh′ən] *noun*, that which one owns, property

pos·si·bil·i·ty [pǒs′ə-bǐl/ĭ-tē] *noun*, likelihood, probability, chance

pos·si·ble [pǒs′ə-bəl] *adjective*, what may happen or exist

post [pōst] *noun*, 1) a piece of wood or metal placed in the ground as a support 2) a place where a person is stationed, a job or responsibility 3) sending mail through the post office, *verb*, 4) to make known by putting notices or flyers in public places 5) to station at a place

post·age [pō′stǐj] *noun*, *no plural*, the amount of money paid for something sent through the mail

post·card [pōst′kärd′] *noun*, a small note card with a written message sent through the mail

post·er [pō′stər] *noun*, a large advertisement usually hung on a wall in a public place

pos·ter·i·ty [pǒ-stěr′ĭ-tē] *noun*, the future generation, descendents

post·hu·mous [pǒs′chə-məs] *adjective*, occurring after death

post·pone [pōst-pōn′] *verb*, to put off, to defer to a later time

post·script [pōst′skrǐpt′] *noun*, 1) a note added to a signed letter 2) an addition to a book

pos·tu·late [pǒs′chə-lāt′] *noun*, 1) a self-evident truth, *verb*, 2) to presume, theorize, speculate

pos·ture [pǒs′chər] *noun*, a stance, an unnatural attitude, position

pot [pǒt] *noun*, a container, usually round made for cooking

pot·ash [pǒt′ǎsh′] *noun*, wood ashes, potassium hydrochloride

po·tas·si·um [pə-tǎs′e-əm] *noun*, 1) a soft, white metallic element of the alkali group, 2) Vitamin K

po·ta·to [pə-tā′tō] *noun*, an underground starchy vegetable

po·tent [pōt′nt] *adjective*, powerful, effective, mighty

po·ten·tial [pə-těn′shəl] *noun*, the capability someone has to accomplish something

po·tion [pō′shən] *noun*, a dose of a liquid with magical powers

pot·pour·ri [pō′pōō-rē′] *noun*, any miscellaneous grouping

pot·ter·y [pǒt′ə-rē] *noun*, *no plural*, ceramic dishes and pots made of baked clay

pouch [pouch] *noun*, 1) a bag, purse 2) a sack on a marsupial for their young

poul·tice [pōl′tǐs] *noun*, a compress used to heal a bruise or sprain

poul·try [pōl′trē] *noun*, any domestic fowl used as food

pounce [pouns] *verb*, to jump on something, to seize eagerly

pound [pound] *noun*, 1) a form of money in Britain and some other countries 2) a measure of weight equal to 2 cups, 16 oz. 3) a place to keep stray animals *verb*, 4) to crush something by striking it over and over

pour [pôr] *verb*, to flow or cause to flow, as in making a stream

pout [pout] *verb*, to make a long face, to sulk, to mope

pov-er-ty [pŏv′ər-tē] *noun*, the state of being poor, destitute, or without money or resources

pow-der [pou′dər] *noun*, *no plural*, fine grains of matter, like dust

pow-er [pou′ər] *noun*, the ability to do something, strength or force

pow-er-ful [pou′ər-fəl] *adjective*, strong, forceful, mighty

prac-ti-cal [prăk′tĭ-kəl] *adjective*, 1) derived from actual use and experience, virtual 2) given to action rather than to speculation

prac-ti-cal-ly [prăk′tĭk-lē] *adverb*, almost, nearly

prac-tice [prăk′tĭs] *noun*, 1) an exercise 2) an habitual action 3) the work of a profession, *verb*, 4) to perform over and over to learn a skill 5) to do something as a principle of living 6) to work at a profession

prag-mat-ic [prăg-măt′ĭk] *adjective*, practical, matter of fact, using common sense

prai-r-ie [prâr′ē] *noun*, a meadow of grassland with no trees

praise [prāz] *noun*, 1) applause, approval, admiration, *verb*, 2) to say nice things about someone, to applaud, to compliment

prance [prăns] *verb*, to frolic, to dance about in a lively manner

prank [prăngk] *noun*, a playful trick, a joke, a caper

prate [prāt] *verb*, to speak foolishly, to boast idly

pray [prā] *verb*, to talk to God or a god, often asking for something or expressing gratitude

pray-er [prâr] *noun*, words spoken aloud or silently to God

preach [prēch] *verb*, to talk to people about how they should live a better life

preach-er [prē′chər] *noun*, a person who talks about living life according to the words of the Bible, a minister

pre-am-ble [prē′ăm′bəl, prē-ăm′-] *noun*, an introduction or preface

pre-car-i-ous [prĭ-kâr′ē-əs] *adjective*, depending on the will of another, uncertain

pre-cau-tion [prĭ-kô′shən] *noun*, something that is done beforehand to guard against harm, danger, mistakes, or accidents

pre-cede [prĭ-sēd′] *adjective*, to go before, to introduce or preface

prec-e-dent [prĕs′ĭ-dənt] *noun*, 1) an authoritative example 2) preceding in time or rank serving as an example

pre-cept [prē′sĕpt′] *noun*, a principle of conduct

pre-cinct [prē′sĭngkt′] *noun*, a district with certain boundaries

pre-cious [prĕsh′əs] *adjective*, 1) of great value, much loved by someone 2) costly, expensive

prec-i-pice [prĕs′ə-pĭs] *noun*, a very high and steep cliff

pre-cip-i-tate [pri-sĭp′i-tāt′] *adjective*, 1) headlong, rash, *noun*, 2) a solid formed in a solvent in which it will not dissolve and settles as particles, *verb*, 3) to condense from vapor and fall to the earth's surface like snow or rain

pre-cip-i-ta-tion [prĭ-sĭp′ĭ-tā′shən] *noun*, water that falls as rain or snow from the atmosphere

pre-cip-i-tious [prĭ-sĭp′ĭ- tious] *adjective*, 1) very steep 2) hasty, done without careful thought

pre-cise [prĭ-sīs′] *adjective*, exact, accurate, clearly expressed

pre-ci-sion [prĭ-sĭzh′ən] *adjective*, accuracy, exactness

pre-clude [prĭ-klōōd′] *verb*, to prevent from happening, to hinder, to make impossible

pre-co-cious [prĭ-kō′shəs] *adjective*, showing skills at an earlier age than usual

pre-cur-sor [prĭ-kûr′sər] *noun*, forerunner, predecessor

pred-a-tor [prĕd′ə-tər, -tôr′] *noun*, an animal that eats other animals

pred-e-ces-sor [prĕd′ĭ-sĕs′ər] *noun*, one that comes before another in business or sequence

pre-dic-a-ment [prĭ-dĭk′ə-mənt] *noun*, a stressful position, dilemma, or situation

pred-i-cate [prĭ-dĭk′ət] *noun,* the part of a sentence or clause containing a verb and stating something about the subject

pre-dict [prĭ-dĭkt′] *verb*, to make a reasonable statement about what might happen, to foretell

pre-dic-tion [prĭ-dĭk′shən] *noun*, foretelling the future, prophecy

pre-di-lec-tion [prĕd′l-ĕk′shən] *noun*, an inclination toward something, preference

pre-dom-i-nance [prĭ-dŏm′ə-nəns] *noun*, power over someone

pre-em-i-nent [prē-ĕm′ə-nənt] *noun*, distinction above others, outstanding, superior

pref-ace [prĕf′ĭs] *noun*, an explanation to the reader at the beginning of a book

pre-fer [prĭ-fûr′] *verb*, to like one thing better than another

pref-er-ence [prĕf′ər-əns] *noun*, one thing that is liked more than another, inclination

pre-fix [prē′fĭks′] *noun*, letters added at the front of a word to alter the meaning

preg-nant [prĕg′nənt] *adjective*, having a child or offspring developing in the body

pre-his-tor-ic [prē′hĭ-stôr′ĭk] *adjective*, a time prior to recorded history

prej-u-dice [prĕj′ə-dĭs] *noun*, a strong feeling against something

prel-ude [prĕl′yōōd′] *noun*, the introduction, forerunner

pre-ma-ture [prē′mə-tyŏŏr′] *adjective*, too early, undeveloped

pre-mier [prĭ-mîr′] *adjective*, a head of government in many nations, such as Russia

pre-miere [prĭ-mîr′] *noun*, the first public showing or display

pre-mi-um [prē′mē-əm] *noun*, 1) a bonus given as an inducement to purchase products 2) the amount usually paid in installments by a policy holder for coverage under a contract

pre-mo-ni-tion [prē′mə-nĭsh′ən] *noun*, a dream or image in which one sees what is to come

prep-a-ra-tion [prĕp′ə-rā′shən] *noun*, the act of doing something beforehand to get ready for something

pre-pare [prĭ-pâr′] *verb*, to make or get ready for something

pre-pon-der-ance [prĭ-pŏn′dər-əns] *adjective*, superiority of weight, influence, overwhelming power

prep-o-si-tion [prĕp′ə-zĭsh′ən] *noun*, a word used before a noun or pronoun to indicate where or to express connections and relationships

pre-pos-ter-ous [prĭ-pŏs′tər-əs] *adjective*, absurd, ridiculous

pre-req-ui-site [prē-rĕk′wĭ-zĭt] *noun*, an essential condition, required beforehand

pre-rog-a-tive [prĭ-rŏg′ə-tĭv] *noun*, an exclusive or peculiar right or privilege of a certain rank

pres-age [prĕs′ĭj] *verb*, to foretell

pre-scribe [prĭ-skrīb′] *verb*, to give directions to guide someone

pre-scrip-tion [prĭ-skrĭp′shən] *noun*, a written direction for preparation of a medicine

pres-ence [prĕz′əns] *noun*, the act or state of being present

pre-sent [prĕz′ənt] *adjective*, 1) not past or future, now 2) in attendance, being in a certain place *noun*, 3) the present time, right now 4) a gift, *verb*, 5) to

show, to perform 6) to introduce one person to another 7) to give as a gift

pres-en-ta-tion [prĕz′ən-tā′shən] *noun*, exhibition, demonstration, display or lecture

pre-ser-va-tion [prĕ-zûr-vā′shən] *noun*, protection from harm, danger, or rot

pre-serve [prĭ-zûrv′] *noun*, 1) an area for the protection of wildlife and natural resources, *verb*, 2) to keep something in its original form, to protect

pre-serves [prĭ-zûrvz′] *noun plural*, fruits preserved in syrup

pre-side [prĭ-zīd′] *verb*, to control, to lead, to manage, to oversee

pres-i-dent [prĕz′ĭ-dənt] *noun*, 1) the elected leader of the United States government 2) the head of a university, college or corporation

press [prĕs] *noun*, 1) the newspaper business or media generated news stories, *verb*, 2) to push on steadily with pressure 3) trying to get someone to do something 4) pushing something to cause an effect 5) to iron out the wrinkles in clothing

pres-sure [prĕsh′ər] *noun*, the action of a force against an opposing force

pres-tige [prĕ-stēzh′] *noun*, influence derived from past success or reputation

pre-sume [prĭ-zōōm′] *verb*, to assume, to conclude, to suppose

pre-sump-tion [prĭ-zŭmp′shən] *noun*, an assumption

pre-sup-pose [prē′sə-pōz′] *verb*, to assume, to consider beforehand

pre-tend [prĭ-těnd′] *verb*, to fake, to make believe, to imitate

pre-tense [prē′těns′] *noun*, the act of pretending to be or have something you are not

pre-ten-sion [prĭ-těn′shən] *adjective*, when one assumes an air of superiority

pre-text [prē′těkst′] *noun*, a false reason to justify an action

pret-ty [prĭt′ē] *adjective*, 1) attractive, pleasing to the eye, *adverb*, 2) close to, quite, fairly

pre-vail [prĭ-vāl′] *verb*, to command, to control, to win

prev-a-lent [prěv′ə-lənt] *adjective*, widespread, generally accepted

pre-vent [prĭ-věnt′] *verb*, to keep something from happening

pre-ven-tion [prĭ-věn′shən] *noun*, that which hinders or obstructs

pre-view [prē′vyōō′] *noun*, 1) a look at something before it is reproduced, *verb*, 2) to see in advance

pre-vi-ous [prē′vē-əs] *adjective*, existing or occurring earlier, prior, preceding

pre-vi-ous-ly [prē′vē-əs-lē] *adverb*, formerly, at one time, before

prey [prā] *noun*, any animal that serves as food for another animal

price [prīs] *noun*, the cost of something, what you have to pay

prick [prĭk] *verb*, to make a small hole with something sharp

pride [prīd] *noun*, *no plural*, the feeling of doing your personal best, self-respect

priest [prēst] *noun*, a clergyman of the Catholic Church

prim [prĭm] *adjective*, very precise and formal, exceedingly proper

pri-ma-ry [prī′měr′ē] *adjective*, 1) pertaining to elementary education or schools 2) first

prime [prīm] *adjective*, 1) best, choice, excellent, *verb*, 2) to prepare for operation, to make ready

prime min-is-ter [prīm-mĭn′ĭ-stər] *noun*, the head of government in the parliamentary system

prim-i-tive [prĭm′ĭ-tĭv] *adjective*, characterized by the manner of an early time, crude

prince [prĭns] *noun*, 1) the son of a king or queen 2) the ruler of a small country or state

prin-cess [prĭn′sĭs] *noun*, 1) the daughter of a king or queen 2) the wife of a prince

prin-ci-pal [prĭn′sə pəl] *noun*, 1) occupying the first place or rank, most important 2) the person in charge of a school

prin-ci-ple [prĭn′sə-pəl] *noun*, 1) a source or origin 2) a fundamental truth or doctrine

print [prĭnt] *noun*, 1) the size and style of lettering in a book or poster, *verb*, 2) to press words and pictures on paper or cloth by machine 3) to write

print-er [prĭn′tər] *noun*, a device connected to a computer to make paper copies of a document

prior

pri-or [prī′ər] *adjective*, earlier, before, preceding in time

pri-or-i-ty [prī-ôr′ĭ-tē] *noun*, most important

prism [prĭz′əm] *noun*, 1) a three dimensional object with all sides equal 2) a transparent solid that refracts light

pris-on [prĭz′ən] *noun*, a place where criminals are kept while they are punished

pris-on-er [prĭz′ə-nər] *noun*, a person who is guilty of a crime and must serve a sentence of time away from society, living among other criminals

pris-tine [prĭs′tēn′] *adjective*, 1) part of earlier times, primitive 2) unspoiled, spotless

pri-va-cy [prī′və-sē] *noun*, isolation, seclusion, solitude

pri-vate [prī′vĭt] *adjective*, 1) confidential, personal, secret, *noun*, 2) an enlisted soldier

pri-va-tion [prī-vā′shən] *noun*, hardship, want, lack of comfort

priv-i-lege [prĭv′ə-lĭj] *noun*, a peculiar benefit, favor, or advantage of a group

prize [prīz] *noun*, 1) a reward for winning a contest, *verb*, 2) to cherish, to hold dear

prob-a-bil-i-ty [prŏb′ə-bĭl′ĭ-tē] *adjective*, the chance an event will occur, likelihood

prob-a-ble [prŏb′ə-bəl] *adjective*, likely to occur, plausible

prob-a-bly [prŏb′ə-blē] *adverb*, very likely to prove true

pro-bate [prō′bāt′] *noun*, proof before an officer of the county that a will is valid

pro-ba-tion [prō-bā′shən] *noun*, a trial period, an experiment

probe [prōb] *verb*, to explore with a pointed object or tool

prob-lem [prŏb′ləm] *noun*, 1) a dilemma, something that needs to be solved or worked out 2) a question on a test

pro-ce-dure [prə-sē′jər] *noun*, a manner of proceeding in any action, a process, conduct

pro-ceed [prō-sēd′] *verb*, to go onward or forward, to advance

proc-ess [prŏs′ĕs′] *noun*, 1) a method of operation 2) to change by a special treatment

pro-ces-sion [prə-sĕsh′ən] *noun*, people following one another as part of a ceremony

pro-claim [prō-klām′] *verb*, to announce officially, to declare

proc-la-ma-tion [prŏk′lə-mā′shən] *noun*, an announcement

pro-cliv-i-ty [prō-klĭv′ĭ-tē] *noun*, an inclination, a natural tendency

pro-cras-ti-nate [prō-krăs′tə-nāt′] *verb*, to postpone, to put off doing something, to delay

pro-cras-ti-na-tion [prō-krăs′tə-nā′ shən] *noun*, hesitation, delaying, tarrying

prod [prŏd] *verb*, 1) to poke, to stir up, to jab 2) to urge, to nag

prod-i-gal [prŏd′ĭ-gəl] *adjective*, one who is reckless with money

pro-di-gious [prə-dĭj′əs] *adjective*, marvelous, enormous, huge

prod-i-gy [prŏd′ə jō] *noun*, a highly gifted child, a marvel

pro-duce [prə-dōōs′] *noun*, 1) fruits of the harvest, *verb*, 2) to create, to bring forth, to provide 3) to present, to display, to exhibit 4) to cause, to make

pro-duc-er [prə-dōō′sər] *noun*, someone in charge of making a movie or film

prod-uct [prŏd′əkt] *noun*, 1) something that has an economic value such as refined natural resources or a man-made material 2) the outcome of an endeavor 3) the result of multiplying two numbers together

pro-duc-tion [prə-dŭk′shən] *noun*, 1) creation, construction 2) that which is the result of effort

pro-fane [prō-fān′] *adjective*, not sacred, irreverent, secular

pro-fan-i-ty [prō-făn′ĭ-tē] *noun*, cursing, swearing, expletive

pro-fess [prə-fĕs′] *verb*, to lay claim to, to affirm, to declare

pro-fes-sion [prə-fĕsh′ən] *noun*, an employment which needs specialized study and training

pro-fes-sion-al [prə-fĕsh′ə-nəl] *adjective*, 1) engaged in an activity as a paid job 2) highly competent

pro-fes-sor [prə-fĕs′ər] *noun*, a teacher of the highest rank in a university or college

prof-fer [prŏf′ər] *verb*, to offer, to give, to present, to submit

pro-fi-cient [prə-fĭsh′ənt] *adjective*, advanced in any occupation or study, skillful

pro-file [prō′tĭl′] *noun*, a drawing or other representation of a view

prof-it [prŏf′ĭt] *noun*, 1) a monetary gain, *verb*, 2) to be of advantage, to gain, to benefit

prof-li-gate [prŏf′lĭ-gĭt] *adjective*, 1) wasteful 2) licentious

pro-found [prə-found′] *adjective*, 1) intense, intellectual 2) very deep, endless, bottomless

pro-fuse [prə-fyōōs′] *adjective*, existing in large amounts

pro-fu-sion [prə-fyōō′zhən] *noun*, plenty, abundance

prog-e-ny [prŏj′ə-nē] *noun*, children, offspring

prog-no-sis [prŏg-nō′sĭs] *noun*, foretelling the course and termination of a disease

prog-nos-ti-cate [prŏg-nŏs′tĭ-kāt′] *verb*, to predict, to plan for the future, to foretell

pro-gram [prō′grăm′] *noun*, 1) a plan of action 2) a written outline of the order of events in a public exercise presented as a leaflet 3) a set of instructions that tells a computer to do a specific job 4) a planned activity, verb 5) to use create a set of instructions for a computer

pro-gress [prŏg′rĕs′] *noun*, *no plural*, 1) a moving toward a goal, development, *verb*, 2) to go forward, 3) to advance to a higher stage, to improve

pro-gres-sion [prə-grĕsh′ən] *noun*, the act of moving forward

pro-gres-sive [prə-grĕs′ĭv] *adjective*, favoring reform, forward thinking

prohibit

pro-hib-it [prō-hǐb′ǐt] *verb*, to prevent, to forbid, to hinder

pro-hi-bi-tion [prō′ə-bǐsh′ən] *noun*, a law forbidding the sale of alcoholic liquors

proj-ect [prǒj′ĕkt′] *noun*, 1) an activity that requires planning and materials, *verb*, [prō-jĕkt′] 2) to cause an image to be shown on a screen 3) to stick out, to protrude 4) to estimate

pro-jec-tile [prə-jĕk′təl] *noun*, an object propelled through the air

pro-jec-tion [prə-jĕk′shən] *noun*, 1) a bulge, something sticking out 2) a forecast, a prediction

pro-le-tar-i-at [prō′lǐ-târ′ē-ǐt] *noun*, a member of the working class

pro-lif-ic [prə-lǐf′ǐk] *adjective*, abundantly fruitful, plentiful

pro-logue [prō′lôg′] *noun*, an introduction to a play or a story

pro-long [prə-lông′] *verb*, to lengthen, to extend

prom-e-nade [prǒm′ə-nād′] *noun*, 1) a walk in a public place, *verb*, 2) to walk arm in arm

prom-i-nent [prǒm′ə-nənt] *adjective*, important, noticable

prom-ise [prǒm′ǐs] *noun*, 1) a declaration, binding one to do or not to do a specific act, *verb*, 2) to engage to do, to pledge

prom-is-so-ry [prǒm′ǐ-sôr′ē] *adjective*, containing or implying a promise, an informal contract such as an I.O.U. note

pro-mote [prə-mōt′] *verb*, to further, to encourage, to advance

pro-mo-tion [prə-mō′shən] *noun*, advancement in rank, improvement, support

prompt [prǒmpt] *adjective*, 1) without delay, without too much time passing, *verb*, 2) to cause to act, to urge

prompt-ly [prǒmpt′lē] *adverb*, instantly, quickly, without delay

prone [prōn] *adjective*, 1) inclined to, apt 2) lying face down

prong [prông] *noun*, a sharp projecting part, a spike

pro-noun [prō′noun′] *noun*, a word like **he**, **she**, **it**, **they**, used instead of using a noun again

pro-nounce [prə-nouns′] *verb*, 1) to assert, to declare, to proclaim 2) to speak emphasizing proper sounds and accents, to enunciate

pro-nun-ci-a-tion [prə-nŭn′sē-ā′shən] *noun*, the act of saying words with the proper sound and accent

proof [prōof] *noun*, *no plural*, facts which prove something

prop [prǒp] *noun*, 1) an accessory, *verb*, 2) to support, to reinforce 3) to encourage

prop-a-gan-da [prǒp′ə-gǎn′də] *noun*, an effort to spread an idea

prop-a-gate [prǒp′ə-gāt′] *verb*, to multiply, to spread around

pro-pel [prə-pĕl′] *verb*, to impel , to cause to move or continue in motion, to push forward

pro-pel-ler [prə-pĕl′ər] *noun*, blades turned by a motor to move a boat or airplane through water or air

pro·pen·si·ty [prə-pĕn′sĭ-tē] *noun*, a natural inclination, a tendency

prop·er [prŏp′ər] *adjective*, fitting, appropriate, respectable

prop·er noun [prŏp′ər noun] a particular person, place or thing, the first letters is capitalized

prop·er·ly [prŏp′ər-lē] *adverb*, correctly, rightly, absolutely

prop·er·ty [prŏp′ər-tē] *noun*, land, buildings, cars, boats, and other things people own

prop·er·ty tax [prŏp′ər-tē-tăks] *noun*, a certain amount of money paid as a tax on the land and buildings, and cars and boats a person owns

proph·e·sy [prŏf′ĭ-sī′] *noun*, 1) a prediction made after receiving a sign or a vision, *verb*, 2) to predict, to foretell, to foresee

proph·et [prŏf′ĭt] *noun*, 1) a person who predicts what is going to happen in the future 2) a person who claims to be selected by God to lead

pro·phy·lac·tic [pro′fə-lăk′tĭk] *noun*, a medicine that prevents disease, a preventive

pro·pi·tious [prə-pĭsh′əs] *adjective*, favorable conditions

pro·por·tion [prə-pôr′shən] *noun*, the relation of one portion to another in size, the ratio

pro·pos·al [prə-pō′zəl] *noun*, a formal suggestion, an offer

pro·pose [prə-pōz′] *verb*, to offer for consideration, to put forward

prop·o·si·tion [prŏp′ə-zĭsh′ən] *noun*, a plan, a scheme

pro·pri·e·tor [prə-prī′ĭ-tər] *noun*, an owner, one who has legal right to a business

pro·pri·e·ty [prə-prī′ĭ-tē] *noun*, established standards of proper behavior, appropriateness

pro·pul·sion [prə-pŭl′shən] *noun*, driving forward, thrust

prose [prōz] *noun*, ordinary language, not poetry or verse

pros·e·cute [prŏs′ĭ-kyōōt′] *verb*, to enforce the law by legal process, to seek justice for a crime

pros·pect [prŏs′pĕkt′] *noun*, 1) an expectation, a possibility, odds 2) a view, an outlook, *verb*, 3) to explore, to search

pros·pec·tus [prə-spĕk′təs] *noun*, a summary of a plan, an outline

pros·per [prŏs′pər] *verb*, to do well, to become rich, to succeed

pros·per·i·ty [prŏ-spĕr′ĭ-tē] *noun*, material well-being, success

pros·per·ous [prŏs′pər-əs] *adjective*, doing well

pros·the·sis [prŏs-thē′sĭs] *noun*, an artificial device to replace a missing part of the body

pros·trate [prŏs′trāt′] *adjective*, 1) lying down *verb*, 2) to stretch out full on the ground

pro·tect [prə-tĕkt′] *verb*, to guard or defend, to keep from harm

pro·tec·tion [prə-tĕk′shən] *noun*, preservation from loss, injury, or annoyance, safe keeping

pro·té·gé [prō′tə-zhā′] *noun*, one under the care and protection of another, often learning a craft under the guidance of a more experienced person

protein

pro-tein [prō'tēn'] *noun*, a nutrient found in amino acids essential to the growth and repair of animal tissue found in eggs, meat, etc.

pro-test [prə-tĕst'] *noun*, 1) a complaint or formal disagreement, *verb*, 2) to disagree strongly, to object

Prot-es-tant [prŏt'ĭ-stənt] *noun*, *adjective*, a person belonging to a Christian church

pro-to-col [prō'tə-kôl'] *noun*, decorum, formalities, proper manners, a set of rules

pro-ton [prō'tŏn'] *noun*, a particle of matter, a part of an atom

pro-to-type [prō'tə-tīp'] *noun*, original work used as a model by others, an example

pro-trac-tor [prō-trăk'tər-] *noun*, a device for measuring angles on a plane or on paper

pro-trude [prō-trōōd'] *verb*, to stick out, to cause to jut out

proud [proud] *adjective*, a feeling of satisfaction over something one owns, is, or does

proud-ly [proud'lē] *adverb*, feeling a sense of accomplishment after doing your personal best

prove [prōōv] *verb*, 1) to show that something is true with evidence and tests 2) to turn out

prov-e-nance [prŏv'ə-nəns] *noun*, place or source of origin

pro-verb [prŏv'ûrb'] *noun*, a short saying that speaks the truth

pro-vide [prə-vīd'] *verb*, 1) to look out for in advance 2) to furnish

prov-i-dence [prŏv'ĭ-dəns] *noun*, divine direction, foresight

prov-ince [prŏv'ĭns] *noun*, part of a country, with its own government

pro-vin-cial [prə-vĭn'shəl] *adjective*, limited to a small area, parochial

pro-vi-sion [prə-vĭzh'ən] *noun*, requirement, a formal stipulation

pro-voke [prə-vōk'] *verb*, 1) to make someone angry, to annoy, 2) to incite to action

prowl [proul] *verb*, to sneak, to rove about stealthily

prox-im-i-ty [prŏk-sĭm'ĭ-tē] *noun*, nearness, neighborhood, vicinity

prox-y [prŏk'sē] *noun*, 1) a person authorized to act for another 2) a document giving such consent

pru-dent [prōōd'nt] *adjective*, cautious, sagacious, advisory

prune [prōōn] *noun*, 1) a dried plum, *verb*, 2) to cut off branches of a plant

pry [prī] *verb*, 1) to lift off or open by pushing with leverage 2) to snoop, to spy, to search

psalm [säm] *noun*, a sacred song or poem used to praise God

pseu-do-nym [sōōd'n-ĭm'] *noun*, a fictitious name, a pen name

psy-che [sī'kē] *noun*, 1) the soul or spirit 2) the mind's force

psy-chic [sī'k'ĭk] *adjective*, 1) apprently sensitive to supernatural forces 2) a person who predicts the future

psy-chi-a-trist [sī-kī'ə-trĭst] *noun*, a doctor who analyzes and treats mental problems

psy-cho [sī'kē'ō] noun, the mind or mental processes

psy-chol-o-gy [sī-kŏl′ɔ-jē] *noun*, the study of mental states, the mind and its processes

psy-cho-sis [sī-kō′sĭs] *noun*, a major mental disorder in which the personality is very seriously disorganized and one's sense of reality is usually altered

pto-maine [tō′mān′] *noun*, an alkaloid from decomposing animals that is usually poisonous

pub-lic [pŭb′lĭk] *adjective*, 1) open to everyone, *noun*, 2) the people constituting a community

pub-li-ca-tion [pŭb′lĭ-kā′shɔn] *noun*, published material

pub-lic-i-ty [pŭ-blĭs′ĭ-tē] *noun*, public notice and attention

pub-lish [pŭb′lĭsh] *verb*, to print and sell a manuscript

pub-lish-er [pŭb′lĭ-shɔr] *noun*, one who creates and offers for sale books, magazines, or newspapers

pud-ding [pŏŏd′ĭng] *noun*, a custard made of milk, sugar and eggs boiled together

pud-dle [pŭd′l] *noun*, a small pool of water on the ground

puff [pŭf] *noun*, 1) a quick burst of air, smoke, etc. *verb*, 2) to make short quick breaths of air

pu-is-sant [pwĭs′ɔnt] *adjective*, powerful, strong, potent

pul-chri-tude [pŭl′krĭ-tōōd′] *noun*, beauty, loveliness, charm

pull [pŏŏl] *noun*, 1) a force, a power, strength, *verb*, 2) to move something toward oneself through grasping and drawing with force 3) to put on

pul ley [pŏŏl′ē] *noun*, a wheel used to transmit power by means of a band, rope, or chain

pul-mo-nar-y [pŏŏl′mɔ-nĕr′ē] *adjective*, affecting the lungs

pulp [pŭlp] *noun*, 1) a soft, moist, sticky mass of fibers made up of wood, straw, etc. and used to make paper and paperboard 2) the soft moist part of fruit that is left after the seeds and peels are removed

pul-pit [pŏŏl′pĭt] *noun*, an elevated desk or platform in a church for a preacher or orator

pul-sate [pŭl′sāt′] *verb*, to throb

pulse [pŭls] *noun*, a heart beat

pul-ver-ize [pŭl′vɔ-rīz′] *verb*, to reduce to a fine powder or dust

pum-mel [pŭm′ɔl] *verb*, to beat

pump [pŭmp] *noun*, 1) a machine for making liquid or gas move by putting air into something or to extract water or other liquid from the ground using a special lever, *verb*, 2) to draw up using up and down action

pump-kin [pŭmp′kĭn] *noun*, a large orange gourd-like fruit, used in cooking

punch [pŭnch] *noun*, 1) a hit aimed squarely with a fist 2) a fruit drink, *verb*, 3) to hit someone very hard with a fist

punc-tu-al [pŭngk′chōō-ɔl] *adjective*, on time

punc-tu-al-i-ty [pŭngk′chōō-ăl′ĭ-tē] *adverb*, being prompt, making a point of being on time

punctuate

punc-tu-ate [pŭngk′chōo-āt′] *verb*, to add proper signs and marks of grammar to writing

punc-tu-a-tion [pŭngk′chōo-ā′shən] *noun*, *no plural*, signs like ,, : , ? and ! used in writing so that the reader emphasizes certain ideas expressed on paper

punc-ture [pŭngk′chər] *noun*, 1) perforation with something pointed, *verb*, 2) to penetrate, to pierce, to make a hole

pun-dit [pŭn′dĭt] *noun*, a critic, a commentator, an expert

pun-gent [pŭn′jənt] *adjective*, powerful or strong odor or flavor

pun-ish [pŭn′ĭsh] *verb*, to discipline, to reprove, to correct

pun-ish-ment [pŭn′ĭsh-mənt] *noun*, 1) a penalty 2) rough or injurious treatment inflicted for an offense

pu-ny [pyōo′nē] *adjective*, insignificant, tiny, weak

pu-pa [pyōo′pə] *noun*, the inactive stage of development of an insect before reaching the adult, often in a cocoon or a cell

pu-pil [pyōo′pəl] *noun*, 1) a boy or girl being taught by a teacher 2) a black dot, the expanding and contracting opening in the iris of the eye, in the middle of the eye that receives light

pup-pet [pŭp′ĭt] *noun*, a small doll that looks like a person or an animal that is moved by wires or with hands on a small stage

pup-py [pəpē] *noun*, a young dog

pur-chase [pûr′chĭs] *noun*, 1) something that has been paid for, an acquisition, *verb*, 2) to acquire for a price, to buy

pure [pyōor] *adjective*, without anything mixed into it, clean, unpolluted, spotless

pur-ga-to-ry [pûr′gə-tôr′ē] *noun*, 1) a place where a sinner makes amends 2) limbo

purge [pûrj] *verb*, 1) to clean by removing impurities 2) to remove all criminal charges from public record

pu-ri-fy [pyōor′ə-fī′] *verb*, to make clean, to free from imperfection

pu-ri-ty [pyōor′ĭ-tē] *noun*, cleanliness, pureness, innocence

pur-loin [pər-loin′] *verb*, to steal

pur-ple [pûr′pəl] *adjective*, 1) the color of violets, *noun*, 2) a color made by mixing red and blue pigments

pur-pose [pûr′pəs] *noun*, the reason for which something exists or has been done

purse [pûrs] *noun*, 1) a small hand bag to hold money and personal items 2) prize money from a race

pur-sue [pər-sōo′] *verb*, to follow with a view to overtake, to persecute, to capture

pur-suit [pər-sōot′] *noun*, an aim, an objective, a search

pur-vey-or [pər-vā′ər] *noun*, someone who provides food

push [pōosh] *noun*, 1) a shove, a rigorous effort, *verb*, 2) to press or lean against, so as to move

put [pōot] *verb*, 1) to move, to place 2) to impose, to assign

pu-trid [pyoo'trĭd] *adjootivo*, foul, rotten, decayed, disgusting

put-ty [pŭt'ē] *noun*, an adhesive, glue, compound to seal something

puz-zle [pŭz'əl] *noun*, 1) a picture cut into many pieces to be put back together 2) a game designed to make it difficult for you to finish, *verb*, 3) to exercise one's mind 4) to perplex

pyg-my [pĭg'mē] *noun*, a dwarf, a very small person in Africa

pyr-a-mid [pĭr'ə-mĭd] *noun*, 1) a solid shape with a square base and pointed top, whose faces are triangles with a common corner 2) huge monuments in the desert of Egypt, built as burial vaults for ancient Egyptian kings

py-ro-ma-ni-ac [pī'rō–mā'ē–ak'] *noun*, a person who likes to set fires and watch them burn

Q

quack [kwăk] *noun*, 1) an imposter, a fake, *vcrb*, 2) to make noises like a duck

quad-ri-lat-er-al
[kwŏd'rə-lăt'ər-əl] *noun*, a four-sided polygon

quad-ru-ped [kwŏd'rə-pĕd'] *noun*, a four-footed animal

quad-ru-ple [kwŏ-droo'pəl] *verb*, to multiply by four

quaff [kwŏf] *verb*, to drink with enthusiasm

quag-mire [kwăg'mīr'] *noun*, a bog, a marsh, muddy soil

quail [kwăl] *noun*, 1) a game bird that lives in the woods, *verb*, 2) to cower in fear

quaint [kwānt] *adjective*, pleasing in an unusual way, peculiar, odd

quake [kwāk] *verb*, to shake, to shudder, to tremble, to quiver

qual-i-fi-ca-tion
[kwŏl'ə-fĭ-kā'shən] *noun*, special training or knowledge

qual-i-fy [kwŏl'ə-fī'] *verb*, 1) to meet the set criteria 2) to make less harsh or strict

qual-i-ty [kwŏl'ĭ-tē] *noun*, 1) a characteristic that distinguishes one person or thing from another 2) a degree of excellence

qualm [kwäm] *noun*, misgiving, remorse, uneasiness

quan-ti-ty [kwŏn'tĭ-tē] *noun*, an amount of something

quar-an-tine [kwôr'ən-tēn'] *noun*, 1) separation of people with a contagious disease, *verb*, 2) to be separated from society while suffering from an infectious disease in order to prevent the disease from spreading

quar-rel [kwôr'əl] *noun*, 1) an angry dispute, *verb*, 2) to argue or disagree, to fight with words

quar-ry [kwôr'ē] *noun*, 1) a deep pit where stone is cut out of the gound to use for buildings 2) prey, an animal that is being hunted

quart [kwôrt] *noun*, a liquid measurement equal to 32 ounces, 1.13 liters, ¼ of a gallon, 2 pints

quarter

quar-ter [kwôr′tər] *noun*, 1) a coin worth 25 cents 2) one of four equal parts, one fourth

quar-ters [kwôr′tərz] *noun, plural*, a place where people live, especially if they live where they work

quar-tet [kwôr-tĕt′] *noun*, a group of musicians or singers, also, a piece of music for four instruments or voices

quartz [kwôrts] *noun*, a mineral compound of silica

queen [kwēn] *noun*, 1) the wife of the king 2) any woman who rules a country born to that title, a female monarch 3) any woman who is very important

queer [kwîr] *adjective*, odd, different in a strange way

quell [kwĕl] *verb*, to put down, to quiet, to suppress, to pacify

quench [kwĕnch] *verb*, 1) to satisfy one's thirst or appetite 2) to extinguish, to put out

que-ry [kwîr′ē] *noun*, 1) a question, *verb*, 2) to doubt or question, to interrogate

quest [kwĕst] *noun*, a search, a journey, an exploration

ques-tion [kwĕs′chən] *noun*, 1) an inquiry, *verb*, 2) to ask, to inquire 3) to doubt, to quiz

ques-tion mark [kwĕs′chən-märk] *noun*, the sign ? used at the end of a sentence which asks a question

ques-tion-naire [kwĕs′chə-nâr′] *noun*, a survey submitted to obtain information, a printed set of questions

queue [kyōō] *noun*, a line of people waiting for something

quib-ble [kwĭb′əl] *verb*, to equivocate, to play with words

quick [kwĭk] *adjective*, very fast,

quick-en [kwĭk′ən] *verb*, to hurry, to rush, to hasten, to accelerate

quick-ly [kwĭk′lē] *adverb*, in a hurry, fast, promptly

qui-et [kwī′ĭt] *adjective*, 1) making little or no sound, not moving , still, *noun*, 2) silence

qui-et-ly [kwī′ĭt- lē] *adverb*, calmly, peacefully, silently

quill [kwĭl] *noun*, 1) a large feather from a bird's tail or wing 2) a sharp spine of a porcupine

quilt [kwĭlt] *noun*, a blanket made by sewing small pieces of fabric together in a design

quince [kwĭns] *noun*, a bitter fruit resembling a large yellow apple

quin-tes-sence [kwĭn-tĕs′əns] *noun*, the purest and highest essence of something

quip [kwĭp] *noun*, a taunting remark, a witty remark

quit [kwĭt] *verb*, to give up, to surrender, to depart, to leave

quite [kwīt] *adverb*, completely, entirely, actually, really

quiv-er [kwĭv′ər] *noun*, 1) a case for holding arrows 2) a trembling, *verb*, 2) to shake a little, to tremble nervously

quix-ot-ic [kwĭk-sŏt′ĭk] *adjective*, romantically idealistic

quiz [kwĭz] *noun*, 1) a small test, *verb*, 2) to ask a few questions

quo-rum [kwôr′əm] *noun*, the number of members of any body legally necessary to transact business

quo-ta [kwō′tə] *noun*, the amount, quantity, proportion

quo-ta-tion [kwō-tā′shən] *noun*, 1) words spoken or written lifted from their context 2) the naming or publishing of the current prices of stocks, bonds, etc., the price named

quote [kwōt] *verb*, to say or write something that has been said before by another person

quo-tient [kwō′shənt] *noun*, the product from the division of one number by another

R

rab-bi [răb′ī] *noun*, the leader or teacher of the Jewish religion

rab-bit [răb′ĭt] *noun*, a small furry animal with long ears and long back legs that burrows holes and lives underground

rab-ies [rā′bēz] *noun*, disease caused by organisms called a virus that attacks the nervous system

rac-coon [ră-kōōn′] *noun*, a large black and white nocturnal rodent that lives in trees

race [rās] *noun*, 1) a competitive event, a contest 2) a part of humanity, an ethnic background, *verb*, 3) to run in a dash or compete in a contest

ra-cial [rā′shəl] *adjective*, pertaining to ethnic differences

rac-ism [rā′sĭz′əm] *noun*, narrow-mindedness, intolerance, bigotry

rack [răk] *noun*, 1) a frame on which things are hung or kept, *verb*, 2) to cause pain

rack-et [răk′ĭt] *noun*, 1) a light bat with a netted hoop 2) a loud or confused noise

ra-dar [rā′där] *noun, no plural*, the ability to find the position of something using radio waves

ra-di-ant [rā′dē-ənt] *adjective*, shining, luminous, bright

ra-di-ate [rā′dē-āt′] *verb*, to give off energy or rays of light

ra-di-a-tor [rā′dē-ā′tər] *noun*, a device used to cool a liquid

rad-i-cal [răd′ĭ-kəl] *adjective*, unconventional, odd

ra-di-o [rā′dē-ō] *noun*, 1) the use of electromagnetic waves to carry messages without the use of wires, *verb*, 2) to send or transmit messages in this manner

ra-di-o-act-ive waste [rā′dē-ōăk′tĭvwāst] *noun*, waste left over from creating nuclear power or atomic energy which gives off radiant energy in rays or particles by the disintegration of the atomic nuclei such as found in radium and uranium

ra-di-um [rā′dē-əm] *noun*, a metallic element found in minute quantities, capable of spontaneously emitting rays

ra-di-us [rā′dē-əs] *noun*, the distance from the center of a circle to its perimeter

raft [răft] *noun*, large pieces of wood joined to make a flat floating surface

raft-er [răf′tər] *noun*, a crossbeam

rag [răg] *noun*, 1) an old torn garment 2) a piece of cloth used to clean, polish or dust

rage [rāj] *noun*, fierce anger that continues with great force

raid [rād] *noun*, 1) a surprise attack, *verb*, 2) to invade, to attack, to assault

rail [rāl] *noun*, 1) a bar extending horizontally between two posts as in a fence or railroad ties, *verb*, 2) to scold, to rant and rave

rail-ing [rā'lǐng] *noun*, a fence or partition to keep people or animals from straying into places they should not go

rail-road [rāl'rōd'] *noun*, a road or track built with parallel steel rails and used by trains

rain [rān] *noun*, 1) part of a weather pattern when water droplets fall from the sky *verb*, 2) to fall as water in drops from the sky 3) to fall like rain

rain-bow [rān'bō'] *noun*, an arc-shaped spectrum of colors seen in the sky, caused by sunlight refracted by raindrops

rain-coat [rān'kōt'] *noun*, a coat that protects a person from getting wet

rain-fall [rān'fôl'] *noun*, the amount of water falling within a given time or area

raise [rāz] *noun*, 1) an increase in salary, *verb*, 2) to lift up, to elevate 3) to grow or cultivate

rai-sin [rā'zǐn] *noun*, a dried grape

rake [rāk] *noun*, 1) a long-handled tool with teeth used to gather leaves on the ground, *verb*, 2) to use a tool to gather fallen leaves or to smooth soil

ral-ly [răl'ē] *noun*, 1) a mass meeting, an assembly, a gathering, *verb*, 2) to restore, to recover, to renew 3) to counter attack

ram [răm] *noun*, a male sheep

ram-ble [răm'bəl] *verb*, 1) to wander in a leisurely manner 2) to chatter, to babble

ram-i-fi-ca-tion [răm'ə-fǐ-kā'shən] *noun*, 1) branching out, a diversion 2) a complicated outcome of a statement or plan

ramp [rămp] *noun*, a slanted walk or roadway that connects a lower to a higher place

ram-page [răm'pāj'] *noun*, a rage, violent behavior, a tantrum

ramp-ant [răm'pənt] *adjective*, unruly, furious, unrestrained

ram-part [răm'pärt', -pərt] *noun*, a defensive mound of earth

ran [răn] *past tense* of **run**

ranch [rănch] *noun*, a rural estate where livestock are raised

ran-cid [răn'sǐd] *adjective*, rotten, an unpleasant smell or taste

ran-cor [răng'kər] *noun*, bitterness, hatred, malice, ill will

ran-dom [răn'dəm] *adjective*, without order or logic

range [rānj] *noun*, 1) a line of mountains or hills 2) an extensive variety of different things 3) the distance something can travel on its own

rang-er [rān'jər] *noun*, an enforcement agent assigned to patrol a certain region

rank [răngk] *adjective*, 1) bad smell, *noun*, 2) a class thought of as higher or lower than other groups, *verb*, 3) to classify in a group 4) to arrange in a row

ran-kle [răng′kəl] *verb*, to make someone annoyed and mad

ran-sack [răn′săk′] *verb*, to search a house thoroughly

ran-som [răn′səm] *noun*, the release of a person in return for payment

rant [rănt] *verb*, to talk wildly, to speak bombastically

rap [răp] *verb*, 1) to knock, to tap, to thump 2) to talk, to chat

rap-id [răp′ĭd] *adjective*, very fast, quick, swift, often, speedy

rap-id-ly [răp′ĭd-lē] *adverb*, quickly, hurriedly, swiftly

rap-ids [răp′ĭdz] *noun*, *plural*, a place in the river where the river descends creating swift currents producing white water

rap-ture [răp′chər] *noun*, joy, delight, bliss, exhilaration

rare [râr] *adjective*, unusual, uncommon, hard to come by

rare-ly [râr′lē] *adverb*, once in a great while, very seldom

ras-cal [răs′kəl] *noun*, a deceitful person, a mischievous child

rash [răsh] *adjective*, 1) acting quickly without thinking about the results, reckless, *noun*, 2) a patch of red spots on the skin, indicating an allergy

rasp-ber-ry [răz′běr′ē] *noun*, a red or purple berry that grows on a bush

rat [răt] *noun*, 1) a small rodent, larger than a mouse, that lives on grain 2) an informer

rate [rāt] *noun*, 1) a relative amount 2) the speed of something, *verb*, 3) to evaluate, to rank, to grade, to consider

rath-er [răth′ər, rä′thər] *adjective*, preferable, instead, somewhat

rat-i-fy [răt′ə-fī′] *verb*, to approve formally, to endorse, to confirm

ra-tio [rā′shē-ō′] *noun*, the relation between quantity, degree or rate between one thing and another

rati-oci-na-tion [răsh′ē-ŏs′ə-nā′shən] *noun*, reasoning logically, the process of exact thinking

ra-tion [răsh′ən, rā′shən] *noun*, 1) a fixed amount of something that is given or allowed, *verb*, 2) to limit the amount of resources to each person or group

ra-tion-al [răsh′ə-nəl] *adjective*, reasonable, intelligent, sensible

ra-tion-al-i-za-tion [răsh′ə-nə-lĭ-zā′shən] *noun*, bringing into conformity with reason, logical thinking

ra-tion-al-ize [răsh′ə-nə-līz′] *verb*, to explain away, to make excuses, to justify

rat-tle [răt′l] *noun*, 1) a toy with beads inside that makes a noise when shaken, *verb*, 2) to shake, to clatter, to move noisily

rau-cous [rô′kəs] *adjective*, rough in sound, harsh, strident

rav-age [(răv′ĭj] *verb*, to plunder, to destroy or wreck, to ruin

rave

rave [rāv] *verb*, to speak enthusiastically about something

rav-en-ous [răv′ə-nəs] *adjective*, extremely hungry

ra-vine [rə-vēn′] *noun*, a long, deep ditch or valley in the earth with steep sides, a gorge

raw [rô] *adjective*, 1) uncooked, bloody 2) something in its natural, unadulterated state 3) cold and damp

ray [rā] *noun*, 1) a thin beacon of light 2) part of a line that has an endpoint and goes on and on in one direction 3) a trace, hint

ray-on [rā′ŏn] *noun*, a fine cloth that looks like glossy silk

raze [rāz] *verb*, to level to the ground, to destroy completely

ra-zor [rā′zər] *noun*, a keen edged cutting instrument especially used for shaving

reach [rēch] *noun, no plural*, 1) the distance that can be attained 2) grasp, *verb*, 3) to stretch out to touch or take something 4) to get to a place, to arrive at

re-act [rē-ăkt′] *verb*, to act because of something that has happened

re-ac-tion [rē-ăk′shən] *noun*, a direct response

re-ac-tion-ar-y [rē-ăk′shə-něr′ē] *adjective*, someone who is against progress

read [rēd] *verb*, to look at words and understand them

read-i-ly [rěd′ə-lē] *adverb*, easily, willingly, without hesitating

read-i-ness [rěd′ē-nĭs] *adjective*, willingness, eagerness, ease

re-ad-just [rē′ə-jŭst′] *verb*, to adapt, to fine tune

read-y [rěd′ē] *adjective*, 1) willing, able, prepared 2) at hand

re-al [rē′əl, rēl] *adjective*, factual, actually existing, true

re-al-ism [rē′ə-lĭz′əm] *noun*, a philosophy that regards external objects as the most fundamentally real things, and perceptions or ideas as secondary

re-al-ist [rē′ə-lĭst] *noun*, 1) someone with a practical outlook 2) an attempt to make art and literature resemble life

re-al-i-ty [rē-ăl′ĭ-tē] *noun*, fact, truth, real things, actuality

re-al-i-za-tion [rē′ə-lĭ-zā′shən] *noun*, a perception, an awareness

re-al-ize [rē′ə-līz′] *verb*, 1) to understand, to make real, to become aware of 2) to achieve

re-al-ly [rē′ə-lē′] *adverb*, truly, very, genuinely, indeed

realm [rělm] *noun*, region, sphere, domain or province, kingdom

ream [rēm] *noun*, in the paper business, 500 sheets of paper

reap [rēp] *verb*, to gather the harvest by cutting

rear [rîr] *adjective*, 1) at the back, behind, *noun*, 2) the back part, *verb*, 3) to raise children or livestock until they grow up

rea-son [rē′zən] *noun*, 1) the answer or explanation given as part of a belief 2) a cause for acting, thinking, or feeling a special way, *verb*, 3) to think things through to present an opinion, to conclude, to infer

rea-son-a-ble [rē′zə-nə-bəl] *adjective*, governed by reason, not excessive, logical

rea-son-a-bly [rē′zə-nə-blē] *adverb*, adequately, fairly, sufficiently, logically

rea-son-ing [rē′zə-nǐng] *noun*, the thought process, logic

re-as-sure [rē′ə-shoor′] *verb*, to help feel safe and comfortable

re-as-sur-ance [rē′ə-shoor′əns] *noun*, restoring confidence

re-bate [rē′bāt′] *noun*, a deduction offered on a purchase in the form of a refund

re-bel [rĕb′əl] *noun*, 1) someone who fights against the leadership of a government, *verb*, 2) to defy any authority, to revolt

re-bel-lion [rǐ-bĕl′yən] *noun*, a revolt, resistance, mutiny

re-bel-lious [rǐ-bĕl′yəs] *adjective*, someone who resists the law, defying authority

re-bound [rē′bound′] *verb*, 1) to bounce back, to move like a boomerang 2) to recover

re-buff [rǐ-bŭf′] *noun*, 1) a sharp rejection, a snub, *verb*, 2) to drive back or repel 3) to refuse bluntly, to reject, to snub

re-build [rē-bǐld′] *verb*, to repair, to put in working order

re-but-tal [rǐ-bŭt′l] *noun*, an argument introduced by the other side in a debate

re-cal-ci-trant [rǐ-kăl′sǐ-trənt] *adjective*, obstinately stubborn

re-call [rǐ-kôl′] *verb*, 1) to summon or call back, 2) to remember

re-cant [rǐ-kănt′] *verb*, to withdraw a previous statement

re-ca-pit-u-late [rē′kə-pǐch′ə-lāt′] *verb*, to repeat the principal points in a program

re-cede [rǐ-sēd′] *verb*, to move back, to retreat, to withdraw

re-ceipt [rǐ-sēt′] *noun*, a written acknowledgment that something was received

re-ceive [rǐ-sēv′] *verb*, to take in, to come into possession of, accept

re-cent [rē′sənt] *adjective*, something that happened a little while ago, prior to the present

re-cent-ly [rē′sənt-lē] *adverb*, a short while ago

re-cep-ta-cle [rǐ-sĕp′tə-kəl] *noun*, 1) a container 2) a contact device in an electrical outlet

re-cep-tion [rǐ-sĕp′shən] *noun*, 1) a greeting, a welcome 2) a social gathering 3) receiving television or radio wave frequencies

re-cess [rē′sĕs′] *noun*, 1) a short intermission 2) a space formed by indentation, a niche

re-ces-sion [rǐ-sĕsh′ən] *noun*, an economic slow down characterized by high unemployment

re-cid-i-vism [rǐ-sǐd′ə-vǐz′əm] *noun*, habitual return to crime

rec-i-pe [rĕs′ə-pē′] *noun*, a list of ingredients and directions for preparing something

re-cip-i-ent [rǐ-sǐp′ē-ənt] *noun*, the person who accepts something

reciprocal

re-cip-ro-cal [rĭ-sĭp′rə-kəl] *adjective*, mutual, exchangeable, interacting, given in return

re-cip-ro-cate [rĭ-sĭp′rə-kāt′] *verb*, to return the favor for something done or given, to respond in kind

re-cit-al [rĭ-sīt′l] *noun*, a program of music or dance before an audience

re-cite [rĭ-sīt′] *verb*, to repeat from memory, to narrate in detail

reck-less [rĕk′lĭs] *adjective*, careless and dangerous

reck-on [rĕk′ən] *verb*, to come to terms with, to settle matters

re-claim [rĭ-klām′] *verb*, to bring back, to restore, to recover

re-cline [rĭ-klīn′] *verb*, to lean back

rec-luse [rĕk′lōōs′] *noun*, a hermit

rec-og-ni-tion [rĕk′əg-nĭsh′ən] *noun*, 1) acknowledgment of something done or given 2) acknowledgment of acquaintance

rec-og-nize [rĕk′əg-nīz′] *verb*, 1) to acknowledge formally 2) to identify as previously seen or known 3) to greet, to accept

re-coil [rĭ-koil′] *verb*, to retreat, or drawback, to shrink back

rec-ol-lect [rĕk′ə-lĕkt′] *verb*, to call to mind, to remember

rec-ol-lec-tion [rĕk′ə-lĕk′shən] *noun*, something remembered

rec-com-mend [rĕk′ə-mĕnd′] *verb*, to present favorably, to urge or suggest, to advise

re-com-men-da-tion [rĕk′ə-mĕn-dā′shən] *noun*, a suggestion for what is most suitable

rec-om-pense [rĕk′əm-pĕns′] *noun*, 1) compensation, payment, *verb*, 2) to pay for service received

rec-on-cil-able [rĕk′ən-sī′lə-bəl, rĕk′ən-sī′-] *adjective*, capable of being restored to friendship

re-con-cile [rĕk′ən-sīl′] *verb*, 1) to restore to friendship 2) to settle a quarrel 3) to be resigned to accept things as they are

rec-on-dite [rĕk′ən-dīt′] *adjective*, hard to understand, profound, hidden from view, abstruse

re-con-nais-sance [rĭ-kŏn′ə-səns] *noun*, a survey of the enemy by soldiers, reconnoitering

re-con-struct [rē′kən-strŭkt′] *verb*, to put something together or make it again, to rebuild

re-cord [rĭ-kôrd′,rĕk′ərd] *noun*, 1) a written account of what happened 2) a plastic disk on which sounds are recorded, *verb*, 3) to write down something that has happened 4) to register on a disk in a permanent form

re-cord-er [rĭ-kôr′dər] *noun*, 1) an office worker, a secretary 2) a wooden or plastic flute played like a whistle

re-count [rĭ-kount′] *verb*, 1) to tell a story, to narrate 2) to count again

re-course [rē′kôrs′] *noun*, resorting to help when in trouble

re-cov-er [rĭ-kŭv′ər] *verb*, 1) to get back to a normal state, to get well, to recuperate 2) to get back what was lost or stolen

re-cov-er-y [rĭ-kŭv′ə-rē] *noun*, a return to good health

roo re a tion [rĕk′rē-ā′shən] *noun*, sports or play as a form of enjoyable relaxation

re-crim-i-na-tion [rĭ-krĭm′ə-nā′shən] *noun*, an accusation in response to another, a countercharge

re-cruit [rĭ-krōōt′] *noun*, 1) a new member who agrees to join a group, *verb*, 2) to enlist, to attract new members

rec-tan-gle [rĕk′tăng′gəl] *noun*, a flat shape with four straight sides and four right angles, the opposite sides of which are parallel

rec-ti-fy [rĕk′tə-fī′] *verb*, to correct, to make better

rec-ti-tude [rĕk′tĭ-tōōd′] *noun*, uprightness, moral virtue

re-cu-per-ate [rĭ-kōō′pə-rāt′] *verb*, to recover, to restore to health

re-cur [rĭ-kûr′] *verb*, to return again and again as an event

re-cur-rent [rĭ-kûr′ənt] *adjective*, returning repeatedly or coming again to mind

re-cy-cle [rē-sī′kəl] *verb*, to process materials so they can be made into new products

red [rĕd] *adjective*, 1) crimson, cherry, ruby, *noun*, 2) one of the three primary colors: blue, yellow and red

re-deem [rĭ-dēm′] *verb*, 1) to recover, 2) to buy back 3) to exchange 4) to fulfill

red-o-lent [rĕd′l-ənt] *adjective*, 1) fragrant, a pleasant odor 2) strongly reminiscent

re-dress [rĭ-drĕs′] *verb*, to set right, to make amends for, to remedy

re-duce [rĭ-dōōs′] *verb*, to diminish, to make smaller or use less

re-duc-tion [rĭ-dŭk′shən] *noun*, 1) the act of making less 2) the amount by which something is diminished

re-dun-dant [rĭ-dŭn′dənt] *adjective*, superfluous, excessively wordy, repetitious

reed [rēd] *noun*, 1) a small, thin, flat piece of wood, metal, or plastic used in the mouthpiece of some musical instruments, such as the clarinet 2) a tall sturdy grass that grows in the water

reef [rēf] *noun*, a ridge of sand, rocks, or coral, off shore but close to the water's surface

reek [rēk] *verb*, to give off an odor

reel [rēl] *noun*, 1) a spool that turns, winding or unwinding a fishing line 2) a Scottish dance *verb*, 3) to feel happy, elated with excitement

re-enact [rē′ĕn-ăkt′] *verb*, to perform as if for the first time

re-fer [rĭ-fûr′] *verb*, 1) to recommend someone go to see someone for help 2) to use a resource for help

ref-er-ee [rĕf′ə-rē′] *noun*, a sports official with final authority for conducting a game

ref-er-ence [rĕf′ər-əns] *noun*, 1) a specific direction of the attention 2) a written statement of the qualifications of another 3) a resource such as a, dictionary, encyclopedia, thesaurus

refine

re-fine [rĭ- fīnd] *verb*, to reduce to a fine, unmixed, or pure state by removing all unwanted matter

re-fined[rĭ-fīn′d] *adjective*, 1) in a pure state 2) having good manners and good taste

re-fin-er-y [rĭ-fī′nə-rē] *noun*, a factory where resources like oil or sugar are made ready for use

re-flect [rĭ-flĕkt′] *verb*, 1) to throw or cast back the sun's rays 2) to think, to ponder, to meditate

re-flec-tion [rĭ-flĕk′shən] *noun*, 1) an image bounced back from a shiny surface 2) an object seen in a mirror 3) serious thought, thinking back on something

re-flec-tor [rĭ-flĕk′tər] *noun*, a polished surface that reflects light, heat or sound

re-flex [rē′flĕks′] *adjective*, mechanical, unthinking, habitual

re-form [rĭ-fôrm′] *noun*, 1) a change, an improvement, *verb*, 2) to correct, to revise, to renew

re-form-a-to-ry [rĭ-fôr′mə-tôr′ē] *noun*, a jail or prison

re-frac-tion [rĭ-frăk′shən] *noun*, the bending of a ray of light

re-frain [rĭ-frān′] *noun*, 1) a chorus, a verse, *verb*, 2) to abstain, to keep oneself from doing something

re-fresh [rĭ-frĕsh′] *verb*, to revive with rest or food, to renew

re-fresh-ment [rĭ-frĕsh′mənt] *noun*, food and drink

re-frig-er-a-tor [rĭ-frĭj′ə-rā′tər] *noun*, an appliance that preserves food in cool temperatures

ref-uge [rĕf′yo͞oj] *noun*, a safe place, a place to hide

ref-u-gee [rĕf′yo͞o-jē′] *noun*, an exile, someone forced to leave his country

re-fund [rĭ-fŭnd′] *noun*, 1) reimbursement, repayment, *verb*, 2) to give back, to reimburse, to repay

re-fur-bish [rē-fûr′bĭsh] *verb*, to repair and make useful

re-fus-al [rĭ-fyo͞o′zəl] *noun*, a denial, a refusal

ref-use [rĭ-fyo͞oz′] *noun*, 1) a general term for solid waste materials, also called garbage or trash, *verb*, 2) to deny, not to allow or agree, to decline to do

re-fute [rĭ-fyo͞ot′] *verb*, to prove false, to disprove, to rebut

re-gain[rĭ- gān] *verb*, to get back

re-gal [rē′gəl] *adjective*, royal, majestic, stately, splendid

re-gale [rĭ-gāl′] *verb*, to entertain

re-gard [rĭ-gärd′] *noun, plural*, 1) respect, concern, *verb*, 2) to think of or see 3) to relate to

re-gard-ing [rĭ-gär′dĭng] *preposition*, about, concerning

re-gard-less [rĭ-gärd′lĭs] *adverb*, without concern for problems or objections, despite, although

re-gat-ta [rĭ-gä′tə] *noun*, a boat or yacht race

re-gen-er-ate [rĭ-jĕn′ə-rāt′] *verb*, to renew, to reconstitute

re-gen-er-a-tion [rĭ-jĕn′ə-rā′shən] *noun*, a spiritual rebirth

re-gime [rā-zhēm′] *noun*, character of government or of a prevailing social system

relax

reg-i-men [rĕj/ə-mən] *noun*, a systematic plan usually to improve health

reg-i-ment [rĕj/ə-mənt] *noun*, 1) an infantry unit 2) to systematize

re-gion [rē/jən] *noun*, an indefinite area, a territory, a district

reg-is-ter [rĕj/ĭ-stər] *noun*, 1) an entry in a book or record, *verb*, 2) to enter one's name on the list, catalogue, record

reg-is-trar [rĕj/ĭ-strär/] *noun*, a keeper of records

reg-is-tra-tion [rĕj/ĭ-strā/shən] *noun*, enrollment

re-gret [rĭ-grĕt/] *noun*, 1) an apology, a feeling of remorse, *verb*, 2) to feel sadness for doing something wrong

re-gret-ta-ble [rĭ-grĕt/ə-bəl] *adjective*, unfortunate, sad

reg-u-lar [rĕg/yə-lər] *adjective*, habitual, customary, routine

reg-u-lar-i-ty [rĕg/yə-lăr/ĭ-tē] *noun*, *no plural*, uniformity, constancy, on a regular basis

reg-u-late [rĕg/yə-lāt/] *verb*, to control or direct by a rule

reg-u-la-tion [rĕg/yə-lā/shən] *noun*, a rule of conduct, a law

re-gur-gi-tate [rē-gûr/jĭ-tāt/] *verb*, to spit out food that has been swallowed, to vomit

re-ha-bil-i-tate [rē/hə-bĭl/ĭ-tāt/] *verb*, to restore to proper condition, i.e., good health

re-hears-al [rĭ-hûr/səl] *noun*, a practice performance

re-hearse [rĭ-hûrs/] *verb*, to practice in preparation for a performance, to try out

reign [rān] *noun*, 1) the period of time when a king or queen rules, *verb*, 2) to rule or govern

re-im-burse [rē/ĭm-bûrs/] *verb*, to make restoration, to repay

rein [rān] *noun*, 1) a strap of a bridle for governing a horse or other animal, *verb*, 2) to pull back or control, to check

rein-deer [rān/dîr/] *noun*, a large deer of arctic regions used to pull a cart or sled

re-in-force [rē/ĭn-fôrs/] *verb*, to strengthen, to stiffen, to fortify

re-it-er-ate [rē-ĭt/ə-rāt/] *verb*, to repeat, to say or do again

re-ject [rĭ-jĕkt/] *verb*, to refuse to accept or use

re-joice [rĭ-jois/] *verb*, to celebrate, to be joyful, to delight

re-ju-ve-nate [rĭ-jōō/və-nāt/] *verb*, to make more lively or youthful

re-lapse [rĭ-lăps/] *noun*, 1) a set back 2) to return to a former state, to regress, to revert

re-late [rĭ-lāt/] *verb*, to tell, to connect in thought and meaning

re-la-tion [rĭ-lā/shən] *noun*, 1) a member of the same family 2) an association or friendship

re-la-tion-ship [rĭ-lā/shən-shĭp/] *noun*, 1) the association between things, the affect one thing has on another 2) kinship

rel-a-tive [rĕl/ə-tĭv] *adjective*, 1) in relation to or compared to, *noun*, 2) a person connected by blood or marriage, kin

re-lax [rĭ-lăks/] *verb*, 1) to rest, to be at ease 2) to make less rigid

relaxation

re-lax-a-tion [rē′lăk-sā′shən] *noun*, no plural, a time of rest or ease, leisure, recreation

re-lay [rē′lā] *verb*, 1) to send, to give out, to beam 2) to convey

re-lease [rĭ-lēs′] *noun*, 1) freedom from confinement, *verb*, 2) to let go, to set free, to liberate, to untie 3) to relieve

rel-e-gate [rĕl′ĭ-gāt′] *verb*, to banish, to consign to an inferior position, place or condition

re-lent [rĭ-lĕnt′] *verb*, to become less strict, to become more forgiving

rel-e-van-cy [rĕl′ə-vəns-ē] *noun*, reference to the case at hand

re-li-a-ble [rĭ-lī′ə-bəl] *adjective*, dependable, trustworthy

re-li-ance [rĭ-lī′əns] *adjective*, confidence, something dependent on something else

rel-ic [rĕl′ĭk] *noun*, that which remains or is left, anything valued as a memento

re-lief [rĭ-lēf′] *noun*, no plural, 1) assistance, aid, help 2) comfort, ease, cheer 3) the contour of the front of a building

re-lieve [rĭ-lēv′] *verb*, to free from worry, to alleviate, to ease

re-lig-ion [rĭ-lĭj′ən] *noun*, possessing beliefs concerning the nature and purpose of the universe and the supernatural

re-li-gious [rĭ-lĭj′əs] *adjective*, 1) possessing pious beliefs in a God or gods 2) dedicated, devout

re-lin-quish [rĭ-lĭng′kwĭsh] *verb*, to abandon, to leave alone

rel-ish [rĕl′ĭsh] *noun*, 1) a condiment made of vegetables and herbs 2) great enjoyment, *verb*, 3) to savor, to appreciate, to like, to enjoy, to delight in

re-luc-tance [rĭ-lŭk′təns] *noun*, unwillingness or aversion marked by hesitation

re-luc-tant [rĭ-lŭk′tənt] *adjective*, unwilling to participate

re-ly [rĭ-lī′] *verb*, to depend confidently, to trust

re-main [rĭ-mān′] *verb*, to stay

re-main-der [rĭ-mān′dər] *noun*, 1) the fraction left over after a number has been divided 2) what is left over, remnant, residue

re-mains [rĭ-mānz′] *noun*, *plural*, parts which are left behind exposed to air, a corpse

re-make [rē-māk′] *noun*, something that has been redone or given a different form

re-mark [rĭ-märk′] *noun*, 1) something spoken, *verb*, 2) to take notice of, to observe

re-mark-a-ble [rĭ-mär′kə-bəl] *adjective*, uncommon, extraordinary, unusual

re-mark-a-bly [rĭ-mär′kə-blē] *adverb*, notably, especially

re-me-di-al [rĭ-mē′dē-əl] *adjective*, intended to improve poor skills

rem-e-dy [rĕm′ĭ-dē] *noun*, 1) a cure 2) a solution to the problem

re-mem-ber [rĭ-mĕm′bər] *verb*, to keep in your mind, to not forget

re-mem-brance [rĭ-mĕm′brəns] *noun*, a recollection, a memory

ro-mind [rĭ mīnd′] *verb*, to help someone remember

rem-i-nisce [rĕm′ə-nĭs′] *verb*, to think back or talk about past experiences, to recollect

rem-i-nis-cence [rĕm′ə-nĭs′əns] *noun*, the act of recalling the past, recollection, memory

rem-i-nis-cent [rĕm′ə-nĭs′ənt] *adjective*, suggestive, remindful

re-miss [rĭ mĭs′] *adjective*, negligent, careless, neglectful

re-mit [rĭ-mĭt′] *verb*, to send money usually as a payment

re-mit-tance [rĭ-mĭt′ns] *noun*, the sending of money, bills, etc, money transmitted

rem-nant [rĕm′nənt] *noun*, something left over

re-mon-strate [rĭ-mŏn′strāt′] *verb*, to plead in protest, to argue repeatedly in opposition

re-morse [rĭ-môrs′] *noun*, deep regret for wrongdoing

re-mote [rĭ-mōt′] *adjective*, far away, a great distance from everyone, slight, aloof

re-mov-al [rĭ-mōō′vəl] *noun*, to take something away

re-move [rĭ-mōōv′] *verb*, to take and move somewhere else

re-mu-ner-a-tion [rĭ-myōō′nə-rā′shən] *noun*, compensation, reward

ren-ais-sance [rĕn′ĭ-säns′] *noun*, a rebirth, revival, renewal

rend [rĕnd] *verb*, 1) to split, to tear apart with violence 2) to disturb

rend-er [rĕn′dər] *verb*, to cause to become, to provide, to perform

ren-dez-vous [rän′də-vōō′] *noun*, a meeting place, an appointment

ren-di-tion [rĕn-dĭsh′ən] *noun*, the artistic interpretation of a song or dance and how it is performed

ren-e-gade [rĕn′ĭ-gād′] *noun*, a person who deserts a cause to join another, an outlaw

re-new [rĭ-nōō′] *verb*, 1) to bring up to date 2) to start again

re-new-al [rĭ-nōō′əl] *noun*, a new start, recurrence, a revival

re-nounce [rĭ-nouns′] *verb*, to abandon, to discontinue, to disown, to repudiate

ren-o-vate [rĕn′ə-vāt′] *verb*, to make repairs, to redecorate

re-nown [rĭ-noun′] *adjective*, fame, widespread recognition

rent [rĕnt] *noun*, 1) money paid to use property, *verb*, 2) to pay someone to use something that they own, to lease

re-pair [rĭ-pâr′] *noun*, 1) the result of renewing or reconditioning something, *verb*, 2) to fix or mend, to make new again

re-par-a-tion [rĕp′ə-rā′shən] *noun*, compensation demanded by a victorious nation from a defeated nation, amends

rep-ar-tee [rĕp′ər-tē′,] *noun*, a clever reply

re-pay [rĭ-pā′] *verb*, to give someone money owed to them

re-peal [rĭ-pēl′] *noun*, 1) retraction, withdrawal, *verb*, 2) to cancel

re-peat [rĭ-pēt′] *verb*, to cause to happen again, to duplicate

repeatedly

re-peat-ed-ly [rĭ-pē′tĭd-lē] *adverb*, said or done again and again

re-pel [rĭ-pĕl′] *verb*, to drive back, to oppose, to ward off

re-pel-lent [rĭ-pĕl′ənt] *adjective*, offensive, disgusting, repugnant

re-pent [rĭ-pĕnt′] *verb*, to express regret, to feel contrite

re-pent-ance [rĭ-pĕn′təns] *noun*, sorrow for what one has done or omitted to do, regret

re-per-cus-sion [rē′pər-kŭsh′ən, rĕp′ər-] *noun*, the effect of something said or done

rep-er-toire [rĕp′ər-twär′] *noun*, a list of musical scores which a company or a person has thoroughly rehearsed and is prepared to perform

rep-e-ti-tion [rĕp′ĭ-tĭsh′ən] *noun*, doing or saying something over and over

re-place [rĭ-plās′] *verb*, 1) to take the place of 2) to make good

re-place-ment [rĭ-plās′mənt] *noun*, a person or thing that takes the place of another, a substitute

re-plen-ish [rĭ-plĕn′ĭsh] *verb*, to fill again, to supply anew

re-plete [rĭ-plēt′] *adjective*, filled to capacity, abundantly supplied

rep-li-ca [rĕp′lĭ-kə] *noun*, a copy

re-ply [rĭ-plī′] *noun*, 1) an answer, a response, *verb*, 2) to give an answer, to reply

re-port [rĭ-pôrt′] *noun*, 1) an oral or written account containing information in an organized form, *verb*, 2) to give an account of something

re-port-er [rĭ-pôr′tər] *noun*, 1) a person who reports legal proceedings or legislative debates 2) a person who gathers information and writes reports for a newspaper, magazine, etc.

re-pose [rĭ-pōz′] *noun*, 1) a state of calm *verb*, 2) to be in a state of rest or relaxation

re-pos-i-to-ry [rĭ-pŏz′ĭ-tôr′ē] *noun*, a storehouse, a vault where things are kept

rep-re-hen-si-ble [rĕp′rĭ-hĕn′sə-bəl] *verb*, deserving blame or censure, rebuke, wicked, deceitful

rep-re-sent [rĕp′rĭ-zĕnt′] *verb*, 1) to portray, to stand for something 2) to act or speak for someone or something

rep-re-sen-ta-tion [rĕp′rĭ-zĕn-tā′shən] *noun*, something that expresses a point of view or represents something else, a portrayal

rep-re-sen-ta-tive [rĕp′rĭ-zĕn′tə-tĭv] *adjective*, 1) typically characteristic, *noun*, 2) one acting in the place of another

re-press [rĭ-prĕs′] *verb*, to check, to overpower, to keep down

re-prieve [rĭ-prēv′] *noun*, to postpone an execution

rep-ri-mand [rĕp′rə-mănd′] *verb*, to censure, to scold

re-pris-al [rĭ-prī′zəl] *noun*, retaliation, an act short of war by which a nation seeks to redress a wrong committed against it by another nation

re-proach [rĭ-prōch′] *noun*,
1) blame, censure, *verb*, 2) to
blame someone, to criticize

re-pro-duce [rē′prə-dōōs′] *verb*,
1) to produce offspring or create
babies 2) to make a copy of
something, to duplicate

re-prove [rĭ-prōōv′] *verb*, to
reprimand someone for doing
something wrong, to correct
someone, to rebuke, to chide

rep-tile [rĕp′tĭl] *noun*, cold-
blooded, egg laying vertebrate,
such as a lizard or snake

re-pub-lic [rĭ-pŭb′lĭk] *noun*,
government in which people
elect their representatives

re-pub-li-can [rĭ-pŭb′lĭ-kən] *noun*,
a person who advocates a
republican government, one who
believes in government by
elected by representatives

Re-pub-li-can Par-ty *noun*, A U.S.
political party that developed in
the 1850s from those who
opposed slavery and that elected
Abraham Lincoln as the first
Republican president

re-pu-di-ate [rĭ-pyōō′dē-āt′] *verb*,
to disown, to renounce, to reject

re-pug-nant [rĭ-pŭg′nənt]
adjective, disgusting, vulgar,
offensive, objectionable

re-pulse [rĭ-pŭls′] *verb*, to offend

re-pul-sion [rĭ-pŭl′shən] *noun*, a
feeling of aversion or disgust

rep-u-ta-tion [rĕp′yə-tā′shən]
noun, what people generally
think about a person or thing

re-quest [rĭ-kwĕst′] *noun*,
1) something that is asked for,
verb, 2) to ask for something

re-quire [rĭ-kwīr′] *verb*, to have
need of, to insist or compel

re-quire-ment [rĭ-kwīr′mənt] *noun*,
a condition that must be met to
satisfy a need

req-ui-site [rĕk′wĭ-zĭt] *noun*, a
demand, something required

req-ui-si-tion [rĕk′wĭ-zĭsh′ən]
noun, an official written request
for something

re-quite [rĭ-kwīt′] *verb*, to repay, to
seek revenge, to get even

re-scind [rĭ-sĭnd′] *verb*, to cut off
or remove, to cancel or abolish

res-cue [rĕs′kyōō] *noun*, 1) help or
aid offered to save someone,
verb, 2) to aid or save from
danger or confinement

re-search [rĭ-sûrch′] *noun*, no
plural, 1) a careful study
conducted to learn and discover
something new, *verb*, 2) to
investigate or study something,
to make a careful inquiry

re-sem-blance [rĭ-zĕm′bləns]
noun, similarity, likeness

re-sem-ble [rĭ-zĕm′bəl] *verb*, to
have similar qualities and
likeness, to be like

re-sent [rĭ-zĕnt′] *verb*, to feel angry
with someone because they
were unfair, to feel indignant

re-sent-ment [rĭ-zĕnt′mənt] *noun*,
exasperation, ill will, anger

res-er-va-tion [rĕz′ər-vā′shən]
noun, 1) a commitment to hold a
space for someone 2) hesitation,
qualm 3) land the government
gave Indians to live on

reserve

re-serve [rĭ-zûrv′] *noun*,
1) restraint, *verb*, 2) to hold
something for someone

res-er-voir [rĕz′ər-vwär′] *noun*,
1) a place where a large supply
of anything is built up over time
2) a body of water stored for use

re-side [rĭ-zīd′] *verb*, to live, to
inhabit, to remain, to dwell in

res-i-dence [rĕz′ĭ-dəns] *noun*,
living or dwelling in a place for
some time, a home

res-i-dent [rĕz′ĭ-dənt] *noun*,
someone who resides in a place

res-i-den-tial [rĕz′ĭ-dĕn′shəl]
adjective, where people live

re-sid-u-al [rĭ-zĭj′ōō-əl] *adjective*,
effects remaining after the
principal action

res-i-due [rĕz′ĭ-dōō′] *noun*, the
remainder of something

re-sign [rĭ-zīn′] *verb*, 1) to
relinquish, to withdraw from an
office or position 2) to calmly
accept an unpleasant outcome

res-ig-na-tion [rĕz′ĭg-nā′shən]
noun, *no plural*, 1) reluctant
acceptance of something 2) a
formal statement to leave a job

re-signed [rĭ-zīnd′] *adjective*,
unresisting, patiently submissive

re-sil-ient [rĭ-zĭl′yənt] *adjective*, the
ability to return to the same size
and condition after excessive
stress and strain

res-in [rĕz′ĭn] *noun*, in plastics
manufacturing, the different
compounds used to create the
different forms of plastic

re-sist [rĭ-zĭst′] *verb*, to oppose, to
refuse to comply, to withstand

re-sist-ance [rĭ-zĭs′təns] *noun*, the
act of resisting or opposing, any
opposing force

res-o-lute [rĕz′ə-lōōt′] *adjective*,
determined, purposeful, earnest

res-o-lu-tion [rĕz′ə-lōō′shən] *noun*,
a firm decision, a course of
action decided on

re-solve [rĭ-zŏlv′] *noun*,
1) determination, conviction,
verb, 2) to decide to take action
3) to explain, to untangle

res-o-nant [rĕz′ə-nənt] *adjective*,
echoing, resounding, vibrant,
deep in sound

re-sort [rĭ-zôrt′] *noun*, 1) a
luxurious place visited for rest
and relaxation, *verb*, 2) to turn to
for help or support

re-source [rē′sôrs′] *noun*, 1) a
source of help or supply 2) a
supply or form of wealth

re-spect [rĭ-spĕkt′] *noun*, 1) an
aspect 2) consideration for
someone, *verb*, 3) to have a
good opinion of someone, to
look up to, to hold in esteem

re-spect-a-ble [rĭ-spĕk′tə-bəl]
adjective, honorable, well
thought of, worthy of respect

re-spect-ful [rĭ-spĕkt′fəl] *adjective*,
polite, well-mannered, civil

re-spect-ful-ly [rĭ-spĕkt′fə-lē]
adverb, in a civil manner,
courteously, politely

re-spec-tive [rĭ-spĕk′tĭv] *adjective*,
in relation to one another

re-spec-tive-ly [rĭ-spĕk′tĭv-lē]
adverb, for each separately in
precisely the order given

res-pi-ra-tion [rĕs′pə-rā′shən] *noun*, the emission of vapor, exhaling, breathing

res-pite [rĕs′pĭt] *verb*, postponement or delay

re-splend-ent [rĭ-splĕn′dənt] *adjective*, brilliant, lustrous

re-spond [rĭ-spŏnd′] *verb*, to answer, to act in return

re-spond-ent [rĭ-spŏn′dənt] *noun*, one who answers actions in a civil case, the defendant

re-sponse [rĭ-spŏns′] *noun*, an answer, a reaction, something said or done in reply

re-spon-si-bil-i-ty [rĭ-spŏn′sə-bĭl′ĭ-tē] *noun*, trustworthiness, dependability

re-spon-si-ble [rĭ-spŏn′sə-bəl] *adjective*, 1) the willingness to respond appropriately 2) trustworthy, reliable

rest [rĕst] *noun*, 1) a quiet time for relaxation 2) those remaining or left behind, *verb*, 3) to relax and feel at ease 4) to lean or put something on something else

res-tau-rant [rĕs′tər-ənt] *noun*, a public eating establishment

res-ti-tu-tion [rĕs′tĭ-too′shən] *noun*, an agreement as terms of a settlement to pay for loss or damage

rest-less [rĕst′lĭs] *adjective*, not relaxed, eager to do something else, uneasy, fitful, anxious

re-store [rĭ-stôr′] *verb*, 1) to revive 2) to bring back to a former condition, to reinstate 3) to give back, to return

re-strain [rĭ-strān′] *verb*, 1) to hold back with force 2) to limit

re-straint [rĭ-strānt′] *noun*, a control, restriction, a check

re-strict [rĭ-strĭkt′] *verb*, to confine, to keep within limits

re-stric-tive [rĭ-strĭk′tĭv] *adjective*, confining, limiting, inhibiting, uncomfortable

re-sult [rĭ-zŭlt′] *noun*, 1) the product or consequence of an action, the outcome, *verb*, 2) to have been the cause of something, to end up

re-su-me [′rez-ə-mā] *noun*, 1) a summary of personal or work history [rĭ-zoom′] *verb*, 2) to start again after stopping for a period of time

res-ur-rec-tion [rĕz′ə-rĕk′shən] *noun*, 1) the act of rising from the dead 2) renewal, revival

re-sus-ci-tate [rĭ-sŭs′ĭ-tāt′] *verb*, to revive, especially from apparent death, to restore to consciousness

re-tail [rē′tāl′] *verb*, to sell goods directly to the consumer

re-tain [rĭ-tān′] *verb*, 1) to keep in place or hold 2) to have

re-tal-i-a-tion [rĭ-tăl′ē-ā′shən] *noun*, to repay like for like, especially evil for evil

re-tard [rĭ-tärd′] *verb*, to delay the progress of, to hinder

re-ten-tion [rĭ-tĕn′shən] *noun*, 1) holding something 2) having a good memory, retaining

ret-i-cence [rĕt′ĭ-səns] *noun*, not revealing your thoughts or feelings openly

retina

ret-i-na [rĕt′n-ə] *noun*, the light-sensitive colored circle of an eye

re-tire [rĭ-tīr′] *verb*, 1) to withdraw to a place of privacy 2) to remove from active service

re-tire-ment [rĭ-tīr′mənt] *noun*, the period at the end of a career when a person stops working to relax and enjoy their savings

re-tort [rĭ-tôrt′] *verb*, a response

re-tract [rĭ-trăkt′] *verb*, 1) to draw back as claws or fangs 2) to disavow, to recant, to disclaim

re-treat [rĭ-trēt′] *noun*, 1) a place to rest and relax, a place of safety *verb*, 2) to turn around and go back, to withdraw

re-trench [rĭ-trĕnch′] *verb*, to cut down, to economize, to reduce

ret-ri-bu-tion [rĕt′rə-byoo′shən] *noun*, vengeance, compensation, punishment for offenses

re-trieve [rĭ-trēv′] *verb*, 1) to get and bring back 2) to recover

ret-ro-ac-tive [rĕt′rō-ăk′tĭv] *adjective*, that which takes effect from a time in the past

ret-ro-grade [rĕt′rə-grād′] *verb*, going or inclined to go backward

ret-ro-spect [rĕt′rə-spĕkt′] *noun*, looking back on things past

re-turn [rĭ-tûrn′] *noun*, 1) to go to a place and come back from it 2) the income from an investment, *verb*, 3) to give or put something back 4) to go back to the same place 5) to reply

re-use [rē-yooz′] *verb*, to use again, to recycle

re-veal [rĭ-vēl′] *verb*, 1) to make known, to tell, to disclose, to admit 2) to bring into view

re-veil-le [rĕv′əl lē]*noun*, a signal on a bugle, drum, etc. early in the morning to wake soldiers

rev-e-la-tion [rĕv′ə-lā′shən] *noun*, a sign from heaven, a disclosure

rev-el-ry [rĕv′əl-rē] *noun*, boisterous merrymaking

re-venge [rĭ-vĕnj′] *noun*, 1) a form of getting even, retribution, *verb*, 2) to administer punishment

rev-e-nue [rĕv′ə-noo] *noun*, 1) the return from an investment 2) an item of income 3) the taxes collected by a government

re-ver-ber-ate [rĭ-vûr′bə-rāt′] *verb*, to echo, to resound

re-vere [rĭ-vîr′] *verb*, to regard with respect, to admire, to look upon with awe, to honor

rev-er-ence [rĕv′ər-əns] *adjective*, honor or respect given to someone because of position

rev-er-end [rĕv′ər-ənd] *noun*, the title of the leader of a church

rev-er-ie [rĕv′ə-rē] *noun*, a daydream, a musing

re-verse [rĭ-vûrs′] *adjective*, 1) opposite, backward, *noun*, 2) a lever that makes a machine go backward, *verb*, 3) to turn around 4) to evoke or annul

re-vert [rĭ-vûrt′] *verb*, to return to a former habit, practice or belief

re-view [rĭ-vyoo′] *noun*, 1) an examination or inspection 2) a critical essay 3) a periodical, *verb*, 4) to go over or examine critically 5) to look back upon

ribald

re-vile [rĭ-vīl′] *verb*, to denounce using abusive language

re-vise [rĭ-vīz′] *verb*, to review and make changes in order to bring up to date, to correct, to improve

re-vi-sion [rĭ-vĭzh′ən] *noun*, the changed version of writing, or work, or doctrine

re-vive [rĭ-vīv′] *verb*, to bring back to life or to regain strength

re-volt [rĭ-vōlt′] *noun*, 1) a planned attack on a government or its leaders, *verb*, 2) to fight as a mass of rebels against leaders 3) to offend someone by making them feel ill or disgusted

rev-o-lu-tion [rĕv′ə-lōō′shən] *noun*, 1) the motion of a body about a center or axis 2) the overthrow of a government or system by those who are governed, usually by force, a rebellion 3) a radical change

rev-o-lu-tion-ar-y [rĕv′ə-lōō′shə-nĕr′ē] *noun*, an activist who promotes change

re-volve [rĭ-vŏlv′] *verb*, 1) to orbit the way the Earth moves slowly around the sun 2) to rotate 3) to recur in cycles

re-volv-er [rĭ-vŏl′vər] *noun*, a firearm with a cylinder of several chambers to be discharged repeatedly

re-vul-sion [rĭ-vŭl′shən] *noun*, a sickening feeling, a negative reaction

re-ward [rĭ-wôrd′] *noun*, 1) something given to praise good work, kindness or bravery, *verb*, 2) to give a prize in appreciation of good work

rhap-so-dize [răp′sə-dīz′] *verb*, to speak or write enthusiastically

rhap-so-dy [răp′sə-dē] *noun*, delight, happiness, enthusiasm

rhet-o-ric [rĕt′ər-ĭk] *noun*, the art of using language effectively

rheu-ma-tism [rōō′mə-tĭz′əm] *noun*, a painful disease of the muscles and joints, accompanied by swelling and stiffness

rhi-noc-er-os [rī-nŏs′ər-əs] *noun*, a large wild animal with tough skin and two large horns on its nose, which lives in Africa

Rhode Island [rōd-ī′lənd] *noun*, one of 50 United States located on the East Coast, the capital is Providence. The state flower of **Rhode Island** is the violet and the motto is "Hope."

rhom-bus [rŏm′bəs] *noun*, a form with four equal sides in the shape of a diamond

rhu-barb [rōō′bärb′] *noun*, acid leafstalks of a coarse herb, used for sauce or pie

rhyme [rīm] *noun*, 1) correspondence of sounds in words, *verb*, 2) to end the line of a verse with the same sound

rhythm [rĭth′əm] *noun*, 1) repetition of a beat played throughout a musical piece 2) the recurrence of stress or a sound at regular intervals

rib [rĭb] *noun*, one of many narrow bones surrounding the chest

rib-ald [rĭb′əld] *adjective*, wanton, indecent, offensive, vulgar

ribbon

rib-bon [rĭb'ən] *noun*, a narrow fabric usually of silk, used to trim a dress or a present

rice [rīs] *noun*, a grain in the cereal family from a grass-like plant grown in warm climates

rich [rĭch] *adjective*, 1) wealthy, having many resources 2) plentiful, abundant

rich-es [rĭch'ĭz] *noun*, *plural*, treasures, things worth a lot of money, valuable possessions

rid [rĭd] *verb*, to dispose of

rid-dance [rĭd'ns] *noun*, a cleaning up or out, relief or deliverance

rid-dle [rĭd'l] *noun*, 1) a clever question with an unexpected answer, a puzzling thing, *verb*, 2) to pierce with many holes

ride [rīd] *verb*, to travel on an animal or in a vehicle to go somewhere

rid-er [rī'dər] *noun*, 1) modification of a law, by adding a clause to legislation 2) a passenger on a journey

ridge [rĭj] *noun*, a long narrow raised part of the hill, a crest

rid-i-cule [rĭd'ĭ-kyo͞ol'] *noun*, 1) taunts, jeers, *verb*, 2) to sneer at, to mock, to make fun of

ri-dic-u-lous [rĭ-dĭk'yə-ləs] *adjective*, unworthy of serious consideration, absurd

rife [rīf] *adjective*, prevalent, common or frequent in occurrence, widespread

ri-fle [rī'fəl] *noun*, 1) a firearm with a long barrel, *verb*, 2) to search hurriedly through

rift [rĭft] *noun*, an opening, a break

rig [rĭg] *noun*, 1) heavy equipment, 2) a vehicle used to haul large shipments, *verb*, 3) to equip

rig-ging [rĭg'ĭng] *noun*, the ropes used to raise and hold the sails of a ship

right [rīt] *adjective*, 1) of or located to the opposite of left 2) what is fair and good 3) correct, *adverb*, 4) correctly 5) straight to, without stopping, *noun*, 6) a freedom allowed by law

right triangle [rīt-trī'ăng'gəl] *noun*, a triangle that has one right angle in it, the opposite side is the hypotenuse

right-eous [rī'chəs] *adjective*, just, virtuous, acting in a moral way

rig-id [rĭj'ĭd] *adjective*, hard, fixed, immovable, not flexible

rig-or [rĭg'ər] *noun*, severity

rig-or-ous [rĭg'ər-əs] *adjective*, strict, severe discipline

rim [rĭm] *noun*, the often-curved edge of something, a border

rind [rīnd] *noun*, the tough outer skin of fruit or cheese that protects it from air

ring [rĭng] *noun*, 1) small circular band worn on the finger 2) a circular object with a vacant center 3) an area where fights are held 4) a small group 5) the sound created by a bell, *verb*, 6) to make a sound like a bell

rink [rĭngk] *noun*, a playing field, a ring, a smooth floor

rinse [rĭns] *verb*, to wash lightly, to cleanse with water after washing

ri-ot [rī′ət] *noun*, 1) unrestrained fighting, vandalism, *verb*, 2) to fight in an angry crowd

ri-ot-ous [rī′ət-əs] *adjective*, unrestrained, tumultuous

rip [rĭp] *verb*, to tear away

ripe [rīp] *adjective*, completely mature, ready to be eaten, aged

rip-en [rī′pən] *verb*, to grow to maturity or when ready to eat

rip-ple [rĭp′əl] *noun*, 1) a little wave, *verb*, 2) to cause little waves of sound or movement

rise [rīz] *noun*, 1) an increase, *verb*, 2) to stand up 3) to move upward 4) to move in a positive direction 5) to get up out of bed

risk [rĭsk] *noun*, 1) a sense or chance of danger involved with doing something, *verb*, 2) to take a chance of injury or loss

rite [rīt] *noun*, a formal ceremony, a ritual, a custom

rit-u-al [rĭch′ōō-əl] *noun*, a set action or series of actions

ri-val [rī′vəl] *noun*, a competitor

ri-val-ry [rī′vəl-rē] *noun*, a contention, a contest, jealousy

riv-er [rĭv′ər] *noun*, a large natural stream of fresh water that flows into the ocean

riv-et [rĭv′ĭt] *noun*, 1) a metal pin for passing through holes in two or more pieces to hold them together, *verb*, 2) to hold attention firmly, to engross

roach [rōch] *noun*, a cockroach or small insect that eats food

road [rōd] *noun*, a route used for vehicles to travel, an avenue or thoroughfare, a street

roam [rōm] *verb*, to wander about, to travel aimlessly

roar [rôr, rōr] *noun*, 1) a deep angry sound, a loud growl or snarl, *verb*, 2) to growl in a loud voice 3) to laugh loudly

roast [rōst] *noun*, 1) a piece of meat that has been cooked over fire or will be, *verb*, 2) to cook without water over a fire or in an oven, to expose to great heat

rob [rŏb] *verb*, to deprive, to steal from someone, to defraud

rob-ber [rŏb′ər] *noun*, a thief, someone who steals

robe [rōb] *noun*, a piece of clothing that covers most of the body worn for lounging or relaxing

rob-in [rŏb′ĭn] *noun*, a brown song bird with a red breast found in North America

ro-bot [rō′bət] *noun*, a programmed machine designed to do the work of a person

ro-bust [rō-bŭst′] *adjective*, vigorous, strong, healthy

rock [rŏk] *noun*, 1) a hard, natural material of mineral origin, a stone 2) the mineral matter that makes up a large portion of the earth's crust *verb*, 3) to move back and forth or from side to side

rock-et [rŏk′ĭt] *noun*, 1) a missile, a spacecraft, *verb*, 2) to shoot into space 3) to move swiftly

rod [rŏd] *noun*, a thin pole

rode [rōd] *past tense* of **ride**

ro-dent [rōd′nt] *noun*, a small furry four-legged animal, like a squirrel, mouse or rat

rodeo

ro-de-o [rō'dē-ō'] *noun,* a contest for people like cowhands to show their skill

rogue [rōg] *noun,* a scoundrel

role [rōl] *noun,* a part played by an actor, a characterization

roll [rōl] *noun,* 1) a long, drawn out noise 2) a small rounded portion of bread, *verb,* 3) to move along by turning over and over 4) to make something flat by pressing it with a roller

ro-man nu-mer-als [rō-mäɴ'nōō'mər-əlz] *noun, plural,* the number symbols used by Romans 2,500 years ago

ro-mance [rō-mǎns'] *noun,* 1) the state of being in love 2) a story about love between people, *verb,* 3) to court romantically

ro-man-tic [rō-mǎn'tǐk] *adjective,* 1) not based in fact, fanciful 2) thoughts of love and adventure

roof [rōōf] *noun,* 1) the external cover of a building 2) the top of the mouth

rook-ie [rōōk'ē] *noun,* a beginner

room [rōōm] *noun,* 1) one of the parts of a house separated by walls and doors 2) space

roost [rōōst] *noun,* 1) a perch, *verb,* 2) to sleep or rest on a perch

roost-er [rōō'stər] *noun,* a domestic male fowl, a cock

root [rōōt] *noun,* 1) the part of the plant that grows in the ground, it's purpose is to hold it in the earth, to absorb moisture and to store nourishment, *verb,* 2) to dig up with the nose or snout 3) to cheer for a team

rope [rōp] *noun,* a heavy cord

rose [rōz] *noun,* 1) a shrub with a beautiful sweet smelling flower, *verb,* 2) the *past tense* of **rise**

ros-ter [rǒs'tər] *noun,* a list

ros-trum [rǒs'trəm] *noun,* a stage for public speaking, a pulpit

rot [rǒt] *verb,* to decompose, to decay gradually, to spoil

ro-ta-ry [rō'tə-rē] *noun,* rotating parts turning on an axis

ro-tate [rō'tāt] *verb,* to turn around a center or axis, to revolve

ro-ta-tion [rō-tā'shən] *noun,* 1) a revolution, turning in a full circle 2) the growing of different crops in the same place usually in regular order

rote [rōt] *noun,* learning through repetition and memorization

rot-ten [rǒt'n] *adjective,* no good

ro-tun-da [rō-tǔn'də] *noun,* a round building or rooms

rough [rǔf] *adjective,* 1) not smooth, uneven, difficult 2) not calm or gentle 3) unfinished, crude, coarse to the touch

rough-ly [rǔf-lē] *adverb,* approximately

round [round] *adjective,* 1) in the shape of a circle or a ball, circular, *noun,* 2) a circle, an orb, a globe 3) a course, a cycle, a series, *verb,* 4) to turn a bend or corner 5) to express a number to the nearest whole number

round-a-bout [round'ə-bout'] *adjective,* 1) not direct or

straightforward, *noun*, 2) a traffic
circle

rouse [rouz] *verb*, to stimulate, to
spur, to wake up, to excite

rout [rout] noun1) a disorganized
retreat from an attack, *verb*, 2) to
drive out, to defeat decisively

route [ro͞ot, rout] *noun*, a road for
traveling ffrom one place to
another

rou-tine [ro͞o-tēn'] *adjective*,
1) habitual, 2) unoriginal, *noun*,
3) a regular course or procedure

row [rō] *noun*, 1) an arrangement
set in a line 2) a quarrel or fight,
verb, 3) to propel with oars

roy-al [roi'əl] *adjective*, 1) of a king
or queen 2) fit for a king or
queen

roy-al-ty [roi'əl-tē] *noun*, 1) a
member of the monarchy 2) a
payment to the owner for the use
of copyright material

rub [rŭb] *verb*, 1) to create friction
by moving something back and
forth 2) to massage

rub-ber [rŭb'ər] *noun*, *no plural*, a
mix of chemicals to form a
pliable substance

rub-bish [rŭb'ĭsh] *noun*, *no plural*,
refuse, garbage, trash

rub-ble [rŭb'əl] *noun*, pieces or
fragments of large objects

ru-by [ro͞o'bē] *noun*, a precious
stone of deep red

rud-der [rŭd'ər] *noun*, a steering
mechanism at the back of a boat

rud-dy [rŭd'ē] *adjective*, reddish,
healthy-looking

rude [ro͞od] *adjective*, not polite,
unkind, discourteous behavior

ru-di-men-ta-ry [ro͞o'də-měn'tə-rē]
adjective, the first undeveloped
state, unrefined, imperfect

ruf-fi-an [rŭf'ē-ən] *noun*, a person
who is rough and dirty

ruf-fle [rŭf'əl] *noun*, 1) trimming,
frill, *verb*, 2) to make uneasy

rug [rŭg] *noun*, a floor covering
made of woven fibers or wool

rug-ged [rŭg'ĭd] *adjective*,
1) rough and wild 2) full of rocks
with a jagged surface

ruin [ro͞o'ĭn] *noun*, 1) destruction,
damage, *verb*, 2) to destroy

ru-in-ous [ro͞o'ə-nəs] *adjective*,
destructive, harmful

rule [ro͞ol] *noun*, 1) a law, a guide
for conduct or procedure, *verb*,
2) to have power and control
over someone 3) to decree

rul-er [ro͞o'lər] *noun*, 1) someone
who governs a body of people
2) an instrument used to
measure and draw straight lines

rum-ble [rŭm'bəl] *noun*, 1) a loud
sound, like earth moving, *verb*,
2) to make a continuous loud,
low noise, like thunder

ru-mi-nate [ro͞o'mə-nāt'] *verb*,
1) to chew the cud 2) to ponder,
to think about, to meditate

rum-mage [rŭm'ĭj] *noun*, 1) odds
and ends, miscellany, *verb*, 2) to
look for, to rifle through

ru-mor [ro͞o'mər] *noun*, gossip,
common talk, hearsay

run [rŭn] *noun*, 1) the distance
traveled, a journey 2) a score in
a baseball game 3) movement
that is quicker than walking,
verb, 4) to move quickly or swiftly

5) to work or make work 6) to go over 7) to escape, to retreat 8) to ooze or pour out

rung [rŭng] *noun*, 1) a rod on a ladder that is a step, *verb*, 2) *past participle* of **ring**

run-ner [rŭn'ər] *noun*, 1) a long ski on the bottom of a sled used on snow and ice 2) a person who runs errands 3) a carpet or decorative cover placed on a walk way

rup-ture [rŭp'chər] *noun*, 1) a fracture, a breach, *verb*, 2) to break, to fracture, to split

ru-ral [roŏr'əl] *adjective*, having to do with, in, or like farmland, country people, or life in the country, rustic

ruse [roōs] *noun*, a trick, gimmick

rush [rŭsh] *noun*, *no plural*, 1) rapid movement, haste 2) reeds that grow near the water, *verb*, 3) to move quickly or fast as in a hurry 4) to charge, to attack

rust [rŭst] *noun*, *no plural*, 1) a corrosive red-brown substance that forms on iron when it has been exposed to water and oxygen, *verb*, 2) to become covered with the corrosive element 3) to deteriorate

rus-tic [rŭs'tĭk] *adjective*, referring to country people, rural

rus-tle [rŭs'əl] *verb*, to make a soft rubbing sound, to crackle

rut [rŭt] *noun*, a deep narrow groove in the ground

ruth-less [roōth'lĭs] *adjective*, cruel, harsh, merciless

rye [rī] *noun*, a grass with seeds that are made into flour

S

Sab-bath [săb'əth] *noun*, a holy day, a day of rest

sack [săk] *noun*, a large bag made of woven material strong enough to carry things

sa-cred [sā'krĭd] *adjective*, holy, worshipped, religious

sac-ri-fice [săk'rə-fīs'] *noun*, 1) an offering, the surrender of anything, *verb*, 2) to give up something, to forfeit

sac-ro-sanct [săk'rō-săngkt'] *adjective*, most sacred, holy

sad [săd] *adjective*, unhappy, sorrowful, affected by grief

sad-dle [săd'l] *noun*, 1) a seat made of leather that fits over the back of a horse, *verb*, 2) to burden

sa-dis-tic [sə-dĭs'tĭk] *adjective*, pleasure in being cruel

sa-fa-ri [sə-fär'ē] *noun*, a journey into the jungles and plains of Africa, to look at wild animals

safe [sāf] *adjective*, 1) not in danger, protected, secure, *noun*, 2) a vault, a chest, a repository

safe-ty [sāf'tē] *noun*, a way of preventing damage to workers or a machine, protection

sag [săg] *verb*, 1) to hang down, to droop 2) to decline in value

sa-ga [sä'gə] *noun*, any legend, a long drawn out story

sa-ga-cious [sə-gā'shəs] *adjective*, shrewd, wise, knowledgeable

sage [sāj] *noun*, a wise man

said [sĕd] *past tense* of **say**

sail [sāl] *noun*, 1) a large cloth used to catch the wind and move a boat, *verb*, 2) to travel on water 3) to navigate a ship equipped with sails 4) to glide

sail-or [sā′lər] *noun*, a seaman, someone who works on a ship

saint [sānt] *noun*, a person who has lived a religious life and has been recognized by a group of religious leaders for good work

sake [sāk] *noun*, used with **for**, to show purpose or reason

sal-ad [săl′əd] *noun*, a preparation of vegetables, fruit, fish, or meat, dressed with vinegar, oil, etc.

sal-a-ry [săl′ə-rē] *noun*, fixed wages for a year, quarter, or month, for services

sale [sāl] *noun*, 1) the exchange of goods for money 2) when merchandise is sold at a reduced price 3) an auction

sales-man [sālz′mən] *noun*, one whose occupation is to sell goods or merchandise

sales tax [sālz-tăks] *noun*, a tax people pay for purchases

sa-li-ent [sā′lē-ənt] *adjective*, standing out, conspicuous, striking, noticeable, obvious

sa-line [sā′lēn′] *adjective*, salty

sa-li-va [sə-lī′və] *noun*, a fluid secreted in the mouth to help digest food, spit

salm-on [săm′ən] *noun*, a species of fresh-water fish

sa-loon [sə-loon′] *noun*, a bar or tavern, a large public room

salt [sôlt] *noun*, a white crystal compound of chlorine and sodium found in sea water, used to flavor food and preserve meat

sa-lu-bri-ous [sə-loo′brē-əs] *adjective*, promoting health

sal-u-ta-tion [săl′yə-tā′shən] *noun*, a greeting, something uttered

sal-u-tar-y [săl′yə-tĕr′ē] *adjective*, beneficial, wholesome

sa-lute [sə-loot′] *noun*, 1) a sign of respect for a superior officer *verb*, 2) to hold up the right hand to the forehead

sal-vage [săl′vĭj] *noun*, 1) property saved from destruction, *verb*, 2) to save, to recycle, to recover, to rescue

sal-va-tion [săl-vā′shən] *noun*, saved from harm or loss, deliverance from evil

salve [săv] *noun*, a medicinal ointment, a lotion, a balm

same [sām] *adjective*, 1) having the same identifying characteristics, identical 2) not different

sam-ple [săm′pəl] *noun*, 1) a part of anything shown as quality, a specimen, *verb*, 2) to try or test

san-a-to-ri-um [săn′ə-tôr′ē-əm] *noun*, a place where chronically ill patients receive the care they need until they recover

sanc-ti-fy [săngk′tə-fī′] *verb*, to bless, to make holy, to anoint

sanc-tion [săngk′shən] *noun*, 1) coercive measures directed against a nation that has violated international law, *verb*, 2) to approve, to support, to confirm

sanc-tu-ar-y [săngk′choo-ĕr′ē] *noun*, church, a place of refuge

sand

sand [sănd] *noun*, fine grains made of rocks usually found near the sea or in deserts

san-dal [săn′dl] *noun*, a kind of shoe consisting of a sole strapped to the foot

sand-bar [sănd′ bär] *noun*, a ridge of sand formed in a river or along a shore by the action of currents or tides

sand-wich [sănd′wĭch, săn′-] *noun*, slices of bread with something between them such as meat, cheese or jelly

sane [sān] *adjective*, reasonable, sensible, sound in mind

sang [săng] *past tense* of **sing**

san-i-tar-y [săn′ĭ-tĕr′ē] *adjective*, very clean, antiseptic

san-i-ta-tion [săn′ĭ-tā′shən] *noun*, the job of keeping things clean

san-i-ty [săn′ĭ-tē] *noun*, a healthy outlook, a state of being sane

sank [săngk] *verb*, *past tense* of **sink**

sap [săp] *noun*, 1) the fluid in a plant that gives nourishment, *verb*, 2) to take strength from something, to weaken gradually

sapi-ent [sā′pē-ənt] *adjective*, wise, shrewd, showing great wisdom

sap-ling [săp′lĭng] *noun*, a young tree, a sprout of a tree

sap-phire [săf′īr′] *noun*, a precious gemstone of a blue color

sar-casm [sär′kăz′əm] *noun*, scornful remarks, ridicule

ˌcas-tic [sär-kăs′tĭk] *adjective*, ˌnting, satirical, scornful

sar-coph-a-gus [sär-kŏf′ə-gəs] *noun*, a coffin, a casket

sar-dine [sär-dēn′] *noun*, a small herring preserved in olive oil

sash [săsh] *noun*, a wide ribbon worn around the waist or over the shoulder

sat-el-lite [săt′l-īt′] *noun*, 1) a small, heavenly body orbiting around a planet 2) an artificial object launched to orbit the earth or other celestial bodies

sa-ti-ate [sā′shē-āt′] *verb*, to satisfy fully, to supply to excess

sat-ire [săt′īr′] *noun*, a form of writing that makes fun of habits, ideas or customs

sat-is-fac-tion [săt′ĭs-făk′shən] *noun*, the feeling of having what you need and want

sat-is-fac-to-ry [săt′ĭs-făk′tə-rē] *adjective*, sufficient, fulfilling all requirements, adequate

sat-is-fy [săt′ĭs-fī′] *verb*, 1) to be enough or good enough, to meet a need 2) to make sure

sat-u-rate [săch′ə-rāt′] *verb*, to become thoroughly soaked

Sat-ur-day [săt′ər-dē′] *noun*, the seventh day of the week

sauce [sôs] *noun*, a liquid of a variety of ingredients eaten with food to improve its taste

sauc-er [sô′sər] *noun*, a small plate put under a cup to catch the drips

saun-ter [sôn′tər] *verb*, to stroll, to walk slowly, to meander

sau-sage [sô′sĭj] *noun*, minced and seasoned meat, commonly enclosed in an edible casing

sav-age [săv′ĭj] *adjective*, wild, untamed, uncivilized

sa-van-nah [sə-văn′ə] *noun*, a grassy plain that has very few trees in a tropical climate

sa-vant [să-vănt′] *noun*, a scholar, a learned person, a sage

save [sāv] *verb*, 1) to rescue from harm or danger 2) to set aside for future use, to store

sav-ings [sā′vĭngz] *noun, plural, no singular,* money set aside to use in the future, reserve funds

sav-ior [sāv′yər] *noun*, someone who saves others from danger

sa-vor [sā′vər] *noun*, 1) a taste or aroma, *verb*, 2) to taste or enjoy a distinctive flavor, smell or quality, to appreciate

saw [sô] *noun*, 1) a tool with a jagged blade and handle used to cut wood, *verb*, 2) *past tense* of **see** 3) to cut with a serrated blade or saw

say [sā] *verb*, to speak something

say-ing [sā′ĭng] *noun*, a wise statement that is full of truth like a proverb or aphorism

scab [skăb] *noun*, 1) a hard covering of coagulated blood on a wound 2) a worker who stays on the job while others go on strike

scaf-fold [skăf′əld] *noun*, 1) a temporary platform built to hold laborers while working on a building 2) the gallows

scald [skôld] *verb*, 1) to injure or burn with hot liquid 2) to heat to just below the boiling point

scale [skāl] *noun*, 1) a balance to measure weight 2) a range, degree, or progression 3) a protective crust *verb*, 4) to adjust to a standard of measure 5) to climb or ascend

sca-lene tri-an-gle [skā′lēn′ trī′ăng′gəl] *noun*, a triangle with unequal sides

scal-lop [skăl′lŏp]*noun*, 1) a kind of mollusk with two deeply grooved, curved shells, that swims by rapidly snapping its shells together 2) any of a series of curves forming an ornamental edge on cloth, lace, etc.

scalp [skălp] *noun*, 1) the skin and hair of the head, *verb*, 2) to remove the hair from someone

scam-per [skăm′pər] *verb*, to scurry, to run quickly

scan [skăn] *verb*, to look over, to review, to examine closely

scan-dal [skăn′dl] *noun*, an incident which offends conscience or moral feelings

scape-goat [skāp′gōt′] *noun*, someone who bears the blame for others

scar [skăr] *noun*, 1) a mark left where a wound has been, *verb*, 2) to make a deep cut or to cause deep unforgettable pain

scar-ab [skăr′əb] *noun*, a large beetle with a dark shell

scarce [skârs] *adjective*, hard to find or come by, not plentiful

scarce-ly [skârs′lē] *adverb*, with difficulty, barely, hardly

scare [skâr] *noun*, 1) a sudden fright, *verb*, 2) to make someone afraid, to frighten, to terrify

scarf [skärf] *noun, plural,* **scarves,** a triangular or rectangular piece of cloth worn around the head, neck, or shoulders

scat-ter [skăt′ər] *verb,* to throw things everywhere, to disperse

scav-en-ger [skăv′ən-jər] *noun,* collector of garbage, an animal that devours refuse

scene [sēn] *noun,* 1) a setting, a view 2) a specific place 3) a shocking incident, a fight

scen-er-y [sē′nə-rē] *noun, no plural,* the setting of a place or landscape, the panorama

sce-nic [sē′nĭk] *adjective,* full of natural splendors, breathtaking

scent [sĕnt] *noun,* a smell that characterizes things

sched-ule [skĕj′ōōl] *noun,* 1) a written formal list or inventory, *verb,* 2) to arrange tasks to fit into a specific time frame

scheme [skēm] *noun,* 1) a plan, purpose, arrangement, *verb,* 2) to make secret plans, to plot

schol-ar [skŏl′ər] *noun,* a person who studies a particular subject at great length, a student

schol-ar-ship [skŏl′ər-shĭp′] *noun,* money granted to a worthy student to pay for their education

scho-las-tic [skə-lăs′tĭk] *noun,* pertaining to a school or education

school [skōōl] *noun,* 1) a place of instruction 2) a style, manner, method 3) a company of fish

schoon-er [skōō′nər] *noun,* a sailing ship with fore and aft rigging

sci-ence [sī′əns] *noun,* classified knowledge of the physical world

sci-en-tif-ic [sī′ən-tĭf′ĭk] *adjective,* in conformity to the principles of the physical world

sci-en-tist [sī′ən-tĭst] *noun,* a person who studies information about natural phenomena

scis-sors [sĭz′ərz] *noun,* a tool with two blades and handles, pivoted together that is used for cutting

scoff [skŏf] *verb,* to ridicule or make fun of, to deride, to jeer

scold [skōld] *verb,* to angrily tell someone they did something wrong, to reprimand

scoop [skōōp] *noun,* 1) a large spoonful, *verb,* 2) to take some from the whole thing with a spoon or the hands

scoot [skōōt] *verb,* to move quickly

scope [skōp] *noun,* 1) a range of one's mind 2) opportunity to function, capacity

scorch [skôrch] *verb,* to burn lightly leaving a brown stain

score [skôr] *noun,* 1) the points you get on a test or in a game 2) the reason, the purpose 3) a copy of a musical composition showing all parts for instruments and voices 4) a period of twenty years, *verb,* 5) to make points in a game 6) to achieve success

scorn [skôrn] *noun,* 1) disrespect, disdain, hate, *verb,* 2) to act like someone is worthless

scor-pi-on [skôr′pē-ən] *noun,* an arachnid that kills with its poisonous tail

scoun-drel [skoun′drəl] *noun*, a villain, a rascal, a mean person

scour [skour] *verb*, 1) to search an area thoroughly 2) to clean and polish by rubbing

scout [skout] *noun*, a person sent out ahead to obtain information

scowl [skoul] *noun*, 1) an angry, disgusted expression on the face, *verb*, 2) to make an angry expression showing disapproval

scram-ble [skrăm′bəl] *verb*, to move quickly on hands and knees, to hurry along

scrap [skrăp] *noun*, waste with some value, particularly material left over from construction or manufacturing suitable for reprocessing

scrap-book [skrăp′bŏok′] *noun*, a blank book filled with mementos, cards and souvenirs

scrape [skrāp] *noun* 1) a predicament, *verb*, 2) to take something off by rubbing it with a sharp edge 3) to make a grating sound

scratch [skrăch] *noun*, 1) a mark or wound made with something pointed, *verb*, 2) to make marks with something pointed 3) to remove a layer by rubbing

scream [skrēm] *noun*, 1) a loud, shrill cry made in pain or fear, *verb*, 2) to make a sharp cry

screech [skrēch] *noun*, 1) a loud high-pitched noise, *verb*, 2) to make a harsh shrill noise

screen [skrēn] *noun*, 1) a portable covered framework in the nature of a partition 2) a grating of fine wire 3) protection, *verb*, 4) to eliminate applicants

screw [skrōō] *noun*, 1) a cylinder, grooved in an advancing spiral on its surface, *verb*, 2) to turn around and around

scrib-ble [skrĭb′əl] *verb*, to write or draw in an unintelligible manner

scrim-mage [skrĭm′ĭj] *noun*, a football or soccer practice

script [skrĭpt] *noun*, 1) a form of handwriting that connects the letters in a word 2) written words to be spoken from a text

scrip-ture [skrĭp′chər] *noun*, any sacred writing or book

scroll [skrōl] *noun*, 1) a rod with a roll of paper attached, *verb*, 2) to move a cursor smoothly, vertically or sideways, to review data on a computer screen

scrub [skrŭb] *verb*, to rub with a hard brush to clean off a spot

scru-pu-lous [skrōō′pyə-ləs] *adjective*, careful, cautious, exact, punctilious, precise

scru-ti-nize [skrōōt′n-īz′] *verb*, to examine closely and critically

scru-ti-ny [skrōōt′n-ē] *noun*, close examination, minute inspection

sculpt [skŭlpt] *verb*, to make or shape a statue

sculp-tor [skŭlp′tər] *noun*, one who carves or cuts wood or stone into statues

sculp-ture [skŭlp′chər] *noun*, works of art made from stone, clay or metal, a statue

scythe [sīth] *noun*, a long, curved-blade instrument for cutting grass by hand

sea [sē] *noun*, part of an ocean that is partially surrounded by land

sea-gull [sē′gŭl′] *noun*, a bird that lives near the ocean and scavenges for food

seal [sēl] *noun*, 1) an emblem affixed to a document to prove authenticity 2) a mammal with sleek skin, and limbs in the form of flippers, that lives in the water and on land, *verb*, 3) to close tightly so that something cannot be opened

seam [sēm] *noun*, 1) the stitches joining two pieces of cloth together 2) a fissure

search [sûrch] *noun*, 1) a careful investigation, a hunt, *verb*, 2) to look for someone or something

sea-son [sē′zən] *noun*, 1) a special time of year devoted to a certain activity 2) one of the four divisions of the year: fall, winter, spring, summer, *verb*, 3) to flavor or add zest to food

seat [sēt] *noun*, 1) a place to sit or a cushion to sit on 2) a location

se-cede [sĭ-sēd′] *verb*, to withdraw from association or fellowship

se-ces-sion [sĭ-sĕsh′ən] *noun*, withdrawal

se-clu-sion [sĭ-kloo′zhən] *noun*, 1) hiding, isolation 2) privacy

sec-ond [sĕk′ənd] *adjective*, 1) coming directly after the first, *noun*, 2) a very short period of time, a moment, *verb*, 3) to endorse, to support a motion

se-cre-cy [sē′krĭ-sē] *noun*, keeping things quiet without the knowledge of others

se-cret [sē′krĭt] *adjective*, 1) kept from the knowledge of most people, *noun*, 2) something known only to oneself or a few

sec-re-tar-y [sĕk′rĭ-tĕr′ē] *noun*, 1) a person who writes letters, files documents 2) a government officer who is a member of the President's Cabinet

se-crete [sĭ-krēt′] *verb*, to produce a liquid discharge

se-cre-tion [sĭ-krē′shən] *noun*, a fluid emitted from a gland

sec-tion [sĕk′shən] *noun*, a piece of the whole, a portion, a part

sec-tor [sĕk′tər, -tôr′] *noun*, region, area, zone, a distinct part

sec-u-lar [sĕk′yə-lər] *adjective*, worldly, not pertaining to church matters, temporal, earthly

se-cure [sĭ-kyoor′] *adjective*, 1) safe 2) strong and fixed firmly, *verb*, 3) to assure

se-cu-ri-ty [sĭ-kyoor′ĭ-tē] *noun*, 1) safety, assurance, freedom from danger 2) stocks and bonds

se-date [sĭ-dāt′] *adjective*, dignified, composed, calm

sed-a-tive [sĕd′ə-tĭv] *noun*, a tranquilizer, a narcotic

sed-en-tar-y [sĕd′n-tĕr′ē] *adjective*, accustomed to sitting most of the day

sed-i-ment [sĕd′ə-mənt] *noun*, the solid matter that settles to the bottom in a liquid

se-di-tion [sĭ-dĭsh′ən] *noun*, resistance to authority, insubordination

sed-ul-ous-ly [sĕj′ə-ləs-lē] *adjective*, diligently, loyally

see [sē] *verb*, 1) to perceive or acknowledge with the eye 2) to understand, to comprehend 3) to go and look 4) to meet 5) to think about something and to act if necessary

seed [sēd] *noun*, a small grain from which a plant grows

seek [sēk] *verb*, to look for

seem [sēm] *verb*, to appear to be true or probable

seen [sēn] past perfect of **see**

seep [sēp] *verb*, a liquid flowing slowly or leaking through

seg-ment [sĕg'mənt] *noun*, any part which separates from the whole

seg-re-ga-tion [sĕg'rĭ-gā'shən] *noun*, the act of setting groups apart, separation, racial discrimination

seis-mic [sīz'mĭk] *adjective*, pertaining to an earthquake

seize [sēz] *verb*, 1) to grasp suddenly, to take possession of by force

sel-dom [sĕl'dəm] *adjective*, rarely, not often, infrequently

se-lect [sĭ-lĕkt'] *adjective*, 1) first rate, *verb*, 2) to choose, to pick

se-lec-tion [sĭ-lĕk'shən] *noun*, a collection of things chosen

self [sĕlf] *noun*, your person, what you are, individuality

self-ish [sĕl'fĭsh] *adjective*, to think only of oneself and not others

self-ish-ness [sĕl'fĭsh- nĭs] *noun*, pettiness, being small-minded

sell [sĕl] *verb*, 1) to offer in exchange for money 2) to deal in

sem-blance [sŏm'bləns] *noun*, likeness, resemblance, similarity

se-mes-ter [sə-mĕs'tər] *noun*, either of two terms into which the period of instruction is divided in an academic year

sem-i-cir-cle [sĕm'ĭ-sûr'kəl] *noun*, the shape of half a circle

sem-i-co-lon [sĕm'ĭ-kō'lən] *noun*, a mark of punctuation (;) used to separate two independent clauses when there is no conjunction, as *When you make a mistake, admit it; learn from it and don't repeat it. Bear Bryant*

sen-ate [sĕn'ĭt] *noun*, one of the groups that constitutes the legislative government

sen-a-tor [sĕn'ə-tər] *noun*, an elected representative who serves in the Senate

send [sĕnd] *verb*, to cause something or someone to go somewhere, to dispatch

se-nil-i-ty [sĭ-nĭl'ĭ-tē] *noun*, feeble mindedness of old age

sen-ior [sēn'yər] *adjective*, 1) older, *noun*, 2) a student in the final year of a four year course

sen-sa-tion [sĕn-sā'shən] *noun*, 1) a feeling 2) excited interest

sense [sĕns] *noun*, 1) reason or understanding 2) a reasonable meaning 3) a feeling, *verb*, 4) to recognize, to detect

sense-less [sĕns'lĭs] *adjective*, stupid, unconscious

sen-si-bil-i-ty [sĕn'sə-bĭl'ĭ-tē] *noun*, awareness, understanding

sensible

sen-si-ble [sĕn′sə-bəl] *adjective*, reasonable, possessing good sense, smart, perceptive

sen-si-tive [sĕn′sĭ-tĭv] *adjective*, quick to notice or feel, easily affected by slight change

sen-su-ous [sĕn′shoo-əs] *adjective*, exuding sexuality, appealing

sen-tence [sĕn′təns] *noun*, 1) a combination of words which express a thought, beginning with a capital letter, ending with a period 2) the judgment of a court, *verb*, 3) to pass judgment on, to inflict punishment

sen-ti-ment [sĕn′tə-mənt] *noun*, feelings, thoughts, emotions

sen-ti-men-tal [sĕn′tə-mĕn′tl] *adjective*, expressing feelings of love, pity, etc. to excess

sen-ti-nel [sĕn′tə-nəl] *noun*, a soldier set to guard an army from surprise, a sentry

sen-try [sĕn′trē] *noun*, a lookout, guard, watchman, a soldier

sep-a-rate [sĕp′ə-rāt′] *adjective*, 1) not together, not joined, *verb*, 2) to divide, to disconnect, to keep apart

sep-a-ra-tion [sĕp′ə-rā′shən] *noun*, time apart from each other

Sep-tem-ber [sĕp-tĕm′bər] *noun*, the ninth month of the year, having 30 days

sep-tic [sĕp′tĭk] *adjective*, decaying, putrid or toxic, rotten

sep-ul-cher [sĕp′əl-kər] *noun*, a tomb, a burial place

se-quel [sē′kwəl] *noun*, the continuation of a story

se-quence [sē′kwəns] *noun*, a succession, a following or coming after in a series

se-ques-ter [sĭ-kwĕs′tər] *verb*, to go into isolation, to remove, to seclude, to set apart

sere-nade [sĕr′ə-nād′] *verb*, to court, to play music under a window to charm a sweetheart

ser-en-dip-i-tous [sĕr′ən-dĭp′ĭ-t əs] *adjective*, fortunate discoveries made by accident

se-rene [sə-rēn′] *adjective*, calm, tranquil, placid, clear, peaceful

se-ren-i-ty [sə-rĕn′ĭ-tē] *noun*, tranquility, peace

ser-geant [sär′jənt] *noun*, a noncommissioned officer ranking next above a corporal

se-ries [sîr′ēz] *noun*, a number of things connected in a sequence

se-ri-ous [sîr′ē-əs] *adjective*, 1) grave in manner or disposition, earnest, solemn, sincere 2) weighty

se-ri-ous-ly [sîr′ē-əs-lē] *adverb*, thoughtfully, sincerely

ser-mon [sûr′mən] *noun*, a talk given by a religious leader

ser-pent [sûr′pənt] *noun*, a snake

ser-pen-tine [sûr′pən-tēn′] *adjective*, winding, twisting

ser-rat-ed [sĕr′ā′tĭd] *adjective*, having a saw-toothed or jagged edge

se-rum [sîr′əm] *noun*, the watery protein of an animal fluid

serv-ant [sûr′vənt] *noun*, one who works for another especially in a home to perform chores

serve [sûrv] *verb*, 1) to do work for other people, to give assistance or help 2) to offer food to someone 3) to answer a purpose

serv-ice [sûr/vĭs] *noun*, 1) a job that one performs for others 2) a church ceremony

ser-vile [sûr/vəl] *adjective*, subservient, groveling, cringing

ses-sion [sĕsh/ən] *noun*, the sitting of an organized body for the transaction of business, a term

set [sĕt] *noun*, 1) a group of things thought of together, *verb*, 2) to put in a place 3) to make something happen, to begin 4) to sink in the sky below the horizon

set-ting [sĕt/ĭng]] *noun*, 1) the position of something, as a dial, that has been set 2) time and place, environment, etc. of an event, story, play, etc. 3) actual physical surroundings, real or artificial

set-tle [sĕt/l] *verb*, 1) to go and live in a place 2) to make comfortable 3) to come to a mutual agreement, to decide

set-tle-ment [sĕt/l-mənt] *noun*, 1) an agreement 2) a new place for people to live, a colony

sev-en [sĕv/ən] *adjective, noun*, the number 7, one plus six

sev-en-teen [sĕv/ən-tēn/] *adjective, noun*, the number 17, 7 + 10

sev-en-teenth [sĕv/ən-tēnth/] *adjective, noun*, number 17 in order, written 17th

sev-enth [sĕv/ənth] *adjective, noun*, number 7 in order, 7th

sev-en-ti-eth [sĕv/ən-tē-ĭth] *adjective, noun*, number 70 in order, written 70th

sev-en-ty [sĕv/ən-tē] *noun, adjective*, the number 70, 7 X 10

sev-er [sĕv/ər] *verb*, to cut off, to separate, to disconnect

sev-er-al [sĕv/ər-əl] *adjective*, 1) separate or distinct, *pronoun*, 2) being more than two but fewer than many

se-vere [sə-vîr/] *adjective*, 1) strict in judgment or discipline, harsh 2) hard to deal with

se-ver-i-ty [sə-vĕr/ĭ-tē] *noun*, harshness, intensity

sew [sō] *verb*, to bind two pieces of cloth together with a needle and thread, to repair with a thread

sew-age [sōō/ĭj] *noun*, liquid waste from homes and businesses transported away by sewers

sew-er [sōō/ər] *noun*, 1) a gutter, a disposal system 2) one who works with needle and thread

sex [sĕks] *noun*, to be male or female

shab-by [shăb/ē] *adjective*, old, cheap, dirty, falling apart

shack-le [shăk/əl] *noun*, 1) chains, handcuffs, *verb*, 2) to confine, to restrain with chains

shade [shād] *noun, no plural*, 1) shelter from the sun or light, *verb*, 2) to cut off from a bright light 3) to dim or darken

shad-ow [shăd/ō] *noun*, 1) the image cast on a surface when something blocks the light 2) a faint indication

shaft

shaft [shăft] *noun*, 1) a long thin pole 2) a long hole leading to a mine 3) a ray or beam

shake [shāk] *verb*, 1) to move quickly up and down or from side to side 2) to tremble

shall [shăl] *verb*, 1) a word used instead of will with *I* and *we*, to indicate something is going to happen 2) used with *I* and *we* in questions when asking or offering to do something

shal-low [shăl'ō] *adjective*, 1) not deep 2) superficial, with little seriousness or deep thought

sham [shăm] *noun*, a farce

sham-bles [shăm'bəlz] *noun*, *plural*, a scene of disorder

shame [shām] *noun*, 1) dishonor, guilt, humiliation, *verb*, 2) to humiliate or embarrass

sham-poo [shăm-pōo'] *noun*, 1) a liquid soap used to wash hair, *verb*, 2) to wash hair with soap

shape [shāp] *noun*, 1) the outline or form of something, 2) a form or condition in which something exists, *verb*, 3) to mold or give form to something

share [shâr] *noun*, 1) a portion of something after it has been divided, *verb*, 2) to use, experience, or enjoy with others 3) to participate in 4) to disclose to others

shark [shärk] *noun*, a large predatory fish with a huge jaw

sharp [shärp] *adjective*, 1) having a thin cutting edge 2) the ability to see things far away that are small 3) severe or intense, having a strong odor or flavor 4) alert 5) quick and forceful

sharp-en [shär'pən] *verb*, 1) to make a pointed edge 2) to make acute or more sensitive to feeling

sharp-ly [sharp-lē] *adverb*, clearly, suddenly, distinctly

shat-ter [shăt'ər] *verb*, to break into many pieces or fragments

shave [shāv] *verb*, to cut very close

shawl [shôl] *noun*, a long piece of cloth worn over the shoulders and head

she [shē] *pronoun*, the female person or subject in the sentence

sheaf [shēf] *noun*, 1) a quantity of grain bound together 2) any bundle of things such as papers

shear [shîr] *verb*, to cut wool from a sheep, to cut hair, to clip

shears [shîrz] *noun*, *plural*, large-sized scissors

sheathe [shēth] *noun*, a case that holds a sword or dagger

shed [shĕd] *noun*, 1) a hut for tools, *verb*, 2) to let something fall or come off naturally 3) to pour forth, to stream out

sheep [shēp] *noun*, *no plural*, an animal that is kept for meat and wool from its thick, fleecy coat

sheep-ish-ly [shē'pĭsh-lē] *adverb*, with a feeling of embarrassment

sheer [shîr] *adjective*, 1) totally, entirely 2) transparent

sheet [shēt] *noun*, 1) a large flat piece of something such as paper or cloth 2) a rope used to secure a ship's sail

shelf [shĕlf] *noun, plural,* **shelves,** a board attached to a wall to put things on it

shell [shĕl] *noun,* the hard protective covering of fruit, eggs or some fish and reptiles

shel-lac [shə-lăk'] *noun,* a wood finishing such as varnish, lacquer or polyurethane

shell-fish [shĕl'fĭsh'] *noun,* any fish with a hard armor such as crabs, lobsters, or oysters

shel-ter [shĕl'tər] *noun,* 1) a safe place, a place to hide, *verb,* 2) to hide someone, to guard or keep safe from harm, to protect

shep-herd [shĕp'ərd] *noun,* a person who herds and tends sheep, goats, or livestock

sher-bet [shûr'bĭt] *noun,* flavored dessert ice

sher-iff [shĕr'ĭf] *noun,* a law enforcement officer of a county

shib-bo-leth [shĭb'ə-lĭth] *noun,* a slogan, a catchword

shield [shēld] *noun,* 1) a piece of defensive armor carried on the arm, protection, *verb,* 2) to defend or protect 3) to conceal

shift [shĭft] *noun,* 1) a set of people who work together at one time 2) the length of time that one group works, *verb,* 3) to move, to transfer, to displace

shil-ling [shĭl'ĭng] *noun,* English currency equal to a dollar

shim-mer [shĭm'ər] *verb,* to glimmer intermittently, to glisten

shin [shĭn] *noun,* the part of the leg between the knee and the ankle

shine [shīn] *verb,* to give off light

shin-gle [shĭng'gəl] *noun,* a tile made of wood or tar used to protect a roof or wall

ship [shĭp] *noun,* a boat which travels in deep water like the sea

ship-ment [shĭp'mənt] *noun,* the act of sending goods by air, water, or, on the road

shirt [shûrt] *noun,* a garment which covers the upper part of the body consisting of a collar, sleeves, and buttons, similar to a blouse

shiv-er [shĭv'ər] *verb,* to shake from feeling cold or afraid

shoal [shōl] *noun,* 1) a sandbar or piece of rising ground in shallow water 2) a school of fish

shock [shŏk] *noun,* 1) the feeling caused by a horrible unpleasant surprise 2) a pain caused by electricity going through the body, *verb,* 3) to startle, to disturb or surprise

shod-dy [shŏd'ē] *adjective,* not genuine, inferior quality

shoe [shoo] *noun,* an outer covering for the foot consisting of a sole and a covering made of leather, vinyl, or cloth

shoot [shoot] *noun,* 1) new growth, a sprout, *verb,* 2) to discharge a weapon 3) to move quickly, to dart 4) to photograph or film

shop [shŏp] *noun,* 1) a place to go and buy different things that you need, *verb,* 2) to visit stores to make purchases

shore [shôr] *noun,* 1) land bordering water such as a lake or the sea, *verb,* 2) to prop up

short

short [shôrt] *adjective*, 1) the opposite of tall, small 2) not long, brief, concise

short-age [shôr′tĭj] *noun*, not enough, a deficiency

short-en [shôr′tn] *verb*, to cut down

short-en-ing [shôr′tn-ĭng] *noun*, lard or oil used in cooking

shorts [shôrts] *noun*, *plural*, pants worn above the knee

shot [shŏt] *noun*, 1) injection with a hypodermic needle 2) a try, an attempt 3) lead for a shotgun

should [shŏŏd] *verb*, obligated to do something, ought to

shoul-der [shōl′dər] *noun*, 1) part of the body between the neck and the chest, connected to the arms, *verb*, 2) to carry a burden

shouldn't [shŏŏd′nt] the *contraction* of the words **should** and **not**

shout [shout] *noun*, 1) a sudden cry in a loud voice, *verb*, 2) to speak or yell in a loud voice

shove [shŭv] *noun*, 1) a push, *verb*, 2) to push roughly or rudely

shov-el [shŭv′əl] *noun*, 1) a broad scoop with a long handle for lifting dirt, *verb*, 2) to lift things from the ground or another surface with a shovel

show [shō] *noun*, 1) a display in which things are gathered for people to see 2) a performance for an audience, *verb*, 3) to let someone see something

show-er [shou′ər] *noun*, 1) precipitation from clouds in the form of rain 2) a bath in which water is sprayed from a nozzle, 3) a party to honor someone, *verb*, 4) to pour down or fall on 5) to bestow

shred [shrĕd] *noun*, 1) a small amount, *verb*, 2) to tear or cut into small pieces

shrew [shrōō] *noun*, 1) a scolding woman, a nag 2) a mouse-like rodent with a long snout

shrewd [shrōōd] *adjective*, clever in business, sharp-witted

shriek [shrēk] noun, 1) a high-pitched scream, *verb*, 2) to utter a shrill cry, to scream

shrill [shrĭl] *adjective*, having a high-pitched sound, piercing

shrimp [shrĭmp] *noun*, a shellfish that is considered a delicacy

shrine [shrīn] *noun*, 1) a place for worship and keeping sacred relics 2) a saint's tomb

shrink [shrĭngk] *verb*, 1) to withdraw, to pull away from 2) to lessen, to make smaller

shriv-el [shrĭv′əl] *verb*, to contract in size, to shrink and wrinkle

shrub [shrŭb] *noun*, a bush

shrug [shrŭg] *verb*, 1) to raise the shoulders to show uncertainty about something 2) to disregard

shud-der [shŭd′ər] *noun*, a quick, light shaking motion, a shiver

shuf-fle [shŭf′əl] *verb*, 1) to walk dragging your feet 2) to rearrange the order, to mix together like a deck of cards

shun [shŭn] *verb*, to deliberately avoid, to stay away from

shut [shŭt] *verb*, to close, to adjust something so that it is not open

shut-ter [shŭt′ər] *noun*, 1) a wooden cover for a window 2) a mechanical device for opening and closing the aperture of a camera lens to expose the film

shy [shī] *adjective*, bashful, wary

sib-ling [sĭb′lĭng] *noun*, a brother or sister

sick [sĭk] *adjective*, not feeling well

sick-ness [sĭk′nĭs] *noun*, illness, nausea, ailment, disease

side [sīd] *noun*, 1) the right or left portion of the body 2) the surface of something flat that has a top and bottom 3) the boundaries of a surface or image 4) a perspective, a way of looking at something, an aspect

siege [sēj] *noun*, a continued attempt of an army to gain possession around a fortified place to compel its surrender

sieve [sĭv] *noun*, a bowl with holes in the bottom to let water drain out, or used to separate fine matter from the coarser materials

sigh [sī] *noun*, 1) a deep breath indicating that you are tired, sad, etc, *verb*, 2) to let out a deep breath, to exhale

sight [sīt] *noun*, 1) the ability or power to see 2) something worth seeing 3) a scene, an incident

sign [sīn] *noun*, 1) a gesture which sends a message to the person who sees it 2) an indication 3) a plaque with a message, *verb*, 4) to write your name 5) to hire or transfer by written agreement

sig-nal [sĭg′nəl] *noun*, 1) a movement or thing which tells you what to do, *verb*, 2) to warn someone, or send another message through motions

sig-na-ture [sĭg′nə-chər] *noun*, 1) a name written in ink, in cursive, as an endorsement to an agreement 2) the printed sheet so marked as to leave an imprint

sig-net [sĭg′nĭt] *noun*, an emblem

sig-nif-i-cance [sĭg-nĭf′ĭ-kəns] *noun*, *no plural*, the meaning

sig-nif-i-cant [sĭg-nĭf′ĭ-kənt] *adjective*, expressive or suggestive, important

sig-ni-fy [sĭg′nə-fī′] *verb*, to indicate, to signal, to denote

si-lence [sī′ləns] *noun*, *no plural*, 1) complete quiet 2) secrecy

si-lent [sī′lənt] *adjective*, making no sound, quiet, speechless

si-lent-ly [sī′lənt-lē] *adverb*, quietly, without a sound

sil-hou-ette [sĭl′o̅o̅-ĕt′] *noun*, an outline of something against a light background

sil-i-con [sĭl′ĭ-kən, -kŏn′] *noun*, a nonmetallic element, very abundant in nature

silk [sĭlk] *noun*, a fine fabric made by the threads from a silkworm

sill [sĭl] *noun*, the rim on a window

sil-ly [sĭl′ē] *adjective*, not serious, or reasonable, playful, foolish

silt [sĭlt] *noun*, sediment of fine particles that hangs in stagnant water or forms on the bottom left there by running water

sil-ver [sĭl′vər] *adjective*, 1) the color of this metal, *noun*, *no plural*, 2) a soft shiny gray metal used for jewelry, coins, and ornaments

sim-i-an [sĭm′ē-ən] *adjective*, like a monkey or an ape

sim-i-lar [sĭm′ə-lər] *adjective*, somewhat like, nearly, corresponding, resembling

sim-i-lar-i-ty [sĭm′ə-lăr′ĭ-tē] *noun*, likeness, resemblance

sim-i-le [sĭm′ə-lē] *noun*, a phrase comparing unlike subjects using like or as, i.e., *he is as slow as a turtle; she sings like a bird*

sim-ple [sĭm′pəl] *adjective*, 1) easy to understand 2) plain, common, not complicated, not showy

sim-plic-i-ty [sĭm-plĭs′ĭ-tē] *adjective*, freedom from duplicity, absence of excess

sim-pli-fy [sĭm′plə-fī′] *verb*, to make easier to understand

sim-ply [sĭm′plē] *adverb*, only, or merely, absolutely

sim-u-late [sĭm′yə-lāt′] *verb*, to feign, to pretend, to fake

si-mul-ta-ne-ous [sī′məl-tā′nē-əs] *adjective*, occurring at the same time, concurrent

si-mul-ta-ne-ous-ly [sī′məl-tā′nē-əs-lē] *adverb*, happening at the same time

sin [sĭn] *noun*, 1) an act that harms someone, *verb*, 2) to err, to violate a moral principle

since [sĭns] *adverb*, 1) between a moment in the past and now, *conjunction*, 2) because, *preposition*, 3) after, from a certain time until the present

sin-cere [sĭn-sîr′] *adjective*, being in reality what it appears to be, genuine 3) free of hypocrisy

sin-cere-ly [sĭn-sîr′lē] *adverb*, honestly, truly

sin-cer-i-ty [sĭn-sĕr′ĭ-tē] *adverb*, honesty, truthfulness

sin-ew [sĭn′yōō] *noun*, 1) a tendon, a muscle 2) strength, power

sing [sĭng] *verb*, to make music with the voice

singe [sĭnj] *verb*, to scorch or burn the surface or ends

sin-gle [sĭng′gəl] *adjective*, 1) consisting of only one person or thing, alone, *noun*, 2) in baseball, a hit in which the batter reaches first base

sin-gu-lar [sĭng′gyə-lər] *adjective*, 1) when speaking of one, *noun*, 2) unique, particular, individual

sin-is-ter [sĭn′ĭ-stər] *adjective*, dishonest, indicative of lurking evil, wicked, menacing

sink [sĭngk] *noun*, 1) a basin that holds water, *verb*, 2) to go down 3) to become submerged in water 4) to permeate the mind

sin-ner [sĭn′ər] *noun*, one who does wrong to others

sip [sĭp] *noun*, 1) a small amount of liquid swallowed, *verb*, 2) to drink a very small amount

si-phon [sī′fən] *noun*, a bent tube, having one end longer than the other, used for drawing liquids from a higher to a lower level

sir [sûr] *noun*, 1) the title of a knight 2) a respectful term to use when talking to a man

si-ren [sī'rən] *noun*, a device that makes a loud warning sound

sis-ter [sĭs'tər] *noun*, 1) a girl who shares the same parents with a sibling 2) the title for a nun

sit [sĭt] *verb*, to rest in a chair or on the floor, with the back straight

site [sīt] *noun*, a particular piece of land or a building whose location has a specific use

sit-u-ate [sĭch'ōō-āt'] *verb*, to put in place, to position, to locate

sit-u-a-tion [sĭch'ōō-ā'shən] *noun*, 1) circumstances, the state of affairs, a case 2) a position

six [sĭks] *adjective, noun*, the number 6, five plus one

six-teen [sĭk-stēn'] *adjective, noun*, the number 16, six plus ten

six-teenth [sĭk-stēnth'] *adjective, noun*, the number 16 in order, written 16th

sixth [sĭksth] *adjective, noun*, the number 6 in order, written 6th

six-ti-eth [sĭk'stē-ĭth] *adjective, noun*, number 60 in order, 60th

six-ty [sĭks'tē] *adjective*, the number 60, six times ten

size [sīz] *noun*,) the amount of space that something takes up

skate [skāt] *noun*, 1) a runner or set of wheels with a frame to fit the shoe, *verb*, 2) to glide over the ground with shoes fit with a runner or wheels

skel-e-ton [skĕl'ĭ-tn] *noun*, the bones of a person or animal that show its size and structure

skep-tic [skĕp'tĭk] *noun*, a doubter, a cynic, a questioner

skep-ti-cal [skĕp'tĭ-kəl] *adjective*, distrustful, not convinced

sketch [skĕch] *noun*, 1) a drawing that lacks detail, an image, *verb*, 2) to draw in a rough manner

ski [skē] *noun, plural*, **skis**, one of a pair of long, flat, wood or metal runners used for gliding on snow or water *verb*, 2) to slide over snow on blades using poles for balance

skid [skĭd] *noun*, 1) a pallet to elevate something off the ground, *verb*, 2) to slip on a wet surface 3) to lose traction

skill [skĭl] *noun*, having the ability and knowledge to do something

skil-let [skĭl'ĭt] *noun*, a small metal pan with a handle, a frying pan

skill-ful [skĭl'fəl] *adjective*, very good at doing something

skill-ful-ly [skĭl'fə-lē] *adverb*, intelligently, sensibly

skim [skĭm] *verb*, 1) to read over quickly 2) to take off the floating layer 3) to glide in a sail boat

skimp [skĭmp] *verb*, to hold back, to offer small portions

skin [skĭn] *noun*, 1) the covering of the body, or fruit, often covered with hairs, *verb*, 2) to remove the outer layer of something

skip [skĭp] *verb*, 1) to move by alternately hopping or stepping, to move with light steps 2) to omit, to pass over, to miss

skirt [skûrt] *noun*, 1) woman's clothing that hangs from the waist, *verb*, 2) to avoid

skit [skĭt] *noun*, a short play or theatrical performance

skit-tish [skĭt′ĭsh] *adjective*, lively, frisky, nervous

skulk [skŭlk] *verb*, 1) to move slyly and secretly in a sneaking manner 2) to lie in hiding

skull [skŭl] *noun*, the bony structure of the head enclosing the brain

skunk [skŭngk] *noun*, a rodent with black fur distinguished by a white strip that goes down its back and tail and sprays a horrible smell when scared

sky [skī] *noun*, the space above the Earth which can be seen when you look up

sky-scrap-er [skī′skrā′pər] *noun*, a very tall building

slack [slăk] *adjective*, 1) lazy, slow, barely moving 2) a mixture of small pieces of coal, dust, and dirt left from screening coal

slacks [slăks] *noun*, *plural*, pants or trousers for casual wear

slain [slān] *past tense* of **slay**

slam [slăm] *verb*, 1) to fling or put down violently, with a loud noise 2) to shut, to close

slan-der [slăn′dər] *noun*, 1) a malicious, false statement made about a person, *verb*, 2) to lie about someone, to malign

slang [slăng] *noun*, *no plural*, language used in conversation, that is crude, disrespectful, or inappropriate, an expletive

slant [slănt] *verb*, to lean or slope

slap [slăp] *noun*, 1) the blow or hit caused by something flat, *verb*, 2) to hit with something flat, such as an open hand

slate [slāt] *adjective*, 1) a gray color, *noun*, 2) a fine-grained metamorphic rock used as a roof tile or writing tablet with chalk

slaugh-ter [slô′tər] *noun*, *no plural*, 1) a killing of a large number of people or animals, *verb*, 2) to kill animals or people as a group

slave [slāv] *noun*, a person owned as property, subject to the will of his owner

slav-er-y [slā′və-rē] *noun*, *no plural*, the concept of owning people as property

slay [slā] *verb*, to kill or murder

slea-zy [slē′zē] *adjective*, low class

sled [slĕd] *noun*, a wooden device with runners on the bottom used to carry people or things on snow or ice as a vehicle

sleek [slēk] *adjective*, smooth, neat, glossy, well-groomed

sleep [slēp] *noun*, *no plural*, 1) a time of rest, when not awake and alert, *verb*, 2) to rest semi-unconscious with eyes closed

sleet [slēt] *noun*, 1) a combination of ice and rain falling from the sky, *verb*, 2) to shower frozen rain

sleeve [slēv] *noun*, the part of clothing that covers the arm

sleigh [slā] *noun*, a horse drawn vehicle with runners used for carrying people over snow

sleight [slīt] *noun*, skill, cunning

slen-der [slĕn′dər] *adjective*, 1) slim, thin, narrow 2) meager

slice [slīs] *noun*, 1) a piece cut from the whole, a share, *verb*,

2) to cut a flat piece off from a whole

slick [slĭk] *adjective*, 1) a surface that is slippery when wet 2) clever, deceitful

slide [slīd] *noun*, 1) a piece of playground equipment you can sit on and slip on the surface, an image for projection on a screen, *verb*, 3) to move smoothly along a surface, to slip

slight [slīt] *adjective*, of a small degree, of little importance

slim [slĭm] *adjective*, slender, thin, lean, narrow, meager

slime [slīm] *noun*, mire, mud

sling [slĭng] *noun*, 1) a piece of cloth holding something in place, *verb*, 2) to throw

slip [slĭp] *noun*, 1) a piece of paper 2) a garment worn under a dress 3) a mistake 4) a stall to keep something 5) a cutting from a plant, *verb*, 6) to lose your balance and fall off your feet 7) to enter or exit unobserved 8) to escape, to pass from

slip-per [slĭp/ər] *noun*, a light shoe which may be slipped on easily

slip-per-y [slĭp/ə-rē] *adjective*, 1) smooth and slick or slimy, hard to grip 2) devious, not trustworthy, shifty

slit [slĭt] *noun*, 1) a long narrow opening, *verb*, 2) to make a small cut as an opening

slith-er [slĭth/ər] *verb*, to move, walk or slide like a snake

slo-gan [slō/gən] *noun*, a catch phrase, a motto

slope [slōp] *noun*, 1) a surface which is higher on one side than the other, *verb*, 2) to lean on an incline, to slant up or downward

slot [slŏt] *noun*, a long, narrow opening for receiving something

sloth [slôth] *noun*, a lazy person

slov-en-ly [slŭv/ən-lē] *adjective*, untidy, careless in work habits

slow [slō] *adjective*, 1) to move without much speed, not fast 2) behind others, sluggish

slow-ly [slō/lē] *adverb*, to crawl or move sluggishly, not quickly

slug [slŭg] *noun*, 1) a soft, slimy creature without bones or legs that eats plants 2) a false coin, *verb*, 3) to hit with a fist

sluice [slōōs] *noun*, an artificial channel for water with a gate

slum [slŭm] *noun*, a poor neighborhood, a ghetto

slum-ber [slŭm/bər] *noun*, 1) a deep sleep, a long nap, *verb*, 2) to sleep, to doze

slump [slŭmp] *noun*, 1) a drop, a decline, a decrease, *verb*, 2) to sink, to slouch, to stoop

slur [slûr] *noun*, 1) a disrespectful remark, *verb*, 2) to insult, to offend 3) to garble, to speak unintelligibly

slush [slŭsh] *noun*, partially melting snow or ice

sly [slī] *adjective*, clever and deceiving, calculating

smack [smăk] *noun*, 1) a kiss, a pat, a peck, *verb*, 2) to hit with a hand as a slap 3) to put the lips together after a tasty meal

small [smôl] *adjective*, 1) little, not big 2) mean-spirited, petty

smaller

small-er [smôlّər] *adjective*, not as big, shorter, less, fewer

small-est [smôl′ĕst] *adjective*, tiny, very little

smart [smärt] *adjective*, 1) intelligent, bright 2) well dressed, attractive, fashionable, *verb*, 3) to feel a painful, stinging sensation

smash [smăsh] *verb*, to break violently into many pieces

smat-ter-ing [smăt′ər-ĭng] *noun*, slight knowledge, a few facts

smell [smĕl] *noun*, 1) the identifying scent that distinguishes something, *verb*, 2) to use one of the five senses to recognize a scent

smelt [smĕlt] *verb*, to melt in a furnace, to purify an ore

smile [smīl] *noun*, 1) an expression formed by the upward curve of the mouth, to show pleasure, amusement, etc., 2) to look pleased, happy, or amused

smirk [smûrk] *noun*, a twisted smile, a smug expression

smog [smŏg] *noun*, a mixture of pollutants, principally ground-level ozone, produced by chemical reactions in the air

smoke [smōk] *noun*, 1) visible fumes, *verb*, 2) to puff or inhale the vapor from a lit cigarette, 3) to make fumes come from fire

smol-der [smōl′dər] *verb*, 1) to burn without flame 2) anger, liable to break out at any moment

smooth [smo͞oth] *adjective*, 1) even, level, without bumps 2) calm, composed, unruffled

smoth-er [smŭth′ər] *verb*, to hide or suppress, to suffocate

smudge [smŭj] *noun*, 1) a dirty mark, a smear, *verb*, 2) to make dirty with streaks, to blur

smug-gle [smŭg′əl] *verb*, to bring things across borders secretly or illegally to avoid tariffs or border police

snack [snăk] *noun*, 1) food eaten between meals, *verb*, 2) to eat when you are hungry

snail [snāl] *noun*, a slug in a spirally coiled shell

snake [snāk] *noun*, 1) a cold-blooded reptile without legs that slithers on the ground, *verb*, 2) to move like a snake by slithering and sliding

snap [snăp] *noun*, 1) the sharp sound of something breaking 2) a clothing fastener like a button that locks together, *verb*, 3) to make a crackling sound 4) to try to nip or bite someone

snare [snâr] *noun*, 1) a trap that entangles its victim, *verb*, 2) to trap with a noose, to entangle

snarl [snärl] *verb*, 1) to make an angry noise with bared teeth 2) to talk in a vicious tone

snatch [snăch] *verb*, to take something directly from someone in a rough manner

sneak [snēk] *noun*, 1) a cheater, a rascal, *verb*, 2) to creep, to slink

sneer [snîr] *verb*, to laugh at someone to make fun of them

sneeze [snēz] *noun*, to blow air through the nose and mouth without warning

sniff [snĭf] *verb*, to breathe in, to inhale, to get a whiff, to smell

snif-fle [snĭf′əl] *verb*, to gasp as if to hold back tears

snob [snŏb] *noun*, someone who thinks he is better than others

snore [snôr] *verb*, to make a loud guttural noise in the nose or throat when sleeping

snout [snout] *noun*, the part of an animal's head projecting forward containing the nose and jaws

snow [snō] *noun, no plural*, 1) precipitation that forms in the cloud as ice and falls to the ground as white crystals, *verb*, 2) a flurry of crystals or snowflakes falling to the earth from the sky

snug [snŭg] *adjective*, close fitting, comfortable, cozy, compact

so [sō] *adverb*, 1) in such a way, to such a point 2) also 3) very, very much 4) therefore 5) in order that 6) the same thing 7) used to show agreement 8) factual

soak [sōk] *verb*, to leave something immersed in liquid for awhile

soap [sōp] *noun*, a substance used for cleaning, manufactured as bars, flakes, or liquid, mixed with water

soar [sôr] *verb*, to fly or ascend quickly and easily upward

sob [sŏb] *verb*, to cry aloud in large gasps, to weep convulsively

so-ber [sō′bər] *adjective*, serious, somber, not gay or laughing

so-bri-e-ty [sə-brī′ĭ-tē] *noun*, self restraint, recovery from abusing alcohol, not drunk

so-bri-quet [sō′brĭ-kā′] *noun*, a nickname, a pet name

soc-cer [sŏk′ər] *noun, no plural*, a game of football as played in South America and Europe

so-cial [sō′shəl] *adjective*, pertaining to men as living in society, friendly, gregarious

so-cial-ism [sō′shə-lĭz′əm] *adjective*, a communist philosophy of equal sharing

so-ci-e-ty [sə-sī′ĭ-tē] *noun*, a group of persons associated together

so-ci-ol-o-gy [sō′sē-ŏl′ə-jē] *noun*, the science of the development of human society

sock [sŏk] *noun*, 1) a short stocking made of soft material to cover the foot, *verb*, 2) to punch

sock-et [sŏk′ĭt] *noun*, any device that holds a complementary part

sod [sŏd] *noun*, earth, dirt, soil

so-da [sō′də] *noun*, a carbonated beverage flavored with syrup

so-di-um [sō′dē-əm] *noun*, a silver-white, metallic element of the alkali group, also known as salt

so-fa [sō′fə] *noun*, a long couch, usually upholstered and having a back and arms

soft [sôft] *adjective*, 1) tender 2) not hard 3) low volume, not loud 4) smooth or silky

soft-en [sô′fən] *verb*, 1) to ease, to relax, 2) to melt

soft-ly [sôft′lē] *adverb*, 1) quietly 2) mildly, gently

soft-ware [sôft′wâr′] *noun*, instructions that allow a computer to do specific tasks

soil [soil] *noun*, 1) the earth where plants and organisms grow, the top layer of the earth, *verb*, 2) to make something dirty

so-journ [sō′jûrn′] *noun*, 1) a brief stay, *verb*, 2) to stay temporarily

sol-ace [sŏl′ĭs] *noun*, comfort in trouble, or sorrow, or distress

so-lar [sō′lər] *adjective*, referring to or relating to the sun

sold [sōld] *verb*, *past tense* of **sell**

sol-der [sŏd′ər] *noun*, a metal or a metallic alloy used to join by fusing metallic surfaces together

sol-dier [sōl′jər] *noun*, a man or woman enlisted in the army

sole [sōl] *adjective*, 1) single, one *noun*, 2) the part of the shoe on which the bottom of the foot rests 3) an edible flat fish

sole-ly [sōl′lē] *adverb*, the only one

sol-emn [sŏl′əm] *adjective*, serious, grave, formal and dignified

so-le-noid [sō′lə-noid′] *noun*, a cylindrical round coil

so-lic-it [sə-lĭs′ĭt] *verb*, to ask someone to buy something or commit themselves

so-lic-i-tor [sə-lĭs′ĭ-tər] *noun*, the law officer of a city or government

sol-id [sŏl′ĭd] *adjective*, 1) not hollow, hard, firm, *noun*, 2) any substance that cannot flow, takes up space and has a definite shape and volume

sol-id-ify [sə-lĭd′ə-fī′] *verb*, to change from liquid to solid

so-lil-o-quy [sə-lĭl′ə-kwē] *noun*, the act of talking to one's self, a monologue in a drama

sol-i-taire [sŏl′ĭ-târ′] *noun*, 1) a gem set by itself 2) a card game involving one person

sol-i-tar-y [sŏl′ĭ-tĕr′ē] *adjective*, living or being by one's self, single, alone, secluded

sol-i-tude [sŏl′ĭ-tōōd′] *noun*, state of being alone, a lonely place

so-lo [sō′lō] *noun*, 1) something accomplished by one person 2) an unaccompanied performance

sol-stice [sŏl′stĭs] *noun*, either of two times a year when the sun is farthest from the equator, June 21 and December 22

sol-u-ble [sŏl′yə-bəl] *adjective*, something that dissolves

so-lu-tion [sə-lōō′shən] *noun*, 1) a liquid containing another substance dissolved in it 2) the answer found

solve [sŏlv] *verb*, to find the answer by studying the problem

sol-vent [sŏl′vənt] *adjective*, 1) debt free, able to pay one's debts, *noun*, 2) a usually liquid substance in which another substance can dissolve

som-ber [sŏm′bər] *adjective*, gloomy, serious, melancholy

some [sŭm] *adjective*, 1) an amount of, not all, *pronoun*, 2) referring to people or things without saying exactly who or what

some-bod-y [sŭm′bŏd′ē] *pronoun*, any person, an unknown or unnamed individual

some-how [sŭm′hou′] *adverb*, in some unknown way

some-one [sŭm′wŭn′] *pronoun*, a person or an individual

some-place [sŭm′plās′] *noun*, a location, somewhere

som-er-sault [sŭm′ər-sôlt′] *noun*, the act of turning upside down with your head between your legs as though rolling in a ball

some-thing [sŭm′thĭng] *pronoun*, an unknown amount or identity

some-time [sŭm′tīm′] *adverb*, a time in the past or future

some-times [sŭm′tīmz′] *adverb*, occasionally, not always

some-what [sŭm′hwŏt′] *adverb*, slightly, to some degree

some-where [sŭm′hwâr′] *adverb*, in or to, in an unspecified space

som-nam-bu-list [sŏm-năm′byə-lĭst] *noun*, a sleepwalker

son [sŭn] *noun*, a male child, or offspring

song [sông] *noun*, 1) a piece of music with words 2) poetry

son-net [sŏn′ĭt] *noun*, a poem, fourteen lines in iambic pentameter

soon [sōōn] *adverb*, something that will happen in a short time from now, promptly, quickly

soon-er [sōō′nər] *adjective*, before long, earlier than

soot [sōōt] *noun*, *no plural*, a black powder separated from fuel during combustion, smoke residue, cinders, ash

soothe [sōōth] *verb*, 1) to ease or comfort 2) to quiet, to pacify

so-phis-ti-ca-tion [sə-fĭs′tĭ-kā′shən] *noun*, intelligence, social grace, elegance, style, good taste

soph-o-more [sŏf′ə-môr] *noun*, a student in his second year of a four-year course

so-pran-o [sə-prăn′ō] *noun*, a singer who can reach the high notes in music

sor-cer-ess [sôr′sər-ĭs] *noun*, a magician, a witch

sor-did [sôr′dĭd] *adjective*, filthy, base, vile, squalid, selfish

sore [sôr, sōr] *adjective*, 1) hurting, painful, *noun*, 2) a painful, injured place on the body

so-ror-i-ty [sə-rôr′ĭ-tē] *noun*, a society or club of girls or women

sor-row [sŏr′ō] *noun*, sadness

sor-ry [sŏr′ē] *adjective*, feeling pity or sorrow, regret

sort [sôrt] *noun*, 1) a special kind, *verb*, 2) to separate into different categories, to classify

sought [sôt] *past tense* of **seek**

soul [sōl] *noun*, the part of you that is not body, and that some people think does not die with your body, the spirit of a person

sound [sound] *adjective*, 1) healthy, strong 2) deep or undisturbed, *noun*, 3) something heard from transmitted vibrations, *verb*, 4) to make a noise

soup

soup [so͞op] *noun*, a liquid food made by boiling meat, fish, or vegetables and seasonings

sour [sour] *adjective*, 1) having a sharp, biting, acid taste, tart, tangy, 2) soured, curdled

source [sôrs] *noun*, 1) the thing or place from which something comes 2) someone who provides information 3) a reference book

south [south] *adjective,* just opposite the north

South America [south-ə-měr'ĭ-kə] *noun*, one of the seven continents, containing 5.9% of the world's population

South Carolina [south-kăr'ə-lī'nə] *noun*, one of the 50 United States, located in the Southeast, the capital is Columbia. The state flower of **South Carolina** is the yellow jasmine, and the motto is "Prepared in mind and resources." or "While I breathe I hope."

South Dakota [south-də-kō'tə] *noun*, one of the 50 United States, located in the Northwest, the capital is Pierre. The state flower of **South Dakota** is the pasque flower and the motto is "Under God the people rule."

sou-ve-nir [so͞o'və-nîr'] *noun*, that which serves as a reminder, a keepsake, a memento

sov-er-eign [sŏv'ər-ĭn] *adjective*, highest in power, chief

sow *noun*, 1) [sou*]* *noun*, an adult female pig, [sō] *verb*, 2) to scatter seeds over the ground where they will grow to produce a crop

soy-bean [soi'bēn'] *noun*, a bean plant grown for its edible, nutritious seeds

space [spās] *noun*, 1) the limitless three-dimensional area all around 2) an empty place or unoccupied time

space-ship [spās'shĭp'] *noun*, a rocket orbiting the earth

spa-cious [spā'shəs] *adjective*, vast in extent, roomy, sizeable

spade [spād] *noun*, 1) a small hand-held shovel 2) one of the four suits in a deck of cards

spa-ghet-ti [spə-gĕt'ē] *noun*, a variety of macaroni made in cords of small diameter

span [spăn] *noun*, a stretch, the measure, the distance

spare [spâr] *adjective*, 1) kept in addition to what is already available, *verb*, 2) to give something extra, to share 3) to omit, to leave out

spark [spärk] *noun*, 1) a tiny burning particle, *verb*, 2) to stimulate, to set in motion

spar-kle [spär'kəl] *verb*, to shine with bright points of light

spark plug [spärk'plŭg'] *noun*, a device with two electrodes between which an electric jump spark is made

spar-row [spăr'ō] *noun*, a small brownish-gray bird

sparse [spärs] *adjective*, not thick, thinly scattered or distributed

spasm [spăz'əm] *noun*, a seizure, a fit, a convulsive movement

spa-tial [spā'shəl] *adjective*, relating to space

spat-u-la [spăch′ə-lə] *noun*, an instrument with a broad blade used for spreading or mixing

spawn [spôn] *verb*, to lay eggs

spay [spā] *verb*, to remove the reproductive organs, to castrate

speak [spēk] *verb*, to say words aloud, to talk, to express ideas

speak-er [spē′kər] *noun*, 1) the one talking 2) an orator, a lecturer

spear [spîr] *noun*, a long thin weapon with a pointed end

spe-cial [spĕsh′əl] *adjective*, 1) individual, peculiar, particular, different from the others 2) extra nice, distinct 3) having a particular function or purpose

spe-cial-ist [spĕsh′ə-lĭst] *noun*, one who studies a subject at great length, an expert, an authority

spe-cial-ize [spĕsh′ə-līz′] *verb*, to focus on a particular profession

spe-cies [spē′shēz] *noun*, *plural*, 1) a distinct sort, kind, or variety 2) a group of living things that can breed together

spe-cif-ic [spĭ-sĭf′ĭk] *noun*, special, explicit, precise, peculiar

spec-i-fy [spĕs′ə-fī′] *verb*, to designate, to name explicitly, to indicate, to point out in detail

spec-i-men [spĕs′ə-mən] *noun*, a part of anything to show the quality of the whole

spe-cious [spē′shəs] *adjective*, something false that appears to be true, deceptively attractive

speck [spĕk] *noun*, a small piece or particle of something

spec-ta-cle [spĕk′tə-kəl] *noun*, 1) a public scene that attracts a lot of attention 2) a display, a show

spec-ta-cles [spĕk′tə-kəlz] *noun*, *plural*, glasses for the eyes to improve vision set in a frame that rests on the nose and ears

spec-tac-u-lar [spĕk-tăk′yə-lər] *adjective*, impressive, amazing, breath-taking, dramatic

spec-ta-tor [spĕk′tā′tər] *noun*, one who looks on and watches, an observer, a bystander

spec-ter [spĕk′tər] *noun*, any object of dread, a ghost, an apparition

spec-tro-scope [spĕk′trə-skōp′] *noun*, an optical instrument

spec-trum [spĕk′trəm] *noun*, a broad range or sequence, especially of light separated into its constituent colors

spec-u-late [spĕk′yə-lāt′] *verb*, 1) to gamble, to buy and sell on the market 2) to consider, to contemplate, to hypothesize

spec-u-la-tion [spĕk′yə-lā′shən] *noun*, theory, hypothesis, conjecture, contemplation

speech [spēch] *noun*, 1) a long talk usually prepared in advance 2) language, words, dialect

speed [spēd] *noun*, 1) the rate at which something moves, *verb*, 2) to quicken, to hasten

speed-om-e-ter [spĭ-dŏm′ĭ-tər] *noun*, an instrument for indicating speed or velocity

spell [spĕl] *noun*, 1) a charm that captivates some and holds their attention 2) a short period of time, *verb*, 3) to indicate the correct arrangement of letters in a word 4) to be a sign of

spell-ing [spĕl′ĭng] *noun*, the correct use of the proper letters composing a word

spend [spĕnd] *verb*, 1) to give money for something 2) to use or consume energy or time

spent [spĕnt] *past tense* of **spend**

sphere [sfīr] *adjective*, 1) a social position, *noun*, 2) a ball or globe

spher-i-cal [sfīr′ĭ-kəl] *adjective*, globular, round like a ball

spice [spīs] *noun*, a seed or root of a plant used to add flavor to food

spi-der [spī′dər] *noun*, a bug that uses threads from its body to make a web to capture insects

spill [spĭl] *noun*, 1) a fall, *verb*, 2) to accidentally allow a liquid to flow out of a container

spin [spĭn] *verb*, 1) to whirl quickly 2) to twist into a thread from wool or other natural fibers

spin-ach [spĭn′ĭch] *noun*, an edible green leafy vegetable

spine [spīn] *noun*, the long row of bones in your back

spi-ral [spī′rəl] *noun*, helical, like the thread of a screw

spire [spīr] *noun*, the pointed top of a tower or steeple

spir-it [spĭr′ĭt] *noun*, 1) a mysterious part of you which is not the body, the soul 2) an eager state of mind, enthusiasm 3) a supernatural being such as a ghost or a fairy 4) an alcoholic drink such as liquor

spir-it-u-al [spĭr′ĭ-chōō-əl] *adjective*, airy, motivated by the soul, holy, religious

spit [spĭt] *noun*, 1) saliva, *verb*, 2) to spray water or saliva out of the mouth

spite [spīt] *noun*, *no plural*, hatred, feelings of malice, wanting to hurt or annoy another person

splash [splăsh] *noun*, 1) the sound made when a solid falls into liquid, *verb*, 2) to make a wave of water in a pool

splen-did [splĕn′dĭd] *adjective*, excellent, magnificent, very fine

splice [splīs] *verb*, to insert a shoot, to join, to graft, to unite

splint [splĭnt] *noun*, a board used to keep a thing from bending, a way of protecting a broken limb

splin-ter [splĭn′tər] *noun*, a thin piece of wood split off from a larger piece, a sliver

split [splĭt] *noun*, 1) a tear or a break, *verb*, 2) to break lengthwise 3) to share

spoil [spoil] *verb*, 1) to damage or injure, to ruin 2) to become rotten or decayed 3) to overindulge or corrupt by coddling someone

spoke [spōk] *noun*, 1) one of the bars joining the rim of a wheel to the center to support weight, *verb*, 2) *past tense* of **speak**

sponge [spŭnj] *noun*, 1) a substance that absorbs water, used to clean and wipe 2) a primitive marine animal having a soft elastic skeleton with many pores, *verb*, 3) to live off the generosity of others

spon-sor [spŏn′sər] *noun*, 1) a patron, supporter, mentor, backer, *verb*, 2) to offer financial support for a program

spon-ta-ne-i-ty [spŏn′tə-nē′ĭ-tē] *noun*, acting at the spur of the moment, impromptu

spon-ta-ne-ous [spŏn-tā′nē-əs] *adjective*, 1) acting on impulse, a result of natural law 2) energy

spool [spool] *noun*, a round object used to wind thread or wire

spoon [spoon] *noun*, a utensil consisting of a shallow bowl with a long handle attached to it, used for eating or stirring

spoon-ful [spoon′fool′] *noun*, the quantity that sits in a spoon

spo-rad-ic [spə-răd′ĭk] *adjective*, occurring irregularly

spore [spōr] *noun*, a cell that reproduces itself such as fungus, fern, or bacterium

sport [spōrt] *noun*, 1) games and exercises done for pleasure 2) a rascal 3) a teammate

spot [spŏt] *noun*, 1) a small mark, drop, or blemish 2) a location, *verb*, 3) to see something

spouse [spous] *noun*, a partner in marriage, husband or wife

spout [spout] *noun*, 1) the lip of a container from which liquid is poured, *verb*, 2) to spurt, to discharge, to gush forth

sprain [sprān] *verb*, to strain a body part by twisting it, causing it to swell

sprawl [sprôl] *verb*, to stretch, to spread out, to extend

spray [sprā] *noun*, 1) liquid dispersed in very fine drops 2) a small branch of flowers or foliage, *verb*, 3) to blow or scatter liquid in very fine drops

spread [sprĕd] *verb*, 1) to cover a surface with a thin layer 2) to unfold or stretch out 3) to circulate, to disseminate 4) to extend over a large area

spring [sprĭng] *noun*, 1) a river or pond coming up from the ground 2) a piece of wire twisted into a spiral 3) the season following winter, when plants begin to grow, *verb*, 4) to jump 5) to come from 6) to grow

sprin-kle [sprĭng′kəl] *verb*, 1) to spatter, to disperse in drops 2) to drizzle 3) to dust lightly

sprint [sprĭnt] *noun*, 1) a short fast run, *verb*, 2) to dash at top speed

sprock-et [sprŏk′ĭt] *noun*, a projection shaped so as to engage with a chain

sprout [sprout] *verb*, to grow out of a seed, to start to grow

spruce [sproos] *noun*, one of the softwood evergreen trees

sprung [sprŭng] *past tense* of **spring**

spry [sprī] *adjective*, vigorous, quick, energetic, agile

spun [spŭn] *past tense* of **spin**

spur [spûr] *noun*, 1) a short side track connecting with the main railroad 2) a sharp blade on the back of a boot used to urge horses to run faster 3) an impetus, a cause to action, *verb*, 4) to urge, to goad, to stimulate

spurious

spu-ri-ous [spyŏŏr′ē-əs] *adjective*, counterfeit, false, not genuine

spurn [spûrn] *verb*, to reject, to scorn, to despise, to shun

spy [spī] *noun*, *plural*, **spies** 1) an agent hired to secretly obtain information *verb*, 2) to see or catch sight of 3) to keep secret watch

squad [skwŏd] *noun*, a small group of soldiers who work, train, and fight together 2) a sports team

squad-ron [skwŏd′rən] *noun*, armed military aircraft

squal-id [skwŏl′ĭd] *adjective*, dirty through neglect, foul, filthy

squan-der [skwŏn′dər] *verb*, to spend money or resources without being accountable

square [skwâr] *noun*, 1) a surface with four equal sides and right angle corners 2) an open area in the center of town surrounded by stores and businesses

square number [skwâr- nŭm′bər] *noun*, the product of two equal factors, e.g., 12 x 12 = 144

squash [skwŏsh] *noun*, 1) a vegetable that grows on a vine 2) a game similar to racquetball, *verb*, 3) to repress 4) to flatten by pressing or from pressure

squat [skwŏt] *adjective*, 1) wide, stocky, *verb*, 2) to stoop

squeak [skwēk] *noun*, 1) a very sharp, high-pitched sound, *verb*, 2) to make a short high-pitched sound

squeal [skwēl] *noun*, 1) a shrill cry, *verb*, 2) to make such a sound 3) to turn informer

squeeze [skwēz] *verb*, to press hard upon 2) to put pressure on to extract liquid 3) to force one's way 4) to crowd

squid [skwĭd] *noun*, a sea creature similar to an octopus

squint [skwĭnt] *verb*, to scrunch one's eyes to strain to see

squirm [skwûrm] *verb*, to wiggle

squir-rel [skwûr′əl, skwŭr′-] *noun*, a small rodent with a bushy tail that lives in trees

sta-bil-i-ty [stə-bĭl′ĭ-tē] *adjective*, firmness, constancy, strength

sta-ble [stā′bəl] *adjective*, 1) firm, steady, *noun*, 2) a building in which horses are kept

stac-ca-to [stə-kä′tō] *adjective*, music played in a quick, abrupt manner

stack [stăk] *noun*, 1) a large pile arranged in some sort of order 2) a chimney, *verb*, 3) to pile up

sta-di-um [stā′dē-əm] *noun*, an open arena where concerts, sports, or events are held

staff [stăf] *noun*, a long stick carried in the hand for support

stag [stăg] *noun*, a male deer

stage [stāj] *noun*, 1) a raised floor or platform in a theatre or auditorium 2) a period of time or a step in development

stage-coach [stāj′kōch′] *noun*, a carriage on wheels pulled by horses on a fixed route

stag-ger [stăg′ər] *verb*, to stand or walk unsteadily, to reel

stag-nant [stăg′nənt] *adjective*, not moving or flowing, motionless

stag-nate [stăg′nāt′] *verb*, to be or become stagnant, motionless, to become impure or foul

staid [stād] *adjective*, sober, sedate

stain [stān] *noun*, 1) a mark that changes the appearance of something, a blot, *verb*, 2) to make a strong mark that cannot be removed 3) to disgrace

stair [stâr] *noun*, a step connecting different levels, *plural*, **stairs,** a series or flight of steps

stake [stāk] *noun*, 1) a pointed post in the ground 2) a gamble, a risk

stale [stāl] *adjective*, 1) old, dry, not fresh, tasteless 2) dull, bored

stale-mate [stāl′māt′] *noun*, a deadlock, a situation in which no side may take action

stalk [stôk] *noun*, 1) the long part of a plant that supports leaves or flowers, *verb*, 2) to follow someone with the intention of harming them 3) to pursue prey

stall [stôl] *noun*, 1) a small open room, as in a barn or a market place, *verb*, 2) to stop due to a mechanical failure

stal-lion [stăl′yən] *noun*, a male horse used for breeding

stal-wart [stôl′wərt] *adjective*, 1) sturdy, strong 2) brave 3) firm, steadfast

stam-i-na [stăm′ə-nə] *noun*, the power to endure, strength

stamp [stămp] *noun*, 1) a small piece of paper purchased to put on an envelope or package to send it through the mail 2) the imprint left from a device used to leave a mark, *verb*, 3) to mark with a special sign or design 4) to set the foot down heavily

stam-pede [stăm-pēd′] *verb*, to rush wildly in a group

stance [stăns] *noun*, 1) posture 2) political or social position

stand [stănd] *verb*, 1) to be your feet 2) to take a position 3) to mean or signify, to represent

stand-ard [stăn′dərd] *adjective*, 1) regular, official, basic, *noun*, 2) a fixed quality by which things are compared

stands [stăndz] *noun*, *plural*, the bleachers where spectators watch sports events

stan-za [stăn′zə] *noun*, a verse in a poem, a song, or a refrain

sta-ple [stā′pəl] *noun*, 1) principle commodity, an essential element 2) a wire used to attach things together such as cloth or paper, *verb*, 3) to bond two things together with staples applied by a stapler

star [stär] *noun*, 1) a point of light that can be seen in the sky at night 2) a five-pointed shape, *verb*, 3) to stand out in a positive way, to be outstanding

star-board [stär′bərd] *adjective*, the right-hand side of a ship as one faces the bow

starch [stärch] *noun*, a carbohydrate, that turns into sugar in the body

stare [stâr] *verb*, to look at someone or something with a steady gaze, to glare

stark [stärk] *adjective*, extremely simple or severe, bleak

start

start [stärt] *noun*, 1) an act of beginning, *verb*, 2) to begin

star-tle [stär'tl] *verb*, to surprise, to greet unexpectedly, to shock

star-va-tion [stär-vā'shən] *noun*, to suffer from hunger and lack of food or nourishment

starve [stärv] *verb*, to be hungry, unfed, deprived of food

state [stāt] *noun*, 1) the condition of something 2) a mood 3) a group of people living under an independent government, that is part of a country or federal union which governs itself as a republic or commonwealth, *verb*, 5) to say, to declare

state-ment [stāt'mənt] *noun*, 1) a spoken or written commitment 2) a summary of an account showing the balance

states-man [stāts'mən] *noun*, a leader of government

stat-ic [stăt'ĭk] *noun*, applicable to electricity not in motion

sta-tion [stā'shən] *noun*, a stopping place for the convenience of passengers, a depot

sta-tion-ar-y [stā'shə-nĕr'ē] *adjective*, fixed in a place, not changing, not moving

sta-tion-er-y [stā'shə-nĕr'ē] *noun*, writing paper, pens, and ink

sta-tis-tic [stə-tĭs'tĭk] *noun*, a fact stated as a number or in tables

stat-ue [stăch'ōō] *noun*, replica of a figure, real or imaginary made of plaster, bronze, marble, etc.

stat-ure [stăch'ər] *noun*, 1) a person's status or place in the community 2) the height of a person or animal

sta-tus [stā'təs] *noun*, position, high standing, prestige

stat-ute [stăch'ōōt] *noun*, a law enacted by a legislature

stat-u-to-ry [stăch'ə-tôr'ē] *adjective*, authorized, made as a law, regulated by statute

stay [stā] *verb*, to continue to be

stead-fast [stĕd'făst'] *adjective*, firmly fixed or established, unwavering, constant

stead-i-ly [stĕd'ə-lē] *adverb*, constantly, continually, regularly

stead-y [stĕd'ē] *adjective*, 1) regular 2) firm, immovable

steak [stāk] *noun*, a thick flat piece of meat or fish

steal [stēl] *verb*, 1) to take or carry away without permission 2) to move or pass very quietly without making noise

stealth [stĕlth] *noun*, secrecy, sneakiness, surreptitious

steam [stēm] *noun*, 1) the vapor created by boiling water, *verb*, 2) to cook using the intense heat of steam 3) to expose to steam

steel [stēl] *noun*, a hard metal made of specially treated iron, used in machines, knives, hardware, etc.

steep [stēp] *adjective*, 1) having a sharp incline or slope, *verb*, 2) to soak in liquid, to saturate

stee-ple [stē'pəl] *noun*, a free-standing column or tower

steer [stîr] *noun*, 1) a form of long horned cattle, *verb*, 2) to drive, to fly, to conduct, or navigate

318

stel-lar [stĕl/ər] *adjective*, 1) star-like, referring to heavenly bodies, celestial 2) outstanding

stem [stĕm] *noun*, 1) the stalk of a plant that supports the flower and leaves, *verb*, 2) to develop from 3) to stop the flow of

sten-cil [stĕn/səl] *noun*, a thin sheet with perforations in the form of a design through which ink or paint may be forced

step [stĕp] *noun*, 1) a stair 2) the movement with a foot 3) one of a series of events in a program, *verb*, 4) to walk or go on foot

ster-e-o [stĕr/ē-ō/] *noun*, an electronic device that makes sounds or plays music

ster-e-o-type [stĕr/ē-ə-tīp/] *noun*, 1) a typical example or pattern 2) a conventional, oversimplified conception

ste-rile [stĕr/əl, -īl/] *adjective*, clean, antiseptic, germ free

ster-i-lize [stĕr/ə-līz/] *verb*, 1) to render incapable of germination, 2) to disinfect, to clean

ster-ling [stûr/lĭng] *adjective*, 1) genuine, superior, excellent, of the highest quality *noun*, 2) made of pure silver

stern [stûrn] *adjective*, 1) unsympathetic, firm, strict 2) the back of the boat

steth-o-scope [stĕth/ə-skōp/] *noun*, an instrument used to convey to the ear, sounds produced by the body, especially in the chest

stew [stoo] *noun*, 1) a thick soup, *verb*, 2) to cook in liquid

stew-ard [stoo/ərd] *noun*, 1) one who watches over something 2) one in charge of provisions and dinner arrangements

stew-ard-ess [stoo/ər-dĭs] *noun*, a woman who serves passengers on an airplane, a flight attendant

stick [stĭk] *noun*, 1) a short branch or twig, *verb*, 2) to make something adhere to a surface 3) to push in or out 4) to stay with something, to persevere

stiff [stĭf] *adjective*, 1) something that cannot be moved or bent easily 2) difficult or hard to accomplish 3) sore

stiff-en [stĭf/ən] *verb*, to harden, to brace, to become rigid

stig-ma [stĭg/mə] *noun*, 1) the apex of a flower pistil where pollen is placed 2) a disgraceful blot

stig-ma-tize [stĭg/mə-tīz/] *verb*, to brand, to mark as wicked

still [stĭl] *adjective*, 1) without movement, *adverb*, 2) up to this or that time 3) even so

still-ness [stĭl/nĭs] *noun*, the state of being still or without sound

stim-u-late [stĭm/yə-lāt/] *verb*, to rouse to action, to excite

stim-u-lus [stĭm/yə-ləs] *noun*, an incentive, an impetus

sting [stĭng] *noun*, 1) the pain or wound of an insect or bug bite 2) a sharp or smarting pain 3) the attack of an insect on its prey or an enemy

stin-gy [stĭn/jē] *adjective*, not generous, miserly

stink

stink [stǐngk] *noun*, 1) an unpleasant or awful odor, *verb*, 2) to give off a bad smell

sti-pend [stī'pěnd'] *noun*, payment given for services

stip-u-late [stǐp'yə-lāt'] *verb*, to bargain, to specify as a condition of an agreement

stir [stûr] *verb*, to mix or blend

stir-ring [stûr'ǐng] *adjective*, moving, touching, exciting

stitch [stǐch] *noun*, 1) a needle and thread, piercing cloth and then coming out again to form a link of thread in a fabric 2) a loop added to a knitting needle, *verb*, 3) to sew, to mend

stock [stǒk] *noun*, goods kept on hand, merchandise

stock-ade [stǒ-kād'] *noun*, a barricade, a fence, an obstacle

stock-hold-er [stǒk'hōl'dər] *noun*, an owner of stocks or shares in a corporation

stock-ing [stǒk'ǐng] *noun*, a sheer leg covering made of nylon

sto-ic [stō'ǐk] *noun*, one who is indifferent to pleasure or pain, stern, impassive, cold

stoke [stōk] *verb*, to provide with fuel, to feed abundantly

stole [stōl] *past tense* of **steal**

stom-ach [stǔm'ək] *noun*, a large muscular bag in the body that receives food, digests some of it, and passes it on, to the intestines

stone [stōn] *noun*, 1) a small piece of rock, *verb*, 2) to pelt or kill

stool [stōol] *noun*, 1) a seat with three or four legs and no back 2) a bowel movement

stoop [stōop] *verb*, 1) to bend or squat the body over forwards 2) to lower oneself, to condescend

stop [stǒp] *verb*, 1) to end, to make something come to an end 2) to prevent something from happening, moving, etc. 3) to complete the action

stor-age [stôr'ǐj] *noun*, the act of keeping things for future use

store [stōr] *noun*, 1) supply of things saved for use later 2) a shop, a place to buy things, *verb*, 3) to put away for later use

stork [stôrk] *noun*, a large bird with long legs and a large beak

storm [stôrm] *noun*, a period of high winds, possibly thunder and lightning, rain, or snow

sto-ry [stōr'ē] *noun*, 1) telling of events with words spoken or written in a book 2) an account of something either true or fictitious, a report, a description 3) the floor of a building

stout [stout] *adjective*, 1) short, heavy-set 2) resolute, firm

stove [stōv] *noun*, an appliance which is heated and used for cooking or heating

stow [stō] *verb*, to store, to put away for future use

straight [strāt] *adjective*, 1) not curved, *adverb*, 2) without going anywhere else or doing anything else 3) moving on a path that is unchanged 4) without delay, *noun*, 5) a poker hand of 5 cards in consecutive order

straight-en [strāt'n] *verb*, to fix or arrange in order

strain [strān] *noun*, 1) the change of a body produced by an external force 2) a new species or breed 3) a suggestion, a hint, a trace, *verb*, 4) to cause stress, to stretch to reach

strait [strāt] *noun*, a narrow channel between two bodies of water, an inlet

strand [strănd] *noun*, 1) seashore, waterfront 2) a piece of something long and thin like a rope or a piece of hair

strange [strānj] *adjective*, unusual, odd, unfamiliar, exotic

strange-ly [strānj'lē] *adverb*, unusually, seldom, rarely

stran-ger [strān'jər] *noun*, a person you do not know, an outsider

stran-gle [străng'gəl] *verb*, 1) to kill by suffocating 2) to suppress

strap [străp] *noun*, 1) a narrow piece of leather, plastic, cloth, etc, used for fastening something, *verb*, 2) to fasten something on with a tie

strat-e-gy [străt'ə-jē] *noun*, a plan

strat-o-sphere [străt'ə-sfîr'] *noun*, the upper atmosphere extending 12-30 miles above the earth's surface, the ozone

stra-tum [strā'təm] *noun*, *plural* **strata**, a layer of the earth's surface, sedimentary rock

straw [strô] *noun*, 1) a dry stem 2) something that people use to suck a drink out of a glass

straw-ber-ry [strô'běr'ē] *noun*, the edible red berry of a small plant, that grows on the ground

stray [strā] *adjective*, 1) anything that does not seem to be part of a group, *verb*, 2) to wander away from home or the rest of the group 3) to digress

streak [strēk] *noun*, 1) a long mark like a band or a stripe, *verb*, 2) to draw stripes on something in a wild pattern

stream [strēm] *noun*, 1) a small river, a small body of running water 2) a steady or continuous flow, *verb*, 3) to flow, to pour

street [strēt] *noun*, a public paved road as in a town or city

strength [strĕngkth] *noun*, power, capacity for exertion or endurance, force in numbers

strength-en [strĕngk'thən] *verb*, to reinforce, to make stronger

stren-u-ous [strĕn'yōo-əs] *adjective*, characterized by vigorous exertion, difficult

stress [strĕs] *noun*, 1) anxiety, tension, *verb*, 2) to apply force to cause strain 3) to emphasize

stretch [strĕch] *noun*, 1) an expanse, a range or reach, *verb*, 2) to exaggerate 3) to extend across a given space 4) to extend one's body or limbs to feel limber

stretch-er [strĕch'ər] *noun*, a framework consisting of two poles with a cloth fastened between them used to carry an injured person

strict [strĭkt] *adjective*, close adherence to the rules

stride

stride [strīd] *noun*, 1) a large step or movement, *verb*, 2) to step

stri-dent [strīd'nt] *adjective*, loud and harsh in sound, grating

strike [strīk] *noun*, 1) an unsuccessful attempt by a batter to hit a ball 2) a protest of wages that stops work in order to bargain for better working conditions, *verb*, 3) to hit or attack 4) to refuse to work because of a pay dispute 5) to discover, to uncover 6) to eliminate 7) to find, to reach

string [strĭng] *noun*, 1) a thin twine made by twisting several threads together 2) a fine piece of wire used in some musical instruments, *verb*, 3) to thread a bead onto a string

strin-gent [strĭn'jənt] *adjective*, strict, inflexible, exacting

stripe [strīp] *noun*, a long thin line

strive [strīv] *verb*, to exert oneself, to try, to make a strenuous effort

stroke [strōk] *noun*, 1) a mild heart attack, *verb*, 2) to caress, to rub

stroll [strōl] *verb*, to walk leisurely

strong [st rŏng] *adjective*, 1) able to take stress or strain 2) intense in degree 3) physically powerful

struck [strŭk] *verb*, *past tense* of **strike**

struc-ture [strŭk'chər] *noun*, 1) the framework of something, 2) a complete building

strug-gle [strŭg'əl] *noun*, 1) the fight, the effort, *verb*, 2) to continue to endure set backs

strut [strŭt] *verb*, to swagger, to walk with bravado

stub-born [stŭb'ərn] *adjective*, unwilling to give in or compromise, obstinate

stuck [stŭk] *verb*, *past tense* of **stick**

stu-dent [stood'nt] *noun*, a person enrolled at a school or college

stud-y [stŭd'ē] *noun*, 1) a room to read and write 2) a subject or area of learning, *verb*, 3) to apply the mind to the effort to learn by reading and thinking

stuff [stŭf] *noun*, 1) substance, material, *verb*, 2) to fill by crowding, to push or crowd in

stum-ble [stŭm'bəl] *verb*, to walk unsteadily so that you appear to be about to fall, to trip while running 2) to come upon unexpectedly 3) to stammer

stump [stŭmp] *noun*, 1) what is left of a tree after it has been cut down, *verb*, 2) to perplex

stun [stŭn] *verb*, to astonish, to amaze, to confound, to shock

stunt [stŭnt] *noun*, 1) a performance, a skit, an act, *verb*, 2) to suppress, to retard the growth of something

stu-pen-dous [stoo-pĕn'dəs] *adjective*, astonishing, wonderful, amazing

stu-por [stoo'pər] *noun*, a state of apathy, daze, a lack of awareness

stur-dy [stûr'dē] *adjective*, very strongly built, durable

stut-ter [stə'tər] *verb*, to speak with difficulty, to stammer

sty [stī] *noun*, 1) a painful red swelling on the end of an eyelid 2) a pig pen

style [stīl] *noun*, 1) the fashion or design 2) elegance or flair

sty-mie [stī′mē] *verb*, to present an obstacle, to stump, to hinder

suave [swäv] *adjective*, smoothly, agreeable, courteous, polite

sub-due [səb-dōō′] *verb*, to calm down, to bring under control

sub-ject [sŭb′jĭkt] *adjective*, 1) owing obedience to 2) likely to be affected by, *noun*, 3) an area of study 4) a person under the authority or control of another 5) in a sentence the word about which the predicate makes a statement, *verb*, 6) to expose to

sub-jec-tive [səb-jĕk′tĭv] *adjective*, based on personal feelings or opinions

sub-lime [sə-blīm′] *adjective*, great, noble, majestic, superior

sub-lim-i-nal [sŭb-lĭm′ə-nəl] *adjective*, affecting the subconscious, below the threshold of consciousness

sub-ma-rine [sŭb′mə-rēn′] *noun*, a naval warship armed with torpedoes and missiles that operates under water

sub-merge [səb-mûrj′] *verb*, to put or sink under water

sub-mis-sive [səb-mĭs′ĭv] *adjective*, to take orders without questioning authority

sub-mit [səb-mĭt′] *verb*, 1) to put something forward for someone else's reaction 2) to give in to someone or something

sub-or-di-nate [sə-bôr′dn-ĭt] *adjective*, 1) being in a lower rank or class, subject to another's authority *noun*, 2) one lower in rank, inferior

sub-poe-na [sə-pē′nə] *noun*, a writ commanding a person listed in it to appear in court

sub-scribe [səb-scrīb′] *verb*, 1) to sign up for something 2) to give permission or consent

sub-scrip-tion [səb-skrĭp′shən] *noun*, money paid as a form of membership for service

sub-se-quent [sŭb′sĭ-kwĕnt′] *adjective*, following, after

sub-ser-vi-ent [səb-sûr′vē-ənt] *adjective*, useful in an inferior capacity, subordinate

sub-side [səb-sīd′] *verb*, to settle down to become calm

sub-si-dize [sŭb′sĭ-dīz′] *verb*, 1) to add to 2) to provide financial aid

sub-si-dy [sŭb′sĭ-dē] *noun*, direct financial aid by the government

sub-stance [sŭb′stəns] *noun*, the material something is made of

sub-stan-tial [səb-stăn′shəl] *adjective*, 1) strong 2) having considerable property

sub-stan-ti-ate [səb-stăn′shē-āt′] *verb*, to verify, to support

sub-stan-tive [sŭb′stən-tĭv] *adjective*, essential, pertaining to

sub-sti-tute [sŭb′stĭ-tōōt′] *noun*, 1) a person or thing put in place of another, a replacement *verb*, 2) to act in place of another

sub-ter-fuge [sŭb′tər-fyōōj′] *noun*, a device or plan by which one can hide an objective

subterranean

sub-ter-ra-ne-an [sŭb′tə-rā′nē-ən] *adjective*, 1) under the earth's surface 2) hidden, secret

sub-tle [sŭt′l] *adjective*, difficult to to detect, not obvious, slight

sub-tle-ty [sŭt′l-tē] *noun*, cunning, delicately understated

sub-tract [səb-trăkt′] *verb*, to take away one number from another

sub-trac-tion [səb-trăk′shən] *noun*, an equation in which one number is taken from another

sub-urb [sŭb′ûrb′] *noun*, a residential community on the outskirts of a city or town

sub-ur-ban [sə-bûr′bən] *adjective*, pertaining to a smaller district next to a city or town

sub-ver-sive [səb-vûr′sĭv] *adjective*, tending to overthrow or ruin, corruption

sub-way [sŭb′wā′] *noun*, an underground electric train or urban transit system

suc-ceed [sək-sēd′] *adjective*, to attain a desired object or goal

suc-cess [sək-sĕs′] *noun*, a person who accomplishes a difficult task or meets a goal

suc-cess-ful [sək-sĕs′fəl] *adjective*, gaining a desired object or goal

suc-ces-sion [sək-sĕsh′ən] *noun*, sequence, order, descent

suc-ces-sive [sək-sĕs′ĭv] *adjective*, following one after another in a line or series, consecutive

suc-ces-sor [sək-sĕs′ər] *noun*, someone appointed to a title or position to replace another

suc-cinct [sək-sĭngkt′] *adjective*, concise, terse, brief, to the point

suc-cor [sŭk′ər] *noun*, aid, help, assistance, relief

suc-cu-lent [sŭk′yə-lənt] *adjective*, 1) juicy 2) delicious, tasty

suc-cumb [sə-kŭm′] *verb*, 1) to yield, to give way 2) to die

such [sŭch] *pronoun*, 1) of this or that kind 2) used in some phrases to mean like

suck [sŭk] *verb*, to draw into the mouth by action of the lips and tongue when inhaling

suc-tion [sŭk′shən] *noun*, the pulling force of a partial vacuum

sud-den [sŭd′n] *adjective*, when something happens unexpectedly

sud-den-ly [sŭd′n-lē] *adverb*, happening at once without warning, unexpectedly

sue [soō] *verb*, to ask a court to solve a problem legally

suede [swād] *noun*, a leather made when the flesh, or underside of the leather is buffed or sandpapered to produce a nap

suf-fer [sŭf′ər] *verb*, 1) to feel pain or hurt 2) to tolerate, to allow

suf-fer-ing [sŭf′ər-ĭng] *noun*, enduring pain and sadness

suf-fice [sə-fīs′] *verb*, 1) to be enough for 2) to satisfy a need

suf-fi-cient [sə-fĭsh′ənt] *adjective*, adequate for the purpose

suf-fix [sŭf′ĭks] *noun*, letters added to the end of a word, to change the meaning

suf-fo-cate [sŭf′ə-kāt′] *verb*, 1) to omother, to choke 2) to kill by depriving of oxygen

suf-frage [sŭf′rĭj] *noun*, the right to vote, a vote

sug-ar [shŏŏg′ər] *noun*, a sweet substance made from sugar cane or sugar beets and used in food products

sug-gest [səg-jĕst′] *verb*, 1) to bring up or call to mind, to propose for consideration 2) to imply, to indicate

sug-ges-tion [səg-jĕs′chən] *noun*, 1) a proposal, an idea, advice, a recommendation 2) a slight trace, a hint, an implication

su-i-cide [sŏŏ′ĭ-sīd′] *noun*, the act of taking one's own life

suit [sŏŏt] *noun*, 1) a set of clothes made from the same fabric, *verb*, 2) to adapt, to perform

suit-a-ble [sŏŏ′tə-bəl] *adjective*, fitting, proper, appropriate

suit-case [sŏŏt′kās′] *noun*, a rectangular piece of luggage

suite [swēt] *noun*, a number of rooms connected together

suit-or [sŏŏ′tər] *noun*, a beau, a man who courts a woman

sul-fur [sŭl′fər] *noun*, a nonmetallic yellow element used in gunpowder, matches and medicine

sulk [sŭlk] *verb*, to pout and feel angry or sorry for yourself

sul-len [sŭl′ən] *adjective*, silent from anger or hurt, moody, indulging in self-pity

sul-ly [sŭl′e] *verb*, 1) to disgrace, to tarnish someone's character 2) to soil, to stain

sul-try [sŭl′trē] *adjective*, sweltering, hot and humid

sum [sŭm] *noun*, the total of different amounts added together

sum-ma-ry [sŭm′ə-rē] *noun*, a shorter version of an article

sum-ma-tion [sə-mā′shən] *noun*, the act of finding the total

sum-mer [sŭm′ər] *noun*, the third season of the year, between spring and autumn

sum-mit [sŭm′ĭt] *noun*, 1) the top leaders, the highest point 2) the top of a mountain

sum-mon [sŭm′ən] *verb*, 1) to call, to send for by command 2) to gather, to call forth

sum-mons [sŭm′ənz] *noun*, a formal letter requesting a response in court

sump-tu-ous [sŭmp′chŏŏ-əs] *adjective*, luxurious, splendid

sun [sŭn] *noun*, the central star of the solar system around which the planets revolve which gives off light, heat and energy

sun-dae [sŭn′dē] *noun*, a dish of ice cream covered with toppings such as chocolate syrup, nuts and whipped cream

Sun-day [sŭn′dē] *noun*, the first day of the week, observed as the Sabbath by most Christians

sun-dry [sŭn′drē] *adjective*, various, more than one or two

sun-flow-er [sŭn′flou′ər] *noun*, a plant with large yellow-rayed flower heads that produces edible seeds that yield an oil

sun-rise [sŭn′rīz′] *noun*, the early morning, the crack of dawn

sun-set [sŭn′sĕt′] *noun*, close of the day, twilight

sun-shine [sŭn′shīn′] *noun*, *no plural*, bright light, day light

su-per [soo′pər] *adjective*, 1) outstanding, exceptionally fine, 2) great, extreme or excessive

su-perb [soo-pûrb′] *adjective*, exceptional, extraordinary

su-per-cil-i-ous [soo′pər-sĭl′ē-əs] *adjective*, lofty with pride, haughty, contemptuous

su-per-fi-cial [soo′pər-fĭsh′əl] *adjective*, 1) relating to the surface or appearance only 2) actions thoughtlessly done, insincere, shallow

su-per-flu-ous [soo-pûr′floo-əs] *adjective*, excessive, more than needed, unnecessary

su-per-in-tend-ent [soo′pər-ĭn-tĕn′dənt] *noun*, one having oversight and direction of some place or agency

su-pe-ri-or [soo-pîr′ē-ər] *adjective*, 1) beyond power or influence of another 2) greater in number or amount 3) above average

su-per-mar-ket [soo′pər-mär′kĭt] *noun*, a large store with shelves that have a variety of household products, a large grocery store

su-per-nat-u-ral [soo′pər-năch′ər-əl] *adjective*, beyond what is explainable by natural law, metaphysical

su-per-sede [soo′pər-sēd′] *adjective*, to come to take the place of something that is not as modern, efficient,or appropriate

su-per-son-ic [soo′pər-sŏn′ĭk] *adjective*, faster than sound

su-per-sti-tion [soo′pər-stĭsh′ən] *noun*, reverence for that which is unknown or mysterious

su-per-sti-tious [soo′pər-stĭsh′əs] *adjective*, awe of that which is unknown or mysterious based on an irrational belief

su-per-vise [soo′pər-vīz′] *verb*, to direct, to watch over

su-per-vi-sion [soo′pər-vĭzh′ən] *noun*, *no plural*, overseeing someone's work

su-per-vi-sor [soo′pər-vī′zər] *noun*, a person who oversees a department of workers

sup-per [sŭp′ər] *noun*, dinner, a meal eaten in the evening

sup-ple [sŭp′əl] *adjective*, 1) flexible, pliant, bending easily without breaking 2) limber

sup-ple-ment [sŭp′lə-mənt] *noun*, a part added, an appendix

sup-ply [sə-plī′] *noun*, 1) a resource, *verb*, 2) to provide something needed

sup-port [sə-pôrt′, -pōrt′] *noun*, 1) aid, assistance 2) an abutment, a brace, a stay, *verb*, 3) to advocate, to back, to uphold 4) to provide food and clothing and other necessities

sup-pose [sə-pōz′] *verb*, to hold that something is true, to assume that something is true

sup-po-si-tion [sŭp′ə-zĭsh′ən] *noun*, presumption, theory, principle

sup-press [sə-prĕs′] *verb*, to subdue, to quell, to inhibit, to keep from being known

su-preme [sōō-prēm′] *adjective*, highest in authority, highest in degree, above all

Su-preme Court [sōō-prēm′kôrt] *noun*, the most important court in the United States, consisting of 9 members appointed by the President

sure [shōōr] *adjective*, best, convinced, certain beyond question, having no doubt

sure-ly [shōōr′lē] *adverb*, certainly

surf [sûrf] *noun, no plural*, 1) the waves of the sea as they hit the shores, *verb*, 2) to ride a surfboard 3) to search the Internet on a computer

sur-face [sûr′fəs] *noun*, 1) a plane, the outside or topside face 2) the top of the water, *verb*, 3) to rise to the top of a body of water

sur-feit [sûr′fĭt] *noun*, 1) excess *verb*, 2) to over-indulge, to give to use in excess

surge [sûrj] *noun*, 1) a rush, a flow, *verb*, 2) to swell, to pour out

sur-geon [sûr′jən] *noun*, one whose profession it is to cure diseases or injuries by performing an operation

sur-ger-y [sûr′jə-rē] *noun*, an operation when a doctor cuts into a person's body with instruments to help cure them

sur-ly [sûr′lē] *adjective*, rude, cross, bad-tempered, grumpy

sur-mise [sər-mīz′] *noun*, 1) a guess, speculation, likelihood, *verb*, 2) to assume, to guess, to suppose, to conjecture

sur-mount [sər-mount′] *verb*, to be overcome, to prevail over

sur-name [sûr′nām′] *noun*, a person's last name

sur-pass [sər-păs′] *verb*, to exceed, to do better, to go beyond

sur-plus [sûr′pləs, -plŭs′] *noun*, the amount that is more than needed

sur-prise [sər-prīz′] *noun*, 1) something sudden and unexpected, *verb*, 2) to cause to feel astonished

sur-ren-der [sə-rĕn′dər] *verb*, to give up, to yield

sur-rep-ti-tious [sûr′əp-tĭsh′əs] *adjective*, kept secret (especially if it would not be approved of), hidden, unauthorized

sur-ro-gate [sûr′ə-gĭt] *adjective*, substitute, replacement

sur-round [sə-round′] *verb*, to encircle, to enclose on all sides

sur-round-ings [sə-roundĭngs] *noun, plural,* the conditions or things around a person or place

sur-veil-lance [sər-vā′ləns] *noun*, a close watch over something

sur-vey [sər-vā′] *noun*, 1) a study, a poll, a review, *verb*, 2) to examine, to inspect, to watch

sur-vey-or [sər-vā′ər] *noun*, 1) one who collects data 2) one whose business it is to measure land

sur-viv-al [sər-vī′vəl] *noun, no plural*, what one needs to stay alive or exist

sur-vive [sər-vīv′] *verb*, to continue to exist, to live longer

sur-vi-vor [sər-vīv′ər] *noun*, the one to make it when the others died or failed

sus-cep-ti-ble [sə-sĕp′tə-bəl] *adjective*, capable of being affected emotionally

sus-pect [sə-spĕkt′] *noun*, 1) a person who is believed to have done something wrong, *verb*, 2) to suppose that something is true

sus-pend [sə-spĕnd′] *verb*, 1) to hang 2) to stop temporarily

sus-pend-ers [sə-spĕn′dərz] *noun*, two adjustable bands or straps arranged to pass over the shoulders to hold the trousers up

sus-pense [sə-spĕns′] *noun, no plural*, a pause or delay which leaves people anxious

sus-pen-sion [sə-spĕn′shən] *noun*, a delay, postponement

sus-pi-cion [sə-spĭsh′ən] *noun*, 1) distrust, doubt, 2) trace

sus-pi-cious [sə-spĭsh′əs] *adjective*, having a feeling that something is wrong, distrustful

sus-tain [sə-stān′] *verb*, to bear, to hold up, to keep going

sus-te-nance [sŭs′tə-nəns] *noun*, that which supports life, a food or nourishment

su-ture [soo′chər] *noun*, stitches sewn to hold the cut edges of a wound or incision

swag-ger [swăg′ər] *verb*, to walk in a boastful and proud manner

swal-low [swŏl′ō] *noun*, 1) a small bird with a tail split into two parts, *verb*, 2) to consume food through the mouth into the stomach, to take in

swamp [swŏmp, swômp] *noun*, 1) wet, boggy ground which is always soft, wet land, *verb*, 2) to overwhelm with too much of something, to inundate

swan [swŏn] *noun*, a large white bird with a long neck that lives in the water and on land

swap [swŏp] *verb*, to exchange

swarm [swôrm] *noun*, 1) a large group of insects or bugs, *verb*, 2) to travel in a large group, to teem, to crowd

swarth-y [swôr′thē] *adjective*, having a dark complexion

swat [swŏt] *verb*, to hit, to whack

sway [swā] *verb*, to swing gently

swear [swâr] *verb*, 1) to curse 2) to promise, to make a solemn declaration

sweat [swĕt] *noun*, 1) moisture which comes out of the skin due to exertion, *verb*, 2) to give off water through the skin

sweat-er [swĕt′ər] *noun*, a wool or woven garment worn over the top of the body

sweep [swēp] *noun*, 1) a continuous search, *verb*, 2) to clean or clear with a brush or broom

sweet [swēt] *adjective*, 1) tasting like sugar or honey 2) a pleasant or kind personality 3) having a pleasant smell

swell [swĕl] *verb*, to become larger

swel-ter [swĕl'tər] *verb*, to be tired by the heat, to perspire, to sweat

swept [swĕpt] *past tense* of **sweep**

swerve [swûrv] *verb*, to move suddenly to one side when you are moving along

swift [swĭft] *adjective*, very fast or quick to act, nimble, prompt

swlm [swĭm] *noun*, 1) the act of staying afloat or traveling in water, *verb*, 2) to move through the water by using movements of the body

swin-dle [swĭn'dl] *verb*, to cheat, to deceive or defraud

swing [swĭng] *noun*, 1) a seat hanging on ropes or chains, *verb*, 2) to move freely from a fixed point, to pivot, to turn

swirl [swûrl] *noun*, 1) a spiral, *verb*, 2) to turn in a circular motion

switch [swĭch] *noun*, 1) a device that can be used to turn something on or off, *verb*, 2) to exchange 3) to turn something on or off 4) to change as in direction, to shift, to transfer

swiv-el [swĭv'əl] *verb*, to turn or pivot on a bolt or pin

swol-len [swō'lən] *adjective*, inflamed, puffed up, enlarged

swoon [swōōn] *noun*, 1) a fainting spell, *verb*, 2) to faint

swoop [swōōp] *verb*, to fly down very quickly like a bird

sword [sôrd] *noun*, a weapon similar to a knife with a very long blade

swore [swôr] *past tense* of **swear**

syl-la-ble [sĭl'ə-bəl] *noun*, a combination of letters indicating a sound in a word

syl-lo-gism [sĭl'ə-jĭz'əm] *noun*, logical formula using a major premise, a minor premise leading to a conclusion

sym-bol [sĭm'bəl] *noun*, anything that stands for or represents something else

sym-met-ri-cal [sĭ-mĕt'rĭ-kəl] *adjective*, alike on both sides, proportional

sym-me-try [sĭm'ĭ-trē] *noun*, the balance of things on opposite sides, excellence of proportion

sym-pa-thet-ic [sĭm'pə-thĕt'ĭk] *adjective*, kind, warm, compassionate, tender

sym-pa-thize [sĭm'pə-thīz'] *verb*, to feel sorry for another, to share in a feeling

sym-pa-thy [sĭm'pə-thē] *noun*, the understanding of another person's feelings, pity

sym-pho-ny [sĭm'fə-nē] *noun*, a musical composition performed by an orchestra

symp-tom [sĭm'təm] *noun*, a sign indicating the presence of an illness or something

syn-a-gogue [sĭn'ə-gŏg'] *noun*, a Jewish house of worship, a temple

syn-chro-nic-i-ty [sĭng'krə-nĭs'ĭ-tē] *noun*, to do something that is similarly timed

syn-chro-nize [sĭng'krə-nīz'] *verb*, to agree in time, to move together, simultaneously

syn-di-cate [sĭn′dĭ-kĭt] *verb*, a network of businesses that sell news to the media

syn-o-nym [sĭn′ə-nĭm′] *noun*, a word that means the same as another

syn-op-sis [sĭ-nŏp′sĭs] *noun*, a general view of a whole, an abstract or summary

syn-the-sis [sĭn′thĭ-sĭs] *noun*, combining parts into a whole

syn-thet-ic [sĭn-thĕt′ĭk] *adjective*, produced by artificial processes, not real or genuine

sy-ringe [sə-rĭnj′] *noun*, an instrument with a needle used to inject a fluid into the blood stream through a vein

syr-up [sĭr′əp] *noun*, a sugar liquid

sys-tem [sĭs′təm] *noun*, a network of things working together as a functioning unit

sys-tem-at-ic [sĭs′tə-măt′ĭk] *adjective*, methodical, proceeding according to method

T

ta-ble [tā′bəl] *noun*, 1) a piece of furniture with a flat top and legs used for placing things on or using as a work space 2) a list, often using lines or boxes to arrange facts

tab-leau [tăb′lō′] *noun*, a scene of persons in costume remaining silent and motionless

ta-ble-cloth [tā′bəl-klôth′] *noun*, a decorative cloth spread over the top of a table

tab-let [tăb′lĭt] *noun*, a hard flat piece or block of something

ta-boo [tə-boo′] *adjective*, 1) forbidden, banned by religion or custom, *noun*, 2) a restriction, a ban or prohibition

tab-u-late [tăb′yə-lāt′] *verb*, to arrange in column forms

tac-it [tăs′ĭt] *adjective*, implied or indicated, but not expressed

tac-i-tur-ni-ty [tăs′ĭ-tûr′ nĭ-tē] *adjective*, habitually silent, not given to conversation

tack [tăk] *noun*, a small nail with a broad, flat head on it

tack-le [tăk′əl] *noun*, 1) ropes and pulleys arranged for hoisting or pulling 2) equipment used for fishing 3) downing a player 4) a football player, *verb*, 5) to undertake, to get down to business to solve a problem 6) to bring to the ground

tact [tăkt] *noun*, *no plural*, to do or say the right thing at the right time, diplomacy

tact-ful [tăkt′fəl] *adjective*, discreet, careful, prudent

tac-tic [tăk′tĭk] *noun*, a maneuver

tac-tile [tăk′təl, -tīl′] *adjective*, referring to the sense of touch

tag [tăg] *noun*, 1) a small identifying card or label 2) a game children play in which one player chases the others, *verb*, 3) to follow along

tail [tāl] *adjective*, 1) coming from behind, *noun*, 2) the part of an animal which sticks out at the end of its back

tai-lor [tā′lər] *noun*, one who cuts out and makes clothes

taint [tānt] *noun*, 1) a trace of something bad, *verb*, 2) to contaminate, to corrupt

take [tāk] *verb*, 1) to get hold of something 2) to carry something or go with someone to another place 3) to swallow something 4) to travel 5) to accept

tak-en [tā′kən] *adjective*, 1) held, seized 2) accepted

tale [tāl] *noun*, a story

tal-ent [tăl′ənt] *noun*, a natural ability, aptitude

tal-is-man [tăl′ĭs-mən] *noun*, an amulet or lucky charm

talk [tôk] *verb*, to speak or be able to speak, to consult or confer

talk-a-tive [tô′kə-tĭv] *adjective*, inclined to talk a lot, loquacious

tall [tôl] *adjective*, above average height, high

tal-ly [tăl′ē] *noun*, 1) a mark made to keep score or to count, *verb*, 2) to keep track of an account

tal-on [tăl′ən] *noun*, a claw, especially of a bird of prey

tame [tām] *adjective*, 1) trained to live with man, not wild, *verb*, 2) to make a wild animal obedient and friendly to people

tan [tăn] *adjective*, 1) light brown, tawny 2) to convert into leather

tan-gent [tăn′jənt] *noun*, a straight line that touches a curve without intersecting it

tan-ge-rine [tăn′jə-rēn′] *noun*, a variety of a small-sized orange

tan-gi-ble [tăn′jə-bəl] *adjective*, capable of being touched, real

tank [tăngk] *noun*, 1) a large container to hold liquid or gas fuel 2) an armed vehicle used in combat 3) the metal box in the back of the car to hold gasoline

tan-ta-lize [tăn′tə-līz′] *verb*, to tease, to tempt, to promise by offering a reward

tan-ta-mount [tăn′tə-mount′] *adjective*, equal in value

tan-trum [tăn′trəm] *noun*, an exaggerated display of anger, a fit of irritability, bad temper

tap [tăp] *noun*, 1) the faucet attached to a pipe to release liquid or gas, *verb*, 2) to hit or touch lightly 3) to drain by making a hole 4) to draw from

tape [tāp] *noun*, 1) a narrow piece of cloth or other material, *verb*, 2) to bind or secure with an adhesive material 3) to record

tap-er [tā′pər] *verb*, to decrease in amount or size by becoming narrower or smaller

tap-es-try [tăp′ĭ-strē] *noun*, a heavy, decorative, woven fabric used especially for wall hangings

tap-i-o-ca [tăp′ē-ō′kə] *noun*, cassava, a coarse granular preparation used in puddings

tar [tär] *noun*, a thick black liquid made from heating coal or wood

ta-ran-tu-la [tə-răn′chə-lə] *noun*, a hairy, large, poisonous spider

tar-get [tär′gĭt] *noun*, 1) somebody or something aimed at 2) an objective, a goal, *verb*, 3) to make the focus or object of something

tar-iff [tär′ĭf] *noun*, a tax on goods exported or imported

tarnish

tar-nish [tär′nĭsh] *verb*, 1) to dull the luster of metal 2) to taint

tart [tärt] *adjective*, 1) sour to the taste, *noun*, 2) a piece of pastry with fruit cooked on top of it

task [tăsk] *noun*, a chore or small job that must be done

tas-sel [tăs′əl] *noun*, a pendant ornament ending in a tuft of loose threads

taste [tāst] *noun*, 1) a preference, liking 2) the sense that distinguishes the flavor of things placed in the mouth 3) a flavor itself, *verb*, 4) to sample a food by taking it in the mouth

tat-too [tă-tōō′] *noun*, a design on the skin made using a needle filled with dye

taught [tôt] *past tense* of **teach**

taunt [tônt] *verb*, to tease or make fun of someone, to ridicule

taut [tôt] *adjective*, stretched tight

tau-tol-o-gy [tô-tŏl′ə-jē] *noun*, needless repetition of an idea in different words

taw-dry [tô′drē] *adjective*, cheap and showy or flashy, gaudy

tax [tăks] *noun*, 1) a sum of money to be paid to the government imposed by the elected leaders, *verb*, 2) to put a fee on service or goods that are given to the government

tax-i [tăk′sē] *noun*, a car for hire to take people from one place to another

tax-i-der-mist [tăk′sĭ-dûr′mĭst] *noun*, one who prepares dead animals to look life-like

tea [tē] *noun*, 1) prepared dried leaves of a plant 2) a small meal or snack in the afternoon 3) a cup of a beverage made with leaves steeped in hot water

teach [tēch] *verb*, to show someone how to do something

teach-er [tē′chər] *noun*, a person whose occupation is to instruct

team [tēm] *noun*, 1) persons working or playing together as a group 2) two or more animals harnessed together to pull a vehicle

tear [tîr] *noun*, 1) a drop of water that comes out of the eye 2) a hole or cut in material, *verb*, 3) to make a hole in material by pulling on it

tease [tēz] *verb*, to make fun of someone, to annoy

tea-spoon [tē′spōōn′] *noun*, a small spoon used to measure

tech-ni-cal [tĕk′nĭ-kəl] *adjective*, having knowledge of a mechanical or scientific subject

tech-ni-cian [tĕk-nĭsh′ən] *noun*, a person who works with machines or instruments

tech-nique [tĕk-nēk′] *noun*, a procedure used to perform a task

tech-nol-o-gy [tĕk-nŏl′ə-jē] *noun*, the use of science to produce useful things for practical purposes that improve life

te-di-ous [tē′dē-əs] *adjective*, tiresome, dull, boring

tel-e-phone [tĕl′ə-fōn′] *noun*, 1) an instrument for reproducing sounds at a distance, *verb*, 2) to call to someone on an instrument that communicates voices through airwaves or wires

tel-e-scope [tĕl′ĭ-skōp′] *noun*, an optical instrument for viewing distant objects

tel-e-vi-sion [tĕl′ə-vĭzh′ən] *noun*, a set used to transmit visual images onto a screen

tell [tĕl] *verb*, 1) to speak to someone, to inform, to narrate 2) to deduce, to differentiate

tell-er [tĕl′ər] *noun*, a bank employee who handles customer transactions

tem-per [tĕm′pər] *noun*, 1) a person's state of mind, mood, *verb*, 2) to tone down, to moderate, to bring under control

tem-per-a-ment [tĕm′prə-mənt] *noun*, the physical and mental character of an individual

tem-per-ance [tĕm′pər-əns] *noun*, habitual moderation of the appetites and passions

tem-per-a-ture [tĕm′pər-ə-chŏŏr′] *noun*, the degree of heat or cold

tem-ple [tĕm′pəl] *noun*, 1) a holy building 2) the part of the head above and in front of the ear

tem-po [tĕm′pō] *noun*, the rate of speed of a musical passage

tem-po-ral [tĕm′pər-əl] *adjective*, not lasting forever, limited by time, the present

tem-po-rar-y [tĕm′pə-rĕr′ē] *adjective*, intended to last a short period of time, not permanent

tempt [tĕmpt] *verb*, to entice someone to do something unwise or wrong, to provoke

temp-ta-tion [tĕmp-tā′shən] *noun*, an instant urge or desire

ten [tĕn] *noun*, the number 10, one plus nine

te-na-cious [tə-nā′shəs] *adjective*, holding fast, stubborn

te-nac-i-ty [tə-năs′ĭ-tē] *noun*, firmness, persistency

ten-ant [tĕn′ənt] *noun*, someone who lives in a house or apartment, an occupant

tend [tĕnd] *verb*, 1) to be likely to, to do something habitually 2) to take care of something

ten-den-cy [tĕn′dən-sē] *noun*, inclination, propensity, leaning

tend-er [tĕn′dər] *adjective*, 1) kind and gentle 2) sensitive to touch or movement 3) cooked so that the food is easy to eat, *noun*, 4) a car attached to a train for carrying food and water

ten-der-ness [tĕn′dər-nĭs] *noun*, affection, gentleness

ten-e-ment [tĕn′ə-mənt] *noun*, a building divided into flats

ten-et [tĕn′ĭt] *noun*, doctrine, dogma, belief, conviction

Ten-nes-see [tĕn′ĭ-sē′] *noun*, one of the 50 United States located in the South, the capital city is Nashville. The state flower of **Tennessee** is the iris, and the motto is "Agriculture and commerce."

ten-nis [tĕn′ĭs] *noun*, a game played on a court by two or four people in which a ball is hit over a net with rackets

tenor

ten-or [tĕn′ər] *noun*, 1) a tendency, a trend 2) the highest range of the male singing voice

tense [tĕns] *adjective*, 1) full of excitement 2) tightly stretched, taut, *noun*, 3) the form of a verb that shows when the action happens – past, present, or future

ten-sion [tĕn′shən] *noun*, 1) act of stretching, 2) mental or nervous state or condition of strain

tent [tĕnt] *noun*, a shelter of canvas or nylon, supported by poles

ten-ta-cle [tĕn′tə-kəl] *noun*, a long, arm-like structure growing out of an animal's body, used for movement or catching food

ten-ta-tive [tĕn′tə-tĭv] *adjective*, experimental, based on trials

tenth [tĕnth] *adjective*, the number after nine in series, written 10th

ten-u-ous [tĕn′yo͞o-əs] *adjective*, weak and unconvincing

ten-ure [tĕn′yər] *noun*, the period of time during which an office is held, occupation

te-pee [tē′pē] *noun*, a cone shaped tent in which some Indians live

tep-id [tĕp′ĭd] *adjective*, 1) not hot or cold, lukewarm 2) showing little enthusiasm

term [tûrm] *noun*, 1) a fixed amount of time 2) an expression or form of language 3) a condition or stipulation

ter-min-al [tûr′mə-nəl] *adjective*, 1) end, final, concluding, *noun*, 2) a depot where buses or trains make connections 3) a conducting circuit arranged for connection in an electrical circuit

ter-mi-nate [tûr′mə-nāt′] *verb*, to end, to finish, to cancel

ter-mi-na-tion [tûr′mə-nā′shən] *noun*, the ending

ter-mi-nol-o-gy [tûr′mə-nŏl′ə-jē] *noun*, vocabulary used in a specialized subject

ter-race [tĕr′ĭs] *noun*, 1) a level area cut out from the side of a hill 2) a flat area outside a house

ter-rain [tə-rān′] *noun*, the features of an area of land

ter-rar-i-um [tə-râr′ē-əm] *noun*, a transparent container in which land animals or plants are kept

ter-res-tri-al [tə-rĕs′trē-əl] *adjective*, of the earth

ter-ri-ble [tĕr′ə-bəl] *adjective*, appalling, dreadful

ter-rif-ic [tə-rĭf′ĭk] *adjective*, awesome, wonderful

ter-ri-fy [tĕr′ə-fī′] *verb*, to fill or overwhelm with fear or horror

ter-ri-to-ry [tĕr′ĭ-tôr′ē] *noun*, a portion of land belonging to someone else, a region

ter-ror [tĕr′ər] *adjective*, fear

terse [tûrs] *adjective*, concise, abrupt, a short answer

ter-ror-ist [tĕr′ər] *noun,* one who uses violence to intimidate

tes-sel-la-tion [tĕs′ə-lā′shən] *adjective*, a mosaic pattern

test [tĕst] *noun*, 1) a trial 2) an examination to assess the level of knowledge of a subject, *verb*, 3) to try something out to see how it works 4) to examine

tes-ta-ment [tĕs′tə-mənt] *noun,*1) a will 2) scripture from the Bible

tes-ti-fy [tĕs′tə-fī′] *verb*, to establish some fact, under oath to serve as evidence

tes-ti-mo-ny [tĕs′tə-mō′nē] *noun*, the statement of a witness under oath, evidence or proof

tet-a-nus [tĕt′n-əs] *noun*, a painful, often fatal, infectious disease, marked by painful spasms of the muscles, frequently of the jaw

teth-er [tĕth′ər] *noun*, 1) a cord, a link, a supply line, *verb*, 2) to tie up with a rope, to hitch, to fasten

Tex-as [tĕk′səs] *noun*, one of the 50 United States located in the Southwest, the capital city is Austin. The state flower of **Texas**, is the bluebonnet, and the motto is "Friendship."

text [tĕkst] *noun*, the words used in a book, a written work

text-book [tĕkst′bŏŏk′] *noun*, an instruction book, a manual

tex-tile [tĕks′tīl′] *noun*, fabrics such as cotton, wool, linen, silk, rayon, and polyester

tex-ture [tĕks′chər] *noun*, the feel or appearance of something – soft, smooth, rough, etc.

than [thăn] used as a *conjunction*, to introduce the second part of a comparison

thank [thăngk] *verb*, to express gratitude and appreciation

thank-ful [thăngk′fəl] *adjective*, to be grateful, to show appreciation or praise

thanks [thăngks] *noun*, an acknowledgment of a kindness, favor, or the like

Thanks-giv-ing [thăngks-gĭv′ĭng] *noun*, a national holiday celebrated the fourth Thursday in November

that [thăt] *pronoun, plural*, **those**, 1) the one singled out 2) used instead of which 3) used to join two parts of a sentence 4) so 5) used to show the result

that's [thăts] the *contraction* of the words **that** and **is**

thatch [thăch] *noun*, bundles of straw woven together

thaw [thô] *verb*, to pass from a frozen to a liquid state

the [thē before a vowel, thə before a consonant] *article*, a word that usually goes before a noun

the-a-ter [thē′ə-tər] *noun*, a building where dramatic performances are presented

the-at-ri-cal [thē-ăt′rĭ-kəl] *adjective*, dramatic, eloquent

thee [thē] *pronoun*, the objective case of thou

theft [thĕft] *noun*, the act or instance of stealing

their [thâr] *pronoun*, belonging to them, a form of the possessive case of **they** used attributively, e.g., *their school*

theirs [thârz] *pronoun*, showing personal ownership

them [thĕm] *pronoun*, the objective case of **they** , *plural*, **them-selves**, the same people, animals, or things mentioned in the sentence as the subject

theme [thĕm] *noun*, the subject on which one writes or speaks

then

then [thĕn] *adverb*, 1) at another time, not now 2) afterwards, next 3) if that is true

the-ol-o-gy [thē-ŏl′ə-jē] *noun*, the science of God or of religion

the-o-rem [thē′ər-əm] *noun*, a principle, a theoretical proposition, a thesis

the-o-ret-i-cal [thē′ə-rĕt′ĭ-kəl] *adjective*, depending on conjecture, speculative

the-o-ry [thē′ə-rē] *noun*, an abstract plan, an hypothesis

ther-a-peu-tic [thĕr′ə-pyōō′tĭk] *adjective*, curative, healing, good for personal growth and health

ther-a-py [thĕr′ə-pē] *noun*, exercises and treatment designed to rehabilitate a person

there [thâr] *adverb*, 1) referring to that place 2) referring to at that moment

there's [thârz] the *contraction* of the words **there** and **is**

there-fore [thâr′fôr′] *adverb*, for that reason, as a result

ther-mal [thûr′məl] *adjective*, pertaining to heat

ther-mo-dy-nam-ics [thûr′mō-dī-năm′ĭks] *noun*, the relationship between heat and other forms of energy

ther-mom-e-ter [thər-mŏm′ĭ-tər] *noun*, a device for measuring how hot or cold something is

ther-mos [thûr′məs] *noun*, a vacuum bottle for keeping liquids hot or cold for hours

ther-mos-tat [thûr′mə-stăt′] *noun*, a mechanical device used to control temperature

the-sau-rus [thĭ-sôr′əs] *noun*, a dictionary of synonyms and antonyms

these [thēz] *pronoun, adjective,* the *plural* of **this**

the-sis [thē′sĭs] *noun*, an essay presented by a candidate for a degree or diploma

they [thā] *pronoun*, the *plural* of **he, she** or **it**

they'll [thāl] the *contraction* of the words **they** and **will**

they're [thâr] the *contraction* of the words **they** and **are**

thick [thĭk] *adjective*, 1) occupying much space in depth or from side to side, measuring between sides 2) a dense fluid

thief [thēf] *noun, plural,* **thieves,** one who steals

thigh [thī] *noun*, the thick part of the leg above the knee and below the hip

thim-ble [thĭm′bəl] *noun*, a metal cap put over the finger to keep it from being pricked by a needle

thin [thĭn] *adjective*, 1) not thick, slender 2) lacking volume or density 3) sparse, insufficient, inadequate, flimsy

thing [thĭng] *noun*, 1) an object, a creature, a form of life 2) conditions 3) an act or event

think [thĭngk] *verb*, 1) to form or have on the mind 2) to use the power of reason 3) to believe, to suppose

third [thûrd] *adjective, noun*, the number three in order after second, written 3rd

thirst [thûrst] *noun, no plural*, the need to drink something

thirst-y [thûr′stē] *adjective*, needing something to drink

thir-teen [thûr-tēn′] *adjective, noun*, the number 13, 3+10

thir-teenth [thûr-tēnth′] *adjective, noun*, number 13 in order, 13th

thir-ti-eth [thûr′tē-ĭth] *adjective, noun*, number 30 in order, 30th

thir-ty [thûr′tē] *adjective, noun*, the number 30, ten times three

this [thĭs] *adjective*, 1) being the one present, near or just mentioned 2) being the one nearer or last mentioned, *adverb* 3) the thing the speaker is talking about, *pronoun*, 4) the one nearer than that one in time or space 5) what is in the present or being talked about

this-tle [thĭs′əl] *noun*, a plant with prickly leaves and stems and a purple flower

thorn [thôrn] *noun*, a sharp projection on a stem

thor-ough [thûr′ō] *adjective*, complete, perfect, absolute

thor-ough-ly [thûr′ō-lē] *adverb*, completely done

those [thōz] *pronoun*, the ones over there, the ones further away than this one

thou [thou] you

though [thō] *adverb*, 1) however, *conjunction*, 2) although

thought [thôt] *noun*, 1) an idea, the process of thinking 2) intention 3) attention, *verb*, 4) the *past tense* of **think**

thought-ful [thôt′fəl] *adjective*, showing consideration for others, kind, discreet

thou-sand [thou′zənd] *noun, adjective*, the number 1,000, ten times 100

thread [thrĕd] *noun*, 1) a fine string made of cotton, linen, or silk, *verb*, 2) to wind through openings 3) to pass a thread through the eye of a needle

threat [thrĕt] *noun*, a warning, that one may do harm

threat-en [thrĕt′n] *verb*, to torment, to scare, to pose a danger

three [thrē] *adjective, noun*, the number 3, one plus two, 3

thresh-old [thrĕsh′ōld′] *noun*, a piece of timber which lies under a door, an entrance

thrift [thrĭft] *noun*, the practice of being careful with money

thrift-y [thrĭf′tē] *adjective*, careful about money, economical

thrill [thrĭl] *noun*, 1) an excited feeling, *verb*, 2) to fill with excitement

thrive [thrīv] *verb*, 1) to grow abundantly 2) to prosper, to flourish, to succeed

throat [thrōt] *noun*, the passage inside of the neck attached to the mouth, lungs, and stomach

throb [thrŏb] *verb*, to beat strongly, to pulsate steadily

throne [thrōn] *noun*, a special chair for a king or queen

throng [thrông, thrŏng] *noun*, a crowd of people, a multitude

throt-tle [thrŏt′l] *noun*, 1) a lever or pedal that helps an engine start

through

and run, *verb*, 2) to strangle, to
suppress 3) to regulate the
speed of an engine

through [thrōō] *adjective*,
1) finished, *adverb*, 2) from one
side or end of something to the
other, *preposition*, 3) in one side
and out the other 4) by the
agency of, by way of, via
5) among or between 6) past or
beyond, in the midst of

through-out [thrōō-out′]
preposition, all over, from end to
end, from inside and out

throw [thrō] *noun*, 1) the distance
something is tossed, cast or
projected, *verb*, 2) to toss, fling,
or hurl something through the air

thrust [thrŭst] *verb*, to push
suddenly and hard

thud [thŭd] *noun*, a dull sound
made when something heavy
falls and lands

thumb [thŭm] *noun*, the short,
thick finger on the hand which is
separate from the others

thun-der [thŭn′dər] *noun, no
plural*, the loud sound heard in
the sky during a storm

Thurs-day [thûrz′dē] *noun*, the fifth
day of the week

thus [thŭs] *adverb*, in this way

thy [thī] *pronoun*, your

thyme [tīm] *noun*, a pungent
aromatic plant used in seasoning

tick [tĭk] *noun*, 1) the sound made
by a clock 2) a check mark 3) a
small parasite that sucks blood
from animals and people, *verb*,
4) to make a soft, steady,
rhythmic sound 5) to check off

things on a list that fit a certain
criteria

tick-et [tĭk′ĭt] *noun*, 1) the ballot of
a political party 2) an admission
3) a fine 4) a price tag

tick-le [tĭk′əl] *noun*, 1) a tingling
sensation, *verb*, 2) to touch a
person lightly to make them
laugh 3) to delight, to amuse

tid-al [tīd′l] *adjective*, action of the
sea caused by the tides

tide [tīd] *noun*, regular rise and fall
of the ocean caused by the pull
of the sun and the moon

ti-dy [tī′dē] *adjective*, 1) neat and
orderly 2) substantial, more than
enough, *verb*, 3) to make neat
and well organized

tie [tī] *noun*, 1) a narrow piece of
cloth used as a man's dress
accessory worn around the neck
with a shirt, a necktie 2) a bond
3) a standoff, *verb*, 4) to fasten
something with string or rope
5) to come out equal in a contest

tier [tîr] *noun*, one of several levels

ti-ger [tī′gər] *noun*, a fierce animal,
one of the big cats, which has
yellow fur with black stripes

tight [tīt] *adjective*, 1) so close in
structure that air cannot pass
through 2) drawn close together

tight-en [tīt′n] *verb*, to draw closer
together, to squeeze

tight-ly [tīt′lē] *adverb*, pulled
closely together, tautly

tile [tīl] *noun*, a flat piece of baked
clay that has been painted with
glaze or linoleum used as a floor
covering

till [tĭl] *adverb*, 1) before, up to, *noun*, 2) a cash box, a place to store money, *verb*, 3) to plow

till-er [tĭl′ər] *noun*, a handle used to steer a boat

tilt [tĭlt] *verb*, to make something lean so that it is not straight

tim-ber [tĭm′bər] *noun*, a piece of wood, lumber, hardwood

tim-bre [tăm′bər] *noun*, quality of a musical tone produced by a musical instrument

time [tīm] *noun*, 1) minutes, hours, days, weeks, months, years, etc. 2) a limited duration 3) a period or event 4) a certain hour or part of the day 5) a moment, *verb*, 6) to measure how long it takes to do something 7) a number multiplied by another

time-ly [tīm′lē] *adjective*, prompt, well-timed, favorable

tim-id [tĭm′ĭd] *adjective*, shy, afraid, uncertain, hesitant

tim-id-i-ty [tĭm′ĭ-dĭ-tē] *noun*, lack of self-confidence or courage

tim-or-ous [tĭm′ər-əs] *adjective*, fearful and hesitant

tin [tĭn] *noun, no plural*, a soft white metal mixed with alloys

tinc-ture [tĭngk′chər] *noun*, a slight quality added to anything, a trace or tinge, pigment

tin-gle [tĭng′gəl] *verb*, 1) to get excited 2) to have a prickling sensation

tin-ker [tĭng′kər] *verb*, to fool around, to dabble, to putter

tin-sel [tĭn′səl] *noun*, showy or flashy decorations

tint [tĭnt] *noun*, 1) the color, shade, hue, *verb*, 2) to color, to shade

ti-ny [tī′nē] *adjective*, very small

tip [tĭp] *noun*, 1) a point, a peak 2) a hint, advice, a pointer 3) compensation for a service, gratuity, *verb*, 4) to tilt, to list, to lean to one side, to slant 5) to give someone money for a small service 6) to cause something to fall over and become unbalanced

tip-toe [tĭp′tō′] *noun*, 1) the tip of the toe, *verb*, 2) to walk on toes so that the step is not heard

ti-rade [tī′rād′] *noun*, extended scolding, denunciation

tire [tīr] *noun*, 1) a rubber, air-filled part of a car or bicycle wheel that cushions the ride, *verb*, 2) to make someone feel that he needs to rest 3) to become bored, fatigued

tir-ed [tīrd] *adjective*, feeling sleepy, needing rest

tis-sue [tĭsh′ōō] *noun*, very thin paper that feels soft

ti-tan-ic [tī-tăn′ĭk] *adjective*, gigantic, of great size or power

tithe [tīth] *noun*, a payment of one tenth of an income given to the church

ti-tle [tīt′l] *noun*, 1) the name of a story, a book, a film, etc. 2) a word used in front of a person's name 3) a sport's championship

to [tōō; tə when unstressed] *adverb*, 1) in a direction toward *preposition*, 2) in the direction of 3) as far as 4) on or against 5) until 6) used to show why 7) used with the infinitive of a

toad

verb 8) for the purpose of, in order to 9) belonging to

toad [tōd] *noun*, an animal that looks like a frog but does not live in water

toast [tōst] *noun*, 1) sliced bread broiled to make it crisp, *verb*, 2) to praise someone when raising your drink in a glass 3) to brown by the heat of a fire

to-bac-co [tə-băk′ō] *noun*, the dried leaves of a plant used for smoking and chewing

to-bog-gan [tə-bŏg′ən] *noun*, a very long, flat-bottomed sled used to glide on snow

to-day [tə-dā′] *adverb*, 1) on or for this very day, *noun*, 2) modern times, present day, contemporary

toe [tō] *noun*, 1) one of the five digits at the end of the foot 2) the part of a shoe or sock that covers this end of the foot

tof-fee [tô′fē] *noun*, a hard, chewy candy made of caramel candy, brown sugar and butter

to-ga [tō′gə] *noun*, Roman outer robe of free born men

to-geth-er [tə-gĕth′ər] *adverb*, 1) at the same time 2) in conjunction, with each other, in cooperation

toil [toil] *verb*, to work very hard

toi-let [toi′lĭt] *noun*, an instrument to flush human waste into a sewage system, a bathroom

to-ken [tō′kən] *noun*, 1) a sign or symbol or gesture to indicate something 2) a souvenir 3) a coin used as a currency for travel

told [tōld] *past tense* of **tell**

tol-er-ance [tŏl′ər-əns] *noun*, compassion, open-mindedness

tol-er-ant [tŏl′ər-ənt] *noun*, broad minded, liberal, accepting

toll [tōl] *noun*, 1) the charge for a privilege or a service 2) the number lost or taken, *verb*, 3) to ring a bell slowly

to-ma-to [tə-mā′tō] *noun*, a red berry with seeds and a pulpy fruit eaten as a vegetable

tomb [tōōm] *noun*, a sacred place where a dead person is buried

tomb-stone [tōōm′stōn′] *noun*, the carved stone with an inscription identifying the person on a grave

tome [tōm] *noun*, a large volume

to-mor-row [tə-môr′ō] *adverb* 1) the day after today, *noun*, 2) sometime in the future

ton [tŭn] *noun*, the weight of measure of a very heavy quantity, e.g., 2,000 pounds

tone [tōn] *noun*, 1) the sound of a voice or a musical instrument 2) manner, expression

tongs [tôngz] *noun*, *plural*, (pair of) a tool with two legs used to pick up or to hold something

tongue [tŭng] *noun*, 1) the organ of speech covered by taste buds 2) the flap of leather or cloth under the lacing of a shoe 3) the language spoken 4) dialect

ton-ic [tŏn′ĭk] *noun*, a refreshing drink that invigorates

to-night [tə-nīt′] *adverb*, 1) the night following today, *noun,* 2) on or during the night of today

too [tōō] *adverb*, 1) also 2) more than is needed or wanted

took [tŏŏk] *past tense* of **take**

tool [tōol] *noun*, an instrument used to do work or make repairs

tooth [tōoth] *noun*, *plural* **teeth**, 1) a white bony material that grows in the mouth, set in sockets around the jaw, used for chewing 2) the projections on a blade

tooth-ache [tōoth′āk′] *noun*, a pain in the mouth due to an infection from a tooth

top [tŏp] *adjective*, 1) best, first, chief, *noun*, 2) the highest part of something 3) the lid or cover of something 4) a toy that spins quickly on a point

to-paz [tō′păz′] *noun*, a precious stone, usually yellow or tan

top-ic [tŏp′ĭk] *noun*, the subject of a conversation, speech, or essay

to-pog-ra-phy [tə-pŏg′rə-fē] *noun*, detailed representation of the features of a region

top-ple [tŏp′əl] *verb*, to make or become unsteady and fall over

torch [tôrch] *noun*, an instrument that gives off a very hot flame

tor-ment [tôr′mĕnt′] *noun*, 1) abuse, agony, chaos, *verb*, 2) to torture, to annoy, to abuse, to afflict with mental suffering

tor-na-do [tôr-nā′dō] *noun*, a storm with a strong wind which spins very fast, a violent windstorm

tor-pe-do [tôr-pē′dō] *noun*, a self-propelled underwater missile containing explosives fired through the water from a ship to destroy another ship

tor-pid [tôr′pĭd] *adjective*, dormant, dull, lethargic

tor-rent [tôr′ənt] *noun*, a fast flow of water or energy

tor-ren-tial [tô-rĕn′shəl] *adjective*, a rushing, violent stream of water

tor-rid [tôr′ĭd] *adjective*, 1) passionate 2) tropical, sweltering, oppressively hot

tor-so [tôr′sō] *noun*, the trunk of a statue with head and limbs missing, the upper part of the human body

tort [tôrt] *noun*, a civil wrong, independent of a contract

tor-toise [tôr′tĭs] *noun*, a very large turtle that lives on the land

tor-tu-ous [tôr′chōo-əs] *adjective*, winding, full of curves

tor-ture [tôr′chər] *noun* 1) the act of causing great pain or suffering 2) distress of mind or body, *verb*, 3) to inflict pain on someone mercilessly, in order to dominate and control

toss [tôs, tŏs] *verb*, 1) to throw 2) to move about up and down

to-tal [tōt′l] *adjective*, 1) making up the whole, *noun*, 2) the sum of numbers in addition, entire

to-tal-ly [tōt′l-ē] *adverb*, wholly, entirely, completely

touch [tŭch] *noun*, 1) one of the five senses that communicates texture, temperature, and density to the brain through feeling, *verb*, 2) to make physical contact with something or someone

tough [tŭf] *adjective*, 1) yielding to force without breaking, strong 2) brave 3) difficult to chew

tour [tŏŏr] *noun*, 1) a journey that ends where it starts, *verb*, 2) to make a trip through a place

tour-ist [tŏŏr'ĭst] *noun*, a person traveling for pleasure

tour-na-ment [tŏŏr'nə-mənt] *noun*, a set number of contests that includes many teams or players and produces one winner

tow [tō] *verb*, to pull or haul with a rope or a chain

to-ward [tôrd] *preposition*, 1) in the direction of, in relation to 2) facing from the opposite direction

tow-el [tou'əl] noun, a piece of cloth or paper used for wiping or drying

tow-er [tou'ər] *noun*, 1) a tall building or structure that stands above the rest 2) a turret or spire attached to a building or fortress, *verb*, 3) to stand or reach above everything

town [toun] *noun*, buildings creating a hamlet, larger than a village and smaller than a city

tox-ic [tŏk'sĭk] *adjective*, poisonous, harmful

toy [toi] *noun*, an ornament or article that children play with

trace [trās] *noun*, 1) a small amount of something, *verb*, 2) to draw an image using paper to duplicate it 3) to try to follow the path of someone by using evidence that indicates what they are doing or have done

track [trăk] *noun*, 1) a mark left by something that has passed 2) a path or roadway, *verb*, 3) to follow or trace, to trail

trac-ta-ble [trăk'tə-bəl] *adjective*, 1) obedient, willing, compliant 2) easily shaped, malleable

trac-tion [trăk'shən] *noun*, adhesive friction of being drawn or pulled, the grip of the wheels on the ground

trac-tor [trăk'tər] *noun*, a machine used to plow and to till soil

trade [trād] *noun*, *no plural*, 1) the exchange of goods 2) a form of business or enterprise 3) a specific type of work that requires training, *verb*, 4) to buy and sell goods, to barter

tra-di-tion [trə-dĭsh'ən] *noun*, a custom or belief passed within families or other groups from one generation to another

tra-di-tion-al [trə-dĭsh'ə-nəl] *adjective*, following a custom that has been handed down through generations

traf-fic [trăf'ĭk] *noun*, 1) commerce, trade, the interchange of goods 2) the movement of cars and people on streets or of planes and ships

trag-e-dy [trăj'ĭ-dē] *noun*, 1) drama that deals with sad or terrible themes, as opposed to comedy 2) a fatal or unfortunate event

trag-ic [trăj'ĭk] *adjective*, very sad, dreadful, unfortunate

trail [trāl] *noun*, 1) the marks or evidence left behind in a place by someone or something that was there earlier, *verb*, 2) to follow someone, to track

train [trān] *noun*, 1) railroad cars for people or freight pulled by an engine, *verb*, 2) to teach someone or yourself to do something difficult that is considered a skill

train-ing [trā′nĭng] *noun*, preparation, instruction

trait [trāt] *noun*, a distinguishing characteristic or feature

trai-tor [trā′tər] *noun*, one who betrays a cause or any trust

tra-jec-to-ry [trə-jĕk′tə-rē] *noun*, a path taken by a projectile, or a flying object in its flight

tramp [trămp] *noun*, a person with no home or job who travels from place to place begging, a vagrant

tram-ple [trăm′pəl] *verb*, to crush into the ground, to walk heavily on something

trance [trăns] *noun*, a dream-like state of deep relaxation

tran-quil [trăng′kwəl] *adjective*, calm, peaceful, quiet, serene

tran-quil-li-ty [trăng-kwĭl′ĭ-tē] *noun*, calmness, composure

tran-quil-iz-er [trăng′kwə-līz′ər] *noun*, a sleeping pill, sedative

trans-ac-tion [trăn-săk′shən] *noun*, the doing of any business

tran-scend [trăn-sĕnd′] *verb*, to rise above and beyond the ordinary limits, to surpass, to exist independent of

tran-scen-den-tal [trăn′sĕn-dĕn′tl] *adjective*, beyond understanding, supernatural, spiritual

trans-con-ti-nen-tal [trăns′kŏn-tə-nĕn′tl] *adjective*, spanning a continent

tran-scribe [trăn-skrīb′] *verb*, to write out a spoken message

tran-script [trăn′skrĭpt′] *noun*, a written copy of a broadcast or a student's academic record

trans-fer [trăns-fûr′] *noun*, 1) the act of moving something from one place to another, *verb*, 2) to convey from one place to another

trans-fer-a-ble [trăns-fûr′ə-bəl] *noun*, capable of being moved from one place to another

trans-form [trăns-fôrm′] *verb*, 1) to change the form or appearance of something 2) to glorify

trans-form-er [trăns-fôr′mər] *noun*, a device that transfers electrical energy from one circuit to another

trans-fu-sion [trăns-fyo͞o′zhən] *noun*, the introduction into a person's bloodstream of blood from another

trans-gres-sion [trăns-grĕsh′ən] *noun*, violation of law, a going beyond some limit

tran-sient [trăn′shənt] *adjective*, of short duration, not permanent

tran-sis-tor [trăn-zĭs′tər] *noun*, an electrical device like a radio that sends and amplifies voices

tran-sit [trăn′sĭt] *noun*, 1) a passage 2) the state of being carried 3) a surveyor's instrument for measuring angles

tran-si-tion [trăn-zĭsh′ən] *noun*, going from one state of action or position to another

tran-si-tive [trăn′sĭ-tĭv] *adjective*, when the action of a verb is done to something or somebody

tran-si-to-ry [trăn′sĭ-tôr′ē] *adjective*, temporary, brief, lasting only a short time

trans-late [trăns-lāt′] *verb*, to pass along the message from one language to another

trans-la-tion [trăns-lā′shən] *noun*, the conversion of a message into another language

trans-lu-cent [trăns-lōō′sənt] *adjective*, a material that lets light in diffusively, but cannot be seen through

trans-mis-sion [trăns-mĭsh′ən] *noun*, 1) the apparatus by which the power is transmitted from high-speed motor power to the wheels 2) the sending of pictures or sounds through the air, as by radio or television

trans-mit [trăns-mĭt′] *verb*, 1) to send information over wires or air waves 2) to convey or send from one person or place to another 3) to pass along

trans-mit-ter [trăns-mĭt′ər] *noun*, the part of a telegraph or telephone instrument used to send a message

trans-mute [trăns-myōōt′] *verb*, to change, to convert from one substance to another

trans-par-ent [trăns-pâr′ənt] *adjective*, easily or capable of being seen through, clear

tran-spire [trăn-spīr′] *verb*, 1) to exhale 2) to happen, to occur

trans-plant [trăns-plănt′] *verb*, 1) to take out of the ground to plant somewhere else 2) a medical operation that exchanges a body organ

trans-port [trăns-pôrt′] *noun*, 1) a means of carrying people or goods, *verb*, 2) to carry

trans-por-ta-tion [trăns′pər-tā′shən] *noun*, the act of carrying things from one place to another

trans-pose [trăns-pōz′] *verb*, 1) to switch 2) to put into a different key in music

trap [trăp] *noun*, 1) a device used to capture someone or something 2) a strategy used to capture or entrap someone, *verb*, 3) to capture something or someone so that they cannot escape

tra-peze [tră-pēz′] *noun*, a short horizontal bar suspended by two parallel ropes, one at each end

trap-e-zoid [trăp′ĭ-zoid′] *noun*, a closed figure of four sides, two sides are parallel but unequal in length

trash [trăsh] *noun*, something considered worthless that is thrown away, garbage

trau-mat-ic [trou′măt′ĭk] *adjective*, upsetting, stressful, disturbing

tra-vail [trə-vāl′] *noun*, 1) painful labor, hard work 2) anguish

trav-el [trăv′əl] *noun*, 1) taking a trip, seeing the world, *verb*, 2) to go from one place to another 3) to be transmitted

trav-erse [trə-vûrs′] *verb*, to cross in traveling, to pass over

trawl-er [trô/lər] *noun*, a fishing boat which drags a cone-shaped net across the floor of the ocean

tray [trā] *noun*, a flat shallow receptacle with raised edges on which things can be carried

treach-er-ous [trĕch/ər-əs] *adjective*, dangerous

trea-cle [trē/kəl] *noun*, syrup obtained in refining sugar

tread [trĕd] *noun*, 1) the part touching the ground, *verb*, 2) to stand on, to walk on, to step

trea-son [trē/zən] *noun*, *no plural*, the crime of helping the enemy of a group or country one is loyal to

treas-ure [trĕzh/ər] *noun*, 1) an accumulation of wealth such as money or jewels, *verb*, 2) to regard as precious, to cherish

treas-ur-er [trĕzh/ər-ər] *noun*, one who is in charge of the disbursement of money

treas-ur-y [trĕzh/ə-rē] *noun*, a place to store and control money such as a bank

treat [trēt] *noun*, 1) something that gives pleasure or enjoyment, *verb*, 2) to behave toward 3) to deal with, to serve 4) to give medicine as a doctor

trea-tise [trē/tĭs] *noun*, an article treating a subject systematically and thoroughly

treat-ment [trēt/mənt] *noun*, 1) handling, processing 2) therapeutic care

trea-ty [trē/tē] *noun*, a formal agreement between two or more nations

tree [trē] *noun*, a large plant with a trunk, branches, and leaves

trek [trĕk] *verb*, to travel with hardship, a difficult journey

trem-ble [trĕm/bəl] *verb*, to shake, to feel nervous, to quiver

tre-men-dous [trĭ-mĕn/dəs] *adjective*, 1) marvelously great 2) very large 3) extraordinary

trem-or [trĕm/ər] *noun*, trembling, involuntary shaking of the body

trem-u-lous [trĕm/yə-ləs] *adjective*, quivering, wavering

trench [trĕnch] *noun*, a long narrow ditch, dug into the earth

trench-ant [trĕn/chənt] *adjective*, 1) keen, cutting 2) sarcastic, critical, mean-spirited

trench-er-man [trĕn/chər-mən] *noun*, a person with a hearty appetite

trend [trĕnd] *noun*, the popular course, direction, tendency

trep-i-da-tion [trĕp/ĭ-dā/shən] *noun*, fear, apprehension

tres-pass [trĕs/pəs] *noun*, 1) an intrusion, *verb*, 2) to encroach on another's right 3) to unlawfully enter property of another

tri-al [trī/əl] *noun*, 1) when people in a court of law decide whether a person is guilty of a crime 2) a test to see if something is good or bad 3) suffering or adversity

tri-an-gle [trī/ăng/gəl] *noun*, a plane figure with three sides and three angles

tri-an-gu-lar [trī-ăng/gyə-lər] *adjective*, having three points like a triangle

tribe

tribe [trīb] *noun*, a group of people descended from a common ancestor who practice the same traditions, customs, and rituals, lead by a chief, a clan

trib-u-la-tion [trĭb′yə-lā′shən] *noun*, distress, suffering

tri-bu-nal [trī-byoō′nəl] *noun*, a court or forum for justice

trib-u-tar-y [trĭb′yə-tĕr′ē] *adjective*, 1) subsidiary, *noun*, 2) a stream or river that flows into a larger river

trib-ute [trĭb′yoōt] *noun*, a gesture to show respect for someone, an accolade

trick [trĭk] *noun*, 1) a clever prank, a sly or ingenious feat, *verb*, 2) to deceive by cunning

trick-le [trĭk′əl] *verb*, to flow in a small, gentle stream

tri-cy-cle [trī′sĭk′əl] *noun*, a light three-wheeled vehicle

tried [trīd] *past tense* of **try**

tri-fle [trī′fəl] *noun*, 1) a small amount, *verb*, 2) to play or toy

tri-fling [trī′flĭng] *adjective*, of little value or importance

trig-ger [trĭg′ər] *noun*, 1) the firing mechanism on a gun, *verb*, 2) to set something off

trig-o-nom-e-try [trĭg′ə-nŏm′ĭ-trē] *noun*, measuring the sides and angles of triangles

tril-lion [trĭl′yən] *noun*, one million million: 1,000,000,000,000

tril-o-gy [trĭl′ə-jē] *noun*, a novel or play in three separate works that are closely related

trim [trĭm] *noun*, 1) ornaments or decorations, *verb*, 2) to decorate 3) to cut back to make tidy

tri-o [trē′ō] *noun*, a set of three

trip [trĭp] *noun*, 1) a journey, a jaunt, an excursion, a pilgrimage, *verb*, 2) to skip, to stumble 3) to release a lever suddenly

tri-ple [trĭp′əl] *adjective*, three-way, multiplied three times

tri-pod [trī′pŏd′] *noun*, a stand or support with three legs

trite [trīt] *adjective*, 1) trivial, insignificant 2) hackneyed

tri-umph [trī′əmf] *noun*, 1) exultation over success, *verb*, 2) to gain victory

tri-um-phant [trī-ŭm′fənt] *adjective*, feeling thrilled and happy about winning

triv-i-a [trĭv′ē-ə] *noun*, trifles, unimportant matters

triv-i-al [trĭv′ē-əl] *adjective*, of little worth or importance

trol-ley [trŏl′ē] *noun*, a public bus that travels on a train track

troop [troōp] *noun*, 1) a collection of people 2) a body of cavalry

tro-phy [trō′fē] *noun*, something as a prize or award, given to show success in an activity

trop-ic [trŏp′ĭk] *noun*, a place between the two imaginary lines that run parallel above and below the equator, where it is hot and humid all year long

trop-i-cal [trŏp′ĭ-kəl] *adjective*, temperatures of a jungle or warm climate near the equator

trot [trŏt] *verb*, to keep at a steady pace, to canter, to gallop

trou-ble [trŭb′əl] *noun*, 1) a problem, a difficulty 2) a dangerous or difficult situation 3) extra work or effort, *verb*, 4) to impose on 5) to distress

troupe [trōop] *noun*, a troop or company of musicians or performers

trou-sers [trou′zərz] *noun, plural*, loose fitting pants

trout [trout] *noun*, a small fresh-water fish in the salmon family

trow-el [trou′əl] *noun*, 1) a hand-held spade 2) a tool with a flat blade used to apply mortar or cement

tru-ant [trōo′ənt] *noun*, 1) absent from school without good reason or permission 2) neglectful

truce [trōos] *noun*, a peace agreement, cease-fire

truck [trŭk] *noun*, a large, heavy vehicle with at least four wheels used to transport heavy materials or large quantities

true [trōo] *adjective*, 1) honest, real, based on fact 2) loyal

tru-ism [trōo′ĭz′əm] *noun*, a self-evident obvious truth

tru-ly [(trōo′lē] *adverb*, in fact or in truth, sincerely, really

trump [trŭmp] *verb*, 1) to fabricate or invent 2) to beat someone's hand in bridge

trum-pet [trŭm′pĭt] *noun*, a horn, one of the brass instruments with several keys and a flaring bell

trunk [trŭngk] *noun*, 1) a chest, a storage box 2) the main stem of a tree 3) a compartment in a car 4) the snout of an elephant

trust [trŭst] *noun*, 1) belief in someone's goodness and integrity, *verb*, 2) to believe that someone will do as they say

trust-ee [trŭ-stē′] *noun*, one entrusted to administer the property of another

truth [trōoth] *noun*, the facts, what actually happened, reality

try [trī] *verb*, 1) to attempt, to make an effort 2) to sample

try-ing [trī′ĭng] *adjective*, difficult, straining one's patience

tryst [trĭst] *noun*, an appointed meeting, a rendezvous

tsu-nami [tsōo-nä′mē] *noun*, a giant, fast-moving ocean wave produced by an earthquake

tub [tŭb] *noun*, a container used to take a bath or wash clothes

tu-ba [tōo′bə] *noun*, the lowest-pitched of the brass instruments

tube [tōob] *noun*, 1) a pipe made of metal, plastic 2) a glass usually used to conduct liquids or gases

tu-ber-cu-lo-sis [tōo-bûr′kyə-lō′sĭs] *noun*, a disease due to the presence of small granular tumors in an organ marked by coughing

tuck [tŭk] *noun*, 1) a pleat, fold or gather, *verb*, 2) to wrap snugly

Tues-day [tōoz′dē] *noun*, the third day of the week

tuft [tŭft] *noun*, a cluster, a clump

tug [tŭg] *verb*, to jerk, to yank, to pull with force or effort

tu-i-tion [tōo-ĭsh′ən] *noun*, the price paid for instruction

tu-lip [tōō′lĭp] *noun*, a flower grown from a bulb in a variety of colors, in the shape of a cup

tulle [tōōl] *noun*, a thin, fine net of acetate, silk or rayon, often used for veils or a tutu

tum-ble [tŭm′bəl] *verb*, 1) to turn over and over 2) to fall down

tu-mult [tōō′mŭlt′] *noun*, commotion, a riot, noise

tu-mul-tu-ous [tōō-mŭl′chōō-əs] *adjective*, wild, chaotic

tu-na [tōō′nə] *noun*, a large fish that lives in the ocean

tun-dra [tŭn′drə] *noun*, the vast treeless plains in Siberia and arctic North America

tune [tōōn] *noun*, 1) musical notes arranged as a medley, *verb*, 2) to put the right amount of tension on a stringed instrument so that it gives a certain sound 3) to be in sync, to put in harmony

tung-sten [tŭng′stən] *noun*, a hard, brittle, whitish-gray metal with an extremely high melting point at 6100 degrees Fahrenheit

tun-nel [tŭn′əl] *noun*, 1) a long passageway dug underground, *verb*, 2) to dig, to burrow

tur-ban [tûr′bən] *noun*, a man's headdress having no brim

tur-bid [tûr′bĭd] *adjective*, muddy, having the sediment disturbed

tur-bine [tûr′bĭn] *noun*, a machine that uses the gas from liquid to turn a shaft

tur-bu-lence [tûr′byə-ləns] *noun*, 1) wind currents that move very quickly 2) confusion, excited activity

tur-bu-lent [tûr′byə-lənt] *adjective*, 1) agitated, violent, stormy 2) full of disorder

tu-reen [tōō-rēn′] *noun*, a deep table dish for holding soup

tur-key [tûr′kē] *noun*, a bird of the pheasant family, originally found wild in North America

tur-moil [tûr′moil′] *adjective*, a state of great confusion, agitation or disturbance

turn [tûrn] *noun*, 1) a chance or opportunity to participate 2) a bend, a twist or a bend in the road 3) a reversal, *verb*, 4) to cause to rotate or revolve 5) to change or to transform

tur-nip [tûr′nĭp] *noun*, a thick, edible, roundish root in the mustard family, eaten when boiled

tur-pen-tine [tûr′pən-tīn′] *noun*, a thin flammable oil made from certain pine trees used as a solvent to thin paint

tur-quoise [tûr′kwoiz′] *noun*, a bluish green or greenish gray mineral used as a gem

tur-tle [tûr′tl] *noun*, a reptile with a soft body protected by a hard shell covering, it carries his house on his back

tusk [tŭsk] *noun*, a long pointed tooth, as of an elephant or walrus

tu-tor [tōō′tər] *noun*, a private teacher

tweed [twēd] *noun*, a soft, flexible fabric made of wool

tweez-ers [twē′zərz] *noun*, *plural*, a pincer-like tool for picking up small things

twelfth [twĕlfth] *adjective*, the ordinal of twelve, written 12th

twelve [twĕlv] *noun, adjective*, the number 12, the number after eleven

twen-ti-eth [twĕn′tē-ĭth] *adjective*, the number 20 in order, 20th, the ordinal of 20

twen-ty [twĕn′tē] *adjective, noun*, the number 20, ten times two

twice [twīs] *adverb*, two times, in double amount or degree

twig [twĭg] *noun*, a small outshoot of a branch or stem

twi-light [twī′lĭt′] *noun*, the light as the sun sets from the west

twin [twĭn] *adjective*, 1) two of the same, matched 2) an identical couple 3) either of two offspring brought forth at birth

twine [twīn] *noun*, 1) a strong cord of threads twisted together, *verb*, 2) to twist together

twinge [twĭnj] *verb*, to feel a sharp physical or mental pain

twin-kle [twĭng′kəl] *verb*, to sparkle, to shimmer, to flicker

twins [twĭnz] *noun, plural*, two children born at the same time from the same mother

twirl [twûrl] *verb*, to whirl or spin in a circle, to rotate rapidly

twitch [twĭch] *verb*, to jerk or make spastic movements

two [tōō] *adjective, noun*, the number that follow one, written 2, one plus one

type [tīp] *noun*, 1) the letters in different fonts used to print words 2) category, sort, *verb*,

3) to use a keyboard to write words printed on a computer

type-writ-er [tīp′rī′tər] *noun*, an instrument for writing by means of type

ty-phoid [tī′foid′] *noun*, a fever which eats up the walls of the intestines causing internal bleeding

ty-phoon [tī-fōōn′] *noun*, a cyclone in the region of the Philippines or the China Sea

typ-i-cal [tĭp′ĭ-kəl] *adjective*, representing something by a model, characteristic

ty-rant [tī′rənt] *noun*, an absolute ruler who is usually cruel

U

u-biq-ui-tous [yōō-bĭk′wĭ-təs] *adjective*, being everywhere at the same time, omnipresent

UFO [yōō′ĕf-ō′] *noun*, **U**nidentified **F**lying **O**bject, a thing in the sky that seems too strange to be real

ug-ly [ŭg′lē] *adjective*, revolting to look at, unattractive

ul-cer [ŭl′sər] *noun*, a sore on the skin filled with pus and infection that is painful, a lesion

ul-te-ri-or [ŭl-tîr′ē-ər] *adjective*, intentionally concealed

ul-ti-mate [ŭl′tə-mĭt] *adjective*, 1) final, supreme 2) farthest

ul-ti-mate-ly [ŭl′tə-mĭt-lē] *adverb*, finally, at the end, totally

ul-ti-ma-tum [ŭl′tə-mā′təm] *noun*, a final proposition or condition offered to end a dispute

um-brage [ŭm′brĭj] *noun*, resentment, anger, a sense of injury or insult, offense

um-brel-la [ŭm-brĕl′ə] *noun*, a covering held in the hand as protection from the rain

um-pire [ŭm′pīr′] *noun*, the judge or referee in a baseball game

un-a-ble [ŭn-ā′bəl] *adjective*, not capable of doing something

un-alienable [ŭn-āl′yə-nə-bəl] *adjective*, cannot be taken away

u-nan-i-mous [yŏŏ-năn′ə-məs] *adjective*, being of one mind, showing complete agreement

u-nan-i-mous-ly [yŏŏ-năn′ə-məs-lē] *adverb*, with all voters voting the same way

un-as-sum-ing [ŭn′ə-sŏŏ′mĭng] *adjective*, modest, simple, plain

un-a-void-a-ble [ŭn′ə-voi′də-bəl] *adjective*, inevitable

un-bear-a-ble [ŭn-bâr′ə-bəl] *adjective*, not capable of being endured, intolerable

un-bri-dled [ŭn-brīd′ld] *adjective*, not restrained, uninhibited

un-can-ny [ŭn-kăn′ē] *adjective*, strange, mysterious, seeming to have a supernatural basis

un-cer-tain-ty [ŭn-sûr′tn-tē] *noun*, doubtfulness, not reliable

un-cle [ŭng′kəl] *noun*, the brother of one of your parents, or the husband of the sister of one of your parents

un-com-fort-a-ble [ŭn-kŭm′fər-tə-bəl] *adjective*, uneasy, causing discomfort

un-com-mon [ŭn-kŏm′ən] *adjective*, not usual, unique, odd

un-con-cern [ŭn′kən-sûrn′] *adjective*, indifference, lack of interest, freedom from anxiety

un-con-scion-a-ble [ŭn-kŏn′shə-nə-bəl] *adjective*, unscrupulous, something done that shows no conscience, excessive, unreasonable

un-con-scious [ŭn-kŏn′shəs] *adjective*, not knowing what is happening, lacking awareness

un-cov-er [ŭn-kŭv′ər] *verb*, 1) to take something from on top of something 2) to find out

un-der [ŭn′dər] *adjective*, 1) less than 2) working for or obeying, *preposition*, 3) below, beneath the surface

un-der-es-ti-mate [ŭn′dər-ĕs′tə-māt′] *verb*, to undervalue, to minimize

un-der-go [ŭn′dər-gō′] *verb*, 1) to experience 2) to suffer or endure

un-der-grad-u-ate [ŭn′dər-grăj′ŏŏ-ĭt] *noun*, a student at a college who has not received a bachelor's degree

un-der-ground [ŭn′dər-ground′] *adjective*, 1) in the recesses of the earth 2) in secrecy

un-der-growth [ŭn′dər-grōth′] *noun*, *no plural*, thickly growing plants underneath trees

un-der-line [ŭn′dər-līn′] *verb*, to put a line under a word or words

un-der-neath [ŭn′dər-nēth′] *adverb*, down from below

un-der-rate [ŭn′dər-rāt′] *verb*, to evaluate too low, to undervalue

un-der-stand [ŭn′dər-stănd′] *verb*, 1) to grasp the nature of 2) to know what something means

un-der-take [ŭn′dər-tāk′] *verb*, to take upon oneself as a task

un-der-tak-er [ŭn′dər-tā′kər] *noun*, one whose business is to take charge of funerals

un-der-tak-ing [ŭn′dər-tā′kĭng] *noun*, a duty, an obligation, a job, a task

un-der-wear [ŭn′dər-wâr′] *noun*, the garments worn next to the skin under outside clothing

un-der-write [ŭn′dər-rīt′] *verb*, to insure, to guarantee

un-do [ŭn-dōō′] *verb*, 1) to untie or unfasten 2) to reverse or annul

un-doubt-ed-ly [ŭn-dou′tĭd-lē] *adverb*, certainly, indeed

un-du-late [ŭn′jə-lāt′] *verb*, to move with a wave-like motion

un-earth [ŭn-ûrth′] *verb*, to dig up

un-eas-y [ŭn-ē′zē] *adjective*, a little afraid, worried, uncomfortable

un-em-ployed [ŭn′ĕm-ploid′] *adjective*, having no paid work

un-equal [ŭn-ē′kwəl] *adjective*, unmatched, unparalleled

un-e-quiv-o-cal [ŭn′ĭ-kwĭv′ə-kəl] *adjective*, plain, obvious

un-err-ing-ly [ŭn-ûr′ĭng-lē] *adverb*, correctly, precisely, infallibly, accurately

un-e-ven [ŭn-ē′vən] *adjective*, not level or flat, not uniform

un-ex-pect-ed [ŭn′ĭk-spĕk′tĭd] *adjective*, sudden, coming without warning, unforeseen

un-fair [ŭn-fâr′] *adjective*, unjust, unethical, biased, dishonest

un-faltering [ŭn-fôl′tər-ĭng] *adjective*, steadfast

un-fas-ten [ŭn-făs′ən] *verb*, to undo, to detach, to separate

un-fit [ŭn-fĭt′] *adjective*, made unsuitable, not prepared or adapted, not competent

un-fold [ŭn-fōld′] *verb*, 1) to open out 2) to explain, to evolve

un-for-tu-nate [ŭn-fôr′chə-nĭt] *adjective*, unlucky, regrettable

un-for-tu-nate-ly [ŭn-fôr′chə-nĭt-lē] *adverb*, having bad luck, unsuccessful

un-friend-ly [ŭn-frĕnd′lē] *adjective*, not nice, unkind

un-grate-ful [ŭn-grāt′fəl] *adjective*, thankless

un-hap-py [ŭn-hăp′ē] *adjective*, dissatisfied, not content, sad

un-health-y [ŭn-hĕl′thē] *adjective*, 1) ill, sickly 2) food or habits that make a person feel tired

u-ni-form [yōō′nə-fôrm′] *adjective*, 1) unvaried, regular, constant, *noun*, 2) clothes worn for a special job or school

u-ni-form-i-ty [yōō′nə-fôrm′ĭ-tē] *noun*, sameness, consistency, identical with others

u-ni-fy [yōō′nə-fī′] *verb*, to combine, to integrate, to connect

u-ni-lat-er-al [yōō′nə-lăt′ər-əl] *adjective*, one sided

un-im-ag-i-na-tive [ŭn-ĭ-măj′ə-nə-tĭv] *adjective*, uninspired, common, everyday

un-impeach-a-ble [ŭn′ĭm-pē′chə-bəl] *adjective*, blameless and exemplary

unimportant

un-im-por-tant [ŭn′ĭm-pôr′tnt]
adjective, 1) trivial, trite
2) extraneous, irrelevant

un-in-hib-it-ed [ŭn′ĭn-hĭb′ĭ-tĭd]
adjective, not restrained by
convention, free and easy

un-in-tel-li-gi-ble
[ŭn′ĭn-tĕl′ĭ-jə-bəl] *adjective*, not
capable of being understood

un-ion [yōōn′yən] *noun*, 1) a
coming together 2) a group of
people who join to support a
cause 3) a combination, **Union**
4) the army fighting for northern
states during the Civil War

u-nique [yōō-nēk′] *adjective*, single
in kind or excellence

u-ni-son [yōō′nĭ-sən] *noun*, unity
of pitch, complete accord

u-nit [yōō′nĭt] *noun*, 1) a complete
set 2) a specific amount, a form
of measurement 3) a single
entity

u-nite [yōō-nīt′] *verb*, to join, to
connect, to put together as one

United States
[yōō-nī′tĭd-stāts-ŭv-ə-mĕr′ĭ-kə]
noun, the country made up of
the land between the Pacific
Ocean and the Atlantic Ocean,
between Canada and Mexico,
including Alaska and Hawaii, the
capital, is the District of
Columbia

u-ni-ver-sal [yōō′nə-vûr′səl]
adjective, mutual understanding,
totally accepted everywhere

u-ni-verse [yōō′nə-vûrs′] *noun*, all
existing things including the
earth and all of space

u-ni-ver-si-ty [yōō′nə-vûr′sĭ-tē]
noun, an institution of higher

learning empowered to confer
degrees in the arts and sciences

un-just [ŭn-jŭst′] *adjective*, unfair,
biased, unworthy

un-kempt [ŭn-kĕmpt′] *adjective*, a
messy, uncared for appearance

un-kind [ŭn-kīnd′] *adjective*,
indifferent, unfeeling, rude

un-known [ŭn-nōn′] *adjective*,
1) unfamiliar 2) unexplored

un-less [ŭn-lĕs′] *adjective*, under
different conditions, or else

un-like [ŭn-līk′] *adjective*,
dissimilar, different

un-load [ŭn-lōd′] *verb*, 1) to take
something off a vehicle such as
cargo 2) to dispose of

un-luck-y [ŭn-lŭk′ē] *adjective*,
unsuccessful, unfortunate

un-mis-tak-a-ble [ŭn′mĭ-stā′kə-bəl]
adjective, clear, obvious

un-mis-take-a-bly
[ŭn′mĭ-stā′kə-blē] *adverb*,
undoubtedly, obviously

un-nec-es-sar-y [ŭn-nĕs′ĭ-sĕr′ē]
adjective, uncalled for, needless

un-ob-tru-sive [ŭn′əb-trōō′sĭv]
adjective, not noticeable

un-pleas-ant [ŭn-plĕz′ənt]
adjective, disagreeable

un-prec-e-dent-ed
[ŭn-prĕs′ĭ-dĕn′tĭd] *adjective*,
novel, unparalleled

un-pre-pare-ed [ŭn′prĭ-pârd′]
adjective, unaware, not ready

un-rav-el [ŭn-răv′əl] *verb*, to
untangle, to unwind, to unfold

un-rea-son-a-ble [ŭn-rē′zə-nə-bəl]
adjective, absurd, illogical, not
guided by sound judgment

un-re-li-a-ble [ŭn′rĭ-lī′ə-bəl] *adjective*, not dependable

un-ru-ly [ŭn-rōō′lē] *adjective*, disobedient, lawless

un-safe [ŭn-sāf′] *adjective*, hazardous, dangerous, risky

un-sat-is-fac-to-ry [ŭn-săt′ĭs-făk′tə-rē] *adjective*, not good enough, inadequate

un-scru-pu-lous [ŭn-skrōō′pyə-ləs] *adjective*, unprincipled, devious, deceptive

un-seem-ly [ŭn-sēm′lē] *adjective*, unbecoming, inappropriate

un-so-phis-ti-cat-ed [ŭn′sə-fĭs′tĭ-kā′tĭd] *adjective*, innocent, showing inexperience

un-stead-y [ŭn-stĕd′ē] *adjective*, 1) not safe 2) unsure, wavering

un-suit-a-ble [ŭn-sōō′tə-bəl] *adjective*, inappropriate, unsatisfactory, something that does not fit in, irregular

un-sure [ŭn-shŏŏr] *adjective*, uncertain, doubtful

un-ten-a-ble [ŭn-tĕn′ə-bəl] *adjective*, not able to be maintained or supported against criticism

un-ti-dy [ŭn-tī′dē] *adjective*, messy, cluttered, not orderly

un-tie [ŭn-tī′] *verb*, to unfasten a string or rope, to loosen

un-til [ŭn-tĭl′] *conjunction*, 1) up to the time that, or when, *preposition*, 2) up to the time of, as far as, before

un-to-ward [ŭn-tôrd′] *adjective*, unfortunate, annoying

un-true [ŭn-trōō′] *adjective*, false, incorrect, deceptive, disloyal

un-u-su-al [ŭn-yōō′zhōō əl] *adjective*, strange, odd

un-veil [ŭn-vāl′] *verb*, to remove the covering from something

un-well [ŭn-wĕl′] *adjective*, ill, sick, upset, ailing

un-wield-y [ŭn-wēl′dē] *adjective*, not easily carried, bulky

un-will-ing [ŭn-wĭl′ĭng] *adjective*, reluctant, resistant, averse

un-wind [ŭn-wīnd′] *verb*, 1) to undo something, to loosen 2) to relax, to get rid of tension

un-wise [ŭn-wīz′] *adjective*, not reasonable or sensible

un-wit-ting [ŭn-wĭt′ĭng] *adjective*, unintentional, not knowing

un-wrap [ŭn-răp′] *verb*, to remove the protective covering on a package or product

up [ŭp] *adverb*, 1) to put in a higher place, *preposition*, 2) to position something so that it is standing 3) toward

up-braid [ŭp-brād′] *verb*, to scold, to reproach, to criticize

up-heav-al [ŭp-hē′vəl] *noun*, an eruption, a change, a quake

up-hold [ŭp-hōld′] *verb*, to maintain, to support, to sustain

up-hol-ster-y [ŭp-hōl′stə-rē] *noun*, furniture with stuffing, springs, covers or trim

up-lift [ŭp-lĭft′] *noun*, 1) upgrade, restoration, *verb*, 2) to raise up 3) to improve socially or morally

up-on [ə-pŏn′] *adverb*, 1) on, *preposition*, 2) on top of something

upper

up-per [ŭp′ər] *adjective*, 1) in a higher position, further up 2) the part of the shoe above the sole

up-right [ŭp′rīt′] *adjective*, 1) straight up and down 2) righteous, honest, honorable

up-set [ŭp-sĕt′] *verb*, 1) to knock over 2) to make unhappy or worried 3) to spoil something that was planned, to disrupt

up-stairs [ŭp′stârz′] adverb, 1) up the steps, *noun*, *plural*, 2) the next level, the upper level

up-ward [ŭp′wərd] *adjective*, to a higher place or position

u-ra-ni-um [yŏŏ-rā′nē-əm] *noun*, a rare radioactive, metallic element found in certain minerals used in nuclear weapons

ur-ban [ûr′bən] *noun*, characteristic of a city

ur-bane [ûr-bān′] *adjective*, suave, refined, elegant, sophisticated, charming, courteous, polite

ur-chin [ûr′chĭn] *noun*, a needy or mischievous child

urge [ûrj] *noun*, 1) a strong wish, *verb*, 2) to try to make someone do something, to push along

ur-gen-cy [ûr′jən-sē] *adverb*, calling for quick action

ur-gent [ûr′jənt] *adjective*, pressing, calling for immediate attention or action, insistent

us [ŭs] *pronoun*, the person who is speaking, and the others mentioned in the sentence, the objective case of **we**

us-age [yŏŏ′sĭj] *noun*, a long continued practice, a custom

use [yŏŏz] *noun*, 1) a purpose, *verb*, 2) to find a purpose for something, to utilize

used to [yŏŏst-tŏŏ] *adjective*, 1) knowing what something or someone is like, familiar 2) something done in the past but is not done now

use-ful [yŏŏs′fəl] *adjective*, helpful, serviceable

use-less [yŏŏs′lĭs] *adjective*, hopeless, valueless, vain

u-su-al [yŏŏ′zhŏŏ-əl] *adjective*, something that happens regularly, not uncommon

u-su-al-ly [yŏŏ′zhŏŏ-əl-lē] *adverb*, almost always, frequently

u-surp [yŏŏ-sûrp′] *verb*, to seize, to take possession of by force or without right or authority

u-sur-pa-tion [yŏŏ′sər-pā′shən] *noun*, the act of seizing power and rank of another

u-su-ry [yŏŏ′zhə-rē] *noun*, interest in excess of a legal rate

Utah [yŏŏ′tô′] *noun*, one of the 50 United States, the capital is Salt Lake City. The state flower of **Utah** is the sego lily; and the motto is "Industry."

u-ten-sil [yŏŏ-tĕn′səl] *noun*, a tool, a dining instrument

u-til-i-ty [yŏŏ-tĭl′ĭ-tē] *noun*, a company that provides products such as gas, water, or electricity

u-ti-lize [yŏŏt′l-īz′] *verb*, to make use of something

ut-most [ŭt′mōst′] *adjective*, the furthest or most extreme

u-to-pi-a [yŏŏ-tō′pē-ə] *noun*, heaven on earth, an ideal place

ut-ter [ŭt′ər] *verb*, to speak

ut-ter-ance [ŭt′ər-əns] *noun*, vocal expression, articulation, speech

ut-ter-ly [ŭt′ər-lē] *adverb*, completely, entirely, without doubt, totally, absolutely

V

va-can-cy [vā′kən-sē] *noun*, 1) emptiness 2) an unfilled place, job or position 3) an opening

va-cant [vā′kənt] *adjective*, empty

va-cate [vā′kāt′] *verb*, 1) to leave, to empty, to abandon 2) to annul

va-ca-tion [vā-kā′shən] *noun*, time away from work for rest, amusement, and relaxation

vac-ci-nate [văk′sə-nāt′] *verb*, to inoculate with a vaccine as a form of protection

vac-ci-na-tion [văk′sə-nā′shən] *noun*, a remedy which is the injection of the virus itself

vac-cine [văk-sēn] *noun*, a weakened germ of a virus used to protect a person from the often fatal or debilitating effects of a virus

vac-Il-late [văs′ə-lāt′] *verb*, to change one's mind often, to waffle, to waver

vac-u-um [văk′yoo-əm] *noun*, 1) the absolute absence of matter 2) an appliance used to rid carpets of dust and litter 3) a kind of bottle that keeps liquids hot or cold, such as a thermos

vag-a-bond [văg′ə-bŏnd′] *noun*, a tramp, an outcast, a vagrant

va-grant [vā′grənt] *adjective*, 1) wandering, begging, *noun*, 2) one who wanders around outside from place to place

vague [vāg] *adjective*, not clearly understood, indistinct

vain [vān] *adjective*, 1) conceited, too proud of the way one looks 2) fruitless, unsuccessful

vale [vāl] *noun*, valley, lowland

val-en-tine [văl′ən-tīn′] *noun*, a love poem, a card expressing love and affection

val-et [văl′ĭt] *noun*, a manservant who takes care of the clothes and personal needs of his employer

val-iant [văl′yənt] *adjective*, full of courage, brave

val-iant-ly [văl′yənt-lē] *adverb*, unafraid of danger, boldly, courageously, bravely

val-id [văl′ĭd] *adjective*, 1) significant, sound 2) legally effective or binding

val-i-date [văl′ĭ-dāt′] *verb*, to confirm, to ratify, to substantiate

va-lid-i-ty [vŭ-lĭ′dĭ-tē] *noun*, confirmation that proves something is what it says it is

val-ley [văl′ē] *noun*, a region of low land situated between hills or mountains, a dale

val-or [văl′ər] *noun*, bravery, courage, boldness

val-u-a-ble [văl′yoo-ə-bəl] *adjective*, precious, of considerable worth, costly

val-ue [văl′yoo] *noun*, 1) what something is worth, what someone will pay, *verb*, 2) to

355

think that something is important and meaningful 3) to say how much something is worth on the market, to rate

valve [vălv] *noun*, any device by which the flow of liquid, air, or gas may be regulated

van [văn] *noun*, a small, covered truck carrying goods or passengers or animals

van-dal-ism [văn′dl-ĭz′əm] *noun*, willful destruction of property

vane [vān] *noun*, a piece of metal or cloth set up high to swing with the wind to tell which way the wind is blowing

va-nil-la [və-nĭl′ə] *noun*, a flavoring made from the beans of the vanilla plant

van-ish [văn′ĭsh] *verb*, to disappear, to dissolve, to end

van-i-ty [văn′ĭ-tē] *noun*, 1) too proud of oneself 2) a small table for putting on makeup

van-quish [văng′kwĭsh] *verb*, to conquer, to overcome, to overpower in battle

van-tage [văn′tĭj] *noun*, the position giving an advantage

va-por [vā′pər] *noun*, 1) condensation 2) a substance in the gaseous state such as fog

var-i-a-ble [vâr′ē-ə-bəl] *noun*, changeable, liable to vary

var-i-ance [vâr′ē-əns] *noun*, degree of difference, disagreement

var-i-a-tion [vâr′ē-ā′shən] *noun*, a change in form, position, or condition

vari-ed [vâr′ēd] *adjective*, changing, various, mixed

va-ri-e-ty [və-rī′ĭ-tē] *noun*, many different things, assortment

var-i-ous [vâr′ē-əs] *adjective*, , several different kinds, diverse

var-nish [vär′nĭsh] *noun*, 1) a liquid that hardens into a clear, tough film, *verb*, 2) to paint with a clear protective sealant

var-si-ty [vär′sĭ-tē] *adjective*, a principal team in sports representing a school or college

var-y [vâr′ē] *verb*, to change

vase [vās] *noun*, a decorated pot for cut flowers or for decoration

vas-sal [văs′əl] *noun*, 1) in feudalism, one who held land of a superior lord 2) one subordinate to another

vast [văst] *adjective*, limitless, expansive, very great in size, quantity or degree, widespread

vat [văt] *noun*, a large container for liquids, a barrel

vaude-ville [vôd′vĭl′] *noun*, a theatrical performance with music, songs, and dance

vault [vôlt] *noun*, 1) a room constructed to protect its contents, *verb*, 2) to jump or leap over with hands holding a pole

veer [vîr] *verb*, to change in direction or position

veg-e-ta-ble [vĕj′tə-bəl] *noun*, an edible plant grown for food

veg-e-tate [vĕj′ĭ-tāt′] *verb*, to live in a monotonous, inactive way

veg-e-ta-tion [vĕj′ĭ-tā′shən] *noun*, plant growth, foliage, flowers

ve-he-ment [vē′ə-mənt] *adjective*, fervent, impassioned, fiery

ve-hi-cle [vē′ĭ-kəl] *noun*, something used to carry or transport people or things

veil [vāl] *noun*, a piece of transparent material worn to hide or protect the face, a cover

vein [vān] *noun*, 1) one of the vessels which conveys blood back to the heart 2) a crack in a rock filled with mineral matter

vel-lum [vĕl′əm] *noun*, a form of paper made out of animal skin that will hold ink

ve-loc-i-ty [və-lŏs′ĭ-tē] *noun*, speed, rapidity of motion

vel-vet [vĕl′vĭt] *noun*, *no plural*, a type of cloth with a soft surface

ven-det-ta [vĕn-dĕt′ə] *noun*, revenge for a dispute

ven-dor [vĕn′dər] *noun*, someone who sells something, a merchant

ve-neer [və-nîr′] *noun*, 1) a thin layer of finished wood, glued on a cheap surface 2) a superficial show of quality

ven-er-a-ble [vĕn′ər-ə-bəl] *adjective*, deserving high respect

ven-er-a-tion [vĕn′ə-rā′shən] *noun*, deep, respectful love, adoration

venge-ance [vĕn′jəns] *noun*, retribution, revenge, reprisal

ve-ni-al [vē′nē-əl] *adjective*, capable of being forgiven

ven-i-son [vĕn′ĭ-sən] *noun*, deer meat used for food

venn di-a-gram [vĕn-dĭ′ə-grăm′] *noun*, a tool to indicate the relationship of elements

ven-om [vĕn′əm] *noun*, poison stored in some animals

ven-om-ous [vĕn′ə-məs] *adjective*, poisonous, deadly, toxic

vent [vĕnt] *noun*, a small opening or outlet to let out air

ven-ti-late [vĕn′tl-āt′] *verb*, to cause fresh air to circulate through, to admit air into

ven-tril-o-quist [vĕn-trĭl′ə-kwĭst] *noun*, one who can make a voice seem to come from another person or thing

ven-ture [vĕn′chər] *noun*, 1) doing something that involves the risk of a loss *verb*, 2) to dare to go, to do or to say

ven-tur-ous [vĕn′chər-əs] *adjective*, daring, bold

ven-ue [vĕn′yōō] *noun*, an agreed place where something will take place, the scene of an event

ve-rac-i-ty [və-răs′ĭ-tē] *noun*, habitual observance of truth, truthfulness, accuracy

ve-ran-da [və-răn′də] *noun*, a long porch with a roof along the outside of a building

verb [vûrb] *noun*, the word expressing action in a sentence

ver-ba-tim [vər-bā′tĭm] *adverb*, word for word, literal

ver-bi-age [vûr′bē-ĭj] *noun*, a pompous array of words

ver-dant [vûr′dnt] *adjective*, green with vegetation

ver-dict [vûr′dĭkt] *noun*, the decision of a jury given to the court, a judgment or decision

verge [vûrj] *noun*, 1) the point beyond which something begins,

verify

the brink, *verb*, 2) to tend to incline

ver-i-fy [vĕr′ə-fī′] *verb*, to prove to be true, to confirm, to ascertain

ver-i-si-mil-i-tude [vĕr′ə-sĭ-mĭl′ĭ-to͞od′] *noun*, appearance of truth, likelihood

ver-i-ty [vĕr′ĭ-tē] *noun*, truth, reality, a statement that is true

ver-mi-cel-li [vûr′mĭ-chĕl′ē] *noun*, a pasta dried in a slender tube form, like spaghetti

ver-mic-u-lite [vər-mĭk′yə-līt′] *noun*, slivers of mica that expand when heated, used for insulation, and water absorption

Ver-mont [vər-mŏnt′] *noun*, one of the 50 United States located in New England, the capital is Montpelier. The state flower of **Vermont** is the red clover, the motto is "Freedom and unity."

ver-nal [vûr′nəl] *adjective*, of or occurring in spring

ver-sa-tile [vûr′sə-təl′] *adjective*, having the capability of doing many different things

verse [vûrs] *noun*, 1) lines of writing which have a rhythm often a rhyme 2) a few lines of this from a longer piece called a poem 3) a small part of the Bible, the Jewish Koran, or Talmud

ver-sion [vûr′zhən] *noun*, a description from a particular point of view, a standpoint

ver-sus [vûr′səs] *preposition*, against, in contrast with

ver-te-brate [vûr′tə-brĭt] *noun*, an animal with a backbone

ver-tex [vûr′tĕks′] *noun*, 1) the point where two planes intersect to form an angle 2) the highest point

ver-ti-cal [vûr′tĭ-kəl] *adjective*, straight up and down, perpendicular to the horizon

verve [vûrv] *noun*, enthusiasm, liveliness, energy, vitality

ver-y [vĕr′ē] *adjective*, 1) the same 2) the right or appropriate one, *adverb*, 3) to emphasize the word to make it stronger

ves-sel [vĕs′əl] *noun*, 1) a hollow utensil for holding anything 2) a boat 3) a channel for delivering blood, a vein or capillary

vest [vĕst] *noun*, a sleeveless top worn over a shirt with pockets

ves-ti-bule [vĕs′tə-byo͞ol′] *noun*, foyer, lobby, entry way

ves-tige [vĕs′tĭj] *noun*, a trace or visible sign of something gone

vet-er-an [vĕt′ər-ən] *noun*, experienced, old in service, especially in military life

vet-er-i-nar-i-an [vĕt′ər-ə-nâr′ē-ən] *noun*, a doctor who specializes in animal health and surgery

ve-to [vē′tō] *noun*, 1) a denial, a rejection, *verb*, 2) to deny, to reject, to turn down

vex [vĕks] *verb*, to annoy, to distress, to irritate

vex-a-tion [vĕk-sā′shən] *noun*, irritation, a cause of trouble or disquiet, annoyance

vi-a [vī′ə, vē′ə] *preposition*, traveling through, by way of

vi-a-ble [vī'ə-bəl] *adjective*, capable of maintaining life

vi-a-duct [vī'ə-dŭkt'] *noun*, a bridge for carrying a road, resting on masonry arches, often in water to allow boats through

vi-and [vī'ənd] *noun*, food, provision

vi-brate [vī'brāt'] *verb*, 1) to shake, to quiver or tremble 2) to echo, to reverberate, to move to and fro

vi-bra-tion [vɪ-brā'shən] *noun*, the movement caused by shaking

vi-car-i-ous-ly [vī-kâr'ē-əs-lē] *adverb*, acting as a substitute, done in place of another

vice [vīs] *noun*, a weakness, personal faults or foibles

vice president [vīs'prĕz'ĭ-dənt] *noun*, the person chosen to replace the president

vi-cin-i-ty [vĭ-sĭn'ĭ-tē] *noun*, the region near or close by

vi-cious [vĭsh'əs] *adjective*, corrupt, wicked, mean

vi-cis-si-tude [vĭ-sĭs'ĭ-tōod'] *noun*, change or succession from one thing to another

vic-tim [vĭk'tĭm] *noun*, 1) someone who suffers from an illness or action 2) a person who is deceived or cheated

vic-to-ri-ous [vĭk-tôr'ē-əs] *adjective*, conquering, triumphant in war, winning

vic-to-ry [vĭk'tə-rē] *noun*, winning a contest or a battle, a triumph

vict-uals [vĭt'lz] *noun*, *plural*, food for human beings, provisions

vid-e-o [vĭd'ē-ō'] *noun*, film for showing on a television set

vie [vī] *verb*, to contend, to strive in competition, to struggle

view [vyōo] *noun*, 1) ideas, beliefs, opinion 2) something you see

vig-i-lance [vĭj'ə-ləns] *noun*, watchfulness, caution

vi-gnette [vĭn-yĕt'] *noun*, a scene depicting a moment in time

vig-or [vĭg'ər] *noun*, physical or mental strength, stamina, energy

vig-or-ous [vĭg'ər-əs] *adjective*, exhibiting strength, powerful, energetic, intense, robust

vig-or-ous-ly [vĭg'ər-əs-lē] *adverb*, very fast, with a great deal of energy, healthy, spirited

vile [vīl] *adjective*, disgusting

vil-i-fy [vĭl'ə-fī'] *verb*, to slander, to malign, to slur, to revile

vil-lage [vĭl'ĭj] *noun*, a group of houses that form a community, usually smaller than a town

vil-lain [vĭl'ən] *noun*, one capable or guilty of great crimes, a rascal

vin-di-cate [vĭn'dĭ-kāt'] *verb*, to support or maintain as true, to free from suspicion

vin-dic-tive [vĭn-dĭk'tĭv] *adjective*, revengeful, retaliatory, mean

vine [vīn] *noun*, a name given to some plants with climbing stems

vin-e-gar [vĭn'ĭ-gər] *noun*, a sour liquid made by fermentation of wine or cider

vi-o-late [vī'ə-lāt'] *verb*, 1) to break the rules, to disregard as a promise 2) to break in on

vi-o-lence [vī'ə-ləns] *noun*, commotion, disorder, outrage, brutality, intense force

violent

vi-o-lent [vī′ə-lənt] *adjective*, brutal, vicious, forceful, rough

vi-o-lent-ly [vī′ə-lənt-lē] *adverb*, harshly, with destructive force

vi-o-let [vī′ə-lĭt]) *adjective*, 1) the color that is a combination of blue and red, *noun*, 2) a purple flower that grows wild as a ground cover

vi-o-lin [vī′ə-lĭn′] *noun*, one of the small stringed instruments played with a bow

vi-o-lin-ist [vī′ə-lĭn′ĭst] *noun*, a person who plays a violin

vi-per [vī′pər] *noun*, a poisonous snake, a serpent

vir-gin [vûr′jĭn] *adjective*, pure, chaste, unused

Vir-gin-i-a [vər-jĭn′yə] *noun*, one of the 50 United States located in the Southeast, the capital is Richmond. The state flower of **Virginia** is the flowering dogwood and the motto is "Ever thus to tyrants."

vir-ile [vîr′əl] *adjective*, manly, showing masculine strength

vir-tue [vûr′chōō] *noun*, uprightness, moral excellence

vir-tu-ous [vûr′chōō-əs] *adjective*, righteous, honest, moral

vi-rus [vī′rəs] *noun*, an group of infectious submicroscopic agents that cause various diseases in plants or animals

vis-age [vĭz′ĭj] *noun*, the face, countenance, or look of a person

vis-cer-al [vĭs′ər-əl] *adjective*, felt in one's inner organs

vis-cous [vĭs′kəs] *adjective*, thick and sticky in consistency

vise [vīs] *noun*, a clamp, clasp, grip

vis-i-ble [vĭz′ə-bəl] *adjective*, as seen by the eye, in view

vi-sion [vĭzh′ən] *noun*, 1) something imagined, as in a dream, 2) a look into the future, unusual foresight 3) eyesight

vi-sion-ar-y [vĭzh′ə-nĕr′ē] *noun*, existing only in the imagination

vis-it [vĭz′ĭt] *noun*, 1) a social call, an appointment, *verb*, 2) to go to see someone 3) to chat casually

vis-i-tor [vĭz′ĭ-tər] *noun*, one who comes and goes to see another

vi-sor [vī′zər] *noun*, a sunshade or shield to block out glare

vi-su-al [vĭzh′ōō-ə-l] *adjective*, of or used in seeing, pleasing to the sight

vi-su-al-ize [vĭzh′ōō-ə-līz′] *verb*, 1) to imagine 2) to see something in the mind

vi-tal [vīt′l] *adjective*, necessary to life, important, indispensable

vi-tal-i-ty [vī-tăl′ĭ-tē] *noun*, spirit, energy, the capacity to develop

vi-ta-min [vī′tə-mĭn] *noun*, nutrients that give the body nourishment to help balance the metabolism

vi-ti-ate [vĭsh′ē-āt′] *verb*, to spoil the effect of something, to make less effective or imperfect

vit-ri-ol-ic [vĭt′rē-ŏl′ĭk] *adjective*, mean, causing bad feelings

vi-tu-per-a-tive [vī-tōō′pər-ə-tĭv] *adjective*, abusive, scolding

vi-va-cious [vĭ-vā′shəs] *adjective*, lively, sprightly, energetic

viv-id [vĭv′ĭd] *adjective*, easy to see, life-like, bright, colorful

vo-cab-u-lar-y [vō-kăb′yə-lĕr′ē] *noun*, the words of a language

vo-cal [vō′kəl] *adjective*, 1) voiced, outspoken 2) expressed by singing 3) relating to the sound made by the voice

vo-ca-tion [vō-kā′shən] *noun*, a job, employment or occupation, a profession

vogue [vōg] *adjective*, fashionable, in style, popular

voice [vois] *noun*, 1) the sounds coming through a person's mouth made by the respiratory system 2) to express an idea in writing or speaking

void [void] *noun*, an empty space

vol-ca-no [vŏl-kā′nō] *noun*, an opening in the earth's crust where melted rock, lava, gases, and ash are thrust onto the land

vo-li-tion [və-lĭsh′ən] *noun*, the act of making a conscious choice

vol-ley [vŏl′ē] *noun*, 1) a barrage, a bombardment, *verb*, 2) to return a ball before it hits the ground

vol-ley-ball [vŏl′ē-bôl′] *noun*, *no plural*, a game in which a large ball is knocked back and forth across a net, by hand

volt [vōlt] *noun*, 1) a measure of electricity, the unit of electromotive force 2) a turning movement of a horse, sideways around a center

vol-ume [vŏl′yōōm] *noun*, 1) a single book, *no plural*, 2) the space something occupies 3) the amount of sound something makes, loudness of a sound

vo-lu-mi-nous [və-lōō′mə-nəs] *adjective*, bulky, large

vol-un-tar-y [vŏl′ən-tĕr′ē] *adjective*, proceeding from the will, to give or perform freely

vol-un-teer [vŏl′ən-tîr′] *noun*, 1) one who offers his services of his own free will, *verb*, 2) to give freely of your time

vo-lup-tu-ous [və-lŭp′chōō-əs] *adjective*, shapely, full in form

vom-it [vŏm′ĭt] *noun*, 1) something from the stomach that comes out of the mouth, *verb*, 2) to throw up, to regurgitate food

vo-ra-cious [vô-rā′shəs] *adjective*, 1) someone who has a large appetite 2) exceedingly eager

vor-tex [vôr′tĕks′] *noun*, whirlpool, a whirling mass of water

vote [vōt] *noun*, 1) a choice made during an election, *verb*, 2) to decide by general consent

vot-er [vōt′ər] *noun*, a person registered to participate in an election

vouch [vouch] *verb*, to certify, to assure, to provide proof

vouch-er [vou′chər] *noun*, a document exchangeable for certain goods or services

vow [vou] *noun*, 1) an oath, a solemn pledge, *verb*, 2) to promise something important

vow-el [vou′əl] *noun*, the letters – **a,e,i,o,u**, and sometimes **y**

voy-age [voi′ĭj] *noun*, a long journey by sea, water, air, or space from one place to another

vul-gar [vŭl′gər] *adjective*, rude or rough in behavior, taste, etc, lacking good taste or refinement

vul-ner-a-ble [vŭl′nər-ə-bəl] *adjective*, capable of being easily harmed or injured

vul-ture [vŭl′chər] *noun*, a large bird that eats as a scavenger of dead animals

W

wade [wād] *verb*, to walk through a substance such as water or snow

waf-fle [wŏf′əl] *noun*, 1) a cake baked in an iron skillet, *verb*, 2) to change one's mind often

waft [wäft] *verb*, to move or be moved lightly over water or air, to drift

wag [wăg] *verb*, to move or cause to move briskly from side to side or up and down

wage [wāj] *noun*, 1) money paid for work or services, salary, *verb*, 2) to carry on (a war or campaign)

wa-ger [wā′jər] *noun*, the amount of money or property risked in an uncertain event, a bet

wag-on [wăg′ən] *noun*, a vehicle with four wheels that is pulled

waif [wāf] *noun*, a homeless child or animal, an orphan

wail [wāl] *verb*, to make a long cry showing sadness or pain, to sob

waist [wāst] *noun*, the part of the body between the ribs and the hips where the stomach is

wait [wāt] *noun*, 1) a time of anticipation, *verb*, 2) to expect, to anticipate, to be ready

wait-er [wā′tər] *noun*, a person hired to serve meals

waive [wāv] *verb*, to give up temporarily, to yield

waiv-er [wā′vər] *noun*, the act of giving up a right or claim

wake [wāk] *noun*, 1) the ripple of waves created by the motion of a boat, *verb*, 2) to stop sleeping, to be aroused from sleep

walk [wôk] *noun*, 1) a journey on foot, *verb*, 2) to take one step at a time, to proceed along

wall [wôl] *noun*, 1) a partition made of bricks or stone that separates space 2) one of the sides of a room or building, *verb*, 3) to divide, to partition

wal-let [wŏl′ĭt] *noun*, a small flat case for money, cards, etc., usually carried in a pocket

wal-low [wŏl′ō] *verb*, to tumble in the mud 2) move slowly

wall-pa-per [wôl′pā′pər] *noun*, *no plural*, decorative paper used to cover walls of a room

wal-nut [wôl′nŭt′] *noun*, 1) a hard, dark-colored wood, valuable for furniture 2) the nut or seed from the walnut tree in a hard shell

wal-rus [wôl′rəs] *noun*, a sea animal like the sea lion and the seal, with outside ears and tusks

waltz [wôlts] *verb*, a dance with four beats per measure

wand [wŏnd] *noun*, a baton, a rod, a fairy's magic stick

wan-der [wŏn′dər] *verb*, 1) to travel from place to place with no plan or purpose in mind 2) to slip easily off the subject

wane [wān] *verb*, to grow gradually smaller or decrease in strength, to decline, to dwindle

wan-gle [wăng′gəl] *verb*, to bring about by manipulation or trickery, to scheme

want [wŏnt] *noun*, 1) a need, lack, not having something necessary, *verb*, 2) to desire or feel a need for something, to require

wan-ton [wŏn′tən] *adjective*, unruly, wild, excessive

war [wôr] *noun*, a deadly conflict

war-ble [wôr′bəl] *verb*, to sing melodiously, to trill as a bird

ward [wôrd] *noun*, 1) a child in the care of someone other than his family 2) a district, a division, *verb*, 3) to fend off, to avert

war-den [wôrd′n] *noun*, the chief administrator of a prison

ward-robe [wôr′drōb′] *noun*, a closet of clothes

ware [wâr] *noun*, a product, merchandise, stock

ware-house [wâr′hous′] *noun*, a storehouse for wares or goods

war-i-ly [wâr′ĭ-lē] *adverb*, in a watchful and suspicious way

warm [wôrm] *adjective*, 1) a temperature between hot and cold, moderately hot, *verb*, 2) to add heat to make something no longer cold

warmth [wôrmth] *noun*, 1) friendship, 2) bodily heat

warn [wôrn] *verb*, 1) to inform someone that something bad will happen or of impending danger 2) to admonish, to exhort

warn-ing [wôr′nĭng] *noun*, the act of telling someone to proceed with caution, notification

warp [wôrp] *verb*, 1) to twist out of shape, to distort 2) to pervert

war-rant [wôr′ənt] *noun*, 1) a written request by a judge to make an arrest, *verb*, 2) to be sure of something, to justify

war-ran-ty [wôr′ən-tē] *noun*, a guarantee that a contract will be carried out by a manufacturer

war-ri-or [wôr′ē-ər] *noun*, a man engaged in war, a soldier

wart [wôrt] *noun*, a small growth or lump that looks like a blemish on skin often caused by a virus

war-y [wâr′ē] *adjective*, very cautious, on guard, watchful

was [wŭz] *verb*, *past tense* of **be**, used in the 3rd singular, **he**, **she** or **it**

wash [wŏsh] *noun*, 1) a batch of clothes that are to be or have been washed, *verb*, 2) to clean with soap and water

wash-er [wŏsh′ər] *noun*, 1) a machine for washing clothes or dishes 2) a round piece of metal put under a bolt to reinforce it

Wash-ing-ton [wŏsh′ĭng-tən] *noun*, one of the 50 United States located in the Northwest, the capital is Olympia. The state flower of **Washington** is the coast rhododendron and the motto is "By and by."

wasn't

wasn't [wŭz′ənt] the *contraction* of the words **was** and **not**

wasp [wŏsp] *noun*, a flying insect like a bee, the female inflicts the sting

waste [wāst] *adjective*, 1) useless, *noun*, 2) anything discarded that is not considered useful, *verb*, 3) to throw away, to spend or use carelessly, to squander

waste-ful [wāst′fəl] *adjective*, squandering or spending in a needless manner

waste-wa-ter [wāst′wô′tər] *noun*, water that has been used either to manufacture a product or in the home, which requires treatment and purification before it can be used again

watch [wŏch] *noun*, 1) a small clock worn on the wrist or hung from a chain, *verb*, 2) to observe, to look at attentively 3) to guard, to be on the lookout

wa-ter [wô′tər] *noun*, 1) a molecule made of one oxygen atom and two hydrogen atoms, that covers 75% of the earth's surface, *verb*, 2) to moisten or soak with water 3) to dilute

wa-ter-fall [wô′tər-fôl′] *noun*, a cascade of water coming down from a precipice or cliff

wa-ter-way [wô′tər-wā′] *noun*, a body of water that ships can use

wa-ter-wheel [wô′tər-hwēl] *noun*, a wheel turned by water running against or falling on paddles or steps, used as a source of power

watt [wŏt] *noun*, a measure of electrical power equivalent to one joule per second

wave [wāv] *noun*, 1) a breaker, a surge, surf, *verb*, 2) to greet

wa-ver [wā′vər] *verb*, 1) to be unsteady and show signs of falling or giving way 2) to be indecisive

wax [wăks] *noun*, a substance made from fats and oils that melts when heated

way [wā] *noun*, 1) the manner, custom, style 2) means, process 3) a passage, a road

way-ward [wā′wərd] *adjective*, unruly, disobedient, willful

we [wē] *plural, pronoun*, referring to one or more people, including oneself and others

weak [wēk] *adjective*, not strong, fragile, feeble, lacking strength

weak-ness [wēk′nĭs] *noun*, inclination, tendency

wealth [wĕlth] *noun*, riches, abundance of property

wealth-y [wĕl′thē] *adjective*, rich

wean [wēn] *verb*, 1) to accustom a baby not to nurse 2) to give up a cherished activity or habit

weap-on [wĕp′ən] *noun*, an instrument used for attack or defense in combat

wear [wâr] *noun*, 1) the diminished value caused by use, *verb*, 2) to put on, to carry on the body or over the body 3) to exhibit a certain expression on the face 4) to diminish through friction 5) to cause someone to be weary or exhausted 6) to impair by use

wear-y [wîr′ē] *adjective*, 1) tired, fatigued, physically or mentally exhausted 2) bored or resigned

weath-er [wĕth′ər] *noun*, 1) the condition of the atmosphere with regard to temperature, moisture, wind, etc., *verb*, 2) to endure the elements and the conditions outside in the atmosphere

weath-er-ing [wĕth′ər-ĭng] *noun*, the effects of the elements such as wind and water on rock surfaces, and homes or buildings

weave [wēv] *verb*, 1) to interlace threads into cloth 2) to wind or curve in and out

web [wĕb] *noun*, an entanglement, a mesh, an intricate network

web-li-og-ra-phy [wĕb′lē-ŏg′rə-fē] a bibliography of Internet sites used for research

we'd [wēd] the *contraction* of the words **we** and **would**

wed [wĕd] *verb*, to join in marriage

wed-ding [wĕd′ĭng] *noun*, the ceremony when two people are married

wedge [wĕj] *noun*, 1) a flat edge used to split objects or to lift them up 2) a chunk or a block of something, *verb*, 3) to force something to split apart 4) to press in closely, to cramp

Wednes-day [wĕnz′dē, -dā′] *noun*, the fourth day of the week

weed [wēd] *noun*, 1) an unwanted or unwelcome plant, *verb*, 2) to remove as being undesirable

week [wēk] *noun*, the seven days between Sunday and Saturday

weep [wēp] *verb*, 1) to cry, to shed tears 2) to grieve, to mourn 3) to exude liquid

weigh [wāt] *verb*, to measure the heaviness of someone or something by use of a scale

weight [wāt] *noun*, 1) the force with which a body is attracted to the earth or other celestial bodies 2) how heavy a thing is

weight-less [wāt′lĭs] *adjective*, having little or no weight

weird [wîrd] *adjective*, strange

wel-come [wĕl′kəm] *verb*, to receive gladly or hospitably

weld [wĕld] *verb*, 1) to join or connect by fusing two metals with heat 2) to unite

wel-fare [wĕl′fâr′] *noun*, assistance from the government, a state of well-being, health, happiness

well [wĕl] *adjective*, 1) healthy, strong, fit, *adverb*, 2) in a thoroughly manner, *noun*, 3) a narrow, deep hole made in the ground to reach water, oil, or natural gas, *verb*, 4) to rise to the surface and flow out

welt [wĕlt] *noun*, a large blister caused by heat or a beating

went [wĕnt] past participle of **go**

were [wûr] *past tense* of the *verb* **to be** used with **we**, **you** and **they**

west [wĕst] *noun*, the direction in which the sunsets

west-ern [wĕs′tərn] *adjective*, of or typical of Europe and the Americas

West Vir-gin-i-a [wĕst- vər-jĭn′yə] *noun*, one of the 50 United

States, located in the Southeast, the capital is Charleston. The state flower of **West Virginia** is the great rhododendron, and the motto is "Mountaineers are always free."

wet [wĕt] *adjective*, 1) covered with water, moistened, *verb*, 2) to soak with water

wet-lands [wĕt'lăndz'] *noun*, *plural*, a habitat of swamps and marshes for wildlife

whale [hwāl] *noun*, the largest animal in the sea, it is not a fish, it feeds its young with milk

wharf [hwôrf] *noun*, a dock along a shore where boats moor and wait to load or unload

what [hwŏt, hwŭt, wôt] *adjective*, 1) used to ask about the identity of a person, object, or matter 2) how remarkable, *adverb*, 3) how, in what way? *pronoun*, 4) which thing, an event, etc. 5) used to ask a question

what-ev-er [hwŏt-ĕv'ər] *pronoun*, anything that, so what

what's [hwŏts] the *contraction* of the words **what** and **is**

wheat [hwēt] *noun*, one of the cereal plants used to make flour

whee-dle [hwēd'l] *verb*, to coax

wheel [hwēl] *noun*, 1) a circular frame or disk attached to an axis that rolls, *verb*, 2) to move on rollers or wheels, to turn

wheel-bar-row [hwēl'băr'ō] *noun*, a hand cart with three wheels

when [hwĕn] *adverb*, at what time

when-ev-er [hwĕn-ĕv'ər] *adjective*, any time, no matter when

where [hwâr] *adverb*, 1) to or toward a certain place 2) at or in what place

wher-ev-er [hwâr-ĕv'ər] *adjective*, at or any place at all

whet [hwĕt] *verb*, 1) to sharpen by friction 2) to stimulate, to stir

wheth-er [hwĕth'ər] *conjunction*, used to express two choices

which [hwĭch] *noun*, the one, that

while [hwīl] *noun*, a period of time

whim-per [hwĭm'pər] *verb*, to pout, to whine, to cry

whim-si-cal [hwĭm'zĭ-kəl] *adjective*, capricious, given to fanciful notions, playful

whine [hwīn] *verb*, 1) to make a high and sad sound 2) to complain in an annoying manner

whip [hwĭp] *noun*, 1) an instrument made with a handle attached to a long lash made of leather or rope used to hit animals, *verb*, 2) to strike with a lash, to flog 3) to beat to a froth 4) to defeat

whirl [hwûrl] *verb*, to move or make something move around and around very fast

whisk [hwĭsk] *noun*, 1) a cooking utensil used to mix ingredients, *verb*, 2) to move quickly

whisk-er [hwĭs'kər] *noun*, 1) hair growing on the sides of a man's face 2) one of the long stiff hairs that grow near the mouth of dogs, cats, rats, etc.

whis-per [hwĭs'pər] *noun*, 1) a murmur, *verb*, 2) to speak very softly, to murmur quietly

whis-tle [hwĭs'əl] *noun*, 1) an instrument that makes a shrill,

wind

musical sound, *verb*, 2) to make a clear, high-pitched sound by forcing breath through the teeth or by pursing the lips, or using a device

white [hwīt] *adjective*, the color of snow, the absence of pigment

whit-tle [hwĭt′l] *verb*, 1) to shape by carving or sculpting 2) to reduce gradually, to diminish

who [hoo] *pronoun*, 1) the person or people 2) that 3) what persons?

who-ev-er [hoo-ĕv′ər] *pronoun*, any one that

whole [hōl] *adjective*, 1) total, complete, *noun*, 2) the total amount of a thing or entity

whole-some [hōl′səm] *adjective*, sound, healthy, beneficial

whom [hoom] *pronoun*, objective case for **who**

whose [hooz] *pronoun*, of whom, possessive case of who

why [hwı] *adverb*, 1) for what reason or purpose, *noun*, 2) the cause or interaction

wick [wĭk] *noun*, the string in a candle or oil lamp that burns the flame, the fuse

wick-ed [wĭk′ĭd] *adjective*, evil, very bad, sinful, vicious

wide [wīd] *adjective*, 1) broad, expansive 2) to be fully open or accessible, of great scope

wid-ow [wĭd′ō] *noun*, a woman whose husband is dead

wid-ow-er [wĭd′ō-ər] *noun*, a man whose wife is dead

width [wĭdth] *noun*, the distance across, the breadth

wield [wēld] *verb*, to control, to sway, to manage, to use

wife [wīf] *noun*, *plural*, **wives,** a married woman

wig [wĭg] *noun*, a covering for the head, hair from other people or animals, a toupee, a hairpiece

wig-gle [wĭg′əl] *verb*, to move around, to squirm

wild [wīld] *adjective*, untamed or domesticated, a natural state

wil-der-ness [wĭl′dər-nĭs] *noun*, a tract of land undeveloped and uninhabited by people

wild-life [wīld′līf′] *noun*, any species of animals living in their natural habitat

will [wĭl] *noun*, 1) power in the mind or character, what we want to do 2) a declaration by a person concerning their estate, *verb*, 3) used with other verbs to show something is going to happen 4) used in questions when asking to do something

will-ful [wĭl′fəl] *adjective*, 1) determined, intentional, deliberate 2) obstinate, stubborn

will-ing [wĭl′ĭng] *adjective*, ready, given or done gladly

wil-low [wĭl′ō] *noun*, a tree with long drooping branches

wilt [wĭlt] *verb*, 1) to wither, to lose freshness 2) to lose strength

wil-y [wī′lē] *adjective*, sly, clever

win [wĭn] *verb*, 1) to achieve victory over others 2) to receive an award for a performance

wind [wĭnd] *noun*, 1) currents of air moving quickly with force, [wīnd] *verb*, 2) to wrap around over and

window

over 3) to turn round and round, to move in curves and bends, not a straight line

win-dow [wĭn′dō] *noun*, 1) a pane of glass 2)an opening with a transparent cover that allows light in

win-dow-sill [wĭn′dō-sĭl′] *noun*, a shelf or ledge below a window

wine [wīn] *noun*, an alcoholic drink made from fermented grapes

wing [wĭng] *noun*, 1) one of the two limbs of a bird or insect with which it flies 2) a side projection of an airplane 3) an extension of a building

wink [wĭngk] *noun*, 1) one eye closed and one eye open as a gesture of approval, *verb*, 2) to close and open one eye quickly

win-now [wĭn′ō] *verb*, to sift, to separate good parts from bad

win-some [wĭn′səm] *adjective*, agreeable, gracious, engaging

win-ter [wĭn′tər] *noun*, the first season of the year, between autumn and spring, when the earth is farthest from the sun

wipe [wīp] *verb*, to make dry or clean with a cloth

wire [wīr] *noun*, 1) a metal thread or strand, *verb*, 2) to connect

Wis-con-sin [wĭs-kŏn′sĭn] *noun*, one of the 50 United States located in the North, the capital city is Madison. The state flower of **Wisconsin** is the violet, and the motto is "Forward."

wis-dom [wĭz′dəm] *noun*, learning and the capacity to use it

wise [wīz] *adjective*, showing good judgment, intelligent

wish [wĭsh] *noun*, 1) a desire that is beyond your reach, *verb*, 2) to desire, to long for, to want

wist-ful [wĭst′fəl] *adjective*, hopeful, yearning, longing

wit [wĭt] *noun*, cleverness, quickness of mind, ingenuity

witch [wĭch] *noun*, a woman who is believed to have magic powers

with [wĭth] *preposition*, 1) in the company of 2) using it 3) having 4) because of 5) next to

with-draw [wĭth-drô′] *verb*, to retreat, to go back on or to take back an offer, to remove

with-drawn [wĭth-drôn′] *adjective*, 1) taken back, removed 2) shy, introverted, retiring

with-er [wĭth′ər] *verb*, to shrivel, to fade, to lose freshness

with-hold [wĭth-hōld′] *verb*, to restrain, to hold back

with-in [wĭth-ĭn′] *adverb*, 1) inside, *preposition*, 2) in, not beyond

with-out [wĭth-out′] *adverb*, 1) outside, *preposition*, 2) lacking, wanting, not having

wit-ness [wĭt′nĭs] *noun*, 1) a spectator, an onlooker, a person who sees something, *verb*, 2) to see, to observe, to hear

wiz-ard [wĭz′ərd] *noun*, someone who performs sorcery and magic

woe [wō] *noun*, self-pity, sadness

wolf [wŏolf] *noun*, *plural*, **wolves**, a wild dog similar to a coyote

wom-an [wŏom′ən] *noun*, *plural*, **women**, a female, a lady

won-der [wŭn′dər] *noun*, 1) a feeling of surprise and

admiration, amazement, *verb*,
2) to express a wish to know

won-der-ful [wŭn′dər-fəl] *adjective*,
extra special, very good,
remarkable, marvelous

won-drous [wŭn′drəs] *adjective*,
amazing, astonishing, marvelous

wont [wônt] *adjective,* 1) apt or
likely, *noun,* 2) custom, habitual
procedure

won't [wōnt] the *contraction* of the
words **will** and **not**

wood [wŏŏd] *noun,* 1) the material
which comes from trees 2) a
small forest

wood-land [wŏŏd′lənd] *noun,* the
forest, land covered with trees

wood-peck-er [wŏŏd′pĕk′ər] *noun,*
a black and white bird with a red
head that pecks at wood with its
bill to find bugs to eat

wood-winds [wŏŏd′wĭndz′] *noun,*
musical instruments, usually
made of wood or metal, that you
blow into or use a reed to play
such as a clarinet

wool [wŏŏl] *noun,* the, soft, thick
fur on a sheep often used for
yarn or fabric

word [wûrd] *noun,* 1) speech,
sound or symbol used to
communicate 2) a message 3) a
promise 4) news, information

work [wûrk] *noun,* 1) a job, a form
of labor, a duty 2) a deed, an
accomplishment, *verb,* 3) to do a
job, to labor, to perform a duty

world [wûrld] *noun,* the Earth and
its people and all living things

world-ly [wûrld′lē] *adjective,*
known all over, cosmopolitan

worm [wûrm] *noun,* a thin creature
without bones or legs that lives
in the earth

wor-ry [wûr′ē] *verb,* to fret, to show
concern, to feel anxious

worse [wûrs] *adjective,* to go from
bad to a more damaged
condition, inferior, less good or
well

wor-ship [wûr′shĭp] *noun,*
1) ardent devotion, *verb,* 2) to
pray to or show reverence or
respect for someone

worth [wûrth] *noun,* the value or
importance of something

worth-less [wûrth′lĭs] *adjective,*
without worth, valueless

wor-thy [wûr′thē] *adjective,*
admirable, deserving, noble

would [wŏŏd] future perfect tense
of the *verb* **be**

wouldn't [wŏŏd′nt] the *contraction*
of the words **would** and **not**

wound [wōŏnd] *noun,* 1) an injury,
verb, 2) to injure, to hurt 3) to
disturb or upset someone

wrap [răp] *noun,* 1) a removable
covering, *verb,* 2) to cover with a
substance usually to protect
something, to enclose

wrath [răth] *noun,* anger, fury

wreak [rēk] *verb,* to produce rage,
to perpetuate, to inflict

wreath [rēth] *noun,* a ring of
flowers and leaves

wreck [rĕk] *noun,* 1) the remains of
something partially destroyed
like a car, building, or ship, *verb,*
2) to destroy or damage
something, to tear down

wren

wren [rĕn] *noun*, a brown-grey bird that lives in the south

wrench [rĕnch] *noun*, 1) a tool used to grip a bolt or a nut 2) a forcible twist, *verb*, 3) to pull or turn suddenly with a violent twist, to damage or injure

wrest [rĕst] *verb*, 1) to pull away 2) to take away by force, to seize, to wrench away

wres-tle [rĕs′əl] *verb*, to struggle hand to hand, to grapple

wretch [rĕch] *noun*, a vile, disgusting person

wrig-gle [rĭg′əl] *verb*, to squirm or twist like a worm, to writhe

wring [rĭng] *verb*, to twist, to squeeze by twisting tightly

wrin-kle [rĭng′kəl] *noun*, 1) a crease or fold, *verb*, 2) to pucker into folds and creases

wrist [rĭst] *noun*, the joint between the hand and the forearm

write [rīt] *verb*, to use an instrument such as a pencil to draw symbols to communicate

writer [rī′tər] *noun*, author, journalist, newsperson

writhe [rīth] *verb*, to twist or move as if in pain, to thrash

writ-ten [rĭt′n] *verb*, 1) *past participle* of **write**, *adjective*, 2) expressed in writing

wrong [rông] *adjective*, 1) in error, mistaken, incorrect 2) contrary to morality or laws

wrote [rōt] *verb*, *past tense* of **write**

Wy-o-ming [wī-ō′mĭng] *noun*, one of the 50 United States, located in the Northwest, the capital is Cheyenne. The state flower of **Wyoming** is the indian paintbrush and the motto is "Equal rights."

X

xeno-phile [zĕn′ə-fīl′] *noun*, one attracted to foreign people, manners, and styles

xeno-pho-bi-a [zĕn′ə-fō′bē-ə] *noun*, fear and hatred of foreigners or strangers

xy-lem [zī′ləm] *noun*, the system of a woody tissue that transports water in a plant

xy-log-ra-phy [zī-lŏg′rə-fē] *noun*, the art of engraving on wood

x-ray [ĕks′rā′] *noun*, 1) a photograph of a part of the inside of your body, *verb*, 2) to take a picture of the inside of the body

xy-lo-phone [zailəfoun] *noun*, a percussion instrument played by striking horizontal wooden bars with small wooden hammers

Y

yacht [yät] *noun*, a boat used either for private pleasure or as a vessel of state to convey people from one place to another

yam [yăm] *noun*, a sweet potato, the root of a potato plant

yard [yärd] *noun*, 1) a length of measure equal to 36 inches 2) the lawn or property around someone's house

yarn [yärn] *noun*, 1) knitting thread, spun wool 2) a story, a fictional account

yawn [yôn] *verb*, to open the mouth wide and breathe deeply as if tired or bored

year [yîr] *noun*, 365 days, or each cycle that the earth rotates around the sun divided, into 12 months, 52 weeks, and 4 seasons

yearn [yûrn] *verb*, to strive, to long for, to desire something

yeast [yēst] *noun*, a fungus which produces fermentation, used as a leavening agent in dough

yell [yĕl] *verb*, to shout, to scream

yel-low [yĕl′ō] *noun*, one of the primary colors, the color of corn

yen [yĕn] *noun*, a longing, an urge

yes [yĕs] *interjection*, a word of agreement, an affirmative reply

yes-ter-day [yĕs′tər-dā′] *adverb*, 1) on the day before today, *noun*, 2) the day before today

yet [yĕt] *conjunction*, 1) nevertheless, *adverb*, 2) until now

yield [yēld] *verb*, 1) to give way to, to submit, to surrender 2) to produce, to supply, to give forth

yo-gurt [yō′gərt] *noun*, a dairy product that is thicker than milk and has a slightly sour taste

yolk [yōk] *noun*, the yellow and principal part inside an egg

yon-der [yŏn′dər] *adjective*, distant, far-off, faraway

you [yo͞o] *pronoun*, the person or persons spoken to

you'd [yo͞od] the *contraction* of the words **you** and **would**

you'll [yo͞ol] the *contraction* of the words **you** and **will**

young [yŭng] *adjective*, the early stage of life, not old

young-ster [yŭng′stər] *noun*, a very young person, a child

your [yo͞or] *pronoun*, belonging to you

you're [yo͞or] the *contraction* of the words, **you** and **are**

yours [yo͞orz, yôrz, yōrz] *pronoun*, belonging to you

your-self [yo͞or-sĕlf′] *pronoun*, a form of you for emphasis when the object of a verb and the subject are the same

youth [yo͞oth] *noun*, a young person, an adolescent

Z

za-ny [zā′nē] *adjective*, crazy, whimsically comical

zap [zăp] *verb*, to hit a jolt of electricity or a powerful punch

zeal [zēl] *noun*, ardor in pursuit of anything, fervor, eagerness

zeal-ous [zĕl′əs] *adjective*, enthusiastic, eager, devoted, marked by passionate support for a person, cause or purpose

ze-bra [zē′brə] *noun*, an African wild animal like a horse which has brown and white stripes all over its body

ze-bu [zi′:bju] *noun*, *plural*, Zebu cattle, a domestic ox found in East Asia and India that has a large hump over the shoulders and loose skin with hanging folds

Zen Buddhism [zĕn- bo͞o′dĭz′əm] *noun*, a faith in which Buddha is the embodiment of the superior

zenith

man and followers seek
enlightenment through
meditation and intuition instead
of the traditional scriptures

ze-nith [zē'nĭth] *noun*, the point
directly overhead in the sky, the
summit, the highest point

zeph-yr [zĕf'ər] *noun*, a gentle
breeze, the west wind

zep-pe-lin [zĕp'əlin] *noun*, a type
of rigid airship resembling an
enormous balloon that has a
fabric covered rigid metal
framework and is driven through
the air by engines installed
underneath the airship

ze-ro [zîr'ō] *noun, plural,* **zeros** *or*
zeroes, 1) the numberical
symbol 0 2) nothing 3) the
temperature on a scale
indicated by this symbol

zest [zĕst] *noun*, feeling of
enjoyment, excitement

zig-zag [zĭg'zăg] *adjective*,
1) having a jagged course,
defined by sharp angles, adverb,
in or by a line that has short
sharp turns or angles *noun*,
3) one of a series of short sharp
turns or angles on a course,
verb, 4) to form into a line that
has short sharp turns or angles

zil-lion [zĭl'yən] *noun*, an
indeterminately huge number

zinc [zĭngk] *noun*, a bluish white
metallic element often mixed
with other metals

zin-nia [zĭn'iə] *noun*, a summer
garden flower grown for its long
lasting colorful flowers

zip code [zĭp'koud] *noun*, a nine
digit number that defines a
postal delivery area in the United
States

zip-per [zĭp'ər] *noun*, a slide
fastener for clothing, briefcases,
and other objects, with two sets
of interlocking teeth

zith-er [zĭth'ər] *noun*, a musical
instrument consisting of strings
stretched over a flat body that is
played by strumming or plucking
the strings with fingers or a pick

zo-diac [zō'diăk] *noun*, an
imaginary place in the heavens
that includes the paths of the
planets, divided into 12
constellations, each with their
own special name or symbol that
interact with each other

zom-bie [zŏm'bi] *noun*, a person
who is believed to have died and
been brought back to life without
speech or free will

zone [zōn] *noun*, a division of an
area that differs or is
distinguished in some respect
from adjoining areas

zoo [zoō] *noun*, a place where
different animals are kept for
people to look at

zo-ol-o-gy [zō-ŏl'ə-jē] *noun*, the
science of animals

zuc-chi-ni [zoō-kē'-nē] *noun*, a
type of squash with green skin,
shaped like a cylinder

zy-gote [zī'gōt'] *noun*, the single
cell resulting from the union of
an egg and a sperm

The Longest Word
in the English Language

Methionylglutaminylarginyltyrosylglutamylserylleucylphenylalanylalanyl-
glutaminylleucyllysylglutamylarginyllysylglutamylglysylalanylphenylalanylvalyl
Prolylphenylalanylyalylthreonylleucylglcycylaspartylprolylglicylisoleucy-
glutamylglutaminlserylleucyllysylisoleucylaspartylthreonylleucylisoleu-
cylglutamylalanylglyclyalanylaspartylalanylleucyglutamylleucylgluycyliso-
leucylproluylphenylalanyserylaspartyprolylleucelalanylaspartylglycylprolylthrec
Nylisolleucyglutaminylasparaginylalanythreonylleucylarginylalanylphenylalany
Lalanylalanylglycylvalylthreonylprolylalanylglutaminylcysteinylphenylalanyl-
Glglutamylmethionylleucyalanylleucylisoleucylarginylglutaminyllysylhistidyl-
Prolyuthreonylisoleucylprolylisoleucylglycylleucylleucylmethionyltyrosylalany-
Lasbaraginylleucylvalylphenylalanylsparaginyyllysylglycylisoleucylaspartyl-
Glutamylphenylalanylyltyrosylalanylglutaminylcysteinylglutamyllysylvalyl-
Glycylvalylspartylserylvalylleucylvallalanylaspartylvalylprolylvalvlglutaminyl-
Glutamylserylalanylprolylphenylalalrginylglutaminylalanylalanyllleucylarginyl-
Histidylasparaginylvalylalalprolylisoleucylphenylalanylisoleucylcysteinylproly-
Prolylaspartylalanylaspartylaspartyspartyleucylleucylarginylglutaminylisoleucy
Lalanylseryltyroslglycylarginylglycyltyrosylthreonyltyrosylleucylleucylsery-
larginlalanylglycylvalylthreonylglycylalanylglutamylaspartasparaginylarginyla-
nylalanylleucylprolylleucylaspaaginylhistidylleucylvalylalanyllysylleucylly-
sylglutamyltyrosylasparagimylalanylalanyprolylprolylleucylglutaminylglycyl-
phenlalanylglycylisoleyucylserylalanylprolylaspartylglutaminylvalyllysylalany-
lalanylisoleucylalspartylalanylglycylalanylalanylglycylalanylasoleucylse-
rylglycylserylalanylisoleucylbalyllysylisoleucylisoleucylglutamylglutaminyl-
histidylasparaginlylisoleucylglutamylpronylglu-0-tamyllysylmethionylluecy-
lalanylalanyoeucyllysylvalylphenylalanylvalylglutamilylprolylmethionylly-
sylalanylalanylthreonylarginylserine

This word consists of 1,909 letters. It is the term for the formula
C1289H2051N343O375S8. A Tryptophan synthetase A protein, an
enzyme that has 267 amino acids.

Weights and Measures

ENGLISH

Length

12 inches	=	1 foot
3 feet	=	1 yard
5280 feet	=	1 mile
1760 yards	=	1 mile

Area

144 square inches	=	1 square foot
9 square feet	=	1 square yard
4840 square yards	=	1 acre
640 acres	=	1 square mile

Volume

1728 cubic inches	=	1 cubic foot
27 cubic feet	=	1 cubic yard

Capacity (Dry)

2 pints	=	1 quart
8 quarts	=	1 peck
4 pecks	=	1 bushel

Capacity (Liquid)

16 fluid ounces	=	1 pint
2 pints	=	1 quart
4 quarts	=	1 gallon (8 pints)

Mass

16 ounces	=	1 pound (7000 grains)
20 cwt	=	1 ton
2000 lbs	=	1 ton

Troy Weights

12 ounces	=	1 pound (5760 grains)

Measures

16 fluid ounces	=	1 pint

METRIC

Length

1 millimeter	=	1000 micrometers
1 centimeter	=	10 millimeters
1 meter	=	1000 millimeters
1 meter	=	100 centimeters
1 kilometer	=	1000 meters

Area

1 square centimeter	=	100 square millimeters
1 square meter	=	10,000 square centimeters
1 square meter	=	1,000,000 square millimeters
1 square kilometer	=	1,000,000 square meters

Volume

1 milliliter	=	1 cubic centimeter
1 liter	=	1000 milliliters
1 liter	=	0.001 cubic meter

Mass

1 gram	=	1000 milligrams
1 kilogram	=	1000 grams
1 metric ton	=	1000 kilograms

Volume

1 cubic inch (in^3) = 16.39 cubic centimeters (cm^3)

1,728 cubic inches = 1 cubic foot = 0.02832 cubic meters (m^3)

27 cubic feet (ft^3) = 1 cubic yard (y^3) = 0.7646 cubic meters

Temperature Conversions

°C Celsius = (5/9 °F) –32   °F Fahrenheit = (9/5 °C) +32

Square Measure

100 sq. meters = 1 sq. decameter   = 119.6 sq. yards

100 sq. decameters = 1 sq. hectometer = 2.471 acres

100 sq. hectometers = 1 sq. kilometer = 0.386 sq. miles or
                                                          247.1 acres

Words for Large Numbers

Term	Calculation	# of Zeros
Ten	10 Ones	1
One Hundred	100 Ones	2
One Thousand	1,000 Ones	3
One Million	1,000 Thousands	6
One Billion	1,000 Millions	9
One Trillion	1,000 Billions	12
One Quadrillion	1,000 Trillions	15
One Quintillion	1,000 Quadrillions	18
One Sextillion	1,000 Quintillions	21
One Septillion	1,000 Sextillions	24
One Octillion	1,000 Septillions	27
One Nonillion	1,000 Octillions	30
One Decillion	1,000 Nonillion	33

Big Words

HIPPOPOTOMONSTRASESQUIPPEDALIOPHOBIA
The fear of long words.

PNEUMONOULTRAMICROSCOPICSILICOVOLCANOCONIOSIS
This word is forty-five letters and its definition is a lung disease caused by breathing in certain particles.

ANTITRANSUBSTANTIATIONALIST
One who doubts the validity of transubstantiation.

FLOCCINAUCINIHILIPILIFICATION
The estimation of a thing as worthless.

ANTIDISESTABLISHMENTARIANISM
Opposition of those who oppose the link between Church and State.

SUPERCALIFRAGILISTICEXPIALIDOCIOUS
The word to say when you don't know what to say.

Common Standard International Unit Symbols

km	=	kilometer
m	=	meter
dm	=	decimeter
cm	=	centimeter
mm	=	millimeter

$m^3 = L$	=	cubic decimeter = Liter
m^3	=	cubic meter
mg = T	=	megagram
kg	=	kilogram
g	=	gram
mg	=	milligram

ks	=	kilosecond
s	=	second
ms	=	millisecond
us	=	microsecond

Standard International Factor Prefixes

10^{24}	yotta	Y	septillion
10^{21}	zeta	Z	sextillion
10^{18}	exa	E	quintillion
10^{15}	peta	P	quadrillion
10^{12}	tera	T	trillion
10^{9}	giga	G	billion
10^{6}	mega	M	million
10^{3}	kilo	k	thousand
10^{2}	hecto	h	hundred
10^{1}	dcka	da	ten
10^{-1}	deci	d	tenth
10^{-2}	centi	c	hundredth
10^{-3}	milli	m	thousandth
10^{-6}	micro	u	millionth
10^{-9}	nano	n	billionth
10^{-12}	pico	p	trillionth
10^{-15}	femto	f	quadrillionth
10^{-18}	atto	a	quintillionth
10^{-21}	zepto	z	sextillionth
10^{-24}	yocto	y	septillionth

Periodic Table of the Elements

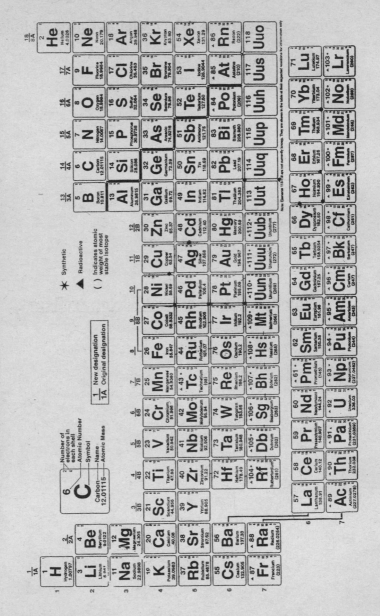

Multiplication Table

x	1	2	3	4	5	6	7	8	9	10	11	12
1	1	2	3	4	5	6	7	8	9	10	11	12
2	2	4	6	8	10	12	14	16	18	20	22	24
3	3	6	9	12	15	18	21	24	27	30	33	36
4	4	8	12	16	20	24	28	32	36	40	44	48
5	5	10	15	20	25	30	35	40	45	50	55	60
6	6	12	18	24	30	36	42	48	54	60	66	72
7	7	14	21	28	35	42	49	56	63	70	77	84
8	8	16	24	32	40	48	56	64	72	80	88	96
9	9	18	27	36	45	54	63	72	81	90	99	108
10	10	20	30	40	50	60	70	80	90	100	110	120
11	11	22	33	44	55	66	77	88	99	110	121	132
12	12	24	36	48	60	72	84	96	108	120	132	144

Prefix Table

one	uni	unicorn, unilateral, universal
	mon, mono	monarchy, monotone, monochromatic
two	bi	bicycle, binoculars, bifocals, biceps
three	tri	triangle, trilogy, triplet, triceratops
four	quad	quadruped, quadrant, quadruplet
	tetra	tetrahedron, tetrad, tetragon, tetrapod
five	penta	pentagon, pentathlon, pentagram,
	quint	quintuplet, quintet, quintile
six	hexa	hexagon, hexagram, hexahedron
	sext	sextuplet, sextet, sextuple
seven	hepta	heptathlon, heptad, heptahedron,
	sept	septuplet, septuple, septennial
eight	oct	octave, octopus, octagon, octogenarian
nine	nona *before a vowel*	nonagon, nonet
ten	deca *before a vowel*	decade, decibel, decimal, decimeter
hundred	cent	century, centennial, centigrade
thousand	kilo	kilogram, kilometer, kilobyte, kilobit,
million	mega	megabyte, megahertz, megaton
billion	giga	gigabyte, gigawatt, gigaflop, gigaton

Roman Numerals

I	1
II	2
III	3
IV	4
V	5
VI	6
VII	7
VIII	8
IX	9
X	10
XX	20
XXX	30
XL	40
L	50
LX	60
LXX	70
LXXX	80
XC	90
C	100
CC	200
CD	400
D	500
DC	600
DCC	700
DCCC	800
CM	900
M	1,000
$\overline{V}$	5,000
$\overline{X}$	10,000
$\overline{L}$	50,000
$\overline{C}$	100,000
$\overline{D}$	500,000
$\overline{M}$	1,000,000

The United States Flag

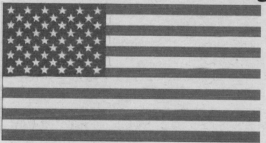

Betsey Ross sewed the first American flag in May, 1776. No one wrote down the story of why the United States decided to use stars and stripes when the design was chosen for our new nation. The only record indicates that the United States flag was first authorized by the Second Continental Congress on June 14, 1777. It said: "Resolved That the Flag of the United States be 13 stripes alternate red and white, that the Union be 13 stars white in a blue field representing a new constellation." This date is now observed as "Flag Day" throughout America.

The flag has changed 26 times since 1777 – each time a new state joined the Union. The flag was first modified in 1795 to have 15 stars and 15 stripes to include Vermont and Kentucky. In 1818, when Tennessee, Ohio, Louisiana, Indiana and Mississippi became states, the flag was designed to have 20 stars and 13 stripes. At that time, Congress decreed that the flag should have 13 stripes, and that new admissions to the Union should be recognized with a new star. Since then, the only change has been the adding of new stars. The 50-star flag was raised for the first time at 12:01 a.m. on July 4, 1960, at Fort McHenry National Monument, when Hawaii joined the Union.

Civics Lesson

Civics is the study of government and laws. Laws are made to maintain order, mutual respect and peace by defining people's rights and responsibilities toward society. They are agreed upon by people and enforced by governments. Most of the laws we use are based on English law, which was based on a judge's ruling in a dispute. This decision set a precedent and so any similar violation was considered with the most recent ruling used as a guide or common practice. These decisions created what is known as common law. Since these laws do not cover all situations, the elected officials created their own laws, known as statute law.

There are three branches of government: legislative, executive and judicial.

The **Legislative** branch: Congress, which is made up of the Senate and the House of Representatives. Congress has the power to make laws, declare war, charge taxes, borrow money, and regulate business between states. To become law, a bill must be approved by both houses, the Senate and the House of Representatives and signed by the President. The **Senate** consists of 100 members, two members from each state, who serve six year terms. The Senate approves or rejects appointees made by the President to his Cabinet and to the Supreme Court and treaties made by the President.

The **House of Representatives** consists of 435 members. Members are elected from their home state based on population. Each member is elected to serve a two year term. The House of Representatives has the responsibility for initiating all bills for raising taxes and determines how money collected in taxes is spent.

The **Executive** branch consists of the President, the Vice President and the members of the President's Cabinet. The President and Vice President are elected together to a four year term by the Electoral College after a popular vote. Duties of the President: chief executive, head of state, and commander-in-chief of the armed forces. The Vice President acts in the President's capacity if the President is unable to perform the duties of the office; presides over the Senate and only votes to break a tie. The Cabinet members are advisors to the President, appointed by the President. All members must be approved by the Senate. The Cabinet consists of the secretaries of the departments of State, Agriculture, Commerce, Defense, Education, Energy, Health and Human Services, Homeland Security, Housing and Urban Development, the Interior, Labor, Transportation, the Treasury, Veterans Affairs, and the Justice Department headed by the Attorney General.

The **Judicial** Branch is made up of the Supreme Court which consists of the Chief Justice and eight Associate Justices, who make the law of the land. Each justice is appointed for life terms after the President's nomination is approved by the Senate. The Supreme Court is responsible for hearing appeals of cases from the federal and state court systems and all matters between individual states. It presides over all cases affecting ambassadors to the United States and public ministers including the president. Courts handle two kinds of disputes: civil and criminal. A civil dispute is between two private citizens; a criminal case is dispute between an individual and the whole community. Our justice system is comprised of courts within 94 Federal Judicial Districts in the 50 states, Washington D.C. and Puerto Rico. Some of the other courts within the Federal Judicial Branch include the U.S. Tax Court, the U.S. Court of International Trade, 13 circuit Courts of Appeals: one Federal Circuit Court, 11 for the districts throughout the states, and one in the District of Columbia.

THE DECLARATION OF INDEPENDENCE
of the Thirteen Colonies In CONGRESS, July 4, 1776

The unanimous Declaration of the thirteen united States of America,

When in the Course of human events, it becomes necessary for one people to dissolve the political bands which have connected them with another, and to assume among the powers of the earth, the separate and equal station to which the Laws of Nature and of Nature's God entitle them, a decent respect to the opinions of mankind requires that they should declare the causes which impel them to the separation.

We hold these truths to be self-evident, that all men are created equal, that they are endowed by their Creator with certain unalienable Rights, that among these are Life, Liberty and the pursuit of Happiness. – That to secure these rights, Governments are instituted among Men, deriving their just powers from the consent of the governed, – That whenever any Form of Government becomes destructive of these ends, it is the Right of the People to alter or to abolish it, and to institute new Government, laying its foundation on such principles and organizing its powers in such form, as to them shall seem most likely to effect their Safety and Happiness. Prudence, indeed, will dictate that Governments long established should not be changed for light and transient causes; and accordingly all experience hath shown, that mankind are more disposed to suffer, while evils are sufferable, than to right themselves by abolishing the forms to which they are accustomed. But when a long train of abuses and usurpations, pursuing invariably the same Object evinces a design to reduce them under absolute.Despotism, it is their right, it is their duty, to throw off such Government, and to provide new Guards for their future security. --Such has been the patient sufferance of these Colonies; and such is now the necessity which constrains them to alter their former Systems of Government. The history of the present King of Great Britain [George III] is a history of repeated injuries and usurpations, all having in direct object the establishment of an absolute Tyranny over these States. To prove this, let Facts be submitted to a candid world.

He has refused his Assent to Laws, the most wholesome and necessary for the public good.

He has forbidden his Governors to pass Laws of immediate and pressing importance, unless suspended in their operation till his Assent should be obtained; and when so suspended, he has utterly neglected to attend to them.

He has refused to pass other Laws for the accommodation of large districts of people, unless those people would relinquish the right of Representation in the Legislature, a right inestimable to them and formidable to tyrants only.

He has called together legislative bodies at places unusual, uncomfortable, and distant from the depository of their public Records, for the sole purpose of fatiguing them into compliance with his measures.

He has dissolved Representative Houses repeatedly, for opposing with manly firmness his invasions on the rights of the people.

He has refused for a long time, after such dissolutions, to cause others to be elected; whereby the Legislative powers, incapable of Annihilation, have returned to the People at large for their exercise; the State remaining in the mean time exposed to all the dangers of invasion from without, and convulsions within.

He has endeavored to prevent the population of these States; for that purpose obstructing the Laws for Naturalization of Foreigners; refusing to pass others to encourage their migrations hither, and raising the conditions of new Appropriations of Lands.

He has obstructed the Administration of Justice, by refusing his Assent to Laws for establishing Judiciary powers.

He has made Judges dependent on his Will alone, for the tenure of their offices, and the amount and payment of their salaries.

He has erected a multitude of New Offices, and sent hither swarms of Officers to harass our people, and eat out their substance.

He has kept among us, in times of peace, Standing Armies without the consent of our legislatures.

He has affected to render the Military independent of and superior to the Civil power.

He has combined with others to subject us to a jurisdiction foreign to our constitution and unacknowledged by our laws; giving his Assent to their Acts of pretended Legislation:

For Quartering large bodies of armed troops among us:

For protecting them, by a mock Trial, from punishment for any Murders which they should commit on the Inhabitants of these States:

For cutting off our Trade with all parts of the world:

For imposing Taxes on us without our Consent:

For depriving us, in many cases, of the benefits of Trial by Jury:

For transporting us beyond Seas to be tried for pretended offences:

For abolishing the free System of English Laws in a neighbouring Province, establishing therein an Arbitrary government, and enlarging its Boundaries so as to render it at once an example and fit instrument for introducing the same absolute rule into these Colonies:

For taking away our Charters, abolishing our most valuable Laws, and altering fundamentally the Forms of our Governments:

For suspending our own Legislatures, and declaring themselves invested with power to legislate for us in all cases whatsoever.

He has abdicated Government here, by declaring us out of his Protection and waging War against us.

He has plundered our seas, ravaged our Coasts, burnt our towns, and destroyed the lives of our people.

He is at this time transporting large Armies of foreign Mercenaries to complete the works of death, desolation and tyranny, already begun with circumstances of Cruelty and perfidy scarcely paralleled in the most barbarous ages, and totally unworthy the Head of a civilized nation.

He has constrained our fellow Citizens taken Captive on the high Seas to bear Arms against their Country, to become the executioners of their friends and Brethren, or to fall themselves by their Hands.

He has excited domestic insurrections amongst us, and has endeavored to bring on the inhabitants of our frontiers, the merciless Indian Savages, whose known rule of warfare, is an undistinguished destruction of all ages, sexes and conditions.

In every stage of these Oppressions We have Petitioned for Redress in the most humble terms: Our repeated Petitions have been answered only by repeated injury. A Prince whose character is thus marked by every act which may define a Tyrant, is unfit to be the ruler of a free people.

Nor have We been wanting in attentions to our British brethren. We have warned them from time to time of attempts by their legislature to extend an unwarrantable jurisdiction over us. We have reminded them of the circumstances of our emigration and settlement here. We have appealed to their native justice and magnanimity, and we have conjured them by the ties of our common kindred to disavow these usurpations, which, would inevitably interrupt our connections and correspondence. They too have been deaf to the voice of justice and of consanguinity. We must, therefore, acquiesce in the necessity, which denounces our Separation, and hold them, as we hold the rest of mankind, Enemies in War, in Peace Friends.

We, therefore, the Representatives of the united States of America, in General Congress, Assembled, appealing to the Supreme Judge of the world for the rectitude of our intentions, do, in the Name, and by the Authority of the good People of these Colonies, solemnly publish and declare, That these United Colonies are, and of Right ought to be Free and Independent States; that they are Absolved from all Allegiance to the British Crown, and that all political connection between them and the State of Great Britain, is and ought to be totally dissolved; and that as Free and Independent States, they have full Power to levy War, conclude Peace, contract Alliances, establish Commerce, and to do all other Acts and Things which Independent States may of right do. And for the support of this Declaration, with a firm reliance on the protection of divine Providence, we mutually pledge to each other our Lives, our Fortunes and our sacred Honor.

The signers of the Declaration represented the new states as follows:

Connecticut:

Roger Sherman, Samuel Huntington, William Williams, Oliver Wolcott

Delaware:

Caesar Rodney, George Read, Thomas McKean

Georgia:

Button Gwinnett, Lyman Hall, George Walton

Maryland:

Samuel Chase, William Paca, Thomas Stone, Charles Carroll of Carrollton

Massachusetts:

John Hancock, Samuel Adams, John Adams, Robert Treat Paine, Elbridge Gerry

New Hampshire:

Josiah Bartlett, William Whipple, Matthew Thornton

New Jersey:

Richard Stockton, John Witherspoon, Francis Hopkinson, John Hart, Abraham Clark

New York:

William Floyd, Philip Livingston, Francis Lewis, Lewis Morris

North Carolina:

William Hooper, Joseph Hewes, John Penn

Pennsylvania:

Robert Morris, Benjamin Rush, Benjamin Franklin, John Morton, George Clymer, James Smith, George Taylor, James Wilson, George Ross

Rhode Island:

Stephen Hopkins, William Ellery

South Carolina:

Edward Rutledge, Thomas Heyward, Jr., Thomas Lynch, Arthur Middleton, Jr.

Virginia:

George Wythe, Richard Henry Lee, Thomas Jefferson, Benjamin Harrison, Thomas Nelson, Jr., Francis Lightfoot Lee, Carter Braxton

* * * *

The United States Constitution

Preamble

We the People . . .

of the United States, in Order to form a more perfect Union, establish Justice, insure domestic Tranquility, provide for the common defense, promote the general Welfare, and secure the Blessings of Liberty to ourselves and our Posterity, do ordain and establish this Constitution for the United States of America.

Article. I. *Adopted 1787*

Section. 1.
All legislative Powers herein granted shall be vested in a Congress of the United States, which shall consist of a Senate and House of Representatives.

Section. 2.
The House of Representatives shall be composed of Members chosen every second Year by the People of the several States, and the Electors in each State shall have the Qualifications requisite for Electors of the most numerous Branch of the State Legislature.

No Person shall be a Representative who shall not have attained to the Age of twenty five Years, and been seven Years a Citizen of the United States, and who shall not, when elected, be an Inhabitant of that State in which he shall be chosen.

Representatives and direct Taxes shall be apportioned among the several States which may be included within this Union, according to their respective Numbers, which shall be determined by adding to the whole Number of free Persons, including those bound to Service for a Term of Years, and excluding Indians not taxed, three fifths of all other Persons.

The actual Enumeration shall be made within three Years after the first Meeting of the Congress of the United States, and within every subsequent Term of ten Years, in such Manner as they shall by Law direct. The Number of Representatives shall not exceed one for every thirty Thousand, but each State shall have at Least one Representative; and until such enumeration shall be made, the State of New Hampshire shall be entitled to choose three, Massachusetts eight, Rhode Island and Providence Plantations one, Connecticut five, New York six, New Jersey four, Pennsylvania eight, Delaware one, Maryland six, Virginia ten, North Carolina five, South Carolina five and Georgia three.

When vacancies happen in the Representation from any State, the Executive Authority thereof shall issue Writs of Election to fill such Vacancies.

The House of Representatives shall chuse their Speaker and other Officers; and shall have the sole Power of Impeachment.

Section. 3.

The Senate of the United States shall be composed of two Senators from each State, chosen by the Legislature thereof, for six Years; and each Senator shall have one Vote.

Immediately after they shall be assembled in Consequence of the first Election, they shall be divided as equally as may be into three Classes. The Seats of the
Senators of the first Class shall be vacated at the Expiration of the second Year, of the second Class at the Expiration of the fourth Year, and of the third Class at the Expiration of the sixth Year, so that one third may be chosen every second Year; and if Vacancies happen by Resignation, or otherwise, during the Recess of the Legislature of any State, the Executive thereof may make temporary Appointments until the next Meeting of the Legislature, which shall then fill such Vacancies.

No person shall be a Senator who shall not have attained to the Age of thirty Years, and been nine Years a Citizen of the United States, and who shall not, when elected, be an Inhabitant of that State for which he shall be chosen.

The Vice President of the United States shall be President of the Senate, but shall have no Vote, unless they be equally divided.

The Senate shall chuse their other Officers, and also a President pro tempore, in the absence of the Vice President, or when he shall exercise the Office of President of the United States.

The Senate shall have the sole Power to try all Impeachments. When sitting for that Purpose, they shall be on Oath or Affirmation. When the President of the United States is tried, the Chief Justice shall preside: And no Person shall be convicted without the Concurrence of two thirds of the Members present.

Judgment in Cases of Impeachment shall not extend further than to removal from Office, and disqualification to hold and enjoy any Office of honor, Trust or Profit under the United States: but the Party convicted shall nevertheless be liable and subject to Indictment, Trial, Judgment and Punishment, according to Law.

Section. 4.

The Times, Places and Manner of holding Elections for Senators and Representatives, shall be prescribed in each State by the Legislature thereof; but the Congress may at any time by Law make or alter such Regulations, except as to the Places of chusing Senators.

The Congress shall assemble at least once in every Year, and such Meeting shall be on the first Monday in December, unless they shall by Law appoint a different Day.

Section. 5.

Each House shall be the Judge of the Elections, Returns and Qualifications of its own Members, and a Majority of each shall constitute a Quorum to do Business; but a smaller number may adjourn from day to day, and may be authorized to compel the Attendance of absent Members, in such Manner, and under such Penalties as each House may provide.

Each House may determine the Rules of its Proceedings, punish its Members for disorderly Behaviour, and, with the Concurrence of two-thirds, expel a Member.

Each House shall keep a Journal of its Proceedings, and from time to time publish the same, excepting such Parts as may in their Judgment require Secrecy; and the Yeas and Nays of the Members of either House on any question shall, at the Desire of one fifth of those Present, be entered on the Journal.

Neither House, during the Session of Congress, shall, without the Consent of the other, adjourn for more than three days, nor to any other Place than that in which the two Houses shall be sitting.

Section. 6.

The Senators and Representatives shall receive a Compensation for their Services, to be ascertained by Law, and paid out of the Treasury of the United States. They shall in all Cases, except Treason, Felony and Breach of the Peace, be privileged from Arrest during their Attendance at the Session of their respective Houses, and in going to and returning from the same; and for any Speech or Debate in either House, they shall not be questioned in any other Place.

No Senator or Representative shall, during the Time for which he was elected, be appointed to any civil Office under the Authority of the United States which shall have been created, or the Emoluments whereof shall have been increased during such time; and no Person holding any Office under the United States, shall be a Member of either House during his Continuance in Office.

Section. 7.

All bills for raising Revenue shall originate in the House of Representatives; but the Senate may propose or concur with Amendments as on other Bills.

Every Bill which shall have passed the House of Representatives and the Senate, shall, before it become a Law, be presented to the President of the United States; If he approve he shall sign it, but if not he shall return it, with his Objections to that House in which it shall have originated, who shall enter the Objections at large on their Journal, and proceed to reconsider it. If after such Reconsideration two thirds of that House shall agree to pass the Bill, it shall be sent, together with the Objections, to the other House, by which it shall likewise be reconsidered, and if approved by two thirds of that House, it shall become a Law. But in all such Cases the Votes of both Houses shall be determined by Yeas and Nays, and the Names of the Persons voting for and against the Bill shall be entered on the Journal of each House respectively. If any Bill shall not be returned by the President within ten Days (Sundays excepted) after it shall have been presented to him, the Same shall be a Law, in like Manner as if he had signed it, unless the Congress by their Adjournment prevent its Return, in which Case it shall not be a Law.

Every Order, Resolution, or Vote to which the Concurrence of the Senate and House of Representatives may be necessary (except on a question of Adjournment) shall be presented to the President of the United States; and before the Same shall take Effect, shall be approved by him, or being disapproved by him, shall be repassed by two thirds of the Senate and House of Representatives, according to the Rules and Limitations prescribed in the Case of a Bill.

Section. 8.
The Congress shall have Power To lay and collect Taxes, Duties, Imposts and Excises, to pay the Debts and provide for the common Defence and general Welfare of the United States; but all Duties, Imposts and Excises shall be uniform throughout the United States;

To borrow Money on the credit of the United States;

To regulate Commerce with foreign Nations, and among the several States, and with the Indian Tribes;

To establish an uniform Rule of Naturalization, and uniform Laws on the subject of Bankruptcies throughout the United States;

To coin Money, regulate the Value thereof, and of foreign Coin, and fix the Standard of Weights and Measures;

To provide for the Punishment of counterfeiting the Securities and current Coin of the United States;

To establish Post Offices and post Roads;

To promote the Progress of Science and useful Arts, by securing for limited Times to Authors and Inventors the exclusive Right to their respective Writings and Discoveries;

To constitute Tribunals inferior to the supreme Court;

To define and punish Piracies and Felonies committed on the high Seas, and Offences against the Law of Nations;

To declare War, grant Letters of Marque and Reprisal, and make Rules concerning Captures on Land and Water;

To raise and support Armies, but no Appropriation of Money to that Use shall be for a longer Term than two Years;

To provide and maintain a Navy;

To make Rules for the Government and Regulation of the land and naval Forces;

To provide for calling forth the Militia to execute the Laws of the Union, suppress Insurrections and repel Invasions;

To provide for organizing, arming, and disciplining the Militia, and for governing such Part of them as may be employed in the Service of the United States, reserving to the States respectively, the Appointment of the Officers, and the Authority of training the Militia according to the discipline prescribed by Congress;

To exercise exclusive Legislation in all Cases whatsoever, over such District (not exceeding ten Miles square) as may, by Cession of particular States, and the acceptance of Congress, become the Seat of the Government of the United States, and to exercise like Authority over all Places purchased by the Consent of the Legislature of the State in which the Same shall be, for the Erection of Forts, Magazines, Arsenals, dock-Yards, and other needful Buildings; And

To make all Laws which shall be necessary and proper for carrying into Execution the foregoing Powers, and all other Powers vested by this Constitution in the Government of the United States, or in any Department or Officer thereof.

Section. 9.
The Migration or Importation of such Persons as any of the States now existing shall think proper to admit, shall not be prohibited by the Congress prior to the Year one thousand eight hundred and eight, but a Tax or duty may be imposed on such Importation, not exceeding ten dollars for each Person.

The privilege of the Writ of Habeas Corpus shall not be suspended, unless when in Cases of Rebellion or Invasion the public Safety may require it.

No Bill of Attainder or ex post facto Law shall be passed.

No capitation, or other direct, Tax shall be laid, unless in Proportion to the Census or Enumeration herein before directed to be taken.

No Tax or Duty shall be laid on Articles exported from any State.

No Preference shall be given by any Regulation of Commerce or Revenue to the Ports of one State over those of another: nor shall Vessels bound to, or from, one State, be obliged to enter, clear, or pay Duties in another.

No Money shall be drawn from the Treasury, but in Consequence of Appropriations made by Law; and a regular Statement and Account of the Receipts and Expenditures of all public Money shall be published from time to time.

No Title of Nobility shall be granted by the United States: And no Person holding any Office of Profit or Trust under them, shall, without the Consent of the Congress, accept of any present, Emolument, Office, or Title, of any kind whatever, from any King, Prince or foreign State.

Section. 10.
No State shall enter into any Treaty, Alliance, or Confederation; grant Letters of Marque and Reprisal; coin Money; emit Bills of Credit; make any Thing but gold and silver Coin a Tender in Payment of Debts; pass any Bill of Attainder, ex post facto Law, or Law impairing the Obligation of Contracts, or grant any Title of Nobility.

No State shall, without the Consent of the Congress, lay any Imposts or Duties on Imports or Exports, except what may be absolutely necessary for executing it's inspection Laws: and the net Produce of all Duties and Imposts, laid by any State on Imports or Exports, shall be for the Use of the Treasury of the United States; and all such Laws shall be subject to the Revision and Controul of the Congress.

No State shall, without the Consent of Congress, lay any duty of Tonnage, keep Troops, or Ships of War in time of Peace, enter into any Agreement or Compact with another State, or with a foreign Power, or engage in War, unless actually invaded, or in such imminent Danger as will not admit of delay.

Articlo II. *Adopted 1787*

Section. 1.

The executive Power shall be vested in a President of the United States of America. He shall hold his Office during the Term of four Years, and, together with the Vice-President chosen for the same Term, be elected, as follows:

Each State shall appoint, in such Manner as the Legislature thereof may direct, a Number of Electors, equal to the whole Number of Senators and Representatives to which the State may be entitled in the Congress: but no Senator or Representative, or Person holding an Office of Trust or Profit under the United States, shall be appointed an Elector.

The Electors shall meet in their respective States, and vote by Ballot for two persons, of whom one at least shall not be an Inhabitant of the same State with themselves. And they shall make a List of all the Persons voted for, and of the Number of Votes for each; which List they shall sign and certify, and transmit sealed to the Seat of the Government of the United States, directed to the President of the Senate. The President of the Senate shall, in the Presence of the Senate and House of Representatives, open all the Certificates, and the Votes shall then be counted. The Person having the greatest Number of Votes shall be the President, if such Number be a Majority of the whole Number of Electors appointed; and if there be more than one who have such Majority, and have an equal Number of Votes, then the House of Representatives shall immediately chuse by Ballot one of them for President; and if no Person have a Majority, then from the five highest on the List the said House shall in like Manner chuse the President. But in chusing the President, the Votes shall be taken by States, the Representation from each State having one Vote; a quorum for this Purpose shall consist of a Member or Members from two-thirds of the States, and a Majority of all the States shall be necessary to a Choice. In every Case, after the Choice of the President, the Person having the greatest Number of Votes of the Electors shall be the Vice President. But if there should remain two or more who have equal Votes, the Senate shall chuse from them by Ballot the Vice President.

The Congress may determine the Time of chusing the Electors, and the Day on which they shall give their Votes; which Day shall be the same throughout the United States.

No person except a natural born Citizen, or a Citizen of the United States, at the time of the Adoption of this Constitution, shall be eligible to the Office of President; neither shall any Person be eligible to that Office who shall not have attained to the Age of thirty-five Years, and been fourteen Years a Resident within the United States.

In Case of the Removal of the President from Office, or of his Death, Resignation, or Inability to discharge the Powers and Duties of the said Office, the same shall devolve on the Vice President, and the Congress may by Law provide for the Case of Removal,

Death, Resignation or Inability, both of the President and Vice President, declaring what Officer shall then act as President, and such Officer shall act accordingly, until the Disability be removed, or a President shall be elected.

The President shall, at stated Times, receive for his Services, a Compensation, which shall neither be increased nor diminished during the Period for which he shall have been elected, and he shall not receive within that Period any other Emolument from the United States, or any of them.

Before he enter on the Execution of his Office, he shall take the following Oath or Affirmation:-- "I do solemnly swear (or affirm) that I will faithfully execute the Office of President of the United States, and will to the best of my Ability, preserve, protect and defend the Constitution of the United States."

Section. 2.
The President shall be Commander in Chief of the Army and Navy of the United States, and of the Militia of the several States, when called into the actual Service of the United States; he may require the Opinion, in writing, of the principal Officer in each of the executive Departments, upon any Subject relating to the Duties of their respective Offices, and he shall have Power to Grant Reprieves and Pardons for Offenses against the United States, except in Cases of Impeachment.

He shall have Power, by and with the Advice and Consent of the Senate, to make Treaties, provided two thirds of the Senators present concur; and he shall nominate, and by and with the Advice and Consent of the Senate, shall appoint Ambassadors, other public Ministers and Consuls, Judges of the supreme Court, and all other Officers of the United States, whose Appointments are not herein otherwise provided for, and which shall be established by Law: but the Congress may by Law vest the Appointment of such inferior Officers, as they think proper, in the President alone, in the Courts of Law, or in the Heads of Departments.

The President shall have Power to fill up all Vacancies that may happen during the Recess of the Senate, by granting Commissions which shall expire at the End of their next Session.

Section. 3.
He shall from time to time give to the Congress Information of the State of the Union, and recommend to their Consideration such Measures as he shall judge necessary and expedient; he may, on extraordinary Occasions, convene both Houses, or either of them, and in Case of Disagreement between them, with Respect to the Time of Adjournment, he may adjourn them to such Time as he shall think proper; he shall receive Ambassadors and other public Ministers; he shall take Care that the Laws be faithfully executed, and shall Commission all the Officers of the United States.

Section. 4.
The President, Vice President and all civil Officers of the United States, shall be removed from Office on Impeachment for, and Conviction of, Treason, Bribery, or other high Crimes and Misdemeanors.

Article III. *Adopted 1787*

Section. 1.
The judicial Power of the United States, shall be vested in one supreme Court, and in such inferior Courts as the Congress may from time to time ordain and establish. The Judges, both of the supreme and inferior Courts, shall hold their Offices during good Behavior, and shall, at stated Times, receive for their Services a Compensation which shall not be diminished during their Continuance in Office.

Section. 2.
The judicial Power shall extend to all Cases, in Law and Equity, arising under this Constitution, the Laws of the United States, and Treaties made, or which shall be made, under their Authority;-- to all Cases affecting Ambassadors, other public Ministers and Consuls; to all Cases of admiralty and maritime Jurisdiction;-- to Controversies to which the United States shall be a Party;-- to Controversies between two or more States; between a State and Citizens of another State;-- between Citizens of different States; between Citizens of the same State claiming Lands under Grants of different States, and between a State, or the Citizens thereof, and foreign States, Citizens or Subjects.

In all Cases affecting Ambassadors, other public Ministers and Consuls, and those in which a State shall be Party, the Supreme Court shall have original Jurisdiction. In all the other Cases before mentioned, the supreme Court shall have appellate Jurisdiction, both as to Law and Fact, with such Exceptions, and under such Regulations as the Congress shall make.

The Trial of all Crimes, except in Cases of Impeachment, shall be by Jury; and such Trial shall be held in the State where the said Crimes shall have been committed; but when not committed within any State, the Trial shall be at such Place or Places as the Congress may by Law have directed.

Section. 3.
Treason against the United States, shall consist only in levying War against them, or in adhering to their Enemies, giving them Aid and Comfort. No Person shall be convicted of Treason unless on the Testimony of two Witnesses to the same overt Act, or on Confession in open Court.

The Congress shall have Power to declare the Punishment of Treason, but no Attainder of Treason shall work Corruption of Blood, or Forfeiture except during the Life of the Person attainted.

Article. IV. *Adopted 1787*

Section. 1.
Full Faith and Credit shall be given in each State to the public Acts, Records, and judicial Proceedings of every other State. And the Congress may by general Laws prescribe the Manner in which such Acts, Records and Proceedings shall be proved, and the Effect thereof.

Section. 2.
The Citizens of each State shall be entitled to all Privileges and Immunities of Citizens in the several States.

A Person charged in any State with Treason, Felony, or other Crime, who shall flee from Justice, and be found in another State, shall on demand of the executive Authority of the State from which he fled, be delivered up, to be removed to the State having Jurisdiction of the Crime.

No Person held to Service or Labour in one State, under the Laws thereof, escaping into another, shall, in Consequence of any Law or Regulation therein, be discharged from such Service or Labour, but shall be delivered up on Claim of the Party to whom such Service or Labour may be due.

Section. 3.
New States may be admitted by the Congress into this Union; but no new State shall be formed or erected within the Jurisdiction of any other State; nor any State be formed by the Junction of two or more States, or parts of States, without the Consent of the Legislatures of the States concerned as well as of the Congress.

The Congress shall have Power to dispose of and make all needful Rules and Regulations respecting the Territory or other Property belonging to the United States; and nothing in this Constitution shall be so construed as to Prejudice any Claims of the United States, or of any particular State.

Section. 4.
The United States shall guarantee to every State in this Union a Republican Form of Government, and shall protect each of them against Invasion; and on Application of the Legislature, or of the Executive (when the Legislature cannot be convened) against domestic Violence.

Article. V. *Adopted 1787*

The Congress, whenever two thirds of both Houses shall deem it necessary, shall propose Amendments to this Constitution, or, on the Application of the Legislatures of two thirds of the several States, shall call a Convention for proposing Amendments, which, in either Case, shall be valid to all Intents and Purposes, as part of this Constitution, when ratified by the Legislatures of three fourths of the several States, or by Conventions in three fourths thereof, as the one or the other Mode of Ratification may be proposed by the Congress; Provided that no Amendment which may be made prior to the Year One thousand eight hundred and eight shall in any Manner affect the first and fourth Clauses in the Ninth Section of the first Article; and that no State, without its Consent, shall be deprived of its equal Suffrage in the Senate.

Article. VI. *Adopted 1787*

All Debts contracted and Engagements entered into, before the Adoption of this Constitution, shall be as valid against the United States under this Constitution, as under the Confederation.

This Constitution, and the Laws of the United States which shall be made in Pursuance thereof; and all Treaties made, or which shall be made, under the Authority of the United States, shall be the supreme Law of the Land; and the Judges in every State shall be bound thereby, any Thing in the Constitution or Laws of any State to the Contrary notwithstanding.

The Senators and Representatives before mentioned, and the Members of the several State Legislatures, and all executive and judicial Officers, both of the United States and of the several States, shall be bound by Oath or Affirmation, to support this Constitution; but no religious Test shall ever be required as a Qualification to any Office or public Trust under the United States.

Article. VII. *Adopted 1787*

The Ratification of the Conventions of nine States, shall be sufficient for the Establishment of this Constitution between the States so ratifying the Same.

Done in Convention by the Unanimous Consent of the States present the Seventeenth Day of September in the Year of our Lord one thousand seven hundred and Eighty seven and of the Independence of the United States of America the Twelfth. In Witness whereof We have hereunto subscribed our Names.

George Washington - President and deputy from Virginia

New Hampshire - John Langdon, Nicholas Gilman

Massachusetts - Nathaniel Gorham, Rufus King

Connecticut – Wm. Saml. Johnson, Roger Sherman

New York - Alexander Hamilton

New Jersey – Wil: Livingston, David Brearley. Wm. Paterson. Jona: Dayton

Pennsylvania - Benjamin Franklin, Thomas Mifflin, Robt. Morris, Geo. Clymer, Thos. FitzSimons, Jared Ingersoll, James Wilson, Gouverneur Morris

Delaware - Geo. Read, Gunning Bedford Junior, John Dickinson, Richard Bassett, Jaco: Broom

Maryland - James McHenry, Dan of St Thos. Jenifer, Danl Carroll

Virginia - John Blair, James Madison, Junior

North Carolina – Wm. Blount, Richd. Dobbs Spaight, Hugh Williamson

South Carolina - J. Rutledge, Charles Cotesworth Pinckney, Charles Pinckney, Pierce Butler

Georgia - William Few, Abr Baldwin

Attest: William Jackson, Secretary

ARTICLES IN ADDITON TO, AND AMENDMENT OF THE CONSTITUTION OF THE UNITED STATES OF AMERICA, PROPOSED BY CONGRESS, AND RATIFIED BY THE LEGISLATURES OF THE SEVERAL STATES, PURSUANT TO THE FIFTH ARTICLE OF THE ORIGINAL CONSTITUTION.

Article. I.

(Adopted 1791; freedom of religion, speech, press, assembly, and petition.)

Congress shall make no law respecting an establishment of religion, or prohibiting the free exercise thereof; or abridging the freedom of speech, or of the press; or the right of the people peaceably to assemble, and to petition the Government for a redress of grievances.

Article. II.

(Adopted 1791; the right to keep and bear arms.)

A well regulated Militia, being necessary to the security of a free State, the right of the people to keep and bear Arms, shall not be infringed.

Article. III.

(Adopted 1791; prevention of compulsory billeting during peacetime.)

No Soldier shall, in time of peace be quartered in any house, without the consent of the Owner, nor in time of war, but in a manner to be prescribed by law.

Article. IV.

(Adopted 1791; security of person and possessions against search and seizure.)

The right of the people to be secure in their persons, houses, papers, and effects, against unreasonable searches and seizures, shall not be violated, and no Warrants shall issue, but upon probable cause, supported by Oath or affirmation, and particularly describing the place to be searched, and the persons or things to be seized.

Article. V.

(Adopted 1791; prevention of double-jeopardy; right against self-incrimination.)

No person shall be held to answer for a capital, or otherwise infamous crime, unless on a presentment or indictment of a Grand Jury, except in cases arising in the land or naval forces, or in the Militia, when in actual service in time of War or public danger; nor shall any person be subject for the same offense to be twice put in jeopardy of life or limb; nor shall be compelled in any criminal case to be a witness against himself, nor be deprived of life, liberty, or property, without due process of law; nor shall private property be taken for public use, without just compensation.

Article. VI.
(Adopted 1791; Fair speedy, and public trial by jury; right to counsel.)

In all criminal prosecutions, the accused shall enjoy the right to a speedy and public trial, by an impartial jury of the State and district wherein the crime shall have been committed, which district shall have been previously ascertained by law, and to be informed of the nature and cause of the accusation; to be confronted with the witnesses against him; to have compulsory process for obtaining witnesses in his favor, and to have the Assistance of Counsel for his defense.

Article. VII.
(Adopted 1791; right to trial by jury in common law suits.)

In Suits at common law, where the value in controversy shall exceed twenty dollars, the right of trial by jury shall be preserved, and no fact tried by a jury, shall be otherwise re-examined in any Court of the United States, than according to the rules of the common law.

Article. VIII.
(Adopted 1791; prevention of cruel or unusual punishments; and excessive fines.)

Excessive bail shall not be required, nor excessive fines imposed, nor cruel and unusual punishments inflicted.

Article. IX.
(Adopted 1791; protection of rights not enumerated in the Constitution.)

The enumeration in the Constitution, of certain rights, shall not be construed to deny or disparage others retained by the people.

Article. X.
(Adopted 1791; reservation of the rights of individual states.)

The powers not delegated to the United States by the Constitution, nor prohibited by it to the States, are reserved to the States respectively, or to the people.

Article. XI.
(Adopted 1795; delineation of judicial powers of the US in certain cases.)

The Judicial power of the United States shall not be construed to extend to any suit in law or equity, commenced or prosecuted against one of the United States by Citizens of another State, or by Citizens or Subjects of any Foreign State.

Article. XII.
(Adopted 1804; procedures for electing President and Vice President.)

The Electors shall meet in their respective states, and vote by ballot for President and Vice-President, one of whom, at least, shall not be an inhabitant of the same state with themselves; they shall name in their ballots the person voted for as President, and in distinct ballots the person voted for as Vice-President, and they shall make distinct lists of all persons voted for as President, and of all persons voted for as Vice-President and of the number of votes for each, which lists they shall sign and certify, and transmit sealed to the seat of the government of the United States, directed to the President of the Senate;
The President of the Senate shall, in the presence of the Senate and House of Representatives, open all the certificates and the votes shall then be counted;
The person having the greatest Number of votes for President, shall be the President, if such number be a majority of the whole number of Electors appointed; and if no person have such majority, then from the persons having the highest numbers not exceeding three on the list of those voted for as President, the House of Representatives shall choose immediately, by ballot, the President. But in choosing the President, the votes shall be taken by states, the representation from each state having one vote; a quorum for this purpose shall consist of a member or members from two-thirds of the states, and a majority of all the states shall be necessary to a choice. And if the House of Representatives shall not choose a President whenever the right of choice shall devolve upon them, before the fourth day of March next following, then the Vice-President shall act as President, as in the case of the death or other constitutional disability of the President.
The person having the greatest number of votes as Vice-President, shall be the Vice-President, if such number be a majority of the whole number of Electors appointed, and if no person have a majority, then from the two highest numbers on the list, the Senate shall choose the Vice-President; a quorum for the purpose shall consist of two-thirds of the whole number of Senators, and a majority of the whole number shall be necessary to a choice. But no person constitutionally ineligible to the office of President shall be eligible to that of Vice-President of the United States.

Article. XIII.
(Adopted 1865; abolished slavery.)

Section 1. Neither slavery nor involuntary servitude, except as a punishment for crime whereof the party shall have been duly convicted, shall exist within the United States, or any place subject to their jurisdiction.

Section 2. Congress shall have power to enforce this article by appropriate legislation.

Article. XIV.
(Adopted 1868; guarantee of the rights of citizenship.)

Section 1. All persons born or naturalized in the United States, and subject to the jurisdiction thereof, are citizens of the United States and of the State wherein they reside. No State shall make or enforce any law which shall abridge the privileges or immunities of citizens of the United States; nor shall any State deprive any person of life, liberty, or property, without due process of law; nor deny to any person within its jurisdiction the equal protection of the laws.

Section 2. Representatives shall be apportioned among the several States according to their respective numbers, counting the whole number of persons in each State, excluding Indians not taxed. But when the right to vote at any election for the choice of electors for President and Vice-President of the United States, Representatives in Congress, the Executive and Judicial officers of a State, or the members of the Legislature thereof, is denied to any of the male inhabitants of such State, being twenty-one years of age, and citizens of the United States, or in any way abridged, except for participation in rebellion, or other crime, the basis of representation therein shall be reduced in the proportion which the number of such male citizens shall bear to the whole number of male citizens twenty-one years of age in such State.

Section 3. No person shall be a Senator or Representative in Congress, or elector of President and Vice-President, or hold any office, civil or military, under the United States, or under any State, who, having previously taken an oath, as a member of Congress, or as an officer of the United States, or as a member of any State legislature, or as an executive or judicial officer of any State, to support the Constitution of the United States, shall have engaged in insurrection or rebellion against the same, or given aid or comfort to the enemies thereof. But Congress may by a vote of two-thirds of each House, remove such disability.

Section 4. The validity of the public debt of the United States, authorized by law, including debts incurred for payment of pensions and bounties for services in suppressing insurrection or rebellion, shall not be questioned. But neither the United States nor any State shall assume or pay any debt or obligation incurred in aid of insurrection or rebellion against the United States, or any claim for the loss or emancipation of any slave; but all such debts, obligations and claims shall be held illegal and void.

Section 5. The Congress shall have power to enforce, by appropriate legislation, the provisions of this article.

Article. XV.
(Adopted 1870; right to vote regardless of race, color, or previous servitude.)

Section 1. The right of citizens of the United States to vote shall not be denied or abridged by the United States or by any State on account of race, color, or previous condition of servitude.

Section 2. The Congress shall have power to enforce this article by appropriate legislation.

Article. XVI.

(Adopted 1913; right of Congress to levy income taxes.)

The Congress shall have power to lay and collect taxes on incomes, from whatever source derived, without apportionment among the several States, and without regard to any census or enumeration.

Article. XVII.

(Adopted 1913; procedure for electing Senators.)

The Senate of the United States shall be composed of two Senators from each State, elected by the people thereof, for six years; and each Senator shall have one vote. The electors in each State shall have the qualifications requisite for electors of the most numerous branch of the State legislatures.

When vacancies happen in the representation of any State in the Senate, the executive authority of such State shall issue writs of election to fill such vacancies: *Provided*, That the legislature of any State may empower the executive thereof to make temporary appointments until the people fill the vacancies by election as the legislature may direct.

This amendment shall not be so construed as to affect the election or term of any Senator chosen before it becomes valid as part of the Constitution.

Article. XVIII.

(Adopted 1919; introduced prohibition.)

Section 1. After one year from the ratification of this article the manufacture, sale, or transportation of intoxicating liquors within, the importation thereof into, or the exportation thereof from the United States and all territory subject to the jurisdiction thereof for beverage purposes is hereby prohibited.

Section 2. The Congress and the several States shall have concurrent power to enforce this article by appropriate legislation.

Section 3. This article shall be inoperative unless it shall have been ratified as an amendment to the Constitution by the legislatures of the several States, as provided in the Constitution, within seven years from the date of the submission hereof to the States by the Congress.

Article. XIX.

(Adopted 1920; right of women to vote.)

The right of citizens of the United States to vote shall not be denied or abridged by the United States or by any State on account of sex.
Congress shall have power to enforce this article by appropriate legislation.

Article. XX.

(Adopted 1933; presidential term and succession; terms of other offices.)

Section 1. The terms of the President and Vice President shall end at noon on the 20th day of January, and the terms of Senators and Representatives at noon on the 3d day of January, of the years in which such terms would have ended if this article had not been ratified; and the terms of their successors shall then begin.
Section 2. The Congress shall assemble at least once in every year, and such meeting shall begin at noon on the 3d day of January, unless they shall by law appoint a different day.
Section 3. If, at the time fixed for the beginning of the term of the President, the President elect shall have died, the Vice President elect shall become President. If a President shall not have been chosen before the time fixed for the beginning of his term, or if the President elect shall have failed to qualify, then the Vice President elect shall act as President until a President shall have qualified; and the Congress may by law provide for the case wherein neither a President elect nor a Vice President elect shall have qualified, declaring who shall then act as President, or the manner in which one who is to act shall be selected, and such person shall act accordingly until a President or Vice President shall have qualified.
Section 4. The Congress may by law provide for the case of the death of any of the persons from whom the House of Representatives may choose a President whenever the right of choice shall have devolved upon them, and for the case of the death of any of the persons from whom the Senate may choose a Vice President whenever the right of choice shall have devolved upon them.
Section 5. Sections 1 and 2 shall take effect on the 15th day of October following the ratification of this article.
Section 6. This article shall be inoperative unless it shall have been ratified as an amendment to the Constitution by the legislatures of three-fourths of the several States within seven years from the date of its submission.

Article. XXI.

(Adopted 1933; repeal of prohibition, the 18th Amendment.)

Section 1. The eighteenth article of amendment to the Constitution of the United States is hereby repealed.

Section 2. The transportation or importation into any State, Territory, or possession of the United States for delivery or use therein of intoxicating liquors, in violation of the laws thereof, is hereby prohibited.

Section 3. The article shall be inoperative unless it shall have been ratified as an amendment to the Constitution by conventions in the several States, as provided in the Constitution, within seven years from the date of the submission hereof to the States by the Congress

Article. XXII.

(Adopted 1951; limiting Presidents to two terms.)

Section 1. No person shall be elected to the office of the President more than twice, and no person who has held the office of President, or acted as President, for more than two years of a term to which some other person was elected President shall be elected to the office of the President more than once. But this Article shall not apply to any person holding the office of President, when this Article was proposed by the Congress, and shall not prevent any person who may be holding the office of President, or acting as President, during the term within which this Article becomes operative from holding the office of President or acting as President during the remainder of such term.

Section 2. This article shall be inoperative unless it shall have been ratified as an amendment to the Constitution by the legislatures of three-fourths of the several States within seven years from the date of its submission to the States by the Congress.

Article. XXIII.

(Adopted 1961; grants Washington DC residents a vote in the Presidential elections.)

Section 1. The District constituting the seat of Government of the United States shall appoint in such manner as the Congress may direct: A number of electors of President and Vice President equal to the whole number of Senators and Representatives in Congress to which the District would be entitled if it were a State, but in no event more than the least populous State; they shall be in addition to those appointed by the States, but they shall be considered, for the purposes of the election of President and Vice President, to be electors appointed by a State; and they shall meet in the District and perform such duties as provided by the twelfth article of amendment.

Section 2. The Congress shall have power to enforce this article by appropriate legislation.

Article. XXIV.

(Adopted 1964; bars poll (voting) tax in federal elections.)

Section 1. The right of citizens of the United States to vote in any primary or other election for President or Vice President, for electors for President or Vice President, or for

Senator or Representative in Congress, shall not be denied or abridged by the United States or any State by reason of failure to pay any poll tax or other tax.

Section 2. The Congress shall have power to enforce this article by appropriate legislation.

Article. XXV.

(Adopted 1967; order of Presidential succession.)

Section 1. In case of the removal of the President from office or of his death or resignation, the Vice President shall become President.

Section 2. Whenever there is a vacancy in the office of the Vice President, the President shall nominate a Vice President who shall take office upon confirmation by a majority vote of both Houses of Congress.

Section 3. Whenever the President transmits to the President pro tempore of the Senate and the Speaker of the House of Representatives his written declaration that he is unable to discharge the powers and duties of his office, and until he transmits to them a written declaration to the contrary, such powers and duties shall be discharged by the Vice President as Acting President.

Section 4. Whenever the Vice President and a majority of either the principal officers of the executive departments or of such other body as Congress may by law provide, transmit to the President pro tempore of the Senate and the Speaker of the House of Representatives their written declaration that the President is unable to discharge the powers and duties of his office, the Vice President shall immediately assume the powers and duties of the office as Acting President.

Thereafter, when the President transmits to the President pro tempore of the Senate and the Speaker of the House of Representatives his written declaration that no inability exists, he shall resume the powers and duties of his office unless the Vice President and a majority of either the principal officers of the executive department or of such other body as Congress may by law provide, transmit within four days to the President pro tempore of the Senate and the Speaker of the House of Representatives their written declaration that the President is unable to discharge the powers and duties of his office. Thereupon Congress shall decide the issue, assembling within forty eight hours for that purpose if not in session. If the Congress, within twenty one days after receipt of the latter written declaration, or, if Congress is not in session, within twenty one days after Congress is required to assemble, determines by two thirds vote of both Houses that the President is unable to discharge the powers and duties of his office, the Vice President shall continue to discharge the same as Acting President; otherwise, the President shall resume the powers and duties of his office.

Article. XXVI.

(Adopted 1971; right to vote at age eighteen.)

Section 1. The right of citizens of the United States, who are eighteen years of age or older, to vote shall not be denied or abridged by the United States or by any State on account of age.
Section 2. The Congress shall have power to enforce this article by appropriate legislation.

Article. XXVII.

(Adopted 1992; postpones Representatives' pay raises until after new elections.)

No law, varying the compensation for the services of the Senators and Representatives, shall take effect, until an election of Representatives shall have intervened.

* * * * * * *

To find additional information about the Declaration of Independence, visit these sites on the internet:

- National Archives and Records Administration
  http://www.pro.gov.uk/webarchive/
- Library of Congress: http://www.loc.gov/about/sitemap/

To contact The President of the United States visit:

- www.whitehouse.gov or write:

The White House
1600 Pennsylvania Avenue NW
Washington, DC 20500

GEORGE WASHINGTON

1st President. George Washington was born in Westmoreland County, Virginia, on February 22, 1732. His father was a prosperous farmer and his great-grand father emigrated from England to Virginia in the 1650s. Washington had only a basic education and started his first job as a surveyor when he was 16. He acquired Mount Vernon at the age of 21 after his half-brother Lawrence died. At this time, Governor Dinwiddie of Virginia sent Washington on a mission to keep the French out of the Ohio Valley. In 1755, when he was 23, he became commander in chief of the Virginia forces and led them to victory in the French and Indian War. Washington married Martha Custis, a young widow with two children; they did not have any together. In 1774 he served as a delegate to the first Continental Congress. He was appointed commander in chief of the American forces, becoming victorious in 1783. George Washington was named president of the Constitutional Convention in 1787; and in 1789 was elected president of the United States. As the first president, he had to decide how to carry out the duties of the executive branch of the government. Washington felt this position should be devoid of politics and should represent all of the American people. The first cabinet included Thomas Jefferson, Secretary of State; Edmund Randolph, Attorney General; Alexander Hamilton, Secretary of Treasury; Samuel Osgood, Postmaster General; and Henry Knox, Secretary of War. Washington stayed in office two terms and declined to serve a third term. He died at Mount Vernon on December 14, 1799. **Washington was president from 1789-97 and the vice president was John Adams.**

JOHN ADAMS

2nd President. John Adams was born October 30, 1735, in Braintree (later Quincy), Massachusetts. He attended school at a local academy. When he was 15 he enrolled in Harvard College and graduated in 1755. Adams began practicing law three years later. He married Abigail Smith in 1764. They had five children. In 1765 Adams wrote essays in the *Boston Gazette* protesting the Stamp Act imposed by the British government that would tax public documents, newspapers, licenses, insurance policies and playing cards. Adams served in the Continental Congress from 1774 until 1777. He established his reputation as a champion of individual rights. He was one of the first to favor independence from Great Britain and in 1776 he recommended George Washington to be the commander in chief of the new Continental Army. He was sent to France in 1778 and the Netherlands in 1780, where he successfully arranged loan and trade agreements between France, the Netherlands and America. Adams, John Jay and others negotiated a peace treaty with Great Britain in Paris in 1783, ending the Revolutionary War. He served as minister to Great Britain from 1785 until 1788, when he was elected vice president. Adams served as vice president for two terms until he was elected to the presidency in 1796. John and Abigail Adams were the first to occupy the White House. It was undecorated and littered with building debris. Adams served only one term. He lost the election to Thomas Jefferson. He retired to Quincy, Massachusetts, where he died on July 4, 1826. **Adams was president from 1797-1801 and the vice president was Thomas Jefferson.**

THOMAS JEFFERSON

3rd President. Thomas Jefferson was born in Goochland (later Albemarle) County, Virginia, on April 13, 1743. He was born into a wealthy family and tutored at home. Just before he turned 17, he went to the College of William and Mary in Williamsburg, Virginia. Jefferson studied law for five years; he was admitted to the bar when he was 24 and practiced law until the American Revolution closed the courts. In 1772 he married Martha Wayles Skelton; they had six children. In 1776, when he was 33, he was chosen to write the Declaration of Independence. The same year he became a member of the Virginia House of Delegates. He introduced the statute for Religious Freedom in 1777; it passed nine years later. Jefferson served two years as governor of Virginia. In 1782 his wife died; he never remarried. He was elected to the United States Congress in 1783, where he advocated the adoption of the dollar and the decimal system of money. Jefferson was sent by Congress to France in 1784; he eventually succeeded Franklin as minister to Franc. Jefferson left France at the start of the French Revolution in 1789. Jefferson ran against Adams for the presidency and lost by three electoral votes. He became the vice president. In 1800, he ran against Adams again and won the office of president; he served two terms. As president, he bought the Louisiana Territory for $15 million, doubling the size of the United States. In 1819 he chartered the University of Virginia. He died at his home, Monticello, on July 4, 1826. **Jefferson was president from 1801-09 and the vice presidents were Aaron Burr and George Clinton.**

JAMES MADISON

4th President. James Madison was born on March 16, 1751, in Port Conway, Virginia. He grew up on a plantation called Montpelier, where his mother taught him to read and write. When he turned 11 he went off to a boarding school in King and Queen County, Virginia. He loved to read. He attended the college of New Jersey and graduated. In 1776, when Madison was 25, he was elected to the Virginia Convention. He served one year and was defeated when he ran for reelection. He was appointed a member of the Governor's Council, which managed the Revolutionary War efforts. In 1784 he was elected to the Virginia House of Delegates. He married Dolley Payne Todd; they did not have any children together, although Dolley had had two sons by her first husband. Madison attended the Constitutional Convention in Philadelphia, in 1787. His understanding of government made him a leader in creating the Constitution; he advocated a republican form of government in which the people are sovereign but rule through elected representatives. From 1789 to 1797, he was a member of the United States House of Representatives. In 1801, he was appointed secretary of state by Thomas Jefferson. In 1808 he was elected president. At this time, Britain and France were at war. After Britain attacked American ships, Madison reluctantly led our nation into war against Britain. During the War of 1812, the White House was burned by the British. Madison left Washington in 1817 after serving two terms as president. He lived on his plantation, until he died on June 28, 1836. **Madison was president from 1809-17 and the Vice Presidents were George Clinton and Elbridge Gerry.**

JAMES MONROE

5th President. James Monroe was born on April 28, 1758, in Westmoreland County, Virginia. He left home to attend the College of William and Mary when he was 16. He joined the Third Virginia Regiment two years later to fight in the American Revolution. In 1782 he was elected to the Virginia House of Delegates. In 1783 he became a member of the US Congress formed under the Articles of Confederation and served until 1786. He married Elizabeth Kortright in 1786. In 1790 he was elected to the US Senate and served four years, until he was appointed minister to France by George Washington. In 1799 he was elected governor of Virginia. In 1803 Monroe went on a diplomatic mission to France to help negotiate the Louisiana Purchase. President Jefferson appointed Monroe minister to Great Britain until 1807 when he was elected governor again in 1811. The same year he was appointed secretary of state by James Madison as the secretary of war between 1814-1815. In 1816 Monroe was elected President. During his administration he bought Florida from Spain and established the Canadian border. He authored the Monroe doctrine that warned nations in Europe not to take over or set up colonies in North and South America. His presidency was known as the Era of Good Feeling, a period of national optimism, expansion and growth. He left office in 1825 and moved to Loudoun County, Virginia, with his wife. After she died he lived with his daughter in New York City, where he died July 4, 1831. **Monroe was President from 1817-25 and the Vice President was Daniel D. Tompkins.**

JOHN Q. ADAMS

6th President. John Quincy Adams was born July 11, 1767, in Braintree, Massachusetts. He was tutored by his mother and a cousin until leaving with his father for France in 1778. He attended schools in Paris and the University of Leiden in the Netherlands. John Quincy Adams began a diary that he wrote in for over 60 years. He returned from the Netherlands in 1785 to attend Harvard College. He graduated in 1787 and studied law and began to practice in 1790. At the age of 28 he was appointed minister to the Netherlands by George Washington. He married Louisa Johnson and they had three sons and a daughter who died in infancy. He served as the minister to Prussia from 1797 until 1801. Adams was elected to the United States Senate and served from 1803 until 1808. In 1809 President Madison appointed Adams the first American minister to Russia. In 1812 war broke out between the United States and Great Britain. Adams served on the delegation that brought about the Peace Treaty of Ghent in 1814. He later became the minister to Great Britain. In 1817, President Monroe appointed him secretary of state. He negotiated the Transcontinental Treaty of 1819 with Spain, which gave the United States Florida by purchase and settled various boundaries. Adams ran for President in 1824 and won; he served one term. He ran for Congress in 1830 and became an active legislator known for his opposition to slavery. He died, two days after he collapsed on the floor of the House of Representatives on February 23, 1848. **Adams was president from 1825-29 and the vice president was John C. Calhoun.**

ANDREW JACKSON

7th President. Andrew Jackson was born March 15, 1767, in a log cabin in the Waxhaw settlement of South Carolina, a few days after his father's death. He lived with his mother, two older brothers, aunt and uncle. He attended school enough to learn how to read. Jackson left home to fight in the Revolutionary War when he was 13; he was taken prisoner by a British officer. Shortly after he was released, his mother died. Jackson studied law in Salisbury, North Carolina, and passed the bar exam. He moved to Tennessee in 1794 where he married Rachel Donelson Robards. He was elected to the House of Representatives in 1796 as the first representative from Tennessee and then served one year in the United States Senate. He had to return home when his farm failed. In 1802 he was elected major general of the Tennessee militia. In 1814 he defeated the Creek Indians during the War of 1812; he was promoted to major general of the United States Army. In 1815 he successfully fought off the British attack on New Orleans, protecting the Louisiana territory. Jackson was elected governor of the new territory of Florida in 1821. He soon returned to his home in Tennessee where he was elected to the Senate in 1823. Jackson ran for President in 1824 but lost to John Quincy Adams in a close race finally decided by the House of Representatives. In 1828 he was elected President and served two terms. He returned to his home in Nashville, Tennessee, where he lived until he died on June 8, 1845. **Jackson was president from 1829-37 and the vice presidents were John C. Calhoun and Martin Van Buren.**

MARTIN VAN BUREN

8th President. Martin Van Buren was born December 5 1782, in Kinderhook, New York. He was the first president to be born under the American flag. His father owned a tavern that also served as a polling place so he heard politics discussed at an early age. He was a student at the Kinderhook Academy until he graduated at age 14 and took a job in a local law office. At the age of 18 he had a job in a law office in New York City. When he was 21 he returned home to practice law; he was a very successful lawyer. He married Hannah Hoes, his childhood sweetheart, in 1807; together they had five sons. Van Buren was elected to the New York Senate in 1812. Van Buren became a US Senator in 1821, serving until 1829. He was elected governor of New York but resigned when Jackson appointed him secretary of state. He was elected to the office of vice president under Andrew Jackson in 1832. Van Buren was elected president in 1836. He became president in 1837—the same year that the United States entered a major depression. During his administration he argued for an independent treasury, with federal funds kept separate from state banks. Van Buren also opposed the annexation of Texas as part of the United States. He was not reelected in 1840. Van Buren tried again for the presidency in 1848 as a Free Soil candidate and lost to Zachary Taylor. Martin Van Buren died in Kinderhook, New York, in 1862. **Van Buren was president from 1837-41 and the vice president was Richard M. Johnson.**

413

WILLIAM H. HARRISON

9th President. William Henry Harrison was born on February 9, 1773, on his father's plantation in Charles City County, Virginia. His father was one of the signers of the Declaration of Independence and a friend of George Washington. Harrison was taught at home and the Brandon School until he went to Hampden-Sydney College in Virginia. He left college to join the army in 1791-- his father died the same year. In 1795 he married Anna Symmes; they had ten children. Harrison was appointed secretary of the Northwest Territory by President John Adams and served as the delegate to Congress from that region. He was appointed governor of the Indiana Territory, where he served for 12 years. He took millions of acres of land from Native Americans by battle or by treaty. Harrison gained fame as the leader of US troops against Native Americans at the Battle of Tippecanoe in 1811. He defeated the British and Indians at the Battle of the Thames. He moved his family to North Bend, Ohio. In 1816 he was elected to Congress and in 1819 he was elected to the state senate. At the end of that term in 1825 he was elected to the United States Senate. President John Quincy Adams appointed Harrison minister to Columbia in 1828. He offended Columbia President Simon Bolivar and he was recalled by President Jackson in 1829. Harrison returned to his farm in North Bend. He was nominated by the Whig Party to run for president against Martin Van Buren, and lost. Harrison ran for president again four years later and won. He died of pneumonia, April 4, 1841, 30 days after taking office. **Harrison was president from March 4, 1841 to April 4, 1841. His vice president was John Tyler.**

JOHN TYLER

10th President. John Tyler was born on March 29, 1790, in Charles City County, Virginia, on Greenway Plantation. His mother died when he was seven; his father was a judge who was later elected governor of Virginia. In 1802 Tyler entered the preparatory school of the College of William and Mary in Williamsburg. He graduated from the college when he was 17. He went on to study law and in 1811 he began to practice law in Richmond. That same year he was elected to the Virginia House of Delegates and served from 1811 to 1815, from 1823 to 1826, and in 1839. He married Letitia Christian in 1813; they had eight children. In 1816 Tyler was elected to the United States House of Representatives, where he served for five years. He was elected governor of Virginia and served from 1825 to 1827, until he was elected to the United States Senate. He served in the Senate for five years. Tyler was elected Vice President when William Henry Harrison won the presidential election in 1840. A month after Harrison's inauguration, Tyler he took the oath of office as president. His wife died while he was president and two years later he married Julia Gardiner; he was the first president to wed while serving in office. Together they had seven children. President Tyler was instrumental in the annexation of Texas in 1845. As president he established trade between China and the United States. He left office in 1845 and moved to his plantation, Sherwood Forest in Virginia, where he lived with his family until he died on January 18, 1862. **Tyler was president from 1841-45 and since he was completing Harrison's term, there was no vice president**

JAMES K. POLK

11th President. James Knox Polk was born on November 2, 1795, in Mecklenburg, North Carolina. His family moved to Duck River, Tennessee, when he was a child. Polk was too weak to work on the farm so his parents focused on developing his mind. He was taught by tutors and sent to private schools. In 1815 he enrolled in the University of North Carolina. He moved to Tennessee to practice law and in 1821 was elected to the state legislature. On January 1, 1824, he married Sarah Childress; they did not have any children. He was elected to the United States House of Representatives in 1824. He served seven terms, until he was elected governor of Tennessee. Polk served one term as governor. Then he was nominated by the Democrats to run for president. He won and pledged to serve only one term. During Polk's administration, gold was discovered in 1848 in California and thousands of people migrated west. The Department of the Interior was established. Wisconsin, Iowa and Texas became states. Polk negotiated the Minnesota and Oregon boundaries with Britain, making them federal territories. The United States won the Mexican-American War (1846-48) and annexed much of the southwest and California. Polk was known for working long hours, beginning his duties at daybreak and working at his desk until midnight. He was away from the White House only 37 days during his four-year term. He promised voters he would serve only one term as president. He died three months after he left office at his home in Nashville, Tennessee, on June 15, 1849. **Polk was president from 1845-49 and the vice president was George M. Dallas.**

ZACHARY TAYLOR

12th President. Zachary Taylor was born November 24, 1784 near Barboursville, Virginia. His father was a lieutenant colonel in the Revolutionary War. His only formal education was at two small schools. His parents supplemented his education by teaching him at home. He worked on his family's plantation until he left home in 1808 to join the Seventh Infantry Regiment. He married Margaret Mackall South in 1810; they had six children, two daughters died in childhood. Taylor fought in the War of 1812 rising in rank to major in 1812 after a successful defense of Fort Harrison. In 1832 Taylor fought in the Black Hawk War to drive the Sauk Indians out of Illinois. In 1837 he received an honorary commission as brigadier general after he defeated the Seminole Indians in Florida during the Second Seminole War. He was not able to defeat the Indians in 1840; he was relieved of his command and assigned to fight the Indians in the Southwest. He fought as a General in the Mexican War on the Texas-Louisiana border; his army defeated the Mexicans at Palo Alto. His final victory was in the battle of Buena Vista where his troops were outnumbered. He was promoted to major general. The Whig Party nominated Zachary Taylor for president in 1848 and he won. Taylor was a soldier most of his life; he never held political office until he was elected president. He was inaugurated president in March 1849. As president, he tried to use the army to prevent states from withdrawing from the United States. He was president for only one year. On July 4th he attended festivities for the Fourth. He had a stomach ailment after eating that day and he died July 9, 1850. **Taylor was president from 1849-50 and the vice president was Millard Fillmore.**

MILLARD FILLMORE

13th President. Millard Fillmore was born January 7, 1800, in Locke, New York. He spent most of his early life on a farm. He was eager to improve his education and attended a school that was established when he was 19, eventually marrying his 21-year-old teacher, Abigail Powers. Fillmore studied law with County Judge Walter Wood when he was 19. In 1823, Fillmore passed the bar exam and began his law practice in East Aurora, New York. He and Abigail had two children. The family moved to Buffalo, where Fillmore was a very successful lawyer. In 1828 he was elected to the state legislature. In 1832 he was elected to the United States House of Representatives, where he served for 10 years. In 1842, he ran for governor of New York and lost. Fillmore was elected vice president in 1848 and was sworn in as president July 10, 1850, after Zachary Taylor died unexpectedly. During his administration there was a lot of tension between the north and the south over slavery. Many slaves were fleeing to the north. He addressed the slavery issue through the Compromise of 1850 and signed the Fugitive Slave Act. Fillmore tried to prevent the Civil War by urging the northern and southern states to agree on a settlement. He was not nominated for a second term because neither expansionists nor slaveholders were pleased with his policies. After leaving office in 1853, they returned to Buffalo, New York; where his wife died that same year. Fillmore ran again for president in 1856 but was unsuccessful. He married Caroline McIntosh in 1858 and lived in Buffalo until his death on March 8, 1874. **Fillmore was president from 1850-53 and since he was completing Taylor's term, there was no vice president.**

FRANKLIN PIERCE

14th President. Franklin Pierce was born in a log cabin on November 23, 1804, in Hillsborough, New Hampshire. He attended boarding schools. His father was a major in the Revolutionary War and served two terms as governor. In 1820, Pierce enrolled in Bowdoin College in Brunswick, Maine, where he met a lifelong friend, Nathaniel Hawthorne. He went on to study law and was admitted to the bar in 1827. Pierce was elected to the state legislature where he served four years. He married Jane Means Appleton. They had three children, only one son, Benjamin lived past age five. Pierce was elected to two terms in the US House of Representatives and then to the US Senate in 1837. He served four years; he resigned his post because his wife did not like life in Washington, D.C. They returned to Concord, New Hampshire, where he practiced law. In 1847 Pierce enlisted as a private in the Concord Light Infantry. In the Mexican War he rose to brigadier general of volunteers, commanding 2,500 men in Mexico. He could no longer fight after he suffered a leg wound from a fall from his horse. Pierce returned to practice law in Concord. He was nominated by the Democrats to run for president and won. On January 6, shortly before his inauguration, they were in a train wreck that killed their 11 year old son Benjamin. Mrs. Pierce was brokenhearted and lived in seclusion in the White House the entire term. During his presidency, Pierce bought parts of Arizona and New Mexico from Mexico. The Pierces toured Europe after he left office and returned to live in Concord, New Hampshire, where he died on October 8, 1869. **Pierce was president from 1853-57 and the vice president was William R. King, who died before their term even started.**

JAMES BUCHANAN

15th President. James Buchanan was born on April 23, 1791, in a log cabin in Cove Gap, Pennsylvania. He was the second of eleven children. They went to school in Mercersburg, where his father owned a general store. He attended Dickinson College in Carlisle, Pennsylvania, and studied law with James Hopkins in Lancaster. He was a successful lawyer who interrupted his career to join a volunteer company to fight in the War of 1812. Buchanan returned home from the war and won a seat in the state legislature. He returned to his law practice in Lancaster. He served ten years in the US House of Representatives. Andrew Jackson asked him to serve as minister to Russia; he negotiated the first trade agreement between Russia and the United States. Buchanan was elected to the Senate in 1834 and served ten years. President Polk appointed Buchanan secretary of state. He helped to arrange the Treaty of Guadalupe Hidalgo with Mexico in 1848, by which the United States purchased the region extending west from Texas to the Pacific Ocean. He wrote the Oregon Treaty of 1846 that settled the Northwestern boundary between Canada and the United States. Buchanan ran for president in 1852 and lost. He served as minister to Great Britain. He again ran for president in 1856 as a Democrat and won. He never married, so his niece Harriet Lane performed the duties of First Lady. Buchanan ran for a second term and was defeated by Lincoln. Before he left office, seven states seceded from the Union. He returned to his home in Lancaster, Pennsylvania, where he lived until he died June 1, 1868. **Buchanan was president from 1857-61 and the vice president was John C. Breckenridge.**

ABRAHAM LINCOLN

16th President. Abraham Lincoln was born on February 12, 1809, in a log cabin in Hardin County, Kentucky. His parents were uneducated pioneers. His father, Thomas Lincoln, believed that there were better opportunities elsewhere, so the family moved 100 miles to Indiana. Lincoln helped his father, who was a farmer. His mother died when he was nine and his father remarried. He attended school for only a few months but loved to read. In 1830, the family moved to Illinois. He practiced law in Springfield, Illinois, and was very popular in the court circuit. He married Mary Todd in 1842 and they had four boys. Edward died when he was four. In 1847 Lincoln was elected to the United States House of Representatives. He ran for the Senate and lost. He was elected president in 1860 and guided the nation through the Civil War. It was his aim to preserve the union of the states. The Emancipation Proclamation was one of the most important features of his presidency. Designed to help win the war, it freed slaves in the states of the Confederacy, but not those in friendly border states. The Gettysburg Address is his most famous speech. Nearly 8,000 soldiers died in a three-day battle in Gettysburg; and with that speech he tried to bring the nation together in their grief. The Lincolns' son William died in the White House when he was 11. Lincoln was elected to a second term in 1864 and the Civil War ended. April 9, 1865. Five days later Lincoln was shot in the head by John Wilkes Booth of Virginia. He died from that gunshot wound April 15, 1865, in a boarding house across from Ford's Theater. **Lincoln was president from 1861-65; his vice presidents were Hannibal Hamlin and Andrew Johnson.**

ANDREW JOHNSON

17th President. Andrew Johnson was born in Raleigh, North Carolina, on December 29, 1808. His father died when he was three, so his mother and brother worked to support themselves. He did not go to school but he was sent to apprentice with a tailor, where he learned to read. In 1826 when he was 18, he moved to Greenville, Tennessee. He married Eliza McCardle a year later; they had five children. He opened his own tailor shop, where young men in the town frequently stopped by to debate politics and public affairs. He was elected mayor of Greenville in 1834. Johnson was elected to the Tennessee legislature for two terms: from 1835-36 and 1839-40. He served in the U.S. House of Representatives for ten years until he was elected governor in 1853. After serving one term he was voted into office as a U.S. senator until he was elected the military governor of Tennessee during the Civil War. In 1864 he ran as the Republican candidate for vice president and was inaugurated March 4, 1865. When Lincoln was assassinated, he took office on April 15, 1865. In 1868 he was impeached by the House of Representatives, accused of breaking the law by dismissing the secretary of war, Edwin Stanton. He was acquitted in the impeachment trial in 1868. His main accomplishment as president was the purchase of Alaska from Russia. He finished his term as President and returned to Tennessee in March 1869. He was elected to the Senate in 1874 and died of a stroke a year later, July 31, 1875. **Johnson was president, from 1865-69 and since he was completing Lincoln's term, there was no vice president.**

ULYSSES S. GRANT

18th President. Ulysses Simpson Grant was born on April 27, 1822, in Point Pleasant, Ohio. He was born to a pioneer family and became a good horseman. He attended schools in and near Georgetown, Ohio. In 1839 he received an appointment to West Point Academy. He graduated as a second lieutenant, but he did not like the infantry. He wanted to join the cavalry but there were no openings available. He fought in the Mexican-American War from 1846 until 1848 when the war ended. He married Julia Dent and they had four children. In 1854 he resigned from the army. He tried farming and real estate and failed. He became a partner in a family leather business in Galena, Illinois. He returned to join the military when the Civil War broke out in 1861, as colonel of the 21st, Illinois Volunteer Regiment. He captured Vicksburg, Mississippi, in 1863 giving the Union control of the Mississippi River. Lincoln promoted him to lieutenant general and commander of the Union armies. Grant accepted Lee's surrender April 9, 1865, in Appomattox, Virginia. The Congress appointed Grant General of the Armies, the first man to reach this rank since George Washington. He served briefly as secretary of war. Grant was a popular leader after the Civil War. He was elected president in 1868 and served two terms. During his administration the 15th Amendment was ratified, giving African Americans the right to vote. Grant moved to Mount McGregor, New York, and wrote his memoirs. He died on July 23, 1885, one week after he completed his memoirs. **Grant was president, from 1869-77 and the vice presidents were Schuyler Colfax and Henry Wilson.**

RUTHERFORD B. HAYES

19th President. Rutherford Birchard Hayes was born in October 4, 1822, in Delaware, Ohio. His father died just before he was born. He was educated at home and attended private schools. In 1838 he enrolled in Kenyon College in Gambier, Ohio. Hayes graduated in 1842 and then enrolled at Harvard Law School. He graduated in 1845 and was admitted to the Ohio bar. He married Lucy Webb and they had eight children. In 1857 he was elected city solicitor of Cincinnati. When the Civil War started, he joined the Union Army. He was elected to Congress in 1864 but refused to leave the battlefield. Hayes advanced to the rank of major general. He was reelected to Congress in 1866 and served only one year because he was elected governor of Ohio in 1867. He remained in office until 1872 when his term ended. He returned to Spiegel Grove where he practiced law and worked to develop public libraries. He ran again for governor of Ohio in 1876 and won. He was nominated as the Republican candidate for president against Samuel J. Tilden. Hayes won in a close election that was disputed for four months and ultimately decided by an electoral commission. During his administration Hayes, removed all federal troops from the South, ending Reconstruction—the period after the Civil War during which the southern states were reorganized and made part of the Union once again. He tried to promote civil service reform. Hayes did not want to serve a second term and retired to his estate in Spiegel Grove in Fremont, Ohio, where he devoted his time to his philanthropic activities until he died on January 17, 1893. **Hayes was president from 1877-81 and the vice president was William A. Wheeler.**

JAMES A. GARFIELD

20th President. James Abram Garfield was born in Orange, Ohio, on November 19, 1831. He was the last president to be born in a log cabin. His father died when he was two; he had three brothers and sisters living; another brother died before James was born... Since they had to work to help support their family, they could only attend school three months each year. He loved to read. At the age of 17 Garfield left home and worked with Canal boats on the Ohio Canal. He had to return home when he became sick. He attended Williams College in Massachusetts. He graduated and became a teacher at Hiram College, where he had been a student. A year later he became president of the college. He married Lucretia Rudolph in 1858; they had seven children He was elected to the Ohio Senate in 1859 where he served for two years. Garfield volunteered for the Union Army in 1861. He fought in the Civil War battles at Shiloh and Chickamauga. He resigned in 1863 with the rank of Major General, when President Lincoln asked him to run for Congress. In December 1863, at the age of 32, he entered the House of Representatives. He served as a legislator for 17 years and he became minority leader. He was nominated by the Republican Party and was elected president in 1880. During his administration the great railroad expansion reached Texas. James Garfield was shot on July 2, 1881, while waiting for a train, only a few months after he took office. He died 10 weeks later in Elbron, New Jersey, on September 19, 1881. **Garfield was president from March 4, 1881-September 19, 1881 and the vice president was Chester A. Arthur.**

CHESTER A. ARTHUR

21st President. Chester Alan Arthur was born in Fairfield, Vermont, on October 5, 1829. His father was a teacher and minister. Arthur entered Union College in Schenectady, New York, when he was 15. He taught school to pay for his education and graduated with honors in 1848. He then went on to study law, while continuing to teach to support himself. Then in 1853 when he went to New York City, passing the bar in 1854. He took on two very controversial and groundbreaking cases. His law firm gained freedom for eight slaves who had been brought to New York, where the law forbid slavery. He also represented Lizzie Jennings in a segregation case. She was told she was not allowed to ride on a New York City streetcar because she was black; she was awarded $250 in damages. Chester Arthur married Ellen Lewis Herndon in 1859; they had three children. During the Civil War, Arthur was appointed quartermaster general of New York State, supplying food, guns and tents to the soldiers. He became collector of customs for the port of New York from 1871 to 1878. He was elected vice president in 1880. When James Garfield was assassinated only six months after he was sworn in as president, Chester Arthur became president on September 20, 1881. During his administration, Congress passed the Pendleton Act, which helped to eliminate the corruption of political favors and established the Civil Service Commission. After leaving office in 1885, he returned to New York where he died at his home on November 18, 1886. **Arthur was president from 1881-85 and since he was completing the term of James Garfield, there was no vice president.**

GROVER CLEVELAND

22nd and 24th President. (Stephen) Grover Cleveland was born in Caldwell, New Jersey, on March 18, 1837. His family moved to Fayetteville, New York, where he was educated at the Fayetteville Academy. In 1851 they moved to Clinton, New York, where he attended the Clinton Academy. When he was 18 he visited an uncle in Buffalo, New York, who asked for his help in his cattle-breeding business. Cleveland studied law and four years later, was admitted to the bar. In 1863 he became assistant district attorney of Erie County, New York, for two years. His record of honesty and fairness led to his election as sheriff of Erie County; a job he held for three years. In 1881 Cleveland was elected mayor of Buffalo. He was in office one year, when the Democrats nominated him for governor of New York and he won. Two years later he was nominated for president and won. Grover Cleveland married Frances Folsom on June 2, 1886, in a White House ceremony; they had five children. He lost the 1888 presidential election to Benjamin Harrison. He returned to New York where he practiced law. In 1992, he was nominated for president again by the Democrats and won. Cleveland was inaugurated as the 24th president in 1893. After his second term, his party turned to William Jennings Bryan, who lost to William McKinley. After leaving office in 1897, Cleveland moved to Princeton, New Jersey, where he lived until he died on June 24, 1908. **Cleveland was president from 1885-89 and the vice president was Thomas A. Hendricks. He served as president again from 1893-97 and the vice president was Adlai E. Stevenson.**

BENJAMIN HARRISON

23rd President. Benjamin Harrison was born August 20, 1833, in North Bend, Ohio, the grandson of President William Henry Harrison. He was tutored at home and at the age of 14 he entered the Farmer's College near Cincinnati. Two years later he transferred to Miami University at Oxford, Ohio. Harrison went on to study law and he was admitted to the bar. In 1893 Harrison married Caroline Scott; they had two children. He started a law practice in Indianapolis, Indiana. Harrison joined the Union Army in 1862 during the Civil War and earned the position of brigadier general. When the war ended, he returned to his law practice. In 1876 he ran unsuccessfully for governor of Indiana. In 1880 Harrison was elected to the U.S. Senate and served one six-year term. He was elected president in 1888. His wife died in the White House in 1892. During his administration Montana, Idaho, Washington, North and South Dakota, and Wyoming were admitted into the Union. The Sherman Antitrust Act was passed in 1890, which was designed to prevent monopolies. American women were first allowed to vote in Wyoming in 1890. He fortified the navy and established trade policies overseas. Harrison was defeated in the 1892 presidential election by former President Grover Cleveland. After leaving office, Harrison returned to his home in Indianapolis. He married again, in 1896, to Mary Scott Lord Dimmick; they had one child. He practiced law in Indianapolis until he died on March 13, 1901. **Harrison was president from 1889-93 and the vice president was Levi P. Morton.**

WILLIAM MCKINLEY

25th President. William McKinley was born in Niles, Ohio, on January 29, 1843. He attended school in Poland, Ohio, and then went to Allegheny College in Meadville, Pennsylvania. At the age of 17 he left college before he graduated and started teaching in a rural school. The Civil War broke out in 1861. He enlisted as a private in the 23rd Ohio Volunteer Regiment. He was promoted to captain and then brevet major and served under Rutherford B. Hayes. When the Civil War ended in 1865 he returned to Ohio to study law. He opened a law office in 1867 and two years later he was elected county prosecutor. He married Ida Saxton in 1871. They had two daughters both of whom died before age five. His wife suffered from epilepsy and needed special attention. In 1876 McKinley was elected to the House of Representatives, where he served until 1891. In 1892 he was elected governor of Ohio. He served one term and was nominated by the Republican Party to run for president. He won and he was a popular president. He guided the country through the Spanish-American War that lasted less than four months. As a result of the war, Cuba gained its independence from Spain. He became known for the Open Door Policy with China, which initiated the equality of trade with China and respect for its territorial integrity. McKinley was reelected to a second term, but he was assassinated only six months after he was sworn in. He died on September 14, 1901, eight days after being shot at point-blank range, when he was attending a reception in Buffalo, New York. He is buried in Canton, Ohio. **McKinley was president from 1897-1901 and the vice presidents were Garret A. Hobart and Theodore Roosevelt.**

THEODORE ROOSEVELT

26th President. Theodore Roosevelt was born on October 27, 1858, in New York City. He graduated from Harvard University. In 1880 he married Alice Hathaway Lee. He enrolled in Columbia University to study law but dropped out as he lost interest. He was elected to the New York State Assembly. In his third term in 1884, Roosevelt's mother died. A few hours later, his wife died shortly after giving birth to a baby girl. He served to the end of his term, and spent time in the Dakota Territory at his ranch on the Little Missouri River. He married Edith Carow in 1886; they had five children. He accepted an appointment to the United States Civil Service Commission, serving for six years until he was appointed to the New York City Board of Police Commissioners. He resigned from the Police Board to become assistant secretary of the Navy. A year later during the Spanish-American War, he organized and then commanded the first United States Volunteer Cavalry Regiment. In 1899 he was elected governor of New York. Roosevelt was inaugurated vice president of the United States on March 4, 1901, and sworn in as president upon the death of President William McKinley on September 14, 1901. He was easily reelected in 1904. In 1906 he was awarded the Nobel Peace Prize for his efforts in ending the Russo-Japanese War in 1905. He organized the Bull Moose Party to run for president in 1912, but lost to Woodrow Wilson. He wrote his autobiography and then traveled to South America in 1913. Roosevelt died in his sleep at his home in Oyster Bay, New York, on January 6, 1919. **Roosevelt was president from 1901-09 and the Vice president was Charles W. Fairbanks.**

WILLIAM HOWARD TAFT

27th President. William Howard Taft was born in Cincinnati, Ohio, on September 15, 1857. His father was a judge. William was an excellent student. He entered Yale College in 1874 and graduated in 1878. He enrolled at Cincinnati Law School and graduated in 1880 and became a successful lawyer. In 1881 he was appointed assistant prosecutor in a county court. He went on to become an official in the Bureau of the Internal Revenue Service and resigned. In 1886 he married Helen Herron and they had three children. In 1887 he was named a judge on the Ohio Superior Court. In 1890, President Benjamin Harrison appointed Taft to the post of solicitor general of the United States, the second highest position in the Department of Justice. In 1892 he resigned to become a federal circuit judge. In 1901 President William McKinley appointed Taft Governor of the Philippines. In 1904 President Roosevelt appointed Taft secretary of war. In 1908, Taft ran as a Republican and was elected president. He helped establish the 16th Amendment to the Constitution, which allows Congress to collect income tax. He served one term. In the next election he was opposed by Roosevelt and Woodrow Wilson. He retired to Yale University where he was a professor of constitutional law until he was appointed Chief Justice of the United States by President Harding in 1921. His administrative work as a Supreme Court justice is considered his greatest contribution to public service. He retired in 1930 due to poor health and died the same year on March 8 in Washington, D.C. **Taft was president from 1909-13 and the vice president was James S. Sherman.**

WOODROW WILSON

29th President. (Thomas) Woodrow Wilson was born in Staunton, Virginia, on December 28, 1856. He was educated at home; his father was a minister and a teacher. Woodrow enrolled in Davidson College in North Carolina and then the College of New Jersey (later Princeton University). He studied law at the University of Virginia and then attended Johns Hopkins University in Baltimore, where he graduated with a PhD in history and political theory in 1885. He married Ellen Axson in 1885, and they had three daughters. He taught at Bryn Mawr College in Pennsylvania and at Wesleyan University in Connecticut. He later taught at Princeton University and became the president of the university. In 1910 he was elected governor of New Jersey. He was elected president in 1912. As president, Wilson and the Congress reduced tariffs. Ellen Wilson died in 1914; Wilson married Edith Galt at the end of 1915. The United States became involved in World War I after Germany urged Mexico to attack the United States. The armistice was signed on November 11, 1918. After the war, Wilson proposed a League of Nations when he went to Paris to present the 14 Points of Peace and to help write the Versailles Treaty. The idea was accepted in Europe but the Senate defeated the proposal here. Wilson was awarded the Nobel Peace Prize in 1919. He left office in 1921. He died of a stroke while on tour to promote the League of Nations in Washington, D.C. on February 3, 1924. **Wilson was president from 1913-21 and the vice president was Thomas R. Marshall.**

WARREN G. HARDING

29th President. Warren Gamaliel Harding was born in Blooming Grove, Ohio, on November 2, 1865. He helped his father on the farm; attended school became a printer's apprentice at a newspaper owned by his father. He was the oldest of eight children; his father was a doctor. When he was 14, Harding enrolled in Ohio Central College in Iberia. He graduated and took various jobs, earning enough to buy a newspaper, the *Marion Star*, with two friends. His partners left the business and he ran it by himself. He married a widow, Florence Kling De Wolfe, in 1891, who helped him make the newspaper successful. In 1898 he ran as a Republican for the state senate and was elected serving four years. In 1903 he was elected lieutenant governor of Ohio and served for two years. He returned to Marion to work on the *Star*. In 1910 he ran for governor and lost. In 1914 he was elected to the United States Senate and served a full term, and then was elected president in 1920. During his administration the first nonstop transcontinental airplane flight was made and the first commercial radio broadcast took place. During his presidency Harding established a budget system for the federal government but his administration was marred by the Teapot Dome scandal: federal oil reserves were illegally rented to private businesses. In 1923 he and his wife traveled across the country speaking in many cities. He fell ill from food poisoning when he arrived in San Francisco after leaving Alaska. He died suddenly from a heart attack on August 2, 1923. **Harding was president from 1921-23 and the vice president was Calvin Coolidge.**

423

CALVIN COOLIDGE

30th President. Calvin Coolidge was born on July 4, 1872, in Plymouth Notch, Vermont. He was raised on a farm and enrolled in Black River Academy in Ludlow, Vermont, when he was 13. He was admitted to Amherst College in Massachusetts in 1891. After graduation he decided to become a lawyer. He took a job in a law office in Northampton, Massachusetts. While working, he studied for the bar exam and was admitted to the bar in 1897. He opened his own law office in the same town. In 1898 he was appointed city councilman. He married Grace Goodhue in 1905; they had two sons. In 1906 Coolidge was elected to the Massachusetts legislature. Three years later he was voted mayor of Northampton. In 1912 he became a Massachusetts state senator. He was elected Lieutenant Governor of Massachusetts in 1916. Coolidge was elected governor in 1918. He served from 1919 to 1921. He was elected vice president of the United States in 1920. In 1923 he became president of the United States when President Warren Harding died on August 2. The next year he won the presidential election and served the full term. The 18th Amendment, the prohibition against alcohol, was enforced during his presidency. The 1920s were peaceful and prosperous for the United States Coolidge supported tax cuts and opposed U.S. membership in the League of Nations. Coolidge did not want to run for a second term. He retired to Northampton, where he wrote his autobiography and lived a quiet life until he died of a heart attack on January 5, 1933. **Coolidge was President from 1923-29 and the vice president was Charles G. Dawes.**

HERBERT C. HOOVER

31st President. Herbert Clark Hoover was born on August 10, 1874, in West Branch, Iowa. When he was six, his father died of heart failure after contracting pneumonia and his mother died of pneumonia and typhoid fever when he was nine. He moved to Newberg, Oregon, to live with his uncle, Dr. Henry Minthorn. He attended a Quaker academy there. When he was 16, he enrolled in Stanford in Palo Alto, California where he studied geology. He graduated in 1895 and worked in the goldfields of California. In 1897 a British company hired Hoover to manage its gold mines in Australia. He returned home and married Lou Henry in 1899; the couple then moved to China. They and their two sons traveled widely during the next 15 years as he worked on engineering projects. Hoover was in London as Chairman of the American Relief Committee during World War I. He also served on the Commission for Relief in Belgium. President Warren G. Harding appointed Hoover Secretary of Commerce in 1921. Nominated for president in 1928, Hoover won in a landslide victory. As president he worked to improve the standards of radio broadcasting, aviation and housing. During his administration the stock market crashed in 1929, leading to the Great Depression. He established a few programs to combat the crisis, but he opposed aid through federal bureaucracy, so he was blamed for the problems of the Depression so he was defeated in the 1932 election. He died on October 20, 1964, in New York City, at the age of 90. **Hoover was president from 1929-33 and the vice president was Charles Curtis.**

FRANKLIN D. ROOSEVELT

32nd President. Franklin Delano Roosevelt was born on January 30, 1882, in Hyde Park, New York. He was tutored by a governess and he took frequent trips to Europe. He attended Groton School in Massachusetts, graduated in 1903 from Harvard University, and attended Columbia University Law School in New York. He married Eleanor Roosevelt, a distant cousin, in 1905 and together they had six children. He passed the bar and joined a law firm on Wall Street. In 1910 he was elected to the New York Senate. He was 28 years old. President Woodrow Wilson appointed Roosevelt Assistant Secretary of the Navy three years later in 1913. At his vacation home on Campobello Island, New Brunswick, Canada he contracted polio, leaving his legs paralyzed for the rest of his life. In 1928 he ran for governor of New York and won. He served two terms; he was nominated by the Democratic Party to run for president in 1932. Roosevelt won in a landslide victory. He helped the nation through the Great Depression by proposing many new government agencies. In 1936 he was elected to a second term. Roosevelt was elected to a third term in 1940. On December 7, 1941, the United States Naval fleet at Pearl Harbor, Hawaii was attacked by the Japanese Air Force. The United States declared war on Japan, Italy and Germany. The United States was embroiled in World War II when Roosevelt was elected to his fourth term as president in 1944. He died in office at Warm Springs, Georgia, on April 12, 1945. **Roosevelt was President from 1933-45 and the Vice Presidents were John N. Garner, Henry A. Wallace and Harry S Truman.**

HARRY S TRUMAN

33rd President. Harry S Truman was born in Lamar, Missouri, on May 8, 1884. Truman hoped to attend West Point but was rejected because of his poor eyesight. He held a variety of jobs before agreeing to return home and work on the family farm. During World War I he enlisted in the army and was sent to France, where he commanded a field artillery battery. He married Bess Wallace in 1919; they had one daughter. Truman opened a men's clothing store that failed. He lost his life's savings and was left $20,000 in debt. He spent 15 years paying it off. He ran for county judge and won. Truman had little knowledge about law so he attended the Kansas City School of Law at night. He served as a judge of the Jackson County Court from 1926 to 1934, when he was elected to the United States Senate. He was elected to two terms as senator but was chosen in 1944 to become Franklin D. Roosevelt's running mate in Roosevelt's historic bid for a fourth term as president. Truman was inaugurated vice president, January 20, 1945, and became president four months later upon the death of Franklin D. Roosevelt on April 12, 1940. Truman proposals for post-war legislation were called the "Fair Deal." He worked hard for equal rights for all citizens of the United States. He was the only president to use the atomic bomb, when the United States attacked Hiroshima and Nagasaki, Japan in 1945, causing Japan to surrender and end World War II. Truman was elected to a second term but decided not to run for office in 1952. He returned to his home in Independence, Missouri, where he devoted his time to the Truman Library. He died on December 26, 1972. **Truman was president from 1945-53 and the vice president was Alben W. Barkley.**

Dwight D. Eisenhower

34th President. Dwight David Eisenhower was born on October 14, 1890, in Denison, Texas. His family moved to Abilene, Kansas, where his father bought a house on a 10-acre farm. He worked on the farm with his four brothers. Everyone called him "Ike". After high school he worked nights at a local creamery. He was accepted into West Point, graduated in 1915, commissioned as a second lieutenant. A year later he married Mamie Geneva Doud. They had two sons. General Douglas MacArthur asked Eisenhower to assist him in planning the defense of the Philippines from 1935 to 1939. In 1942 Eisenhower became the commanding general of the American Forces in the European theater and the Commander in Chief of the Allied forces in North Africa, commanding British and American troops. A year later he was promoted to 4-star general. On June 6, 1944, also known as D-Day, he was promoted to General of the Army. In May of 1945, the German army surrendered. Eisenhower retired from the army in 1948 and became the president of Columbia University. In 1950, he was named Commander of NATO Forces in Europe. Eisenhower was nominated by the Republicans to run for president and won; he served two terms. While president, he had a severe heart attack in 1955. During his administration he was engaged in foreign policy, ending the Korean War, and negotiating with China, Cuba and Russia. He enforced the Supreme Court's decision to integrate schools. Eisenhower died on March 28, 1969, at Walter Reed Hospital in Washington D.C. **Eisenhower was president from 1953-61 and the vice president was Richard M. Nixon.**

John F. Kennedy

35th President. John Fitzgerald Kennedy was born on May 29, 1917, in Brookline, Massachusetts; the second of nine children. He attended private schools and attended Harvard University. The summer of his freshman year he traveled to London where he fell ill with jaundice. He briefly attended Princeton University before returning to Harvard and graduating with honors in 1940. When the Japanese attacked Pearl Harbor, Kennedy signed up with the navy. As a lieutenant, he commanded a patrol torpedo, or PT, boat, which sank in 1943. He helped rescue his crew and was awarded a Purple Heart. He was elected to Congress in 1946 in a Boston district and re-elected twice. In 1952 he was elected senator from Massachusetts. In 1953 he married Jacqueline Bouvier. They had three children. Kennedy was sworn in as president in 1961. His administration was marked by the invasion of the Bay of Pigs in Cuba, in which anti-Castro Cubans invaded Cuba but failed to complete their mission. Kennedy succeeded in forcing the Soviet Union to remove missiles from Cuba and in keeping troops in Berlin to prevent the spread of Communism. Kennedy supported the Civil Rights movement led by Martin Luther King, Jr. He advocated improved medical care for the elderly and space exploration. Kennedy initiated the Peace Corps, an organization of volunteers who carry education and skills to underdeveloped countries. Kennedy was assassinated while traveling in a motorcade through Dallas, Texas, on November 22, 1963. **Kennedy was president from 1961-63 and the vice president was Lyndon B. Johnson.**

LYNDON B. JOHNSON

36th President. Lyndon Baines Johnson was born near Johnson City, Texas, on August 27, 1908. He attended public schools and enrolled in San Marcos College. He graduated in 1930. He taught for one year in the Texas schools and left to enter politics. He worked for a congressman and was then appointed director of the National Youth Administration. In 1934 he married Claudia Alta Taylor, better known as Lady Bird. They had two daughters. Johnson was elected to the United States House of Representatives in 1937. He joined the navy when the Japanese attacked Pearl Harbor on December 7, 1941, and fought in the Pacific theater. He returned from the war in July 1942 when President Roosevelt ordered all members of Congress in military service to return to their duties. In 1948 he was elected to the Senate and became the Democratic majority leader in 1954. He was elected vice president when John F. Kennedy won the presidential election in 1960. Johnson took the oath of office after Kennedy was assassinated in Dallas, Texas, in 1963. During his administration, Congress passed laws on civil rights, poverty and conservation. Johnson ran for President in 1964 and won. He was known for creating the "Great Society" that promoted equal rights for all and provided health insurance for the elderly. He decided not to run for re-election in 1968 because of the national turmoil of the Vietnam War, which escalated during his administration. He returned to his ranch in Texas, where he died on January 22, 1973. **Johnson was president from 1963-69 and the vice president was Hubert H. Humphrey.**

RICHARD M. NIXON

37th President. Richard Milhous Nixon was born on January 9, 1913, in Yorba Linda, California. His family moved to Whittier, California, where he and his four brothers attended public school and worked at his father's store. He enrolled in Whittier College when he was 17. In 1934, Nixon received a scholarship to Duke University Law School in North Carolina. After graduation, he tried to get a job with a law firm in New York, but he was turned down every time and returned to Whittier, California, where he met and married Thelma Catherine Ryan, nicknamed Pat. They had two daughters. Nixon joined the navy in 1942 rising to lieutenant commander by the end of the war. He was elected to Congress in 1946 and served there until he was elected to the United States Senate in 1950. In 1960 he was elected vice president under Eisenhower. Nixon ran for president in 1960 and lost against Kennedy. Two years later, he ran for governor of California and lost. He was nominated for president by the Republican Party in 1968 and won. Nixon began bringing troops home from Vietnam. In his second term the war ended with the fall of Saigon. During his administration the Apollo 11 space flight landed two men on the moon. Nixon rebuilt ties with China after 21 years of silence. The *Washington Post* began investigating the illegal activities of Nixon and his aides during the 1972 election campaign and the break-in at the Watergate Hotel. In 1974 he faced impeachment and resigned as president. He retired to his home in San Clemente, California where he died on April 22, 1994. **Nixon was president from 1969-74 and the vice presidents were Spiro T. Agnew and Gerald R. Ford.**

GERALD R. FORD

38th President. Gerald Rudolph Ford was born on July 14, 1913, in Omaha, Nebraska. His family moved to Grand Rapids, Michigan, where he attended school. He was a popular student and athlete– he played football in high school and college at the University of Michigan. Ford graduated from Yale law school and was admitted to the bar. He joined the navy in 1942 to fight in World War II; he was promoted to the rank of lieutenant commander and remained on active duty until 1946. After the war he ran for a seat in Congress and won. He spent 25 years in the United States House of Representatives. Ford married Elizabeth Bloomer Warren in 1948; they had four children. In 1973, after the resignation of Vice President Spiro T. Agnew, President Nixon asked Ford to be the vice president. A year later, Ford replaced Nixon as president, when Nixon resigned his presidency because of the Watergate scandal. Ford is the only president who was not elected to the office. As president, Ford gave Nixon a pardon, "for all offenses against the United States." The act made him unpopular with many people. Ford, who was a Republican, had many differences with the Democrat-controlled Congress. He vetoed more than 60 bills. He was successful with his foreign policies– he championed détente, and peace among nations, especially between the United States and the Soviet Union. Ford tried to bring the nation together after Nixon left the White House, but he lost his bid for a second term in 1976 by a narrow margin. The Fords retired to California. Gerald Ford died in Rancho Mirage on December 26, 2006. **Ford was president from 1974-77 and the vice president was Nelson A. Rockefeller.**

JAMES E. CARTER, JR.

39th President. James Earl Carter, Jr. was born on October 1, 1924, in Plains, Georgia. Carter grew up on a peanut farm. He left home to attend the United States Naval Academy at Annapolis, Maryland. He graduated in 1946. He served in the navy for seven years and returned home to run the family business. He married Rosalynn Smith in 1946, they had four children. Carter served on the school board and educational advisory boards. He was a strong advocate for civil rights. In 1962 he was elected to the Georgia Senate and served one term. He ran for governor of Georgia in 1970 and won. In 1976 he was elected president as a Democrat. As president he helped to write the Camp David Accords, a peace treaty between Egypt and Israel. He helped negotiate the Salt II treaty with the Soviet Union. During his administration Carter was criticized for the poor economy and gas shortages that meant long lines at gas pumps. In 1979, a group of Iranian students took the staff of the United States Embassy hostage. Efforts to negotiate the release of the 52 hostages in Iran consumed the later part of his term. He was not successful and this was perceived as weakness and made him unpopular. He was defeated in the 1980 election. After his term as president, Carter started the Carter Center to introduce democracy throughout the world. In 2002 he was awarded the Nobel Peace Prize. Carter and his wife Rosalynn live in Plains, Georgia. They have actively promoted humanitarian programs and peace throughout the world since he left the office of President. **Carter was president from 1977-81 and the vice president was Walter F. Mondale.**

RONALD W. REAGAN

40th President. Ronald Wilson Reagan was born on February 6, 1911, in Tampico, Illinois. He attended public schools and enrolled in Eureka College in Illinois, where he studied economics and sociology. After graduating in 1932 he worked as a radio announcer in Iowa. In 1937 he became an actor, appearing in more than 50 movies during his 27 year career. In 1940 he married Jane Wyman, they had a daughter and adopted a son. Their marriage ended in divorce in 1948. Reagan joined the United States Army Reserve in 1937. During World War II, he served with the Army Air Forces, narrating patriotic movies. In 1952 he married actress Nancy Davis; they had a daughter and son. Reagan ran for governor of California as a Republican and won. He was elected president in a landslide victory over Jimmy Carter in 1980. Moments after he was sworn into office, the hostages were released in Iran. During his administration he set out to strengthen military defense. He tried to stop inflation and improve business growth by instituting supply-side economics, which called for cutting taxes and government programs, but resulted in high budget deficits. In 1981 Reagan was wounded in an assassination attempt. During his second term, the Berlin Wall came down, uniting East and West Germany which had been divided since World War II. His administration was criticized for the sale of weapons to Iran in exchange for hostages and the use of money to aid rebels in Nicaragua. Reagan retired to Bel Air, California and died there on June 6, 2004. **Reagan was president from 1981-89 and the vice president was George H. W. Bush.**

GEORGE H. W. BUSH

41st President. George Herbert Walker Bush was born on June 12, 1924, in Milton, Massachusetts. He attended private schools in Connecticut and Phillips Academy in Andover, Massachusetts. In 1942 he served in the navy as a pilot during World War II and received the Distinguished Flying Cross after being shot down over the Pacific in 1944. He married Barbara Pierce in 1945. They had six children; one died of leukemia when she was four. In 1948 he graduated from Yale University. He started a development company, which dealt in Texas oil and gas properties. Bush tried running for the Senate and lost. He was elected to the House of Representatives in 1966. He served as the ambassador to the United Nations and head of the Central Intelligence Agency. In 1974, he was appointed by President Ford as the U.S. liaison officer to the People's Republic of China. He served eight years as vice president when Reagan was elected president in 1980. Bush was elected President in 1988. In 1989, he ordered an invasion of Panama to remove the country's leader, General Manuel Noriega. In 1990, Iraq invaded Kuwait and President Bush led the worldwide forces against Iraq in the Persian Gulf War. During his administration, Bush supported democratization in the Soviet Union, which dissolved in 1991, and in Eastern Europe. He raised taxes to combat budget deficits. His popularity diminished in late 1991 because of the economic recession. He lost the election to Bill Clinton. George Bush and his wife Barbara retired to Texas. **Bush was president from 1989-93 and the vice president was J. Danforth Quayle.**

WILLIAM J. CLINTON

42nd President. William Jefferson Clinton was born William Jefferson Blythe IV on August 19, 1946, in Hope, Arkansas. His father had died in a traffic accident a few months earlier. His mother married Roger Clinton and he took that family name while in high school. He attended public schools in Arkansas. He moved to Washington, D.C. to attend Georgetown University. In 1968, he won a Rhodes Scholarship to Oxford University in Oxford, England. He received a law degree from Yale University in 1973. Clinton returned to Arkansas and ran for Congress and lost. He married Hillary Rodham; they have one daughter. In 1976, Clinton was elected Arkansas attorney general. He ran for governor of Arkansas in 1978 and won. He lost his bid for a second term, but regained the office four years later. He served until he won the presidency against incumbent George Bush in 1992. As president, Clinton reduced the national debt. He promoted international trade and persuaded Congress to pass the North American Free Trade Agreement (NAFTA) between the United States, Canada and Mexico. Clinton was reelected in 1996. He supported use of NATO forces to remove Serbian troops from Kosovo in 1999. He improved relations with Russia and China. During his second term, in 1998, Clinton was the second president impeached by Congress. He was accused of giving false court testimony, tried in the Senate and found not guilty. Clinton and his wife Hillary live in New York. Hillary became a U.S. Senator from New York and then secretary of state under Obama. **Clinton was president from 1993-2001 and the vice president was Albert Gore, Jr.**

GEORGE W. BUSH

43rd President. George Walker Bush was born on July 6, 1946, in New Haven, Connecticut, the son of the 41st president, George H.W. Bush. He grew up in Midland Texas, where he attended public and private schools. He received a bachelor's degree from Yale University in 1968, and then served as an F-102 fighter pilot in the Texas Air National Guard. He enrolled in Harvard Business School and received a Master of Business Administration in 1975. He married Laura Welch; they have twin daughters. Bush started an oil company and in 1989 bought the Texas Rangers baseball franchise. He served as general manager and partner of the team, in 1989 until he was elected governor of Texas in 1994. Bush was elected president in 2000. After being sworn in as president in 2001, President Bush has signed into law initiatives to improve public schools by raising standards requiring accountability, and strengthening local control. He signed tax relief that lowered the income tax rate. He increased pay and benefits for America's military. After the attacks of September 11, 2001, Bush created the Office of Homeland Security to protect Americans against terrorism. The United States invaded first Afghanistan and then Iraq, but failed during Bush's two terms to find Osama bin Laden, the terrorist leader of al-Qaeda, who was responsible for the 9/11 attacks. Bush and his wife Laura retired to Dallas, Texas. **Bush was president from 2001-2009 and the vice president was Richard B. Cheney.**

BARACK H. OBAMA

44th President, Barack Hussein Obama was born on August 4, 1961, in Honolulu, Hawaii. His parents divorced and his mother then married an Indonesian, so Obama lived in Indonesia from age six to 10. His mother was concerned about his education, though, so she sent him back to Hawaii to live with his grandparents. He graduated from Columbia University in New York City in 1983. He worked as a community organizer in Chicago before enrolling in Harvard Law School, graduating in 1991. The next year, he married Michelle Robinson; they have two daughters. Obama was elected to the Illinois state senate in 1996 and served for eight years. He was elected to the U.S. Senate in 2004. In 2008, Obama was elected president. He was the first African-American president of the United States. He inherited a troubled country, with the economy in a recession and wars in Afghanistan and Iraq. Obama followed through with President Bush's plan to bail out the banks. Obama worked for nuclear arms control, signing an agreement to reduce stockpiles of nuclear weapons in the US and Russia. He also advocated a major reform to the nation's health insurance system. After receiving intelligence describing the whereabouts of Osama bin Laden, the leader of al-Qaeda responsible for the September 11, 2011, attacks on the U.S., Obama ordered an operation that resulted in bin Laden's death on May 1, 2011. He was awarded the Nobel Peace Prize in 2009. Following his reelection in 2012, he has worked on issues such as gun control, troop withdrawal from Iraq and Afghanistan and improving the quality of life for veterans. **Obama became president January 20, 2009 and the vice president is Joseph Biden.**

Washington, DC
The Nation's Capital

The President of the United States lives in the White House at 1600 Pennsylvania Avenue in Washington, DC. Washington DC is the capital of the United States. It became the capital of the United States in 1800, when the federal government moved from Philadelphia. The city was named after George Washington. It was built to be the legislative, administrative, and judicial center of the United States.

There are 715 libraries—only 118 fewer than New York City. The Residence Bill of July 16, 1790, established the federal district which was first called the Territory of Columbia and the federal city, the City of Washington. The name changed to the District of Columbia in 1793. The first act passed by the District's first legislative assembly on August 3, 1871, created the corporate seal of the District of Columbia. The present system of government (since 1975) provides for an elected mayor and city council, but reserves for Congress veto power over the budget and legislation and direct control over most of the federal buildings and monuments. The 23rd Amendment (1961) to the Constitution gave inhabitants the right to vote in presidential elections.

Statistics of our Nation's Capital
Size 61 square miles
Population 646,449
Great Seal Justice, who is a woman, is shown on the seal hanging a wreath on a statue of George Washington.
Motto Justia Omnibus, Justice for all
Flower American beauty rose
Bird Woodthrush
Tree Scarlet Oak

The Fifty United States

Britain's American colonies broke with the mother country in 1776 and were recognized as the new nation of the United States of America following the Treaty of Paris in 1783. During the 19th and 20th centuries, 37 new states were added to the original 13 as the nation expanded across the North American continent and acquired a number of overseas possessions. The two most traumatic experiences in the nation's history were the Civil War (1861-65) and the great Depression of the 1930s. Buoyed by victories in World Wars I and II and the end of the Cold War in 1991, the US remains the world's most powerful nation-state. The economy is marked by steady growth, low unemployment and inflation, and rapid advances in technology.

From the CIA Factbook, 2013-14

Size: 3,794,100 square miles   **Population:** 316,668,567

Motto "In God We Trust", adopted July 30, 1956. The original motto adopted September 9, 1776, was:
"E Pluribus Unum" (Out of many, one).

The Great Seal The Great Seal of the United States shows an American bald eagle with a ribbon in its mouth bearing the Latin words 'e pluribus unum". In its talons are the arrows of war and an olive branch of peace. On the back of the Great Seal is an unfinished pyramid with an eye (the eye of Providence) above it. The seal was approved by Congress on June 20, 1782.

Bird Eagle, adopted June 20, 1782

Song "The Star Spangled Banner," written by Francis Scott Key in 1814, was adopted by Congress as the National anthem in 1931.

Flower Rose, chosen by President Ronald Reagan when he was in office.

Alabama (AL)

Alabama comes from an Indian word for "tribal town."

Capital	Montgomery
Size	52,419 square miles
Population	4,833,722
Statehood	December 14, 1819; 22nd State
Motto	"We Dare Defend Our Rights"
Tree	Southern Pine
Bird	Yellowhammer
Flower	Camellia
Song	"Alabama," by Julia S. Tutwiler Music by Edna Goeckel Gussen

Alaska (AK)

Alaska comes from alakshak, the Eskimo word meaning "peninsula" or "land that is an island."

Capital	Juneau
Size	663,267 square miles
Population	735,132
Statehood	January 3, 1959, 49th State
Motto	"North to the Future"
Tree	Sitka Spruce
Bird	Willow Ptarmigan
Flower	Forget-Me-Not
Song	"Alaska's Flag" by Marie Drake Music by Elinor Dusenbury

NOTE: The abbreviations following the state name are U.S. Postal abbreviations.

Arizona (AZ)

The Grand Canyon State

Arizona comes from a Pima Indian word "Arizonac", meaning "little spring place."

Capital	Phoenix
Size	114,006 square miles
Population	6,626,624
Statehood	February 14, 1912 48th State
Motto	"Ditant Deus (God Enriches)"
Tree	Palo Verde
Bird	Cactus Wren
Flower	Saguaro Cactus Blossom
Song	"Arizona" by Margaret Rowe Clifford Music by Maurice Blumenthal

Arkansas (AR)

The Land of Opportunity

Arkansas is a variation of Quapaw, the name of an Indian tribe, which means "south wind."

Capital	Little Rock
Size	53,182 square miles
Population	2,959,373
Statehood	June 15, 1836 25th State
Motto	"Regnat Populus" (The People Rule)
Tree	Southern Pine
Bird	Mockingbird
Flower	Apple Blossom
Songs	"Arkansas," Music and Words by Wayland Holyfield "Oh, Arkansas," Music and Words by Terry Rose & Gary Klaff

California (CA)

California was named by Spanish explorers after an imaginary island in the story, *Las Sergas de Esplandian*, by Garcia Ordonez de Montalvo, circa 1500.

Capital	Sacramento
Size	163,696 square miles
Population	38,332,521
Statehood	September 9, 1850, 31st State
Motto	"Eureka" (I have found it)
Tree	California Redwood
Bird	California Quail
Flower	California Poppy
Song	"I Love You, California"

Colorado (CO)

Colorado is based on the Spanish word meaning "reddish color". It was the name early Spanish explorers gave to the Colorado River, which originates in the state.

Capital	Denver
Size	104,100 square miles
Population	5,268,367
Statehood	August 1, 1876, 38th State
Motto	"Nil Sine Numine" (Nothing without providence)"
Tree	Colorado Blue Spruce
Bird	Lark Bunting
Flower	Columbine
Song	"Where the Columbines Grow" by A.J. Flynn

Connecticut (CT)

Connecticut comes from an Algonquin Indian word Quinnehtukqut, meaning "beside the long tidal river."

Capital	Hartford
Size	5,544 square miles
Population	3,596,080
Statehood	January 9, 1788 5th State
Motto	"Quitranstulit Sustined" (He who, transplanted, sustains)
Tree	White Oak
Bird	American Robin
Flower	Mountain Laurel
Song	"Yankee Doodle"

Delaware (DE)

Delaware is named after Sir Thomas West, Baron La Warr, the English governor of Virginia in colonial times.

Capital	Dover
Size	2,489 square miles
Population	925,749
Statehood	December 7, 1787, 1st State
Motto	"Liberty and Independence"
Tree	American Holly
Bird	Blue Hen Chicken
Flower	Peach Blossom
Song	"Our Delaware"

Florida (FL)

Florida, means "feast of flowers or flowery" in Spanish. The territory was named by the explorer Ponce de Leon, who discovered it on Easter.

Capital	Tallahassee
Size	65,755 square miles
Population	19,552,860
Statehood	March 3, 1845, 27th State
Motto	"In God We Trust"
Tree	Sabal Palmetto
Bird	Mockingbird
Flower	Orange Blossom
Song	"Swanee River" ("Old Folks at Home") by Stephen Foster

Georgia (GA)

Georgia was named after King George II of England, who granted the settlers the right to create a colony there in 1732.

Capital	Atlanta
Size	59,425 square miles
Population	9,992,167
Statehood	January 2, 1788 4th State
Motto	"Wisdom, Justice, and Moderation"
Tree	Live Oak
Bird	Brown Thrasher
Flower	Cherokee Rose
Song	"Georgia" by Robert Loveman; music by Lollie Belle Wylie

Hawaii (HI)

The Aloha State

Hawaii comes from Hawaiki, or Owhyhee, the native Polynesians' word for "homeland."

Capital	Honolulu
Size	10,931 square miles
Population	1,404,054
Statehood	August 21, 1959, 50th State
Motto	"The Life of the Land is Preserved by Righteousness"
Tree	Kukui
Bird	Hawaiian Goose
Flower	Yellow Hibiscus
Song	"Our Own Hawaii" by King Kalakaua Music by Henry Berger

Idaho (ID)

The Gem State

Idaho is an invented name whose meaning is unknown. It may have come from a Kiowa Apache name for the Comanche Indians.

Capital	Boise
Size	83,574 square miles
Population	1,612,136
Statehood	July 3, 1890, 43rd State
Motto	"It Endures Forever" (Esto Perpetua)
Tree	Western White Pine
Bird	Mountain Bluebird
Flower	Syringa
Song	"Here We Have Idaho"

Illinois (IL)

Illinois comes from Illini, an Algonquin Indian word meaning "tribe of superior men" or "warriors."

Capital	Springfield
Size	57,918 square miles
Population	12,882,135
Statehood	December 3, 1818, 21st State
Motto	"State Sovereignty, National Union"
Tree	White Oak
Bird	Cardinal
Flower	Meadow Violet
Song	"Illinois"

Indiana (IN)

the Hoosier State

Indiana means "land of the Indians."

Capital	Indianapolis
Size	36,420 square miles
Population	6,570,902
Statehood	December 11, 1816, 19th State
Motto	"The Crossroads of America"
Tree	Tulip Tree
Bird	Cardinal
Flower	Peony
Song	"On the Banks of the Wabash Far Away" by Paul Dresser

Iowa (IA)

Iowa comes from an Indian word meaning "this is the place" or "the Beautiful land."

Capital	Des Moines
Size	56,276 square miles
Population	3,090,416
Statehood	December 28, 1846, 29th State
Motto	"Our Liberties We Prize and Our Rights We Will Maintain"
Tree	Oak
Bird	American Goldfinch
Flower	Wild Rose
Song	"The Song of Iowa" by Major S.H.M. Byers To the tune of "O Tannenbaum"

Kansas (KS)

Kansas comes from the name of a Sioux Indian word meaning, "people of the south wind."

Capital	Topeka
Size	82,282 square miles
Population	2,893,957
Statehood	January 29, 1861, 34th State
Motto	"To the Stars Through Difficulty"
Tree	Cottonwood
Bird	Western Meadowlark
Flower	Sunflower
Song	"Home on the Range" by Dr. Brewster M. Higley; music by Daniel Kelly

Kentucky (KY)

From an Iroquoian word "Ken-tah-ten", meaning "land of tomorrow."

Capital	Frankfort
Size	40,411 square miles
Population	4,395,295
Statehood	June 1, 1792, 15th State
Motto	"United We Stand, Divided We Fall"
Tree	Tulip Poplar
Bird	Cardinal
Flower	Goldenrod
Song	"My Old Kentucky Home" by Stephen Foster

Louisiana (LA)

Louisiana is named in honor of Louis XIV of France.

Capital	Baton Rouge
Size	51,840 square miles
Population	4,625,470
Statehood	April 30, 1812, 18th State
Motto	"Union, Justice, and Confidence"
Tree	Bald Cypress
Bird	Brown Pelican
Flower	Magnolia
Song	"Song of Louisiana" by Vashti R. Stopher

Maine (ME)

The Pine Tree State

Maine was first used to distinguish the mainland from the offshore islands. It has been considered a complement to Henrietta Maria, queen of Charles I of England. She was said to have owned the province of Mayne in France.

Capital	Augusta
Size	35,385 square miles
Population	1,328,302
Statehood	March 15, 1820, 23rd State
Motto	"Dirigo (I Lead)"
Tree	White Pine
Bird	Black Capped Chickadee
Flower	White Pine Cone and Tassel
Song	"State of Maine Song" by Roger Vinton Snow

Maryland (MD)

The Old Line State

Maryland was named in honor of Queen Henrietta Maria, who granted the right to establish an English colony there.

Capital	Annapolis
Size	12,407 square miles
Population	5,928,814
Statehood	April 28, 1788, 7th State
Motto	"Strong Deeds, Gentle Words"
Tree	White Oak
Bird	Baltimore Oriole
Flower	Black-Eyed Susan
Song	"Maryland, My Maryland" by James R. Randall

Massachusetts (MA)

The Bay State

Massachusetts is named after the Massachusett tribe of Native Americans, meaning "at or about the great hill."

Capital	Boston
Size	10,555 square miles
Population	6,692,824
Statehood	February 6, 1788, 6th State
Motto	"By The Sword We Seek Peace, But Peace Only Under Liberty"
Tree	American Elm
Bird	Black Capped Chickadee
Flower	Mayflower
Song	"All Hail to Massachusetts"

Michigan (MI)

The Wolverine State

Michigan comes from the Chippewa Indian words "mica gama" meaning "great or large lake," referring to Lake Michigan.

Capital	Lansing
Size	96,705 square miles
Population	9,895,622
Statehood	January 26, 1837, 26th State
Motto	"If You Seek a Pleasant Peninsula, Look About You"
Tree	White Pine
Bird	Robin
Flower	Apple Blossom
Song	"Michigan, My Michigan"

Minnesota (MN)

The Land of 10, 000 Lakes

Minnesota comes from a Dakota Sioux Indian word meaning "sky-tinted water."

Capital	Saint Paul
Size	86,943 square miles
Population	5,420,380
Statehood	May 11, 1858, 32nd State
Motto	"Star of the North"
Tree	Red (Norway) Pine
Bird	Common Loon
Flower	Lady Slipper
Song	"Hail Minnesota"

Mississippi (MS)

The Magnolia State

Mississippi comes from an Indian word meaning "Father of Waters."

Capital	Jackson
Size	48,430 square miles
Population	2,991,207
Statehood	December 10, 1817, 20th State
Motto	"By Valor and Arms"
Tree	Magnolia
Bird	Mockingbird
Flower	Magnolia Blossom
Song	"Go Mississippi"

Missouri (MO)

The Show Me State

Missouri is named after the Algonquin Indian tribe; it means "town of the large canoes."

Capital	Jefferson City
Size	69,709 square miles
Population	6,044,171
Statehood	August 10, 1821, 24th State
Motto	"Let the Welfare of the People be the Supreme Law"
Tree	Flowering Dogwood
Bird	Bluebird
Flower	White Hawthorn Blossom
Song	"Missouri Waltz" by J.R. Shannon

Montana (MT)

The Treasure State

Montana was chosen from a Latin dictionary by J.M. Ashley. It is a Latinized Spanish word meaning "mountainous."

Capital	Helena
Size	147,046 square miles
Population	1,015,165
Statehood	November 8, 1889, 41st State
Motto	"Gold and Silver"
Tree	Ponderosa Pine
Bird	Western Meadowlark
Flower	Bitterroot
Song	"Montana" by Charles C. Cohen Music by Joseph E. Howard

Nebraska (NE)

Nebraska comes from an Oto Indian word meaning "flat river" or "broad water," their name for the Platte River.

Capital	Lincoln
Size	77,358 square miles
Population	1,868,516
Statehood	March 1, 1867, 37th State
Motto	"Equality Before the Law"
Tree	Cottonwood
Bird	Western Meadowlark
Flower	Goldenrod
Song	"Beautiful Nebraska"

Nevada (NV)

Nevada was given the name by Spanish explorers. It is the Spanish word meaning "snowcapped," referring to the Sierra Nevada Mountains.

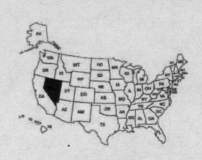

Capital	Carson City
Size	110,567 square miles
Population	2,790,136
Statehood	October 31, 1864, 36th State
Motto	"All for our Country"
Tree	Single-Leaf Pinon
Bird	Mountain Bluebird
Flower	Sagebrush
Song	"Home Means Nevada"

New Hampshire (NH)

The Granite State

New Hampshire comes from the English county of Hampshire.

Capital	Concord
Size	9,283 square miles
Population	1,323,459
Statehood	June 21, 1788, 9th State
Motto	"Live Free or Die"
Tree	White Birch
Bird	Purple finch
Flower	Purple Lilac
Song	"Old New Hampshire" by John F. Holmes; music by Maurice Hoffman

New Jersey (NJ)

The Garden State

New Jersey was named for the English Channel Isle of Jersey.

Capital	Trenton
Size	8,721 square miles
Population	8,899,339
Statehood	December 18, 1787, 3rd State
Motto	"Liberty and Prosperity"
Tree	Red Oak
Bird	American Goldfinch
Flower	Violet
Song	*None Listed*

New Mexico (NM)

Land of Enchantment

New Mexico was given its name by 16th-century Spaniards in Mexico.

Capital	Santa Fe
Size	121,598 square miles
Population	2,085,287
Statehood	January 6, 1912, 47th State
Motto	"It Grows as it Goes"
Tree	Nut Pine
Bird	Roadrunner
Flower	Yucca
Song	"O Fair New Mexico" by Elizabeth Garrett

New York (NY)

The Empire State

New York was named in honor of the Duke of York and Albany after the English took it from Dutch settlers.

Capital	Albany
Size	54,556 square miles
Population	19,651,127
Statehood	July 26, 1788, 11th State
Motto	"Excelsior"
Tree	Sugar Maple
Bird	Bluebird
Flower	Rose
Song	"I Love New York"

North Carolina (NC)

The Tar Heel State

North Carolina, the northern part of the English colony of Carolana, was named in honor of Charles I of England.

Capital	Raleigh
Size	53,819 square miles
Population	9,848,060
Statehood	November 21, 1789, 12th State
Motto	"To Be Rather Than to Seem"
Tree	Southern Pine
Bird	Cardinal
Flower	Flowering Dogwood
Song	"The Old North State" by William Gaston

North Dakota (ND)

The Peace Garden State

North Dakota is named after the Sioux tribe, meaning "allies."

Capital	Bismark
Size	70,704 square miles
Population	723,393
Statehood	November 2, 1889, 39th State
Motto	"Liberty and Union, Now and Forever, One and Inseparable"
Tree	American Elm
Bird	Western Meadowlark
Flower	Wild Prairie Rose
Song	"North Dakota Hymn" by James W. Foley Music by C.S. Putnam

Ohio (OH)

The Buckeye State

Ohio comes from an Iroquoian word meaning "great river."

Capital	Columbus
Size	44,828 square miles
Population	11,570,808
Statehood	March 1, 1803, 17th State
Motto	"With God All Things Are Possible"
Tree	Ohio Buckeye
Bird	Cardinal
Flower	Red Scarlet Carnation
Song	"Beautiful Ohio"

Oklahoma (OK)

The Sooners State

Oklahoma comes from two Choctaw Indian words meaning "red people."

Capital	Oklahoma City
Size	69,903 square miles
Population	3,850,568
Statehood	November 16, 1907, 46th State
Motto	"Labor Conquers all Things"
Tree	Redbud
Bird	Scissor-Tailed Fly Catcher
Flower	Mistletoe
Song	"Oklahoma" by R. Rogers and O. Hammerstein

Oregon (OR)

The Beaver State

Oregon's name origin is unknown, however, it is generally accepted that the name, first used by Jonathan Carver in 1778, was taken from the writings of Major Robert Rogers, an English army officer.

Capital	Salem
Size	98,381 square miles
Population	3,930,065
Statehood	February 14, 1859, 33rd State
Motto	"She Flies With Her Own Wings"
Tree	Douglas Fir
Bird	Western Meadowlark
Flower	Oregon Grape
Song	"Oregon, My Oregon," by J.A. Buchman Music By Henry B. Murtagh

Pennsylvania (PA)

The Keystone State

Pennsylvania means "Penn's Woodland," the name given to the colony founded by Admiral Sir William Penn, father of William Penn.

Capital	Harrisburg
Size	46,058 square miles
Population	12,773,801
Statehood	December, 12, 1787, 2nd State
Motto	"Virtue, Liberty and Independence"
Tree	Hemlock
Bird	Ruffed Grouse
Flower	Mountain Laurel
Song	"Pennsylvania"

Rhode Island (RI)

The Ocean State

Rhode Island's name comes from the Greek Island of Rhodes.

Capital	Providence
Size	1,545 square miles
Population	1,051,511
Statehood	May 29, 1790, 13th State
Motto	"Hope"
Tree	Red Maple
Bird	Rhode Island Red
Flower	Wood Violet
Song	"Rhode Island" by T. Clark Brown

South Carolina (SC)

The Palmetto State

South Carolina, the southern part of the English colony of Carolana, was named in honor of Charles I of England.

Capital	Columbia
Size	32,020 square miles
Population	4,774,839
Statehood	May 23, 1788, 8th State
Motto	"While I Breathe, I Hope"
Tree	Palmetto
Bird	Carolina Wren
Flower	Yellow Jessamine
Song	"Carolina" by Henry Timrod Music by Anna Custis Burgess

South Dakota (SD)

The Mount Rushmore State

South Dakota comes from a Sioux Indian word meaning "ally" or "friend."

Capital	Pierre
Size	77,121 square miles
Population	844,877
Statehood	November 2, 1889; 40th State
Motto	"Under God the People Rule"
Tree	Black Hills Spruce
Bird	Ring-necked Pheasant
Flower	Pasque flower
Song	"Hail, South Dakota"

Tennessee (TN)

The Volunteer State

Tennessee comes from "Tanasi," the name of Cherokee Indian villages on the Little Tennessee River.

Capital	Nashville
Size	42,146 square miles
Population	6,495,978
Statehood	June 1, 1796, 16th State
Motto	"Agriculture and Commerce"
Tree	Tulip Tree
Bird	Mockingbird
Flower	Iris
Songs	"Tennessee Waltz" (1965); "My Homeland, Tennessee" (1925); "When It's Iris Time in Tennessee" (1935); "My Tennessee" (1955); "Rocky Top" (1982); "Tennessee" (1992)

Texas (TX)

The Lone Star State

Texas comes from a word meaning "friends" or "allies," used by the Spanish to describe some of the American Indians living there.

Capital	Austin
Size	268,581 square miles
Population	26,448,193
Statehood	December 29, 1845; 28th State
Motto	"Friendship"
Tree	Pecan
Bird	Mockingbird
Flower	Bluebonnet
Song	"Texas, Our Texas," by William Marsh and Gladys Y. Wright

Utah (UT)

The Beehive State

Utah comes from the Ute tribe, meaning "people of the mountains."

Capital	Salt Lake City
Size	84,904 square miles
Population	2,900,872
Statehood	January 4, 1896, 45th State
Motto	"Industry"
Tree	Blue Spruce
Bird	California Gull
Flower	Sego Lily
Song	"Utah, We Love Thee" by Evan Stephens

Vermont (VT)

Vermont comes from the French "vert mont," meaning "green mountain."

Capital	Montpelier
Size	9,615 square miles
Population	626,630
Statehood	March 4, 1791; 14th State
Motto	"Freedom and Unity"
Tree	Sugar Maple Tree
Bird	Hermit Thrush
Flower	Red Clover
Song	"These Green Mountains" by Diane Martin

Virginia (VA)

Virginia is named in honor of Elizabeth, "Virgin Queen" of England.

Capital	Richmond
Size	42,774 square miles
Population	8,260,405
Statehood	June 25, 1788, 10th State
Motto	"Thus Always to Tyrants"
Tree	Dogwood
Bird	Cardinal
Flower	Flowering Dogwood
Song	"Carry Me Back to Old Virginia" by James A. Bland

Washington (WA)

Washington is named in honor of George Washington, the first president of the United States.

Capital	Olympia
Size	71,300 square miles
Population	6,971,406
Statehood	November 11, 1889; 42nd State
Motto	"By and By"
Tree	Western Hemlock
Bird	Willow Goldfinch
Flower	Rhododendron
Song	"Washington My Home" by Mrs. Helen Davis

West Virginia (WV)

West Virginia was named by the people of western Virginia, who formed their own government during the Civil War.

Capital	Charleston
Size	24,231 square miles
Population	1,854,304
Statehood	June 20, 1863, 35th State
Motto	"Mountaineers Are Always Free"
Tree	Sugar Maple
Bird	Cardinal
Flower	Rhododendron
Song	"West Virginia Hills"

Wisconsin (WI)

The Badger State

Wisconsin comes from a Chippewa name that is believed to mean "grassy place."

Capital	Madison
Size	65,499 square miles
Population	5,742,713
Statehood	May 29, 1848; 30th State
Motto	"Forward"
Tree	Sugar Maple
Bird	Robin
Flower	Violet
Song	"On Wisconsin" by Dr. Phillip A. Forsbeck Music by William T. Purdy

Wyoming (WY)

The Equality State

Wyoming is named after the Delaware Indian word, meaning "mountains and valleys alternating"; the same as the Wyoming Valley in Pennsylvania.

Capital	Cheyenne
Size	97,818 square miles
Population	582,658
Statehood	July 10, 1890, 44th State
Motto	"Equal Rights"
Tree	Cottonwood
Bird	Western Meadowlark
Flower	Indian Paintbrush
Song	"Wyoming State Song" by Charles E. Winter Music by George E. Knapp

MAPS OF THE WORLD

The World

Total area: 510.072 million sq km (316.96 million sq mi).

Land area: 148.94 million sq km (92.55 million sq mi).

Water area: 361.132 million sq km (224.41 million sq mi).
Note: 70.8% of the world is water, 29.2% is land.

The Four Oceans:
Pacific Ocean: 64,186,300 square miles; 12,925 feet deep   **Atlantic Ocean:** 33,420,000 square miles; 11,730 feet deep   **Indian Ocean:** 28,350,500 square miles; 12,598 feet deep   **Arctic Ocean:** 5,105,700 square miles; 3,407 feet deep

- **Terrain:** Highest elevation is Mt. Everest at 8,850 m (29,035 ft) and lowest land depression is the Dead Sea at –411 m (–1,349 ft) below sea level.

- **Land use:** Arable land: 10%. Permanent crops: 1%. Meadows and pastures: 26%. Forests and woodlands: 32%. Other: 31% (1993 est.). Irrigated land: 2,481,250 sq km (1,541,849 sq mi).

* **Note:** *The maps of the world and the seven continents are from The World Factbook 2003.*

The World's Largest Bodies of Water

Sea	Location	Square Miles
South China	between mainland Asia & the Philippines	1,149
Caribbean	east of Central America	1,068
Mediterranean	between Europe and Africa	971
Bering	north of the Pacific, between Alaska & Russia	875
Gulf of Mexico	south of eastern US, east of Mexico	596
Sea of Okhotsk	south of eastern Russia, north of Japan	590
East China & Yellow	east of mainland China, north of South China and south of Okhotsk	482

The World's Longest Rivers

River	Location	Miles
Nile	Egypt	4,145
Amazon	Brazil	4,008
Yangtze	China	3,964
Mississippi-Missouri	United States	3,748
Yenisey-Angara	Russia	3,448
Huang-He	China	3,395
Ob-Irtysh	Russia	3,361
Zaire/ Congo	Zaire/ Congo	2,901
Mekong	Vietnam/ Cambodia	2,796
Parana-Plate	Argentina	2,796
Amur	Russia	2,734
Lena	Russia	2,734
Mackenzie	Canada	2,634
Niger	Nigeria/ Niger/ Mali	2,597
Murray-Darling	Australia	2.330
Volga	Russia	2,299
Zambezi	Mozambique/ Zimbabwe / Zambia	2,199

ASIA

Asia measures 16,990,000 square miles and holds 61% of the world's population. Asia is comprised of many countries including Russia, China, Mongolia, Iran and India.

AUSTRALIA

Australia, the only continent that is also a country, measures 2,978,000 square miles. It is in the Southern Hemisphere and holds .5% of the world's population.

AFRICA

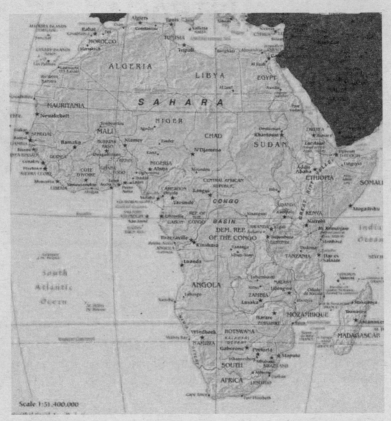

Africa measures 11,657,000 square miles and holds 12.7% of the world's population. The equator goes right through the middle of Africa.

NORTH AMERICA

North America measures 9,348,000 square miles. The United States and Canada are the only two countries in North America which holds 7.9% of the world's population.

SOUTH AMERICA

South America measures 6,885,000 square miles and is in the
Southern Hemisphere. South America contains 5.9% of the
world's population.

ANTARCTICA

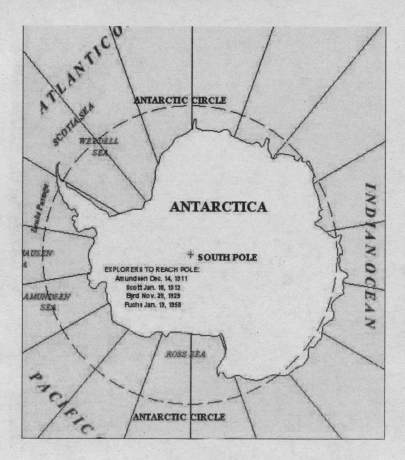

Located south of the Antarctic Circle, Antarctica is 5,404,000 square miles. Antarctica the coldest and windiest place on earth, there are no indigenous inhabitants, but there are seasonally staffed research stations. The Antarctic Treaty governs the continent of Antarctica.

EUROPE

Europe is 4,051,000 square miles and holds 12% of the world's population. Many countries make up the continent of Europe including France, Italy and Germany.

Facts About Countries & Locations

The information gathered here is derived from

The World Factbook 2013-2014 compiled by the Central Intelligence Agency

AFGHANISTAN
Location: Southern Asia, north and west of Pakistan, east of Iran
Area: 250,000 sq mi (652,230 sq km)
Area – comparative: slightly smaller than Texas
Population: 31,108,077
Population growth rate: 2.25%
Nationality: noun: Afghan(s), adjective: Afghan
Ethnic groups: Pashtun 42%, Tajik 27%, Hazara 9%, Uzbek 9%, Aimak 4%, Turkmen 3%, Baloch 2%, others 4%
Religions: Sunni Muslim 80%, Shi`a Muslim 19%, other 1%
Languages: Afghan Persian (Dari) 50%, Pashtu 35%, Turkic languages 11%, 30 minor languages 4%
Government type: Islamic republic
Capital: Kabul
Budget: revenues: $2.243 billion, expenditures: $3.963 billion   **Currency:** afghani (AFA)

ALBANIA
Location: Southeastern Europe, bordering the Adriatic Sea and Ionian Sea, between Greece and Serbia and Montenegro
Area: 11,099 sq mi (28,748 sq km)
Area – comparative: slightly smaller than Maryland
Population: 3,011,405
Population growth rate: 0.29%
Nationality: noun: Albanian(s), adjective: Albanian
Ethnic groups: Albanian 95%, Greek 3%, other 2% (Vlach, Roma (Gypsy), Serb, Macedonian, Bulgarian)
Languages: Albanian (official- derived from Tosk dialect), Greek, Vlach, Romani, Slavic dialects
Religions: Muslim 70%, Albanian Orthodox 20%, Roman Catholic 10%
Government type: parlimentary democracy
Capital: Tirana
Budget: revenues: $3.262 billion, expenditures: $ 3.669 billion
Currency: lek (ALL)

ALGERIA
Location: Northern Africa, bordering the Mediterranean Sea, between Morocco and Tunisia
Area: 919,591 sq mi (2,381,741 sq km)
Area- comparative: slightly less than 3.5 times the size of Texas
Population: 38,087,812
Population growth rate: 1.9%
Nationality: noun: Algerian(s), adjective: Algerian
Ethnic groups: Arab-Berber 99%, European less than 1%
Languages: Arabic (official), French, Berber dialects
Religions: Sunni Muslim (state religion) 99%, Christian and Jewish 1%
Government type: republic
Capital: Algiers
Budget: revenues: $79.32 billion, expenditures: $4.29 billion   **Currency:** Algerian dinar (DZD)

AMERICAN SAMOA
Location: Oceania, group of islands in the South Pacific Ocean half way between Hawaii and New Zealand
Area: 77 sq mi (199 sq km)
Area-comparative: slightly larger than Washington, DC
Population: 54,719
Population growth rate: -0.4%
Nationality: noun: American Samoan(s), adjective: American Samoan
Ethnic groups: native Pacific Islander 91.6%, Asian 2.8%, white 1.1%, mixed 4.2%, other 0.3%
Language: Samoan 90.6% (closely related to Hawaiian and other Polynesian languages), English 2.9%, Tongan 2.4%, other Pacific islander 2.1%, other 2%
Religion: Christian Congressionalist 50%, Roman Catholic 20%, Protestant and other 30%
Government: NA
Capital: Pago Pago
Budget: revenues $155.4 million (37%-local, 63% US Grants) expenditures: $183.6 million, capital $NA
Currency: US dollar (USD)

ANDORRA
Location: Southwestern Europe, between France and Spain
Area: 180 sq mi (468 sq km)
Area –comparative: 2.5 times the size of Washington, DC
Population: 85,293
Population growth rate: 0.22%
Nationality: noun: Andorran(s), adjective: Andorran
Ethnic groups: Spanish 43%, Andorran 33%, Portuguese 11%, French 7%, other 6%
Languages: Catalan (official), French, Castilian, Portuguese
Religion: Roman Catholic (predominant)
Government type: parliamentary democracy
Capital: Andorra la Vella
Budget: revenues: $403 million, expenditures: $470 million   **Currency:** euro (EUR)

ANGOLA
Location: Southern Africa, bordering the South Atlantic Ocean, between Namibia and Democratic
        Republic of the Congo
Area: 481,351 sq mi (1,246,700 sq km)
Area-comparative: slightly less than twice the size of Texas
Population: 18,565,269
Population growth rate: 2.78%
Nationality: noun: Angolan(s), adjective: Angolan
Ethnic groups: Ovimbundu 37%, Kimbundu 25%, Bakongo 13%, Mestico 2%, European 1%, other 22%
Languages: Portuguese (official), Bantu and other African languages
Religions: indigenous beliefs 47%, Roman Catholic 38%, Protestant 15%
Government: Republic; multiparty presidential regime
Capital: Luanda
Budget: revenues: $56.07 billion; expenditures: $42.26 billion
Currency: kwanza (AOA)

ANGUILLA (overseas territory of the UK)
Location: islands between the Caribbean Sea and the North Atlantic Ocean, east of Puerto Rico
Area: 35 sq mi (91 sq km)
Area-comparative: about one half the size of Washington, DC
Population: 15,754
Population growth rate: 2.11%

Nationality: noun: Anguillan(s), adjective: Anguillan
Ethnic groups: black (predominant) 90.1%, mixed mulatto 4.0%, white 3.7%, other 1.5%
Religions: Anglican 29%, Methodist 23.9%, other Protestant 30.2%, Catholic 5.7%, other 5.2%, unspecified 4.3%
Languages: English (official)
Government: NA (overseas territory of the UK)
Capital: The Valley
Budget: revenues: $22.8 million, expenditures: $22.5 million   **Currency:** East Caribbean dollar (XCD)

ANTIGUA AND BARBUDA
Location: islands between the Caribbean Sea and North Atlantic Ocean, east-southeast of Puerto-Rico
Area: 171 sq mi (total 443 sq km)
Area-comparative: 2.5 times the size of Washington, DC
Population: 90,156
Population growth rate: 1.26%
Nationality: noun: Antiguan(s), Barbudan(s), adjective: Antiguan, Barbudan
Ethnic groups: black 91%, mixed 4.4%, white 1.7%, other 2.9%
Languages: English (official), local dialects
Religions: Anglican 25.7%, Seventh Day Adventist 12.3%, Pentecostal 10.6%, Moravian 10.5%, Roman Catholic 10.4%, Methodist 7.9%, Baptist 4.9%, Church of God 4.5%, other Christian 5.4%, other 7.8%
Government type: constitutional parliamentary democracy
Capital: Saint John's
Budget: revenues: $229.5 million, expenditures: $293.4 million
Currency: East Caribbean dollar (XCD)

ARGENTINA
Location: Southern South America, bordering the South Atlantic Ocean, between Chile and Uruguay
Area: 1,073,500 sq mi (2,780,400 sq km)
Area-comparative: slightly less than three tenths the size of the US
Population: 42,610,981
Population growth rate: 0.98%
Nationality: noun: Argentinc(s), adjective: Argentine
Ethnic groups: white (mostly Spanish and Italian) 97%, mestizo, or other nonwhite groups 3%
Languages: Spanish (official), Italian, English German, French
Religions: Roman Catholic 92%, Protestant 2%, Jewish 2%, other 4%
Government type: republic
Capital: Buenos Aires
Budget: revenues: $117.5 billion, expenditures $132.8 billion
Currency: Argentine peso (ARS)

ARMENIA
Location: Southwestern Asia, east of Turkey
Area: 11,484 sq mi (29,743 sq km)
Area-comparative: slightly smaller than Maryland
Population: 2,974,184
Population growth rate: 0.14%
Nationality: noun: Armenian(s), adjective: Armenian
Ethnic groups: Armenian 97.9%, Yezidi (Kurd) 1.3%, Russian 0.5%, other 0.3%
Languages: Armenian 97.7%, Yezidi 1%, Russian 0.9%, other 0.4%
Religions: Armenian Apostolic 94.7%, other Christian 4%, Yezidi 1.3%
Government type: republic
Capital: Yerevan
Budget: revenues: $2.2 billion, expenditures: $2.507 billion   **Currency:** dram (AMD)

ARUBA (part of the Kingdom of the Netherlands)
Location: Caribbean, island in the Caribbean Sea, north of Venezuela
Area: 69.5 sq mi (180 sq km)
Area-comparative: slightly larger than Washington, DC
Population: 109,153
Population growth rate: 1.39%
Nationality: noun: Aruban(s), adjective: Aruban: Dutch
Ethnic groups: mixed white/ Caribbean Amerindian 80%, other 20%
Languages: Papiomento (a Spanish-Portuguese-Dutch-English dialect) 66.3%, Spanish 12.6%, English (widely spoken) 7.7%, Dutch (official) 5.8%, other 7.5%
Religions: Roman Catholic 80.8%, Evangelist 4.1%, Protestant 2.5%, Jehovah's Witnesses 1.5%, Methodist 1.2%, Jewish 0.2%, other 9.7%
Government type: parliamentary democracy
Capital: Oranjestad
Budget: revenues: $568.4 million, expenditures: $735 million   **Currency:** Aruban guilder/florin (AWG)

AUSTRALIA
Location: Oceania, continent between the Indian Ocean and the South Pacific Ocean
Area: 2,988,900 sq mi (7,741,220 sq km)
Area-comparative: slightly smaller than the US contiguous 48 states
Population: 22,262,501
Population growth rate: 1.11%
Nationality: noun: Australian(s), adjective: Australian
Ethnic groups: white 92%, Asian 7%, aboriginal and other 1%
Languages: English (official) 78.5%, Chinese 2.5%, Italian 1.6%, Greek 1.3%, Arabic 1.2%, other 15.2%
Religions: Catholic 25.8%, Anglican 18.7%, other Christian 19.3%, other 17.5%, none 18.7%
Government type: federal parliamentary democracy
Capital: Canberra
Budget: revenues: $516.3 billion, expenditures: $528.3 billion   **Currency:** Australian dollar (AUD)

AUSTRIA
Location: Central Europe, north of Italy and Slovenia
Area: 32,383 sq mi (83,871 sq km)
Area-comparative: slightly smaller than Maine
Population: 8,221,646
Population growth rate: 0.02%
Nationality: noun: Austrian(s), adjective: Austrian
Ethnic groups: Austrians 91.1%, former Yugoslavs 4%, other 4.9%
Language: German (official), Turkish, Serbian, Slovene, Croatian, Hungarian
Religions: Roman Catholic 73.6%, Protestant 4.7%, Muslim 4.2%, other 17.5%
Government type: federal republic
Capital: Vienna
Budget: revenues: $191.7 billion, expenditures: $204.1 billion
Currency: euro (EUR)

AZERBAIJAN
Location: Southwestern Asia, bordering the Caspian Sea, between Iran and Russia
Area: 33,436 sq mi (86,600 sq km)
Area-comparative: slightly smaller than Maine
Population: 9,590,159
Population growth rate: 1.01%
Nationality: noun: Azerbaijani(s), adjective: Azerbaijani

Ethnic groups: Azeri 90.6%, Dagestani 2.2%, Russian 1.8%, Armenian 1.5% , other 3.9%
Languages: Azerbaijani (Azeri) 90.3%, Lezgi 2.2%, Russian 1.8%, Armenian 1.5%, other 4.3%
Religions: Muslim 93.4%, Russian Orthodox 2.5%, Armenian Orthodox 2.3%, other 1.8%
Government type: republic
Capital: Baku (Baki)
Budget: revenues: $23.25 billion, expenditures: $25.55 billion   **Currency:** Azerbaijani manta (AZM)

THE BAHAMAS
Location: Caribbean, chain of islands in the North Atlantic Ocean, northeast of Cuba
Area: 5,359 sq mi (13,880 sq km)
Area-comparative: slightly smaller than Connecticut
Population: 319,031
Population growth rate: 0.89%
Nationality: noun: Bahamian(s), adjective: Bahamian
Ethnic groups: black 85%, white 12%, Asian and Hispanic 3%
Languages: English (official), Creole
Religions: Baptist 35.4%, Anglican 15.1%, Roman Catholic 13.5%, Pentecostal 8.1%, Methodist 4.2%,
        Church of God 4.8%, other Christian 15.2%, other 3.7%
Government type: constitutional parliamentary democracy
Capital: Nassau
Budget: revenues: $1.6 billion, expenditures: $1.8 billion, & capital expenditures of $130 million
Currency: Bahamian dollar (BSD)

BAHRAIN
Location: Middle East, east of Saudi Arabia
Area: 293 sq mi (760 sq km)
Area-comparative: 3.5 times the size of Washington, DC
Population: 1,281,332
Population growth rate: 2.57%
Nationality: noun: Bahraini(s), adjective: Bahraini
Ethnic groups: Bahraini 62.4%, non-Bahraini 37.6%
Languages: Arabic (official), English, Farsi, Urdu
Religions: Muslim (Shi'a and Sunni) 81.2%, Christian 9%, other 9.8%
Government type: constitutional monarchy
Capital: Manama
Budget: revenues: $8.466 billion, expenditures: $8.911 billion
Currency: Bahraini dinar (RHD)

BANGLADESH
Location: Southern Asia, bordering the Bay of Bengal, between Burma and India
Area: 55,598 sq mi (143,998 sq km)
Area-comparative: slightly smaller than Iowa
Population: 163,654,860
Population growth rate: 1.59%
Nationality: noun: Bangladeshi(s), adjective: Bangladeshi
Ethnic groups: Bengali 98%, other 2%
Languages: Bangla (official), English
Religions: Muslim 83%, Hindu 16%, other 1%
Government type: parliamentary democracy
Capital: Dhaka
Budget: revenues: $13.98 billion, expenditures: $19.62 billion
Currency: taka (BDT)

BARBADOS

Location: Caribbean, island in the North Atlantic Ocean, northeast of Venezuela
Area: 166 sq mi (430 sq km)
Area-comparative: 2.5 times the size of Washington, DC
Population: 288,725
Population growth rate: 0.34%
Nationality: noun: Barbadian(s) or Bajan, adjective: Barbadian or Bajan
Ethnic groups: black 93%, white 3.2%, East Indian 1%, other .2%
Languages: English (official)
Religions: Protestant 63.4%, Roman Catholic 4.2%, other Christian 7%, other 4.6%, none 20.6%
Government type: parliamentary democracy
Capital: Bridgetown
Budget: revenues: $1.3 billion, expenditures: $1.5 billion   **Currency:** Barbadian dollar (BBD)

BELARUS

Location: Eastern Europe, east of Poland
Area: 80,154 sq mi (207,600 sq km)
Area-comparative: slightly smaller than Kansas
Population: 9,625,888
Population growth rate: -0.18%
Nationality: noun: Belarusian(s), adjective: Belarusian
Ethnic groups: Belarusian 81.2%, Russian, 11.4%, Polish 3.9%, Ukrainian 2.4%, and other 1.1%
Languages: Belarusian (official), Russian (official); other (Polish and Ukranian)
Religions: Eastern Orthodox 80%, other (including Roman Catholic, Protestant, Jewish and Muslim) 20%
Government type: republic in name, although in fact a dictatorship
Capital: Minsk
Budget: revenues: $21.42 billion, expenditures: $22.04 billion
Currency: Belarusian ruble (BYB/BYR)

BELGIUM

Location: Western Europe, bordering the North Sea, between France and Netherlands
Area: 11,786 sq mi (30,528 sq km)
Area-comparative: about the size of Maryland
Population: 10,444,268
Population growth rate: 0.05%
Nationality: noun: Belgian(s), adjective: Belgian
Ethnic groups: Fleming 58%, Walloon 31%, mixed or other 11%
Languages: Dutch 60%, French 40%
Religions: Roman Catholic 75%, other (including Protestant) 25%
Government type: federal parliamentary democracy under a constitutional monarch
Capital: Brussels
Budget: revenues: $227.3 billion, expenditures: $243.2 billion
Currency: euro (EUR)

BELIZE

Location: Middle America, bordering the Caribbean Sea, between Guatemala and Mexico
Area: 8,867 sq mi (22,966 sq km)
Area-comparative: slightly smaller than Massachusetts
Population: 334,297
Population growth rate: 1.97%
Nationality: noun: Belizean(s), adjective: Belizean
Ethnic groups: Mestizo 48.7%, Creole 24.9%, Maya 10.6%, Garifuna 6.1%, other 9.7%

Languages: English (official), Spanish, Mayan, Garifuna, Creole, German
Religions: Roman Catholic 49.0%, Protestant 27%, other 14%, none 9.4%
Government type: parliamentary democracy
Capital: Belmopan
Budget: revenues: $450 million, expenditures: $450 million   **Currency:** Belizean dollar (BZD)

BENIN

Location: Western Africa, bordering the Bight of Benin, between Nigeria and Togo
Area: 43,482 sq mi (112,620 sq km)
Area-comparative: slightly smaller than Pennsylvania
Population: 9,877,292
Population growth rate: 2.84%
Nationality: noun: Beninese (singular and plural), adjective: Beninese
Ethnic groups: Fon and related 39.2%, Adja and related 15.2%, Yoruba and related 12.3%, Bariba and related 9.2%, Peulh and related 7%, Ottamari and related 6.1%, Yoa-Lokpa and related 4%, Dendi and related 2.5%, other 1.6% (includes Europeans)
Languages: French (official), Fon and Yoruba, tribal languages (at least six major ones in north)
Religions: Christian 42.8%, Muslim 24.4%, Vodoun 17.3%, other 15.5%
Government type: republic
Capital: Porto-Novo(official capital) ; Cotonou is the seat of government
Budget: revenues: $1.403 billion, expenditures: $1.683 billion
Currency: Communaute Financiere Africaine franc (XOF)

BERMUDA (overseas territory of the UK)

Location: North America, group of islands in the North Atlantic Ocean, east of South Carolina (US)
Area: 20.5 sq mi (53.3 sq km)
Area-comparative: about one third the size of Washington, DC
Population: 69,467
Population growth rate: 0.55%
Nationality: noun, Bermudian(s), adjective, Bermudian
Ethnic groups: black 54.8%, white 34.1%, mixed 6.4%, other 4.3%
Languages: English (official), Portuguese
Religions: Anglican 23%, Roman Catholic 15%, African Methodist Episcopal 11%, other Protestant 18%, none 21%, other 12%
Government type: parliamentary; self-governing territory
Capital: Hamilton
Budget: revenues: $973.2 million, expenditures: $1.115 billion   **Currency:** Bermudian dollar (BMD)

BOLIVIA

Location: Central South America, southwest of Brazil
Area: 424,162 sq mi (1,098,581 sq km)
Area-comparative: slightly less than three times the size of Montana
Population: 10,461,053
Population growth rate: 1.63%
Nationality: noun: Bolivian(s), adjective: Bolivian
Ethnic groups: Quechua 30%, Mestizo 30%, Aymara 25%, white 15%
Languages: Spanish (official), Quechua (official), Aymara (official)
Religions: Roman Catholic 95%, Protestant (Evangelical Methodist) 5%
Government type: republic
Capital: La Paz
Budget: revenues: $12.6 billion, expenditures: $12.2 billion   **Currency:** boliviano (BOB)

BOSNIA AND HERZEGOVINA
Location: Southeastern Europe, bordering the Adriatic Sea and Croatia
Area: 19,767 sq mi (51,197 sq km)
Area-comparative: slightly smaller than West Virginia
Population: 3,875,723
Population growth rate: -0.1%
Nationality: noun: Bosnian(s), Herzegovinian(s); **adjective:** Bosnian, Herzegovinian
Ethnic groups: Bosniak 48%, Serb 37.1%, Croat 14.3%, other 0.6%
Languages: Croatian, Serbian, Bosnian
Religions: Muslim 40%, Orthodox 31%, Roman Catholic 15%, other 14%
Government type: emerging federal democratic republic
Capital: Sarajevo
Budget: revenues: $7.887 billion; expenditures: $8.521 billion   **Currency:** marka (BAM)

BOTSWANA
Location: Southern Africa, north of South Africa
Area: 224,607 sq mi (581,730 sq km)
Area-comparative: slightly smaller than Texas
Population: 2,127,825
Population growth rate: 1.35%
Nationality: noun: Motswana (singular); Batswana (plural); **adjective:** Motswana; Batswana
Ethnic groups: Tswana (or Setswana) 79%, Kalanga 11%, Basarwa 3%, other including Kgalagadi 7%
Languages: English (official), Setswana, Kalanga, Sekgalagadi
Religions: Christian 71.6%, Badimo 6%, none 20.6%, other 1.8% .
Government type: parliamentary republic
Capital: Gaborone
Budget: revenues: $5.496 billion; expenditures: $5.398 billion   **Currency:** pula (BWP)

BRAZIL
Location: Eastern South America, bordering the Atlantic Ocean
Area: 3,285,618 sq mi (8,511,965 sq km)
Area-comparative: slightly smaller than the US
Population: 201,009,622
Population rate growth: 0.83%
Nationality: noun: Brazilian(s), **adjective:** Brazilian
Ethnic groups: white (Portuguese, German, and Italian) 53.7%, mulatto 38.5%, black 6.2%, other 1.6%
Languages: Portuguese (official), Spanish, English, French
Religions: Roman Catholic 73.6%, Protestant 15.4%, Spiritualist 1.3%, Bantu/voodoo 0.3%, other 1.8%,
          none 7.6%
Government type: federal republic
Capital: Brasilia
Budget: revenues: 911.4 billion; expenditures: 846.6 billion   **Currency:** real (BRL)

BRITISH VIRGIN ISLANDS (overseas territory of the UK)
Location: Caribbean, between the Caribbean Sea and the North Atlantic Ocean, east of Puerto Rico
Area: 58 sq mi (151 sq km)
Area-comparative: about 0.9 times the size of Washington, DC
Population: 31,912
Population growth rate: 2.4%
Nationality: noun: British Virgin Islander(s); **adjective:** British Virgin Islander
Ethnic groups: black 82%, white 6.8%, Indian, and mixed 11.2%
Language: English (official)
Religions: Protestant 86%, Roman Catholic 10%, other 2%, none 2%

Government type: NA (overseas territory of the UK)
Capital: Road Town
Budget: revenues: $300 million; expenditures: $300 million   **Currency:** US dollar (USD)

BRUNEI

Location: Southeastern Asia, bordering the South China Sea and Malaysia
Area: 2,225 sq mi (5,765 sq km)
Area-comparative: slightly smaller than Delaware
Population: 415,717
Population growth rate: 1.67%
Nationality: noun: Bruneian(s); adjective: Bruneian
Ethnic groups: Malay 66.3%, Chinese 11.2%, indigenous 3.4%, other 19.1%
Languages: Malay (official), English, Chinese
Religions: Muslim (official) 67%, Buddhist 13%, Christian 10%, indigenous beliefs and other 10%
Government type: constitutional sultanate
Capital: Bandar Seri Begawan
Budget: revenues: $8 billion; expenditures: $3.98 billion   **Currency:** Bruneian dollar (BND)

BULGARIA

Location: Southeastern Europe, bordering the Black Sea, between Romania and Turkey
Area: 42,810 sq mi (110,879 sq km)
Area-comparative: slightly larger than Tennessee
Population: 6,981,642
Population growth rate: -0.81%
Nationality: noun: Bulgarian(s); adjective: Bulgarian
Ethnic groups: Bulgarian 83.9%, Turk 9.4%, Roma 4.7%, other 2%
Languages: Bulgarian (official), secondary languages closely correspond to ethic breakdown
Religions: Bulgarian Orthodox 82.6%, Muslim 12.2%, other 5.2%
Government type: parliamentary democracy
Capital: Sofia
Budget: revenues: $17.19 billion; expenditures: $17.93 billion
Currency: lev (BGN)

BURKINA FASO

Location: Western Africa, north of Ghana
Area: 105,841 sq mi (274,200 sq km)
Area-comparative: slightly larger than Colorado
Population: 17,812,961
Population growth rate: 3.06%
Nationality: noun: Burkinabe (singular and plural); adjective: Burkinabe
Ethnic groups: Mossi over 40%, Gurunsi, Senufo, Lobi, Bobo, Mande, Fulani approx. 60%
Languages: French (official), Sudanic tribal languages spoken by 90%
Religions: Muslim 50%, indigenous beliefs 40%, Christian (mainly Roman Catholic) 10%
Government type: parliamentary republic
Capital: Ouagadougou
Budget: revenues: $2.256 billion; expenditures: $2.693 billion
Currency: Communaute Financiere Africaine franc (XOF)

BURMA

Location: Southeastern Asia, bordering the Andaman Sea and the Bay of Bengal
Area: 261,228 sq mi (676,578 sq km)
Area-comparative: slightly smaller than Texas
Population: 55,167,330

Population growth rate: 1.05%
Nationality: noun: Burmese (singular and plural); adjective: Burmese
Ethnic groups: Burman 68%,Shan 9%, Karen 7%,Rakhine 4%,Chinese 3%, Indian 2%,Mon 2%, other 5%
Languages: Burmese, minority ethnic groups have their own languages
Religions: Buddhist 89%, Christian 4%, Muslim 4%, animist 1%, other 2%
Government type: military junta
Capital: Rangoon
Budget: revenues: $2.234 billion; expenditures: $4.414 billion   **Currency:** kyat (MMK)

BURUNDI

Location: Central Africa, east of Democratic Republic of the Congo
Area: 10,742 sq mi (27,830 sq km)
Area-comparative: slightly smaller than Maryland
Population: 10,888,321
Population growth rate: 3.08%
Nationality: noun: Burundian(s); adjective: Burundian
Ethnic groups: Hutu (Bantu) 85%, Tutsi 14%, Twa 1%
Languages: Kirundi (official), French (official), Swahili
Religions: Roman Catholic 62%, indigenous beliefs 23%, Muslim 10%, Protestant 5%
Government type: republic
Capital: Bujumbura
Budget: revenues: $473.2 million; expenditures: $558.5 million   **Currency:** Burundi franc (BIF)

CAMBODIA

Location: Southeastern Asia, bordering the Gulf of Thailand, between Thailand, Vietnam, and Laos
Area: 69,898 sq mi (181,035 sq km)
Area-comparative: slightly smaller than Oklahoma
Population: 15,205,539
Population growth rate: 1.67%
Nationality: noun: Cambodian(s); adjective: Cambodian
Ethnic groups: Khmer 90%, Vietnamese 5%, Chinese 1%, other 4%
Languages: Khmer (official) 95%, French and English 5%
Religions: Buddhist 96.4%, Muslim 2.1%, other 1.5%
Government type: multiparty democracy under a constitutional monarchy
Capital: Phnom Penh
Budget: revenues: $2.049 billion; expenditures: $2.704 billion   **Currency:** riel (KHR)

CAMEROON

Location: Western Africa, bordering the Bight of Biafra, between Equatorial Guinea and Nigeria
Area: 183,519 sq mi (475,440 sq km)
Area-comparative: slightly larger than California
Population: 20,549,221
Population growth rate: 2.04%
Nationality: noun: Cameroonian(s); adjective: Cameroonian
Ethnic groups: Cameroon Highlanders 31%, Equatorial Bantu 19%, Kirdi 11%, Fulani 10%, Northwestern Bantu 8%, Eastern Nigritic 7%, other African 13%, non-African less than 1%
Languages: 24 major African language groups, English (official), French (official)
Religions: indigenous beliefs 40%, Christian 40%, Muslim 20%
Government type: republic; multiparty presidential regime
Capital: Yaounde
Budget: revenues: $5.243 billion; expenditures: $5.61 billion
Currency: Communaute Financiere Africaine franc (XAF)

CANADA
Location: Northern North America, bordering the North Atlantic Ocean, Arctic Ocean and North Pacific Ocean, north of the 48 mainland states of the U.S.
Area: 3,850,790 sq mi (9,984,670 sq km)
Area-comparative: somewhat larger than the U.S.
Population: 34,568,211
Population growth rate: 0.77%
Nationality: noun: Canadian(s); adjective: Canadian
Ethnic groups: British Isles origin 28%, French origin 23%, other European 15%, other (primarily Asian) 6%, Amerindian 2%, mixed background 26%
Languages: English (official), French (official)
Religions: Roman Catholic 42.6%, Protestant 23.3%, other Christian 4.4%, Muslim 1.9%, other 27.8%
Government type: a federation and a parliamentary democracy
Capital: Ottawa
Budget: revenues: $679.3 billion; expenditures: $746.8 billion   **Currency:** Canadian dollar (CAD)

CAPE VERDE
Location: Western Africa, group of islands in the North Atlantic Ocean, west of Senegal
Area: 1,556 sq mi (4,033 sq km)
Area-comparative: slightly larger than Rhode Island
Population: 531,046
Population growth rate: 1.41%
Nationality: noun: Cape Verdean(s); adjective: Cape Verdean
Ethnic groups: Creole 71%, African 28%, European 1%
Language: Portuguese (official), Crioulo (a blend of Portuguese and West African words)
Religion: Roman Catholic (infused with indigenous beliefs), Protestant
Government type: republic
Capital: Praia
Budget: revenues: $539.2 million; expenditures: $724.4 million   **Currency:** Cape Verdean escudo

CAYMAN ISLANDS (overseas territory of the UK)
Location: Caribbean, island group in Caribbean Sea, nearly one half of the way from Cuba to Honduras
Area: 101 sq mi (264 sq km)
Area-comparative: 1.5 times the size of Washington, DC
Population: 53,737
Population growth rate: 2.19%
Nationality: noun: Caymanian(s); adjective: Caymanian
Ethnic groups: mixed 40%, white 20%, black 20%, various other 20%
Language: English 95%, Spanish 3.2%, other 1.8%
Religions: Church of God 26%, United Church (Presbyterian and Congregational) 11.8%, Roman Catholic 11%, Baptist 8.7%, Seventh Day Adventist 8.2%, Anglican 5.7%, Pentecoastal 5.3%, other 23.2%
Government type: British crown colony
Capital: George Town
Budget: revenues: $723.4 million, expenditures: $742.8 million   **Currency:** Caymanian dollar (KYD)

CENTRAL AFRICAN REPUBLIC
Location: Central Africa, north of Democratic Republic of the Congo
Area: 240,471 sq mi (622,984 sq km)
Area-comparative: slightly smaller than Texas
Population: 5,166,510
Population growth rate: 2.14%
Nationality: noun: Central African(s); adjective: Central African

Ethnic groups: Baya 33%, Banda 27%, Mandjia 13%, Sara 10%, Mboum 7%, M'Baka 4%,Yakoma 4%, other 2%

Language: French (official), Sangho (lingua franca and national language), tribal languages

Religion: indigenous beliefs 35%, Protestant 25%, Roman Catholic 25%, Muslim 15%

Government type: republic

Capital: Bangui

Budget: revenues: $335.1 million; expenditures: $352.2 million

Currency: Communaute Financiere Africaine franc (XAF)

CHAD

Location: Central Africa, south of Libya

Area: 495,624 sq mi (1,284,000 sq km)

Area-comparative: slightly more than 3 times the size of California

Population: 11,193,452

Population growth rate: 1.95%

Nationality: noun: Chadian(s); adjective: Chadian

Ethnic groups: Sara 27.7% Arab 12.3% Mayo-Kebbi 11.5%, Kanem-Bornu 9%, Ouaddai 8.7%, Hadjarai 6.7%, Tandjile 6.5%, Gorane 6.3%, Fitri- Batha 4.7%, other 6.7%

Languages: French (official), Arabic (official), Sara, over 120 different languages and dialects

Religions: Muslim 53.1%, Catholic 20.1%, Protestant 14.2%, animist 7.3%, atheist 3.1%, other 2.2%

Government type: republic

Capital: N`Djamena

Budget: revenues: $2.831 billion; expenditures: $3.348 billion

Currency: Communaute Financiere Africaine franc (XAF)

CHILE

Location: Southern South America, bordering the South Atlantic Ocean and South Pacific Ocean, between Argentina and Peru

Area: 291,932 sq mi (756,102 sq km)

Area-comparative: slightly smaller than twice the size of Montana

Population: 17,216,945

Population growth rate: 0.86%

Nationality: noun: Chilean(s); adjective: Chilean

Ethnic groups: white and white-Amerindian 95.4%, Mapuche 4%, other 0.6%

Language: Spanish (official), Mapudungun, German, English

Religions: Roman Catholic 70%, Evangelical 15.1%, Jehovah's Witness 1.1%, other Christian 1%, other 4.6%, none 8.3%

Government type: republic

Capital: Santiago

Budget: revenues: $59.49 billion; expenditures: $55.73 billion

Currency: Chilean peso (CLP)

CHINA (PEOPLE'S REPUBLIC OF CHINA)

Location: Eastern Asia, bordering the East China Sea, Korea Bay, Yellow Sea, and South China Sea, between North Korea and Vietnam

Area: 3,704,426 sq mi (9,596,961 sq km)

Area-comparative: slightly smaller than the US

Population: 1,349,585,838

Population growth rate: 0.46%

Nationality: noun: Chinese (singular and plural); adjective: Chinese

Ethnic groups: Han Chinese 91.5%, Zhuang, Uyghur, Hui, Yi, Tibetan, Miao, Manchu, Mongol, Buyi, Korean, and other nationalities 8.5%

Languages: Standard Chinese or Mandarin (official), Yue, Wu, Minbei, Minnan, Xiang, Gan, Hakka

dialects, minority languages
Religions: Majority is Atheist, Daoist (Taoist), Buddhist, Christian 3%- 4%, Muslim 1%-2%
Government type: Communist state
Capital: Beijing
Budget: revenues: $1.865 trillion; expenditures: $2 trillion
Currency: yuan (CNY)

COLOMBIA
Location: Northern South America, bordering the Caribbean Sea, between Panama and Venezuela,
     bordering the North Pacific Ocean, between Ecuador and Panama
Area: 439,619 sq mi (1,138,910 sq km)
Area-comparative: slightly less than 3 times the size of Montana
Population: 45,745,783
Population growth rate: 1.1%
Nationality: noun: Colombian(s); adjective: Colombian
Ethnic groups: mestizo 58%, white 20%, mulatto 14%, black 4%, mixed-Amerindian 3%, Amerindian 1%
Language: Spanish (official)
Religions: Roman Catholic 90%, other 10%
Government type: republic, executive branch dominates government structure
Capital: Bogota
Budget: revenues: $104.2 billion; expenditures: $106 billion
Currency: Colombian peso (COP)

COMOROS
Location: Southern Africa, group of islands in the Mozambique Channel, about two-thirds of the way
     between northern Madagascar and northern Mozambique
Area: 862 sq mi (2,235 sq km)
Area-comparative: slightly more than 12 times the size of Washington, DC
Population: 752,228
Population growth rate: 1.97%
Nationality: noun: Comoran(s); adjective: Comoran
Ethnic groups: Antalote, Cafre, Makoa, Oimatsaha, Sakalava
Languages: Arabic (official), French (official), Shikomoro (a blend of Swahili and Arabic)
Religions: Sunni Muslim 98%, Roman Catholic 2%
Government type: republic
Capital: Moroni
Budget: revenues: $126.8 million; expenditures: $130.4 million
Currency: Comoran franc (KMF)

CONGO, DEMOCRATIC REPUBLIC OF THE (ZAIRE)
Location: Central Africa, northeast of Angola
Area: 905,354 sq mi (2,344,858 sq km)
Area-comparative: slightly less than one-fourth the size of the US
Population: 75,507,308
Population growth rate: 2.54%
Nationality: noun: Congolese (singular and plural); adjective: Congolese or Congo
Ethnic groups: Over 200 African ethnic groups the majority are Bantu, the four largest tribes-Mongo,
     Luba, Kongo, and the Mangbetu-Azande- make up about 45% of the population
Languages: French (official), Lingala, Kingwana (a dialect of Kiswahili or Swahili), Kikongo, Tshiluba
Religions: Roman Catholic 50%, Protestant 20%, Kimbanguist 10%, Muslim 10%, other 10%
Government type: republic
Capital: Kinshasa

Budget: revenues: $3.383 billion; expenditures: $4.057 billion
Currency: Congolese franc (KMF)

CONGO, REPUBLIC OF THE
Location: Western Africa, bordering the South Atlantic Ocean, between Angola and Gabon
Area: 132,012 sq mi (342,000 sq km)
Area-comparative: slightly smaller than Montana
Population: 4,492,689
Population growth rate: 2.86%
Nationality: noun: Congolese (singular or plural); adjective: Congolese or Congo
Ethnic groups: Kongo 48%, Sangha 20%, Teke 17%, M'Bochi 12%, Europeans and other 3%
Languages: French (official), Lingala and Monokutuba, many local languages and dialects
Religions: Christian 50%, animist 48%, Muslim 2%
Government type: republic
Capital: Brazzaville
Budget: revenues: $8.05 billion; expenditures: $5.93 billion
Currency: Communaute Financiere Africaine franc (XAF)

COSTA RICA
Location: Central America, bordering both the Caribbean Sea and the North Pacific Ocean, between Nicaragua and Panama
Area: 19,724 sq mi (51,100 sq km)
Area-comparative: slightly smaller than West Virginia
Population: 4,695,942
Population growth rate: 1.27%
Nationality: noun: Costa Rican(s); adjective: Costa Rican
Ethnic groups: white and mestizo 94%, black 3%, Amerindian 1%, Chinese 1%, other 1%
Language: Spanish (official), English
Religions: Catholic 76.3%, Evangelical 13.7%, Jehovah's Witness 1.3%, Protestant 0.7%, other 8%
Government type: democratic republic
Capital: San Jose
Budget: revenues: $6.949 billion; expenditures $8.937 billion
Currency: Costa Rican colon (CRC)

COTE d'IVOIRE
Location: Western Africa, bordering the North Atlantic Ocean, between Ghana and Liberia
Area: 124,469 sq mi (322,460 sq km)
Area-comparative: slightly larger than New Mexico
Population: 22,400,835
Population growth rate: 2%
Nationality: noun: Ivorian(s); adjective: Ivoirian
Ethnic groups: Akan 42.1%, Voltaiques or Gur 17.6%, Northern Mandes 16.5%, Krous 11%, Southern Mandes 10%, other 2.8%
Languages: French (official), 60 native dialects with Dioula the most widely spoken
Religions: Muslim 38.6%, Christian 32.8%, indigenous 11.9%, none 16.7%
Government type: republic; multiparty presidential regime
Capital: Yamoussoukro
Budget: revenues: $4.391 billion; expenditures $6.129 billion
Currency: Communaute Financiere Africaine franc (XOF)

CROATIA
Location: Southeastern Europe, bordering the Adriatic Sea, between Bosnia, Herzegovina, and Slovenia
Area: 21,851 sq mi (56,594 sq km)

Area-comparative: slightly smaller than West Virginia
Population: 4,483,804
Population growth rate: -0.076%
Nationality: noun: Croat(s), Croatian(s); adjective: Croatian
Ethnic groups: Croat 89.6%, Serb 4.5%, other 5.9% (including Bosniak, Hungarian, Slovene, Czech, and Roma)
Languages: Croatian 96.1%, Serbian 1%, other 2.9%
Religions: Roman Catholic 87.8%, Orthodox 4.4%, other Christian 0.4%, Muslim 1.3%, other 6.1%
Government type: parliamentary democracy
Capital: Zagreb
Budget: revenues: $19.3 billion; expenditures: $20.99 billion
Currency: Croatian kuna (HRK)

CUBA
Location: Caribbean, island between the Caribbean Sea and the North Atlantic Ocean, south of Florida
Area: 42,791 sq mi (110,860 sq km)
Area-comparative: slightly smaller than Pennsylvania
Population: 11,061,886
Population growth rate: -0.13%
Nationality: noun: Cuban(s); adjective: Cuban
Ethnic groups: white 65.1%, mulatto and mestizo 24.8%, black 10.1%
Language: Spanish (official)
Religions: nominally 85% Roman Catholic prior to Castro assuming power; Protestants, Jehovah's Witnesses, Jews and Santeria are represented
Government type: Communist state
Capital: Havana
Budget: revenues: $47 billion; expenditures: $49.7 billion
Currency: Cuban peso (CUP)

CYPRUS
Location: Middle East, island in the Mediterranean Sea, south of Turkey
Area: 3,571 sq mi (9,250 sq km)
Area-comparative: about 0.6 times the size of Connecticut
Population: 1,155,403
Population growth rate: 1.52%
Nationality: noun: Cypriot(s); adjective: Cypriot
Ethnic groups: Greek 77%, Turkish 18%, other 5%
Languages: Greek, Turkish, English
Religions: Greek Orthodox 78%, Muslim 18%, other (including Maronite and Armenian Apostolic) 4%
Government type: republic
Capital: Nicosia
Budget: revenues: $9.645 billion; expenditures: $10.59 billion
Currency: Greek Cypriot area: Cypriot pound, Turkish Cypriot area: Turkish lira (CYP: TRL)

CZECH REPUBLIC
Location: Central Europe, southeast of Germany
Area: 30,403 sq mi (78,866 sq km)
Area-comparative: slightly smaller than South Carolina
Population: 10,162,921
Population growth rate: -0.15%
Nationality: noun: Czech(s); adjective: Czech
Ethnic groups: Czech 63.7%, Moravian 4.9%, Slovak 1.4%, other 30%
Language: Czech (official), Slovak

Religions: Roman Catholic 10.3%, Protestant .8%, other and unspecified 54.6%, none 34.2%
Government type: parliamentary democracy
Capital: Prague
Budget: revenues: $81.08 billion; expenditures: $87.25 billion
Currency: Czech koruna (CZK)

DENMARK
Location: Northern Europe, bordering the Baltic Sea and the North Sea, on a peninsula north of Germany
Area: 16,634 sq mi (43,094 sq km)
Area-comparative: slightly less than twice the size of Massachusetts
Population: 5,556,452
Population growth rate: 0.23%
Nationality: noun: Dane(s); adjective: Danish
Ethnic groups: Scandinavian, Inuit, Faroese, German, Turkish, Iranian, Somali
Languages: Danish (official), Faroese, Greenlandic, German
Religions: Evangelical Lutheran 95%, other (includes Protestant and Roman Catholic) 3%, Muslim 2%
Government type: constitutional monarchy
Capital: Copenhagen
Budget: revenues: $176.5 billion; expenditures: $188.9 billion
Currency: Danish krone (DKK)

DJIBOUTI
Location: Eastern Africa, bordering the Gulf of Aden and the Red Sea, between Eritrea and Somalia
Area: 8,957.6 sq mi (23,200 sq km)
Area-comparative: slightly smaller than Massachusetts
Population: 792,198
Population growth rate: 2.26%
Nationality: noun: Djiboutian(s); adjective: Djiboutian
Ethnic groups: Somali 60%, Afar 35%, French, Arab, Ethiopian and Italian 5%
Languages: French (official), Arabic (official), Somali, Afar
Religions: Muslim 94%, Christian 6%
Government type: republic
Capital: Djibouti
Budget: revenues: $485.6 million; expenditures: $502 million
Currency: Djiboutian franc (DJF)

DOMINICA
Location: Caribbean, island between the Caribbean Sea and the North Atlantic Ocean, about one-half of the way between Puerto Rico and Trinidad and Tobago
Area: 290 sq mi (754 sq km)
Area-comparative: slightly more than 4 times the size of Washington, DC
Population: 73,286
Population growth rate: 0.22%
Nationality: noun: Dominican(s); adjective: Dominican
Ethnic groups: black 86.8%, mixed 8.9%, Carib Amerindian 2.9%, white 0.8%, other 0.7%
Languages: English (official), French patois
Religions: Roman Catholic 61.4%, Seventh Day Adventist 6%, Pentecostal 5.6%, Baptist 4.1%, Methodist 3.7%, Church of God 1.2%, Jehovah's Witnesses 1.2%, other Christian 7.7%, Rastafarian 1.3%, other or unspecified 1.6%, none 6.1%
Government type: parliamentary democracy
Capital: Roseau
Budget: revenues: $148.1 million; expenditures: $185.2 million
Currency: East Caribbean dollar (XCD)

DOMINICAN REPUBLIC
Location: Caribbean, eastern two-thirds of the island of Hispaniola, between the Caribbean Sea and the North Atlantic Ocean, east of Haiti
Area: 18,792 sq mi (48,670 sq km)
Area-comparative: slightly more than twice the size of New Hampshire
Population: 10,219,630
Population growth rate: 1.28%
Nationality: noun: Dominican(s); adjective: Dominican
Ethnic groups: Mixed 73%, white 16%, black 11%
Language: Spanish (official)
Religions: Roman Catholic 95%, other 5%
Government type: democratic republic
Capital: Santo Domingo
Budget: revenues: $8.338 billion; expenditures: $13.07 billion
Currency: Dominican peso (DOP)

ECUADOR
Location: Western South America, bordering the Pacific Ocean at the Equator
Area: 109,454 sq mi (283,560 sq km)
Area-comparative: slightly smaller than Nevada
Population: 15,439,429
Population growth rate: 1.4%
Nationality: noun: Ecuadorian(s): adjective: Ecuadorian
Ethnic groups: mestizo 71.9%, Montubio 7.4%, Afroecuadorian 7.2%, Amerindian 7%, white 6.1%, other .4%
Languages: Spanish (official), Amerindian languages (Quechua, Shuar)
Religions: Roman Catholic 95%, other 5%
Government type: republic
Capital: Quito
Budget: revenues: $15.9 billion; expenditures: $20.1 billion
Currency: US dollar (USD)

EGYPT
Location: Northern Africa, bordering the Mediterranean Sea, between Libya and the Gaza Strip
Area: 386,560 sq mi (1,001,450 sq km)
Area-comparative: slightly more than three times the size of New Mexico
Population: 85,294,388
Population growth rate: 1.88%
Nationality: noun: Egyptian(s); adjective: Egyptian
Ethnic groups: Egyptians 99.6%, other 0.4%
Languages: Arabic (official), English, French
Religions: Muslim (primarily Sunni) 90%, Coptic 9%, other Christian 1%
Government type: republic
Capital: Cairo
Budget: revenues: $56.64 billion; expenditures: $83.24 billion
Currency: Egyptian pound (EGP)

EL SALVADOR
Location: Central America, bordering the North Pacific Ocean, between Guatemala and Honduras
Area: 8,121 sq mi (21,040 sq km)
Area-comparative: slightly smaller than Massachusetts
Population: 6,108,590
Population growth rate: 0.29%

Nationality: noun: Salvadoran(s); adjective: Salvadoran
Ethnic groups: mestizo 96.3%, white 12.7%, Amerindian 1%,
Languages: Spanish (official), Nahua
Religions: Roman Catholic 57.1%, Protestant 21.2%, Jehovah's Witnesses 1.9%, Mormon 0.7%, other 2.3%, none 16.8%
Government type: republic
Capital: San Salvador
Budget: revenues: $4.835 billion; expenditures: $5.534 billion
Currency: US dollar (USD)

ERITREA

Location: Eastern Africa, bordering the Red Sea, between Djibouti and Sudan
Area: 45,406 sq mi (117,600 sq km)
Area-comparative: slightly larger than Pennsylvania
Population: 6,233,682
Population growth rate: 2.36%
Nationality: noun: Eritrean(s); adjective: Eritrean
Ethnic groups: nine recognized ethnic groups: Tigrinya 55%, Tigre 30%, Saho 4%, Kunama 2%, Rashaida 2%, Bilen 2%, other (Afar, Beni, Amir, Nera) 5%
Languages: Tigrinya (official), Arabic (official), English (official), Afar, Tigre, Kunama, other Cushitic languages
Religions: Muslim, Coptic Christian, Roman Catholic, Protestant
Government type: transitional government
Capital: Asmara (Asmera)
Budget: revenues: $838.8 million; expenditures: $1.19 billion
Currency: nakfa (ERN)

ESTONIA

Location: Eastern Europe, bordering the Baltic Sea and Gulf of Finland, between Latvia and Russia
Area: 17,457 sq mi (45,226 sq km)
Area-comparative: slightly smaller than New Hampshire and Vermont combined
Population: 1,266,375
Population growth rate: -0.66%
Nationality: noun: Estonian(s) adjective: Estonian
Ethnic groups: Estonian 68.7%, Russian 25.6%, Ukrainian 2.1%, Belarusian 1.2%, Finn 0.8% other 1.6%
Languages: Estonian (official), Russian
Religions: Evangelical Lutheran 13.6%, Orthodox 12.8%, Other Christian (including Methodist, Seventh-Day Adventist, Roman Catholic, Pentecostal) 1.4%, unaffiliated 34.1%, unspecified 32%, none 6.1%
Government type: parliamentary republic
Capital: Tallinn
Budget: revenues: $7.915 billion; expenditures: $8.439 billion
Currency: Estonian kroon (EEK)

ETHIOPIA

Location: Eastern Africa, west of Somalia
Area: 426,370 sq mi (1,104,300 sq km)
Area-comparative: slightly less than twice the size of Texas
Population: 93,877,025
Population growth rate: 2.9%
Nationality: noun: Ethiopian(s); adjective: Ethiopian
Ethnic groups: Oromo 34.5%, Amara 26.9%, Somalie 6.2%, Tigraway 6.1%, Sidama 4%, Gurage 2.5%, Welaita 2.3%, Hadiya 1.7%, Affar 1.7%, Gamo 1.5%, Gedeo 1.3%, other 11.3%
Languages: Amarigna (official), Oromingo (official regional),Somaligna, Tigrigna (official regional),

Sidamigna, Wolayitigna, Guaragigna, other local languages, English (official foreign language) Arabic (official)
Religions: Orthodox 43.5%, Muslim 33.9%, Protestant 18.6%), traditional 2.6%, Catholic 0.7%, other 0.7%
Government type: federal republic
Capital: Addis Ababa
Budget: revenues: $6.079 billion; expenditures: $7.219 billion
Currency: birr (ETB)

FIJI
Location: Oceania, island group in the South Pacific Ocean, 2/3's of the way from Hawaii to New Zealand
Area: 7,052 sq mi (18,270 sq km)
Area-comparative: slightly smaller than New Jersey
Population: 896,758
Population growth rate: 0.73%
Nationality: noun: Fijian(s); adjective: Fijian
Ethnic groups: Fijian 57.3%, Indian 37.6%, Rotuman 1.2%, other 3.9% (primarily European, Pacific Islanders, Chinese)
Language: English (official), Fijian (official), Hindustani
Religion: Christian 64.5%, Hindu 27.9%, Muslim 6.3%, Sikh 0.3%, other 1%
Government type: republic
Capital: Suva
Budget: revenues: $1.004 billion; expenditures: $1.172 billion
Currency: Fijian dollar (FJD)

FINLAND
Location: Northern Europe, bordering the Baltic Sea, Gulf of Bothnia, and Gulf of Finland
Area: 130,560 sq mi (338,145 sq km)
Area-comparative: slightly smaller than Montana
Population: 5,266,114
Population growth rate: 0.06%
Nationality: noun: Finn(s); adjective: Finnish
Ethnic groups: Finn 93.4%, Swede 5.6%, Russian 0.5%, Estonian 0.3%, Roma 0.1%, Sami 0.1%
Languages: Finnish 91.2% (official), Swedish 5.5% (official), Sami- and Russian-speaking minorities 3.3%
Religions: Lutheran Church of Finland 82.5%, Orthodox Church 1.1%, other Christian 1.1%, other 0.1%, none 15.1%
Government type: republic
Capital: Helsinki
Budget: revenues: $129.4 billion; expenditures: $134 billion
Currency: euro (EUR)

FRANCE
Location: Western Europe, bordering the Bay of Biscay and English Channel, between Belgium and Spain, southeast of the UK; bordering the Mediterranean Sea, between Italy and Spain
Area: 212,940 sq mi (551,500 sq km)
Area-comparative: slightly less than twice the size of Texas
Population: 65,951,611
Population growth rate: 0.47%
Nationality: noun: Frenchman (men), Frenchwoman (women); adjective: French
Ethnic groups: Celtic and Latin with Teutonic Slavic, North African, Indochinese, Basque minorities
Language: French (official)
Religions: Roman Catholic 83%-88%, Muslim 5%-10%, Protestant 2%, Jewish 1%, unaffiliated 4%
Government type: republic

Capital: Paris
Budget: revenues: $1.341 trillion; expenditures: $1.458 trillion
Currency: euro (EUR)

GABON
Location: Western Africa, bordering the Atlantic Ocean at the Equator, between Republic of the Congo
and Equatorial Guinea
Area: 103,319 sq mi (267,667 sq km)
Area-comparative: slightly smaller than Colorado
Population: 1,640,286
Population growth rate: 1.96%
Nationality: noun: Gabonese (singular and plural); adjective: Gabonese
Ethnic groups: Bantu tribes including four major tribal groups; Fang, Bapounou, Nzebi and Obamba,
other Africans and Europeans
Languages: French (official), Fang, Myene, Nzebi, Bapounou/Eschira, Bandjabi
Religions: Christian 55%-75%, animist, Muslim less than 1%
Government type: republic; multiparty presidential regime
Capital: Libreville
Budget: revenues: $5.395 billion; expenditures: $4.277 billion
Currency: Communaute Financiere Africaine franc (XAF)

GAMBIA
Location: Western Africa, bordering the North Atlantic Ocean and Senegal
Area: 4,362 sq mi (11,300 sq km)
Area-comparative: slightly less than twice the size of Delaware
Population: 1,883,051
Population growth rate: 2.29%
Nationality: noun: Gambian(s); adjective: Gambian
Ethnic groups: African (including Mandinka, Fula, Jola, Serahuli, and Wolof) 99%, non-African 1%
Languages: English (official), Mandinka, Wolof, Fula
Religions: Muslim 90%, Christian 8%, indigenous beliefs 2%
Government type: republic
Capital: Banjul
Budget: revenues: $206.3 million; expenditures: $257.1 million
Currency: dalasi (GMD)

GAZA STRIP
Location: Middle East, bordering the Mediterranean Sea, between Egypt and Israel
Area: 139 sq mi (360 sq km)
Area-comparative: slightly more than twice the size of Washington, DC
Population: 1,763,387
Population growth rate: 3. 01%
Nationality: noun: NA; adjective: NA
Ethnic groups: Palestinian Arab
Languages: Arabic, Hebrew, English
Religions: Muslim (predominantly Sunni) 99.3%, Christian 0.7%
Government type: NA
Capital: NA
Budget: revenues: $2.1 billion; expenditures: $3.2 billion   **Currency:** new Israeli shekel (ILS)

GEORGIA
Location: Southwestern Asia, bordering the Black Sea, between Turkey and Russia
Area: 26,904 sq mi (69,700 sq km)

Area-comparative: slightly smaller than South Carolina
Population: 4,555,911
Population growth rate: 0.33%
Nationality: noun: Georgian(s); adjective: Georgian
Ethnic groups: Georgian 83.8%, Azeri 6.5%, Armenian 5.7%, Russian 1.5%, other 2.5%
Languages: Georgian 71% (official), Russian 9%, Armenian 7%, Azeri 6%, other 7%
Religions: Christian 83.9%, Muslim 9.9%, Armenian-Gregorian 3.9%,Catholic 0.8%,other 0.8%,none 0.7%
Government type: republic
Capital: T`bilisi
Budget: revenues: $4.1 billion; expenditures: $4.8 billion
Currency: lari (GEL)

GERMANY
Location: Central Europe, bordering the Baltic Sea and North Sea, between the Netherlands and Poland
Area: 137,810 sq mi (357,021 sq km)
Area-comparative: slightly smaller than Montana
Population: 81,147,265
Population growth rate: -0.19%
Nationality: noun: German(s); adjective: German
Ethnic groups: German 91.5%,Turkish 2.4%, other 6.1%
Language: German (official)
Religion: Protestant 34%, Roman Catholic 34%, Muslim 3.7%, unaffiliated or other 28.3%
Government type: federal republic
Capital: Berlin
Budget: revenues: $1.511 trillion; expenditures: $1.507 trillion
Currency: euro (EUR)

GHANA
Location: Western Africa, bordering the Gulf of Guinea, between Cote d'Ivoire and Togo
Area: 92,098 sq mi (238,533 sq km)
Area-comparative: slightly smaller than Oregon
Population: 25,199,609
Population growth rate: 2.19%
Nationality: noun: Ghanaian(s); adjective: Ghanaian
Ethnic groups: Akan 45.3%, Mole-Dagbon 16.6%, Ewe 13.9%, Ga-Dangme 7.4%, Gurma 3.6%, Guan 4%, , Grusi 2.5%, Mande-Busanga 1.1%, other 1.6%
Language: English (official), African languages (including Asante, Ewe, Fante, Boron and Dagomba)
Religion: Christian 71.2%, (Pentecostal/Charismatic 28.3%, Protestant 18.4%, Catholic 13.1%, other 11.4%), Muslim 17.6%, traditional 5.2%, other 0.8%, none 5.2%
Government type: constitutional democracy
Capital: Accra
Budget: revenues: $8.375 billion; expenditures: $10.74 billion
Currency: cedi (GHC)

GREECE
Location: Southern Europe, bordering the Aegean Sea, Ionian Sea, and the Mediterranean Sea
Area: 50,949 sq mi (131,957 sq km)
Area-comparative: slightly smaller than Alabama
Population: 10,772,967
Population growth rate: 0.04%
Nationality: noun: Greek(s); adjective: Greek
Ethnic groups: Greek 93%, other 7%
Languages: Greek 99% (official), other (including French and English) 1%

Religions: Greek Orthodox 98%, Muslim 1.3%, other 0.7%
Government type: parliamentary republic
Capital: Athens
Budget: revenues: $108.7 billion; expenditures: $128 billion   **Currency:** euro (EUR)

GRENADA
Location: Caribbean island between the Caribbean Sea and Atlantic Ocean, north of Trinidad and Tobago
Area: 133 sq mi (344 sq km)
Area-comparative: twice the size of Washington, DC
Population: 109,590
Population growth rate: 0.52%
Nationality: noun: Grenadian(s); adjective: Grenadian
Ethnic groups: black 82%, mixed black and European 13%, European and East Indian 5%
Language: English (official), French patois
Religion: Roman Catholic 53%, Anglican 13.8%, other Protestant 33.2%
Government type: parliamentary democracy
Capital: Saint George`s
Budget: revenues: $175.3 million; expenditures: $215.9 million
Currency: East Caribbean dollar (XCD)

GUAM
Location: Oceania, an island in the Pacific Ocean, about 3/4 of the way from Hawaii to the Phillipines.
Area: 210.04 sq. mi. (544 sq. km)
Area-comparative: three times the size of Washington, DC
Population: 160,378
Population growth rate: .34%
Nationality: noun: Guamanian(s) (US citizens); adjective: Guamanian
Ethnic Groups: Chamorro 37.1%, Filipino 26.3%, other Pacific Islander 11.3%, white 6.9%, other Asian 6.3%, other ethnic origin or race 2.3%, mixed 9.8% (2000 census)
Languages: English 38.3%, Chamorro 22.2%, Philippine languages 22.2%, other Pacific island languages 6.8%, Asian languages 7%, other languages 3.5% (2000 census)
Religions: Roman Catholic 85%, other 15%
Government Type: NA
Capital: Hagatna (Agana)
Budget: revenues: $942.6 million; expenditures: $1.082 billion
Currency: US dollar (USD)

GUATEMALA
Location: Central America, bordering the North Pacific Ocean, between El Salvador and Mexico, and bordering the Gulf of Honduras (Caribbean Sea) between Honduras and Belize
Area: 42,031 sq mi (108,890 sq km)
Area-comparative: slightly smaller than Tennessee
Population: 14,373,472
Population growth rate: 1.91%
Nationality: noun: Guatemalan(s); adjective: Guatemalan
Ethnic groups: Mestizo and European 59.4%, K'iche 9.1%, Kaqcuikel 8.4%, Mam 7.9%, Q'eqchi 6.3%, other Mayan 8.6%, indigenous non-Mayan 0.2%, other 0.1%
Languages: Spanish 60%, Amerindian languages 40%
Religions: Roman Catholic, Protestant, indigenous Mayan beliefs
Government type: constitutional democratic republic
Capital: Guatemala City
Budget: revenues: $5.799 billion; expenditures: $7.091 billion
Currency: quetzal (GTQ) US dollar (USD), others allowed

GUINEA

Location: Western Africa, bordering the North Atlantic Ocean, between Guinea-Bissau and Sierra Leone
Area: 94,901 sq mi (245,857 sq km)
Area-comparative: slightly smaller than Oregon
Population: 11,176,026
Population growth rate: 2.64%
Nationality: noun: Guinean(s); adjective; Guinean
Ethnic groups: Peuhl 40%, Malinke 30%, Soussou 20%, smaller ethnic groups 10%
Language: French (official), tribal languages
Religion: Muslim 85%, Christian 8%, indigenous beliefs 7%
Government type: republic
Capital: Conakry
Budget: revenues: $1.235 billion; expenditures: $1.61 billion
Currency: Guinean franc (GNF)

GUINEA-BISSAU

Location: Western Africa, bordering the North Atlantic Ocean, between Guinea and Senegal
Area: 13,942 sq mi (36,120 sq km)
Area-comparative: slightly less than three times the size of Connecticut
Population: 1,660,870
Population growth rate: 1.95%
Nationality: noun: Guinean(s); adjective Guinean(s)
Ethnic groups: African 99% (includes Balanta 30%, Fula 20%, Manjaca 14%, Mandinga 13%, Papel 7%), European and mulatto less than 1%
Languages: Portuguese (official), Crioulo, African languages
Religion: Muslim 50%, indigenous beliefs 40%, Christian 10%
Government type: republic
Capital: Bissau
Budget: revenues: $134.6 million; expenditures: $169.4 million
Currency: Communaute Financiere Africaine franc (XOF)

GUYANA

Location: Northern South America, bordering North Atlantic Ocean, between Suriname and Venezuela
Area: 82,978 sq mi (214,970 sq km)
Area-comparative: slightly smaller than Idaho
Population: 793,903
Population growth rate: -0.21%
Nationality: noun: Guyanese (singular and plural); adjective: Guyanese
Ethnic groups: East Indian 43.5%, black 30.2%, mixed 16.7%, Amerindian 9.1%, other 0.5%
Languages: English, Amerindian dialects, Creole, Hindi, Urdu
Religions: Hindu 28.4%, Pentecostal 16.9%, Roman Catholic 8.1%, Anglican 6.9%, Seventh Day Adventist 5%, Methodist 1.7%, Jehovah Witness 1.1%, other Christian 17.7%, Muslim 7.2%, other 8.6%
Government type: republic
Capital: Georgetown
Budget: revenues $628.7 million; expenditures: $793.1 million
Currency: Guyanese dollar (GYD)

HAITI

Location: Caribbean, western one-third of the island of Hispaniola, west of the Dominican Republic
Area: 10,711 sq mi (27,750 sq km)
Area-comparative: slightly smaller than Maryland
Population: 9,893,934
Population growth rate: 0.99%

Nationality: noun: Haitian(s); adjective: Haitian
Ethnic groups: black 95%, mulatto and white 5%
Languages: French (official), Creole (official)
Religions: Roman Catholic 80%, Protestant 16%, none 1%, other 3%
Government type: republic
Capital: Port-au-Prince
Budget: revenues: $1.001 billion; expenditures: $1.114 billion
Currency: gourde (HTG)

HONDURAS

Location: Central America, bordering the Caribbean Sea, between El Salvador and Nicaragua
Area: 43,267 sq mi (112,090 sq km)
Area-comparative: slightly larger than Tennessee
Population: 8,448,465
Population growth rate: 1.79%
Nationality: noun: Honduran(s); adjective: Honduran
Ethnic groups: mestizo (mixed Amerindian and European) 90%, Amerindian 7%, black 2%, white 1%
Languages: Spanish (official), Amerindian dialects
Religions: Roman Catholic 97%, Protestant 3%
Government type: democratic constitutional republic
Capital: Tegucigalpa
Budget: revenues: $3.339 billion; expenditures: $4.044 billion
Currency: lempira (HNL)

HUNGARY

Location: Central Europe, northwest of Romania
Area: 35,910 sq mi (93,030 sq km)
Area-comparative: slightly smaller than Indiana
Population: 9,939,470
Population growth rate: - 0.2%
Nationality: noun: Hungarian(s); adjective: Hungarian
Ethnic groups: Hungarian 92.3%, Roma 1.9%, other or unknown 5.8%
Languages: Hungarian 93.6%, other or unspecified 6.4%
Religion: Roman Catholic 51.9%, Calvinist 15.9%, Lutheran 3%, Greek Catholic 2.6%, other Christian 1%, other or unspecified 11.1%, unaffiliated 14.5%
Government type: parliamentary democracy
Capital: Budapest
Budget: revenues $55.05 billion; expenditures: $58.55 billion
Currency: forint (HUF)

ICELAND

Location: Northern Europe, island between the Greenland Sea and the North Atlantic Ocean
Area: 39,758 sq mi (103,000 sq km)
Area-comparative: slightly smaller than Kentucky
Population: 315,281
Population growth rate: 0.66%
Nationality: noun, Icelander(s); adjective, Icelandic
Ethnic groups: a mixture of descendents of Norse and Celts 94%, population of foreign origin 6%
Languages: Icelandic, English, Nordic languages, German widely spoken
Religions: Lutheran Church of Iceland 80.7%, Roman Catholic Church 2.5%, Reykjavik Free Church 2.4%, Hafnarfjorour Free Church 1.6%, other 3.6%, unaffiliated 3%, other or unspecified 6.2%
Government type: constitutional republic
Capital: Reykjavik

Budget: revenues: $5.463 billion, expenditures: $5.775 billion
Currency: Icelandic krona (ISK)

INDIA

Location: Southern Asia, bordering the Arabian Sea and the Bay of Bengal, between Burma and Pakistan
Area: 1,269,219 sq mi (3,287,263 sq km)
Area-comparative: slightly more than one-third the size of the United States
Population: 1,220,800,359
Population growth-rate: 1.28%
Nationality: noun, Indian(s); adjective: Indian
Ethnic groups: Indo-Aryan 72%, Dravidian 25%, Mongoloid and other 3%
Language: Hindi 41%, Bengali 8.1%, Telugu 7.2%, Marathi 7%, Tamil 5.9%, Urdu 5.9%, Gujarati 4.5%,
Kannada 3.7%, Malayalam 3.2%, Oriya 3.2%, Punjabi 2.8%, Assamese 1.3%, Maithili 1.2%, other 5.9%
Religions: Hindu 80.5%, Muslim 13.4%, Christian 2.3%, Sikh 1.9%, other 1.8%, unspecified 0.1%
Government type: federal republic
Capital: New Delhi
Budget: revenues: $171.5 billion; expenditures: $281 billion
Currency: Indian rupee (INR)

INDONESIA

Location: Southeastern Asia, group of islands between the Indian Ocean and the Pacific Ocean
Area: 735,358 sq mi (1,904,569 sq km)
Area-comparative: slightly less than three times the size of Texas
Population: 251,160,124
Population growth rate: 0.99%
Nationality: noun: Indonesian(s); adjective: Indonesian
Ethnic groups: Javanese 40.6%, Sundanese 15%, Madurese 3.3%, Minangkabau 2.7%,
Betawi 2.4%, Bugis 2.4%, Banten 2%, Banjar 1.7%, other or unspecified 29.9%
Languages: Bahasa Indonesia (official modified form of Malay), English, Dutch, Javanese, local dialects
Religions: Muslim 86.1%, Protestant 5.7%, Roman Catholic 3%, Hindu 1.8%, other or unspecified 3.4%
Government: republic
Capital: Jakarta
Budget: revenues: $164 billion; expenditures: $180.9 billion
Currency: Indonesian rupiah (IDR)

IRAN

Location: Middle East, bordering the Gulf of Oman, the Persian Gulf, and the Caspian Sea, between Iraq
and Pakistan
Area: 636,371 sq mi (1,648,195 sq km)
Area-comparative: slightly smaller than Alaska
Population: 79,853,900
Population growth rate: 1.24%
Nationality: noun: Iranian(s), adjective: Iranian
Ethnic groups: Persian 61%, Azeri 16%, Kurd 10%, Arab 3%, Lur 6%, Baloch 2%, Arab 2%,Turkmen and
Turkic tribes 2%, other 1%
Languages: Persian (official) 53%, Turkic and Turkic dialects 18%, Kurdish 10%, Gilaki and Mazandarani
7%, Luri 6%, Balochi 2%, Arabic 2%, other 2%
Religions: Shi'a Muslim 89%, Sunni Muslim 9%, other 2% (Zoroastrian, Jewish, Christian, Baha'i)
Government type: theocratic republic
Capital: Tehran
Budget: revenues: $131.2 billion; expenditures: $92.63 billion
Currency: Iranian rial (IRR)

IRAQ

Location: Middle East, bordering the Persian Gulf, between Iran and Kuwait
Area: 169,235 sq mi (438,317 sq km)
Area-comparative: slightly more than twice the size of Idaho
Population: 31,858,481
Population growth rate: 2.29%
Nationality: noun, Iraqi(s); adjective: Iraqi
Ethnic groups: Arab 75%-80%, Kurdish 15%-20%,Turkoman, Assyrian or other 5%
Languages: Arabic (official), Kurdish (official in Kurdish regions), Turkmen and Assyrian
Religions: Muslim 97% (Shi'a 60% - 65%, Sunni 32% - 37%), Christian or other 3%
Government type: parliamentary democracy
Capital: Baghdad
Budget: revenues: $104.4 billion; expenditures: $98.49 billion
Currency: Iraqi dinar (NID)

IRELAND

Location: Western Europe, island in the North Atlantic Ocean, west of Great Britain
Area: 27,128 sq mi (70,280 sq km)
Area-comparative: slightly larger than West Virginia
Population: 4,775,982
Population growth rate: 1.16%
Nationality: noun: Irishman(men), Irishwoman(women), Irish (collective plural); adjective: Irish
Ethnic groups: Irish 87.4%, other white 7.5%, Asian 1.3%, black 1.1%, mixed 1.1%, unspecified 1.6%
Languages: English (official), Irish (official)
Religions: Roman Catholic 87.4%, Church of Ireland 2.9%, other Christian 1.9%, other 3.6%, none 4.2%
Government type: republic, parliamentary democracy
Capital: Dublin
Budget: revenues: $71.57 billion; expenditures: $88.97 billion
Currency: euro (EUR)

ISRAEL

Location: Middle East, bordering the Mediterranean Sea, between Egypt and Lebanon
Area: 8,017 sq mi (20,770 sq km)
Area-comparative: slightly smaller than New Jersey
Population: 7,707,042
Population growth rate: 1.5%
Nationality: noun: Israeli(s); adjective: Israeli
Ethnic groups: Jewish 76.4% (of which Israel-born 67.1%, Europe/America-born 22.6%, Africa-born 5.9%
Asia-born 4.2%) non-Jewish 23.6% (primarily Arab)
Languages: Hebrew (official), Arabic, English
Religions: Jewish 75.6%, Muslim 16.9%, Arab Christian 2%, Druze 1.7%, other 3.8%
Government type: parliamentary democracy
Capital: Jerusalem
Budget: revenues: $62.64 billion: expenditures: $72 billion
Currency: new Israeli shekel (ILS)

ITALY

Location: Southern Europe, peninsula extending into the central Mediterranean Sea, northeast of Tunisia
Area: 116,348 sq mi (301,340 sq km)
Area-comparative: slightly larger than Arizona
Population: 61,482,297
Population growth rate: 0.34%
Nationality: noun: Italian(s); adjective: Italian

492

Ethnic groups: Italian, small clusters of German, French, Slovene, and Albanian
Languages: Italian (official), German, French, Slovene
Religions: Christian 80% (overwhelmingly Roman Catholic), Atheist and Agnostic 20%
Government type: republic
Capital: Rome
Budget: revenues: $956.6 billion; expenditures: $1.014 trillion
Currency: euro (EUR)

JAMAICA

Location: Caribbean, island in the Caribbean Sea, south of Cuba
Area: 4,242 sq mi (10,991 sq km)
Area-comparative: slightly smaller than Connecticut
Population: 2,909,714
Population growth rate: 0.7%
Nationality: noun: Jamaican(s); adjective: Jamaican
Ethnic groups: black 91.2%, mixed 6.2%, other or unknown 2.6%
Language: English (official), English patois
Religion: Protestant 62.5%, Roman Catholic 2.6%, other or unspecified 14.2%, none 20.9%
Government type: constitutional parliamentary democracy and a Commonwealth realm
Capital: Kingston
Budget: revenues: $3.83 billion: expenditures: $4.764 billion
Currency: Jamaican dollar (JMD)

JAPAN

Location: Eastern Asia, island chain between the North Pacific Ocean and the Sea of Japan, east of the Korean Peninsula
Area: 145,914 sq mi (377,915 sq km)
Area-comparative: slightly smaller than California
Population: 127,253,075
Population growth rate: -0.1%
Nationality: noun: Japanese (singular and plural); adjective: Japanese
Ethnic groups: Japanese 98.5%, Korean 0.5%, Chinese 0.4%, other 0.6%
Language: Japanese (official)
Religion: observe both Shintoism 83.9% and Buddhism 71.4%, Christian 2%, other 7.8%
Government type: constitutional monarchy with a parliamentary government
Capital: Tokyo
Budget: revenues. $2.025 trillion; expenditures: $2.57 trillion
Currency: yen (JPY)

JORDAN

Location: Southwestern Asia, northwest of Saudi Arabia. Between Israel and Iraq
Area: 34,495 sq mi (89,342 sq km)
Area-comparative: slightly smaller than Indiana
Population: 6,482,081
Population growth rate: 0.14%
Nationality: noun: Jordanian(s); adjective: Jordanian
Ethnic groups: Arab 98%, Circassian 1%, Armenian 1%
Languages: Arabic (official), English
Religions: Sunni Muslim 92%, Christian 6%, other 2% (several small Shi'a Muslim and Druze populations)
Government type: constitutional monarchy
Capital: Amman
Budget: revenues: $6.378 billion; expenditures: $8.39 billion
Currency: Jordanian dinar (JOD)

KAZAKHSTAN
Location: Central Asia, northwest of China
Area: 1,052,090 sq mi (2,724,900 sq km)
Area-comparative: slightly less than four times the size of Texas
Population: 17,736,896
Population growth rate: 1.2%
Nationality: noun: Kazakhstani(s); adjective: Kazakhstani
Ethnic groups: Kazakh (Qazaq) 63.1%, Russian 23.7%, Ukrainian 2.1%, Uzbek 2.8%, German 1.1%, Tatar 1.3% Uygur 1.4%, other 4.5%
Language: Russian (official), Kazakh (official)
Religion: Muslim 70.2%, Russian Orthodox 23.9%, Protestant 2.3%, other 3.6%
Government type: republic; authoritarian presidential rule, with little power outside the executive branch
Capital: Astana
Budget: revenues: $43.08 billion; expenditures: $48.04 billion
Currency: tenge (KZT)

KENYA
Location: Eastern Africa, bordering the Indian Ocean, between Somalia and Tanzania
Area: 224,081 sq mi (580,367 sq km)
Area-comparative: slightly more than twice the size of Nevada
Population: 44,037,656
Population growth rate: 2.27%
Nationality: Kenyan(s); adjective: Kenyan
Ethnic groups: Kikuyu 22%, Luhya 14%, Luo 13%, Kalenjin 12%, Kamba 11%, Kisii 6%, Meru 6%, other African 15%, non-African 1%
Language: English (official), Kiswahili (official), numerous indigenous languages
Religion: Christian 82.5%, Muslim 11.1%, indigenous beliefs 1.6%, other 1.7%, none 2.4%
Government type: republic
Capital: Nairobi
Budget: revenues: $7.375 billion; expenditures: $9.3 billion
Currency: Kenyan shilling (KES)

KIRIBATI
Location: a group of islands in the Pacific Ocean, about one-half of the way from Hawaii to Australia
Area: 313 sq mi (811 sq km)
Area-comparative: four times the size of Washington, DC
Population: 100,743
Population growth rate: 1.249%
Nationality: noun: I-Kiribati (singular and plural); adjective: I-Kiribati
Ethnic groups: Micronesian 98.8%, other 1.2%
Language: I-Kiribati, English (official)
Religion: Roman Catholic 55%, Protestant 36%, Mormon 3.1%, Baha'I 2.2%, Seventh Day Adventist 1.9%, other 1.8%
Government type: republic
Capital: Tarawa
Budget: revenues: $55.52 million; expenditures: $ 107.1 million
Currency: Australian dollar (AUD)

KOREA, NORTH
Location: Eastern Asia, northern half of the Korean Peninsula bordering the Korea Bay and the Sea of Japan, between China and South Korea
Area: 46,541 sq mi (120,540 sq km)
Area-comparative: slightly smaller than Mississippi

Population: 24,720,407
Population growth rate: 0.53%
Nationality: noun: Korean(s); adjective: Korean
Ethnic groups: racially homogeneous; there is a small Chinese community and a few ethnic Japanese
Language: Korean (official)
Religion: traditional Buddhist and Confucianist, some Christians and syncretic Chondogyo
Government type: Communist state one-man dictatorship
Capital: Pyongyang
Budget: revenues: $3.2 billion; expenditures: $3.3 billion
Currency: North Korean won (KPW)

KOREA, SOUTH

Location: Eastern Asia, southern half of the Korean Peninsula bordering Yellow Sea and Sea of Japan
Area: 38,502 sq mi (99,720 sq km)
Area-comparative: slightly larger than Indiana
Population: 48,955,203
Population growth rate: 0.18%
Nationality: noun: Korean; adjective: Korean
Ethnic groups: homogeneous (except for about 20,000 Chinese)
Languages: Korean, English widely taught in junior high and high school
Religions: Christian 31.6%, Buddhist 24.2%, other or unknown 0.9%, none 43.3%
Government type: republic
Capital: Seoul
Budget: revenues: $250.6 billion; expenditures: $243.9 billion
Currency: South Korean won (KRW)

KUWAIT

Location: Southwestern Asia, the Middle East, bordering the Persian Gulf, between Iraq and Saudi Arabia
Area: 6,878 sq mi (17,820 sq km)
Area-comparative: slightly smaller than New Jersey
Population: 2,695,316
Population growth rate: 1.79%
Nationality: noun: Kuwaiti(s); adjective: Kuwaiti
Ethnic groups: Kuwaiti 45%, other Arab 35%, South Asian 9%, Iranian 4%, other 7%
Languages: Arabic (official), English widely spoken
Religions: Muslim 85% (Shi'a 30%, Sunni 70%), other (includes Christian, Hindu, and Parsi) 15%
Government type: constitutional emirate
Capital: Kuwait
Budget: revenues: $106.9 billion; expenditures: $69.18 billion
Currency: Kuwaiti dinar (KD)

KYRGYZSTAN

Location: Central Asia, west of China, south of Kazakhstan
Area: 77,201 sq mi (199,951 sq km)
Area-comparative: slightly smaller than South Dakota
Population: 5,548,042
Population growth rate: 0.97%
Nationality: noun: Kyrgyzstani(s); adjective: Kyrgyzstani
Ethnic groups: Kyrgyz 64.9%, Uzbek 13.8%, Russian 12.5%, Dungan 1.1%, Ukrainian 1%, Uygur 1%, other 5.7%,
Languages: Kyrgyz (official), Russian (official), Uzbek, Dungun
Religions: Muslim 75%, Russian Orthodox 20%, other 5%
Government type: republic

Capital: Bishkek
Budget: revenues: $1.741 billion; expenditures: $2.223 billion
Currency: som (KGS)

LAOS
Location: Southeastern Asia, northeast of Thailand, west of Vietnam
Area: 91,405 sq mi (236,800 sq km)
Area-comparative: slightly larger than Utah
Population: 6,695,166
Population growth rate: 1.63%
Nationality: noun: Lao(s) or Laotian(s); adjective: Lao or Laotian
Ethnic groups: Lao 55%, Khmou 11%, Hmong 8%, other (over 100 minor ethnic groups) 26%
Languages: Lao (official), French, English and various other ethnic languages
Religions: Buddhist 67%, Christian 1.5%, other and unspecified 31.5%
Government type: Communist state
Capital: Vientiane
Budget: revenues: $2.066 billion; expenditures: $2.258 billion
Currency: kip (LAK)

LATVIA
Location: Eastern Europe, bordering the Baltic Sea, between Estonia and Lithuania
Area: 24,931 sq mi (64,589 sq km)
Area-comparative: slightly larger than West Virginia
Population: 2,178,443
Population growth rate: -0.61%
Nationality: noun: Latvian(s); adjective: Latvian
Ethnic groups: Latvian 59.3%, Russian 27.8%, Belarusian 3.6%, Ukrainian 2.5%, Polish 2.4%, Lithuanian 1.3%, other 3.1%
Languages: Latvian (official) 58.2%, Russian 37.5%, Lithuanian and other 4.3%
Religions: Lutheran 19.6%, Orthodox 15.3%, other Christian 1%, other 0.4%, unspecified 63.7%
Government type: parliamentary democracy
Capital: Riga
Budget: revenues: $9.451 billion; expenditures: $10.18 billion
Currency: Latvian lat (LVL)

LEBANON
Location: Middle East, bordering the Mediterranean Sea, between Israel and Syria
Area: 4,015 sq mi (10,400 sq km)
Area-comparative: about 0.7 times the size of Connecticut
Population: 4,131,583
Population growth rate: -0.04%
Nationality: noun: Lebanese (singular and plural); adjective: Lebanese
Ethnic groups: Arab 95%, Armenian 4%, other 1%
Languages: Arabic (official), French, English, Armenian
Religions: Muslim 59.7%, Christian 39%, other 1.3%
Government type: republic
Capital: Beirut
Budget: revenues: $9.317 billion; expenditures: $12.57 billion
Currency: Lebanese pound (LBP)

LESOTHO
Location: Southern Africa, an enclave of South Africa
Area: 11,717 sq mi (30,355 sq km)

Area-comparative: slightly smaller than Maryland
Population: 1,936,181
Population growth rate: 0.34%
Nationality: noun: Mosotho (singular), Basotho (plural); adjective: Basotho
Ethnic groups: Sotho 99.7%, Europeans, Asians and other 0.3%
Languages: Sesotho (official), English (official), Zulu, Xhosa
Religions: Christian 80%, indigenous beliefs 20%
Government type: parliamentary constitutional monarchy
Capital: Maseru
Budget: revenues: $1.655 billion; expenditures: $1.68 billion
Currency: loti

LIBERIA
Location: Western Africa, bordering the North Atlantic Ocean, between Cote d'Ivoire and Sierra Leone
Area: 42,989 sq mi (111,370 sq km)
Area-comparative: slightly larger than Tennessee
Population: 3,989,703
Population growth rate: 2.56%
Nationality: noun: Liberian(s); adjective: Liberian
Ethnic groups: Kpelle 20.3%, Bassa 13.4%, Grebo 10%, Gio 8%, Mano 7.9%, Kru 6%, Lorma 5.1%, Kissi 4.8%, Gola 4.4%, other 20.1%
Languages: English (official), some 20 tribal languages
Religions: Christian 85.6%, Muslim 12.2%, Traditional 0.6%, other 0.2%, none 1.4%
Government type: republic
Capital: Monrovia
Budget: revenues: $556.8 million; expenditures: $575.7 million
Currency: Liberian dollar (LRD)

LIBYA
Location: Northern Africa, bordering the Mediterranean Sea, between Egypt, Tunisia and Algeria
Area: 679,182 sq mi (1,759,540 sq km)
Area-comparative: slightly larger than Alaska
Population: 6,002,347
Population growth rate: 4.85%
Nationality: noun: Libyan(s); adjective: Libyan
Ethnic groups: Arab-Berber 97%, other (including Greeks, Turks, Maltese, Italians, Egyptians, Pakistanis, Indians, and Tunisians) 3%
Languages: Arabic (official), Italian, English, Berber
Religions: Sunni Muslim 97%, other 3%
Government type: operates under a transitional government
Capital: Tripoli
Budget: revenues: $56.88 billion; expenditures: $51.41 billion
Currency: Libyan dinar (LYD)

LIECHTENSTEIN
Location: Central Europe, between Austria and Switzerland
Area: 62 sq mi (160 sq km)
Area-comparative: about 0.9 times the size of Washington D.C.
Population: 37,009
Population growth rate: 0.81%
Nationality: noun: Liechtensteiner(s); adjective: Liechtenstein
Ethnic groups: Liechtensteiner 65.6%, other 34.4%
Languages: German (official), Alemannic dialect

Religions: Roman Catholic 76.2%, Protestant 7%, unknown 10.6%, other 6.2%
Government type: constitutional monarchy
Capital: Vaduz
Budget: revenues: $1.29 billion; expenditures: $1.372 billion
Currency: Swiss franc (CHF)

LITHUANIA
Location: Eastern Europe, bordering the Baltic Sea, between Latvia and Russia
Area: 25,212 sq mi (65,300 sq km)
Area-comparative: slightly larger than West Virginia
Population: 3,515,858
Population growth rate: -0.28%
Nationality: noun: Lithuanian(s); adjective: Lithuanian
Ethnic groups: Lithuanian 84%, Polish 6.1%, Russian 4.9%, Belarusian 1.1%, other or unspecified 3.6%
Languages: Lithuanian (official), Polish, Russian
Religions: Roman Catholic 79%, Russian Orthodox 4.1%, Protestant (including Lutheran and Evangelical Christian Baptist) 1.9%, other or unspecified 5.5%, none 9.5%
Government: parliamentary democracy
Capital: Vilnius
Budget: revenues: $9.8 billion; expenditures: $10.1 billion
Currency: litas (LTL)

LUXEMBOURG
Location: Western Europe, between France and Germany
Area: 998 sq mi (2,586 sq km)
Area-comparative: slightly smaller than Rhode Island
Population: 514,862
Population growth rate: 1.13%
Nationality: noun: Luxembourger(s); adjective: Luxembourg
Ethnic groups: Luxembourger 63.1%, Portuguese 13.3%, French 4.5%, Italian 4.3%, German 2.3%, other EU 7.3%, other 5.2%
Languages: Luxembourgish, German, French
Religions: Roman Catholic 87%, other (including Protestant,Jews, and Muslims) 13%
Government type: constitutional monarchy
Capital: Luxembourg
Budget: revenues: $23.05 billion; expenditures: $23.56 billion
Currency: euro (EUR)

MACEDONIA
Location: Southeastern Europe, north of Greece
Area: 9,928 sq mi (25,713 sq km)
Area-comparative: slightly larger than Vermont
Population: 2,087,171
Population growth rate: 0.22%
Nationality: noun: Macedonian(s); adjective: Macedonian
Ethnic groups: Macedonian 64.2%, Albanian 25.2%, Turkish 3.9%, Roma (Gypsy) 2.7%, Serb 1.8%, other 2.2%
Languages: Macedonian 66.5%, Albanian 25.1%, Turkish 3.5%, Roma 1.9%, Serbian 1.2%, other 1.8%
Religions: Macedonian Orthodox 64.7%, Muslim 33.3%, other Christian 0.37%, unspecified 1.63%
Government type: parliamentary democracy
Capital: Skopje
Budget: revenues: $2.884 billion; expenditures: $3.255 billion
Currency: Macedonian denar (MKD)

MADAGASCAR

Location: Southern Africa, island in the Indian Ocean, east of Mozambique
Area: 226,597 sq mi (587,040 sq km)
Area-comparative: slightly less than twice the size of Arizona
Population: 22,599,098
Population growth rate: 2.65%
Nationality: noun: Malagasy (singular and plural); adjective: Malagasy
Ethnic groups: Malayo-Indonesian, Cotiers, French, Indian, Creole, Comoran
Languages: French (official), Malagasy (official), English
Religions: indigenous beliefs 52%, Christian 41%, Muslim 7%
Government type: republic
Capital: Antananarivo
Budget: revenues: $1.738 billion; expenditures: $1.907 billion
Currency: Malagasy ariary (MGA)

MALAWI

Location: Southern Africa, east of Zambia, west and north of Mozambique
Area: 45,733 sq mi (118,480 sq km)
Area-comparative: slightly smaller than Pennsylvania
Population: 16,777,547
Population growth rate: 2.74%
Nationality: noun: Malawian(s); adjective: Malawian
Ethnic groups: Chewa 32.6%, Nyanja 5.8%, Tumbuka 8.8%, Yao 13.5%, Lomwe 17.6%, Sena 3.6%, Tonga 2.1%, Ngoni 11.5%, Ngonde 1%, other 3.5%
Languages: Chichewa 57.2% (official), Chinyanja 12.8%, Chiyao 10.1%, Chitumbuka 9.5%, Chisena 2.7%, Chilomwe 2.4%, Chitonga 1.7%, other 3.6%
Religions: Christian 82.7%, Muslim 13%, other 1.9%, none 2.5%
Government type: multiparty democracy
Capital: Lilongwe
Budget: revenues: $1.089 billion; expenditures: $1.373 billion
Currency: Malawian kwacha (MWK)

MALAYSIA

Location: Southeastern Asia, peninsula and northern one-third of the island of Borneo, south of Vietnam
Area: 127,355 sq mi (329,847 sq km)
Area-comparative: slightly larger than New Mexico
Population: 29,628,302
Population growth rate: 1.51%
Nationality: noun: Malaysian(s); adjective: Malaysian
Ethnic groups: Malay 50.4%, Chinese 23.7%, indigenous 11%, Indian 7.1%, others 7.8%
Languages: Bahasa Malaysia (official), English, Chinese, Tamil, Telugu, Malayalam, Panjabi, Thai
Religions: Muslim 60.4%, Buddhist 19.2%, Christian 9.1%, Hindu 6.3%, Confucianism, Taoism, other traditional Chinese religions 2.6%, other or unknown 1.5%, none 0.8%
Government type: constitutional monarchy
Capital: Kuala Lumpur
Budget: revenues: $59.22 billion; expenditures: $75.31 billion
Currency: ringgit (MYR)

MALDIVES

Location: Southern Asia, group of atolls in the Indian Ocean, south-southwest of India
Area: 116 sq mi (300 sq km)
Area-comparative: about 1.7 times the size of Washington D.C.
Population: 393,988

Population growth rate: -0.11%
Nationality: noun: Maldivian(s); adjective: Maldivian
Ethnic groups: South Indians, Sinhalese, Arabs
Languages: Dhivehi (official), English
Religion: Sunni Muslim
Government: republic
Capital: Male
Budget: revenues: $638 million; expenditures: $917 million
Currency: rufiyaa (MVR)

MALI
Location: Western Africa, southwest of Algeria, north of Guinea, Cote d'Ivoire and Burkina Faso
Area: 478,841 sq mi (1,240,192 sq km)
Area-comparative: slightly less than twice the size of Texas
Population: 15,968,882
Population growth rate: 3.01%
Nationality: noun: Malian(s); adjective: Malian
Ethnic groups: Mande 50%, (Bambara, Malinke, Soninke), Peul 17%, Voltaic 12%, Songhai 6%, Tuareg and Moor 10%, other 5%
Languages: French (official), Bambara, numerous African languages
Religions: Muslim 94.8%, Christian 2.4%, Animist 2%, none 0.5%, unspecified 0.3%
Government type: republic
Capital: Bamako
Budget: revenues: $1.391 billion; expenditures: $2.107 billion
Currency: Communaute Financiere Africaine franc (XOF)

MALTA
Location: Southern Europe, islands in the Mediterranean Sea, south of Italy
Area: 122 sq mi (316 sq km)
Area-comparative: slightly less than twice the size of Washington, DC
Population: 411,277
Population growth rate: 0.34%
Nationality: noun: Maltese (singular and plural); adjective: Maltese
Ethnic groups: Maltese
Languages: Maltese (official) 90.2%, English (official) 6%, multilingual 3%, other 0.8%
Religions: Roman Catholic 98%, other 2%
Government type: republic
Capital: Valletta
Budget: revenues: $3.526 billion; expenditures: $3.77 billion
Currency: euro (EUR)

MARSHALL ISLANDS
Location: Oceania, group of atolls and reefs in the North Pacific Ocean, about one-half of the way from Hawaii to Australia
Area: 70 sq mi (181 sq km)
Area-comparative: about the size of Washington D.C.
Population: 69,747
Population growth rate: 1.79%
Nationality: noun: Marshallese (singular and plural); adjective: Marshallese
Ethnic groups: Marshallese 92.1%, mixed Marshallese 5.9%, other 2%
Languages: Marshallese (official) 98.2%, other languages 1.8%, English (official)
Religions: Protestant 54.8%, Assembly of God 25.8%, Roman Catholic 8.4%, Bukot nan Jesus 2.8%, Mormon 2.1%, other Christian 3.6%, other 1%, none 1.5%

Government type: constitutional government in free association with the United States
Capital: Majuro
Budget: revenues: $105.4 million; expenditures: $104.7 million
Currency: United States dollar (USD)

MAURITANIA

Location: Western Africa, bordering the North Atlantic Ocean, between Senegal and Western Sahara
Area: 397,850 sq mi (1,030,700 sq km)
Area-comparative: slightly larger than three times the size of New Mexico
Population: 3,437,610
Population growth rate: 2.29%
Nationality: noun, Mauritanian(s); adjective: Mauritanian
Ethnic groups: mixed Moor/black 40%, Moor 30%, black 30%
Languages: Arabic (official), Pulaar, Soninke, Wolof, French, Hassaniya
Religion: Muslim 100%
Government type: military junta
Capital: Nouakchott
Budget: revenues: $1.568 billion; expenditures: $1.643 billion
Currency: ouguiya (MRO)

MAURITIUS

Location: Southern Africa, island in the Indian Ocean, east of Madagascar
Area: 787 sq mi (2,040 sq km)
Area-comparative: almost 11 times the size of Washington D.C.
Population: 1,322,238
Population growth rate: 0.68%
Nationality: noun: Mauritian(s); adjective: Mauritian
Ethnic groups: Indo-Mauritian 68%, Creole 27%, Sino-Mauritian 3%, Franco-Mauritian 2%
Languages: English (official) less than 1%, Creole 80.5%, French 3.4%, Bhojpuri 12.1%, other 3.7%
Religions: Hindu 48%, Roman Catholic 23.6%, Muslim 16.6%, other Christian 8.6%, other 2.5%, unspecified 0.3%, none 0.4%
Government type: parliamentary democracy
Capital: Port Louis
Budget: revenues: $2.421 billion; expenditures: $2.919 billion
Currency: Mauritian rupee (MUR)

MEXICO

Location: located in the southern part of North America, bordering the Caribbean Sea and the Gulf of Mexico, between Guatemala and the United States
Area: 758,449 sq mi (1,964,375 sq km)
Area-comparative: slightly less than three times the size of Texas
Population: 116,220,947
Population growth rate: 1.07%
Nationality: noun: Mexican(s); adjective: Mexican
Ethnic groups: Mestizo 60%, Amerindian or predominantly Amerindian 30%, white 9%, other 1%
Languages: Spanish only 92.7%, Spanish and indigenous languages (Mayan and Nahuatl dialects) 5.7%, indigenous only 0.8%, unspecified 0.8%
Religions: Roman Catholic 82.7%, Protestant 1.6%, Jehovah's Witnesses 1.4%, other Evangelical Churches 5%, other 1.9%, unspecified 2.7%, none 4.7%
Government type: federal republic
Capital: Mexico (Distrito Federal)
Budget: revenues: $276.2 billion; expenditures: $308.25 billion
Currency: Mexican peso (MXN)

MICRONESIA

Location: Oceania, island group in the North Pacific Ocean, about three-quarters of the way from Hawaii to Indonesia
Area: 271 sq mi (702 sq km)
Area-comparative: four times the size of Washington D.C.
Population: 106,104
Population growth rate: -0.38%
Nationality: noun:Micronesian(s); adjective: Micronesian; Chuukese, Kosraen(s), Pohnpein(s), Yapese
Ethnic groups: Chuukese 48.8%, Pohnpeian 24.2%, Kosraean 6.2%, Yapese 5.2%, Yap outer islands 4.5%, Asian 1.8%, Polynesian 1.5%, other 6.4%, unknown 1.4%
Languages: English (official), Chuukese, Kosrean, Pohpeian, Yapese, Ulithian, Woleaian, Nukuoro, Kapingamarangi
Religions: Roman Catholic 52.7%, Protestant 41.7%, other 3.8%, none or unspecified 0.8%
Government type: constitutional government in free association with the United States
Capital: Palikir
Budget: revenues: $107 million; expenditures: $102 million
Currency: United States dollar (USD)

MOLDOVA

Location: Eastern Europe, northeast of Romania
Area: 13,060 sq mi (33,851 sq km)
Area-comparative: slightly larger than Maryland
Population: 3,619,925
Population growth rate: -1.02%
Nationality: noun: Moldovan(s); adjective: Moldovan
Ethnic groups: Moldavian and Romanian 78.2%, Ukrainian 8.4%, Russian 5.8%, Gagauz 4.4%, Bulgarian 1.9%, and other 1.3%
Languages: Moldovan (official), Russian, Gagauz
Religions: Eastern Orthodox 98%, Jewish 1.5%, Baptist and other 0.5%
Government type: republic
Capital: Chisinau
Budget: revenues: $2.836 billion; expenditures: $2.931 billion
Currency: Moldovan leu (MDL)

MONACO

Location: Western Europe, bordering the Mediterranean Sea on the southern coast of France, near the border with Italy
Area: .75 sq mi (1.95 sq km)
Area-comparative: about 3 times the size of The Mall in Washington, DC
Population: 30,500
Population growth rate: -0%
Nationality: noun: Monegasque(s) or Monacan(s); adjective: Monegasque or Monacan
Ethnic groups: French 47%, Monegasque 16%, Italian 16%, other 21%
Languages: French (official), English, Italian, Monegasque
Religions: Roman Catholic 90%, other 10%
Government type: constitutional monarchy
Capital: Monaco
Budget: revenues: $1.126 billion; expenditures: $1.198 billion
Currency: euro (EUR)

MONGOLIA

Location: Northern Asia, between China and Russia

Area: 603,909 sq mi (1,564,116 sq km)
Area-comparative: slightly smaller than Alaska
Population: 3,226,516
Population growth rate: 1.44%
Nationality: noun: Mongolian(s); adjective: Mongolian
Ethnic groups: Mongol 94.9%, Turkic 5%, other 0.1%
Languages: Khalkha Mongol 90%, Turkic, Russian
Religions: Buddhist Lamaist 50%, Shamanist and Christian 6%, Muslim 4%, none 40%
Government type: parliamentary
Capital: Ulaanbaatar
Budget: revenues: $4.409 billion; expenditures: $5.238 billion
Currency: togrog / tughrik (MNT)

MONTSERRAT
Location: Caribbean, island in the Caribbean Sea, southeast of Puerto Rico
Area: 63.4 sq mi (102 sq km)
Area-comparative: about 0.6 times the size of Washington, DC
Population: 5,189
Population growth rate: 0.48%
Nationality: noun: Montserratian(s) adjective: Montserratian
Ethnic groups: black, white
Languages: English
Religions: Anglican, Methodist, Roman Catholic, Pentecostal, Seventh-Day Adventist, other Christian
denominations
Government: NA
Capital: Plymouth
Budget: revenues: $31.4 million; expenditures: $37.04 million
Currency: East Caribbean dollar (XCD)

MOROCCO
Location: Northern Africa, bordering the North Atlantic Ocean and the Mediterranean Sea, between
Algeria and Western Sahara
Area: 172,368 sq mi (446,550 sq km)
Area-comparative: slightly larger than California
Population: 32,649,130
Population growth rate: 1.04%
Nationality: noun: Moroccan(s); adjective: Moroccan
Ethnic groups: Arab-Berber 99%, other 1%
Languages: Arabic (official), Berber dialects, French
Religions: Muslim 99%, Christian 1%, Jewish about 6,000
Government: constitutional monarchy
Capital: Rabat
Budget: revenues: $25.16 billion; expenditures: $32.3 billion
Currency: Moroccan dirham (MAD)

MOZAMBIQUE
Location: South-eastern Africa, bordering the Mozambique Channel, between South Africa and Tanzania
Area: 308,642 sq mi (799,380 sq km)
Area-comparative: slightly less than twice the size of California
Population: 24,096,669
Population growth rate: 2.44%
Nationality: noun: Mozambican(s); adjective: Mozambican
Ethnic groups: African 99.66%, (Makhuwa, Tsonga, Lomwe, Sena, and others) Europeans 0.06%,

Euro-Africans 0.2%, Indians 0.08%

Languages: Emakhuwa 25.3%, Xichangana 10.3%, Portuguese 10.7% (official), Elomwe 7%, Cisena 7.5%, Echuwabo 5.1%, other Mozambican languages 30.1%, other 4%

Religions: Catholic 28.4%, Muslim 17.9%, Protestant 27.7%, other 7.2%, none 18.7%

Government type: republic

Capital: Maputo

Budget: revenues: $4.37 billion; expenditures: $5.324 billion

Currency: metical (MZM)

NAMIBIA

Location: Southern Africa, bordering the South Atlantic Ocean, between Angola and South Africa

Area: 318,261 sq mi (824,292 sq km)

Area-comparative: slightly more than half the size of Alaska

Population: 2,182,852

Population growth rate: 0.75%

Nationality: noun: Namibian(s); adjective: Namibian

Ethnic groups: black 87.5%, white 6%, mixed 6.5%,

Languages: Afrikaans 60%, German 32%, English 7% (official), indigenous languages 1%:Oshivambo,Herero,Nama

Religions: Christian 80% to 90%, (Lutheran 50% at least), indigenous beliefs 10% to 20%

Government type: republic

Capital: Windhoek

Budget: revenues: $4.481 billion; expenditures: $5.081 billion

Currency: Namibian dollar (NAD)

NAURU

Location: Oceania, island in the South Pacific Ocean, south of the Marshall Islands

Area: 8 sq mi (21 sq km)

Area-comparative: about 0.1 times the size of Washington D.C.

Population: 9,434

Population growth rate: 0.58%

Nationality: noun: Nauruan(s); adjective: Nauruan

Ethnic groups: Nauruan 58%, other Pacific Islander 26%, Chinese 8%, European 8%

Languages: Nauruan (official), English

Religions: Nauru Congregational 35.4%, Roman Catholic 33.2%, Nauru Independent Church 10.4%, other 14.1%, none 4.5%, unspecified 2.4%

Government type: republic

Capital: government offices in Yaren District

Budget: revenues: $13.5 million; expenditures: $13.5 million

Currency: Australian dollar (AUD)

NEPAL

Location: Southern Asia, between China and India

Area: 56,827 sq mi (147,181 sq km)

Area-comparative: slightly larger than Arkansas

Population: 30,430,267

Population growth rate: 1.81%

Nationality: noun: Nepali (singular and plural); adjective: Nepali

Ethnic groups: Chhettri 15.5%, Brahman-Hill 12.5%, Magar 7%, Tharu 6.6%, Tamang 5.5%, Newar 5.4%, Muslim 4.2%, Kami 3.9%, Yadav 3.9%, other 32.7%, unspecified 2.8%

Languages: Nepali 47.8%, Maithali 12.1%, Bhojpuri 7.4%, Tharu (Dagaura/Rana) 5.8%, Tamang 5.1%, Newar 3.6%, Magar 3.3%, Awadhi 2.4%, other 10%, unspecified 2.5%

Religions: Hindu 80.6%, Buddhist 10.7%, Muslim 4.2%, Kirant 3.6%, other 0.9%

Government type: federal democratic republic
Capital: Kathmandu
Budget: revenues: $3.5 billion; expenditures: $4.7 billion
Currency: Nepalese rupee (NPR)

NETHERLANDS

Location: Western Europe, bordering the North Sea, between Belgium and Germany
Area: 16,040 sq mi (41,543 sq km)
Area-comparative: slightly less than twice the size of New Jersey
Population: 16,805,037
Population growth rate: 0.441%
Nationality: noun: Dutchman (men), Dutchwoman (women); adjective: Dutch
Ethnic groups: Dutch 80.7%, EU 5%, Indonesian 2.4%, Turkish 2.2%, Surinamese 2%, Moroccan 2%, Netherlands Antilles & Aruba 0.8%, other 4.8%
Languages: Dutch (official), Frisian (official)
Religions: Roman Catholic 30%, Dutch Reformed 11%, Calvinist 6%, other Protestant 3%, Muslim 5.8%, other 2.2%, none 42%
Government type: constitutional monarchy
Capital: Amsterdam
Budget: revenues: $347.4 billion; expenditures: $386.6 billion
Currency: euro (EUR)

NEW ZEALAND

Location: Oceania, islands in the South Pacific Ocean, southeast of Australia
Area: 103,363 sq mi (267,710 sq km)
Area-comparative: about the size of Colorado
Population: 4,365,113
Population growth rate: 0.85%
Nationality: noun: New Zealander(s); adjective: New Zealand
Ethnic groups: European 56.8%, Asian 8%, Maori 7.4%, Pacific Islander 4.6%, mixed 9.7%, other 13.5%
Languages: English (official), Maori (official), Sign Language, Samoan, French, Hindi, Yue
Religions: Anglican 13.8%, Roman Catholic 12.6%, Presbyterian 10%, Methodist 3%, other Christian 3.8%, Pentecostal 2%, Hindu 1.6%, Maori Christian 1.6%, Baptist 1.4%, Buddhist 1.3%, other religion 2.2%, none 32.2%, other unidentified 9.9%
Government type: parliamentary democracy and a Commonwealth realm
Capital: Wellington
Budget: revenues: $62.64 billion, expenditures: $72.71 billion
Currency: New Zealand dollar (NZD)

NICARAGUA

Location: Central America, bordering both the Caribbean Sea and the North Pacific Ocean, between Costa Rica and Honduras
Area: 50,336 sq mi (130,370 sq km)
Area-comparative: slightly smaller than the state of New York
Population: 5,788,531
Population growth rate: 1.05%
Nationality: noun: Nicaraguan(s); adjective: Nicaraguan
Ethnic groups: mestizo 69%, white 17%, black 9%, Amerindian 5%
Language: Spanish 97.5% (official), Miskito 1.7%, other 0.8%
Religion: Roman Catholic 58.5%, Evangelical 21.6%, Moravian 1.6%, Jehovah's Witness 0.9%, other 1.7%, none 15.7%
Government type: republic
Capital: Managua

Budget: revenues: $2.619 billion; expenditures: $2.56 billion
Currency: gold cordoba (NIO)

NIGER
Location: Western Africa, southeast of Algeria
Area: 489,062 sq mi (1,267,000 sq km)
Area-comparative: slightly less than twice the size of Texas
Population: 16,899,327
Population growth rate: 3.32%
Nationality: noun: Nigerien(s); adjective: Nigerien
Ethnic groups: Haoussa 55.4%, Djerma Sonrai 21%, Tuareg 9.3%, Peuhl 8.5%, Kanouri Manga 4.7%, other 1.2%
Languages: French (official), Hausa, Djerma
Religions: Muslim 80%, remainder indigenous beliefs and Christian
Government type: republic
Capital: Niamey
Budget: revenues: $1.655 billion; expenditures: $1.927 billion
Currency: Communaute Financiere Africaine franc (XOF)

NIGERIA
Location: Western Africa, bordering the Gulf of Guinea, between Benin and Cameroon
Area: 356,574 sq mi (923,768 sq km)
Area-comparative: slightly more than twice the size of California
Population: 174,507,539
Population growth rate: 2.54%
Nationality: noun: Nigerian(s); adjective: Nigerian
Ethnic groups: Hausa and Fulani 29%, Yoruba 21%, Igbo 18%, Ijaw 10%, Kanuri 4%, Ibibio 3.5%, Tiv 2.5%
Languages: English (official), Hausa, Yoruba, Igbo, Fulani
Religions: Muslim 50%, Christian 40%, indigenous beliefs 10%
Government type: federal republic
Capital: Abuja
Budget: revenues: $23.48 billion; expenditures: $31.61 billion
Currency: naira (NGN)

NORWAY
Location: Northern Europe, bordering the North Sea and the North Atlantic Ocean, west of Sweden
Area: 125,021 sq mi (323,802 sq km)
Area-comparative: slightly larger than New Mexico
Population: 4,722,701
Population growth rate: 0.33%
Nationality: noun: Norwegian(s); adjective: Norwegian
Ethnic groups: Norwegian 94.4%, other European 3.6%, other 2%
Language: Bokmal Norwegian (official), Nynorsk Norwegian (official), small Sami and Finnish-speaking minorities
Religions: Church of Norway 85.7%, Pentecostal 1%, Roman Catholic 1%, other Christian 2.4%, Muslim 1.8%, other 8.1%
Government type: constitutional monarchy
Capital: Oslo
Budget: revenues: $282.9 billion; expenditures: $206.7 billion
Currency: Norwegian krone (NOK)

OMAN
Location: Middle East, bordering the Arabian Sea, Gulf of Oman, and the Persian Gulf, between

Yemen and United Arab Emirates
Area: 119,499 sq mi (309,500 sq km)
Area-comparative: slightly smaller than Kansas
Population: 3,154,134
Population growth rate: 2.06%
Nationality: noun: Omani(s); adjective: Omani
Ethnic groups: Arab, Baluchi, Indian, Pakistani, Sri Lankan, Bangladeshi, African
Languages: Arabic (official), English, Baluchi, Urdu, Indian dialects
Religions: Ibadhi Muslim 75%, other including Sunni Muslim, Shi'a Muslim, Hindu 25%
Government type: monarchy
Capital: Muscat
Budget: revenues: $35.55 billion; expenditures: $30.49 billion
Currency: Omani rial (OMR)

PAKISTAN
Location: Southern Asia, bordering the Arabian Sea, between India on the east and Iran and Afghanistan on the west and China in the north
Area: 307,374 sq mi (796,095 sq km)
Area-comparative: slightly less than twice the size of California
Population: 193,238,868
Population growth rate: 1.52%
Nationality: noun: Pakistani(s); adjective: Pakistani
Ethnic groups: Punjabi 44.68%, Pashtun 15.42%, Sindhi 14.1%, Sariakim 8.38%, Muhajirs 7.57%, Balochi 3.57%, other 6.28%
Languages: Punjabi 48%, Sindhi 12%, Siraiki 10%, Pashtu 8%, Urdu (official) 8%, Balochi 3%, Hindko 2%, Brahui 1%, English, Burushaski, and other 8%
Religions: Sunni Muslim 85-90%, Shi'a Muslim 10-15%, other (including Christian and Hindu) 3.6%
Government type: federal republic
Capital: Islamabad
Budget: revenues: $29.51 billion; expenditures: $44.19 billion
Currency: Pakistani rupee (PKR)

PANAMA
Location: Central America, bordering both the Caribbean Sea and the North Pacific Ocean, between Colombia and Costa Rica
Area: 29,120 sq mi (75,420 sq km)
Area-comparative: slightly smaller than South Carolina
Population: 3,559,408
Population growth rate: 1.38%
Nationality: noun: Panamanian(s); adjective: Panamanian
Ethnic groups: mestizo (mixed Amerindian and white) 70%, Amerindian and mixed (West Indian) 14%, white 10%, Amerindian 6%
Languages: Spanish (official), English
Religions: Roman Catholic 85%, Protestant 15%
Government type: constitutional democracy
Capital: Panama City
Budget: revenues: $9.219 billion: expenditures: $10.21 billion
Currency: balboa (PAB)

PAPUA NEW GUINEA
Location: Oceania, group of islands including the eastern half of the island of New Guinea, east of Indonesia
Area: 178,656 sq mi (462,840 sq km)

Area-comparative: slightly larger than California
Population: 6,431,902
Population growth rate: 1.89%
Nationality: noun: Papua New Guinean(s); adjective: Papua New Guinean
Ethnic groups: Melanesian, Papuan, Negrito, Micronesian, Polynesian
Languages: English (official), Tok Pisin (official), Hiri Motu (official), 836 other indigenous languages
Religions: Roman Catholic 27%, Evangelical Lutheran 19.5%, United Church 11.5%, Seventh Day Adventist 11%, Pentecoastal 8.6%, Evangelical Alliance 5.2%, Anglican 3.2%, Baptist 2.5%, other Protestant 8.9%, Bahai 0.3%, indigenous beliefs and other 3.3%
Government type: constitutional parliamentary democracy and a Commonwealth realm
Capital: Port Moresby
Budget: revenues: $2.962 billion; expenditures: $4.942 billion
Currency: kina (PGK)

PARAGUAY
Location: Central South America, northeast of Argentina , southwest of Brazil
Area: 157,005 sq mi (406,750 sq km)
Area-comparative: slightly smaller than California
Population: 6,623,252
Population growth rate: 1.23%
Nationality: noun: Paraguayan(s); adjective: Paraguayan
Ethnic groups: mestizo (mixed Spanish and Amerindian) 95%, other 5%
Languages: Spanish (official), Guarani (official)
Religions: Roman Catholic 89.6%, Protestant 6.2%, other Christian 1.1%, unspecified 1.9%, none 1.1%
Government type: constitutional republic
Capital: Asuncion
Budget: revenues: $4.687 billion; expenditures: $5.122 billion
Currency: guarani (PYG)

PERU
Location: Western South America, bordering the South Pacific Ocean, between Chile and Ecuador
Area: 496,094 sq mi (1,285,220 sq km)
Area-comparative: slightly smaller than Alaska
Population: 29,849,303
Population growth rate: 1%
Nationality: noun: Peruvian(s); adjective: Peruvian
Ethnic groups: Amerindian 45%, mestizo 37%, white 15%, black, Japanese, Chinese, and other 3%
Languages: Spanish (official), Quechua (official), Aymara, minor Amazonian languages
Religions: Roman Catholic 81.3%, Evangelical 12.5%, other 3.3%, unspecified or none 2.9%
Government type: constitutional republic
Capital: Lima
Budget: revenues: $58.15 billion; expenditures: $56.42 billion
Currency: nuevo sol (PEN)

PHILIPPINES
Location: Southeastern Asia, group of islands between the Philippine Sea and the South China Sea, east of Vietnam
Area: 115,800 sq mi (300,000 sq km)
Area-comparative: slightly larger than Arizona
Population: 105,720,644
Population growth rate: 1.84%
Nationality: noun: Filipino(s); adjective: Philippine
Ethnic groups: Tagalog 28.1%, Cebuano 13.1%, Ilocano 9%, Bisaya/Binisaya 7.6%,

Hiligaynon Ilonggo 7.5%, Bikol 6%, Waray 3.4%, other 25.3%
Languages: Filipino (based on Tagalog) and English are official languages; eight major dialects
Religions: Roman Catholic 80.9%, Muslim 5%, Evangelical 2.8%, Iglesia ni Kristo 2.3%,
Aglipayan 2%, other Christian 4.5%, other 1.8%, unspecified 0.6%, none 0.1%
Government type: republic
Capital: Manila
Budget: revenues: $35.96 billion: expenditures: $41.53 billion
Currency: Philippine peso (PHP)

POLAND

Location: Central Europe, east of Germany
Area: 120,696 sq mi (312,685 sq km)
Area-comparative: slightly smaller than New Mexico
Population: 38,383,809
Population growth rate: -0.09%
Nationality: noun: Pole(s); adjective: Polish
Ethnic groups: Polish 96.7%, German 0.4%, Ukrainian 0.1%, Belarusian 0.1% , other and unspecified 2.7%
Language: Polish (official)
Religions: Roman Catholic 89.8%, Eastern Orthodox 1.3%, Protestant 0.3%, other 0.3%, unspecified 8.3%
Government type: republic
Capital: Warsaw
Budget: revenues: $89.47 billion; expenditures: $99.54 billion
Currency: zloty (PLN)

PORTUGAL

Location: Southwestern Europe, bordering the North Atlantic Ocean, west of Spain
Area: 35,556 sq mi (92,090 sq km)
Area-comparative: slightly smaller than Indiana
Population: 10,799,270
Population growth rate: 0.15%
Nationality: noun: Portuguese (singular and plural); adjective: Portuguese
Ethnic groups: homogeneous Mediterranean stock, African
Language: Portuguese (official), Mirandese (official-but locally used)
Religions: Roman Catholic 84.5%, other Christian 2.2%, other 0.3%, unknown 9%, none 3.9%
Government: republic; parliamentary democracy
Capital: Lisbon
Budget: revenues: $94.67 billion; expenditures: $107.4 billion
Currency: euro (EUR)

PUERTO RICO (commonwealth associated with the US)

Location: Caribbean, island between the Caribbean Sea and the North Atlantic Ocean, east of the
Dominican Republic
Area: 5,324 sq mi (13,790 sq km)
Area-comparative: slightly less than three times the size of Rhode Island
Population: 3,674,209
Population growth rate: -0.47%
Nationality: noun: Puerto Rican(s) (United States citizens); adjective: Puerto Rican
Ethnic groups: white 76.2%, black 6.9%, Asian 0.3%, Amerindian 0.2%, mixed 4.4%, other 12%
Languages: Spanish, English
Religions: Roman Catholic 85%, Protestant and other 15%
Government type: commonwealth
Capital: San Juan
Budget: revenues: $6.7 billion; expenditures: $9.6 billion   **Currency:** United States dollar (USD)

QATAR

Location: Middle East, peninsula bordering the Persian Gulf and Saudi Arabia
Area: 4,473 sq mi (11,586 sq km)
Area-comparative: slightly smaller than Connecticut
Population: 2,042,444
Population growth rate: 4.19%
Nationality: noun: Qatari(s); adjective: Qatari
Ethnic groups: Arab 40%, Pakistani 18%, Indian 18%, Iranian 10%, other 14%
Languages: Arabic (official), English
Religions: Muslim 77.5%, Christian 8.5%, other 14%
Government type: emirate
Capital: Doha
Budget: revenues: $62.66 billion; expenditures: $51.19 billion
Currency: Qatari rial (QAR)

ROMANIA

Location: Southeastern Europe, bordering the Black Sea, between Bulgaria and Ukraine
Area: 92,043 sq mi (238,391 sq km)
Area-comparative: slightly smaller than Oregon
Population: 21,790,479
Population growth rate: -0.27%
Nationality: noun: Romanian(s); adjective: Romanian
Ethnic groups: Romanian 89.5%, Hungarian 6.6%, Roma 2.5%, Ukrainian 0.3%, German 0.3%, Russian 0.2%, Turkish 0.2%, other 0.4%
Languages: Romanian (official) 91%, Hungarian 6.7%, Romany (Gypsy) 1.1%, other 1.2%
Religions: Eastern Orthodox 86.8%, Protestant 7.5%, Roman Catholic 4.7%, other, mostly Muslim and unspecified 0.9%, none 0.1%
Government type: republic
Capital: Bucharest
Budget: revenues:$55.67 billion; expenditures: $59.94 billion
Currency: leu (ROL)

RUSSIA

Location: bordering the Arctic Ocean, between Europe and the North Pacific Ocean to the east, Europe is generally divided from Asia by the water which is divided by the Ural mountains, the Ural River and by the Caspian Sea.
Area: 6,601,668 sq mi (17,098,242 sq km)
Area-comparative: approximately 1.8 times the size of the United States
Population: 142,500,462
Population growth rate: -0.02%
Nationality: noun: Russian(s); adjective: Russian
Ethnic groups: Russian 79.8%, Tatar 3.8%, Ukrainian 2%, Bashkir 1.2%, Chuvash 1.1%, other or unspecified 12.1%
Languages: Russian (official), many other minority languages
Religions: Russian Orthodox 15%-20%, Muslim 10%-15%, other Christian 2%
Government type: federation
Capital: Moscow
Budget: revenues: $423.4 billion; expenditures: $423.8 billion
Currency: Russian ruble (RUR)

RWANDA

Location: Central Africa, east of Democratic Republic of the Congo
Area: 10,166 sq mi (26,338 sq km)

Area-comparative: slightly smaller than Maryland
Population: 12,012,620
Population growth rate: 2.7%
Nationality: noun: Rwandan(s); adjective: Rwandan
Ethnic groups: Hutu (Bantu) 84%, Tutsi (Hamitic) 15%, Twa (Pgymy) 1%
Languages: Kinyarwanda (official), universal Bantu vernacular French (official), English (official), Kiswhahilli (Swahili)
Religions: Roman Catholic 56.5%, Protestant 26%, Adventist 11.1%, Muslim 4.6%, indigenous beliefs 0.1%, none 1.7%
Government type: republic, presidential, multiparty system
Capital: Kigali
Budget: revenues: $1.788 billion; expenditures: $1.911 billion
Currency: Rwandan franc (RWF)

SAINT BARTHELEMY

Location: Caribbean, island between the Caribbean Sea and the North Atlantic Ocean; located in the Leeward Islands (northern) group; located approximately 125 miles northwest of Guadeloupe; Saint Barthelemy lies east of the US Virgin Islands
Area: 13 sq mi (21 sq km)
Area-comparative: less than an eighth of the size of Washington, DC
Population: 7,298
Population growth rate: NA
Nationality: NA
Ethnic groups: white, Creole (mulatto), black, Guadeloupe Mestizo (French-East Asia)
Languages: French (primary), English
Religions: Roman Catholic, Protestant, Jehovah's Witnesses
Dependency status: overseas collectivity of France
Capital: Gustavia
Budget: revenues: $NA; expenditures: $NA   **Currency:** euro (EUR)

SAINT KITTS AND NEVIS
Location: Caribbean, islands in the Caribbean Sea, about one-third of the way from Puerto Rico to Trinidad and Tobago
Area: 101 sq mi (261 sq km)
Area-comparative: 1.5 times the size of Washington, D C
Population: 51,134
Population growth rate: 0.8%
Nationality: noun: Kittitian(s), Nevisian(s); adjective: Kittitian, Nevisian
Ethnic groups: predominately black; some British, Portuguese, and Lebanese
Language: English (official)
Religions: Anglican, other Protestant, Roman Catholic
Government type: parliamentary democracy and a Commonwealth realm
Capital: Basseterre
Budget: revenues: $185.2 million; expenditures: $222.2 million   **Currency:** East Caribbean dollar (XCD)

SAINT LUCIA
Location: island between the Caribbean Sea and North Atlantic Ocean, north of Trinidad and Tobago
Area: 238 sq mi (616 sq km)
Area-comparative: 3.5 times the size of Washington, D C
Population: 162,781
Population growth rate: 0.36%
Nationality: noun: Saint Lucian(s); adjective: Saint Lucian

Ethnic groups: black 82.5%, mixed 11.9%, East Indian 2.4%, other or unspecified 3.1%
Languages: English (official), French patois
Religions: Roman Catholic 67.5%, Protestant 18.2%, (Seventh-Day Adventist 8.5%, Pentecostal 5.7%, Anglican 2%, Evangelical 2%), other Christian 5.1%, Rastafarian 2.1%, other 1.1%, unspecified 1.5%, none 4.5%
Government type: parliamentary democracy and a Commonwealth realm
Capital: Castries
Budget: revenues: $185.2 million; expenditures: $222.2 million
Currency: East Caribbean dollar (XCD)

SAINT MARTIN

Location: Caribbean, located in the Leeward Islands (northern) group, French part of the island of Saint Martin in the Caribbean Sea; Saint Martin lies east of the US Virgin Islands and is 186.4 mi southeast of Puerto Rico
Area: 21 sq mi (54.4 sq km)
Area-comparative: more than one-third the size of Washington, DC
Population: 31,264
Population growth rate: NA
Nationality: NA
Ethnic groups: Creole (mulatto), black, Guadeloupe Mestizo (French-East Asia), white, East Indian
Languages: French (official), English, Dutch, French Patois, Spanish, Papiamento (dialect of Netherlands Antilles)
Religions: Roman Catholic, Jehovah's Witnesses, Protestant, Hindu
Dependency status: overseas collectivity of France
Capital: Marigot
Budget: revenues: $NA; **expenditures:** $NA   **Currency:** euro (EUR)

SAINT VINCENT AND THE GRENADINES

Location: Caribbean, islands between the Caribbean Sea and North Atlantic Ocean, north of Trinidad and Tobago
Area: 150 sq mi (389 sq km)
Area-comparative: twice the size of Washington D.C.
Population: 103,220
Population growth rate: -0.3%
Nationality: noun: Saint Vincentian(s) or Vincentians(s); adjective: Saint Vincentian or Vincentian
Ethnic groups: black 66%, mixed 19%, East Indian 6%, European 4%, Carib Amerindian 2%, other 3%
Languages: English, French patois
Religions: Protestant 75%, (Anglican 47%, Methodist 28%), Roman Catholic 13%, other (includes Hindu, Seventh-Day Adventist, other Protestant) 12%
Government type: parliamentary democracy and a Commonwealth realm
Capital: Kingstown
Budget: revenues: $185.2 million; expenditures: $185.2 million   **Currency:** East Caribbean dollar (XCD)

SAMOA

Location: Oceania, group of islands in the South Pacific Ocean, about one-half of the way from Hawaii to New Zealand
Area: 1,093 sq mi (2,831 sq km)
Area-comparative: slightly smaller than Rhode Island
Population: 195,476
Population growth rate: 0.6%
Nationality: noun: Samoan(s); adjective: Samoan
Ethnic groups: Samoan 92.6%, Euronesians (persons of European and Polynesian blood) 7%,

Europeans 0.4%

Languages: Samoan (Polynesian) (official), English

Religions: Protestant 59.9% (Congregationalist 34.8%, Methodist 15%, Assembly of God 6.6%, Seventh-Day Adventist 3.5%), Roman Catholic 19.6%, Mormon/Latter-Day Saints 12.7%, Worship Centre 1.3%, other Christian 4.5%, other 1.9%, unspecified 0.1%

Government type: parliamentary democracy

Capital: Apia

Budget: revenues: $258.6 million; expenditures: $301.7 million   **Currency:** tala (SAT)

SAN MARINO

Location: Southern Europe, an enclave in central Italy

Area: 24 sq mi (61 sq km)

Area-comparative: about 0.3 times the size of Washington, DC

Population: 32,448

Population growth rate: 0.93%

Nationality: noun: Sammarinese (singular and plural); adjective: Sammarinese

Ethnic groups: Sammarinese, Italian

Language: Italian (official)

Religion: Roman Catholic

Government type: republic

Capital: San Marino

Budget: revenues: $667.7 million; expenditures: $694.7 million   **Currency:** euro (EUR)

SAO TOME AND PRINCIPE

Location: Central Africa, islands in the Gulf of Guinea, straddling the Equator, west of Gabon

Area: 372 sq mi (964 sq km)

Area-comparative: more than 5 times the size of Washington, DC

Population: 186,817

Population growth rate: 1.94%

Nationality: Sao Tomean(s); adjective: Sao Tomean

Ethnic groups: mestico, angolares (descendants of Angolan slaves), forros (descendants of freed slaves), servicais (contract laborers from Angola, Mozambique, and Cape Verde), tongas (children of servicais born on the island), Europeans (primarily Portuguese)

Language: Portuguese (official)

Religions: Catholic 70.3%, Evangelical 3.4%, New Apostolic 2%, Adventist 1.8%, other 3.1%, none 19.4%

Government type: republic

Capital: Sao Tome

Budget: revenues: $111.5 million; expenditures: $139.9 million   **Currency:** dobra (STD)

SAUDI ARABIA

Location: Middle East, bordering the Persian Gulf and the Red Sea, north of Yemen

Area: 830,000 sq mi (2,149,690 sq km)

Area-comparative: slightly more than one-fifth the size of the US

Population: 26,939,583 (includes 5,576,076 non-nationals)

Population growth rate: 1.51%

Nationality: noun: Saudi(s); adjective: Saudi or Saudi Arabian

Ethnic groups: Arab 90%, Afro-Asian 10%

Language: Arabic (official)

Religion: Muslim 100%

Government type: monarchy

Capital: Riyadh

Budget: revenues: $314.3 billion; expenditures: $236.3 billion   **Currency:** Saudi riyal (SAR)

SENEGAL
Location: Western Africa, bordering the North Atlantic Ocean, between Guinea-Bissau and Mauritania
Area: 75,955 sq mi (196,722 sq km)
Area-comparative: slightly smaller than South Dakota
Population: 13,300,410
Population rate growth: 2.51%
Nationality: noun: Senegalese (singular and plural); adjective: Senegalese
Ethnic groups: Wolof 43.3%, Pular 23.8%, Serer 14.7%, Jola 3.7%, Mandinka 3%, Soninke 1.1%,
      European and Lebanese 1%, other 9.4%
Languages: French (official), Wolof, Pulaar, Jola, Mandinka
Religions: Muslim 94%, Christian (primarily Roman Catholic) 5%, indigenous beliefs 1%,
Government type: republic
Capital: Dakar
Budget: revenues: $3.307 billion; expenditures: $4.112 billion
Currency: Communaute Financiere Africaine franc (XOF)

SERBIA
Location: Southeastern Europe, between Macedonia and Hungary
Area: 29,905 sq. mi. (77,474 sq km)
Area comparative: slightly smaller than South Carolina
Population: 7,243,007 (does not include the population of Kosovo)
Population growth rate: -0.46%
Nationality: noun: Serb(s); adjective: Serbian
Ethnic groups: Serb 82.9%, Hungarian 3.9%, Romany (Gypsy) 1.4%, Yugoslavs 1.1%, Bosniaks 1.8%,
      Montenegrin 0.9%, other 8%
Languages: Serbian 88.3% (official); Hungarian 3.8%, Bosniak 1.8%, Romany (Gypsy) 1.1%, other 4.1%,
      unknown 0.9%
Religions: Serbian Orthodox 85%, Catholic 5.5%, Muslim 3.2%, Protestant 1.1%, unspecified 2.6%
Government type: republic
Capital: Belgrade (Beograd)
Budget: revenues: $16.69 billion; expenditures: $18.98 billion   **Currency:** Serbian dinar (RSD)

SIERRA LEONE
Location: Western Africa, bordering the North Atlantic Ocean, between Guinea and Liberia
Area: 27,692 sq mi (71,740 sq km)
Area-comparative: slightly smaller than South Carolina
Population: 5,612,685
Population growth rate: 2.3%
Nationality: noun: Sierra Leonean(s); adjective: Sierra Leonean
Ethnic groups: Temne 35%, Mende 31%, Limba 8%, Kono 5%, Kriole 2% (descendents of freed
      Jamaican slaves who settled in the area in the 18th century), Mandingo 2%, Loko 2%, other 15%
      (includes refugees from Liberia's recent civil war, Europeans, Lebanese, Pakistanis, and Indians)
Languages: English (official, regular use limited to literate minority), Mende (principal vernacular in the
      south), Temne (principal vernacular in the north), Krio (English-based Creole, spoke by the
      descendants of freed Jamaican slaves who were settled in the Freetown area, a lingua franca
      and a first language for 10% of the population but understood by 95%)
Religions: Muslim 60%, indigenous beliefs 30%, Christian 10%
Government type: constitutional democracy
Capital: Freetown
Budget: revenues: $527.5 million; expenditures: $685.7 million   **Currency:** leone (SLL)

SINGAPORE
Location: Southeastern Asia, islands between Malaysia and Indonesia

Area: 269 sq mi (697 sq km)
Area-comparative: slightly more than 3.5 times the size of Washington, DC
Population: 5,460,302
Population growth rate: 1.96%
Nationality: noun: Singaporean(s); adjective: Singapore
Ethnic groups: Chinese 76.8%, Malay 13.9%, Indian 7.9%, other 1.4%
Languages: Mandarin 35% (official), English 23% (official), Malay 14.1% (official), Hokkien 11.4%, Cantonese 5.7%, Teochew 4.9%, Tamil 3.2% (official), other Chinese dialects 1.8%, other 0.9%
Religions: Buddhist 42.5%, Muslim 14.9%, Taoist 8.5%, Catholic 4.8%, Hindu 4%, other Christian 9.8%, other 0.7%, none 14.8%
Government type: parliamentary republic
Capital: Singapore
Budget: revenues: $42.47 billion; expenditures: $39.97 billion   **Currency:** Singapore dollar (SGD)

SLOVAKIA
Location: Central Europe, south of Poland
Area: 18,932 sq mi (49,035 sq km)
Area-comparative: about twice the size of New Hampshire
Population: 5,488,339
Population growth rate: 0.09%
Nationality: noun: Slovak(s); adjective: Slovak
Ethnic groups: Slovak 85.8%, Hungarian 9.7%, Roma 1.7%, Ruthenian/Ukrainian 1%, other and unspecified 1.8%
Languages: Slovak 83.9% (official), Hungarian 10.7%, Roma 1.8%, Ukrainian 1%, other or unspecified 2.6%
Religions: Roman Catholic 68.9%, Protestant 10.8%, Greek Catholic 4.1%, other or unspecified 3.2%, none 13%
Government type: parliamentary democracy
Capital: Bratislava
Budget: revenues: $31.39 billion; expenditures: $35.85 billion   **Currency:** Euro (EUR)

SLOVENIA
Location: south Central Europe, Julian Alps between Austria and Croatia
Area: 7,825 sq mi (20,273 sq km)
Area-comparative: slightly smaller than New Jersey
Population: 1,992,690
Population growth rate: -0.21%
Nationality: noun: Slovene(s); adjective: Slovenian
Ethnic groups: Slovene 83.1%, Serb 2%, Croat 1.8%, Bosniak 1.1%, other or unspecified 12%
Languages: Slovenian 91.1% (official), Serbo-Croatian 4.5%, other or unspecified 4.4%, Italian (official, only in municipalities where Italian national communities reside), Hungarian (official, only in municipalities where Hungarian national communities reside)
Religions: Catholic 57.8%, Muslim 2.4%, Orthodox 2.3%, other Christian 0.9%, unaffiliated 3.5%, other or unspecified 23%, none 10.1%
Government type: parliamentary republic
Capital: Ljubljana
Budget: revenues: $20.5 billion; expenditures: $22.59 billion   **Currency:** Euro (EUR)

SOLOMON ISLANDS
Location: Oceania, group of islands in the South Pacific Ocean, east of Papua New Guinea
Area: 11,543 sq mi (28,896 sq km)
Area-comparative: slightly smaller than Maryland

Population: 571,890
Population growth rate: 2.22%
Nationality: noun: Solomon Islander(s); adjective: Solomon Islander
Ethnic groups: Melanesian 94.5%, Polynesian 3%, Micronesian 1.2%, other 1.1%, unspecified 0.2%
Languages: Melanesian, pidgin (in much of the country is lingua franca), English (official but spoken by only 1%-2% of the population); 120 indigenous dialects
Religions: Protestant 73.7% (Church of Melanesia 32.8%, South Seas Evangelical 17%, Seventh-Day Adventist 11.2%, United Church 10.3%, Christian Fellowship Church 2.4%), Roman Catholic 19%, other Christian 4.4%, other 2.4%, unspecified 0.3%, none 0.2%
Government type: parliamentary democracy and a Commonwealth realm
Capital: Honiara
Budget: revenues: $339.7 million; expenditures: $285.4 million   **Currency:** Solomon Islands dollar (SBD)

SOMALIA
Location: Eastern Africa, bordering the Gulf of Aden and the Indian Ocean, east of Ethiopia
Area: 246,135 sq mi (637,657 sq km)
Area-comparative: slightly smaller than Texas
Population: 10,251,568
Population growth rate: 1.67%
Nationality: noun: Somali(s); adjective: Somali
Ethnic groups: Somali 85%, Bantu and other non-Somali 15% (including 30,000 Arabs)
Languages: Somali (official), Arabic (official according to the Transitional Federal Charter), Italian, English
Religion: Sunni Muslim (Islam) 100%
Government type: no permanent national government; transitional, parliamentary federal government
Capital: Mogadishu
Budget: revenues: NA; expenditures: NA   **Currency:** Somali shilling (SOS)

SOUTH AFRICA
Location: Southern Africa, at the southern tip of the continent of Africa
Area: 470,693 sq mi (1,219,090 sq km)
Area-comparative: slightly less than twice the size of Texas
Population: 48,602,098
Population growth rate: -0.45 %
Nationality: noun: South African(s); adjective: South African
Ethnic groups: black African 79%, white 9.6%, colored 8.9%, Indian/Asian 2.5%,
Languages: IsiZulu 23.82%, IsiXhosa 17.64%, Afrikaans 13.35%, Sepedi 9.4%, English 8.2%, Setswana 8.2%, Sesotho 7.93% Xitsonga 4.44%, siSwati 2.66%, Tshivenda 2.28%, isiNdebele 1.59%, other 0.5%
Religions: Protestant 36.6% (Zionist Christian 11.1%, Pentecostal/Charismatic 8.2%, Methodist 6.8%, Dutch Reformed 6.7%, Anglican 3.8%), Catholic 7.1%, Muslim 1.5%, other Christian 36%, other 2.3%, none 15.1%
Government type: republic
Capital: Pretoria (administrative), Cape Town (legislative center), Bloemfontein (judicial center)
Budget: revenues: $95.27 billion; expenditures: $116.5 billion   **Currency:** rand (ZAR)

SPAIN
Location: Southwestern Europe, bordering the Bay of Biscay, Mediterranean Sea, North Atlantic Ocean, and Pyrenees Mountains; southwest of France
Area: 195,124 sq mi (505,370 sq km)
Area-comparative: slightly more than twice the size of Oregon
Population: 47,370,542
Population growth rate: 0.73%
Nationality: noun: Spaniard(s); adjective: Spanish

Ethnic groups: composite of Mediterranean and Nordic types
Languages: Castilian Spanish 74% (official), Catalan 17%, Galician 7%, Basque 2%
Religions: Roman Catholic 94%, other 6%
Government type: parliamentary monarchy
Capital: Madrid
Budget: revenues: $485.1 billion; expenditures: $584.8 billion   **Currency:** euro (EUR)

SRI LANKA

Location: Southern Asia, island in the Indian Ocean, south of India
Area: 25,325 sq mi (65,610 sq km)
Area-comparative: slightly larger than West Virginia
Population: 21,675,648
Population growth rate: 0.89%
Nationality: noun: Sri Lankan(s); adjective: Sri Lankan
Ethnic groups: Sinhalese 73.8%, Sri Lankan Moors 7.2%, Indian Tamil 4.6%, Sri Lankan Tamil 3.9%, other 0.5%, unspecified 10%
Languages: Sinhala 74% (official and national language), Tamil 18% (national language), other 8%
Religions: Buddhist 69.1% (official), Muslim 7.6%, Hindu 7.1%, Christian 6.2%, unspecified 10%
Government type: republic
Capital: Colombo; note - Sri Jayewardenepura Kotte is the legislative capital
Budget: revenues: $8.1 billion; expenditures: $11.8 billion   **Currency:** Sri Lankan rupee (LKR)

SUDAN

Location: North-eastern Africa, bordering the Red Sea, between Egypt and Eritrea
Area: 718,723 sq mi (1,861,484 sq km)
Area-comparative: slightly less than one-fifth the size of the US
Population: 34,847,910
Population growth rate: 1.83%
Nationality: noun: Sudanese (singular and plural); adjective: Sudanese
Ethnic groups: Sudanese Arab 70%, Fur, Beja, Nuba, Fallata
Languages: Arabic (official), English (official), Nubian, Ta Bedawie, Fur
Religions: Sunni Muslim, small Christian minority
Government type: Federal republic ruled by the National Congress Party (NCP), which came to power by military coup in 1989
Capital: Khartoum
Budget: revenues: $4.521 billion; expenditures: $10.07 billion   **Currency:** Sudanese dinar (SDD)

SURINAME

Location: Northern South America, bordering the North Atlantic Ocean, between French Guiana and Guyana
Area: 63,251 sq mi (163,820 sq km)
Area-comparative: slightly larger than Georgia
Population: 566,846
Population growth rate: 1.15%
Nationality: noun: Surinamer(s); adjective: Surinamese
Ethnic groups: Hindustani 37% (also known locally as "East Indians"; their ancestors emigrated from northern India in the latter part of the 19th century), Creole 31% (mixed with white and black), Javanese 15%, Maroons 10% (their African ancestors were brought to the country in the 17th and 18th centuries as slaves and escaped to the interior), Amerindian 2%, Chinese 2%, white 1%, other 2%,
Languages: Dutch (official), English (widely spoken), Sranang Tongo, Caribbean Hindustani, Javanese
Religions: Hindu 27.4%, Protestant 25.2%, Roman Catholic 22.8%, Muslim 19.6%, indigenous beliefs 5%
Government type: constitutional democracy

Capital: Paramaribo
Budget: revenues: $826.6 million; expenditures: $939.7 million   **Currency:** Surinamese guilder (SRG)

SWAZILAND
Location: Southern Africa, between Mozambique and South Africa
Area: 6,704 sq mi (17,364 sq km)
Area-comparative: slightly smaller than New Jersey
Population: 1,403,362
Population growth rate: 1.17%
Nationality: noun: Swazi(s); adjective: Swazi
Ethnic groups: African 97%, European 3%
Languages: English (official, used for government business), siSwati (official)
Religions: Zionist 40%, Roman Catholic 20%, Muslim 10%, other (including Anglican, Baha'i, Methodist, Mormon, Jewish) 30%
Government type: monarchy
Capital: Mbabane; Lobamba is the royal and legislative capital
Budget: revenues: $1.447 billion: expenditures: $1.459 billion   **Currency:** emanlangeni

SWEDEN
Location: Northern Europe, bordering the Baltic Sea, Gulf of Bothnia, Kattegat, and Skagerrak, between Finland and Norway
Area: 173,859 sq mi (450,295 sq km)
Area-comparative: slightly larger than California
Population: 9,119,423
Population growth rate: 0.18%
Nationality: noun: Swede(s); adjective: Swedish
Ethnic groups: indigenous population: Swedes with Finnish and Sami minorities; foreign-born or first-generation immigrants: Finns, Yugoslavs, Danes, Norwegians, Greeks, Turks
Languages: Swedish (official); small Sami-and Finnish-speaking minorities
Religions: Lutheran 87%, other 13% (including Catholic, Orthodox, Baptist, Muslim, Jewish, and Buddhist)
Government: constitutional monarchy
Capital: Stockholm
Budget: revenues: $287.9 billion; expenditures: $289.3 billion   **Currency:** Swedish kronor (SEK)

SWITZERLAND
Location: Central Europe, east of France, north of Italy
Area: 15,937 sq mi (41,277 sq km)
Area-comparative: slightly less than twice the size of New Jersey
Population: 7,996,026
Population growth rate: 0.85%
Nationality: noun: Swiss (singular and plural); adjective: Swiss
Ethnic groups: German 65%, French 18%, Italian 10%, Romansch 1%, other 6%
Languages: German 63.7%, French 20.4%, Italian 6.5%, Serbo-Croatian 1.5%, Albanian 1.3%, Portuguese 1.2%, Spanish 1.1%, English 1%, Romansch 0.5%, other 2.8%
        *Note: German, French, Italian, and Romansch are all national and official languages
Religions: Roman Catholic 41.8%, Protestant 35.3%, Muslim 4.3%, Orthodox 1.8%, other Christian 0.4%, other 1%, unspecified 4.3%, none 11.1%
Government type: formally a confederation but similar in structure to a federal republic
Capital: Bern
Budget: revenues: $212.7 billion; expenditures: $211.1 billion   **Currency:** Swiss franc (CHF)

SYRIA
Location: Middle East, bordering the Mediterranean Sea, between Lebanon and Turkey
Area: 71,479 sq mi (185,180 sq km)
Area comparative: slightly larger than North Dakota
Population: 22,457,336
Population growth rate: 0.15%
Nationality: noun: Syrian(s); adjective: Syrian
Ethnic groups: Arab 90.3%, Kurds, Armenians, other 9.7%
Languages: Arabic (official), Kurdish, Armenian, Aramaic, Circassian (widely understood); French, English (somewhat understood)
Religions: Sunni Muslim 74%, Alawite, Druze, and other Muslim sects 16%, Christian (various sects) 10%, Jewish (tiny communities)
Government type: republic under an authoritarian military-dominated regime
Capital: Damascus
Budget: revenues: $6.511 billion: expenditures: $12.68 billion   **Currency:** Syrian pound (SYP)

TAIWAN
Location: Eastern Asia, islands bordering the East China Sea, Philippine Sea, South China Sea, and Taiwan Strait, north of the Philippines, off the southeastern coast of China.
Area: 13,888 sq. mi. (35,980 sq. km.)
Area-comparative: slightly smaller than Maryland and Delaware combined
Population: 23,299,716
Population growth rate: 0.27%
Nationality: noun: Taiwan (singular and plural) note: example- he or she is from Taiwan; they are from Taiwan; adjective: Taiwan
Ethnic groups: Taiwanese (including Hakka) 84%, mainland Chinese 14%, indigenous 2%
Languages: Mandarin Chinese (official), Taiwanese (Min), Hakka dialects
Religions: mixture of Buddhist and Taoist 93%, Christian 4.5%, other 2.5%,
Government type: multiparty democracy
Capital: Taipei
Budget: revenues: $57.6 billion; expenditures: $64.62 billion   **Currency:** New Taiwan dollar (TWD)

TAJIKISTAN
Location: Central Asia, west of China, south of Kyrgyzstan
Area: 55,237 sq mi (143,100 sq km)
Area-comparative: slightly smaller than Wisconsin
Population: 7,910,041
Population growth rate: 1.79%
Nationality: noun: Tajikstani(s); adjective: Tajikstani
Ethnic groups: Tajik 79.9%, Uzbeck 15.3%, Russian 1.1%, Kyrgyz 1.1%, other 2.6%
Languages: Tajik (official), Russian (widely spoken in government and business)
Religions: Sunni Muslim 85%, Shi'a Muslim 5% other 10%,
Government type: republic
Capital: Dushanbe
Budget: revenues: $2.046 billion; expenditures: $2.066 billion   **Currency:** Tajikistani somoni (TJS)

TANZANIA
Location: Eastern Africa, bordering the Indian Ocean, between Kenya and Mozambique
Area: 365,754 sq mi (947,300 sq km)
Area-comparative: slightly larger than twice the size of California
Population: 48,261,942
Population growth rate: 2.82%
Nationality: noun: Tanzanian(s); adjective: Tanzanian

Ethnic groups: mainland - African 99% (of which 95% are Bantu consisting of more than 130 tribes), other 1% (consisting of Asian, European, and Arab); Zanzibar – Arab, African, mixed Arab and African

Languages: Kiswahili or Swahili (official), Kiunguja (name for Swahili in Zanzibar), English (official, primary language of commerce, administration, and higher education), Arabic (widely spoken in Zanzibar), many local languages

Religions: mainland- Muslim 35%, indigenous beliefs 35%, Christian 30%; Zanzibar- more than 99% Muslim

Government type: republic

Capital: Dar es Salaam (administrative); Dodoma (legislative)

Budget: revenues: $6.075 billion; expenditures: $7.67 billion   **Currency:** Tanzanian shilling (TZS)

THAILAND

Location: Southeastern Asia, bordering the Andaman Sea and the Gulf of Thailand, southeast of Myanmar

Area: 198,117 sq mi (513,120 sq km)

Area-comparative: slightly more than twice the size of Wyoming

Population: 67,448,120

Population growth rate: 0.52%

Nationality: noun: Thai (singular and plural); adjective: Thai

Ethnic groups: Thai 75%, Chinese 14%, other 11%

Languages: Thai, English (secondary language of the elite), ethnic and regional dialects

Religions: Buddhism 94.6%, Muslim 4.6%, Christian 0.7%, other 0.1%

Government type: constitutional monarchy

Capital: Bangkok

Budget: revenues: $63.7 billion; expenditures: $76.6 billion   **Currency:** baht (THB)

TOGO

Location: Western Africa, bordering the Bight of Benin, between Benin and Ghana

Area: 21,919 sq mi (56,785 sq km)

Area-comparative: slightly smaller than West Virginia

Population: 7,154,237

Population growth rate: 2.73%

Nationality: noun: Togolise; adjective: Togolese

Ethnic groups: African (37 tribes; largest and most important are Ewe, Mina, and Kabre) 99%, European and Syrian-Lebanese less than 1%

Languages: French (official, language of commerce), Ewe, Mina, Kabye, Dagomba

Religions: indigenous beliefs 51%, Christian 29%, Muslim 20%

Government type: republic under transition to multiparty democratic rule

Capital: Lome

Budget: revenues: $729.6 million; expenditures: $872.2 million

Currency: Communaute Financiere Africaine franc (XOF)

TONGA

Location: Oceania, group of islands in the South Pacific Ocean, about two-thirds of the way from Hawaii to New Zealand

Area: 288 sq mi (747 sq km)

Area-comparative: four times the size of Washington, DC

Population: 106,322

Population growth rate: 0.14%

Nationality: noun: Tongan(s); adjective: Tongan

Ethnic groups: Polynesian, Europeans

Languages: Tongan, English

Religions: Christian (Free Wesleyan church claims 30,000 adherents)
Government type: constitutional monarchy
Capital: Nuku'alofa
Budget: revenues: $115.1 million; expenditures: $115.1 million   **Currency:** pa'anga (TOP)

TRINIDAD AND TOBAGO
Location: Caribbean, islands between the Caribbean Sea and the North Atlantic Ocean, northeast of
          Venezuela
Area: 1,979 sq mi (5,128 sq km)
Area-comparative: slightly smaller than Delaware
Population: 1,225,225
Population growth rate: -0.09%
Nationality: noun: Trinidadian(s), Tobagonian(s); adjective: Trinidadian, Tobagonian
Ethnic groups: Indian (South Asian) 40%, African 37.5%, mixed 20.5%, other 1 2%, unspecified 0.8%
Languages: English (official), Caribbean Hindustani (a dialect of Hindi), French, Spanish, Chinese
Religions: Roman Catholic 26%, Protestant 25.8%, Hindu 22.5%, Anglican 7.8%, Baptist 7.2%,
          Pentecostal 6.8%, other Christian 5.8%, Muslim 5.8%, Seventh Day Adventist 4%, other
          10.8%, unspecified 1.4%, none 1.9%
Government type: parliamentary democracy
Capital: Port of Spain
Budget: revenues: $7.705 billion; expenditures: $8.341 billion
Currency: Trinidad and Tobago dollar (TTD)

TUNISIA
Location: Northern Africa, bordering the Mediterranean Sea, between Algeria and Libya
Area: 63,153 sq mi (163,610 sq km)
Area-comparative: slightly larger than Georgia
Population: 10,835,873
Population growth rate: 0.95%
Nationality: noun: Tunisian(s); adjective: Tunisian
Ethnic groups: Arab 98%, European 1%, Jewish and other 1%
Languages: Arabic (official), French, Berber
Religions: Muslim 98%, Christian 1%, Jewish and other 1%
Government type: republic
Capital: Tunis
Budget: revenues: $10.63 billion; expenditures: $14.43 billion   **Currency:** Tunisian dinar (TND)

TURKEY
Location: Southeastern Europe and Southwestern Asia, bordering the Black Sea, between Bulgaria and
          Georgia, and bordering the Aagean Sea and the Mediterranean Sea, between Greece and Syria
Area: 302,534 sq mi (783,562 sq km)
Area-comparative: slightly larger than Texas
Population: 80,694,485
Population growth rate: 1.16%
Nationality: noun: Turk(s); adjective: Turkish
Ethnic groups: Turkish 70-75%, Kurdish 18%, other minorities 7-12%
Languages: Turkish (official), Kurdish, other minority languages
Religions: Muslim 99.8% (primarily Sunni), other (mostly Christians and Jews) 0.2%
Government type: republican parliamentary
Capital: Ankara
Budget: revenues: $179.9 billion; expenditures: $200.4 billion   **Currency:** Turkish lira (TRL)

TURKMENISTAN
Location: Central Asia, bordering the Caspian Sea, between Iran and Kazakhstan
Area: 188,406 sq mi (488,100 sq km)
Area-comparative: slightly larger than California
Population: 5,113,040
Population growth rate: 1.15%
Nationality: noun: Turkmen(s); adjective: Turkmen
Ethnic groups: Turkmen 85%, Uzbek 5%, Russian 4%, other 6%
Languages: Turkmen 72% (official), Russian 12%, Uzbek 9%, other 7%
Religions: Muslim 89%, Eastern Orthodox 9%, unknown 2%
Government type: defines itself as a secular democracy and a presidential republic; in actuality displays authoritarian presidential rule, with power concentrated within the presidential administration
Capital: Ashgabat
Budget: revenues: $26.4 billion; expenditures: $26.9 billion   **Currency:** Turkmen manta (TMM)

TURKS AND CAICOS ISLANDS
Location: Caribbean, two islands in the North Atlantic Ocean, southeast of The Bahamas, north of Haiti
Area: 611 sq mi (984 sq km)
Area-comparative: 2.5 times the size of Washington, DC
Population: 47,754
Population growth rate: 2.87%
Nationality: noun: none; adjective: none
Ethnic groups: black 87.6%, white 7.9%, mixed 2.5%, East Indian 1.3%, other 0.7%
Languages: English (official)
Religions: Protestant 72.8%, Baptist 35.8%, Anglican 10%, Methodist 9.3%, Church of God 11.7%, Seventh-Day Adventist 6%, Roman Catholic 11.4%, Jehovah's Witnesses 1.8%, other 14%
Dependency status: overseas territory of the UK
Capital: Grand Turk (Cockburn Town)
Budget: revenues: $417.4 million; expenditures $208.9 million   **Currency:** United States dollar (USD)

UGANDA
Location: East-Central Africa, west of Kenya, east of the Democratic Republic of Congo
Area: 93,065 sq mi (241,038 sq km)
Area-comparative: slightly smaller than Oregon
Population: 34,758,809
Population growth rate: 3.32%
Nationality: noun: Ugandan(s); adjective: Ugandan
Ethnic groups: Baganda 16.9%, Banyokole 9.5%, Basoga 8.4%, Bakiga 6.9%, Iteso 6.4%, Langi 6.1%, Acholi 4.7%, Bagisu 4.6%, Lugbara 4.2%, Bunyoro 2.7%, other 29.6%
Languages: English (official), Ganda/Luganda, Swahili, other Niger-Congo languages, Nilo-Saharan languages, Arabic
Religions: Roman Catholic 41.9%, Protestant 42%, Anglican 35.9%, Pentecostal 4.6%, Seventh-Day Adventist 1.5%, Muslim 12.1%, other 3.1%, none 0.9%
Government type: republic
Capital: Kampala
Budget: revenues: $2.909 billion; expenditures: $3.627 billion   **Currency:** Ugandan shilling (UGX)

UKRAINE
Location: Eastern Europe, bordering the Black Sea, between Poland, Russia, and Moldova in the west and Russia in the east
Area: 233,031 sq mi (603,550 sq km)
Area-comparative: slightly smaller than Texas

Population: 44,573,205
Population growth rate: -0.63%
Nationality: noun: Ukrainian(s); adjective: Ukrainian
Ethnic groups: Ukrainian 77.8%, Russian 17.3%, Belarusian 0.6%, Moldovan 0.5%, Crimean Tatar 0.5%, Bulgarian 0.4%, Hungarian 0.3%, Romanian 0.3%, Polish 0.3%, Jewish 0.2%, other 1.8%
Languages: Ukrainian 67% (official), Russian 24%, other (including Romanian-, Polish-, and Hungarian-speaking minorities) 9%
Religions: Ukrainian Orthodox-Kyiv Patriarchate 50.4%, Ukrainian Orthodox-Moscow Patriarchate 26.1%, Ukrainian Greek Catholic 8%, Ukrainian Autocephalous Orthodox 7.2%, Roman Catholic 2.2%, Protestant 2.2%, Jewish 0.6%, other 3.2%
Government type: republic
Capital: Kyiv (Kiev)
Budget: revenues: $53.07 billion; expenditures: $59.58 billion
Currency: hryvnia (UAH)

UNITED ARAB EMIRATES (UAE)
Location: Middle East, bordering the Gulf of Oman and the Persian Gulf, between Oman and Saudi Arabia
Area: 32,278 sq mi (83,600 sq km)
Area-comparative: slightly smaller than Maine
Population: 5,473,972
Population growth rate: 2.87%
Nationality: noun: Emirati(s); adjective: Emirati
Ethnic groups: South Asian 50%, Emirati 19%, other Arab and Iranian 23%, other (including Westerners and East Asians) 8% *Note: less than 20% are UAE citizens
Languages: Arabic (official), Persian, English, Hindi, Urdu
Religions: Muslim 96% (Shi'a 16%), other (including Christian and Hindu) 4%
Government type: federation with specified powers delegated to the UAE federal government and other powers reserved to member emirates
Capital: Abu Dhabi
Budget: revenues: $130.3 billion; expenditures: $113.8 billion
Currency: Emirati dirham (AED)

UNITED KINGDOM
Location: Western Europe, between the North Atlantic Ocean and the North Sea, northwest of France
Area: 94,058 sq mi (243,610 sq km)
Area-comparative: slightly smaller than Oregon
Population: 63,395,574
Population growth rate: 0.55%
Nationality: noun: Briton(s), British (collective plural); adjective: British
Ethnic groups: English 83.6%, Scottish 8.6%, Welsh 4.9%, Northern Irish 2.9%, black 2%, Indian 1.8%, Pakistani 1.3%, mixed 1.2%, other 1.6%
Religions: Christian (Anglican, Roman Catholic, Presbyterian, Methodist) 71.6%, Muslim 2.7%, Hindu 1%, other 1.6%, unspecified or none 23.1%
Languages: English, Scots, Welsh, Scottish form of Gaelic, Irish, Cornish
Government type: constitutional monarchy and Commonwealth realm
Capital: London
Budget: revenues: $995.9 billion; expenditures: $1.183 trillion   **Currency:** British pound (GBP)

UNITED STATES OF AMERICA
Location: North America, bordering both the North Atlantic Ocean and the North Pacific Ocean, between Canada and Mexico
Area: 3,794,100 sq mi (9,826,675 sq km)

Area-comparative: about half the size of Russia; about three-tenths the size of Africa; about half the size of South America (or slightly larger than Brazil); slightly larger than China; about two and half times the size of western Europe

Population: 316,668,567

Population growth rate: 0.9%

Nationality: noun: American(s); adjective: American

Ethnic groups: white 79.96%, Hispanic 15.1%, black 12.85%, Asian 4.43%, Amerindian and Alaska native 0.97%, native Hawaiian and other Pacific Islander 0.18%, two or more races 1.61%

Languages: English (official) 82.1%, Spanish 10.7%, other Indo-European 3.8%, Asian and Pacific Islander 2.7%, other 0.7%

Religions: Protestant 51.3%, Roman Catholic 23.9%, Mormon 1.7%, other Christian 1.6%, Jewish 1.7%, Buddhist 0.7%, Muslim 0.6%, unaffiliated 12.1% none 4%, other or unspecified 2.5%

Government type: Constitution-based federal republic; strong democratic tradition

Capital: Washington, DC

Budget: revenues: $2.465 trillion; expenditures: $3.649 trillion   **Currency:** United States dollar (USD)

URUGUAY

Location: Southern South America, bordering the South Atlantic Ocean, between Argentina and Brazil

Area: 68,037 sq mi (176,215 sq km)

Area-comparative: slightly smaller than the state of Washington

Population: 3,324,460

Population growth rate: 0.25%

Nationality: noun: Uruguayan(s); adjective: Uruguayan

Ethnic groups: white 88%, mestizo 8%, black 4%, Amerindian (practically nonexistent)

Languages: Spanish, Portunol, Brazilero (Portuguese-Spanish mix on the Brazilian frontier)

Religions: Roman Catholic 47.1%, non-Catholic Christians 11.1%, nondenominational 23.2%, Jewish 0.3%, atheist or agnostic 17.2%, other 1.1%

Government type: constitutional republic

Capital: Montevideo

Budget: revenues: $14.28 billion; expenditures: $15.07 billion   **Currency:** Uruguayan peso (UYU)

UZBEKISTAN

Location: Central Asia, north of Turkmenistan, south of Kazakhstan

Area: 172,696 sq mi (447,400 sq km)

Area-comparative: slightly larger than California

Population: 28,661,637

Population growth rate: 0.94%

Nationality: noun: Uzbekistani; adjective: Uzbekistani

Ethnic groups: Uzbek 80%, Russian 5.5%, Tajik 5%, Kazakh 3%, Karakalpak 2.5%, Tartar 1.5%, other 2.5%

Languages: Uzbek 74.3% (official), Russian 14.2%, Tajik 4.4%, other 7.1%

Religions: Muslim 88% (primarily Sunni), Eastern Orthodox 9%, other 3%

Government type: republic; authoritarian presidential rule, with little power outside the executive branch

Capital: Tashkent

Budget: revenues: $16.39 billion; expenditures: $16.51 billion

Currency: Uzbekistani soum (UZS)

VENEZUELA

Location: Northern South America, bordering the Caribbean Sea and the North Atlantic Ocean, between Colombia and Guyana

Area: 352,051 sq mi (912,050 sq km)

Area-comparative: slightly more than twice the size of California

Population: 28,459,085

Population growth rate: 1.44%
Nationality: noun: Venezuelan(s); adjective: Venezuelan
Ethnic groups: Spanish, Italian, Portuguese, Arab, German, African, indigenous people
Languages: Spanish (official), numerous indigenous dialects
Religions: Roman Catholic 96%, Protestant 2%, other 2%
Government type: federal republic
Capital: Caracas
Budget: revenues: $116.3 billion; expenditures: $175.3 billion
Currency: bolivar (VEB)

VIETNAM

Location: Southeastern Asia, bordering the Gulf of Thailand, Gulf of Tonkin, and South China Sea, alongside China, Laos, and Cambodia
Area: 127,881 sq mi (331,210 sq km)
Area-comparative: slightly larger than New Mexico
Population: 92,477,857
Population growth rate: 1.03%
Nationality: noun: Vietnamese (singular and plural); adjective: Vietnamese
Ethnic groups: Kinh (Viet) 85.7%, Tay 1.9%, Thai 1.8%, Muong 1.5%, Khmer 1.5%, Mong 1.2%, Nung 1.1%, others 5.3%,
Languages: Vietnamese (official), Chinese, English, (increasingly favored as 2nd language), French, Khmer, tribal languages
Religions: Buddhist 9.3%, Catholic 6.7%, Hoa Hao 1.5%, Cao Dai 1.1%, Protestant 0.5%, Muslim 0.1%, none 80.8%
Government type: Communist state
Capital: Hanoi (Ha Noi)
Budget: revenues: $42.14 billion; expenditures: $47.57 billion   **Currency:** dong (VND)

VIRGIN ISLANDS

Location: islands between the Caribbean Sea and the North Atlantic Ocean, east of Puerto Rico
Area: 737 sq mi (1,190 sq km)
Area-comparative: twice the size of Washington, DC
Population: 104,737
Population growth rate: -0.53%
Nationality: noun: Virgin Islander(s); adjective; Virgin Islander
Ethnic groups: black 76.2%, white 13.1%, Asian 1.1%, other 6.1%, mixed 3.5%
Languages: English (official) 74.7%, Spanish or Spanish Creole 16.8%, French or French Creole 6.6%, other 1.9%
Religions: Protestant 59%, Baptist 42%, Roman Catholic 34%, Episcopalian 17%, other 7%
Government type: NA
Capital: Charlotte Amalie
Budget: revenues: $837 million; expenditures: $837 million   **Currency:** U S dollar (USD)

WEST BANK

Location: Middle East, west of Jordan, east of Israel
Area: 2,270 sq. mi. (5,860 sq. km.)
Area-comparative: slightly smaller than Delaware
Population: 2,676,740
Population growth rate: 2.03%
Nationality: noun: NA; adjective: NA
Ethnic groups: Palestinian Arab and other 83%, Jewish 17%
Languages: Arabic, Hebrew (spoken by Israeli settlers and Palestinians), English (widely understood)
Religions: Muslim 75% (predominantly Sunni), Jewish 17%, Christian and other 8%

Government type: Unity government
Capital: Ramallah
Budget: revenues: $2.1 billion; expenditures: $3.2 billion
Currency: new Israeli shekel (ILS); Jordanian dinar (JOD)

YEMEN
Location: Middle East, bordering the Arabian Sea, Gulf of Aden, and Red Sea, between Oman and Saudi Arabia
Area: 203,850 sq mi (527,968 sq km)
Area-comparative: slightly larger than twice the size of Wyoming
Population: 25,408,288
Population growth rate: 2.5%
Nationality: noun: Yemeni(s); adjective: Yemeni
Ethnic groups: predominantly Arab, some Afro-Arab, South Asians, Europeans
Language: Arabic (official)
Religions: Muslim including Shaf'i (Sunni) and Zaydi (Shi'a), small numbers of Jewish, Christian, Hindu
Government type: republic
Capital: Sanaa
Budget: revenues: $7.63 billion; expenditures: $12.01 billion   **Currency:** Yemeni rial (YER)

ZAMBIA
Location: Southern Africa, east of Angola, south of the Democratic Republic of Congo
Area: 290,587 sq mi (752,618 sq km)
Area-comparative: slightly larger than Texas
Population: 14,222,233
Population growth rate: 2.89%
Nationality: noun: Zambian(s); adjective: Zambian
Ethnic groups: African 99.5% (includes Bemba, Tonga, Chewa, Lozi, Nsenga, Tumbuka, Ngoni, Lala, Kaonde, Lunda, and other African groups), other 0.5% (includes Europeans, Asians, and Americans)
Languages: 11 Bantu languages (Bemba (official), English, Nyanja, Kaonda, Lozi, Lunda, Luvale, Tonga, Chewa, Nsenga, 70 indigenous languages
Religions: Christian 50%-75%, Muslim and Hindu 24%-49%, indigenous beliefs 1%
Government type: republic
Capital: Lusaka
Budget: revenues: $4.092 billion; expenditures: $5.369 billion   **Currency:** Zambian kwacha (ZMK)

ZIMBABWE
Location: Southern Africa, between South Africa and Zambia
Area: 150,872 sq mi (390,757 sq km)
Area-comparative: slightly larger than Montana
Population: 13,182,908
Population growth rate: 4.38%
Nationality: noun: Zimbabwean(s); adjective: Zimbabwean
Ethnic groups: African 98% (Shona 82%,Ndebele 14%, other 2%),mixed and Asian 1%, less than 1% white
Languages: English (official), Shona, Sindebele, and numerous other tribal dialects
Religions: syncretic 50%, Christian 25%, indigenous beliefs 24%, Muslim and other 1%
Government type: parliamentary democracy
Capital: Harare
Budget: revenues: $NA; expenditures: $NA   **Currency:** Zimbabwean dollar (ZWD)

The World

Area: 510.072 million sq km;
land: 148.94 million sq km;
water: 361.132 million sq km.
Note: 70.9% of the world's surface is *water*,
29.1% is *land*.

Area-comparative:
land area about 16 times the size of the US
Population: 7,095,217,980
Population growth rate: 1.1%

Languages: Chinese Mandarin 12.44%;
Spanish 4.85%, English 4.83%, Arabic 3.25%,
Hindi 2.68%, Bengali 2.66%, Portuguese 2.62%,
Russian 2.12%,Japanese 1.8%,
Standard German 1.33%, Javanese 1.25%

Religions: Christian 33.39%; (of which Roman
Catholic 16.99%, Protestant 6.15%, Orthodox
3.96%, Anglican 1.26%), Muslim 22.74%, Hindu
13.8%, Buddhist 6.77%, Sikh 0.35%, Jewish
0.22%, Baha'i 0.11%, other religions 10.95%,
non-religious 9.66%, atheists 2.01%

THE PLANETS

THE PLANETS – SUMMARY

	Distance from Sun (000 km)	Diameter (km)	Planet Mass (kg) $E=mc^2$
Mercury	57,910	4,880	3.30e23
Venus	108,200	12,104	4.87e24
Earth	149,600	12,756	5.98e24
Mars	227,940	6,794	6.42e23
Jupiter	778,330	142,984	1.90e27
Saturn	1,426,940	120,536	5.69e26
Uranus	2,870,990	51,118	8.69e25
Neptune	4,497,070	49,532	1.02e26

Energy equals Mass times the speed of light squared.
$E=mc^2 = 0.111 \times 300{,}000{,}000 \times 300{,}000{,}000 =$ **10,000,000,000,000,000 Joules**

There are eight planets that revolve around the sun in our solar system. A planet is a celestial body that is in orbit around the sun, has enough mass to be round, and dominates its orbit. Each planet is the largest body of matter in its neighborhood that shines by reflected light. Like Earth, the other planets do not give off light of their own. When you see a planet shining brightly in the night sky, it is giving off the sun's light. These planets travel around the sun in fixed paths called orbits. A planet's gravitational pull depends on two things: size and density. The term *density* refers to the amount of matter contained in a given space. A block of iron and a block of ice that are equal in size are not equal in weight; the block of iron weighs more than the block of ice. A scientist would say that the iron is more *dense* meaning the block of iron has more matter in it.

The sun is by far the largest object in the solar system. It is about 4.5 billion years old. Since its birth it has used up about half of the hydrogen in its core. It will continue to radiate for another 5 billion years, but eventually it will run out of hydrogen fuel. The sun contains more than 99.8% of the total mass of the solar system (Jupiter contains most of the rest). The sun is composed of 75% hydrogen and 25% helium. The diameter of the sun is 1,392,684 km or 865,374 miles — more than 100 time's Earth's diameter.

Every star in the night sky is the sun of another solar system. Therefore, our sun would look like a small twinkle if you saw it from the planet of another solar system.

MERCURY is the planet closest to the sun and the eighth largest. It was named for Mercury, who in Greek myths was the speedy messenger of the gods. Mercury revolves around the sun in 88 days, faster than any other planet. Its orbit has the shape of an ellipse—a sort of flattened circle. Because of its irregular shape, sometimes it is only about 28,550,000 miles away from the sun, while at other times it is about 43,350,000 miles away. Its diameter is approximately the same as the width of the Atlantic Ocean. Mercury has a surface temperature of about – 9.6 degrees Fahrenheit on its dark side. The planet is surrounded by a thin atmosphere of carbon dioxide. Mercury's pull of gravity is much weaker than Earth's. A man weighing 140 pounds on Earth would weigh about 50 pounds on Mercury. He would be able to jump over an elephant.

VENUS is the second planet from the sun and the sixth largest. It is named the Evening Star because it shines brighter than any other planet or star. Venus travels around the sun in a circular orbit. It revolves around the sun in 225 days. It is almost the same size as the Earth, its diameter is 7,600 miles. Venus' pull of gravity is also nearly the same as the Earth's. A man who weighed 150 pounds on Earth would weigh about 135 pounds on Venus. Venus is the planet closest to the Earth, surrounded by a layer of white clouds composed of sulfuric acid. These clouds completely obscure our view of the surface. A glowing halo of hydrogen surrounds Venus, about 1,800 miles above its surface. The atmosphere of Venus is made up chiefly of carbon dioxide gas. The surface temperature of the planet is about 536 degrees (hot enough to melt lead).

EARTH is the third planet from the sun, about 93 million miles from the sun. It is the fifth largest planet and the densest major body in the solar system. Simply put, the Earth is a ball of rock and metal that is about 4.5 to 4.6 billion years old. The estimated weight of our planet is 6,580,000,000,000,000,000,000 tons.

Three-fourths of Earth's surface is water. One-fifth of the land surface is mountains. Earth travels around the sun in a circular orbit. It takes about 365 days to make one orbit of the sun. It takes almost 24 hours to rotate once on its axis. It is surrounded by a thin atmosphere of nitrogen and oxygen. The oxygen in Earth's atmosphere is produced and maintained by biological processes. Without life there would be no free oxygen. Earth's diameter is 7,913 miles. Everything falls to the ground, since there is a strong pull of gravity. The hottest recorded temperature on Earth is 58 degrees Celsius in Lybia which is 136.4 degrees Fahrenheit, and the coldest was -89 degrees Celsius (-128.2 degrees Fahrenheit) in Vostok, Antarctica where nobody lives. The lowest recorded temperature in an inhabited region is -72 degrees Celsius (-97.6 degrees Fahrenheit) in the Siberian Village of Oymyakon, Russia. The temperature of the Earth's core is believed to be 4,000 degrees Celsius.

MARS is the fourth planet from the sun, about 142 million miles away. It is the seventh largest planet; it takes 687 days to revolve around the sun. Its orbit is an ellipse. Mars is called the Red Planet because it shines in the sky with a reddish color. At its closest, it is 128,500,000 miles from the sun, at its farthest it is 154,500,000 miles. Mars is a small, rocky world that measures 4,200 miles in diameter. It contains the largest volcano in the solar system, Olympus Mons, which is 15 miles high, almost three times higher than Mount Everest, the highest mountain on Earth. Spirit and Opportunity are Rovers sent to Mars to see if life did exist on the planet. The Martian atmosphere is made up mainly of carbon dioxide, there is little if any oxygen. A man weighing 150 pounds on Earth would weigh 57 pounds on Mars. The hottest temperature on Mars is about 70 degrees Fahrenheit on a hot day at the equator, at the poles which are covered with ice in the winter, the temperatures drop to 150 degrees below zero.

JUPITER is the fifth planet from the sun, about 484 million miles away. It is the largest planet; its diameter is almost 11 times the size of the earth. Jupiter takes 11.9 years to revolve around the sun. The planet spins very quickly, it takes less than 10 hours to rotate once. Jupiter radiates more energy into space than it receives from the Sun. It is surrounded by clouds that are thousands of miles deep, composed of 90% hydrogen and 10% helium. The temperature at the top of the cloud layers is about 202 degrees below zero. The gases surrounding the planet are moving at different speeds, creating bands of colors in the cloud layers. The pull of gravity is about two and a half times stronger than Earth's. A man weighing 150 pounds on Earth would weigh about 397 pounds on Jupiter.

SATURN is the sixth planet from the sun, about 888 million miles away. It was the first known planet. Galileo was the first to observe it with a telescope in 1610, since it is a very large planet. It takes nearly 29 years to make one trip around the sun. Saturn is not quite as large as Jupiter. Its diameter is about nine times that of Earth. Saturn rotates very quickly. The planet takes only 10 hours and two minutes to turn once on its axis. Saturn's atmosphere is surrounded by 75% hydrogen and 25% helium. The winds on Saturn blow at about 900 miles an hour—about six times stronger than hurricane-force winds on Earth. Its gravitational pull is a little less than the pull of Earth. Saturn can be distinguished by the flat rings that circle its equator that seem to be composed primarily of water and ice, but they may also include rocky particles with icy coatings.

URANUS is the seventh planet from the sun, about 1.8 billion miles away. It is the third largest, about four times larger than Earth. A year on Uranus, or the time it takes to revolve around the sun, is 84 years on Earth. It spins on its side; its axis is tilted nearly 98 degrees. Observed through a telescope, Uranus appears to be slightly blue, the result of absorption of red light by methane in the upper atmosphere, surrounded by 11 rings that appear as a broad band of a silvery color around its equator. Uranus is composed primarily of rock and various ices. The gravitational pull is a little more than Earth's. A man weighing 150 pounds on Earth would weigh 162 pounds on Uranus.

NEPTUNE is the eighth planet from the sun, about 2.8 billion miles away from it. Pluto's orbit is so eccentric, it sometimes crosses the orbit of Neptune making Neptune the most distant planet from the sun. Its diameter is 30,603 miles, and it takes 165 years to revolve around the sun. Neptune has rapid winds confined to bands of latitude, Neptune's winds are the fastest in the solar system, reaching 2000 km/hour. Like Jupiter and Saturn, Neptune has an internal heat source— it radiates more than twice as much energy as it receives from the sun. Neptune looks like a twin of Uranus. It has almost the same diameter and it also appears as a dim blue-green object with a few bands of color around it. Scientists believe that the surface of the planet is very hot. A man weighing 150 pounds on Earth would weigh about 165 pounds on Neptune.

PLUTO was considered a planet until 2006, when it was reclassified as a dwarf planet by the International Astronomy Union. It was discovered by Clyde Tombaugh at Lowell Observatory in 1930. Pluto is approximately 3.6 billion miles away from the sun. Any atmosphere surrounding Pluto must be frozen. The temperatures probably never rise beyond 348 degrees below zero. Pluto has not been visited by a spacecraft. Its diameter is half the width of the earth. Pluto's orbit is a long ellipse. It rotates in the opposite direction from most of the other eight planets. Pluto is about 35,000,000 miles closer to the sun than Neptune. Pluto's journey around the sun takes about 248.4 earth years.

EXOSPHERE

THERMOSPHERE (to c.700km)

Appleton Layer[F2] (c.300km)

Heaviside Layer[E] (c.100km)

MESOSPHERE (to c.85km)

STRATOSPHERE (to c.50km)

Tropopause (17km)

TROPOSPHERE (to c.17km)

OZONE is a rare molecule consisting of three oxygen atoms. Ninety percent of the ozone in Earth's atmosphere is found in the stratosphere, the atmospheric layer that is between 15 and 50 kilometers above the Earth's surface. This stratospheric ozone is often referred to as the "ozone layer", and plays a vital role in protecting life on Earth by reflecting most of the harmful ultraviolet radiation that comes from the sun back into space.

Clouds

Luke Howard, died in 1864, used four terms to classify the clouds he saw in the sky. These terms still form the basis of cloud categories used today.

Cumulus=heap

Cumulus clouds are white and appear fluffy. They are generally seen in fair weather. The base of a cumulus cloud is relatively low, less than 2,000 meters above the earth's surface.

Cumulonimbus clouds are large cumulus clouds, high above the earth 2,000 -7,000 meters.

Altocumulus look like patches and sheets of rolled clouds- separate or sometimes merged at the height of at 5,000 - 13,700 meters, that produce thunderstorms. They look like ripples or grains of white clouds in regular patterns.

Stratus = layer

Stratus clouds are low, flat gray clouds. They often produce a steady rain. They are anywhere from the earth's surface to 460 meters high.

Stratocumulus are layers of white clouds with dark gray areas above the stratus clouds, 460- 2,000 meters, from the surface of the earth; often producing light rain or snow.

Altostratus clouds are 2,000 -7,000 meters above the earth. **They** are sheets of gray-blue clouds covering the sky, often covering the sun and the moon.

Cirrus=curl

Cirrus clouds are extremely high (more than 5,000 -13,700 meters above the earth's surface) and feathery. They are made of ice crystals and are seen in fair weather.

Cirriocumulus clouds look like grains or ripples of white clouds in regular patterns.

Cirrostratus clouds look like thin layers of clouds covering much of the sky like sheets. They are very high (5,000-13,700 meters).

Nimbus= rain

Nimbostratus are dark heavy clouds usually associated with rain and snow, they cover most of the sky at 900 to 3000 meters above the earth.

Fog is a cloud at ground or sea level.

Weather Proverbs

Red sky at night, sailors' delight, red sky at morning, sailors' take warning.

Rain before seven, fine by eleven.

The sudden storm lasts not three hours.

The Water Cycle

The "Water Cycle" is the term scientists use to refer to the various ways molecules of water travel between the earth and the atmosphere. The water cycle has no beginning and no end; all of the molecules of water in, on, and around the earth are constantly moving and changing. It consists of six main processes: evaporation, transpiration, condensation, precipitation, runoff, and storage.

Evaporation is the transformation of liquid or frozen (solid) water into water vapor, which is a gas. The heat of the sun causes water to evaporate out of the oceans, lakes and rivers, pools and puddles, and even off of your skin when you get sweaty outside on a hot day. When water evaporates from the leaves of plants, it is called **transpiration**. The water that evaporates into the atmosphere forms clouds through the process of **condensation**. This is the coming together of water vapor molecules to form liquid droplets. You can see water condense out of the atmosphere onto the outside of a cold glass on a warm, humid day. When the condensed droplets of water in the clouds become large enough, the force of gravity causes them to fall to the earth as **precipitation**.

Rain is liquid precipitation; forms of frozen precipitation include freezing rain, sleet, and snow. Precipitation that falls on land either soaks deep into the ground, where it is stored as groundwater, or flows into lakes, streams, or rivers as **runoff**. All rivers eventually flow into the oceans, which are the main **storage** sites for earth's liquid water. Much water is also stored in solid form in glaciers and permanent coverings of snow.

Specifications of the Earth

Equatorial Radius: 6378.1 km

Polar radius: 6356.8 km

Age: approximately 4,500,000,000 years

Escape velocity: 11.18 km/sec

Planet year: 365.256 days

Core temperature: approximately 4500 Celsius

Water to land ratio: 71% to 29%

Iceberg Classification

The tip of the iceberg is believed to be about 1/5th to 1/7th of its total size

HEIGHT (meters above water)	NAME	LENGTH (meters)
< 1	Growler	< 5
1 – 4	Bergy Bit	5 – 14
5 – 15	Small	15 – 60
16 – 45	Medium	61 – 120
46 – 75	Large	121 – 200
>75	Very Large	>200

Sign Language

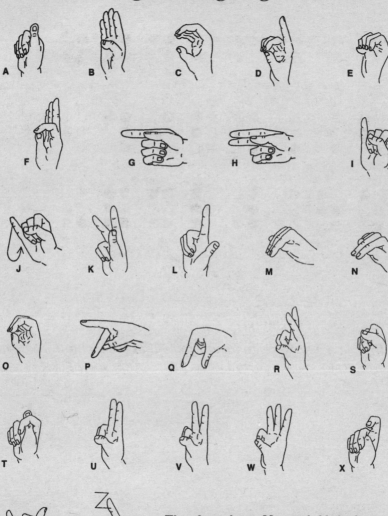

The American Manual Alphabet

Drawings show a side view. In actual practice the letters should face the persons with whom you are communicating.

Braille

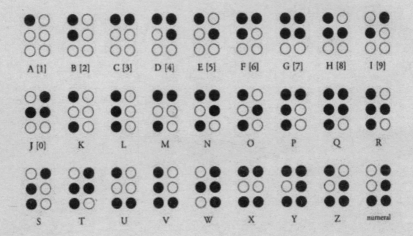

A [1]   B [2]   C [3]   D [4]   E [5]   F [6]   G [7]   H [8]   I [9]

J [0]   K   L   M   N   O   P   Q   R

S   T   U   V   W   X   Y   Z   numeral

"There is a wonder in reading Braille that the sighted will never know: to touch words and have them touch you back."

Jack Fiebig

2015 Calendar

January

Su	Mo	Tu	We	Th	Fr	Sa
				1	2	3
4	5	6	7	8	9	10
11	12	13	14	15	16	17
18	19	20	21	22	23	24
25	26	27	28	29	30	31

February

Su	Mo	Tu	We	Th	Fr	Sa
1	2	3	4	5	6	7
8	9	10	11	12	13	14
15	16	17	18	19	20	21
22	23	24	25	26	27	28

March

Su	Mo	Tu	We	Th	Fr	Sa
1	2	3	4	5	6	7
8	9	10	11	12	13	14
15	16	17	18	19	20	21
22	23	24	25	26	27	28
29	30	31				

April

Su	Mo	Tu	We	Th	Fr	Sa
			1	2	3	4
5	6	7	8	9	10	11
12	13	14	15	16	17	18
19	20	21	22	23	24	25
26	27	28	29	30		

May

Su	Mo	Tu	We	Th	Fr	Sa
					1	2
3	4	5	6	7	8	9
10	11	12	13	14	15	16
17	18	19	20	21	22	23
24	25	26	27	28	29	30
31						

June

Su	Mo	Tu	We	Th	Fr	Sa
	1	2	3	4	5	6
7	8	9	10	11	12	13
14	15	16	17	18	19	20
21	22	23	24	25	26	27
28	29	30				

July

Su	Mo	Tu	We	Th	Fr	Sa
			1	2	3	4
5	6	7	8	9	10	11
12	13	14	15	16	17	18
19	20	21	22	23	24	25
26	27	28	29	30	31	

August

Su	Mo	Tu	We	Th	Fr	Sa
						1
2	3	4	5	6	7	8
9	10	11	12	13	14	15
16	17	18	19	20	21	22
23	24	25	26	27	28	29
30	31					

September

Su	Mo	Tu	We	Th	Fr	Sa
		1	2	3	4	5
6	7	8	9	10	11	12
13	14	15	16	17	18	19
20	21	22	23	24	25	26
27	28	29	30			

October

Su	Mo	Tu	We	Th	Fr	Sa
				1	2	3
4	5	6	7	8	9	10
11	12	13	14	15	16	17
18	19	20	21	22	23	24
25	26	27	28	29	30	31

November

Su	Mo	Tu	We	Th	Fr	Sa
1	2	3	4	5	6	7
8	9	10	11	12	13	14
15	16	17	18	19	20	21
22	23	24	25	26	27	28
29	30					

December

Su	Mo	Tu	We	Th	Fr	Sa
		1	2	3	4	5
6	7	8	9	10	11	12
13	14	15	16	17	18	19
20	21	22	23	24	25	26
27	28	29	30	31		

Holidays

Jan 1	New Year's Day	
Jan 19	Martin Luther King Day	
Feb 14	Valentine's Day	
Feb 16	Presidents' Day	
Apr 5	Easter Sunday	
Apr 13	Thomas Jefferson's Birthday	
May 10	Mothers' Day	
May 25	Memorial Day	
Jun 21	Fathers' Day	
Jul 3	'Independence Day' observed	
Jul 4	Independence Day	
Sep 7	Labor Day	
Oct 12	Columbus Day	
Oct 31	Halloween	
Nov 11	Veterans Day	
Nov 26	Thanksgiving Day	
Dec 24	Christmas Eve	
Dec 25	Christmas Day	
Dec 31	New Year's Eve	

2016 Calendar

January

Su	Mo	Tu	We	Th	Fr	Sa
					1	2
3	4	5	6	7	8	9
10	11	12	13	14	15	16
17	18	19	20	21	22	23
24	25	26	27	28	29	30
31						

February

Su	Mo	Tu	We	Th	Fr	Sa
	1	2	3	4	5	6
7	8	9	10	11	12	13
14	15	16	17	18	19	20
21	22	23	24	25	26	27
28	29					

March

Su	Mo	Tu	We	Th	Fr	Sa
		1	2	3	4	5
6	7	8	9	10	11	12
13	14	15	16	17	18	19
20	21	22	23	24	25	26
27	28	29	30	31		

April

Su	Mo	Tu	We	Th	Fr	Sa
					1	2
3	4	5	6	7	8	9
10	11	12	13	14	15	16
17	18	19	20	21	22	23
24	25	26	27	28	29	30

May

Su	Mo	Tu	We	Th	Fr	Sa
1	2	3	4	5	6	7
8	9	10	11	12	13	14
15	16	17	18	19	20	21
22	23	24	25	26	27	28
29	30	31				

June

Su	Mo	Tu	We	Th	Fr	Sa
			1	2	3	4
5	6	7	8	9	10	11
12	13	14	15	16	17	18
19	20	21	22	23	24	25
26	27	28	29	30		

July

Su	Mo	Tu	We	Th	Fr	Sa
					1	2
3	4	5	6	7	8	9
10	11	12	13	14	15	16
17	18	19	20	21	22	23
24	25	26	27	28	29	30
31						

August

Su	Mo	Tu	We	Th	Fr	Sa
	1	2	3	4	5	6
7	8	9	10	11	12	13
14	15	16	17	18	19	20
21	22	23	24	25	26	27
28	29	30	31			

September

Su	Mo	Tu	We	Th	Fr	Sa
				1	2	3
4	5	6	7	8	9	10
11	12	13	14	15	16	17
18	19	20	21	22	23	24
25	26	27	28	29	30	

October

Su	Mo	Tu	We	Th	Fr	Sa
						1
2	3	4	5	6	7	8
9	10	11	12	13	14	15
16	17	18	19	20	21	22
23	24	25	26	27	28	29
30	31					

November

Su	Mo	Tu	We	Th	Fr	Sa
		1	2	3	4	5
6	7	8	9	10	11	12
13	14	15	16	17	18	19
20	21	22	23	24	25	26
27	28	29	30			

December

Su	Mo	Tu	We	Th	Fr	Sa
				1	2	3
4	5	6	7	8	9	10
11	12	13	14	15	16	17
18	19	20	21	22	23	24
25	26	27	28	29	30	31

Holidays

Jan 1	New Year's Day	May 30	Memorial Day	Nov 11	Veterans Day
Jan 18	Martin Luther King Day	Jun 19	Fathers' Day	Nov 24	Thanksgiving Day
Feb 14	Valentine's Day	Jul 4	Independence Day	Dec 24	Christmas Eve
Feb 15	Presidents' Day	Sep 5	Labor Day	Dec 25	Christmas Day
Mar 27	Easter Sunday	Oct 10	Columbus Day (most regions)	Dec 26	'Christmas Day' observed
Apr 13	Thomas Jefferson's Birthday	Oct 31	Halloween		
May 8	Mothers' Day	Nov 8	Election Day	Dec 31	New Year's Eve